McDougal Littell

SENIOR AUTHORS Rick Billstein
Jim Williamson

McDougal Littell
Evanston, Illinois • Boston • Dallas

AUTHORS

SENIOR AUTHORS

Rick Billstein Department of Mathematical Sciences, University of Montana, Missoula, Montana

Jim Williamson Department of Mathematical Sciences, University of Montana, Missoula, Montana

CONSULTING AUTHORS

Perry Montoya Teacher, Mesa Public Schools, Mesa, Arizona

Jacqueline Lowery Teacher, Indian Queen Elementary School, Fort Washington, Maryland

Dianne Williams Teacher, Booker T. Washington Middle School for International Studies, Tampa, Florida

THE STEM PROJECT *Middle Grades Math Thematics* is based on the field-test versions of The STEM Project curriculum. The STEM Project was supported in part by the

under Grant No. ESI-9150114. Opinions expressed in *Middle Grades Math Thematics* are those of the authors and not necessarily those of the National Science Foundation.

STEM WRITERS

Mary Buck, Clay Burkett, Lynn Churchill, Chris Clouse, Roslyn Denny, William Derrick, Sue Dolezal, Doug Galarus, Paul Kennedy, Pat Lamphere, Nancy Merrill, Perry Montoya, Sallie Morse, Marjorie Petit, Patrick Runkel, Thomas Sanders-Garrett, Richard T. Seitz, Bonnie Spence, Becky Sowders, Chris Tuckerman, Ken Wenger, Joanne Wilkie, Cheryl Wilson, Bente Winston

STEM TEACHER CONSULTANTS

Polly Fite, Jean Howard, Paul Sowden, Linda Tetley, Patricia Zepp

ABOUT THE COVER

The students shown on the back cover are from Thomas Jefferson Middle School in Jefferson City, Missouri.

ISBN 0-395-77499-3   3456789–VH–01 00 99

MIDDLE GRADES

MATH*Thematics*

WELCOME

COURSE GOALS

This course will help you:

- Learn all the important middle grades mathematics concepts and skills that prepare you for high school and beyond.
- Develop the reasoning, problem solving, and communication skills that enable you to apply mathematics to real-life activities.
- Value mathematics and become confident in using it to make decisions in daily life.

SUCCESS THROUGH EXPLORING MATHEMATICS

Theme Approach
You will be learning through thematic modules that connect mathematical concepts to real-world applications.

Active Learning
The lessons in this course will get you actively involved in exploring, modeling, and communicating mathematics using a variety of tools, including technology when appropriate.

Varied Practice and Assessment
The variety of types of practice and assessment will help reinforce and extend your understanding. You will learn to assess your own progress as you go along.

TOOLS for SUCCESS

1

Connecting the Theme *You can tackle any problem if you have the right tools. To solve any real-life problem, you need understanding and strategies. You'll learn to use these universal tools and to assess your mathematical progress.*

Module Features

Assessment Options

PATTERNS and DESIGNS

Connecting the Theme *From tiles to quilts to kites to cars, designers use numbers and geometry to make products sturdy, speedy, or less expensive. You'll discover how patterns in mathematics can be more than just pretty.*

Module Features

Assessment Options

STATISTICAL SAFARI

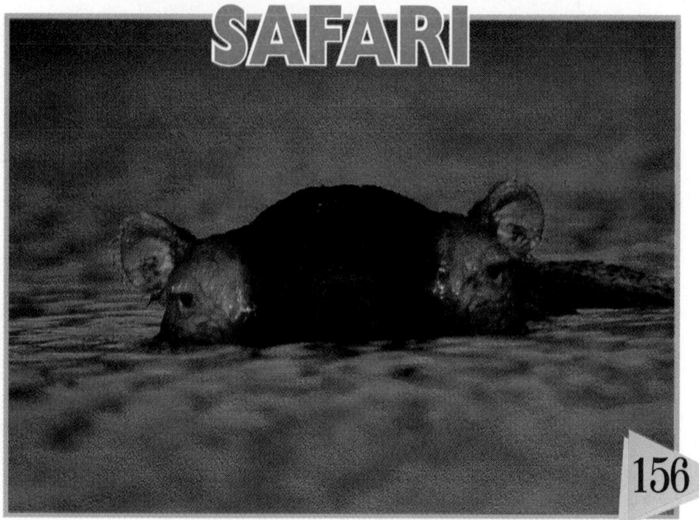

Connecting the Theme *In the field, a biologist watches an animal's movements and records the data. Counting, classifying, and comparing animals can help protect a species. You'll find out how mathematics helps in studying animals.*

Module Features

Assessment Options

MIND GAMES

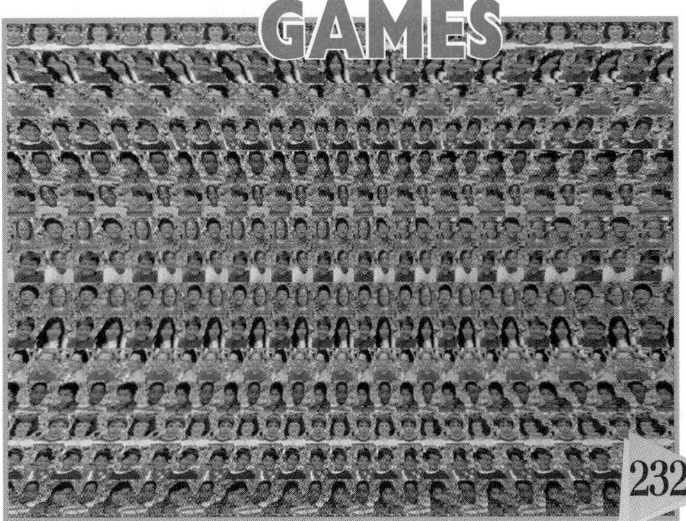

Connecting the Theme *Most games involve a mix of chance and strategy. How can you develop a strategy for winning? You'll play number games, invent puzzles, and run experiments to find the winning edge.*

Module Features

Assessment Options

CREATING THINGS

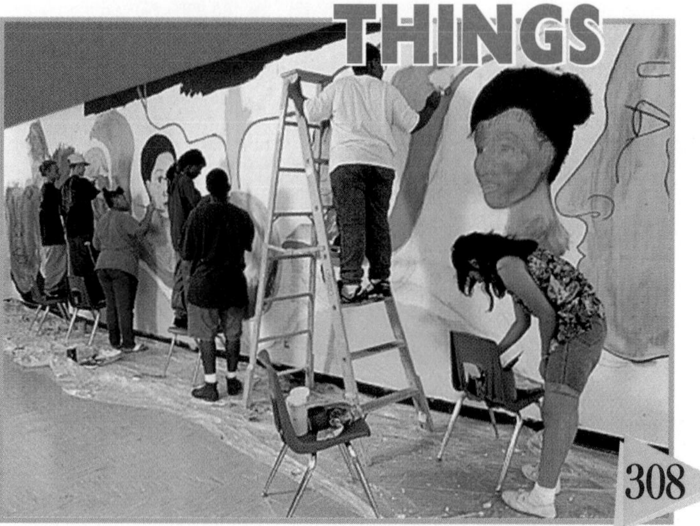

308

Connecting the Theme *Designers give an artistic flair to every type of creation. You'll see how people use mathematics to create everyday objects. You'll also give your personal touch to some creations.*

Module Features

Assessment Options

COMPARISONS and PREDICTIONS

378

Connecting the Theme *In news, sports, or weather, reporters like to compare the fastest, strongest, greatest, and longest. You'll see how artists use scale, and how scientists make predictions.*

Module Features

Assessment Options

WONDERS of the WORLD

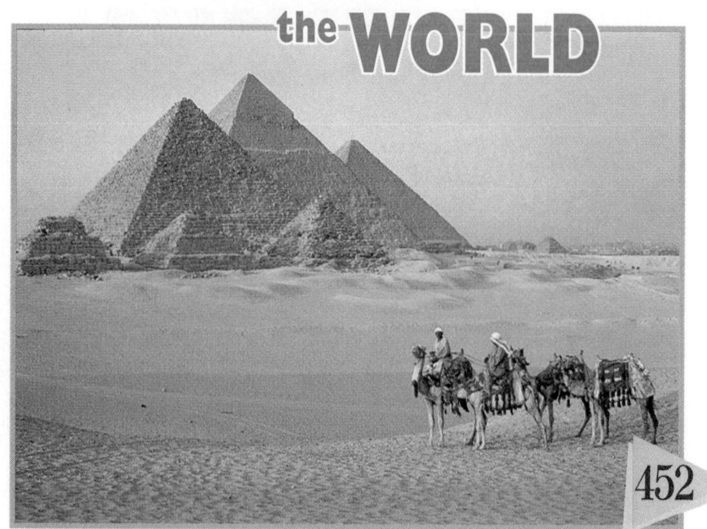

Connecting the Theme *Behind the world's greatest construction projects lie legends of love, fame, competition, and glory. You'll look across centuries and continents to see how engineers use mathematics to build a better marvel.*

Module Features

Assessment Options

OUR ENVIRONMENT

Connecting the Theme *No matter where you live, you can see the power of nature. People depend on the environment for water, food, and energy. You'll learn how to use mathematics to study population growth and conservation.*

Module Features

Assessment Options

STUDENT RESOURCES

COURSE OVERVIEW

THEME APPROACH

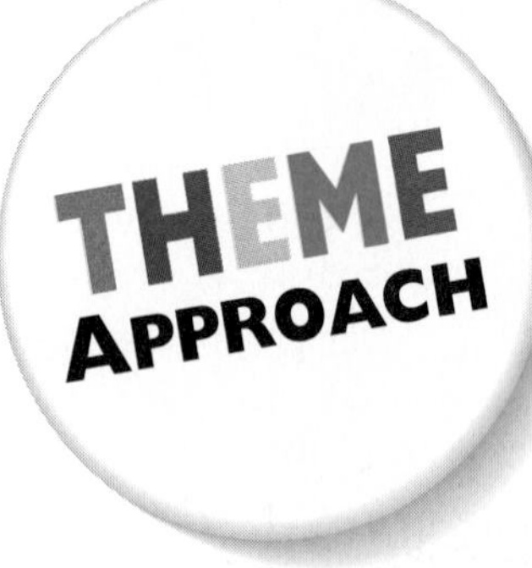

ORGANIZATION OF THE BOOK

This book contains eight modules. To get an overview of the modules and their themes, look at the Table of Contents starting on p. iv.

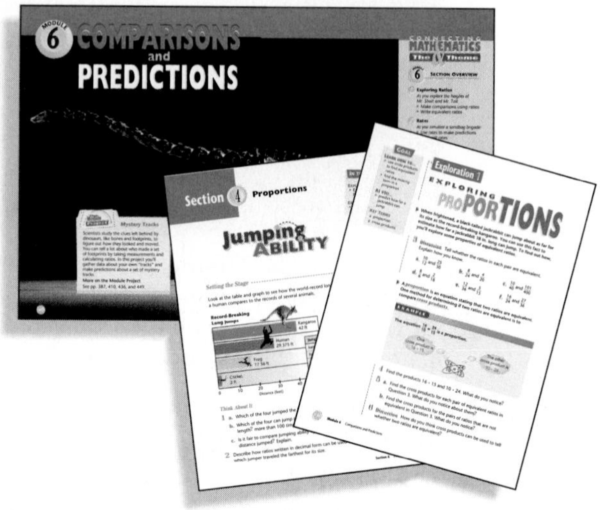

MODULES: 8 per book

Module 1, Module 2, Module 3, Module 4, Module 5, Module 6, Module 7, Module 8

SECTIONS: 5–6 per module

Section 1, Section 2, Section 3, Section 4, Section 5, Section 6

EXPLORATIONS: 1–3 per section

Exploration 1, Exploration 2

PRACTICE: for each exploration

Practice & Application Exercises

MODULE THEME & PROJECT

Each module's theme connects the mathematics you are learning to the real world. *Comparisons and Predictions* is the theme of Module 6. The Module Project that you'll work on is introduced at the beginning of the module.

Connecting Mathematics and the Theme
The math topics you'll be learning and the settings in which you'll be learning them.

MODULE 6
COMPARISONS and PREDICTIONS

The Module Project — Mystery Tracks

Scientists study the clues left behind by dinosaurs, like bones and footprints, to figure out how they looked and moved. You can tell a lot about who made a set of footprints by taking measurements and calculating ratios. In this project you'll gather data about your own "tracks" and make predictions about a set of mystery tracks.

More on the Module Project
See pp. 387, 410, 436, and 449.

378

CONNECTING MATHEMATICS & The Theme

MODULE 6 SECTION OVERVIEW

1 **Exploring Ratios**
As you explore the heights of Mr. Short and Mr. Tall:
- Make comparisons using ratios
- Write equivalent ratios

2 **Rates**
As you simulate a sandbag brigade:
- Use rates to make predictions
- Find unit rates

3 **Using Ratios**
As you find body ratios:
- Write a ratio as a decimal
- Use ratios and scatterplots to make predictions

4 **Proportions**
As you compare the jumping abilities of humans and animals:
- Use cross products to find equivalent ratios
- Write and use a proportion to solve a problem

5 **Geometry and Proportions**
As you look at how artists use

The Module Project
As you learn new math skills, you can apply them to your work on the Module Project. By the end of the module, you'll be able to complete the project and to present your results.

Beginning the Module Project — Mystery Tracks

Imagine searching for evidence of dinosaurs that lived millions of years ago. Do you picture finding a large bone, or even a whole skeleton? Surprisingly, some dinosaurs and other extinct animals are known only from the tracks they left behind. Footprints can provide several clues about an animal such as height, weight, age, and running speed.

Since dinosaur tracks are rare, you'll study your own "tracks" and learn how mathematics can be used to make predictions from them. Be sure to save the data you gather over the next few weeks. To complete the project, you'll try to discover who made a set of mystery tracks.

Measuring and Comparing Lengths Scientists measure dinosaur tracks in several ways. Some ways of measuring the tracks of dinosaurs that walked on two legs are shown.

SET UP
You will need:
- *metric ruler*
- *chalk or large newsprint and marker*

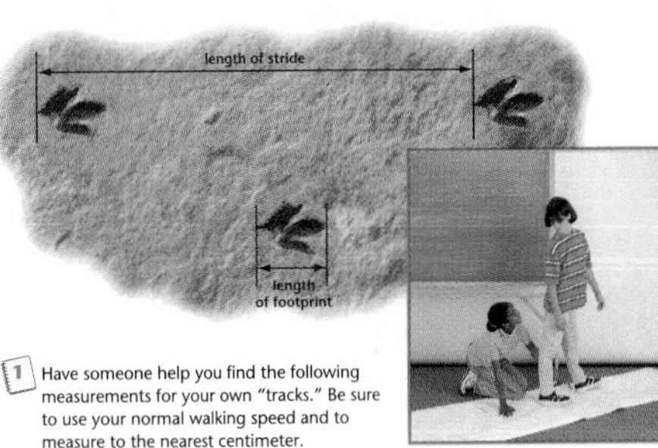

1 Have someone help you find the following measurements for your own "tracks." Be sure to use your normal walking speed and to measure to the nearest centimeter.
- the length of your footprint
- the length of your stride
- your height

2 Write the ratio of the length of your footprint to your height in three ways.

Section 1 Exploring Ratios  387

SECTION OVERVIEW

SECTION ORGANIZATION

The diagram below illustrates the organization of a section:

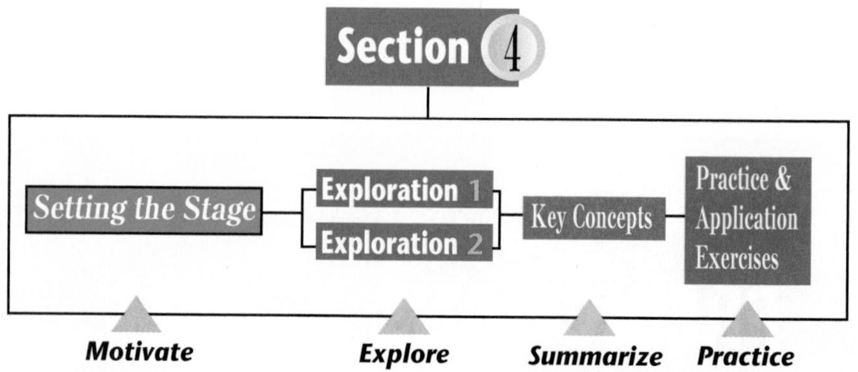

Section Title and Math Focus
The title of Section 4 is *Jumping Ability*. Its math focus is *Proportions*.

Setting the Stage

Look at the table and graph to see how the world-recor[d] a human compares to the records of several animals.

Setting the Stage begins with a reading, graph, activity, or game to introduce the section.

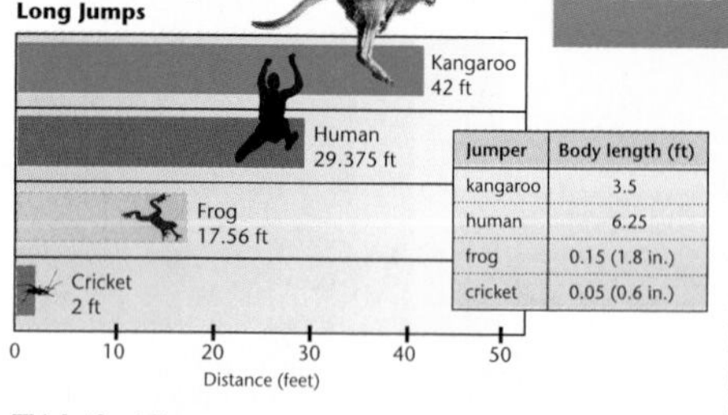

Jumper	Body length (ft)
kangaroo	3.5
human	6.25
frog	0.15 (1.8 in.)
cricket	0.05 (0.6 in.)

Think About It

1 a. Which of the four jumped the farthest?

b. Which of the four can jump more than 10 times its body length? more than 100 times?

c. Is it fair to compare jumping ability by examining just the distance jumped? Explain.

2 Describe how ratios written in decimal form can be used to identify which jumper traveled the farthest for its size.

Section 4 Proportions 413

EXPLORATIONS & KEY CONCEPTS

In the explorations you'll be actively involved in investigating math concepts, learning math skills, and solving problems.

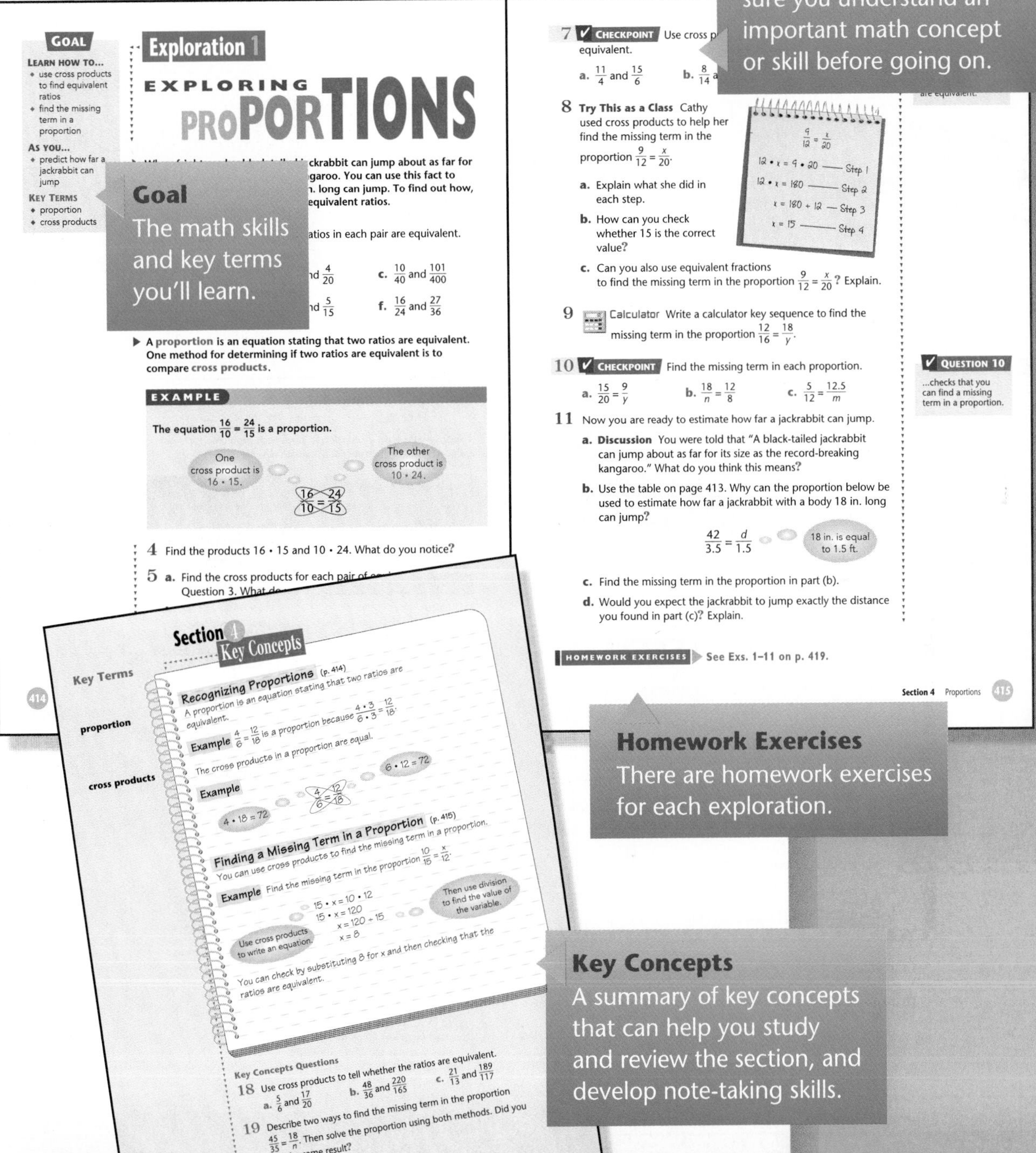

GOAL

LEARN HOW TO...
- use cross products to find equivalent ratios
- find the missing term in a proportion

AS YOU...
- predict how far a jackrabbit can jump

KEY TERMS
- proportion
- cross products

Exploration 1

EXPLORING PROPORTIONS

kangaroo. You can use this fact to ... long can jump. To find out how, ... equivalent ratios.

... atios in each pair are equivalent.

... nd $\frac{4}{20}$ **c.** $\frac{10}{40}$ and $\frac{101}{400}$

... nd $\frac{5}{15}$ **f.** $\frac{16}{24}$ and $\frac{27}{36}$

▶ A **proportion** is an equation stating that two ratios are equivalent. One method for determining if two ratios are equivalent is to compare **cross products**.

EXAMPLE

The equation $\frac{16}{10} = \frac{24}{15}$ is a proportion.

One cross product is 16 • 15.

The other cross product is 10 • 24.

4 Find the products 16 • 15 and 10 • 24. What do you notice?

5 **a.** Find the cross products for each pair of ... Question 3. What do ...

414

7 ✓ CHECKPOINT Use cross p... equivalent.

a. $\frac{11}{4}$ and $\frac{15}{6}$ **b.** $\frac{8}{14}$ a...

8 **Try This as a Class** Cathy used cross products to help her find the missing term in the proportion $\frac{9}{12} = \frac{x}{20}$.

$\frac{9}{12} = \frac{x}{20}$

$12 \cdot x = 9 \cdot 20$ — Step 1

$12 \cdot x = 180$ — Step 2

$x = 180 \div 12$ — Step 3

$x = 15$ — Step 4

a. Explain what she did in each step.

b. How can you check whether 15 is the correct value?

c. Can you also use equivalent fractions to find the missing term in the proportion $\frac{9}{12} = \frac{x}{20}$? Explain.

9 Calculator Write a calculator key sequence to find the missing term in the proportion $\frac{12}{16} = \frac{18}{y}$.

10 ✓ CHECKPOINT Find the missing term in each proportion.

a. $\frac{15}{20} = \frac{9}{y}$ **b.** $\frac{18}{n} = \frac{12}{8}$ **c.** $\frac{5}{12} = \frac{12.5}{m}$

✓ QUESTION 10 ...checks that you can find a missing term in a proportion.

11 Now you are ready to estimate how far a jackrabbit can jump.

a. Discussion You were told that "A black-tailed jackrabbit can jump about as far for its size as the record-breaking kangaroo." What do you think this means?

b. Use the table on page 413. Why can the proportion below be used to estimate how far a jackrabbit with a body 18 in. long can jump?

$\frac{42}{3.5} = \frac{d}{1.5}$ 18 in. is equal to 1.5 ft.

c. Find the missing term in the proportion in part (b).

d. Would you expect the jackrabbit to jump exactly the distance you found in part (c)? Explain.

HOMEWORK EXERCISES ▶ See Exs. 1–11 on p. 419.

Section 4 Proportions 415

Section 4 Key Concepts

Key Terms

proportion

cross products

Recognizing Proportions (p. 414)

A proportion is an equation stating that two ratios are equivalent.

Example $\frac{4}{6} = \frac{12}{18}$ is a proportion because $\frac{4 \cdot 3}{6 \cdot 3} = \frac{12}{18}$.

The cross products in a proportion are equal.

Example $4 \cdot 18 = 72$ $6 \cdot 12 = 72$

Finding a Missing Term in a Proportion (p. 415)

You can use cross products to find the missing term in a proportion.

Example Find the missing term in the proportion $\frac{10}{15} = \frac{x}{12}$.

$15 \cdot x = 10 \cdot 12$

$15 \cdot x = 120$

$x = 120 \div 15$

$x = 8$

Use cross products to write an equation.

Then use division to find the value of the variable.

You can check by substituting 8 for x and then checking that the ratios are equivalent.

Key Concepts Questions

18 Use cross products to tell whether the ratios are equivalent.

a. $\frac{5}{6}$ and $\frac{17}{20}$ **b.** $\frac{48}{36}$ and $\frac{220}{165}$ **c.** $\frac{21}{13}$ and $\frac{189}{117}$

19 Describe two ways to find the missing term in the proportion $\frac{45}{35} = \frac{18}{n}$. Then solve the proportion using both methods. Did you get the same result?

418 Module 6 Comparisons and Predictions

Checkpoint
A place to pause to make sure you understand an important math concept or skill before going on.

Goal
The math skills and key terms you'll learn.

Homework Exercises
There are homework exercises for each exploration.

Key Concepts
A summary of key concepts that can help you study and review the section, and develop note-taking skills.

SECTION OVERVIEW

PRACTICE & APPLICATION

Practice and Application Exercises will give you a chance to practice the skills and concepts in the explorations and apply them in solving many types of problems.

Balanced Practice
These exercises develop numerical and problem solving skills, and the ability to write about and discuss mathematics.

Section 4
Practice & Application Exercises

Find all the equivalent ratios in each list.

1. $\frac{15}{60}, \frac{24}{32}, \frac{75}{300}, \frac{21}{28}, \frac{3.5}{14}$
2. $\frac{6}{7}, \frac{10}{12.5}, \frac{30}{35}, \frac{16}{20}, \frac{40}{45}$

Find the missing term in each proposition.

3. $\frac{3}{12} = \frac{5}{n}$
4. $\frac{4}{24} = \frac{6}{x}$
5. $\frac{5}{15} = \frac{y}{24}$
6. $\frac{s}{7} = \frac{3.5}{1.4}$
7. $\frac{20}{8} = \frac{4.5}{d}$
8. $\frac{5}{m} = \frac{12.5}{40}$
9. $16 : 3 = 64 : r$
10. $p : 15 = 4 : 9$
11. $7 : w = 56 : 40$

12. Choose the proportions that have been set up correctly for solving the problem.

The *Water Arc* in Chicago, Illinois, shoots about 21,000 gal of water over the Chicago River during each 10-minute show. How many gallons of water does it shoot in four minutes?

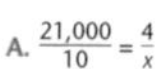
A. $\frac{21,000}{10} = \frac{4}{x}$

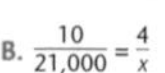
B. $\frac{10}{21,000} = \frac{4}{x}$

C. $\frac{21,000}{10} = \frac{x}{4}$

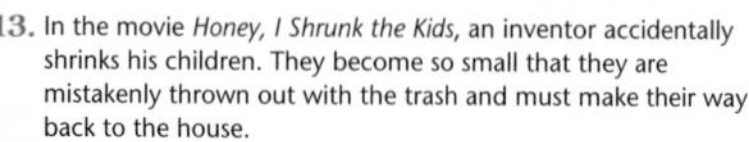

13. In the movie *Honey, I Shrunk the Kids*, an inventor accidentally shrinks his children. They become so small that they are mistakenly thrown out with the trash and must make their way back to the house.

a. **Writing** Nicky explains to the other children, "We are exactly 64 feet from the house, which is the equivalent of 3.2 miles." What does Nicky mean?

b. Nicky can walk one mile in 20 min at his normal height. To predict how long it will take him to walk to the house at his new height, a proportion has been labeled. Fill in the values you know. Use a variable for the value you do not know.

Ratio for 1 mile		Ratio for 3.2 miles
$\frac{\text{distance}}{\text{time}}$	=	$\frac{\text{distance}}{\text{time}}$

c. Find the missing term in your proportion.

14. **Challenge** In Exercise 13 Nicky's height was roughly $\frac{1}{4}$ in. Estimate Nicky's normal height. (Remember that 1 mi = 5280 ft.)

15. **Probability Connection** A die lands on 2 in 5 out of 24 rolls. Find the experimental probability of landing on 2. Use your answer and a proportion to predict the number of times a die will land on 2 in 60 rolls.

420 **Module 6** Comparisons and Predictions

If appropriate, use a proportion to solve each problem. If it is not appropriate to use a proportion, explain why not.

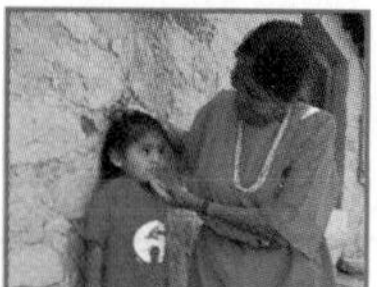

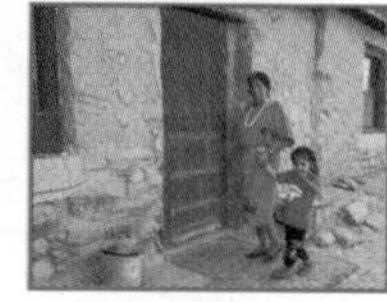

16. Three-year-old Mina is 32 in. tall. Mina grew 4 in. in one year. How tall will Mina be in 18 years?

17. For every 4 steps Mina takes, her grandmother takes 3 steps. How many steps will Mina walk if her grandmother walks 54 steps?

Reflecting on the Section

Be prepared to report on the following topic in class.

18. a. Write a problem about your everyday life that can be solved using a proportion. Be sure your problem is one in which it is appropriate to use a proportion.

b. Solve the problem you wrote for part (a). Be sure to include an explanation of how you solved it.

Oral Report
Exercise 18 checks that you know how to write a proportion to solve a problem.

Spiral Review

19. a. The mean of the ratios for *distance around the thumb to distance around the neck* for some people is 0.26. Write a "nice" fraction that is close to the mean. (Module 6, p. 405)

b. Predict the distance around the neck of a person whose thumb measurement is 3.75 in.

Draw an example of each type of angle. (Module 1, p. 22)

20. acute 21. obtuse 22. straight 23. right

24. Trace the figure. Then find three ways to divide the figure into eight

421

Reflecting on the Section
helps you pull together what you've learned in the form of an oral report, journal writing, visual thinking, research, or a discussion.

ADDITIONAL PRACTICE

At the end of every section, you'll find Extra Skill Practice. You can use these exercises to check that you understand important skills before starting the next section.

Section 4 Extra Skill Practice

Use cross products to tell whether the ratios are equivalent.

1. $\frac{12}{18}$ and $\frac{4}{6}$
2. $\frac{8}{10}$ and $\frac{12}{15}$
3. $\frac{3}{50}$ and $\frac{6}{75}$
4. $\frac{1.5}{3}$ and $\frac{10}{20}$

Find the missing term in each proportion.

5. $\frac{n}{8} = \frac{12}{2}$
6. $x : 5 = 27 : 45$
7. $\frac{9}{13} = \frac{27}{r}$
8. $\frac{8}{12} = \frac{12}{g}$
9. $\frac{d}{4} = \frac{13}{26}$
10. $\frac{2}{n} = \frac{3}{9}$
11. $3 : 8 = k : 20$
12. $\frac{2.5}{5} = \frac{c}{8}$

If appropriate, use a proportion to solve each problem. If it is not appropriate to use a proportion, explain why not.

13. Eight newspapers cost \$3.60. How much will six newspapers cost?

...vhite cars drove past Mark's house from 6:00 to 9:00 A.M. ...many will pass his house in twenty-four hours?

...used four yards of ribbon to make six bows. How many yards ...bon will she need to make ten more bows?

Standardized Testing develops your ability to answer questions in different formats: multiple-choice, open-ended, free response, and performance task.

...ardized Testing ▶ Multiple Choice

...hich values of x and y will the proportion $\frac{x}{25} = \frac{15}{y}$ be correct?

I. $x = 20, y = 20$ II. $x = 12.5, y = 30$ III. $x = 100, y = 5$ IV. $x = 5, y = 75$

A I only B IV only C I and III D II and IV

2. For which problems is it appropriate and correct to find the solution using the proportion $\frac{x}{75} = \frac{10}{45}$?
   I. Darren read 10 pages of a book in 45 minutes. Predict how many pages he can read in 12 minutes.
   II. Sheri bought 10 tapes for the school music library for \$45. If the tapes all have the same price, how many can she buy for \$75?
   III. Elsa drank 10 oz of water after she finished a 45 min. exercise class. How much do you think she will drink after a 75 min class?

A I only B II only C I and III  D II and III

422 **Module 6** Comparisons and Predictions

20. **Writing** Gloria Jones drives 15 mi to work in about h... Write her rate of travel in miles per hour. Why do you... rate is called her "average" speed?

Reflecting ▶ on the Section

Write your response to Exercise 21 in your journal.

21. At top speed, a zebra can run 176 ft in 3 seconds, a r... can run 220 ft in 10 seconds, and a cheetah can run 8... second. Which animal is the fastest? Which is the slow...

Spiral ▶ Review

22. The ratio of triangles to squares is 6 to 10. Make a ske... an equivalent ratio. (Module 6, p. 384)

Calculator **Write each fraction as a decimal rounded to the nearest hundredth.** (Module 3, p. 202)

23. $\frac{5}{6}$
24. $\frac{12}{23}$
25. $\frac{45}{62}$
26. $\frac{84}{116}$

Find the mean for each set of data. (Module 3, p. 202)

27. 75, 86, 73, 80, 86, 80
28. 48, 52, 75, 47, 83, 48

Extension ▶▶

A Doubling Rate

29. Suppose you put \$100 in a bank account where your money doubles every ten years. The table shows how it will grow.

Number of years	0	10	20	30	40
Money in account	\$100	\$200	\$400	\$800	\$1600

Doubling Money in an Account

a. Copy the coordinate grid and plot the data shown in the table. Connect the points in order from left to right.

b. How is the rate of growth for money in the account different from other rates in the section? (*Hint:* Are the ratios of years to money in the account equivalent?)

Section 2 Rates 395

Extension problems challenge you to extend what you have learned and to apply it in a new setting.

TECHNOLOGY OVERVIEW

CALCULATORS & COMPUTERS

There are many opportunities to use calculators, as well as mental-math and paper-and-pencil methods. Special Technology pages show you how to use computer programs to explore concepts and solve problems in the module.

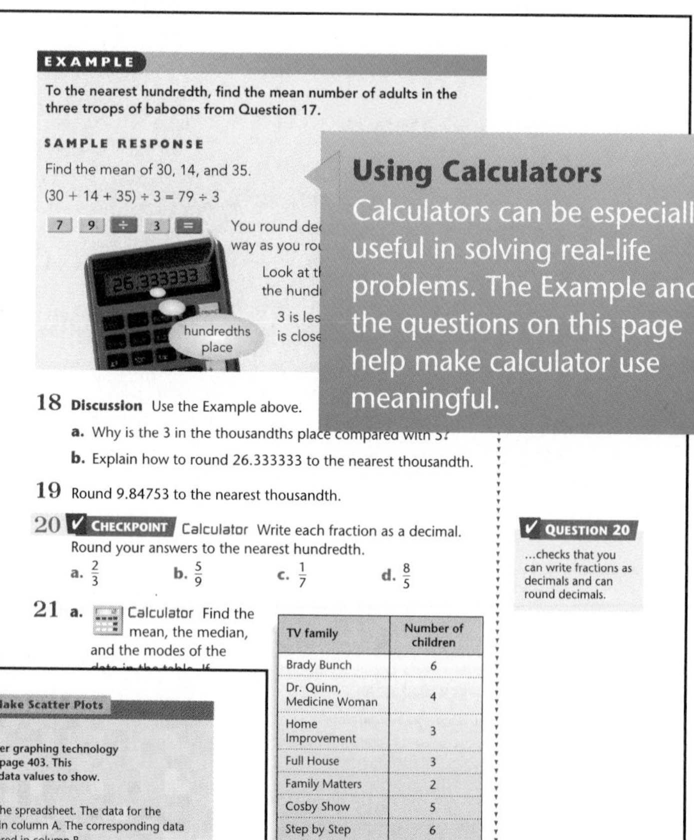

EXAMPLE

To the nearest hundredth, find the mean number of adults in the three troops of baboons from Question 17.

SAMPLE RESPONSE

Find the mean of 30, 14, and 35.

(30 + 14 + 35) ÷ 3 = 79 ÷ 3

7 9 ÷ 3 =

You round de
way as you ro

Look at t
the hund

3 is les
is close

hundredths place

18 **Discussion** Use the Example above.

a. Why is the 3 in the thousandths place compared with 3?

b. Explain how to round 26.333333 to the nearest thousandth.

19 Round 9.84753 to the nearest thousandth.

20 ✓ CHECKPOINT Calculator Write each fraction as a decimal. Round your answers to the nearest hundredth.

a. $\frac{2}{3}$ **b.** $\frac{5}{9}$ **c.** $\frac{1}{7}$ **d.** $\frac{8}{5}$

✓ QUESTION 20

...checks that you can write fractions as decimals and can round decimals.

21 **a.** Calculator Find the mean, the median, and the modes of the

TV family	Number of children
Brady Bunch	6
Dr. Quinn, Medicine Woman	4
Home Improvement	3
Full House	3
Family Matters	2
Cosby Show	5
Step by Step	6

xs. 9–29 on pp. 203–205.

Section 4 Mean, Median, Mode 201

Using Calculators

Calculators can be especially useful in solving real-life problems. The Example and the questions on this page help make calculator use meaningful.

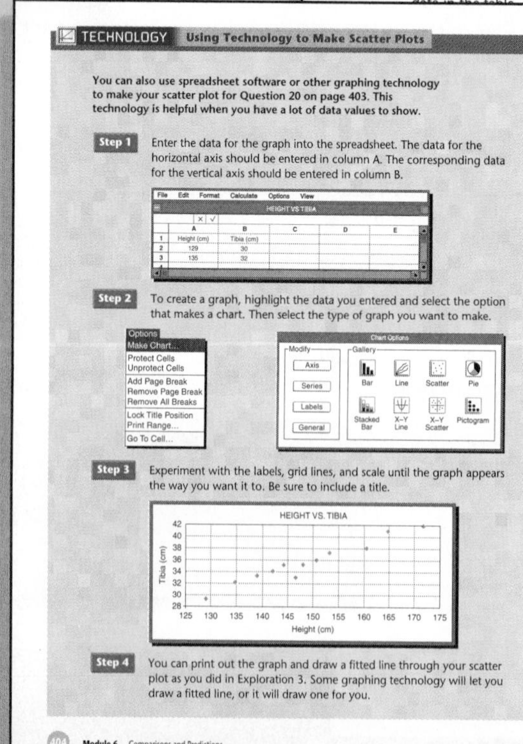

TECHNOLOGY **Using Technology to Make Scatter Plots**

You can also use spreadsheet software or other graphing technology to make your scatter plot for Question 20 on page 403. This technology is helpful when you have a lot of data values to show.

Step 1 Enter the data for the graph into the spreadsheet. The data for the horizontal axis should be entered in column A. The corresponding data for the vertical axis should be entered in column B.

	A	B	C	D	E
1	Height (cm)	Tibia (cm)			
2	129	30			
3	135	32			

Step 2 To create a graph, highlight the data you entered and select the option that makes a chart. Then select the type of graph you want to make.

Step 3 Experiment with the labels, grid lines, and scale until the graph appears the way you want it to. Be sure to include a title.

Step 4 You can print out the graph and draw a fitted line through your scatter plot as you did in Exploration 3. Some graphing technology will let you draw a fitted line, or it will draw one for you.

404 Module 6 Comparisons and Predictions

Using Computers

Technology pages illustrate the use of spreadsheet, graphing, statistical, probability, and drawing software.

ASSESSMENT OVERVIEW

ASSESSMENT & PORTFOLIOS

In each module there are a number of questions and projects that help you check your progress and reflect on what you have learned. These pages are listed under *Assessment Options* in the Table of Contents.

E^2 stands for Extended Exploration — a problem solving project that you'll want to add to your portfolio.

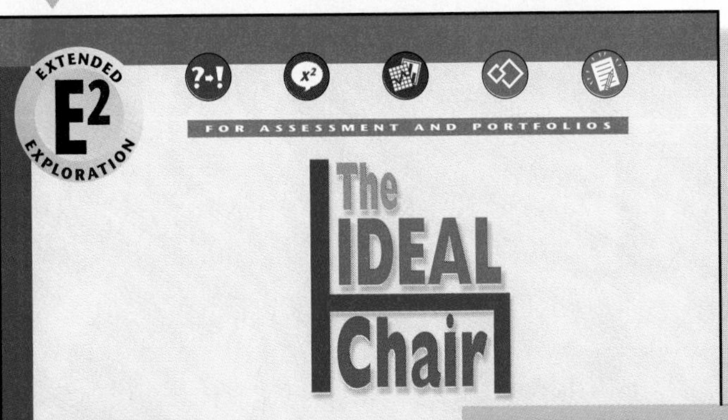
EXTENDED E^2 EXPLORATION

FOR ASSESSMENT AND PORTFOLIOS

The IDEAL Chair

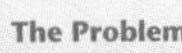
SET UP You will need: • *ruler* • *string*

The Situation

Sometimes it is hard to find a comfortable ch... your classroom are different from the chairs ... The chairs in a restaurant are probably differ... home.

The Problem

Design the ideal school chair for students in ...

Something to Think About

- What things should be considered in designing the ideal school chair for students in your grade level?
- How might you find data for each of the things you will consider?
- What are some ways to keep your ideas and data organized?

Present Your Results

Describe your solution and the methods you used to find it. Show any charts, tables, sketches or models you prepared. Are there other possible solutions? Tell what you tried that worked, and what you tried that did not work. What did you do when you were stuck?

412 Module 6 Comparisons...

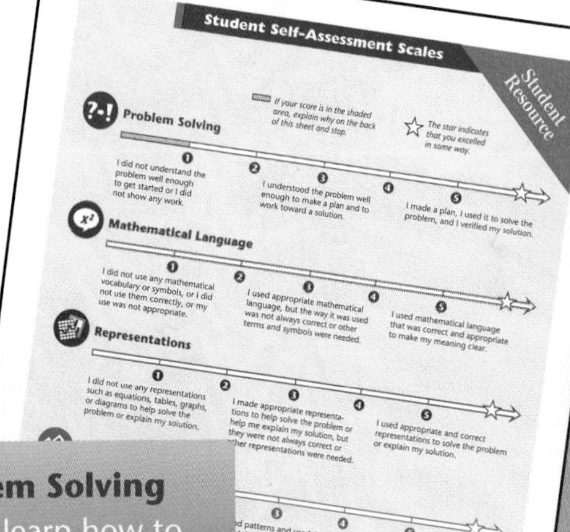
Student Self-Assessment Scales

Student Resource

If your score is in the shaded area, explain why on the back of this sheet and stop.

The star indicates that you excelled in some way.

Problem Solving

1 I did not understand the problem well enough to get started or I did not show any work.
2
3 I understood the problem well enough to make a plan and to work toward a solution.
4
5 I made a plan, I used it to solve the problem, and I verified my solution.

Mathematical Language

1 I did not use any mathematical vocabulary or symbols, or I did not use them correctly, or my use was not appropriate.
2
3 I used appropriate mathematical language, but the way it was used was not always correct or other terms and symbols were needed.
4
5 I used mathematical language that was correct and appropriate to make my meaning clear.

Representations

1 I did not use any representations such as equations, tables, graphs, or diagrams to help solve the problem or explain my solution.
2
3 I made appropriate representations to help solve the problem or help me explain my solution, but they were not always correct or ...her representations were needed.
4
5 I used appropriate and correct representations to solve the problem or explain my solution.

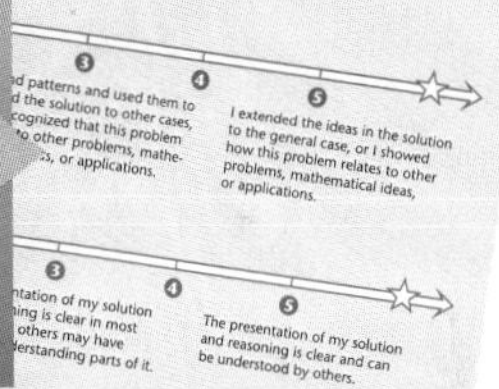
3 ...d patterns and used them to ...d the solution to other cases, ...cognized that this problem ...to other problems, mathe...s, or applications.
4
5 I extended the ideas in the solution to the general case, or I showed how this problem relates to other problems, mathematical ideas, or applications.

3 ...ntation of my solution ...ning is clear in most ... others may have ...erstanding parts of it.
4
5 The presentation of my solution and reasoning is clear and can be understood by others.

Section 2 Lines, Angles, and Triangles 21

Assessing Problem Solving

In Module 1 you'll learn how to use the Student Self-Assessment Scales. They will help you become a better problem solver.

MODULE 6 Review and Assessment

You will need: • *protractor* (Ex. 15)

Write each ratio in three ways. (Sec. 1, Explor. 1)

1. the ratio of red squares to blue squares
2. the ratio of blue squares to white squares

Tell whether or not the ratios are equivalent. (Sec. 1, Explor.1)

3. $\frac{2}{5}$ and $\frac{10}{15}$ 4. 5 : 8 and 15 : 24 5. $\frac{3.3}{2.2}$ and $\frac{12}{8}$

6. At Super Sub, sub sandwiches are sold by the foot and you are charged the same amount for each foot. Suppose a 3-foot-long sub costs $18.00. (Sec. 2, Explor. 1)

Module Review and Assessment

Each module ends with exercises to help you review and assess what you've learned.

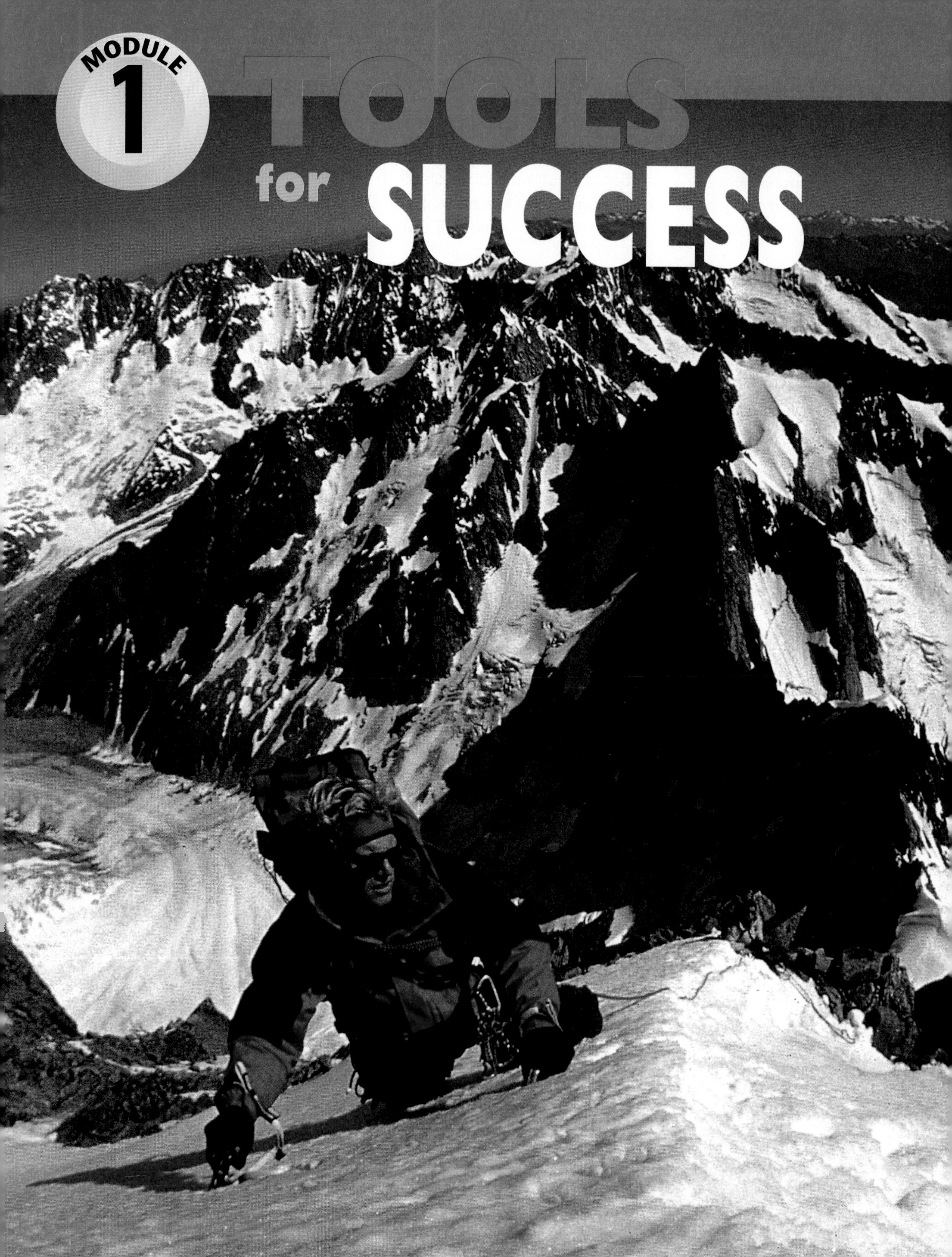
MODULE
1
TOOLS
for SUCCESS

CONNECTING MATHEMATICS & The Theme

MODULE 1 SECTION OVERVIEW

1 Patterns and Sequences

As you use observation tools with animal tracks, comets, and blocks:

- Find a rule to extend a pattern.
- Write a general rule for a sequence.

2 Lines, Angles, and Triangles

As you use language in The China Year *and in a drawing game:*

- Name basic geometric figures.
- Classify angles and triangles.
- Decide when triangles can be formed.

3 A Problem Solving Approach

As you play a card swapping game:

- Learn a 4-step approach to solve problems.
- Use several problem solving strategies.

4 Estimation, Mental Math, or a Calculator

As you choose tools for a school election and an arithmetic race:

- Estimate by rounding.
- Decide when to use estimation, mental math, or a calculator.
- Learn the order of operations.

5 Using Visuals

As you apply teamwork:

- Use visuals to help find solutions.

6 Problem Solving Skills

As you explore problems about the World Cup and about string art:

- Learn to assess and improve your problem solving.

INTERNET
To learn more about the theme:
http://www.mlmath.com

The Module Project: A Puzzling Problem

You'll apply mathematical ideas you have learned as you discover how to solve the *30 Pennies in a Row* problem. You'll explore different approaches that can also help you with the Extended Exploration (E^2) feature in each module and with other problems throughout the year. You'll share your solution in a group presentation.

More on the Module Project

See pp. 27, 39, 62, 72, and 74–75.

Section 1 Patterns and Sequences

IN THIS SECTION

EXPLORATION 1
- Extending Patterns

EXPLORATION 2
- Analyzing Sequences

Observation Tools

Setting the Stage

In this module you'll begin to use several tools that will help you be a successful problem solver. Below, tracker Tom Brown, Jr., tells how his best friend's grandfather Stalking Wolf, an Apache tracker, taught him to solve the mysteries left behind by animal tracks.

> Stalking Wolf gave me the tools to track the mystery to its source.... He taught me to see and to hear...how to know and how to understand....
>
> The vision of the world given me by Stalking Wolf has become a window into time. The more tracks I see, the clearer the picture of the animal becomes until I can see him moving as he moved a minute, an hour, a month before I came along.... I see the animal itself laying down the mystery of its coming and going.

▶ **Examine the animal tracks below carefully. The tracks are drawn to the same scale, about $\frac{3}{8}$ actual size.**

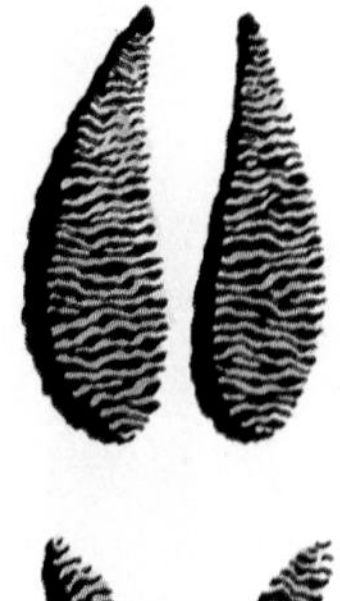

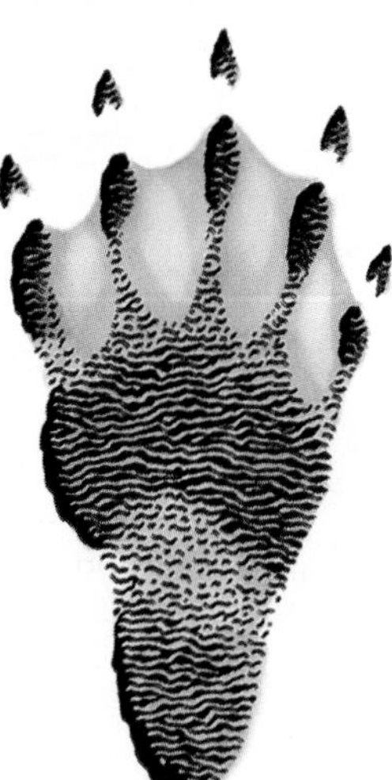

Think About It

1 What are the tools an animal tracker needs?

2 Use the tracks on page 2.

a. How are some of the tracks alike? How are they different?

b. What can you tell about the animals that left these tracks?

c. Guess what animal made each of these tracks.

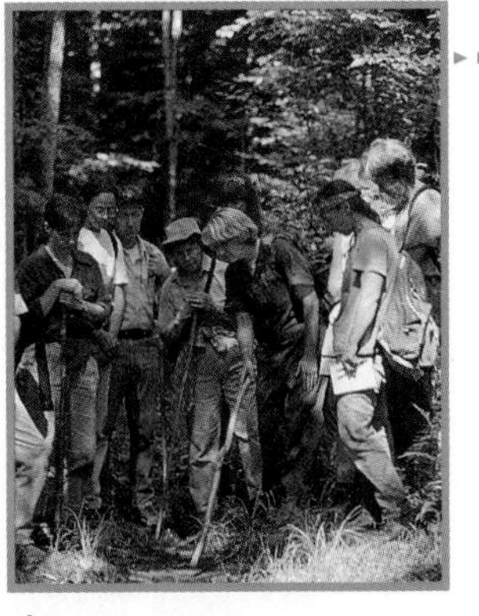

Naturalist Susan Morse trains volunteer trackers. They gather data which is used to protect animals' homes.

▶ **In this section, you'll explore patterns in mathematics and in nature. Like a tracker, you'll need to look carefully to see how shapes and numbers are alike and different.**

Exploration 1

Extending PATTERNS

GOAL

LEARN HOW TO...
- find a rule to extend a pattern
- make a table to organize your work

AS YOU...
- work with pattern blocks and predict comet sightings

KEY TERMS
- rule
- sequence
- term
- term number

SET UP *Work with a partner. You will need pattern blocks.*

3 **a.** Use your pattern blocks to construct the pattern shown below. Extend the pattern to include seven blocks.

b. To create or extend a pattern, you use a **rule**. What is your rule for the pattern above?

4 **a.** Use pattern blocks to create your own pattern.

b. Have your partner extend the pattern by trying to guess your rule and placing the next two blocks.

5 **Discussion** What did you look for when you tried to discover the rule for a pattern?

6 For each of the following:

- Look for a pattern.
- Give the next two entries in the list.
- Explain the rule you used.

The three dots tell you the pattern continues in the same way.

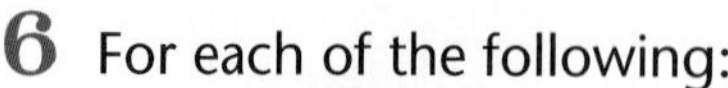

a. 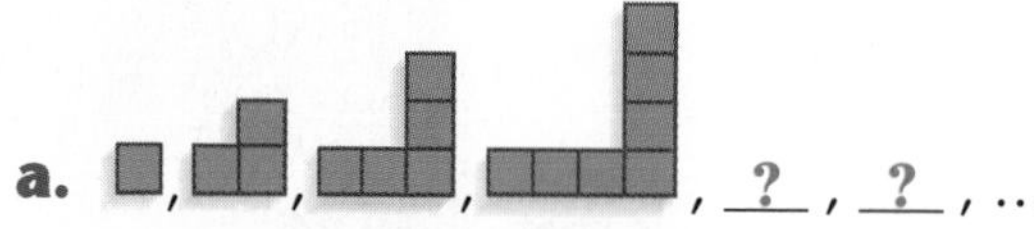 , ?, ?, ...

b. 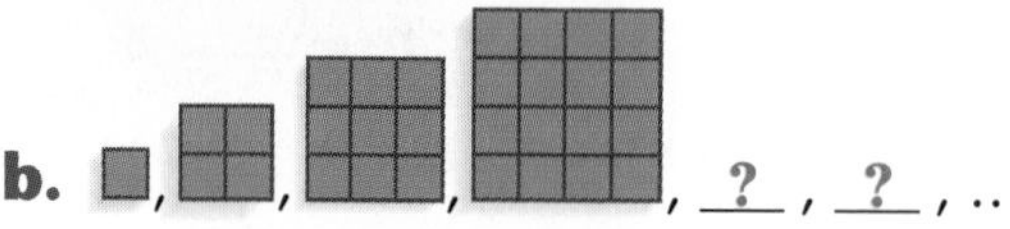 , ?, ?, ...

FOR ▶ HELP with *whole number place value*, see **TOOLBOX, p. 589**

c. 4, 40, 400, 4000, ?, ?, ...

d. 1, 4, 9, 16, ?, ?, ...

e. 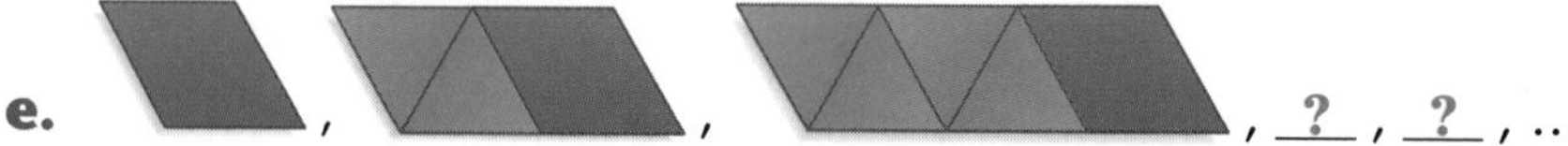 , ?, ?, ...

f. one, ten, hundred, thousand, ?, ?, ...

7 **Discussion** Are any of the patterns in Question 6 related to each other? If so, which ones? Explain.

▶ **Looking at Sequences** **Edmund Halley predicted the return of a comet by discovering a pattern in a list of dates. A comet he saw in 1682 traveled a path similar to that of comets seen by other people in 1456, 1531, and 1607. He put these dates into an ordered list, or a sequence.**

▲ The English astronomer Edmund Halley developed the theory that comets orbit the sun in elliptical paths.

This is a sequence.

8 What pattern do you think Halley saw in the sequence?

9 Halley decided that all the sightings were of the same comet. He successfully predicted the comet would return about every 76 years. When did the comet next return?

▶ **Each number or object in a sequence is called a term and can be labeled with a term number. The term number tells you the order or position of the term in the sequence.**

The **2nd term** in the sequence is **1531**.

1456, **1531**, 1607, 1682, ...

10 What is the next term in the sequence above? What is its term number?

▶ **Using a Table You can use a table to help organize the terms and term numbers of a sequence.**

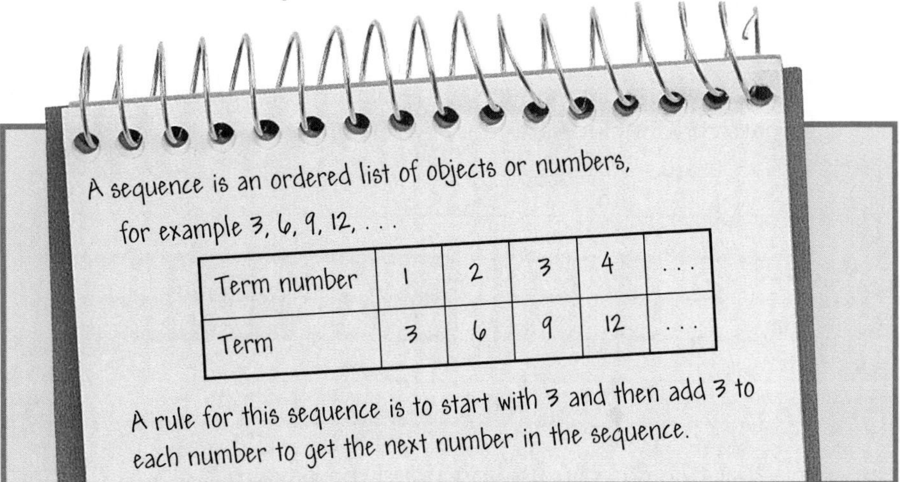
A sequence is an ordered list of objects or numbers, for example 3, 6, 9, 12, . . .

Term number	1	2	3	4	. . .
Term	3	6	9	12	. . .

A rule for this sequence is to start with 3 and then add 3 to each number to get the next number in the sequence.

11 What would be the fifth term in the table above?

12 ✓ **CHECKPOINT** Make a table showing the term numbers and terms of each sequence. Then find the next two terms of each sequence.

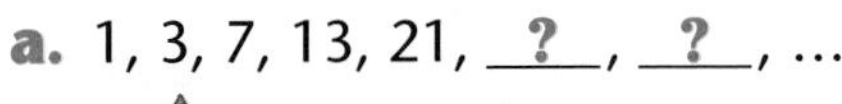
a. 1, 3, 7, 13, 21, ?, ?, ...

b.
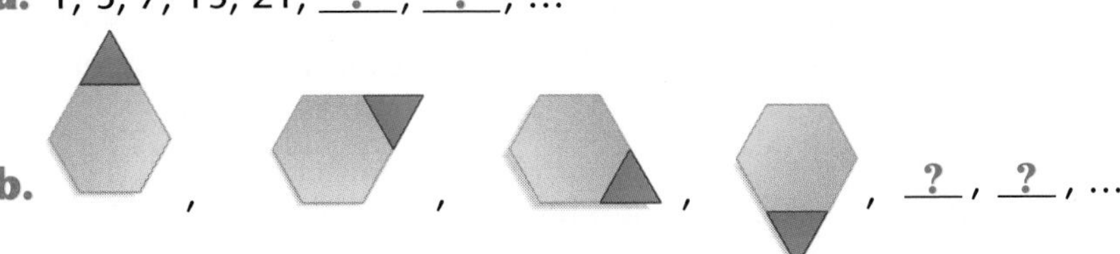
, ?, ?, ...

✓ **QUESTION 12**

...checks that you can set up a table to help you examine and extend a sequence.

13 Patterns in nature are not always exact, for example, the return of Halley's comet. Disturbances along its path cause slight time differences. Halley's comet returns about every 76 years. When may you be able to see it?

HOMEWORK EXERCISES See Exs. 1–9 on pp. 9–10.

GOAL

LEARN HOW TO...
- write a general rule for a sequence

AS YOU...
- explore patterns on grid paper

KEY TERM
- general rule

Exploration 2

ANALYZING SEQUENCES

SET UP *You will need graph paper.*

▶ **A table can help you see the relationship between the term numbers and the terms of a sequence.**

14 **a.** Using graph paper, sketch the pattern below. Extend the pattern to include the next two shapes.

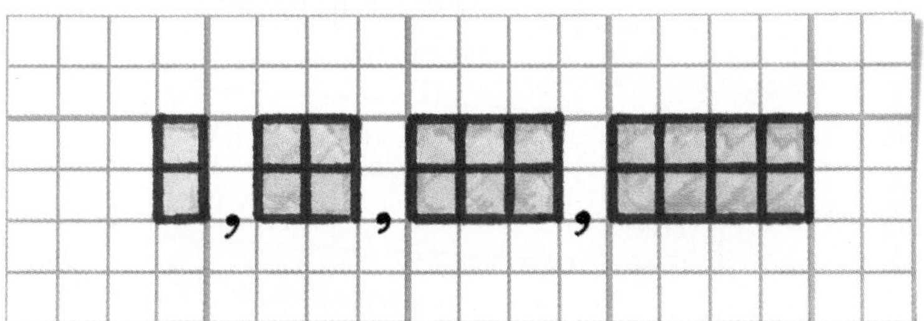

b. What rule did you use to extend the pattern?

15 **a.** You can form a sequence of numbers by counting the blocks in each shape above. Copy and fill in the table.

Term number	1	2	3	4	5	6
Term	2	4	6	?	?	?

b. If the sequence of numbers continues, what is the 7th term? To check, use your rule from Question 14(b) to sketch the shape.

16 **Discussion** How is each term of the table in Question 15 related to its term number?

▶ **Finding a General Rule** **When you describe how to find any term of a sequence you are giving a general rule for the sequence.**

17 Use the general rule you found in Question 16 to find the 100th term of the number sequence.

Use this sequence of shapes to answer Questions 18–23.

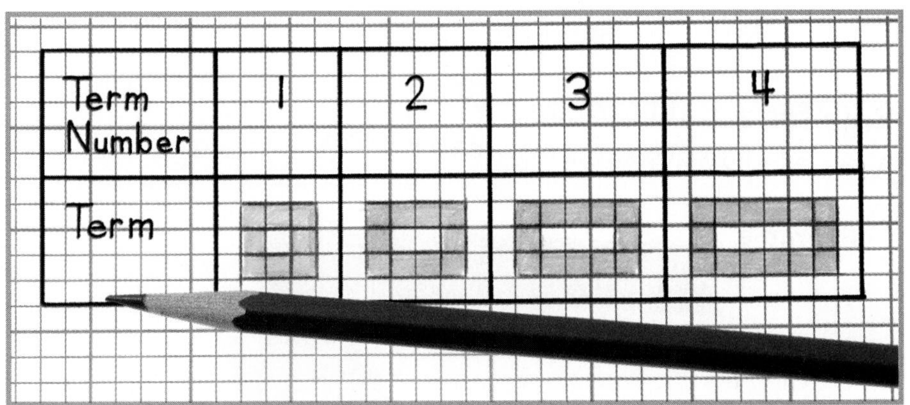

18 Copy the table and extend it to include the next three terms.

19 Look at the third term of the sequence.

a. How many shaded squares are there directly above the white space? directly below the white space? directly above and below the white space?

b. How does the total number of shaded squares directly above and below the white space relate to the term number?

c. How many shaded squares are at the two ends of the third term?

d. Is the number of shaded squares at the ends the same for the other terms?

20 **Try This as a Class** Explain how to sketch the 12th term.

21 A number sequence can be formed by counting the shaded squares in each shape above. Copy and complete the table. Then describe the number sequence that develops.

Term number	1	2	3	4	5	6
Term	8	10	12	?	?	?

22 **Discussion** Describe two ways to find the 20th term of the number sequence above.

23 ✓ **CHECKPOINT** Use the number sequence in Question 21. Write a general rule to find any term from its term number.

✓ **QUESTION 23**

...checks that you can write a general rule for a sequence.

HOMEWORK EXERCISES See Exs. 10–15 on pp. 10–11.

Section 1 Key Concepts

Key Terms

rule

sequence

term

term number

general rule

Rule for a Pattern (pp. 3–4)

A rule tells how to create or extend a pattern.

Example

A rule for this pattern is to repeat .

Sequences (pp. 4–7)

A sequence is an ordered list of numbers or objects.

Example

5, **10**, 15, 20, 25, ...

The **2nd term** in the sequence is **10**.

Each number or object of a sequence is a term.
The position of each term can be labeled with a term number.

A table can help you see how the term numbers and terms of a sequence are related and find a general rule.

Example

Term number	1	2	3	4	5
Term	5	10	15	20	25

general rule:

Term number x 5 = term

or

Start with 5. Add 5 to each term to get the next term.

24 **Key Concept Question** Make a table for the sequence 15, 25, 35, 45, ... Extend it to include the next two terms. Then write a general rule for the sequence.

Section 1 Practice & Application Exercises

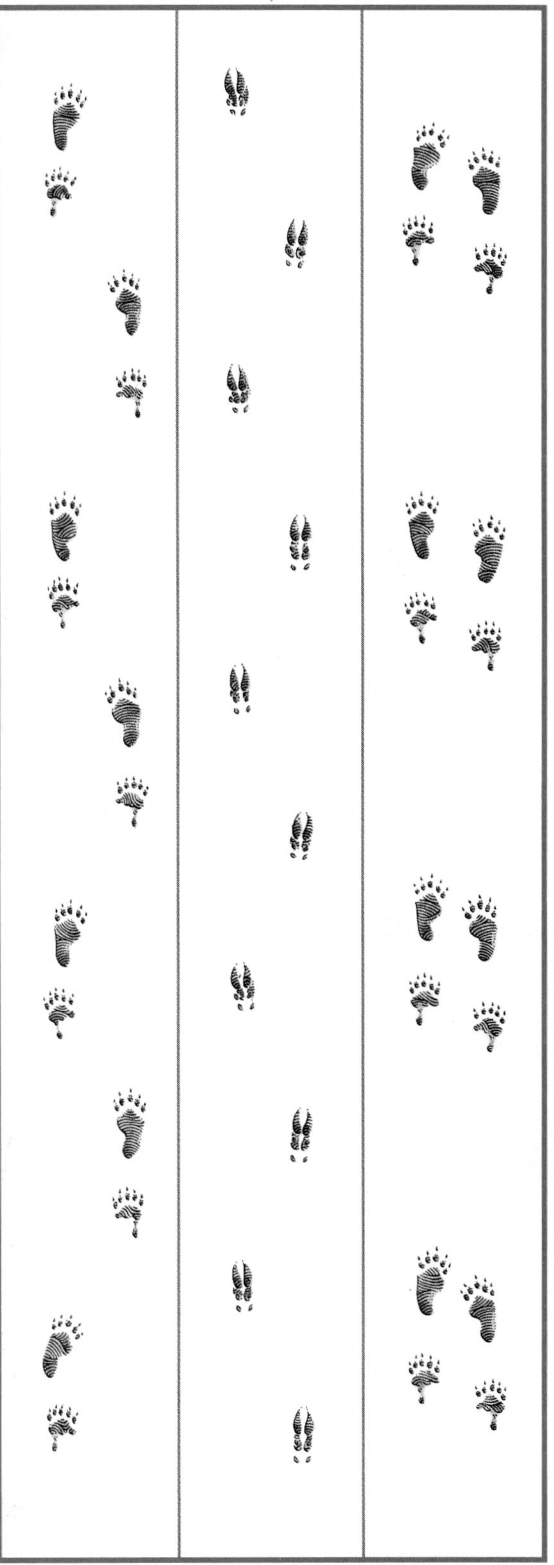

1. a. **Animal Tracking** Guess what animal made each set of tracks. Could any have been made by the same animal? If so, which ones?

   b. There is a repeating pattern of footprints and spaces within each set of tracks. Choose one set of tracks and sketch a section that repeats.

In Exercises 2–5, look for a pattern and replace each __?__ with the correct term. Describe the rule you used for each sequence.

2. 7, 14, 21, 28, __?__, __?__, __?__, __?__, 63

3. 99, 90, 81, 72, __?__, __?__, __?__, __?__, 27

4. $\frac{1}{2}, \frac{1}{4}, \frac{1}{6}, \frac{1}{8}$, __?__, __?__, __?__, __?__, $\frac{1}{18}$

5. •X, Ẋ, X•, X̣, __?__, __?__, __?__, __?__, •X

6. At the end of February Ben began to save for a $240 mountain bike. At that time he had $113 in his savings account. His savings increased to $138 in late March and $163 in late April. If his savings pattern continues, when will he be able to buy the bike?

7. A middle school class schedule forms a sequence. Each period is the same length. The first three periods begin at 7:40 A.M., 8:30 A.M., and 9:20 A.M.

   a. What rule does the class schedule follow?

   b. Make a table showing the term numbers and terms of the sequence of times. Using your rule from part (a), extend the table to find what time 7th period will begin.

8. Jimi and Adam both extended the sequence 2, 4, 8, ... Did they both extend the sequence correctly? Explain.

Jimi

2, 4, 8, 16, 32, 64, 128, ...

Adam

2, 4, 8, 14, 22, 32, 44, ...

9. **Science** Plants and animals are made up of tiny cells you can only see under a microscope. The pictures show a new starfish starting to grow from a single cell. The cell divides to form two cells. Then each of the new cells divides into two cells, and so on.

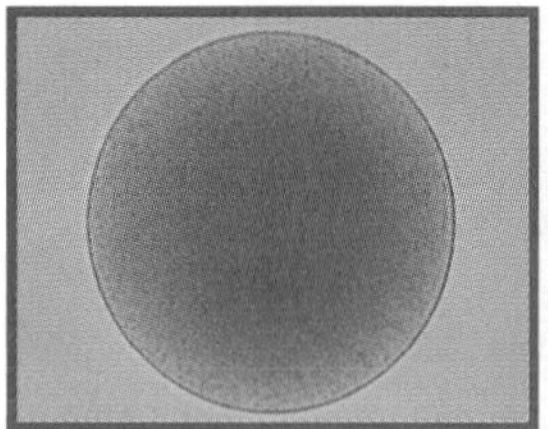
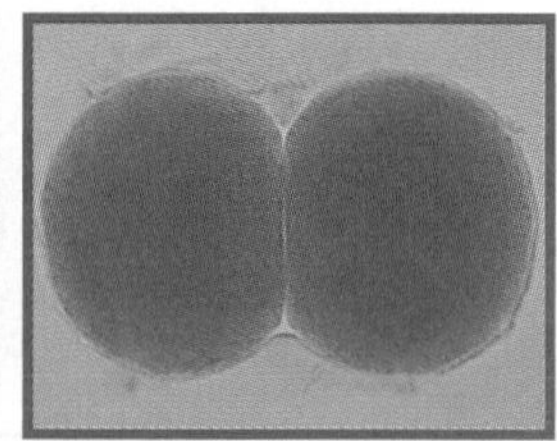
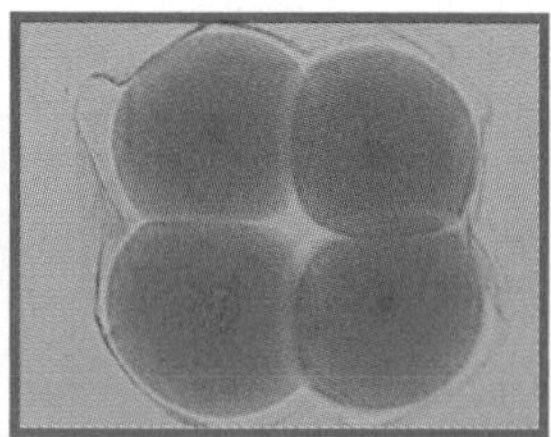
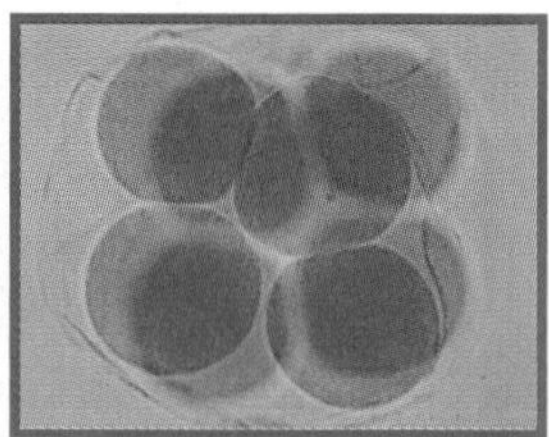

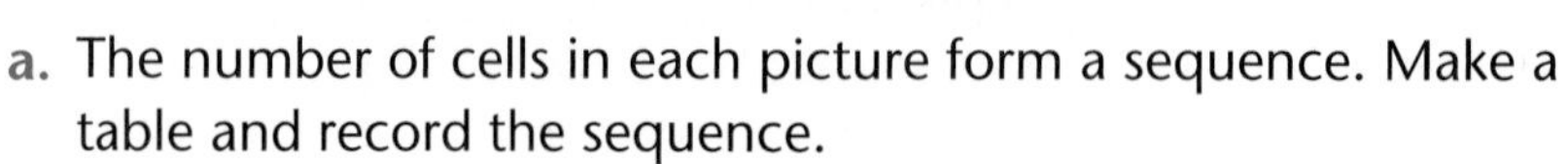

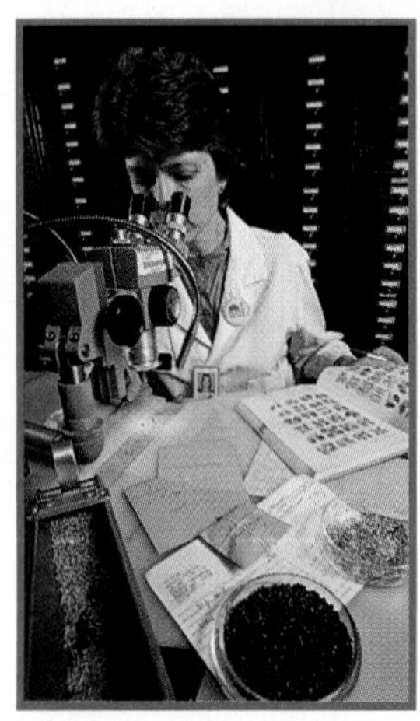

▲ A researcher at the U.S. Department of Agriculture views seed cells under a microscope to monitor development.

a. The number of cells in each picture form a sequence. Make a table and record the sequence.

b. Describe the pattern that develops as the number of cells increases.

c. How many cells would be in the 5th term of the sequence?

10. a. Copy and complete the table.

Term number	1	2	3	4	?	?	?	?
Term	12	24	36	48	?	?	?	?

b. How are the term numbers and terms related?

c. Use your general rule from part (b) to find the 30th term.

11. Repeat parts (a)–(c) of Exercise 10 for the table below.

Term number	1	2	3	4	?	?	?	?
Term	99	98	97	96	?	?	?	?

12. A sequence can be formed by listing the number of toothpicks in each shape below.

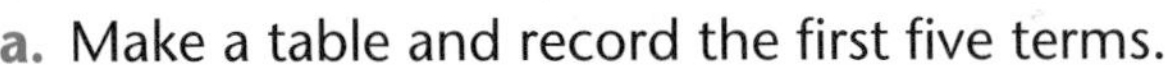

a. Make a table and record the first five terms.

b. Think about the relationship between the terms and the term numbers. Write a general rule for the sequence.

c. How many toothpicks are in the 12th shape?

13. **Visual Thinking** Develop a sequence of objects or shapes to represent this number sequence.

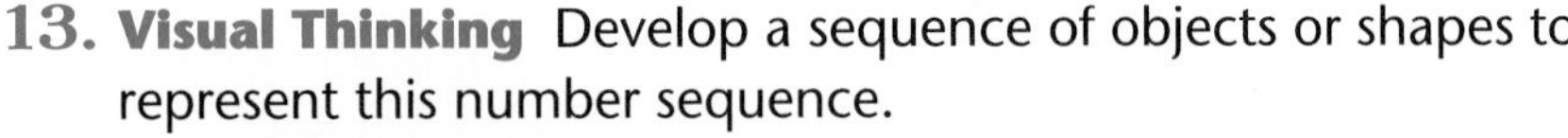

Term number	1	2	3	4	5	6
Term	1	3	5	7	9	11

14. **Challenge** Look back at Exercise 9. Explain how you could find the number of cells in the 25th term.

Reflecting on the Section

Write your response to Exercise 15 in your journal.

15. Write at least one sentence to answer each question below.

a. What are your strengths in mathematics?

b. What do you like most about mathematics?

c. Where do you use mathematics in your everyday life?

d. Describe a pattern of objects or numbers in your everyday life.

Journal

Exercise 15(d) checks that you can observe and describe patterns in everyday life.

Spiral Review

Write each number in words. **(Toolbox, p. 589)**

16. 3672 17. 671,598 18. 23,856

Find each sum or difference. **(Toolbox, pp. 592, 594)**

19. 534 + 682 20. 291 – 156 21. 7256 + 873

22. 5473 – 598 23. 32,567 – 9239 24. 294 + 67 + 141

Draw a picture of each shape.

25. triangle 26. square 27. rectangle

Section 1 Extra Skill Practice

Look for a pattern and replace each ? with the correct term. Describe the rule you used for each sequence.

1. 25, 50, 75, 100, ?, ?, ?, ?, ?, 250
2. 13, 16, 19, 22, ?, ?, ?, ?, ?, 40
3. 144, 132, 120, 108, ?, ?, ?, ?, ?, 36
4. $\frac{1}{3}, \frac{1}{6}, \frac{1}{9}, \frac{1}{12}$, ?, ?, ?, ?, ?, $\frac{1}{30}$
5. 1, 3, 9, 27, ?, ?, ?, ?, 6561

For each sequence, first complete the table. Then write a general rule, and use your rule to find the 40th term.

6.

Term number	1	2	3	4	?	?	?	?
Term	499	498	497	496	?	?	?	?

7.

Term number	10	11	12	13	?	?	?	?
Term	100	110	120	130	?	?	?	?

8.

Term number	1	2	3	4	?	?	?	?
Term	14	16	18	20	?	?	?	?

Study Skills ▸ Getting to Know Your Textbook

When you begin a new course, it is helpful to get to know your textbook. Then you will be able to find information you need quickly.

1. Look through pages xii–xix. Describe two of the features of your textbook that are illustrated in these pages.
2. A section of student resources appears at the back of your textbook. Make a list of all of these resources.
3. Find the Toolbox. Which page of the Toolbox contains help with rounding whole numbers?

Section 2 Lines, Angles, and Triangles

IN THIS SECTION

EXPLORATION 1
- Geometric Language

EXPLORATION 2
- Sides of a Triangle

EXPLORATION 3
- Angles of a Triangle

Language as a Tool

Setting the Stage

Imagine living in a place where people speak a language different from yours. *The China Year,* by Emily Cheney Neville, is a story about Henri, a 13-year-old girl visiting China. One day she visits a post office.

> Henri realized she didn't know how to ask for what she wanted. She waited till the others had left and then moved up to the counter....
>
> Henri put her letter on the counter, pointed to the corner of the envelope for the stamp, and said, "America?"
>
> "Okay." The postmistress went to her drawer and produced not one stamp, but several different rows. She spread them out, clasped her hands, and said, "You like?"
>
> Henri stared. They were so pretty, like miniature paintings.... Henri pointed to the dancers. She held out her hand with change in it, and the lady picked out some fen.... Then they both said "*Xie-xie, xie-xie*" and grinned at each other.
>
> Henri went out and got on her bike, feeling pleased with herself.

Think About It

1 How does Henri communicate with the postmistress?

2 What do you think *xie-xie* (pronounced *she-she*) means?

▶ **Knowing Chinese could have made it easier for Henri to buy stamps. Knowing the appropriate language can also help you learn and share ideas about mathematics.**

GOAL

LEARN HOW TO...
- name basic geometric figures

AS YOU...
- play the game *I Describe, You Draw*

KEY TERMS
- point
- line
- segment
- ray

Exploration 1

Geometric Language

SET UP *Work with a partner. You will need:* • *I Describe, You Draw cards from Labsheet 2A* • *two sheets of unlined paper*

Be sure your partner does not see your card. Be sure you cannot see the drawing.

3 In the game *I Describe, You Draw*, one person describes the design on a card. The other person tries to draw what is described.

Decide who will draw and who will describe. Then play the game with the first card.

4 **a.** How does the drawing compare with the card?

b. Were mathematical words used in the description? If so, did they help? Explain.

▶ **Terms for Geometric Figures** **Special terms and symbols can help you describe geometric figures.**

5 Choose the letter of the best name for each figure.

a. •———→ **A.** line

b. ←———→ **B.** segment

c. •———• **C.** point

d. • **D.** ray

6 **Discussion** Segments and rays are parts of lines. How are lines, rays, and segments alike? How are they different?

▶ **Capital letters are used to name points.**

7 **Discussion** Use the diagram to help explain.

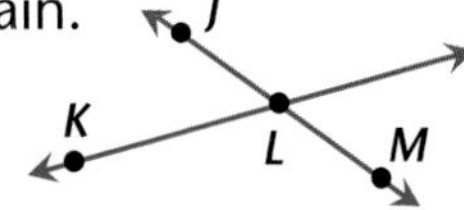

a. Why are two points enough to name a line but one point is not?

b. Are all three letters necessary to name line *JLM*? Explain.

▶ **You can use letters and symbols to name geometric figures.**

EXAMPLE

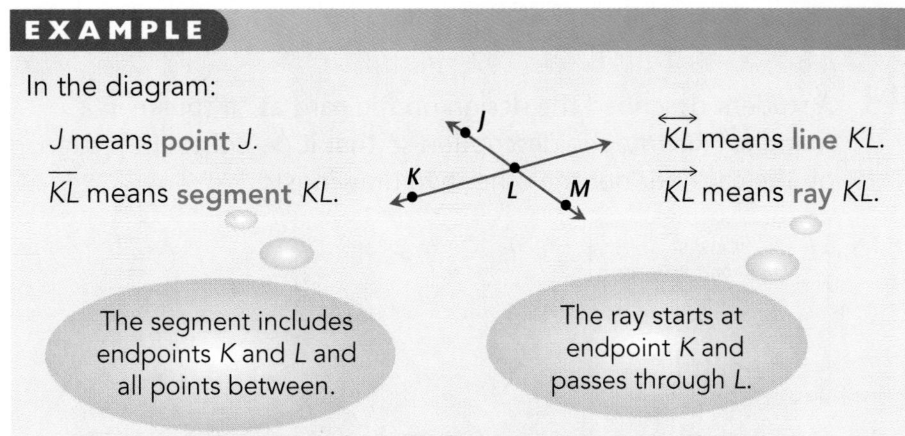

In the diagram:

J means **point** *J*.

$\overline{KL}$ means **segment** *KL*.

$\overleftrightarrow{KL}$ means **line** *KL*.

$\overrightarrow{KL}$ means **ray** *KL*.

The segment includes endpoints *K* and *L* and all points between.

The ray starts at endpoint *K* and passes through *L*.

8 **Try This as a Class** Look at each symbol in red. Do the symbols listed beside it name the same figure? Explain.

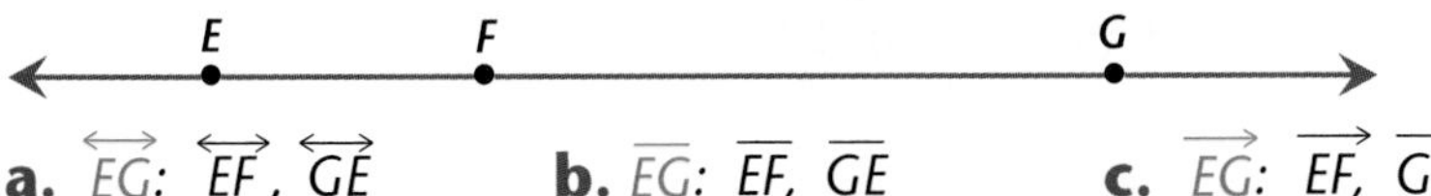

a. $\overleftrightarrow{EG}$: $\overleftrightarrow{EF}$, $\overleftrightarrow{GE}$ **b.** $\overline{EG}$: $\overline{EF}$, $\overline{GE}$ **c.** $\overrightarrow{EG}$: $\overrightarrow{EF}$, $\overrightarrow{GE}$

9 ✓ **CHECKPOINT** Use the correct mathematical term to describe each geometric figure marked on the photo.

...checks that you can identify and name points, lines, segments, and rays.

10 Think about how the geometric terms you learned can help you when playing *I Describe, You Draw*. Switch roles with your partner and use the second card to play another round.

HOMEWORK EXERCISES ▶ **See Exs. 1–6 on pp. 23–24.**

GOAL

LEARN HOW TO...
- classify triangles by the lengths of their sides
- determine when triangles can be formed

AS YOU...
- experiment with sticks of different lengths

KEY TERMS
- equilateral triangle
- isosceles triangle
- scalene triangle

Exploration 2

Sides of a Triangle

SET UP *You will need:* • *Labsheet 2B and scissors or sticks in different sizes* • *Labsheet 2C*

11 A student described the design on the card as "a square in a triangle." Rewrite the description so that it describes the design on the card but not the other two drawings.

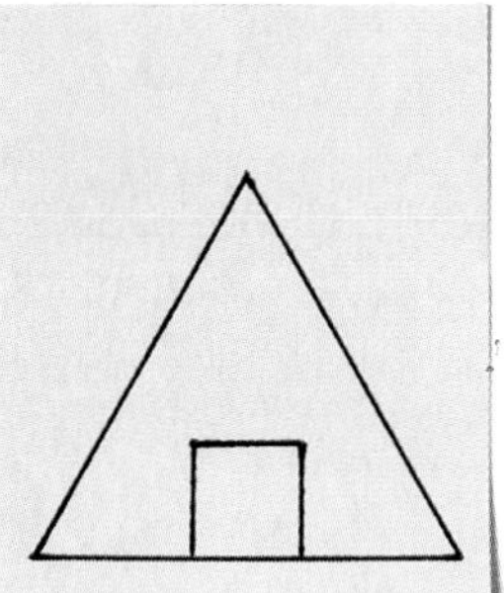

▶ **Types of Triangles The design on the card may be easier to describe if you know more about triangles.**

12 Use the triangles below. Measure the sides if necessary.

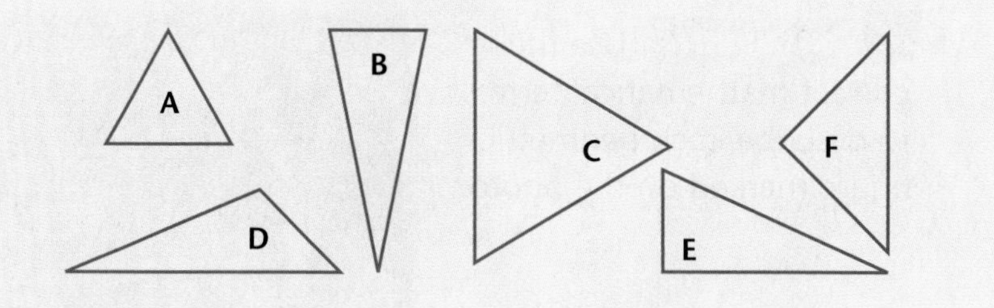

a. Which triangles have three sides of equal length? These are **equilateral triangles**.

b. Which triangles have two or more sides of equal length? These are **isosceles triangles.**

c. Which triangles have no sides of equal length? These are **scalene triangles.**

d. Which triangles can be classified in two ways? Why?

13 What type of triangle is on Card 5 at the top of page 16?

▶ **Constructing Triangles** **You can use sticks of different lengths to examine a variety of triangles.**

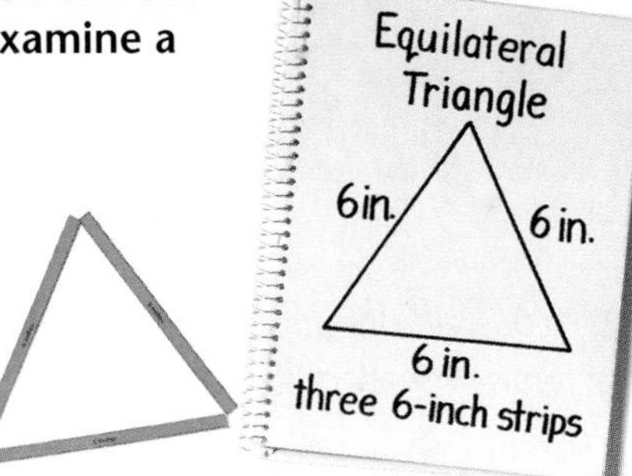

14 ✓ CHECKPOINT **Use Labsheet 2B.** Use *Sticks of Different Sizes* to construct each type of triangle. List the lengths of the sticks you use for each.

a. an isosceles triangle

b. a scalene triangle

c. an equilateral triangle (different from the one shown)

✓ **QUESTION 14**

...checks that you can classify triangles based on the number of sides of equal length.

Use Labsheet 2C for Questions 15 and 16.

15 Using your sticks, decide whether you can form a triangle for each combination of lengths. Sketch each triangle you form and record its type and the lengths of its sides in the *Sides of a Triangle* table.

16 **Try This as a Class** For each combination of sticks, compare the length of the longest side with the sum of the lengths of the two other sides.

a. When does the combination of lengths form a triangle?

b. When is it not possible to form a triangle with the combination of lengths?

c. Write a rule that will help you determine when you can form a triangle.

17 ✓ CHECKPOINT Without using your sticks, decide which combinations of side lengths can form a triangle. Explain.

a. 5 in., 12 in., and 6 in. b. 9 in., 6 in., and 5 in.

✓ **QUESTION 17**

...checks that you understand when a combination of side lengths will form a triangle.

HOMEWORK EXERCISES ▶ **See Exs. 7–15 on p. 24.**

GOAL

LEARN HOW TO...
- identify types of angles
- classify triangles by their angles
- use the mathematical language scale

AS YOU...
- explore geometric figures around you

KEY TERMS
- angle
- vertex
- right angle
- acute angle
- obtuse angle
- straight angle
- acute triangle
- right triangle
- obtuse triangle

Exploration 3

Angles of a Triangle

SET UP *You will need: • Labsheet 2D and 2E • sheet of paper with non-rounded corners*

18 **Discussion** Both triangles at the right are isosceles. What besides side lengths makes them look different?

▶ **Naming and Describing Angles** **You can use an *angle* measurement to describe how the sides of a roof meet. An angle is formed by two rays that have a common endpoint.**

This angle can be named

angle *B* (written $\angle B$)

angle *ABC* (written $\angle ABC$)

angle *CBA* (written $\angle CBA$)

A, B, C

The endpoint of the rays is the vertex of the angle.

19 **Try This as a Class**

a. Explain how the vertex is used in naming an angle.

b. Write all possible names that clearly describe the angle marked in red.

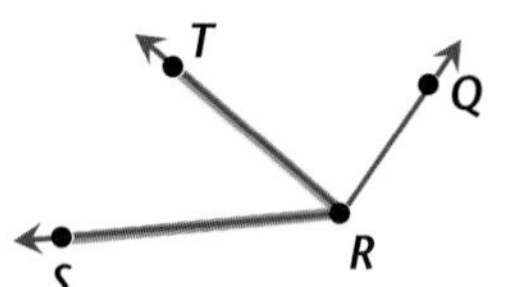

▶ **Look at $\angle ABC$ above. The measure of the opening between its two rays is 90 degrees (written 90°), so $\angle ABC$ is a right angle. The bottom edge and left-hand edge of this page also form a right angle.**

20 Find an example of a right angle in your classroom.

21 Which angles are right angles? Measure with a corner of a sheet of paper.

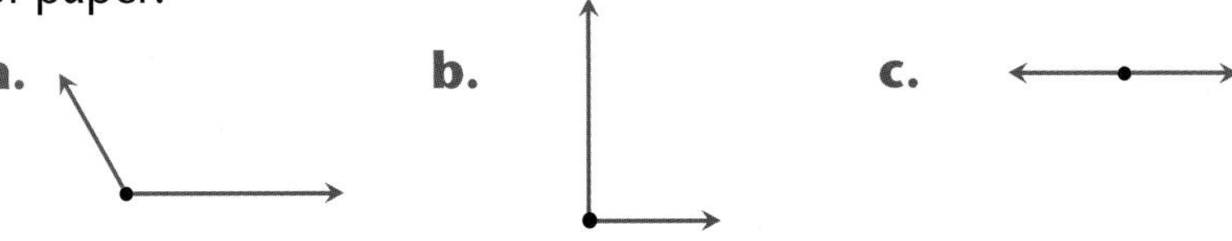

22 Use the definitions on the notebook below. Which angles in Question 21 are acute? obtuse? straight?

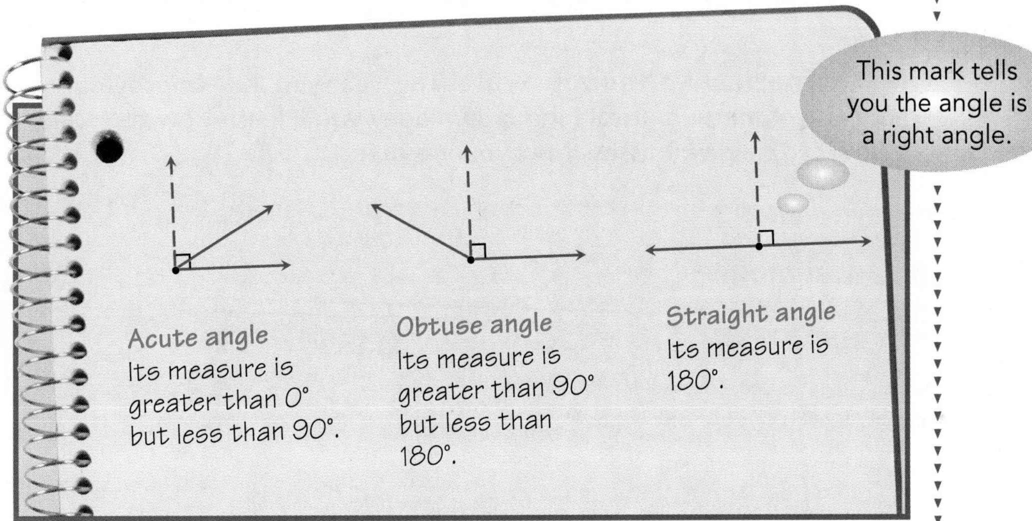

▶ **Classifying Triangles by Angles** **In Exploration 2, you learned to use side lengths to classify triangles. You can also classify triangles by the types of angles they have.**

Use Labsheet 2D for Questions 23 and 24.

23 For each triangle in the *Angles in a Triangle* table, list the names of its angles in the appropriate columns.

24 Use your table to help you answer each question. It will also be helpful to try drawing triangles on a piece of scrap paper.

a. Can a triangle have two right angles? Why or why not?

b. If a triangle has one obtuse angle, what kind of angles will the other two angles be?

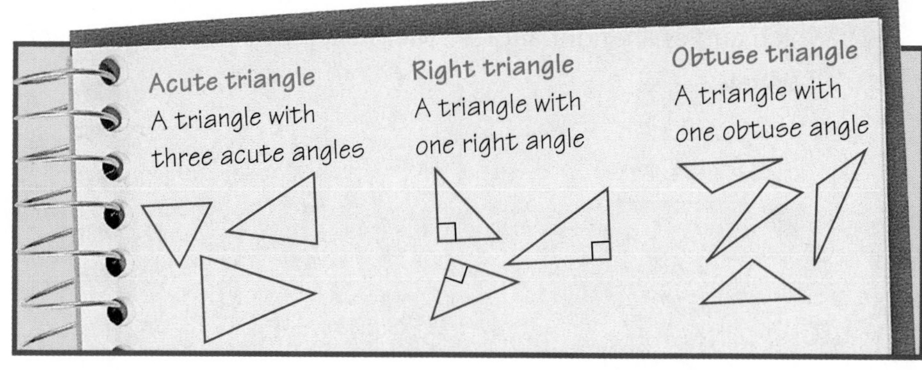

25 After examining a triangle, a student decides it is an acute triangle and a right triangle. Is this possible? Why?

✓ QUESTION 26

...checks that you can classify triangles based on their angles.

26 **✓ CHECKPOINT** **Use Labsheet 2D.** Use the definitions above to classify each triangle. Fill in the last column of the table.

▶ **Mathematical Language Scale This year you'll be improving your use of mathematical language. Today you'll learn how the scale below can help you assess how you are doing.**

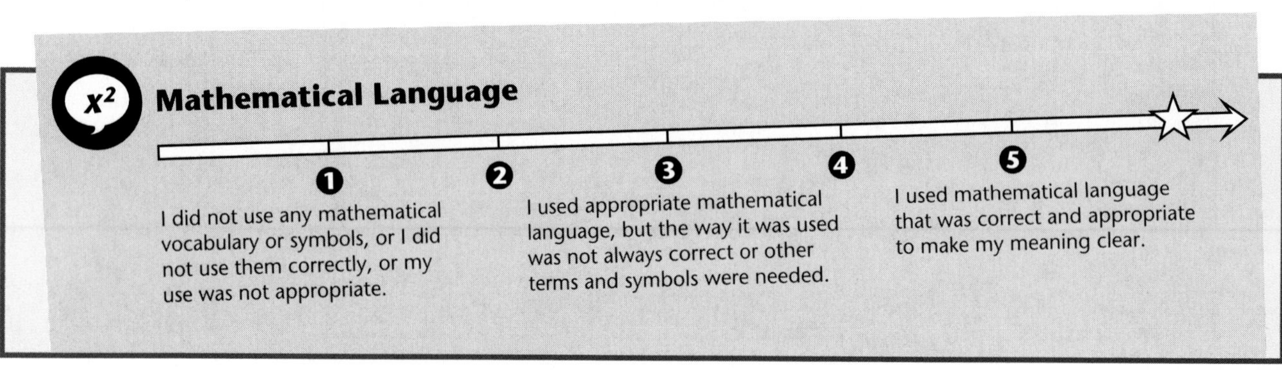

▶ **The scale above is part of the Assessment Scales on page 21 and on Labsheet 2E, which will help you and your teacher think about your work and how to improve it.**

27 **Use Labsheet 2E.** What score would you give this description on the teacher's version of the mathematical language scale? Why?

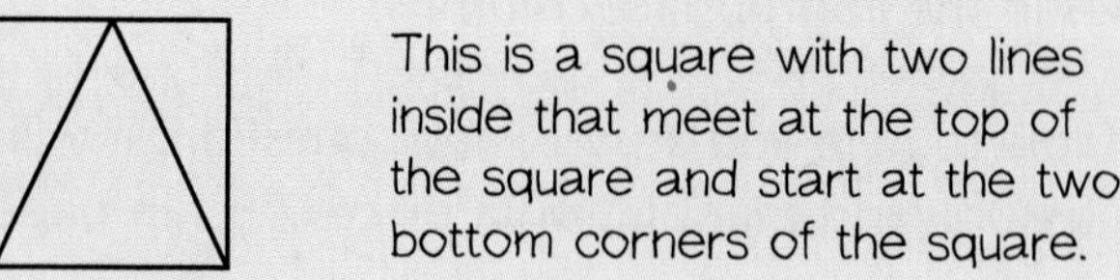

HOMEWORK EXERCISES See Exs. 16–32 on pp. 25–26.

Student Self-Assessment Scales

Student Resource

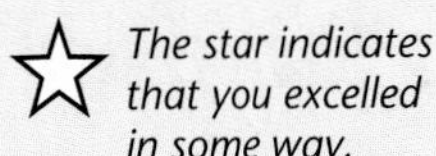

If your score is in the shaded area, explain why on the back of this sheet and stop.

The star indicates that you excelled in some way.

Problem Solving

1 2 3 4 5

I did not understand the problem well enough to get started or I did not show any work.

I understood the problem well enough to make a plan and to work toward a solution.

I made a plan, I used it to solve the problem, and I verified my solution.

Mathematical Language

1 2 3 4 5

I did not use any mathematical vocabulary or symbols, or I did not use them correctly, or my use was not appropriate.

I used appropriate mathematical language, but the way it was used was not always correct or other terms and symbols were needed.

I used mathematical language that was correct and appropriate to make my meaning clear.

Representations

1 2 3 4 5

I did not use any representations such as equations, tables, graphs, or diagrams to help solve the problem or explain my solution.

I made appropriate representations to help solve the problem or help me explain my solution, but they were not always correct or other representations were needed.

I used appropriate and correct representations to solve the problem or explain my solution.

Connections

1 2 3 4 5

I attempted or solved the problem and then stopped.

I found patterns and used them to extend the solution to other cases, or I recognized that this problem relates to other problems, mathematical ideas, or applications.

I extended the ideas in the solution to the general case, or I showed how this problem relates to other problems, mathematical ideas, or applications.

Presentation

1 2 3 4 5

The presentation of my solution and reasoning is unclear to others.

The presentation of my solution and reasoning is clear in most places, but others may have trouble understanding parts of it.

The presentation of my solution and reasoning is clear and can be understood by others.

Section 2 Key Concepts

Key Terms

point

line

ray

segment

equilateral triangle

isosceles triangle

scalene triangle

angle

right

acute

obtuse

straight

vertex

Basic Geometric Figures (pp. 14–15)

Figure	Words	Symbol
A	point A	A
A B	line AB or line BA	$\overleftrightarrow{AB}$ or $\overleftrightarrow{BA}$
A B	ray AB	$\overrightarrow{AB}$
A B	segment AB or segment BA	$\overline{AB}$ or $\overline{BA}$

Classifying Triangles by Sides (pp. 16–17)

All equilateral triangles are also isosceles.

An equilateral triangle has three sides of equal length.	An isosceles triangle has two or more sides of equal length.	A scalene triangle has no sides of equal length.
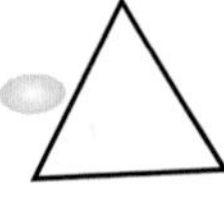		

Triangle Inequality (p. 17)

The sum of the lengths of the shortest two sides of a triangle is greater than the length of the longest side.

Naming and Describing Angles (pp. 18–19)

An angle is formed by two rays that have a common endpoint. The endpoint of the rays is the vertex of the angle. Angles are named by comparing them to a right angle (measure 90°).

28 **Key Concepts Question** A triangle has a 5 in. side and an 11 in. side. Give a possible length for the third side.

Section 2 Key Concepts

Classifying Triangles by Angles (pp. 19–20)

You can also classify a triangle as acute, right, or obtuse by examining its angles. A triangle cannot be formed with a straight angle.

Mathematical Language Scale (p. 20)

To assess your use of mathematical language, ask yourself:

- Was my use of terms and symbols correct? appropriate? Did it help me get my meaning across?
- Are there other mathematical terms or symbols I should have used to make my meaning clearer?

Key Terms

acute triangle

right triangle

obtuse triangle

29 **Key Concepts Question** Sketch each type of triangle.

a. a triangle that is both right and scalene

b. a triangle that is both acute and isosceles

Section 2 Practice & Application Exercises

YOU WILL NEED

For Exs. 7–9:
- ruler

For Ex. 31:
- Labsheet 2E

1. **Korean Writing** Write a description of the character in Box A so that someone can locate its match in Box B.

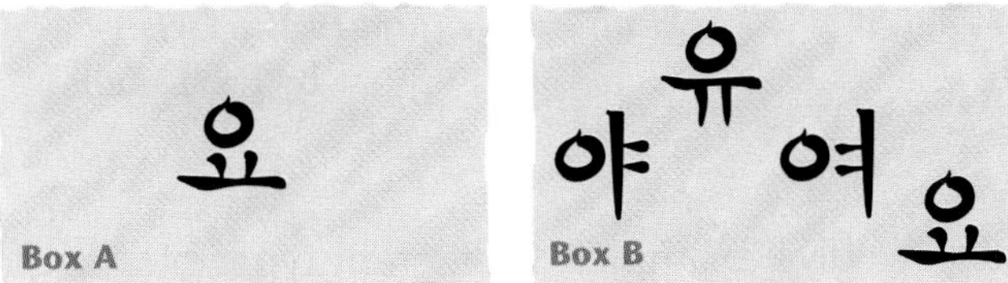

Use the points on the line to write each answer using symbols.

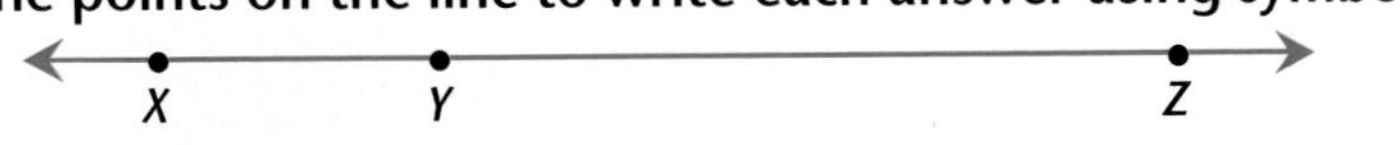

2. Name the line in three ways.

3. Name three different segments. How are they different?

4. Name three different rays. How are they different?

Write *line, segment,* or *ray* to best describe each object.

5. flagpole

6. light from car's headlight

Use a ruler or a straight edge to draw two examples of each type of triangle. Label the sides with their lengths.

7. equilateral

8. isosceles

9. scalene

A triangle has sides of length 20 ft and 15 ft. Tell whether each length *can* or *cannot* be the third side of the triangle.

10. 29 ft

11. 3 ft

12. 5 ft

13. 37 ft

14. Read the story. Then explain Smith's answer to the problem.

Jones said to Smith: "I think I'll sell that piece of land at the bottom of my garden, but I can't make up my mind how much to ask for it. What do you suggest?"

"Well," said Smith, "what are its dimensions?"

Jones drew the following diagram and handed it over.

12 yd, 17 yd, 29 yd

Smith studied the drawing for a second or two, then passed it back. "If your dimensions are right, you won't get so much as a dime for it," he said laughing.

from *Puzzles and Brain Twisters*, by Fred Walls

15. Use the picture to give examples of different types of triangles.

Classify each angle as *right, acute, obtuse,* or *straight.*

16. 

17.

18. 

19. 

20. Suppose you are riding a bike and have to turn a corner that forms a right, an obtuse, or an acute angle.

    a. Which angle must you slow down most for? Why?

    b. Which angle can be turned most safely at a high speed?

    c. Which angle is most commonly found on city streets?

Give two names for each triangle. Classify each according to the measures of its angles and the lengths of its sides.

21. 

22. 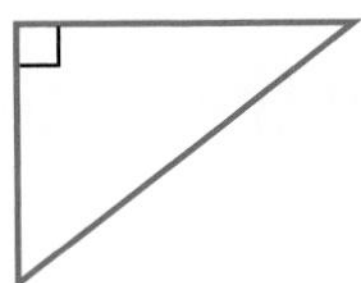

23. 

24. 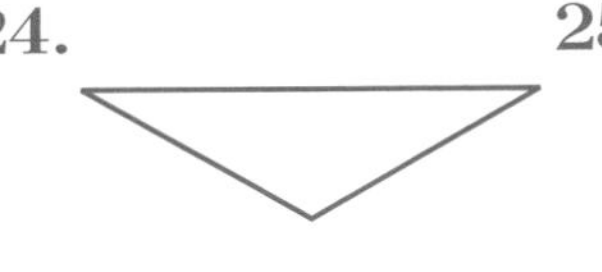

25. 

26. 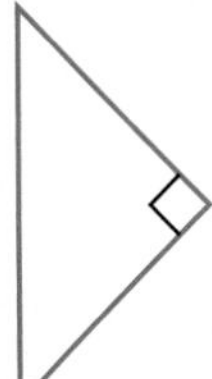

27. **Challenge** *Acute-isosceles* is an example of a combination name for a triangle. A name describing the angles is joined with a name describing the number of equal sides. List all the combination names that can be written. Then explain which names describe triangles that can actually be formed.

Explain what is wrong with each statement.

28. This is $\angle JHI$.

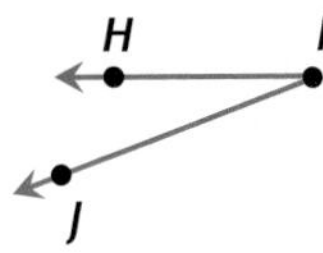
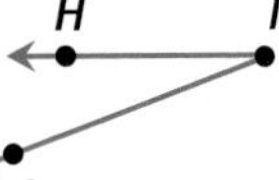

29. This is $\overrightarrow{BC}$.

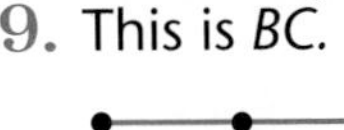
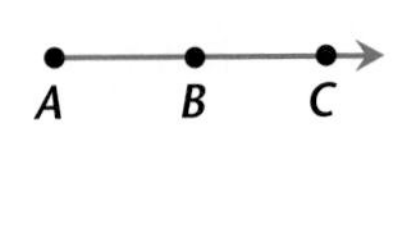

30. This is $\angle G$.

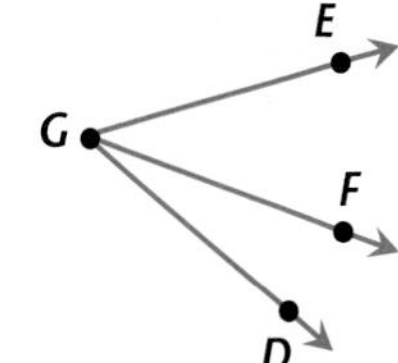

31. a. Will the shop owner know the caller wants to buy the second watch? If not, how can you improve the description?

I want to buy a watch I saw in your shop in New Mexico. The band is silver and there are two blue triangles next to the dial.

b. **Use Labsheet 2E.** What would you score the caller's description on the mathematical language scale on Labsheet 2E? Why?

RESEARCH

Exercise 32 checks that you understand how important mathematical language is in everyday life.

Reflecting on the Section

32. a. Describe ways in which people may need to use words like *line, angle,* or *triangle* in their everyday life or work.

b. What mathematical terms do you use outside of school besides numbers?

Spiral Review

33. In the pattern below, the length of one side of a small square (□) is 1 unit. Find the perimeter of the sixth shape in the pattern. **(Toolbox, p. 599; Module 1, p. 8)**

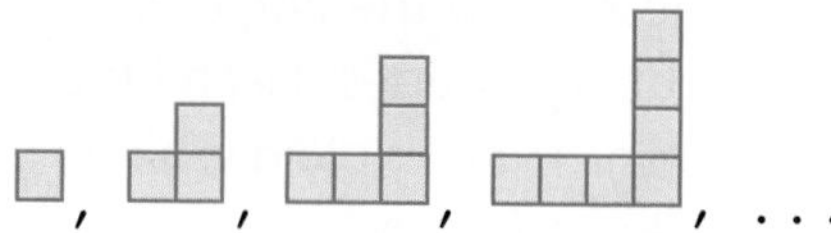

34. Writing What is wrong with the mathematical language in this advertisement: *Special! Two hamburgers for .99¢?* **(Toolbox, p. 592)**

Replace each ? with < , > , or = . **(Toolbox, p. 590)**

35. 84,987 __?__ 85,132

36. 25 thousand __?__ 2500

Change to the given unit of time. **(Toolbox, p. 601)**

37. 50 min = __?__ seconds

38. 3 hours = __?__ min

A Puzzling Problem

SET UP

Work in a group. You will need:

- *Project Labsheet A*

Use Project Labsheet A. Throughout this module you'll explore different ways to approach the *30 Pennies In A Row* problem shown on the labsheet. Plan to keep all your ongoing project work together. To complete the module project, you'll work as a team to present the solution.

1 It will help to study the situation before you try to solve the *30 Pennies in a Row* problem.

a. Read the entire labsheet. Then read *The Situation* again.

b. Breaking *The Situation* into steps can help you understand it. Suppose that in Step 1 you place 30 pennies in a row. What do you do in Step 2? in Steps 3–5?

2 **Focusing on Language and Patterns** You can use a table to look at the patterns the coins create.

a. Copy the table. For Steps 2–5, fill in the pattern using *P, N, D, Q,* and *F* to represent the different coins.

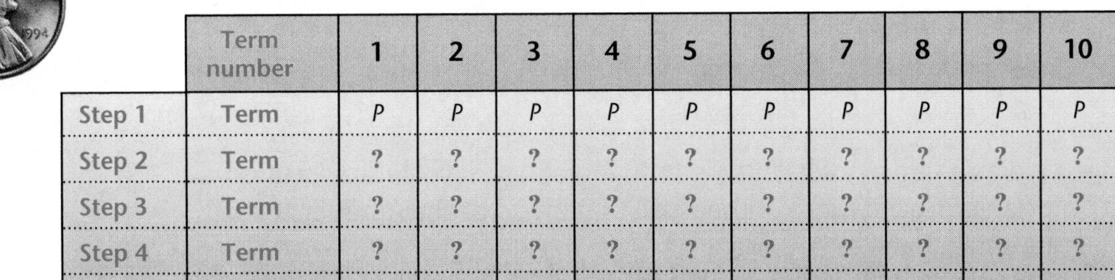

	Term number	1	2	3	4	5	6	7	8	9	10
Step 1	Term	*P*	*P*	*P*	*P*	*P*	*P*	*P*	*P*	*P*	*P*
Step 2	Term	?	?	?	?	?	?	?	?	?	?
Step 3	Term	?	?	?	?	?	?	?	?	?	?
Step 4	Term	?	?	?	?	?	?	?	?	?	?
Step 5	Term	?	?	?	?	?	?	?	?	?	?

b. Use mathematical language to describe the sequence of coins in the row for Step 2.

c. **Discussion** Discuss any relationships you see between each term in the row for Step 3 and its term number.

d. Describe any patterns you see in the rows for Steps 4–5.

Section 2 Extra Skill Practice

Choose the letter of the symbol that matches each term.

1. segment *AB*
2. point *A*
3. line *AB*
4. ray *AB*

A. A
B. $\overleftrightarrow{AB}$
C. $\overrightarrow{AB}$
D. $\overline{AB}$

Tell whether each combination of side lengths *can* or *cannot* form a triangle.

5. 20 ft, 12 ft, 10 ft
6. 8 in., 9 in., 18 in.
7. 15 yd, 6 yd, 6 yd
8. 11 ft, 12 ft, 13 ft

Tell whether each statement is *true* or *false*.

9. A right triangle has one right angle.
10. A scalene triangle has two sides of equal length.
11. An obtuse triangle has one obtuse angle.

Classify each angle as *right, acute, obtuse,* or *straight*.

12. 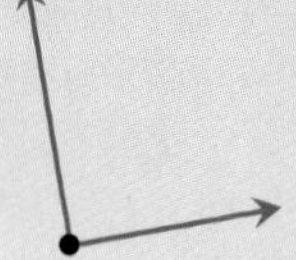

13. 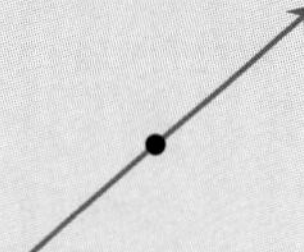

14. 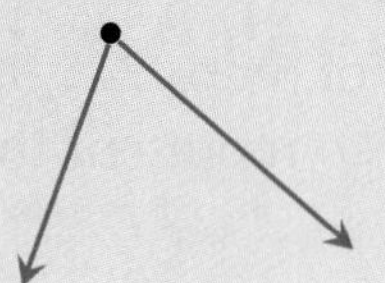

15. 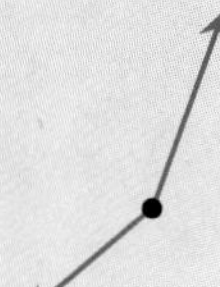

Standardized Testing ▶ Free Response

Find an example of each type of triangle that is formed by putting together two or more of the small triangles. List the numbers of the small triangles you used.

a. right
b. equilateral
c. acute
d. isosceles
e. scalene
f. obtuse

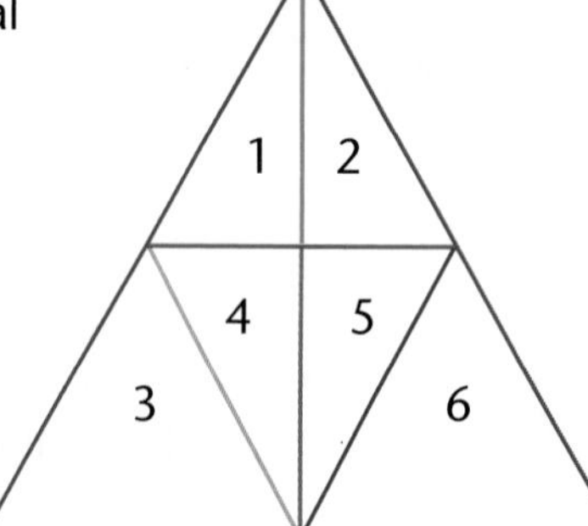

Section 3 A Problem Solving Approach

IN THIS SECTION

EXPLORATION 1
- Understand the Problem

EXPLORATION 2
- Make a Plan

EXPLORATION 3
- Carry Out the Plan and Look Back

Planning Tools

Setting the Stage

SET UP *Work as a class. You will need 9 index cards numbered 1–9.*

One tool for success in mathematics and in life is knowing how to solve a problem. As you play a game called *Card Swappers*, you'll learn a 4-step approach that will help you become a better problem solver.

▶ **As a class, first practice swapping by putting these cards in order from 1 to 9. Try to use as few swaps as possible. Record your swaps.**

CARD SWAPPERS

The object of the game is to put nine cards in order from least to greatest in the fewest swaps possible.

A swap is made by exchanging the positions of two cards.

The challenge is that you must predict the number of swaps needed before you see the order of the cards.

1 2 5 4 8 7 6 3 9

Think About It

1 Do you think the class put the cards in order in the fewest swaps possible? Try swapping another way to see.

2 Do you think the number of swaps needed for different arrangements of the cards will be the same? Try it and see.

GOAL

LEARN HOW TO...
- develop an understanding of a problem

AS YOU...
- play and think about the *Card Swappers* game

Exploration 1

Understand the Problem

SET UP *Work first as a class and then in a group of four. You will need 9 index cards numbered 1–9 for each group.*

▶ **You have had some experience swapping cards. Now you'll use your experience to play the game *Card Swappers.***

You'll need two teams. At the start of each game, the cards should be shuffled and placed facing away from both teams.

First

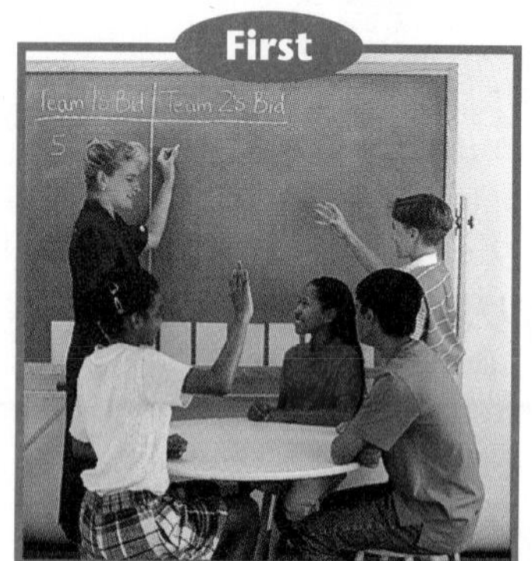

Each team bids the number of swaps they think it may take to put the cards in order.

Next

The cards are turned over so that the numbers can be seen.

Then

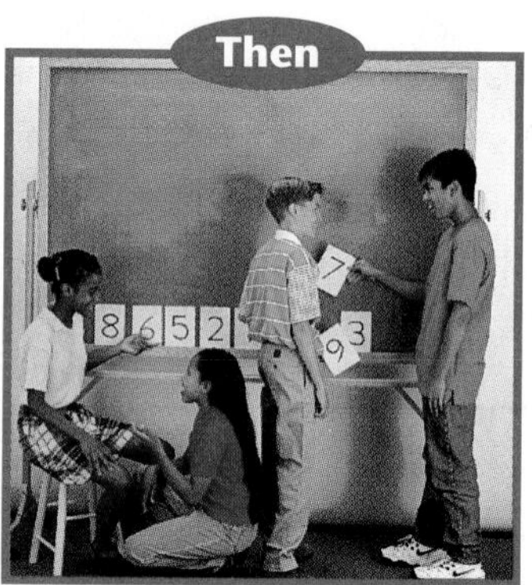

The lowest bidding team puts the cards in order from least to greatest.

If the lowest bidding team uses no more than the number of swaps they bid, then they win. Otherwise the other team wins.

▶ **One way to understand the game better is to play it several times.**

3 Play *Card Swappers* two times with the whole class divided into two teams.

4 **Discussion** When you practiced swapping cards on page 29, you just needed to put the cards in order from least to greatest in the fewest swaps possible. What new challenges did you face when you played the game?

▶ **Now work in your group to think more about bidding.**

5 Split up your group and play *Card Swappers* two times.

6 **a.** If you bid 1 swap each time, will you ever win? Why?

b. If you bid 9 swaps and get the bid, will you win? Why?

c. A bid is called "safe" if you can be sure of always putting the cards in order using that many swaps. What do you think is the lowest safe bid? Why?

d. Would your bid change if you played with fewer cards?

7 **Try This as a Class** Describe the problem you need to solve to be successful at the *Card Swappers* game.

▶ **To *Understand the Problem* is the first step in a 4-step approach to solving problems. As you have played and thought about *Card Swappers,* you have developed an understanding of the problem you'll be solving in Explorations 2 and 3.**

4-Step Approach

1. Understand the Problem

HOMEWORK EXERCISES ▶ See Exs. 1–5 on pp. 36–37.

Exploration 2

Make a Plan

GOAL

LEARN HOW TO...

- make a plan to solve a problem
- use several problem solving strategies

AS YOU...

- begin to solve the problem within *Card Swappers*

SET UP *Work in a group of four. You will need 9 index cards numbered 1–9 for each group.*

▶ **Once you understand the problem you have to solve, the next step is to make a plan for solving it. The plan for solving a problem often involves using problem solving strategies.**

8 **Discussion** List some strategies you remember using to solve problems in mathematics.

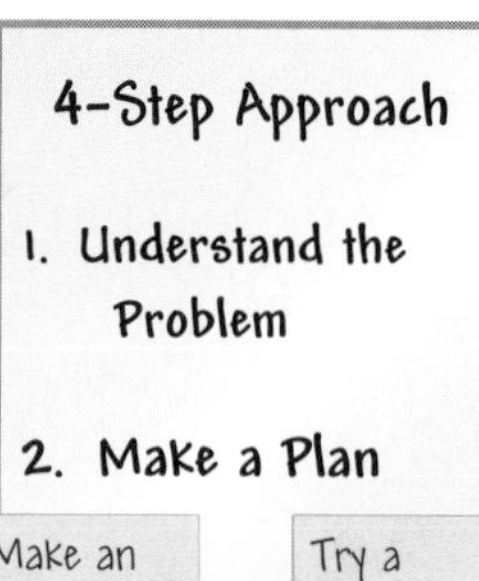

▶ **To find the lowest safe bid in the *Card Swappers* game, you can begin by seeing whether the strategy *try a simpler problem* is helpful. You'll explore what happens as you play with fewer cards.**

9 Imagine playing *Card Swappers* with only one card. How many swaps do you have to make? Explain.

10 Use only the cards numbered 1 and 2.

a. Play *Card Swappers* several times in your group.

b. What seems to be the lowest safe bid for two cards? Remember, this is the least number of swaps you can bid and still be certain of putting the cards in order.

11 Use only the cards 1, 2, and 3. Repeat Question 10.

▶ **Your next step is to check your findings. One way to do this is to *make an organized list.***

12 **a.** List all the possible arrangements for cards 1 and 2.

b. What is the lowest safe bid for two cards?

13 There are six possible arrangements for cards 1, 2, and 3. What are they?

14 **a.** For each arrangement found in Question 13, find the least number of swaps that will put the cards in order. Record your swaps.

b. What is the lowest safe bid for three cards?

Arrangements for cards 1, 2, and 3:

123	1 3 _
213	_ _ _
312	_ _ _

Least number of swaps that will put the cards in order:

123		0 swaps
213	⟶ 123	1 swap

15 Think about your answers to Questions 10 and 11. How does using an organized list help you check your answer?

▶ **So far you have found the lowest safe bid for three cards. In Exploration 3 you'll complete and carry out a plan for bidding successfully in the *Card Swappers* game.**

HOMEWORK EXERCISES ▶ See Exs. 6–9 on p. 37.

Exploration 3

Carry Out the Plan and Look Back

GOAL

LEARN HOW TO...
- carry out a plan
- look back

AS YOU...
- complete the 4-step approach to solve the *Card Swappers* problem

SET UP *Work in a group of four. You will need 9 index cards numbered 1–9 for each group.*

▶ **It looks like trying a simpler problem and making an organized list will help you solve the *Card Swappers* problem. Now you'll see if the strategies *making a table* and *looking for a pattern* are helpful.**

16 Copy the table. Use your results from Exploration 2 to fill in the lowest safe bid for one, two, and three cards.

Number of cards in the game	1	2	3	4
Least number of swaps to safely bid	?	?	?	?

17 **a.** Use your table to predict the lowest safe bid for four cards. Write your prediction in the table.

b. Play the game with four cards. Does it seem as if your prediction was correct? Explain.

c. Make an organized list to check your prediction. Record your swaps as you did for Question 14(a).

18 Suppose you have more than four cards. Would you want to use an organized list to examine what happens? Explain.

19 **Try This as a Class** Think about your work on the *Card Swappers* problem so far.

a. Describe the plan you have developed.

b. Explain what you can do now to find the lowest safe bid for nine cards.

4-Step Approach

1. Understand the Problem
2. Make a Plan

Try a simpler problem

Make an organized list

Make a table

Look for a pattern

3. Carry Out the Plan
4. Look Back

▶ **Now you are ready for the third and fourth steps, which are to *Carry Out the Plan* and *Look Back*. You'll find the lowest safe bid. Then you'll use this result to solve the full problem of how to bid successfully in the *Card Swappers* game.**

20 Use your strategies from Question 19 to carry out the plan. What is the lowest safe bid for nine cards?

21 **Discussion** Look back at your solution to the problem of finding the lowest safe bid in *Card Swappers*.

a. Does your solution seem reasonable? Explain. Do you see any errors in your work?

b. Try to think of another way to find the lowest safe bid for nine cards. If you can, use this method to check your solution to Question 20.

c. Suppose there are 12 cards in the deck. What is the lowest safe bid?

d. What is a general rule you can use to find the lowest safe bid?

22 When playing *Card Swappers*, what would you bid? Why?

▶ **The 4-step problem solving approach will help you tackle other problems. Some problems have many ways to get to a single correct answer. Other problems may have several correct answers. Shown here are some problems you will solve this year.**

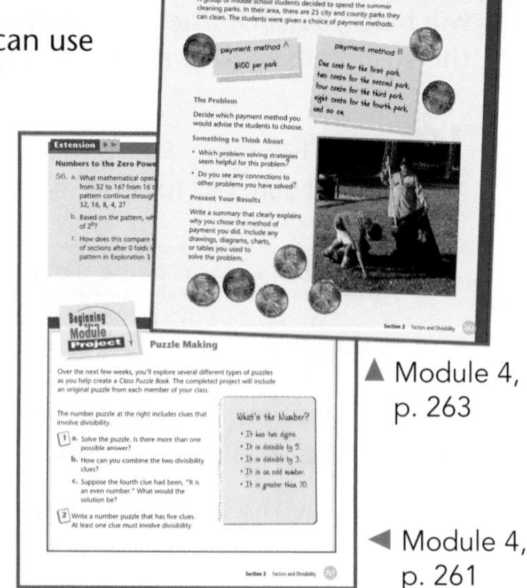

▲ Module 4, p. 263

◀ Module 4, p. 261

HOMEWORK EXERCISES ▶ See Exs. 10–15 on pp. 37–38.

4-Step Approach to Solving Problems

1. Understand the Problem

- Read the problem carefully, probably several times.
- Restate the problem in your own words.
- Identify the important information in the problem.

2. Make a Plan

- You may try several problem solving strategies.

If information is missing, you may need to gather it.

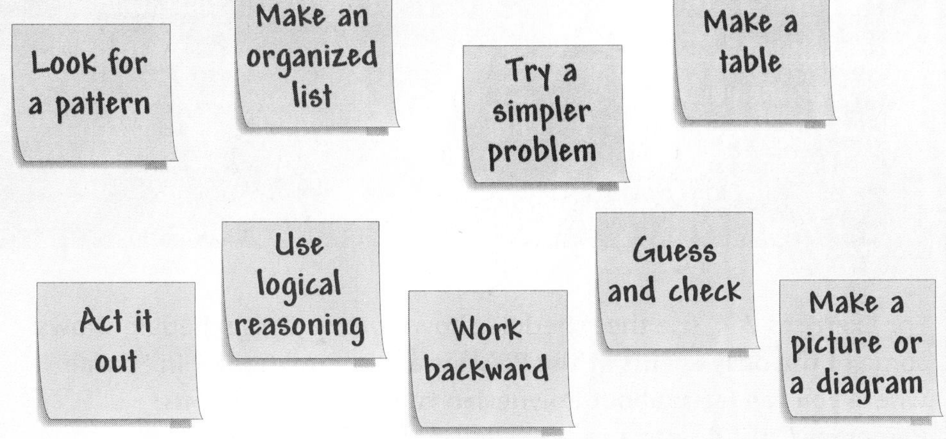

3. Carry Out the Plan

- Solve the problem using the strategies selected.
- You may need to try other strategies.

4. Look Back

- Check that you answered the question being asked.
- Check that your solution seems reasonable.
- Check that your work is accurate.
- Try to find another method. Compare the results.
- Think about other problems you have solved to see if your problem is similar.
- Can you generalize your solution to any situation?

23 **Key Concepts Question** Suppose you play the *Card Swappers* game with 26 cards each showing a letter of the alphabet from A to Z. You must put the cards in alphabetical order. What would be the lowest safe bid?

Section 3 Practice & Application Exercises

YOU WILL NEED

For Ex. 15:
- graph paper (optional)

FOR ▶ HELP with *computing with money*, see **TOOLBOX pp. 592, 595**

For Exercises 1–4 do parts (a)–(c). Do not solve the problems now.

a. **Describe the problem you need to solve.**

b. **State the important information in the problem.**

c. **Identify any information missing from the problem.**

1. An on-line computer service offers two monthly service contracts. Suppose you spend 8 to 10 hours a month on line. Which contract should you choose?

Standard Contract		Frequent User Contract	
Monthly fee	$4.95	Monthly fee	$19.95
Hours included	3	Hours included	20
Additional hours	$2.50	Additional hours	$2.00
		* *Receive a 10% discount when you use over 50 hours of on-line time.*	

For Exercises 2–4, use the schedule shown below. This schedule shows some of the daily events at the Polynesian Cultural Center in Hawaii where you can learn about Polynesian culture and traditions. Remember, just do parts (a)–(c) shown at the top of the page.

DAILY EVENTS

Double Hulled Canoe Tour (15 min) 12:30 – 2:00 and 3:00 – 7:30
Tours leave every 15 min with the last tour at 7:15.

"Ancient Legends of Polynesia" Canoe Pageant (90 min) 2:30

"The Polynesian Odyssey" (45 min) 3:00 4:00 6:00

"The Living Sea" (45 min) 2:00 5:00 7:00

Ali'i Luaua Buffet Dinner 5:15 – 7:00

Canoes carry visitors among the islands at the Polynesian Cultural Center. Polynesians crossed the Pacific in giant catamarans to settle Hawaii and other islands centuries before Columbus ever set sail.

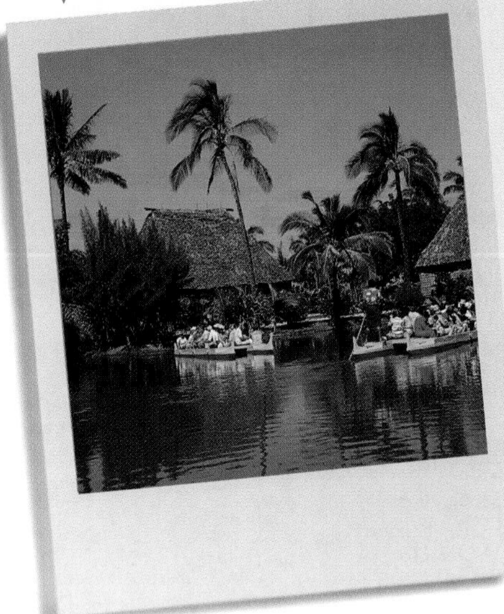

2. Can you attend all the activities and shows listed during one visit?

3. How many times a day is the Canoe Tour given?

4. Suppose you plan to arrive at the Polynesian Center at 2:00 P.M. You want at least 45 minutes for dinner. It takes 10–15 minutes to get to each event. Can you attend all the events listed on page 36? Explain.

5. **Writing** Write a word problem with at least two pieces of extra information. Be sure your problem can be solved.

6. At work Derek must wear a dress shirt, long pants, and a tie. He has three dress shirts (white, blue, and green), two pairs of long pants (tan and black), and two ties (plain and striped). Make an organized list to find how many different outfits he has for work.

▲ The Canoe Pageant uses "dance language" and narration to tell the legends of ancient Polynesia.

7. Solve the problem in Exercise 1.

For Exercises 8 and 9, choose one or more strategies from the list on page 35. Explain how you could use those strategies to solve each problem. You do not need to actually solve it.

8. Marita has to be at school by 8 A.M. It takes her 40 minutes to get up and get dressed in the morning. She needs at least 20 minutes to eat breakfast. Then she has a 15 minute walk to school. What time does Marita need to get up?

9. **Geometry Connection** How many 1-inch equilateral triangles are needed to build a chain of triangles that has a perimeter of 20 in.?

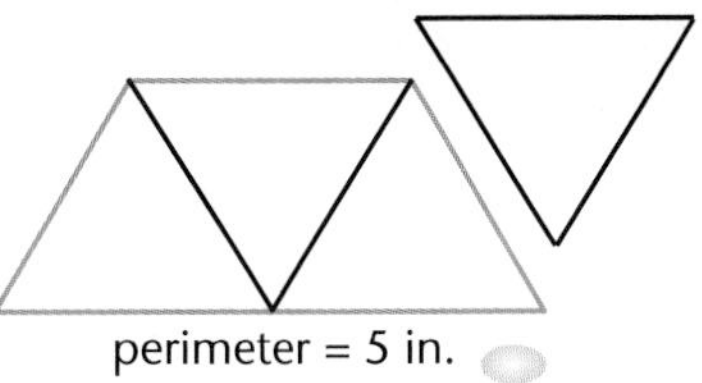

Remember, perimeter is the distance around a figure.

10. Carry out parts (a)–(c) for Exercise 9.

   a. Solve the problem.

   b. Describe the plan you used.

   c. Look back:

      - Did you answer the question asked in the problem?
      - Does your solution seem reasonable? Explain.
      - How can you check your work? Explain.
      - Is the problem similar to other problems you have solved? If so, how is it similar?
      - Can you generalize your solution to a chain of triangles with any perimeter?

Solve each of these problems from pages 36–37.

11. Exercise 3
12. Exercise 4
13. Exercise 8

14. **Challenge** Suppose you have two pots. One pot holds 7 cups and the other holds 4 cups. How can you measure exactly 5 cups of water?

Visual THINKING

Exercise 15 checks that you can use the 4-step approach to solve a problem.

Reflecting on the Section

15. a. Solve the following problem. (*Hint:* graph paper can make it easier to sketch the game board.)

How can five chips be placed on the game board so that each chip does not lie in the same row, column, or any diagonal as any other chip?

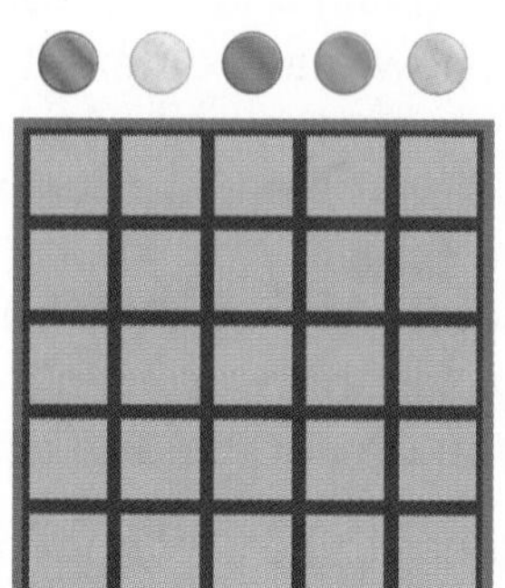

b. Describe your plan.

c. Find at least one other solution.

Spiral Review

Classify each triangle by its angles and sides. (Module 1, pp. 22–23)

16. 

17. 

18. 

Round each number to the given place. (Toolbox, p. 591)

19. 5632 (nearest hundred)
20. $44.99 (nearest ten dollars)
21. $6.72 (nearest dollar)
22. 34,819 (nearest thousand)
23. 896 (nearest ten)
24. 45,031 (nearest hundred)

Mental Math **Multiply.** (Toolbox, p. 598)

25. 100×100
26. $10,000 \times 10$
27. 1000×6
28. 56×10
29. 300×70
30. 726×100
31. 80×400
32. 2000×500
33. $900 \times 70,000$

Career Connection

Programming Developer: Bryan Ellis

Bryan Ellis designs computer programs for the New York Stock Exchange. When Bryan is asked to develop a program, he first gets a clear description of what the customer wants. For example, a customer might want a program that organizes stock orders by price. After Bryan chooses the best way to design the program, he begins writing the computer code.

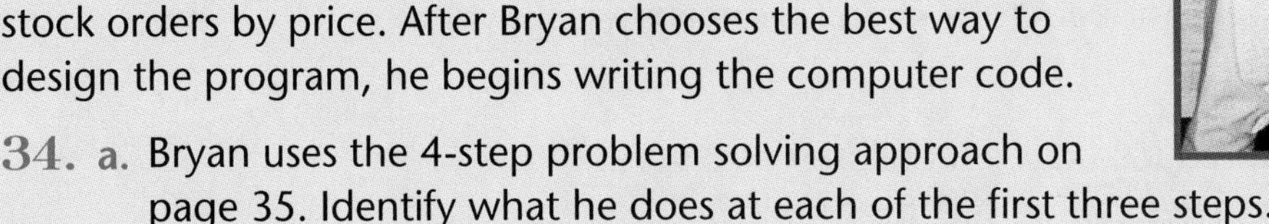

34. a. Bryan uses the 4-step problem solving approach on page 35. Identify what he does at each of the first three steps.

    b. What do you think he might do to look back?

35. Bryan designs programs so that they can be reused. A program used for one request can be changed slightly for another request. Which step is this an example of?

36. Sometimes a request is technically impossible or is against the stock exchange rules. When this happens, Bryan needs to go back to the customer to see if the request can be changed. Which step is this an example of?

A Puzzling Problem

Understanding the Problem Now that you have studied the situation, you need to think about the *30 Pennies in a Row* problem itself.

SET UP

You will need:

- *Project Labsheet A*

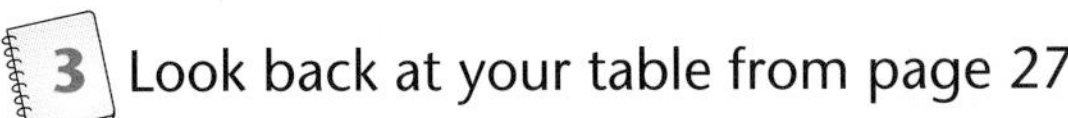

3 Look back at your table from page 27.

   a. Did the coin in position 1 change? in position 2? in position 6?

   b. In which positions do the coins seem to change the most? Why?

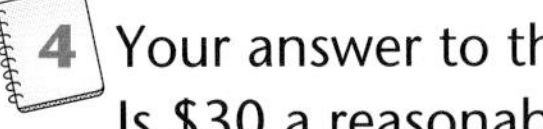

4 Your answer to the problem will be the value of the coins. Is $30 a reasonable answer? is $15? Explain.

Section 3 Extra Skill Practice

Tell whether each problem contains *too much* or *not enough* information. Identify any extra or missing information.

1. Pens cost $1.25, markers $1.50, and pencils $.75. Birgit bought three pencils. If there is no tax, how much did she spend?

2. Sue earns $25 each week for baby-sitting. In how many weeks will Sue have saved $175?

3. The cinema charges a reduced rate for children under 12. If José has $14, how many movies can he see this month?

Solve each problem and describe any strategies you used.

4. Kenesha sold three tickets to the school dance the first day. On each of the next ten days she sold two more tickets than the day before. How many tickets did she sell in all?

5. A library is located 5 mi east of a school. A park is 3 mi east of the school and halfway between the library and a deli. How far is it from the deli to the library?

6. Basketball shots are worth one, two, or three points. In how many different ways can a player score 9 points?

7. Giang has $2.50 left after a shopping trip. She spent $58.50 on purchases, $12.50 on lunch, and $10.00 on travel. How much money did she have before her trip?

8. You saw your friend sorting beads. You asked how many of each color there were and your friend replied this way. "There are 67 beads altogether. There are twice as many white beads as red beads and twice as many green beads as white beads. The number of blue beads is only one more than the number of green beads." How many beads of each color were there?

Standardized Testing ▶ Performance Task

Choose a problem solving strategy you have learned and write a word problem that can be solved using that strategy.

Then present a solution to your problem. Include an explanation of how the strategy you chose can be used to find the solution.

EXTENDED E2 EXPLORATION

FOR ASSESSMENT AND PORTFOLIOS

Estimating Animal Populations

SET UP *You will need the Extended Exploration Labsheet.*

The Situation

Since researchers have no way of controlling the movement of animals in the wild, it can be difficult to make accurate population counts. Often researchers can only make estimates from aerial photographs.

The Problem

Devise a method you can use to estimate the number of geese shown in *Geese Galore* on the labsheet without counting each goose. Then use your method to make an estimate.

Something to Think About

- What is your top-of-the-head guess about whether the number of geese shown is in the *tens*, *hundreds*, *thousands*, or *millions*?
- Have you ever estimated the size of a crowd at a movie or a sports event? If so, what methods did you use?

Present Your Results

Write a summary that clearly explains how you made your estimate of the number of geese in *Geese Galore*. Give your estimate and compare it with your top-of-the-head guess. Include an example of another situation where your method of estimation may be useful.

You'll assess your work on this and other *Extended Exploration* problems using one or more of the assessment scales shown on page 21. You learned how to use the mathematical language scale in Section 2. As you work through the rest of this module, you'll learn how to use the other assessment scales.

Estimation, Mental Math, or a Calculator

IN THIS SECTION

EXPLORATION 1
- Estimating with Rounding

EXPLORATION 2
- Using Mental Math

EXPLORATION 3
- Order of Operations

Choosing Tools

Setting the Stage

Have you ever run for office in a school election? It takes a lot of planning and decision making!

School Election Rules:

1. A maximum of $20 may be spent on each campaign.
2. Each candidate may put up a maximum of 25 posters.
3. Each candidate must deliver a speech about 3 minutes long.

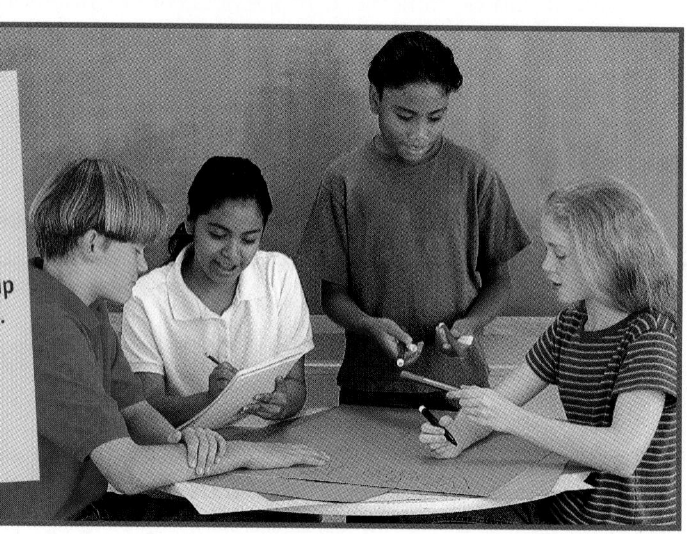

Think About It

1 You have a $20 spending limit. You want to decide whether to create a flier for each student or a poster for each classroom. What other information will help you decide?

2 Why was an estimate used when giving the speech length?

▶ **Making choices and following agreed-on rules are important in mathematics as well as in an election. In this section, you'll choose tools for computation such as estimation, mental math, and a calculator.**

Exploration 1

Estimating With Rounding

GOAL

LEARN HOW TO...
- estimate by rounding
- decide when to use an estimate

AS YOU...
- look at everyday situations

KEY TERMS
- estimate
- round

▶ **When you do not need to know an exact answer, sometimes making an estimate is easier and faster.**

3 **Discussion** For each situation, when will an estimate be useful? When will you need an exact answer?

a. amount you'll be paid for babysitting for three hours

b. the time when the spaghetti you are cooking will be ready

c. the number of students who go to your school

▶ **Estimating Sums and Differences One way to estimate is to round numbers before you add or subtract.**

EXAMPLE

Suppose you are running for office at school. Estimate the number of fliers you'll need for 347 sixth graders, 261 seventh graders, and 493 eighth graders.

SAMPLE RESPONSE

First Round the numbers to the nearest hundred.

Then Use mental math to add.

$$\begin{array}{r} 347 \\ 261 \\ +\ 493 \\ \hline \end{array} \longrightarrow \begin{array}{r} 300 \\ 300 \\ +\ 500 \\ \hline 1100 \end{array}$$

I will need about 1100 fliers.

FOR ▶ HELP with *rounding whole numbers*, and *money*, see **TOOLBOX, p. 591**

4 In the Example, the number 347 was rounded down by almost 50. Together 261 and 493 were rounded up by almost 50.

a. Do you think 1100 is a reasonable estimate? Explain.

b. If all the numbers are rounded to the nearest ten, will the estimated sum be *greater than* or *less than* the exact sum? Explain.

5 Give an example of when you need to know whether your estimate is greater than or less than the exact answer.

6 **a.** Estimate the difference 362 – 29 by rounding the numbers to the nearest ten and then using mental math to subtract.

b. Explain why rounding 362 and 29 to the nearest hundred does not give a reasonable estimate.

c. Explain why rounding 362 to 400 and 29 to 30 does not give a reasonable estimate.

▶ **A diagram can help you understand why a subtraction estimate is greater than or less than the actual difference.**

EXAMPLE

Estimate the difference 346 – 104. Decide whether your estimate is *greater than* or *less than* the exact difference. Explain your thinking.

SAMPLE RESPONSE

I can round both numbers to the nearest ten.

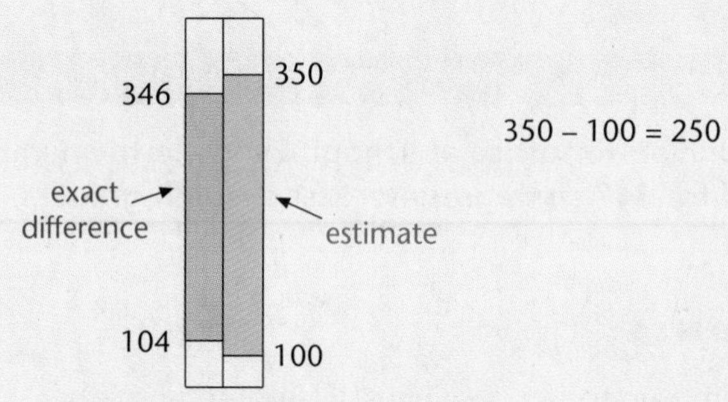

My estimate is greater than the exact difference. Rounding 346 up and rounding 104 down increased the difference.

7 Decide whether your estimate for Question 6(a) is *greater than* or *less than* the exact difference. Explain your thinking.

✓ **QUESTION 8**

...checks that you can estimate sums and differences using rounding.

8 ✓ **CHECKPOINT** Estimate each sum or difference. Decide whether the estimate is *greater than* or *less than* the exact answer or whether it is hard to tell. Explain your thinking.

a. 139 + 57

b. 57 – 49

c. 13,968 – 2,117

d. 291 + 513 + 115

e. 21,281 + 5,260 + 79,346

f. \$38.15 – \$6.78

▶ **Estimating Products** **You can also use rounding to estimate products. Here are two ways students estimated 258 x 6.**

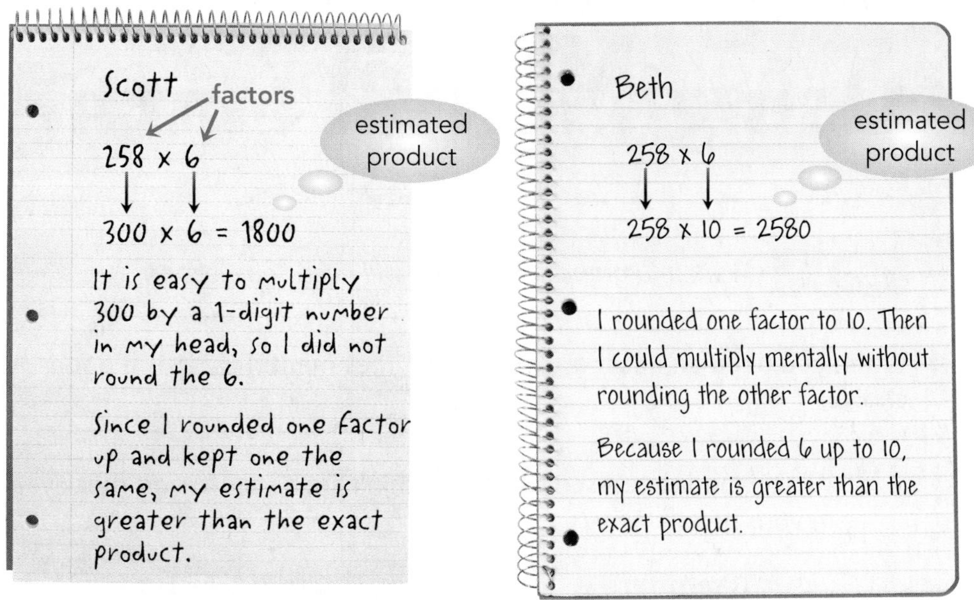

9 **Try This as a Class** Look at the students' work above.

a. Predict which estimate is closer to the exact product.

b. Find 258×6. Which of the two estimates is closer to the exact product?

c. In which estimate was the smaller factor rounded up? By how much did the size of the factor change?

d. In which estimate was the larger factor rounded up? By how much did the size of the factor change?

e. Which method of rounding had a greater effect on the estimate? Why do you think this happened?

10 **a.** Estimate 76×43. Round both factors before multiplying.

b. Is it hard to tell whether your estimate from part (a) is greater than or less than the exact product? Explain.

11 ✓ **CHECKPOINT** Estimate each product. Decide whether the estimate is *greater than* or *less than* the exact product or whether it is hard to tell. Explain your thinking.

a. 13×61 **b.** 63×391 **c.** 224×7

d. 99×55 **e.** 723×118 **f.** 3968×442

✓ **QUESTION 11**

...checks that you know how to use rounding to estimate products.

HOMEWORK EXERCISES See Exs. 1–10 on pp. 51–52.

GOAL

LEARN HOW TO...
- use compatible numbers for mental math
- decide when to use mental math, paper and pencil, or a calculator

AS YOU...
- take part in *The Great Arithmetic Race*

KEY TERM
- compatible numbers

Exploration 2

Using Mental Math

SET UP *Work in a group of four. You will need Labsheet 4A.*

▶ **When you need an exact answer, sometimes mental math is a good choice.**

12 Which candidate's scores do you think are easier to add quickly in your head? Why?

Candidate A	
Room 1	14 votes
Room 2	17 votes
Room 3	16 votes
Room 4	13 votes

Candidate B	
Room 1	19 votes
Room 2	12 votes
Room 3	17 votes
Room 4	14 votes

▶ **Checking for *compatible numbers* can help you add quickly and easily in your head. Compatible numbers are numbers that have sums and products that are easy to find and compute with.**

EXAMPLE

Use mental math to find the sum: 19 + 27 + 11

SAMPLE RESPONSE

19 and 11 are compatible because 30 is easy to compute here.

$19 + 27 + 11 \longrightarrow 30 + 27 = 57$ (19 and 11 combine to 30)

13 For each candidate's list of votes in Question 12, give any pairs of compatible numbers you see.

...checks that you can use compatible numbers for mental math.

14 **CHECKPOINT** Use mental math to find each sum.

a. 40 + 60 + 87 **b.** 42 + 24 + 8 + 26

c. 113 + 76 + 74 + 87 **d.** 17 + 8 + 30 + 75

▶ **Multiplying by Mental Math** **Checking for compatible numbers may also help you multiply quickly in your head. Look for numbers with products that are easy to compute with.**

> **FOR ▶ HELP**
> with *multiplying by tens*, see
> **TOOLBOX, p. 598**

EXAMPLE

Use mental math to find the product $4 \times 7 \times 5$.

SAMPLE RESPONSE

4 and 5 are compatible because it is easy to multiply by 20.

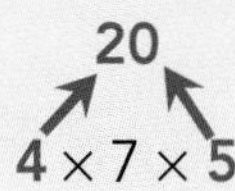

$4 \times 7 \times 5 \longrightarrow 20 \times 7 = 140$

You can easily multiply 7 by 20 in your head.

▶ **Another way to show multiplication is to use a dot between the factors. For example, $4 \times 7 \times 5$ can also be written as $4 \cdot 7 \cdot 5$.**

15 Explain how you can use compatible numbers to find the product $4 \cdot 17 \cdot 25$ by mental math.

16 ✓ **CHECKPOINT** Use mental math to find each product.

a. $2 \cdot 8 \cdot 15$ **b.** $9 \cdot 5 \cdot 4$

c. $25 \cdot 6 \cdot 4 \cdot 4$ **d.** $5 \cdot 9 \cdot 5 \cdot 4$

...checks that you can use compatible numbers for mental math.

▶ **Choosing a Computational Tool** **It is important to know when to use mental math, paper and pencil, or a calculator.** ***The Great Arithmetic Race*** **will help you see which tool to choose for different problems.**

Use Labsheet 4A for Questions 17 and 18.

17 Follow the directions for *The Great Arithmetic Race* to play one round of the game.

18 **Discussion** Use your results from *The Great Arithmetic Race* to help you answer parts (a)–(c).

a. Was the calculator always the quickest tool? Explain.

b. When is it best to use paper and pencil to do the computation?

c. Give an example of when you should use mental math.

HOMEWORK EXERCISES ▶ See Exs. 11–26 on pp. 52–53.

GOAL

LEARN HOW TO...
- follow the order of operations

AS YOU...
- look for patterns in number sentences.

KEY TERMS
- expression
- order of operations

Exploration 3

1. Order 2. Of 3. Operations

SET UP *You will need a calculator.*

▶ **When they solved the problems below, Lydia and Elsa used the same numbers and operations but got different answers.**

19 Are Lydia's and Elsa's answers correct? Explain.

How many feet of fencing are needed to fence in the garden?

How many beads are needed to make the necklace?

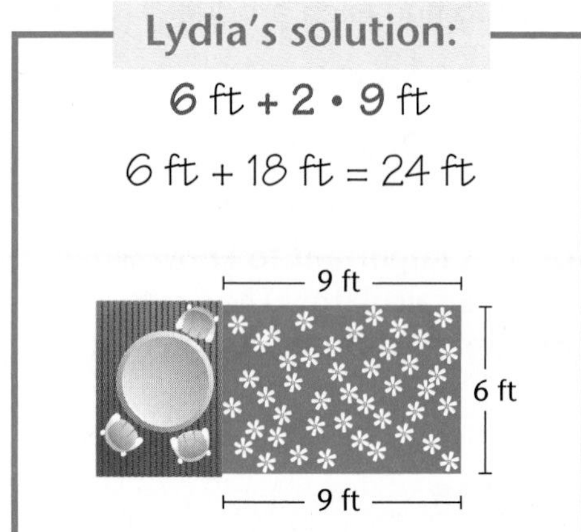

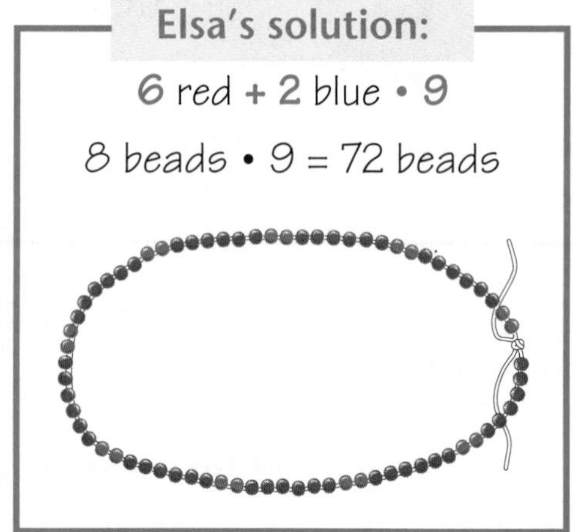

▶ **When they solved their problems, Lydia and Elsa both wrote 6 + 2 • 9. This is an example of a mathematical *expression*. An expression can contain numbers and operation symbols.**

20 What values can you get for the expression 7 + 5 • 3 if you do not know the order in which to perform the operations?

▶ **Mathematics would be very confusing if an expression like 7 + 5 • 3 had more than one value. To understand each other's work, mathematicians have agreed on an order to follow when performing operations. This order is known as the order of operations.**

To answer Questions 21–24, study the number sentences. Each number sentence follows the order of operations.

21 Describe the order in which addition and subtraction are performed to get the answers shown.

$4 + 5 - 3 = 6$ $\quad$ $30 - 10 - 8 = 12$ $\quad$ $16 - 8 + 11 = 19$

22 Describe the order in which multiplication and division are performed to get the answers shown.

$10 \cdot 6 \div 3 = 20$ $\quad$ $24 \div 6 \cdot 2 = 8$ $\quad$ $60 \div 10 \div 2 = 3$

23 Describe the order in which operations are performed to get the answers shown.

$3 \cdot 6 - 5 = 13$ $\quad$ $20 - 6 \cdot 2 = 8$

$30 \div 10 + 5 = 8$ $\quad$ $15 - 4 \cdot 3 + 6 = 9$

24 How do parentheses affect the order in which operations are performed? (*Hint:* Compare these number sentences with the ones in Question 23.)

$3 \cdot (6 - 5) = 3$ $\quad$ $(20 - 6) \cdot 2 = 28$

$30 \div (10 + 5) = 2$ $\quad$ $(15 - 4) \cdot 3 + 6 = 39$

25 **Try This as a Class** Use your results from Questions 21–24. Describe the order of operations in a way that is clear and easy to remember.

26 Look at Elsa's work on page 48. According to the order of operations, the value of $6 + 2 \cdot 9$ is 24, not 72. Rewrite this expression so that it clearly shows what Elsa is thinking.

27 ✓ **CHECKPOINT** Find the value of each expression.

a. $5 + 3 \cdot 2$ $\quad$ **b.** $12 - 8 + 5$ $\quad$ **c.** $25 \cdot 4 \div 2$

d. $6 \cdot 5 - 18 \div 3$ $\quad$ **e.** $6 \cdot (5 - 2) \div 9$ $\quad$ **f.** $4 + (14 - 6)$

✓ **QUESTION 27**

...checks that you can follow the order of operations.

▶ **Although scientific calculators are designed to follow the order of operations, some other calculators are not.**

28 Calculator Use the expressions in Question 23 to see if your calculator follows the order of operations.

HOMEWORK EXERCISES ▶ **See Exs. 27–42 on pp. 53–55.**

Section 4 Key Concepts

Key Terms

Choosing a Method of Computation (p. 43)

Estimation, mental math, paper and pencil, and a calculator are all tools you can use to do computation. The best method to use depends on whether you need an exact answer and on the kinds of numbers you are working with.

Estimation Using Rounding (pp. 43–45)

estimate

round

Rounding can be used to estimate sums, differences, and products when an exact answer is not needed.

Example

247×26

$\downarrow \quad \downarrow$

$250 \times 30 = 7500$

estimated product

Since both factors were rounded up, the estimated product is greater than the exact product.

Mental Math Using Compatible Numbers (pp. 46–47)

compatible numbers

Compatible numbers are numbers that have sums or products that are easy to find and compute with.

Example

$5 \cdot 3 \cdot 5 \cdot 4 \cdot 6 = 100 \cdot 18 = 1800$

(100 groups 5, 5, and 4; 18 groups 3 and 6)

5, 5, and 4 are compatible numbers. Their product, 100, is easy to compute with.

The dot is a symbol for multiplication.

29 **Key Concepts Question** Ann wants to buy three 48¢ pens and one 52¢ ruler at the school store. (There is no tax.)

a. How many dollars does she need to bring to school?

b. Explain what method you used to solve part (a) and why you chose to use that method.

Section 4 Key Concepts

Order of Operations (pp. 48–49)

An expression can contain numbers, operation symbols, and parentheses.

Order of Operations	Example
	$18 - (2 + 4) \cdot 3 + 12$
First Calculate what is inside parentheses.	$18 - (2 + 4) \cdot 3 + 12$ $= 18 - 6 \cdot 3 + 12$
Next Perform multiplication and division in order from left to right.	$= 18 - 6 \cdot 3 + 12$ $= 18 - 18 + 12$
Then Perform addition and subtraction in order from left to right.	$= 18 - 18 + 12$ $= 0 + 12$ $= 12$

Key Terms

expression

order of operations

Key Concepts Questions Find the value of each expression.

30 $10 + 12 \div (3 + 1)$

31 $5 \cdot 3 + 4 - 2 \cdot 6$

Section 4 Practice & Application Exercises

1. a. About how much is the total on the grocery receipt?

   b. Suppose you have exactly $4.80. Without finding an exact total, can you tell if you have enough money to buy the three items? Explain.

1 gal lowfat milk	2.95
1 can of soup	.85
wheat bread	1.09
TOTAL	

2. **Open-ended** Describe two situations when it is appropriate to estimate an answer. Explain your reasoning.

Estimate each answer. Decide whether the estimate is *greater than* or *less than* the exact answer or whether it is hard to tell.

3. $128 + 72$
4. $347 \cdot 42$
5. $58 \cdot 29$
6. $421 - 209$
7. $61 \cdot 992$
8. $794 + 8932$

▲ The abacus is a calculating tool used in China, Japan, and the former Soviet Union.

9. **Russian Abacus** The pictures show a Russian abacus before and after adding two numbers. The first picture shows 542.

5 4 2

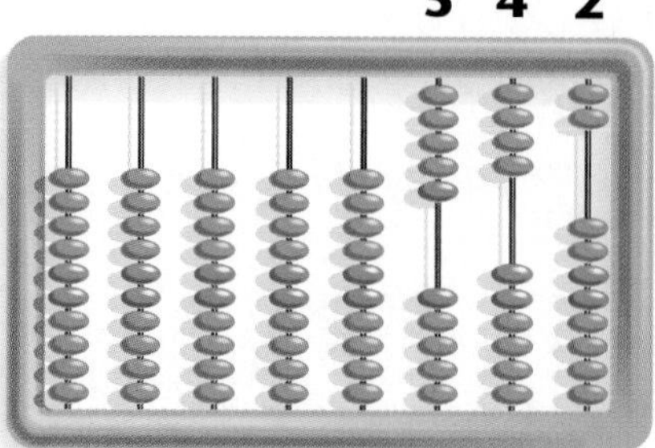

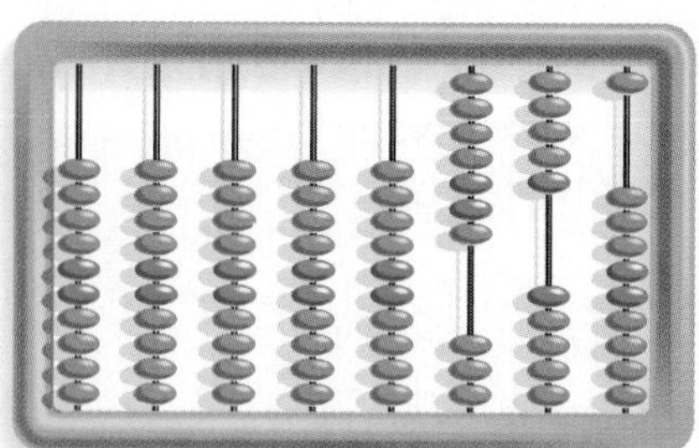

a. Use the beads to estimate about how much was added to 542. Explain how you made your estimate.

b. What number does the second abacus display?

c. Find the exact number that was added to 542 and write the addition sentence.

10. **Presidential Election** The table shows Delaware's results for the 1992 presidential election. Estimate the missing numbers in the table. Then decide whether each estimate is *greater than* or *less than* the exact answer or whether it is hard to tell.

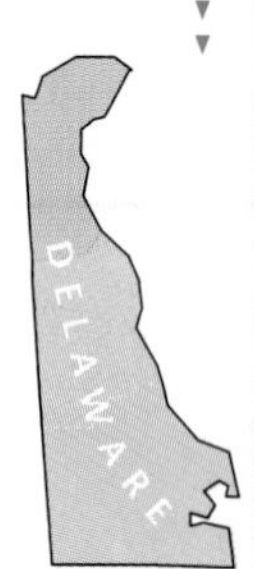

County	Clinton (Democrat)	Bush (Republican)	Perot (Independent)
Kent	15,273	15,571	8,829
New Castle	91,551	66,423	?
Sussex	19,173	?	12,714
TOTALS	?	102,436	59,061

Use compatible numbers to find each answer by mental math.

11. 7 + 15 + 13 + 5

12. 210 + 35 + 65 + 90

13. 2 • 15 • 4

14. 50 + 22 + 3

15. 3 • 4 • 25 • 2

16. 5 • 12 • 2 • 10

Choosing a Method **Find the value of each expression. Which can be done using mental math? Did you use mental math? If not, why?**

17. 3678 + 729 + 534

18. 2 • 8 • 15

19. 7 • 13 • 4

20. 24 + 380 + 56 + 120

Use Exercises 21 and 22 to explore when you can change the order and grouping of numbers. Support each answer with examples.

21. Addition and multiplication are *commutative* because changing the order does not affect a sum or product. Are subtraction and division commutative?

Examples: $3 + 4 = 4 + 3$ and $2 \cdot 6 = 6 \cdot 2$

22. Addition and multiplication are *associative* because changing the grouping does not affect a sum or product. Are subtraction and division associative?

Examples: $(12 + 5) + 9 = 12 + (5 + 9)$

and $(3 \cdot 2) \cdot 7 = 3 \cdot (2 \cdot 7)$

Estimation In Exercises 23–25, explain how to use compatible numbers to estimate each answer.

Example: $26 \cdot 198 \rightarrow 26 \cdot 200 = 5200$ or $26 \cdot 198 \rightarrow 25 \cdot 200 = 5000$

23. $14 \cdot 2 \cdot 39$

24. $24 \cdot 389$

25. $325 + (34 + 40)$

26. Which estimate in the Example is closer to the exact product? How do you know?

27. **Sports** The manager of a track team sets up hurdles for the 400-meter race. The manager writes this expression to find how far apart to place the hurdles.

$$400 - 40 - 45 \div 9$$

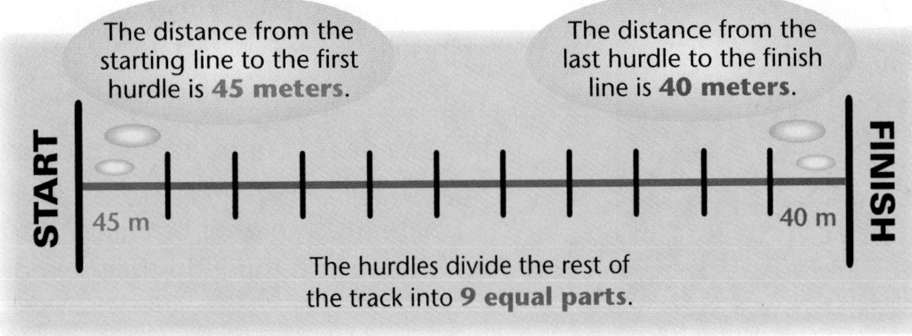

a. Follow the order of operations on page 51 to find the value of the manager's expression.

b. **Writing** Is this answer reasonable? Explain. If not, rewrite the expression. Then find how far apart to place the hurdles.

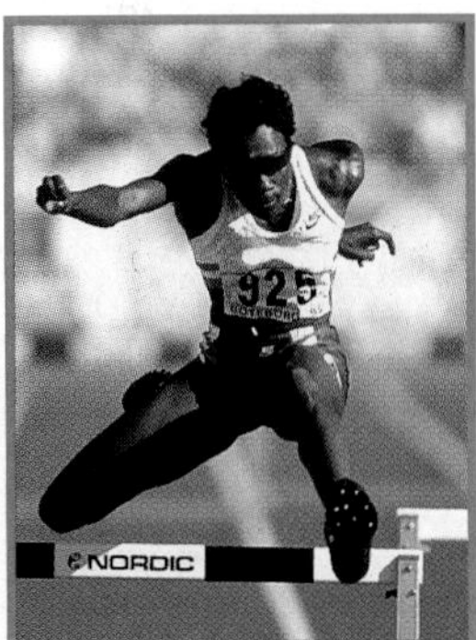

▲ On August 11, 1995, Kim Batten of the United States set the world record for the women's 400-meter hurdles with a time of 52.61 seconds.

Find the value of each expression.

28. $7 + 2 \cdot 3$

29. $4 \cdot 6 + 3 \cdot 4$

30. $6 + (18 - 9) \cdot 2$

31. $12 - 8 \div 4$

32. $80 \div 5 \cdot 4$

33. $(12 + 3) \div 3 + 2$

34. $5 \cdot 4 - 2 \div 2$

35. $(11 + 4) \div 5$

36. $6 \cdot (2 + 4) - 3$

FOR ▶ HELP with *time relationships*, see **TOOLBOX, p. 601**

37. Thomas Fuller thought for about a minute and a half before answering this question:

> "A man has lived 70 years, 17 days, and 12 hours. How many seconds has he lived?"

Then he gave this correct answer: 2,210,500,800 seconds.

When someone else worked it out on paper and got a smaller answer, Fuller told him that he forgot the leap years.

17 of the 70 years the man lived were leap years.

This expression can be used to find Fuller's answer:

12 • (number of seconds in an hour) + 17 • (number of seconds in a day) + 53 • (number of seconds in a year) + 17 • (number of seconds in a leap year)

a. What does the number 53 stand for in the expression?

b. Use mental math to find the **number of seconds in an hour.**

c. Estimate the **number of seconds in a day.**

d. Estimate the **number of seconds in a year.**

e. Can you use the estimate you found in part (d) as your estimate for the **number of seconds in a leap year**? Explain why or why not.

A farmer owns 6 sows.
After a year, each sow has 6 female piglets.
6 6 6 6 6 6
Every year the piglets grow up to be sows and all the sows again have 6 female piglets.
After 8 years, how many sows are there?

38. a. **Challenge** Copy the expression for Fuller's answer. Use your results from Exercise 37 to estimate the value of the expression.

b. How does your estimate compare with Fuller's answer? Is your estimate much higher or lower? If so, why do you think this happened?

◀ Thomas Fuller (1710–1790) was brought from Africa as a slave at age 14. Although he could not read or write, he had extraordinary mental calculating ability. He solved the problem at the left in 10 minutes.

Write an expression to show each set of operations in the correct order.

39. Add 11 and 5. Then divide the sum by 4.

40. Multiply 3 and 5. Then divide 60 by that result.

41. Start with 50. Then subtract the product of 4 and 6.

Reflecting on the Section

Be prepared to report on the following topic in class.

42. a. Choose from the digits 3, 5, 4, 2, and 8. You may not repeat a digit. Copy and fill in the boxes to make the greatest possible product.

	?	?
×		?

b. **Choosing a Method** Describe how you used estimation, mental math, a calculator, or a combination of methods to solve this problem.

Oral Report

Exercise 42 checks that you can choose appropriate computational tools to solve a problem.

Spiral Review

43. In how many different ways can you make 35 cents in change using only nickels, dimes, and quarters? **(Module 1, p. 35)**

Write the next two terms of each sequence. **(Module 1, p. 8)**

44. 9, 13, 17, 21, ...

45. 2, 5, 9, 14, ...

46. A triangle has a perimeter of 12 cm. The length of one side is 5 cm. What is a possible length for each of the other sides? **(Toolbox, p. 599; Module 1, p. 22)**

Extension

Applying Order of Operations

47. Find a sequence of keys that results in each number 1 through 10. You may use only the keys [2], [5], [×], [−], and [=]. You may use each key as many times as you like or not at all.

Example: The key strokes below result in 8.

[5] [×] [2] [−] [2] [=]

Section 4
Extra Skill Practice

Estimate each answer. Decide whether the estimate is *greater than* or *less than* the exact answer or whether it is hard to tell.

1. $229 + 68$
2. $323 - 119$
3. $64 + 42$
4. $137 + 22$
5. $31 \cdot 58$
6. $427 - 212$
7. $158 + 43 + 78$
8. $2362 - 1221$
9. $193 \cdot 13$
10. $12 \cdot 62$
11. $98 \cdot 45$
12. $22{,}352 + 1{,}649$

Use compatible numbers to find each answer by mental math.

13. $12 + 17 + 8 + 3$
14. $6 + 19 + 14 + 211$
15. $32 + 45 + 5 + 8$
16. $140 + 58 + 60 + 42$
17. $5 \cdot 5 \cdot 12 \cdot 4$
18. $2 \cdot 3 \cdot 3 \cdot 25$
19. $15 \cdot 4 \cdot 6 \cdot 5$
20. $20 \cdot 8 \cdot 5 \cdot 3$

Find the value of each expression.

21. $5 + 7 \cdot 3$
22. $6 \cdot 4 + 7 \cdot 2$
23. $15 - 6 \div 3$
24. $60 \div 15 \cdot 5$
25. $10 + 30 \div 6$
26. $42 - 21 \cdot 2$
27. $(10 + 4) \div 7 + 3$
28. $5 + (12 - 4) \cdot 4$
29. $(19 - 10) \cdot 5 - 8$
30. $16 \div 2 \cdot (5 + 3)$
31. $25 - (14 + 3) + 6$
32. $2 \cdot (5 + 8) - 4 \div 2$

Standardized Testing ▶ Multiple Choice

1. Which expression matches this set of directions?
   - First multiply 25 by 9.
   - Next add 16 to the product.
   - Then divide the total by 4.

   A $(16 + 25 \cdot 9) \div 4$
   B $25 \cdot 9 \div 4 + 16$
   C $25 \cdot 9 + 16 \div 4$
   D $16 + (25 \cdot 9) \div 4$

2. Use mental math to decide which expression is equal to $17 + 46 + 13 + 24$.

   A $20 + 60$
   B $46 + 50$
   C $30 + 70$
   D $30 + 50 + 25$

Section 5 Using Visuals

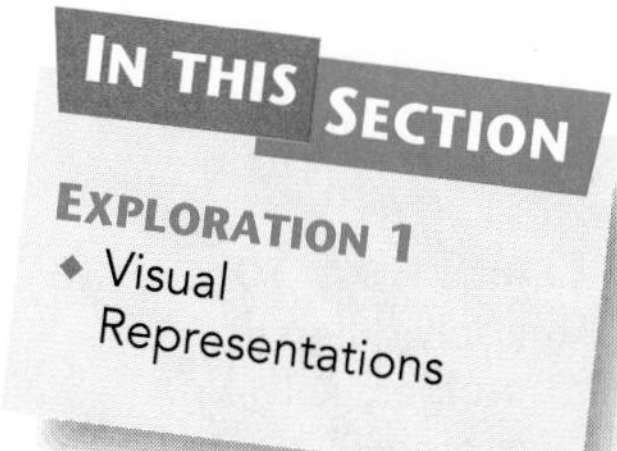

Teamwork as a Tool

Setting the Stage

SET UP *Work in a group of four. You will need* Who's Sitting Where? Clue Cards *from Labsheet 5A.*

Have you ever played basketball? performed in a band or a choir? If so, you already know how important teamwork is. Teamwork is also an important tool for learning mathematics.

▶ **Work as a team to solve the puzzle below. Your group will be given four clues. Each member will get one clue. You may read your clue aloud but may not show it to your team.**

Brad, Marie, Nicole, Saburo, and Tyrone are sitting in a row. Use the clues to figure out who is sitting where.

Think About It

1 What do you think makes a good team? What do you think makes a good team member?

2 Do you think your group worked well together as a team? Why or why not?

GOAL

LEARN HOW TO...

- apply different problem solving strategies
- use the representations scale

AS YOU...

- work as a team to solve a handshake problem

Exploration 1

VISUAL RepresEntations

SET UP *Work in a group. You will need Labsheet 5B.*

3 **Discussion** What problem solving strategies did you use to solve the puzzle on page 57? Did you act out the problem? Was making a table or a diagram helpful? Explain.

▶ **Diagrams, tables, and graphs can help you solve problems and explain solutions. You'll use the representations scale to assess and improve your use of visuals and other representations.**

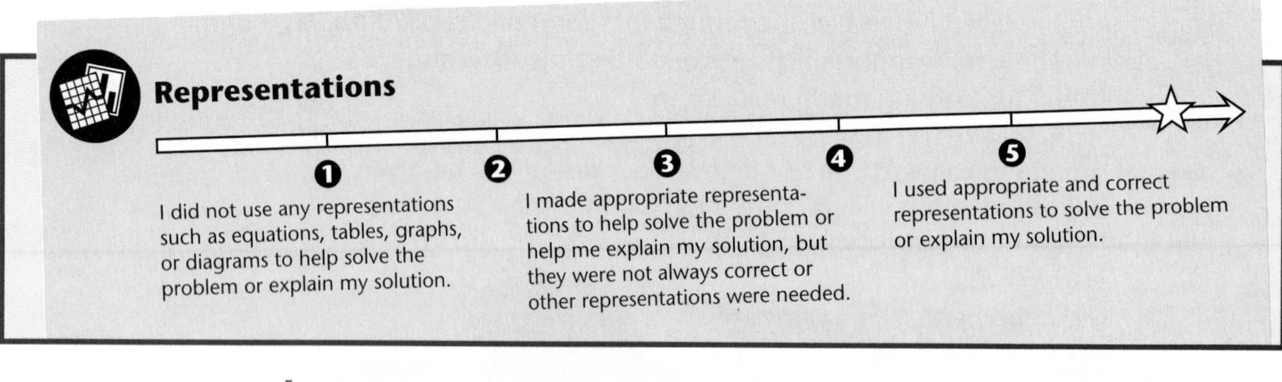

4 Work as a team and use the 4-step approach to solve this problem. Think about how good team skills and visuals can help. Write an explanation that shows how your team solved the problem.

> Five people are hired to work together on a project. As they are introduced, they shake hands with each other exactly one time. How many handshakes take place?

5 If your team used a visual to solve or explain the handshake problem, was it appropriate? Was it correct? Explain why.

6 **Discussion** Explain to the class the visual representations or other problem solving strategies your team used.

7 ✓ **CHECKPOINT** What score would you give your team on the representations scale on page 58? Why?

✓ **QUESTION 7**

...checks that you understand the representations scale.

HOMEWORK EXERCISES ▶ See Exs. 1–9 on pp. 60–62.

Section 5 Key Concepts

Team Skills in Problem Solving (p. 57)

A good team member

- listens carefully to the ideas of others
- communicates well both orally and in writing
- sets goals and works toward them together with the team
- shares responsibility for work

Representations Scale (p. 58)

This scale can be used to assess how well you use equations, tables, graphs, and diagrams to solve a problem.

Ask yourself:

- Was my representation appropriate?
- Was my representation correct?
- Were there any other representations I should have used?

8 **Key Concepts Question Use Labsheet 5B.** To solve the handshake problem, two teams acted it out. On the labsheet are the *Teams' Explanations* of what they did. What score would you give each team on the *Representations Scale*? Explain why.

Section 5 Practice & Application Exercises

1. **Arctic Exploration** In 1995 a team of explorers crossed 2000 mi of sea ice using dog sleds and canoe-sleds. The team traveled from Russia to Canada over the North Pole.

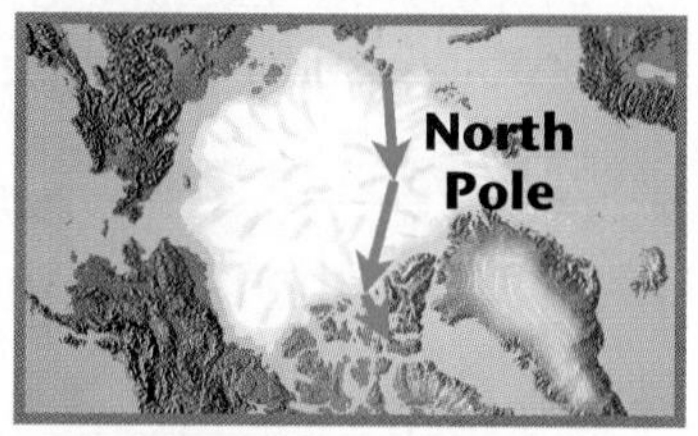

▲ Team Members: Will Steger (United States), Victor Boyarsky (Russia), Julie Hanson (United States), Martin Hignell (Great Britain), Takako Takano (Japan), Ulrik Vedel (Denmark).

The navigator had a doctorate in mathematics. The other team members had the skills of a survival instructor, a paramedic, a dog trainer, an environment researcher, and a writer. Give an example of how two of the team skills listed on page 59 may have been important to this team's success.

2. **Research** Look through the help-wanted ads in the newspaper for ads requiring teamwork skills. Why do you think teamwork skills are important for the jobs you found?

3. **Geometry Connection** Explain why each visual is or is not an appropriate and correct solution to the problem: Draw a segment that divides a square into two right triangles.

a. 

b. 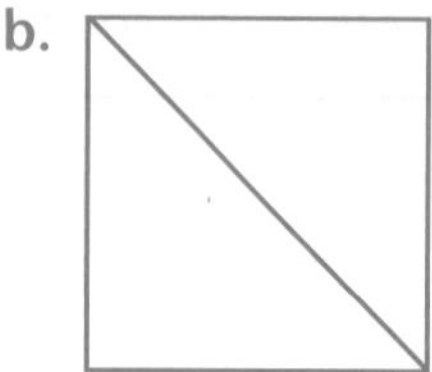

c. 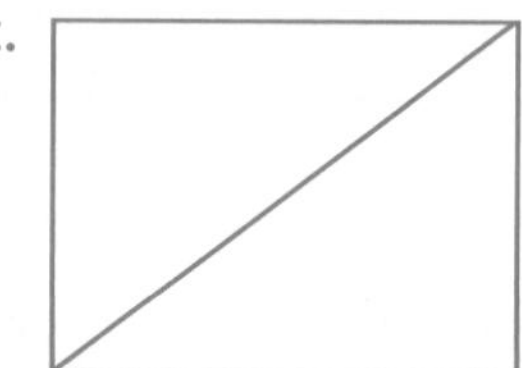

4. **Choosing a Data Display** A sales manager found that 20 gray cars, 40 silver cars, and 100 green cars had been sold. Which graph best displays the sales manager's data? Explain your choice.

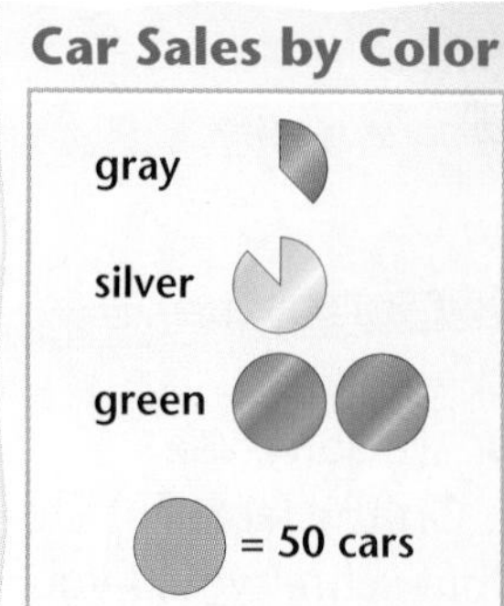

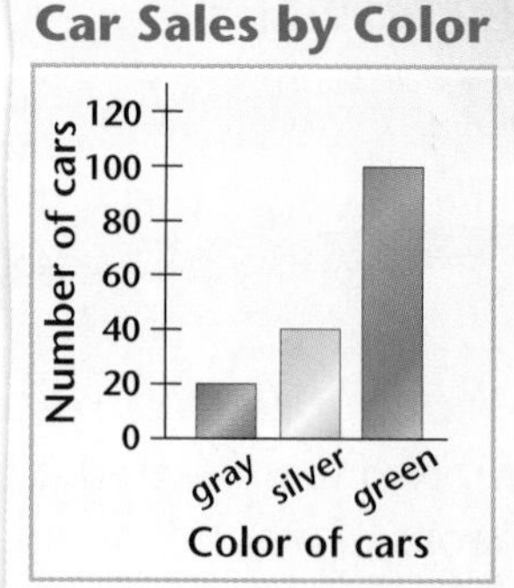

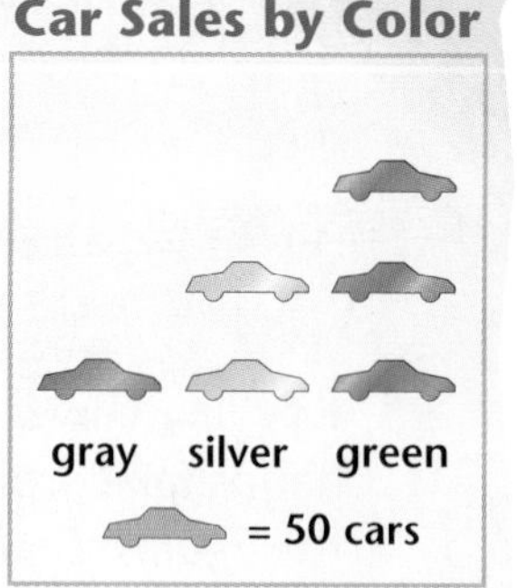

5. Felicia's house is located 2 mi east of the library. The park is 5 mi west of the library. Felicia's school is 3 mi east of the park. How far is it from Felicia's house to the school? Copy and complete the diagram to find the answer.

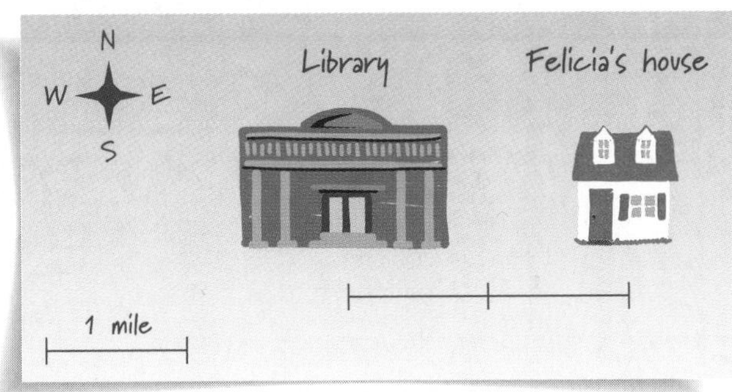

6. a. Half of a boat's crew of 15 men and 15 women could leave to visit a port. The crew lined up. Every ninth person was allowed to leave until half the crew had left. The crew still on the boat were all women. In what order did the crew line up? Show how you found your answer.

   b. Use the representations scale on page 58. What score would you give your solution to part (a)? Why?

7. **Challenge** Use the figure shown.

   a. Trace the figure.

   b. Use two segments to divide the figure into three triangles. One triangle must be both obtuse and isosceles and the other two triangles must be both right and scalene.

   c. Label each triangle to show which type it is.

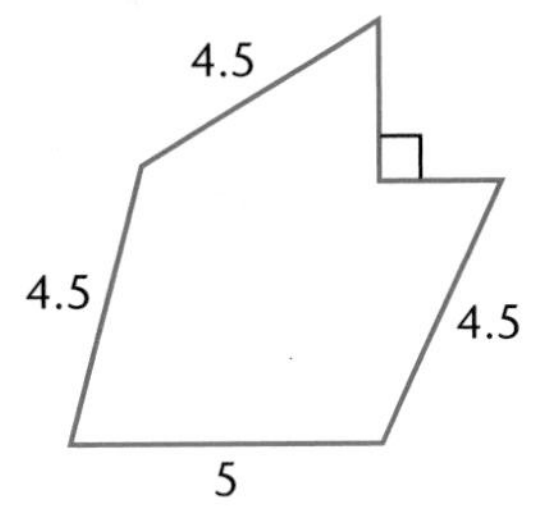

FOR ◀HELP with *classifying triangles*, see **MODULE 1, p. 22**

8. **Home Involvement** Teamwork can help you deal with emergencies and natural disasters such as floods, fires, and earthquakes.

   a. Describe a household emergency and write a plan for everyone's safety. Be sure to include a diagram.

   b. Discuss everyone's role in your plan with your household. Revise the plan if needed.

If a fire occurs and the room door is OPEN

- ✓GET close to the floor. Keep LOW.
- ✓CHECK for smoke and fire.
- ✓If it is safe to leave, COVER your nose and mouth with a cloth (moist if possible). GET LOW and GET OUT quickly.
- ✓If there is SMOKE or FIRE, immediately CLOSE THE DOOR and use an alternate escape route.

Visual THINKING

Exercise 9 checks that you understand how a visual representation can be used to solve problems.

Reflecting on the Section

9. **Create Your Own** Write a word problem that could be solved using one of the visuals shown below.

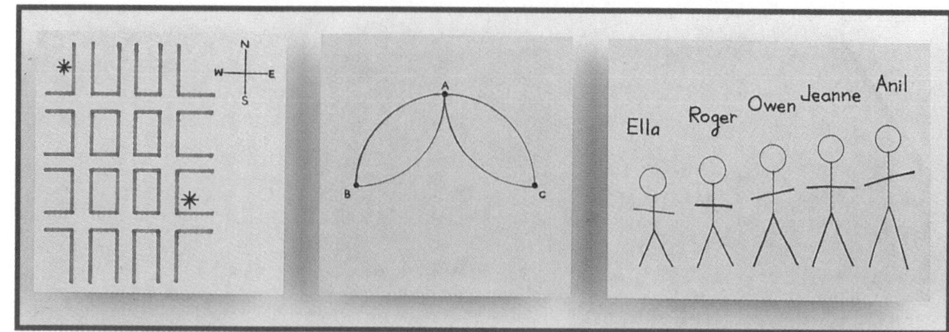

Spiral Review

Find the value of each expression (Module 1, p. 51)

10. $6 \cdot 5 + 13$
11. $54 - 81 \div 9$
12. $144 \div (12 - 8)$

Decide if the given lengths will form a triangle. (Module 1, p. 22)

13. 3 in., 2 in., 6 in.
14. 4 ft, 22 ft, 25 ft

15. Make a table for the sequence 4, 8, 12, 16,.... Extend it to include the next two terms. Then write a general rule for the sequence. (Module 1, p. 8)

A Puzzling Problem

Making and Carrying Out Your Plan Now you'll consider the work you have done on the *30 Pennies in a Row* problem so far.

 **5** **Use Project Labsheet A.** Read *The Problem* again. Choose a strategy or strategies and solve the problem.

 **6** **Use Project Labsheet B.** Score the work you have done so far on the representations and mathematical language scales. How can you improve your scores?

You will need:

- *Project Labsheets A and B*

Section 5 Extra Skill Practice

Show how to use a diagram, a table, or a graph to solve each problem.

1. A school bus travels 3 blocks east, 4 blocks north, 10 blocks west, 2 blocks south, and 1 block east. At this point, the bus is how many blocks north or south of its starting point? How many blocks east or west?

2. An elevator in an office building started at ground level. It rose 5 floors, descended 2 floors, rose 9 floors, descended 3 floors, and rose 7 floors. Which floor is the elevator on?

3. John, Sue, Lisa, and Fernando are student council officers. The council has 4 officers: president, vice president, secretary, and treasurer.
   - John is neither president nor secretary.
   - A boy holds the office of vice president.
   - Sue is not secretary.
   - The names of the treasurer and the vice president have the same number of letters.

   Who is president?

4. The lengths of three sticks are 5 in., 7 in., and 10 in. How can you use these sticks to mark off a length of 8 in.?

5. All six faces of a cube are painted gold. If the cube is cut into 27 smaller cubes, how many cubes have only two gold faces?

Standardized Testing ▶ Multiple Choice

Choose the correct answer to the problem.

There are 2 compact 13-foot long cars and 3 midsize 16-foot long cars parked along a 94-foot long curb. There is equal space between the cars and no space at either end of the curb. How long is the space between cars?

(A) 128 ft (B) 4 ft (C) 5 ft (D) None of these

Section 6 Problem Solving Skills

IN THIS SECTION

EXPLORATION 1
- The Problem Solving Scale

EXPLORATION 2
- The Connections Scale

Using the Tools

Setting the Stage

SET UP *Work in a group.*

The World Cup is a world championship soccer tournament that is held every 4 years and is played over several rounds. In the first round of finals, 24 teams compete against one another. The teams are divided into six groups of four teams. Within each group, each team plays the other three teams once.

▶ **Work as a team to find the total number of games played in the first round of the World Cup finals. Then write up an explanation of your team's solution.**

▶ The World Cup draws a huge audience. In 1990, more than a billion people living on six continents watched the World Cup.

Think About It

1 For each question, explain what your team did when you solved the World Cup problem.

a. Did you make sure everyone understood the problem?

b. Did you make a plan to solve the problem?

c. Did you carry out your plan to find a solution?

d. Did you look back?

▶ **In this section you'll apply assessment tools to improve your problem solving performance.**

Exploration 1

The Problem Solving SCALE

GOAL

LEARN HOW TO...
- use the problem solving scale

AS YOU...
- assess your group's solution to the World Cup problem

SET UP *Work in a group.*

▶ **In Question 1, you saw how well you followed the 4-step approach in solving the World Cup problem. Now see how the problem solving scale below connects to the 4-step approach.**

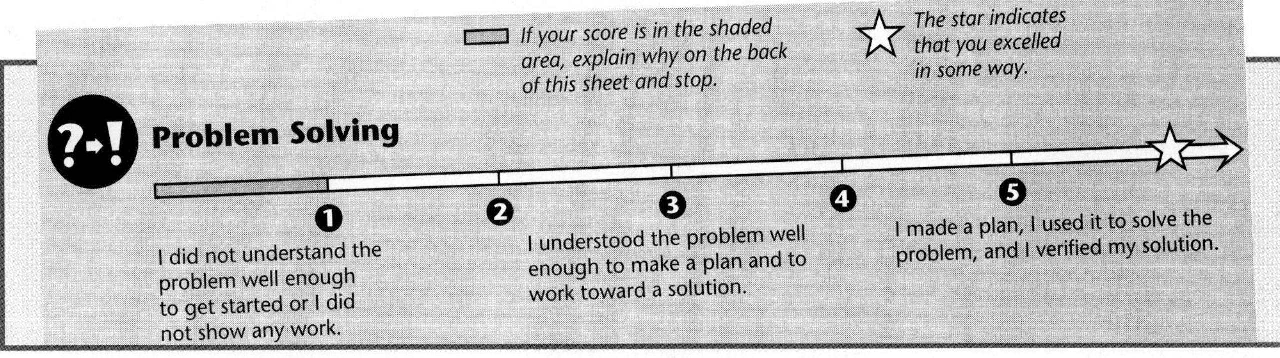

2 If you score a "1" on this scale, you cannot score your work using any of the other assessment scales on page 21. Why?

3 On this scale how can you score a "5"? a "4"?

▶ **Here is Becky's solution to the World Cup problem.**

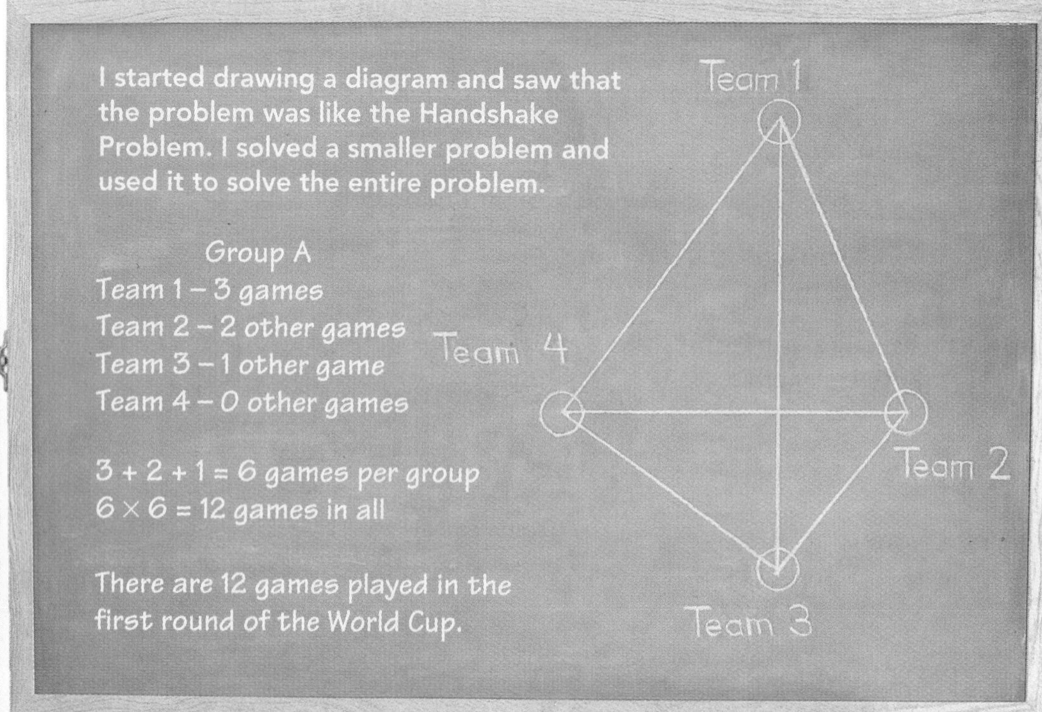

4 Discussion Discuss each question and explain your answer.

a. Do you think Becky understood the World Cup problem?

b. Do you think Becky used a plan to solve the problem?

c. Do you think she looked back?

d. Becky gave herself a "5" on the problem solving scale on page 65. Do you agree with her scoring? Why or why not?

✓ QUESTION 5

...checks that you understand the problem solving scale.

5 ✓ CHECKPOINT Use the problem solving scale on page 65.

a. What score would you give your team's solution to the World Cup problem? Why?

b. What could your team do to improve its score?

HOMEWORK EXERCISES ▶ See Exs. 1–4 on p. 70.

Exploration 2

The Connections Scale

GOAL

LEARN HOW TO...
- extend solutions to the general case
- use the connections scale

AS YOU...
- look for connections between problems you have solved

KEY TERMS
- connections
- general case

▶ **You have made connections by identifying patterns and extending them to other cases. For example, you predicted other appearances of Halley's comet and found the lowest safe bid for playing *Card Swappers* with different numbers of cards.**

6 Describe another connection that you made in this module by identifying and extending a pattern.

▶ **Another type of connection is made when you relate a problem to other problems, mathematical ideas, or applications. When you use the connections scale, you are looking for either type of connection.**

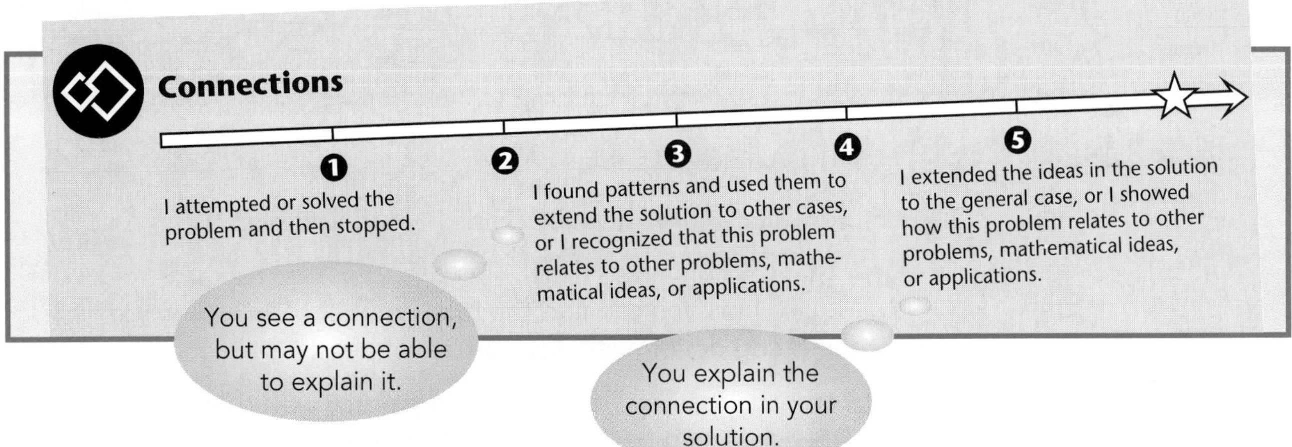

7 **Try This as a Class** Look back at Becky's solution to the World Cup problem at the top of page 66. What score do you think Becky should give her solution on the connections scale? Why?

8 ✓ **CHECKPOINT** Think about your team's solution to the World Cup problem. What score would you give your team on the connections scale? Why?

✓ **QUESTION 8**

...checks that you understand the connections scale.

▶ As you work on the string art problem in Questions 9–12, think about the connections scale.

9 In the design shown, string links each of the six pegs in every way possible. How many linkups are there altogether?

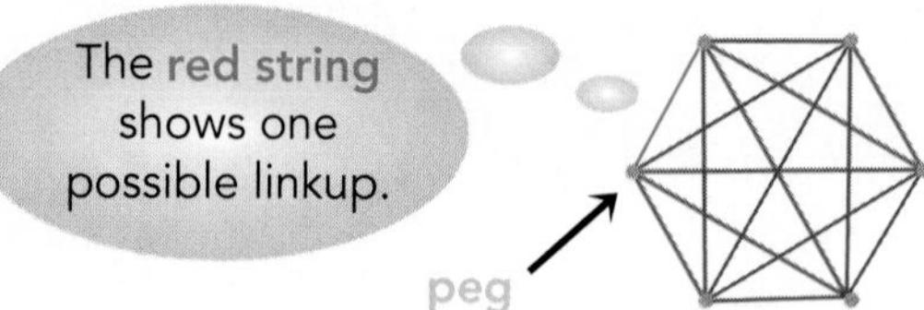

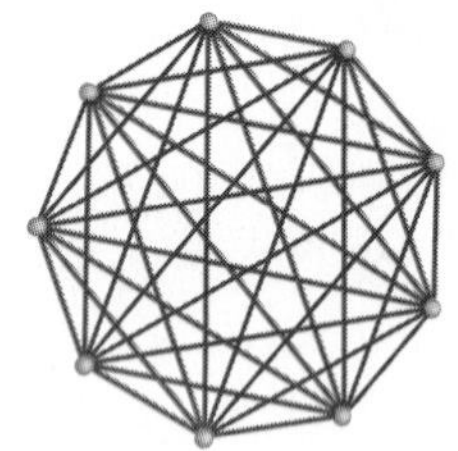

▲ String art designs can be simple or complicated depending on the pattern and the number of pegs used.

10 **Discussion** Is the string design problem related to any other problems you have solved in this module? Explain.

11 Copy and complete the table to find the number of linkups for different numbers of pegs.

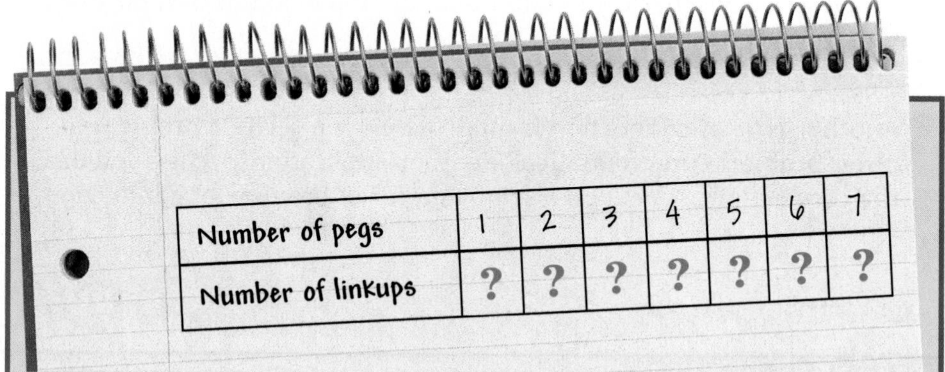

Number of pegs	1	2	3	4	5	6	7
Number of linkups	?	?	?	?	?	?	?

12 **Try This as a Class**

a. How many linkups can be made in a string design with 12 pegs?

b. Explain how you can find the total number of linkups made in a string design with any number of pegs.

c. Compare your method for solving part (b) with those of other class members. If different methods were used, are they all correct?

▶ One way to score a "5" on the connections scale is by extending a solution to the general case. You did this when you found the number of linkups for any number of pegs. You also did this in Section 1 when you wrote a general rule to find any term of a sequence.

HOMEWORK EXERCISES See Exs. 5–7 on pp. 70–71.

Section 6 Key Concepts

Key Terms

Problem Solving Scale (p. 65)

- Did I understand the problem?
- Did I make a plan and get started toward a solution?
- Did I carry out my plan and find a solution?
- Did I look back ? to make sure my work was correct?
  to make sure my answer was reasonable?
  to make sure I answered the right question?
  to try a different method to solve the problem?

Connections Scale (p. 67)

connections

- Did I identify a pattern?
- Did I extend the solution to other cases? to the general case?

general case

- Did I relate the problem to another situation, problem, or mathematical idea?
- Did I clearly show the connections I found?

To extend to the general case, you need to find a rule that will work for any case.

13 **Key Concepts Question** How do you think Sam should score his solution using the problem solving scale on page 65? Why?

Problem:
School buses will be used to take 194 students and 10 adults on a field trip. No more than 60 passengers can be seated on a bus. How many buses will be needed?

Sam's solution:
Since 60 people can fit on a bus, I need to divide the total number of people by 60.

```
    3 R 24
60)204
  -180
    24
```

3 buses will be needed.

Section 6
Practice & Application Exercises

For Exercises 1 and 2, solve each problem and score your solution using the problem solving scale on page 65.

1. A snail starts at the bottom of a well 10 ft deep and crawls up 3 ft each day. Each night the snail slips back 2 ft. How long will it take the snail to reach the top of the well?

2. Use the clues below to find the mystery number.
   - The number is between 0 and 150.
   - If you start with 7 and keep counting by 7s, the number will be on your list.
   - The sum of the digits in the number is 12.
   - The number can be divided evenly by four.

   The sum of the digits in 228 is 2 + 2 + 8 = 12.

FOR ▶ HELP with *whole number multiplication*, see **TOOLBOX, p. 595**

3. a. Find the digit represented by each letter. A letter stands for the same digit throughout the problem. Every letter has a different value.
   b. How can you verify your solution? Explain.

$$\begin{array}{r} CED \\ \times\ GK \\ \hline DD1 \\ +\,257\ \ \\ \hline KK4G \end{array}$$

4. **Challenge** A jeweler has four pieces of gold chain. Each piece has three links. The jeweler wants to join the links to form a closed necklace. Explain how to do this by cutting and rejoining the least number of links.

5. Large stained glass windows are made of panels of colored glass held together by an iron frame.
   a. Suppose a glass panel is 4 ft wide and 10 ft long. About how many feet of iron framing are needed to hold two glass panels stacked vertically as shown? to hold three glass panels stacked vertically?
   b. How can you find how many feet of framing are needed to hold any number of glass panels stacked vertically?
   c. Use the connections scale on page 67. What score would you give your solution to part (b)? Why?

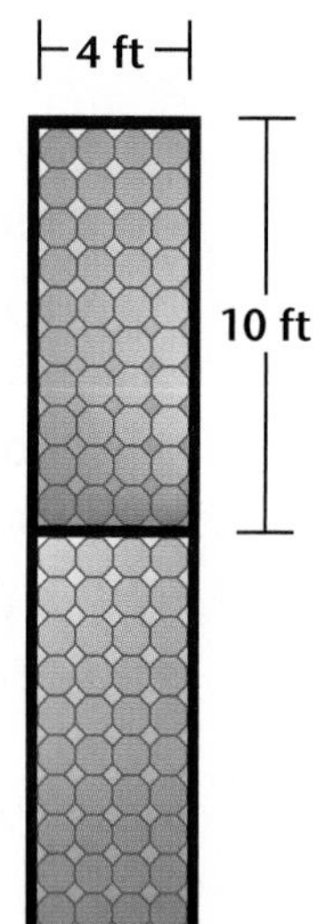

6. **Language Arts** The detective Sherlock Holmes uses clues like these in "The Case of the Itinerant Yeggman" by June Thomson.

December 27, 1894 – Letter arrives at mansion. Professor from Germany wants to visit to study design of buildings.

January 25, 1895 – Professor visits mansion.

July 21, 1895 – Mansion robbed. Among items stolen: priceless prayer book passed down in owner's family.

November 26, 1894 – Letter arrives at old estate. Historian from France wants to visit to study woodwork of rooms.

December 28, 1894 – Historian visits estate.

June 22, 1895 – Estate robbed. Among items stolen: jewelled fan passed down by owner's great grandparents.

October 28, 1894 – Letter arrives at country home. Professor from Chicago wants to visit to study design of floor tiling.

November 27, 1894 – Professor visits country home.

May 24, 1895 – Country home robbed. Among items stolen: gold cup passed down by owner's great grandfather.

a. Describe any patterns that you see in the clues.

b. Holmes learns that the owner of a fourth home received a letter on January 25, 1895, and a visit from a professor on February 24, 1895. He suspects that another break-in may occur. Choose the most likely date. Explain your thinking.

Aug. 15, 1894   July 7, 1895   Aug. 20, 1895   June 5, 1895

Reflecting on the Section

Write your response to Exercise 7 in your journal.

7. The table shows the first four *triangular numbers*.

a. What is a triangular number? Explain how to find the 5th and 6th triangular numbers.

b. What connection can you make between the triangular numbers and other problems you have solved?

1st	2nd	3rd	4th
1	3	6	10
•	• • •	• • • • • •	• • • • • • • • • •

c. Write a rule you can use to find any triangular number.

Journal

Exercise 7 checks that you can make connections as you solve problems.

Spiral Review

8. Jim Tabor needs to fence in a field that is 9 ft wide and 15 ft long. The fence posts must be 3 ft apart. Draw a diagram to help you find how many posts Jim will need. (Module 1, p. 59)

Identify and name each geometric figure. (Module 1, p. 22)

9. 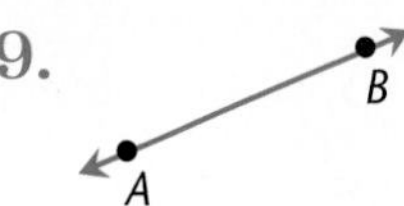

10. C D

11. R S

12. Name all the right angles in the diagram shown at the right. (Module 1, p. 22)

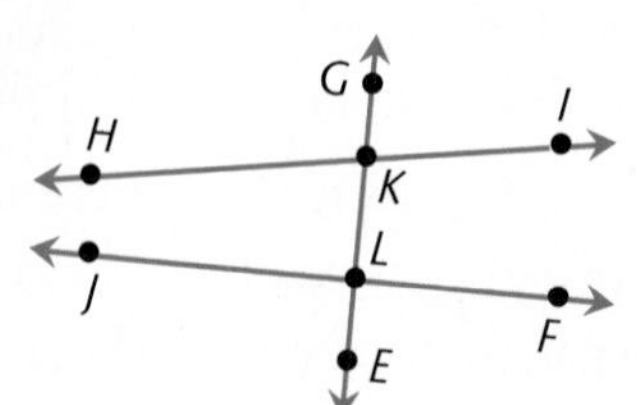

A Puzzling Problem

SET UP

You will need:

- *Project Labsheets A and B*

Verifying and Extending Your Solution Now you'll look back at your answer to the *30 Pennies in a Row* problem.

 7 a. Check that you solved the problem you were given and that your answer is reasonable.

b. Check your work for computational errors.

c. Can you think of any other way to check your answer? If so, explain your method and use it to check your work.

 8 a. What mathematical ideas did you use as you solved the problem? Is this problem like other problems you have solved? Explain.

b. How can you extend the problem to more than 30 coins?

 9 **Use Project Labsheet B.** Score the work you have done so far using the problem solving and connections scales. How can you improve your score?

Section 6
Extra Skill Practice

Solve each problem.

1. A restaurant has two types of tables. One type seats two people and the other seats four. If 28 people are in the restaurant, how many full tables of each type can there be?

2. Tickets to the musical cost $8 for students and $12 for all others. If $520 was earned by the sale of 49 tickets, how many student tickets were sold?

3. The temperature on Sunday was 48°F. On the following day the temperature rose 7 degrees. The next day it fell 5 degrees. On the next two days the temperature rose 3 degrees each day. What was the temperature on Thursday?

4. Walter wants to put a fence around a garden which is 360 ft long and 240 ft wide. If the fence he buys is sold in 12 ft sections, how many sections of fence will Walter need?

5. A number is between 0 and 125, can be divided evenly by 13, and the sum of its digits is 15. Find the number.

6. Six teams compete in an academic challenge. In the first round every team plays one game against each of the other teams. The top three teams go on to the second round where every team plays against each of the other teams twice. In the third round, the top two teams from the second round play against each other twice. What is the least and greatest number of games a team may play?

Standardized Testing ▶ Free Response

Caroline and Juanita are going camping. Their tent weighs 7 pounds. They have 2 sleeping bags which weigh 3 pounds each, a camping stove which weighs 6 pounds, 14 pounds of food and assorted supplies, 15 pounds of water, 10 pounds of clothing, a 1-pound first-aid kit, and a 3-pound lantern.

Can Caroline and Juanita divide their gear so that each person carries the same amount of weight? Explain.

A Puzzling Problem

SET UP

Work in a group.
You will need:
- *Project Labsheets A and B*

Presenting Your Solution As you worked through Module 1, you learned about four different scales that help you assess your work. The last scale you'll learn about is the presentation scale. This scale helps you assess how well you present your solutions.

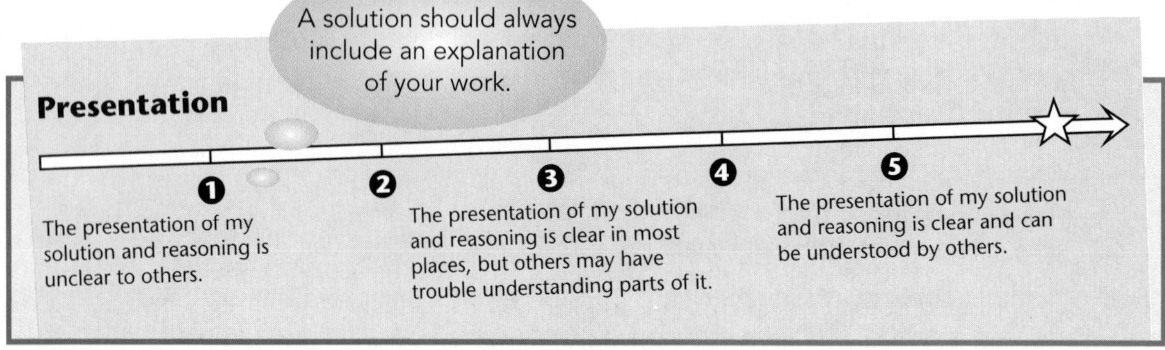

10 **Discussion** How do you think the presentation scale will help you plan your presentation?

To complete the last step in solving the *30 Pennies in a Row* problem, you'll work as a team to present your solution.

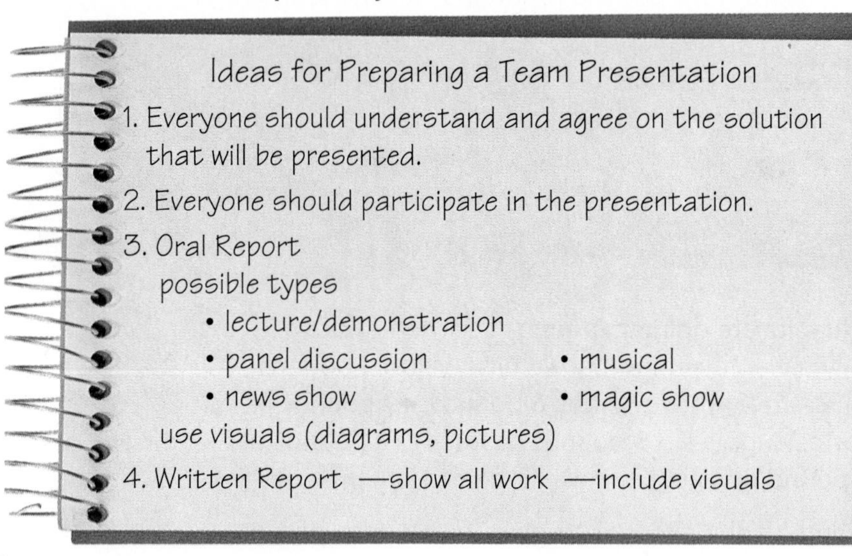

11 What other ideas do you have for preparing a team presentation that you would add to the list on the notebook above?

This team decided to do a lecture/demonstration to present their solution to the *30 Pennies in a Row* problem.

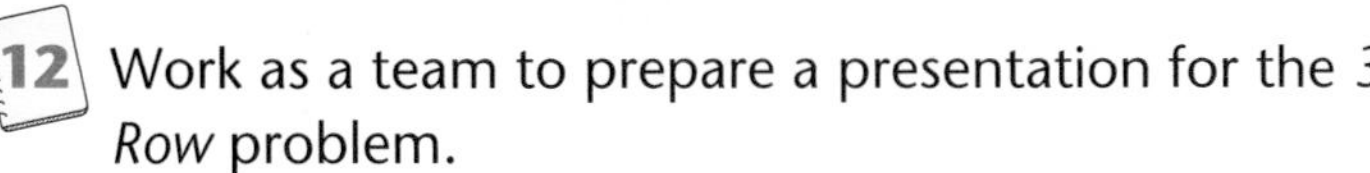

12 Work as a team to prepare a presentation for the *30 Pennies in a Row* problem.

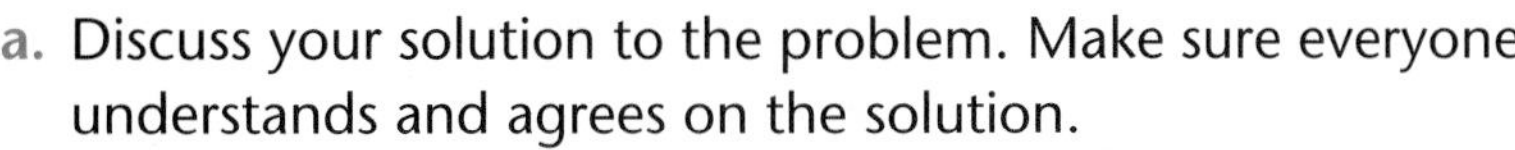

a. Discuss your solution to the problem. Make sure everyone understands and agrees on the solution.

b. Plan how your team will present its solution to the class.

c. Practice your presentation a few times to make sure everyone on your team understands what to do.

13 As a team, present your solution to the rest of the class.

14 **Use Project Labsheet B.** Use the presentation scale to score your team's presentation of the *30 Pennies in a Row* problem.

When you score yourself on an E^2, you score yourself on all the scales that apply to the problem.

MODULE 1 Review and Assessment

For Exercises 1 and 2, replace each ? with the correct term. Describe the rule you used for each sequence. (Sec. 1, Explor. 1)

1. 188, 185, 182, 179, __?__, __?__, __?__, 167
2. 15, 30, 45, 60 __?__, __?__, __?__, 120
3. a. The number of parts in each circle form a sequence of numbers. Make a table and record the first five terms. (Sec. 1, Explor. 1)

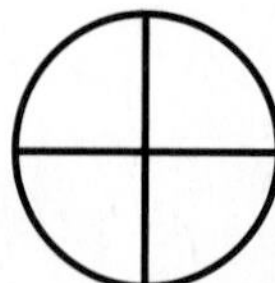
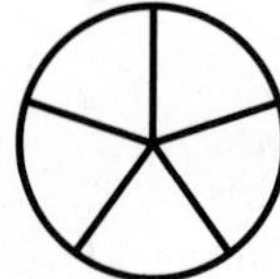

   b. Write a general rule to find any term from its term number. (Sec. 1, Explor. 2)

4. Is it possible to form a triangle with three sticks that are 13 cm, 21 cm, and 9 cm in length? Explain. (Sec. 2, Explor. 2)

If possible, sketch each triangle. (Sec. 2, Explors. 2 and 3)

5. a triangle that is obtuse and isosceles
6. a triangle that is both right and equilateral

For Exercises 7–13, use the diagram at the right. Name an example of each figure. (Sec. 2, Explors. 1 and 3)

7. acute angle
8. segment
9. ray
10. right angle
11. obtuse angle
12. line
13. point

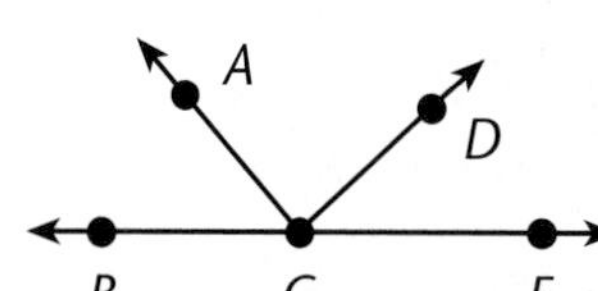

14. In Linda Tetley's 6th grade class, Gail, Lita, and Ben have been chosen to fill the three positions of class president, vice president, and secretary. Make an organized list to find the number of different ways the positions can be filled. (Sec. 3, Explor. 2)

Estimation **For Exercises 15–20, show how to estimate each answer.** (Sec. 4, Explor 1)

15. 42 • 66 **16.** 251 − 188 **17.** 3122 + 890

18. 257 + 34 + 85 **19.** 186 • 12 **20.** 3452 − 2128

21. **Writing** Marco estimated the difference between \$47.98 and \$22.31 to be \$30. Is his estimate *less than* or *greater than* the actual difference? Explain how you can tell without finding the exact difference. (Sec. 4, Explor. 1)

Mental Math **For Exercises 22 – 25, explain how you can use mental math to find each answer.** (Sec. 4, Explor. 2)

22. 67 + 19 + 143 + 31 **23.** 7 • 4 • 5 • 25

24. 5 • 46 • 2 **25.** 34 + 158 + 66

Find the value of each expression. (Sec. 4, Explor. 3)

26. 54 − 63 ÷ 7 **27.** 12 + 7 • 5 **28.** 180 ÷ (5 • 6)

29. 7 + 45 − 22 − 9 **30.** (33 + 8) − (5 + 17)

31. From home, Leon walked 6 blocks east, 5 blocks north, 3 blocks west, and then 7 blocks south on errands. Draw a diagram to show two ways he can get home by walking the fewest blocks. He cannot cut diagonally across any blocks because of buildings. (Sec. 5, Explor. 1)

32. Vina is putting together 1 cm squares as shown. (Sec. 6, Explor. 2)

a. How many squares will she need to build a figure that has a perimeter of 32 cm?

b. Explain how you can extend your solution in part (a) to the general case.

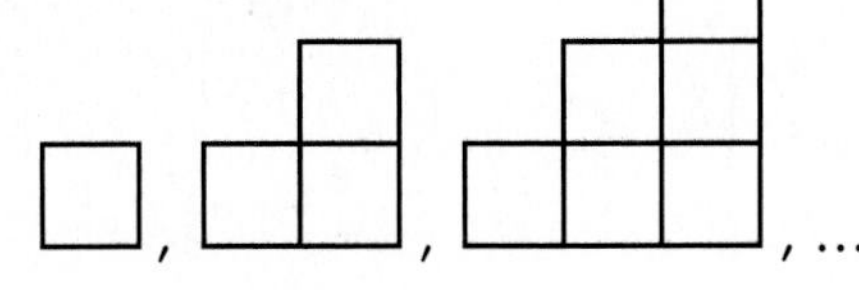

Reflecting on the Module

33. **Writing** Write a letter to an adult member of your family describing the "tools" you have learned about in this module. Discuss how these tools can help you increase your success in mathematics. You may also want to talk about what you liked most and least about the module.

MODULE 2

PATTERNS and DESIGNS

CONNECTING MATHEMATICS & The Theme

MODULE 2

SECTION OVERVIEW

1 **Polygons and Line Symmetry**
As you explore shapes seen in art and in nature:
- Classify shapes
- Identify regular polygons
- Identify lines of symmetry

2 **Fractions and Mixed Numbers**
As you describe kite designs:
- Write a fraction and a mixed number
- Divide a figure into congruent parts
- Use part of a design to create a whole design

3 **Equivalent Fractions**
As you use pattern blocks to make window designs:
- Recognize and find equivalent fractions
- Write a fraction in lowest terms

4 **Transformations**
As you create quilt patch designs:
- Perform a translation, a rotation, and a reflection
- Use transformations to make designs

5 **Understanding Decimals**
As you use base-ten blocks to model Postage Stamp Quilts:
- Read and write decimals
- Compare and order decimals

6 **Decimal Addition and Subtraction**
As you describe changes in the design of a sports car:
- Add and subtract decimals

The Module Project

Pop-Up Art

Pop-ups are made by cutting and folding paper using geometric shapes and patterns. At the end of this module you'll design and create your own pop-up. As you work through the module, you'll learn pop-up techniques and mathematical skills that will help you.

More on the Module Project
See pp. 91, 118, 131, and 152–153.

INTERNET
To learn more about the theme:
http://www.mlmath.com

Section 1 Polygons and Line Symmetry

IN THIS SECTION

EXPLORATION 1
- Naming Shapes

EXPLORATION 2
- Searching for Symmetry

WORLD of Shapes

Setting the Stage

Our world is full of patterns. Some are found in nature and others are made by people. Look at the designs in the photo below.

Think About It

1 **a.** What do you think is pictured in the photo?

b. Describe a shape used in the photo. Is the shape practical? Is it decorative? Explain.

▶ **In this section you'll explore some geometric shapes and their uses in designs found in art and in nature.**

Exploration 1

NAMING SHAPES

SET UP *You will need Labsheet 1A.*

GOAL

LEARN HOW TO...
- identify a polygon
- classify shapes

AS YOU...
- explore shapes used in designs

KEY TERMS
- polygon
- parallel
- quadrilateral
- trapezoid
- parallelogram
- rhombus

▶ **Mathematical terms like polygon can help you describe designs clearly in just a few words.**

These are polygons.

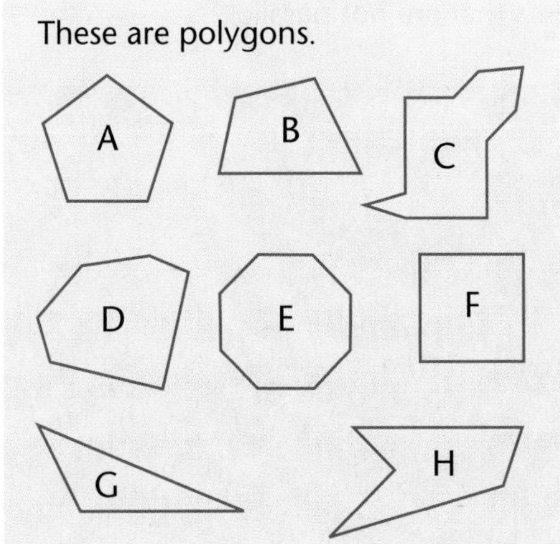

These are *not* polygons.

2 How is each shape on the right different from the polygons on the left? What makes a shape a polygon?

3 **Discussion** Share your answers to Question 2. Decide on and record a class definition of a polygon.

▶ **The word polygon comes from the Greek *poly-* meaning many and *-gon* meaning angles. Polygons have many angles and sides. Many of the words used to classify polygons also come from the Greek word parts at the right.**

Word part	Meaning
tri-	three
quadri-	four
penta-	five
hexa-	six
octa-	eight
deca-	ten
poly-	many
-gon	angle(s)
-lateral	side(s)

4 List three everyday words that use a Greek word part.

5 **Use Labsheet 1A.** Complete the table on *Classifying Polygons* by number of sides. Use the polygons above.

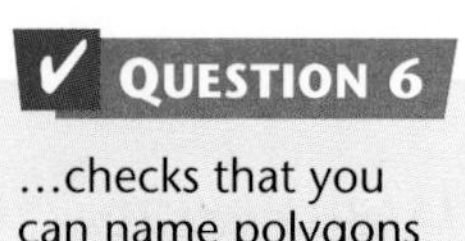

...checks that you can name polygons by number of sides.

6 ✓ CHECKPOINT Write a definition of each term and sketch two examples.

a. quadrilateral b. pentagon c. hexagon

▶ **Polygons with the same number of sides can be classified by the measures of their angles, by the lengths of their sides, or by the number of pairs of *parallel* sides. Two lines on a flat surface are parallel if they do not meet.**

7 a. Describe a pair of segments in the photo below that are parallel.

b. Describe a pair of segments that are not parallel.

▶ **The sides of polygons are segments. You can think of these segments as parts of lines. When two segments are parts of parallel lines, the segments are parallel.**

This polygon has one pair of **parallel sides**.

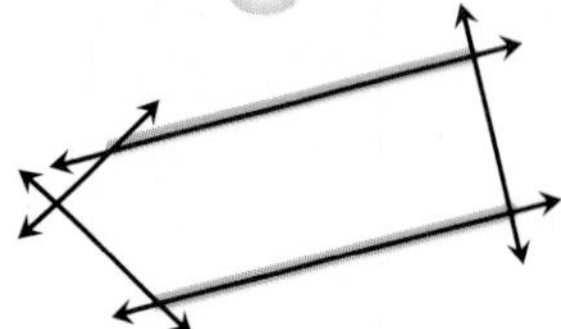

This polygon has two pairs of parallel sides.

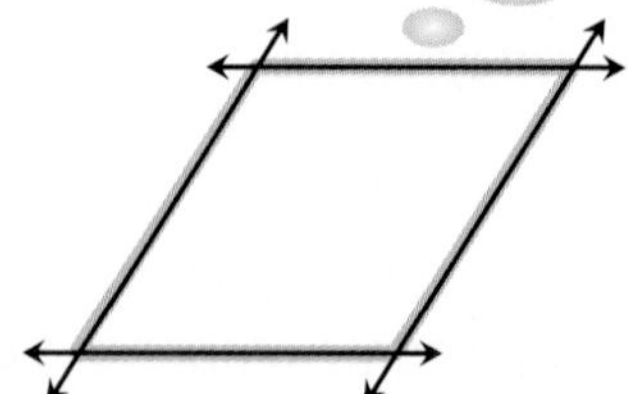

▶ **For Questions 8–12, you'll use the figures below to look at how parallel sides are used to classify quadrilaterals.**

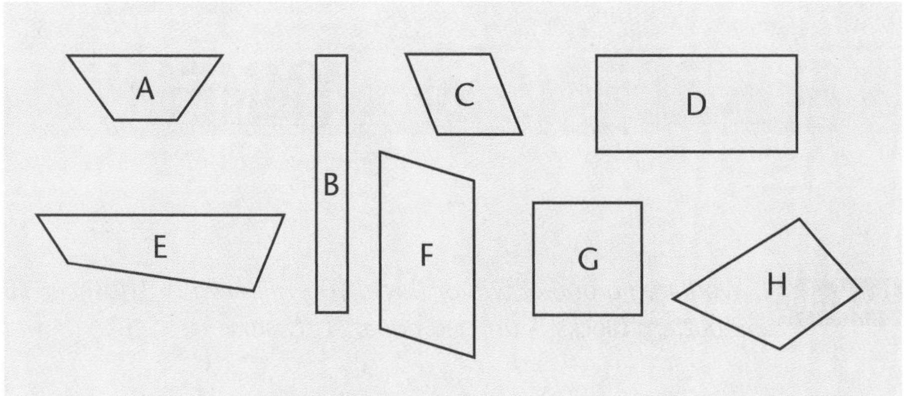

▶ **A quadrilateral that has exactly one pair of parallel sides is a trapezoid.**

8 **a.** Which of the quadrilaterals are trapezoids?

b. Sketch one more trapezoid.

▶ **A quadrilateral that has two pairs of parallel sides is a parallelogram.**

9 **a.** Which of the quadrilaterals are parallelograms?

b. Sketch one more parallelogram.

▶ **A parallelogram with all sides the same length is a rhombus.**

10 **a.** Which of the quadrilaterals are rhombuses?

b. Sketch one more rhombus.

11 Some parallelograms and rhombuses have more specific names.

a. What one name best describes quadrilaterals B, D, and G?

b. What other name describes quadrilateral G?

12 Which quadrilateral does not fit any of the classifications in Questions 8–11? Explain.

13 ✓ **CHECKPOINT** Sketch an example of each quadrilateral.

a. a parallelogram that is not a rhombus

b. a quadrilateral that is not a trapezoid or a parallelogram

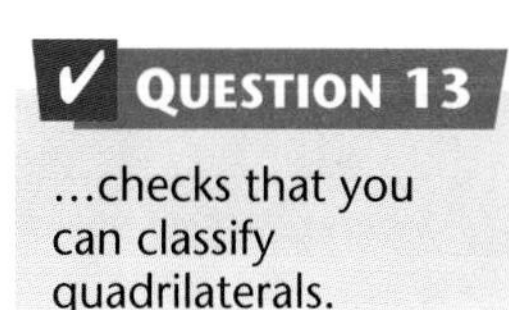

HOMEWORK EXERCISES See Exs. 1–8 on p. 88.

GOAL

LEARN HOW TO...
- identify regular polygons
- identify lines of symmetry

AS YOU...
- create mosaic designs with pattern blocks

KEY TERMS
- regular polygon
- congruent
- line symmetry

Exploration 2

SEARCHING for SYMMETRY

SET UP *Work in a group of two or three. You will need:* • *Labsheet 1B* • *pattern blocks* • *unlined paper* • *scissors*

▶ **There are six different pattern blocks.**

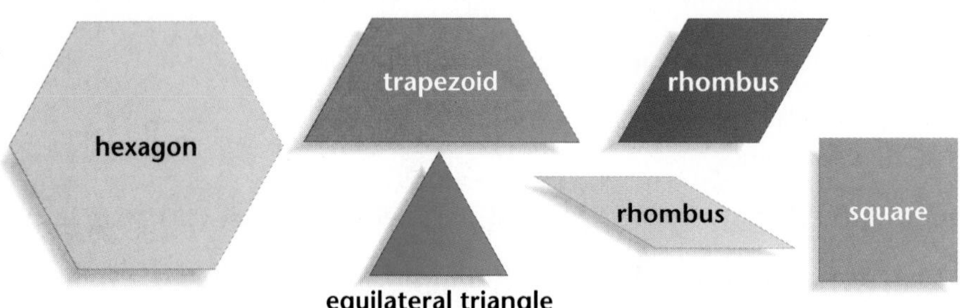

▶ **Geometric shapes, like the pattern blocks, have been used throughout history to create designs. The design below is based on a 13th century Roman tiling.**

14 **a.** Use your pattern blocks to create part of the Roman tile design on top of a sheet of unlined paper. Trace around the outside of the design to form a polygon.

b. How many sides does your polygon have? If you can, give the name of the polygon.

c. Are the sides all the same length?

d. Use the words *acute*, *right*, or *obtuse* to describe the angles in your polygon. Are the angles all the same size?

FOR HELP with *classifying angles*, see **MODULE 1, p. 22**

15 **Discussion** Did any group make a polygon with all the sides the same length and all the angles the same size? If not, find one in the tile design and sketch it or create it with pattern blocks.

▶ **The tile design contains many different polygons. Some of them have special characteristics that make them regular polygons.**

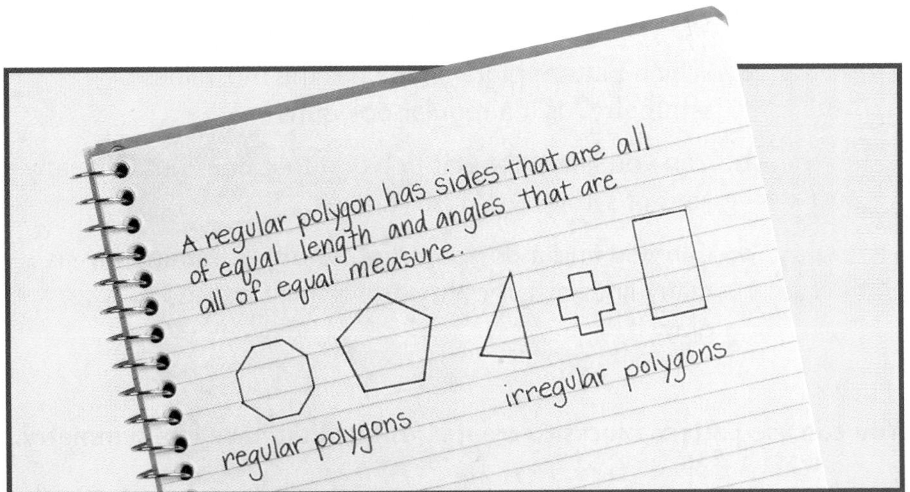

16 Is the polygon you made from pattern blocks in Question 14 regular? Explain how you know.

17 ✓ **CHECKPOINT** Look at the six pattern blocks. Which blocks are shaped like regular polygons? Explain why the other pattern blocks are not regular.

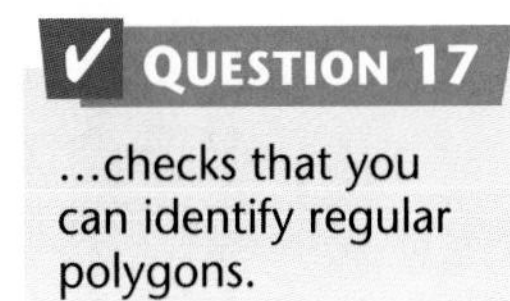

▶ **Special Lines** **The figures below show that the triangle pattern block has an interesting property. When it is traced on paper and cut out, it can be folded in half so that both halves fit exactly on one another.**

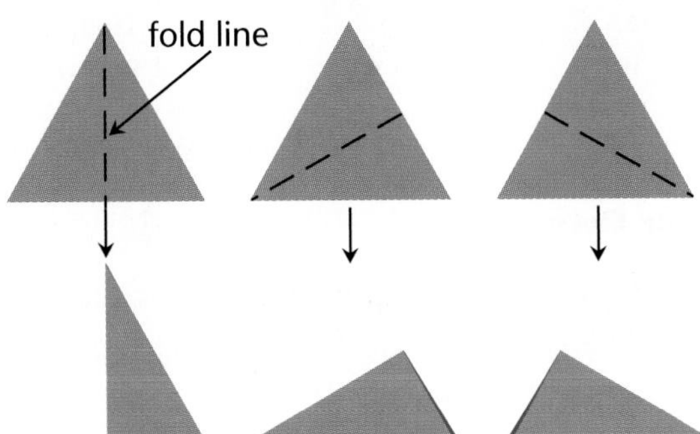

18 **Use Labsheet 1B.** Cut out the *Enlarged Pattern Block Shapes.* Fold each cutout so that the fold divides the cutout into two *congruent parts.* **Congruent** parts have the same size and shape. Make all possible folds.

▶ **If a figure can be folded in half so that the two halves fit exactly on each other, the figure has line symmetry. The fold line is called a *line of symmetry*.**

19 Trace around each pattern block and draw in the lines of symmetry.

20 **Discussion** Use your tracings from Question 19.

a. Which pattern block shape has the most lines of symmetry? Is it a regular polygon?

b. Can you find a regular polygon that does not have any lines of symmetry? If so, draw it.

c. Can you find a polygon that is not regular and has as many lines of symmetry as a regular hexagon? If so, draw it.

▶ **You can use pattern blocks to create designs that have line symmetry.**

This design has no lines of symmetry.

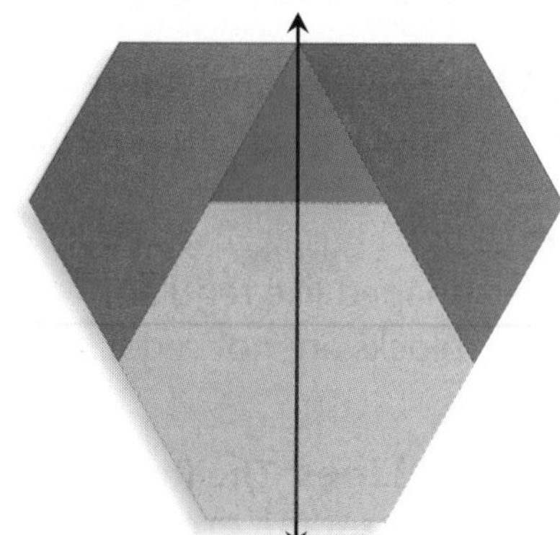

This design has 1 line of symmetry.

21 **Create Your Own**

a. Create a design by arranging pattern blocks on top of a sheet of paper. The design must have at least two lines of symmetry and use at least five pattern blocks.

b. Sketch your design by tracing around each block. Then mark all the lines of symmetry on the drawing.

HOMEWORK EXERCISES ▶ See Exs. 9–18 on pp. 88–90.

Section 1 Key Concepts

Key Terms

Polygons (pp. 81–82)

polygon

A polygon is a closed figure made from segments that are drawn on a flat surface and do not cross.

A polygon can be classified by the number of sides it has.

To review this, use the table on Labsheet 1A.

Quadrilaterals (pp. 82–83)

quadrilateral

parallel

Quadrilaterals can be classified by number of parallel sides. Two lines on a flat surface are parallel if they do not meet.

quadrilateral — 4-sided polygon

trapezoid — 1 pair of parallel sides

parallelogram — 2 pairs of parallel sides

rhombus — a parallelogram with 4 sides of equal length

rectangle — a parallelogram with 4 right angles

square — a parallelogram with 4 right angles and 4 sides of equal length

trapezoid

parallelogram

rhombus

A square is both a rectangle and a rhombus.

Regular Polygons and Line Symmetry (pp. 85–86)

regular polygon

line symmetry

A regular polygon has all angles the same size and all sides the same length.

A figure with line symmetry can be folded in half so that the two congruent parts fit exactly on each other. Congruent parts have the same size and shape. The fold line of the figure is a line of symmetry.

congruent

22 **Key Concepts Question** Explain why each shape is not a polygon.

a. 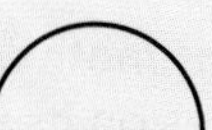

b. 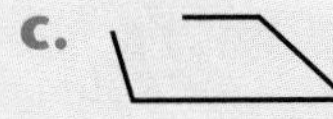

c.

Section 1 Practice & Application Exercises

Is each figure a polygon? If not, explain why not.

1. 

2. 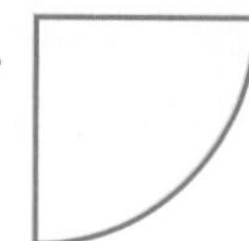

3. 

Name each polygon. Be as specific as possible.

4. 

5. 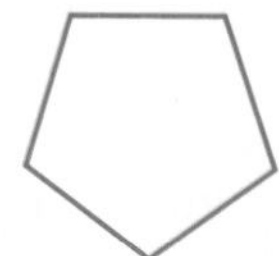

6. 

7. **Probability Connection** Suppose you reached into a bag that contained the shapes from Exercises 1–6 and pulled one out. Do you think it would most likely be a *pentagon*, a *polygon*, or a *quadrilateral*? Explain.

8. **Use Labsheet 1A.** Gem cutters use some common designs to cut stones for jewelry. Follow the directions for identifying and marking different polygons and parallel segments on the *Gem Designs*.

9. Which of the figures in Exercises 4–6 are regular polygons? If a figure is not a regular polygon, explain why not.

10. **Science** Butterflies and moths show symmetry in their wing designs. For some, the bright designs advertise that they are poisonous. For others, the designs help them hide against backgrounds of trees and flowers.

Use Labsheet 1C. Complete the drawing of the butterfly on the *Butterfly Grid* so that the vertical line is a line of symmetry. Color the completed butterfly so that each pair of congruent parts has the same color.

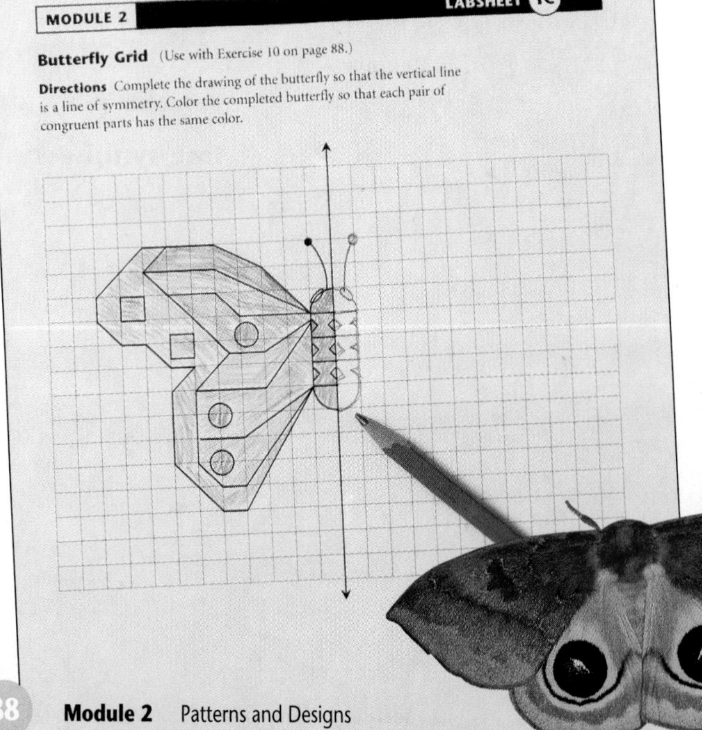

◀ This moth uses false eyes on its wings to scare away predators.

Copy each polygon. Give its most specific name and mark all lines of symmetry.

11. 

12. 

13. 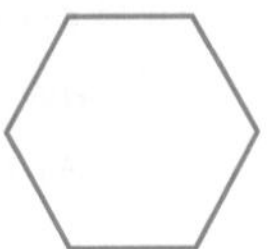

14. **Arts** Follow the steps to create a symmetric design with your name.

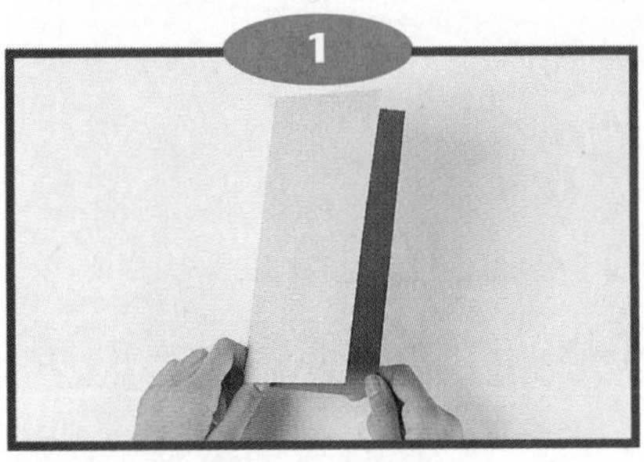

Fold a sheet of paper along a line of symmetry.

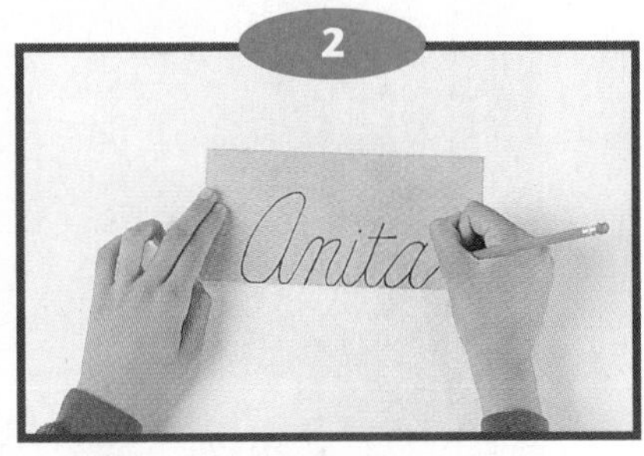

Write your name in script along the fold line. The letters must be attached to each other.

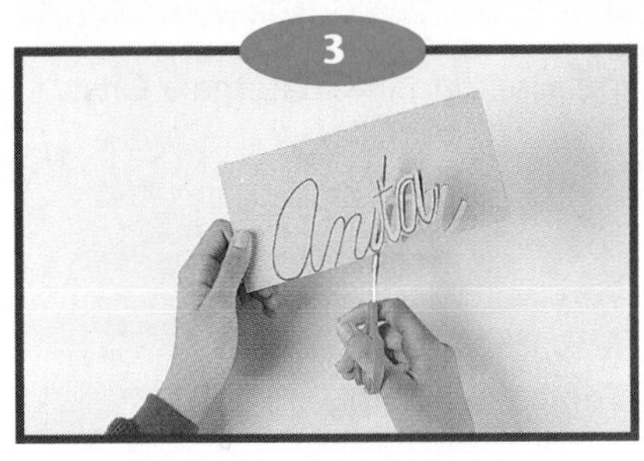

Cut around the letters you have drawn, so that your name has thickness. Cut out the centers of a's, o's, b's and similar letters.

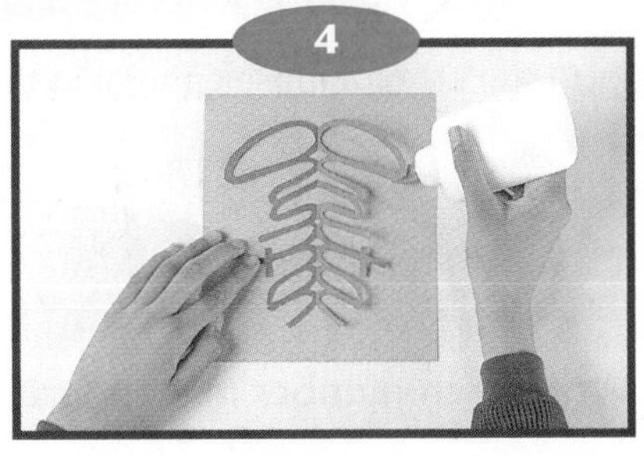

Unfold your design and glue it to a different color piece of paper.

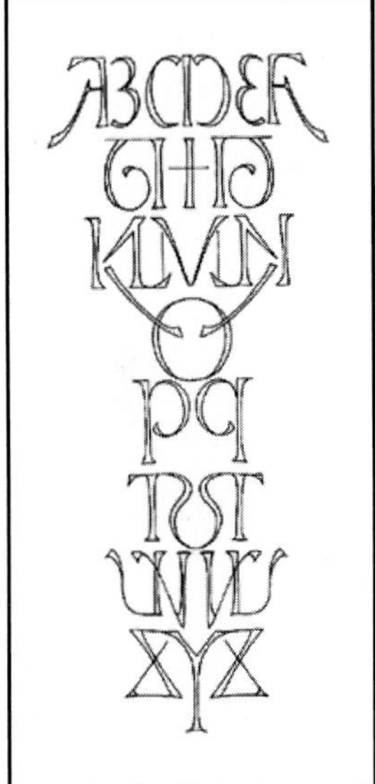

▲ Artist Scott Kim uses symmetry with letters and words. In this design he shows line symmetry in the alphabet.

15. How many lines of symmetry does the design at the right have?

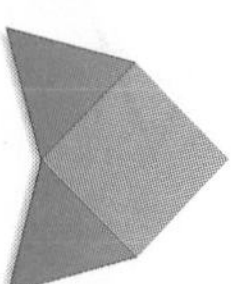

16. How could you rearrange the shapes in Exercise 15 so that the design has two lines of symmetry? Sketch your answer.

17. **Challenge** Is there a way to tell how many lines of symmetry a regular polygon has without actually drawing the polygon? Explain.

Reflecting on the Section

Visual Thinking

Exercise 18 checks that you can apply ideas about polygons.

18. The mural created by artist Carlos Mérida shows many geometric shapes. Draw a design for a mural that fills a whole sheet of paper and includes the following:

- an example of line symmetry
- two different kinds of quadrilaterals
- a regular polygon

▲ Part of a mosaic mural in the Municipal Building in Guatemala City.

Spiral Review

Write each number in standard form. **(Toolbox, p. 589)**

19. eighty-six thousand fifty
20. four thousand seven
21. five hundred thirty-seven
22. one thousand twenty-one

Identify each angle as *acute, obtuse,* or *right*. **(Module 1, p. 22)**

23. 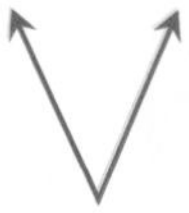
24.

25. 
26.

Each figure has a perimeter of 16 units. Find the missing side lengths. **(Toolbox, p. 599)**

27. 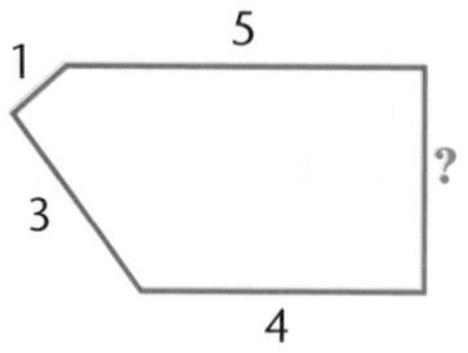 5, 1, 3, 4, ?

28. 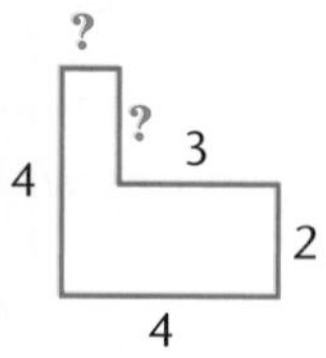 ?, ?, 3, 4, 2, 4

Pop-Up Art

SET UP

You will need:

- *scissors*
- *ruler*
- *construction paper*

Over the next few weeks you'll learn several different pop-up techniques that will help you design and create your own pop-up.

Parallel Segments and Polygons Experiment with the *double-slit* method shown below to create pop-up polygons.

Fold a piece of paper in half. Cut two parallel segments across the fold.

Fold the loose section between the cuts backward and forward.

Open the card. Pull the loose section toward you and close the card.

1. a. What happens when the parallel segments are cut at right angles to the central fold?

   b. What happens when the segments cut are not parallel?

   c. What types of polygons can be formed using the double-slit method? (The segments cut do not have to be parallel.)

Line Symmetry The photo at the right shows how to make a pop-up cutout.

2. a. Design a figure with a fold line that is a line of symmetry. Add tabs to your figure and cut it out. Tape the tabs onto a piece of paper with a central fold as shown.

   b. Experiment with taping the tabs in different positions so that the folded cutout forms different-sized angles. How does changing the angle affect the pop-up?

Align fold line of cutout with fold of paper.

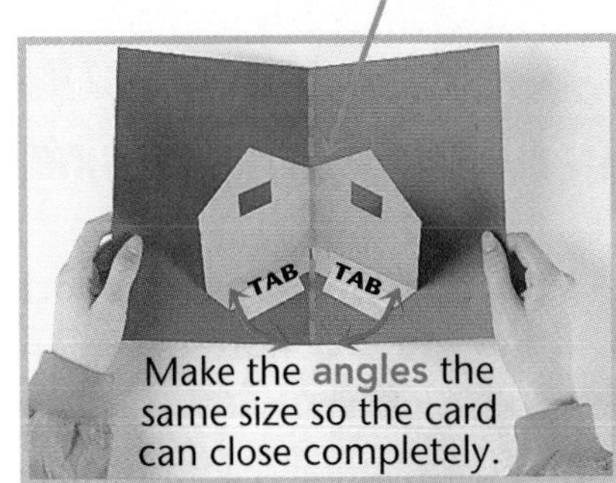

Section 1
Extra Skill Practice

Is each figure a polygon? If not, explain why not.

1.

2. 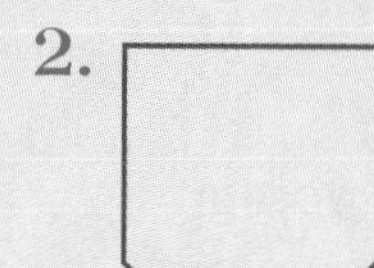

3. 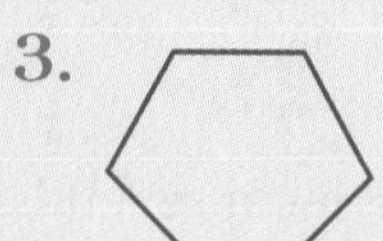

4. 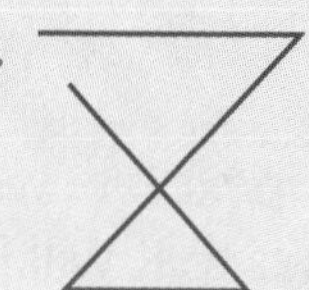

Is each figure a regular polygon? If a figure is not a regular polygon, explain why not.

5. 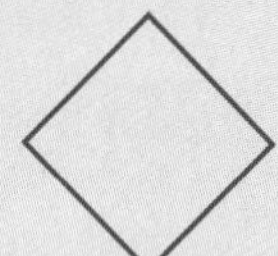

6. 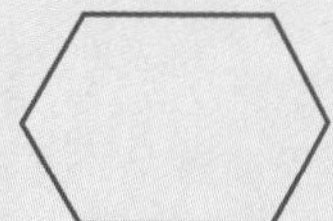

7. 

8. 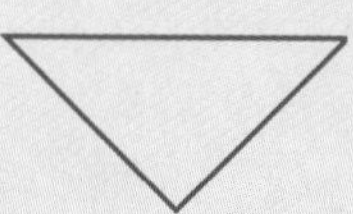

Copy each polygon. Give its most specific name and mark all lines of symmetry.

9. 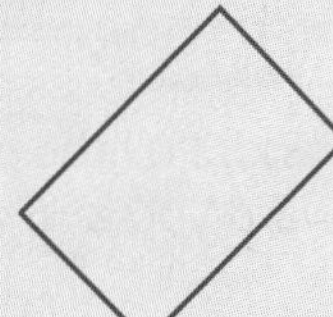

10. 

11. 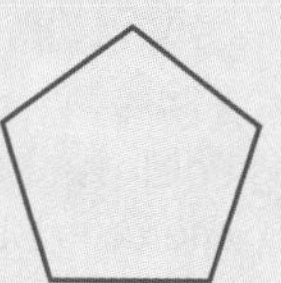

12. 

How many lines of symmetry does each design have?

13. 

14. 

15. 

16. 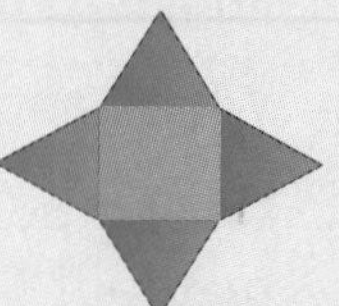

Study Skills Taking Notes

Sometimes it is helpful to include a diagram or another visual representation when you take notes.

1. Look back at the notebook pictured on page 87. What does the quadrilateral diagram illustrate?
2. Make a diagram or a table to organize what you know about angles.

FOR ASSESSMENT AND PORTFOLIOS

Pattern BLOCK Angles

SET UP *You will need pattern blocks or the Extended Exploration Labsheet.*

The Situation

You know that a square has four right (90°) angles and that a straight angle measures 180°.

The Problem

For each polygon in the table, figure out the sum of the measures of the angles without using a measuring tool. How can you find the sum of the measures of the angles of any polygon?

Polygon	Number of sides	Sum of the measures of its angles
triangle	?	?
quadrilateral	?	?
pentagon	?	?
hexagon	?	?
heptagon	7	?
octagon	?	?
nonagon	9	?
decagon	?	?

Something to Think About

- Suppose you start by tracing around each pattern block. How can you find and label the angle measures?
- How can you use pattern blocks to create the polygons in the table? Trace around each polygon you create.

Present Your Results

Describe how you found the angle measures for each polygon in the table. What relationship did you find between the number of sides of a polygon and the sum of the measures of its angles?

Section 2 Fractions and Mixed Numbers

IN THIS SECTION

EXPLORATION 1
- Fractional Parts

EXPLORATION 2
- From Part to Whole

Numbers and Designs

Setting the Stage

The Phantom Tollbooth is a story about a boy named Milo who visits a strange land where he has many adventures. One day he visits an unusual mine owned by the Mathemagician.

The Phantom Tollbooth

by Norton Juster

"Are there any precious stones in it?" asked Milo excitedly.

"PRECIOUS STONES!" [the Mathemagician] roared....And then he leaned over toward Milo and whispered softly, "By the eight million two hundred and forty-seven thousand three hundred and twelve threads in my robe, I'll say there are. Look here."

He reached into one of the carts and pulled out a small object....When he held it up to the light, it sparkled brightly.

"But, that's a five," objected Milo, for that was certainly what it was.

"Exactly," agreed the Mathemagician; "as valuable a jewel as you'll find anywhere. Look at some of the others."

He scooped up a great handful of stones and poured them into Milo's arms. They included all the numbers from one to nine, and even an assortment of zeros....

"So, that's where they come from," said Milo, looking in awe at the glittering collection of numbers. He returned them....as carefully as possible but, as he did, one dropped to the floor with a smash and broke in two....Milo looked terribly concerned.

"Oh, don't worry about that," said the Mathemagician as he scooped up the pieces. "We use the broken ones for fractions."

Think About It

1 What was being mined in the Mathemagician's mine?

2 How many threads are in the Mathemagician's robe? Write your answer in standard form.

▶ **In Section 1, you explored the use of geometry in designs. Now you'll see how numbers are used to create and describe designs.**

Exploration 1

Fractional PARTS

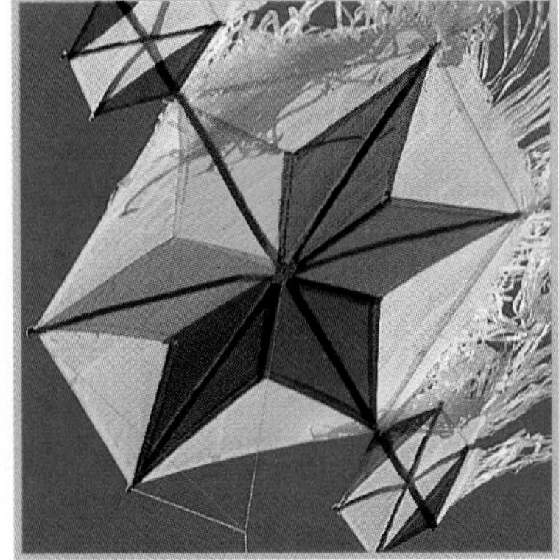

GOAL

LEARN HOW TO...
- write a fraction and a mixed number

AS YOU...
- work with kite designs and pattern blocks

KEY TERMS
- fraction
- numerator
- denominator
- mixed number

SET UP *You will need:* • *Labsheets 2A and 2B* • *pattern blocks*

▶ **Fractions are numbers that can be used to compare part of an object or part of a set with a whole.**

EXAMPLE

The square region is the **whole**.

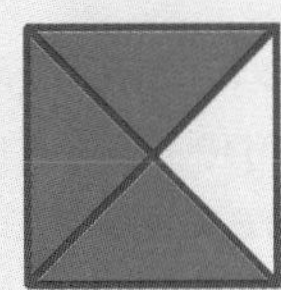

$$\frac{3}{4}$$

The **numerator** tells how many parts to consider.

The **denominator** tells how many equal-sized parts the whole is divided into.

3 of the **4** equal-sized parts are shaded.

3 **Discussion** How can fractions help you describe the design of the kite shown above?

4 Suppose the fraction $\frac{2}{5}$ compares part of a shape with a whole shape.

a. What does the 5 mean?

b. What does the 2 mean?

c. What is the numerator of the fraction?

d. What is the denominator?

5 **Use Labsheet 2A.** Use pattern blocks to complete the table *Relating the Part to the Whole.*

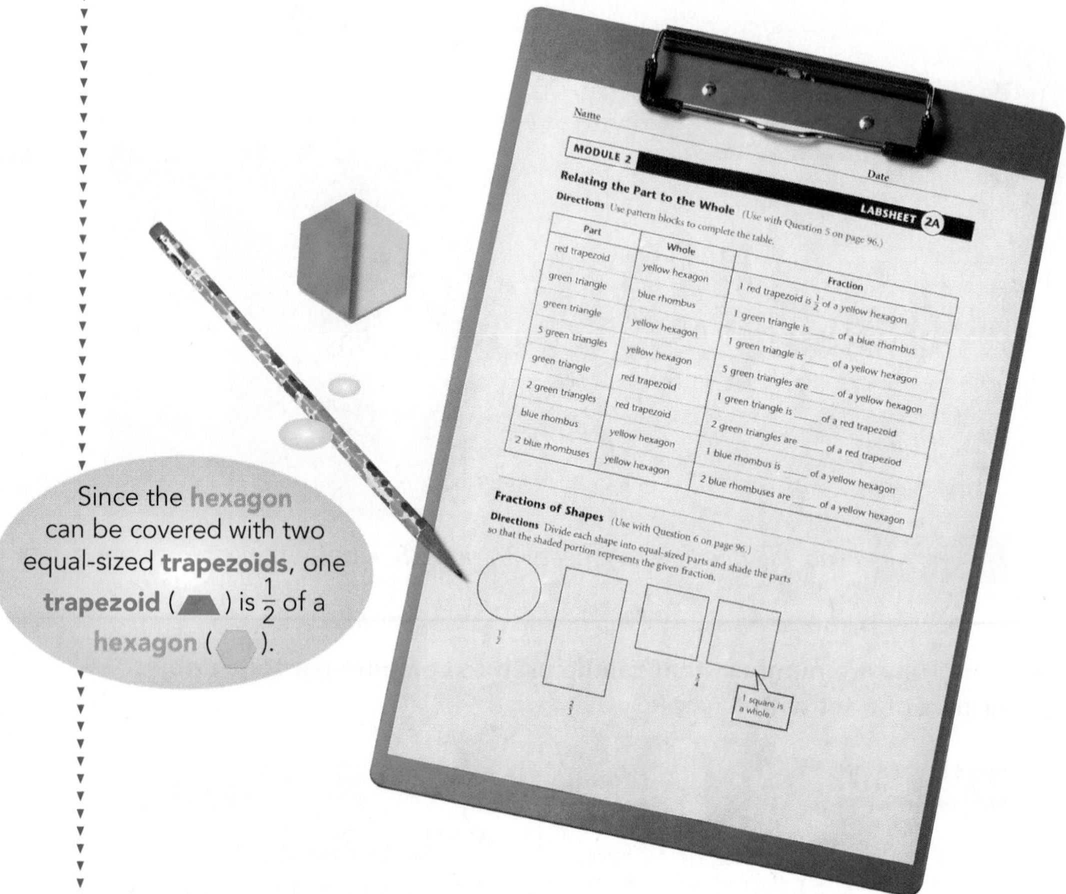
Name

Date

MODULE 2

LABSHEET 2A

Relating the Part to the Whole (Use with Question 5 on page 96.)

Directions Use pattern blocks to complete the table.

Part	Whole	Fraction
red trapezoid	yellow hexagon	1 red trapezoid is $\frac{1}{2}$ of a yellow hexagon
green triangle	blue rhombus	1 green triangle is ___ of a blue rhombus
green triangle	yellow hexagon	1 green triangle is ___ of a yellow hexagon
5 green triangles	yellow hexagon	5 green triangles are ___ of a yellow hexagon
green triangle	red trapezoid	1 green triangle is ___ of a red trapezoid
2 green triangles	red trapezoid	2 green triangles are ___ of a red trapezoid
blue rhombus	yellow hexagon	1 blue rhombus is ___ of a yellow hexagon
2 blue rhombuses	yellow hexagon	2 blue rhombuses are ___ of a yellow hexagon

Fractions of Shapes (Use with Question 6 on page 96.)

Directions Divide each shape into equal-sized parts and shade the parts so that the shaded portion represents the given fraction.

1 square is a whole.

6 **Use Labsheet 2A.** Complete the *Fractions of Shapes* activity. Divide each shape into equal-sized parts and shade the part that represents the given fraction.

7 **Use Labsheet 2B.** Follow the directions to *Cover Each Shape* with pattern blocks and show the given fraction.

✓ QUESTION 8

...checks that you can write a fraction relating a part to a whole.

8 **✓ CHECKPOINT** The drawing at the right shows the design of the kite from page 95. What fraction of the design is white?

▶ **More Than a Whole** **You have mostly worked with fractions that are less than a whole. When the part is more than a whole, you can describe the relationship in two ways.**

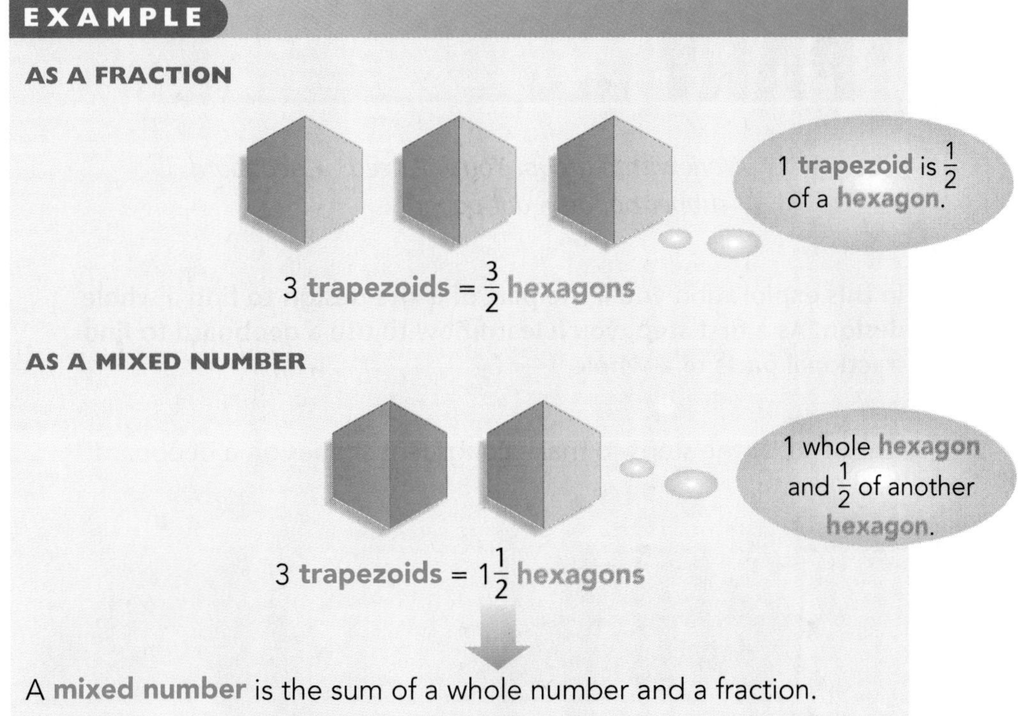

9 **Try This as a Class** Four **triangles** (▲) equal how many **trapezoids** (⏢)? Write your answer in two ways.

10 ✓ **CHECKPOINT** Use the pattern block pictures to write each part to whole relationship.

a. Write the value of the triangles as a fraction.

5 **triangles** (▲) = __?__ **rhombuses** (▰)

b. Write the value of the triangles as a mixed number.

5 **triangles** (▲) = __?__ **rhombuses** (▰)

✓ QUESTION 10

...checks that you can write a fraction that is greater than one whole as a fraction and as a mixed number.

HOMEWORK EXERCISES ▶ **See Exs. 1–12 on pp. 102–103.**

GOAL

LEARN HOW TO...
- divide a figure into congruent parts
- use part of a design to create a whole design

AS YOU...
- work with a geoboard

Exploration 2

From PART to WHOLE

SET UP *Work with a group. You will need:* • *geoboard* • *rubber bands* • *dot paper*

▶ **In this exploration you'll use part of a kite design to find a whole design. As a first step, you'll learn how to use a geoboard to find fractional parts of a whole.**

11 Follow the steps to make congruent shapes on a geoboard.

First

Put a rubber band around the pegs on a geoboard to form the square shown above.

Then

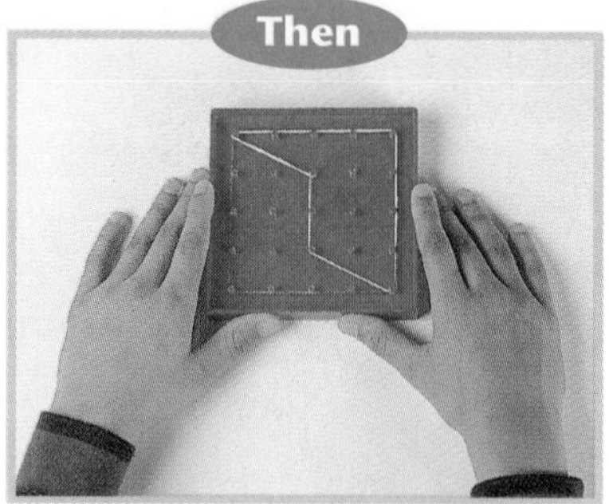

Use another rubber band to divide the square into two congruent parts as shown.

12 **a.** What fraction of the square is each congruent part in Question 11?

b. Find five other ways to divide the square into two congruent parts. Sketch your answers on dot paper.

13 **a.** Construct this rectangle on your geoboard.

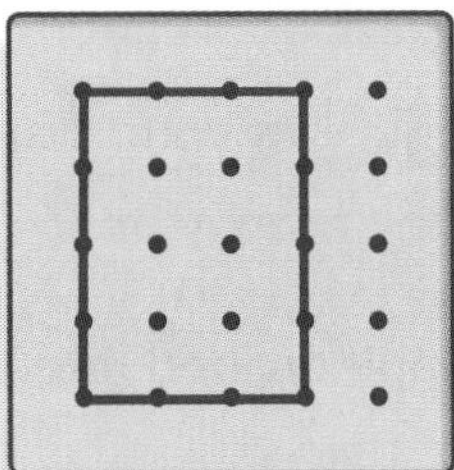

b. Divide the rectangle into four congruent parts. Sketch your answer on dot paper.

c. What fraction of the rectangle is each part?

d. Find other ways to divide the rectangle into four congruent parts. Sketch four more ways on your dot paper.

e. Shade each sketch from parts (b) and (d) to show $\frac{3}{4}$ of the rectangle.

▶ **Creating a Whole** **Now you'll start with part of a design and create a whole design.**

14 This photo shows a fraction of a kite. What other information would you need to be able to create a whole kite design?

15 **a.** Construct the triangle below on your geoboard.

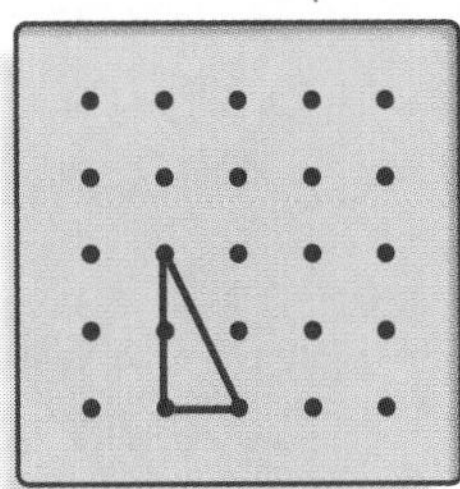

b. Suppose the triangle is $\frac{1}{3}$ of a whole and that a whole can be made using triangles congruent to the one shown. How many triangles are needed to make a whole? How many triangles would you need to add to the original figure?

c. Add congruent triangles to the figure to complete a whole. Record your answer on dot paper.

16 **Discussion** Use your shapes from Question 15.

a. Are everyone's shapes congruent? Explain.

b. Is the original triangle $\frac{1}{3}$ of your shape? of each of the other group's shapes? Why or why not?

✓ QUESTION 17

...checks that you can use congruent parts of a design to create a whole design.

17 **✓ CHECKPOINT** A shape divided into two congruent parts is shown.

a. Construct the following shape on a geoboard.

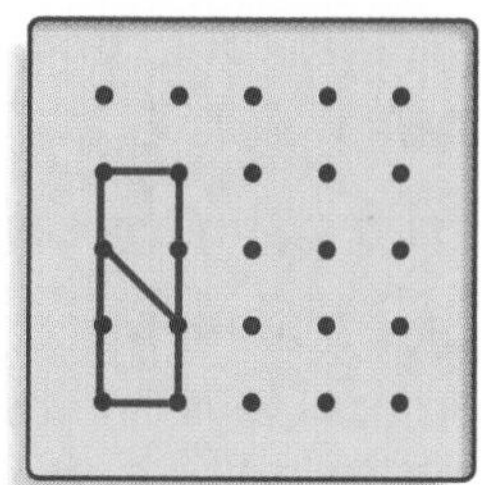

b. Suppose the shape in part (a) is $\frac{2}{5}$ of a whole. What shapes could you add to the figure to complete a whole?

c. Add congruent shapes to the original figure to complete a whole. Record your answer on dot paper.

18 The kite section in the drawing below is $\frac{1}{8}$ of the kite in the photo. Make a sketch to show another possible design that uses the same section as $\frac{1}{8}$ of a whole.

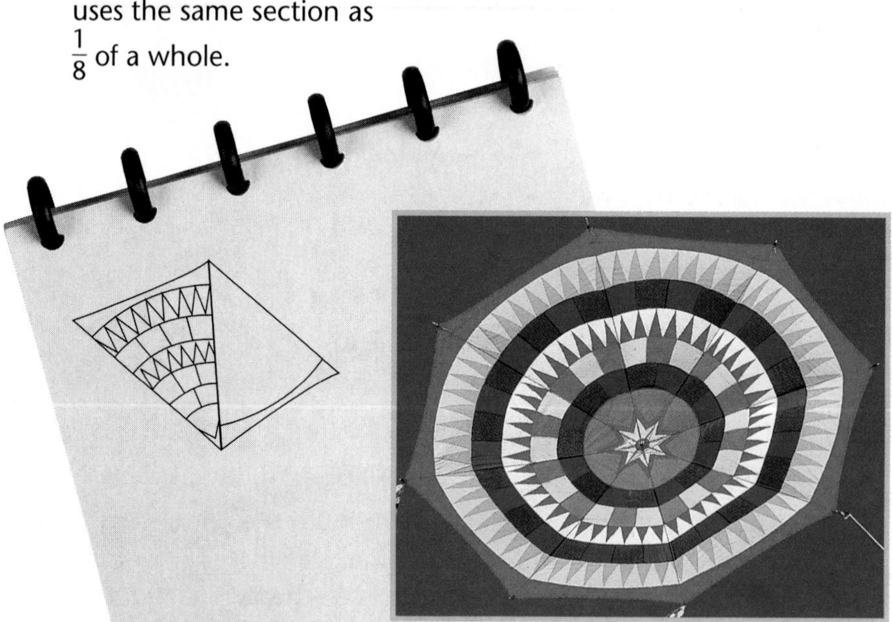

HOMEWORK EXERCISES See Exs. 13–19 on pp. 103–104.

Section 2

Key Concepts

Fractions (pp. 95–97)

A fraction is a number that tells how a part of an object or a set compares with a whole. When a fraction is greater than a whole you can write it in two ways.

Example

As a fraction	As a mixed number
$\frac{4}{3}$ ← numerator ← denominator	$1\frac{1}{3}$
First divide the **whole** into **3 equal-sized** parts. Then consider **4** of the parts.	1 whole and $\frac{1}{3}$ of another whole.

Key Terms

fraction

mixed number

numerator

denominator

Key Concepts Questions For Questions 19–21, tell whether each statement is *true* or *false*. If a statement is false, explain why.

19  $\frac{1}{2}$ of the triangle is shaded.

20  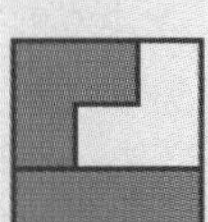 $\frac{2}{3}$ of the square is shaded.

21  $\frac{4}{6}$ of the rectangle is shaded.

22 Suppose these two triangles are $\frac{2}{6}$ of a whole. How many more triangles would you need to make a whole?

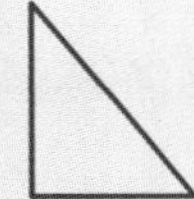 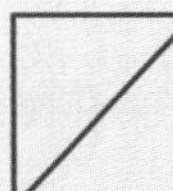

Section 2

Practice & Application Exercises

YOU WILL NEED

For Ex. 16:
- Labsheet 2C

Write a fraction for the shaded part of each figure.

1. 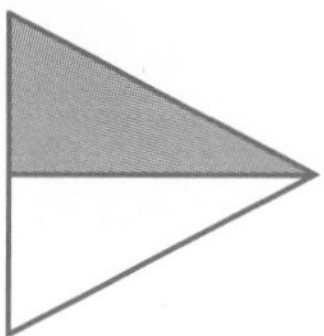

2. 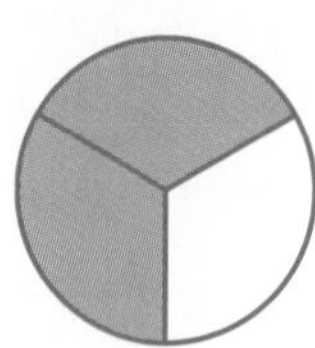

3. 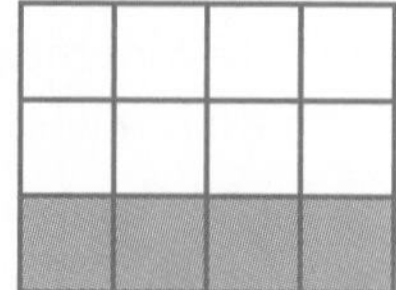

For Exercises 4 and 5, use these sketches of two polygons that were made using pattern blocks. Some blocks in each are shaded.

Polygon A

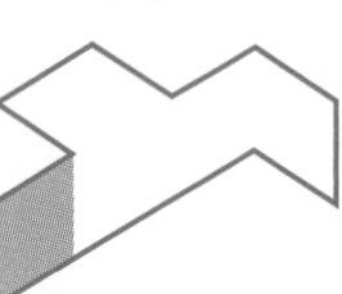

Polygon B

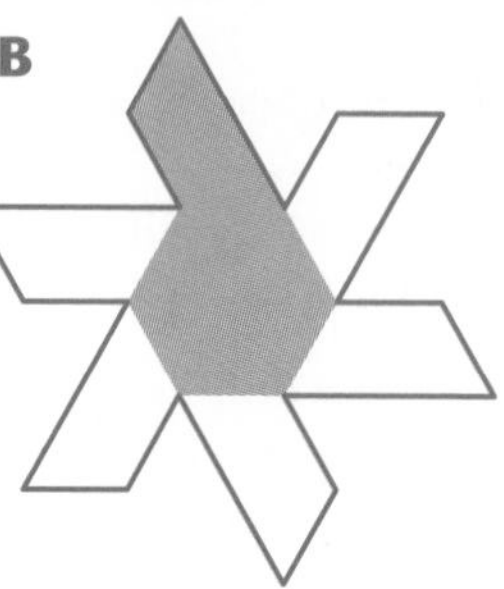

4. What fraction of Polygon A is shaded?

5. a. What fraction of Polygon B is shaded?

   b. What fraction of Polygon B is not shaded?

   c. What do you think the sum of the fractions in parts (a) and (b) would be? Why?

6. **Suppose you have 6 kites that you want to string together with equal distances between them. If you use one long piece of string, what fraction of the string do you need to tie the first 3 kites together? What fraction of the string would you have left? (You may find it helpful to draw a diagram.)**

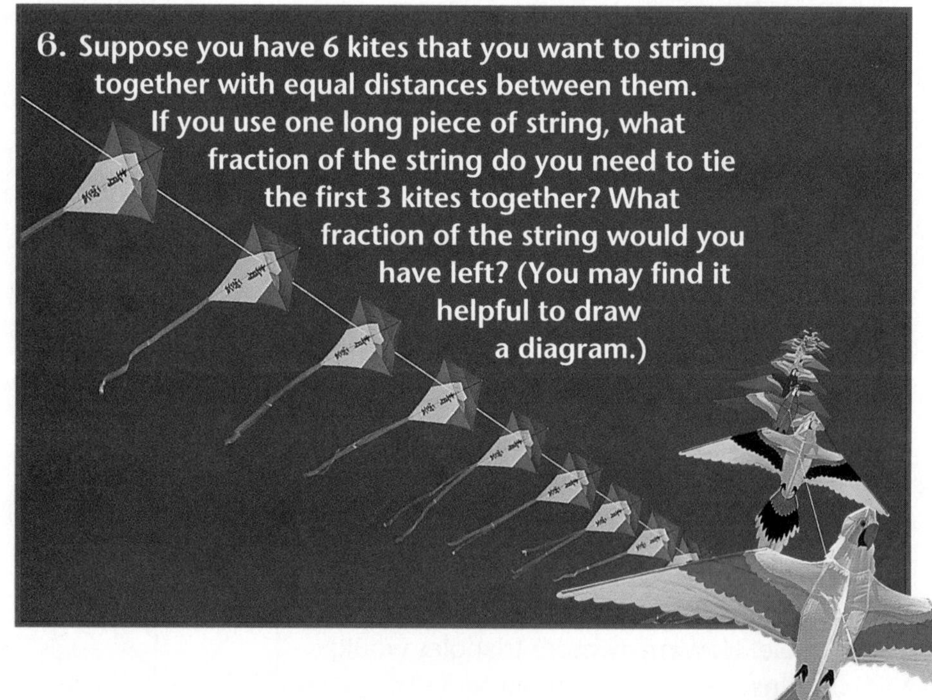

The use of kites can ▶ be traced back to as early as 500 B.C. in China. Kites can be strung together for a decorative effect or for the practical purpose of measuring temperature at different altitudes.

represents the whole. Write each part to whole relationship as a fraction and as a mixed number.

7. 8. 9.

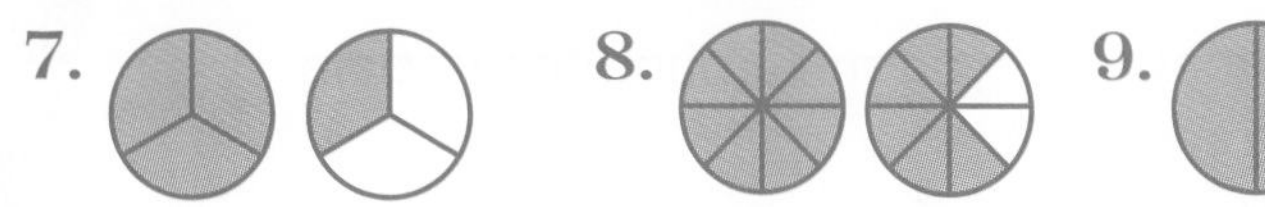

10. The first three terms of a sequence of shapes are shown below. Draw the fourth and fifth terms. Describe the rule you used.

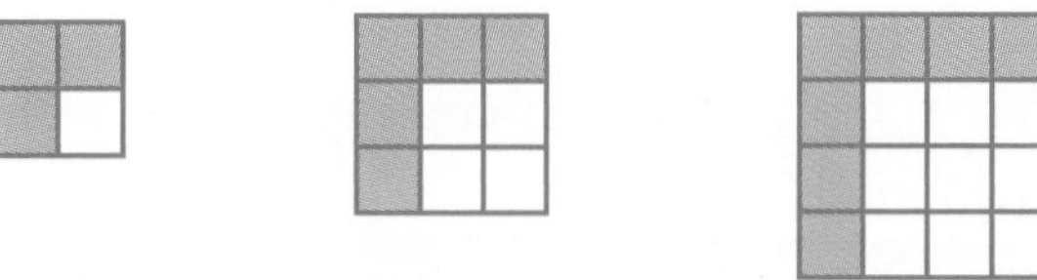

11. Write a fraction for the shaded part of each term from Exercise 10.

12. **Challenge** Can you predict what fraction of the 10th term will be shaded?

For each pair, explain why the shapes are or are not congruent.

13. 14. 15.

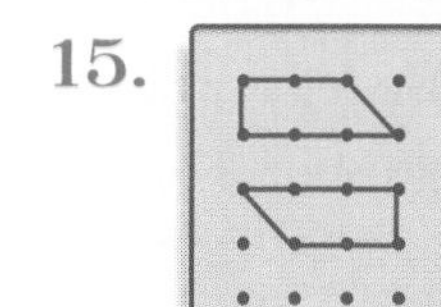

16. **Use Labsheet 2C.** *Fractional Parts on a Geoboard* are shown. Follow the directions to use congruent parts to complete a possible drawing of the whole.

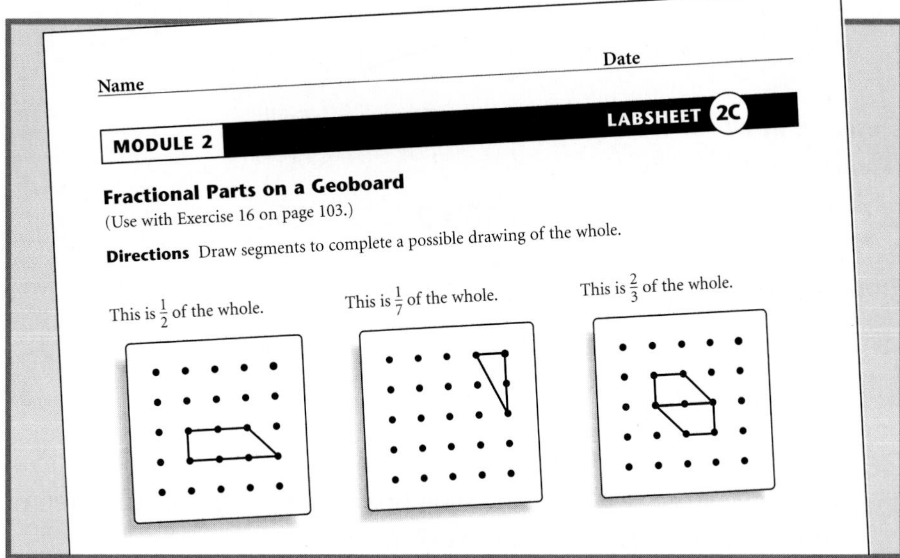

Name

Date

MODULE 2 **LABSHEET 2C**

Fractional Parts on a Geoboard

(Use with Exercise 16 on page 103.)

Directions Draw segments to complete a possible drawing of the whole.

This is $\frac{1}{2}$ of the whole. This is $\frac{1}{7}$ of the whole. This is $\frac{2}{3}$ of the whole.

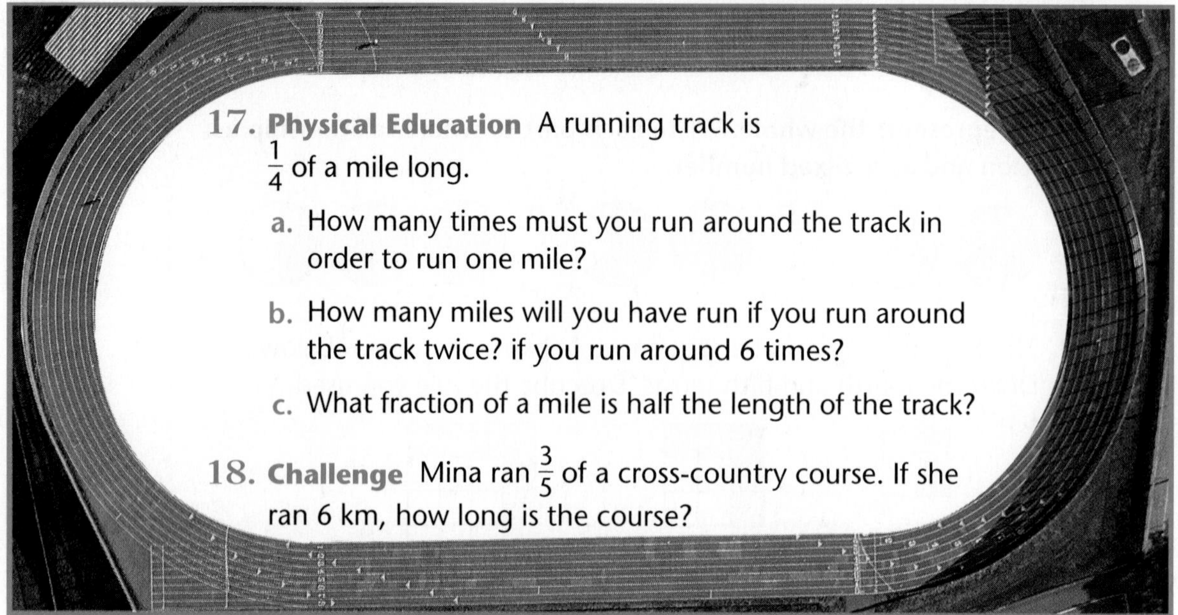

17. **Physical Education** A running track is $\frac{1}{4}$ of a mile long.

a. How many times must you run around the track in order to run one mile?

b. How many miles will you have run if you run around the track twice? if you run around 6 times?

c. What fraction of a mile is half the length of the track?

18. **Challenge** Mina ran $\frac{3}{5}$ of a cross-country course. If she ran 6 km, how long is the course?

Journal

Exercise 19 checks that you understand the meaning of a fraction.

Reflecting on the Section

Write your response to Exercise 19 in your journal.

19. A vase fell and broke into 12 pieces. Jason picked up one of the pieces, but it was not $\frac{1}{12}$ of the vase. How could this be?

Spiral Review

Name each polygon. Be as specific as possible. (Module 2, p. 87)

20. 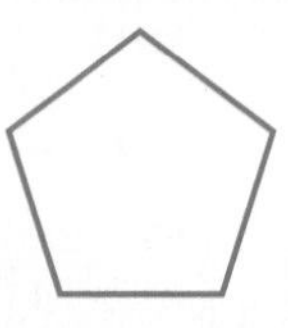

21. 

22. 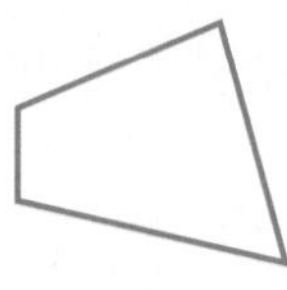

Describe in words how to find the value of each expression. (Module 1, p. 51)

23. $4 \cdot (3 + 2)$

24. $7 + 10 \div 2$

25. $8 - 3 \cdot 2$

Find each product without using a calculator. (Toolbox, p. 598)

26. 17×20

27. 300×53

28. $70{,}000 \times 627$

29. The blue box is to the left of the yellow box. The green box is to the right of the red box. The blue box is to the right of the green box. In what order are the boxes? (Module 1, p. 35)

Career Connection

Drafter: Mark Beckwith

Mark Beckwith uses voice-activated software to draw the plans for buildings. He makes a drawing called a *floor plan* that shows what a building will look like as if seen from above. This floor plan is for a log cabin.

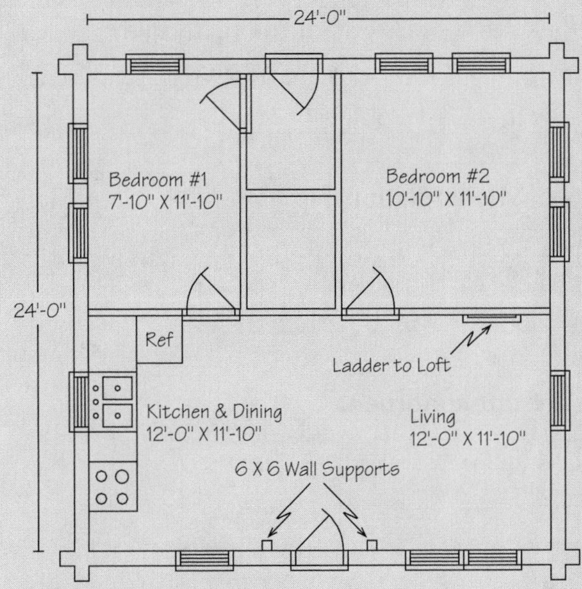

30. About what fraction of the log cabin is taken up by the kitchen, dining room, and living room?

31. Make a sketch of a floor plan for a one-story house that has one third of its space taken up by bedrooms.

Extension 

Visual Puzzles

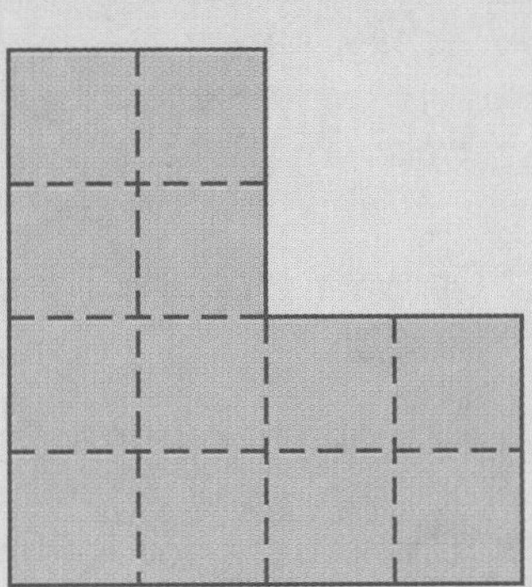

32. a. Copy the figure at the right. If you divide this figure into 4 congruent parts using the grid lines, how many small squares will each congruent part have? Explain how you know.

    b. Use your answer to part (a) to find a way to divide the figure into 4 congruent parts.

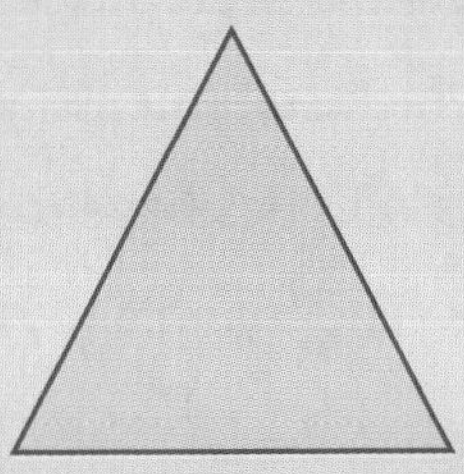

33. a. Trace the equilateral triangle. Find a way to divide the triangle into 4 congruent parts.

    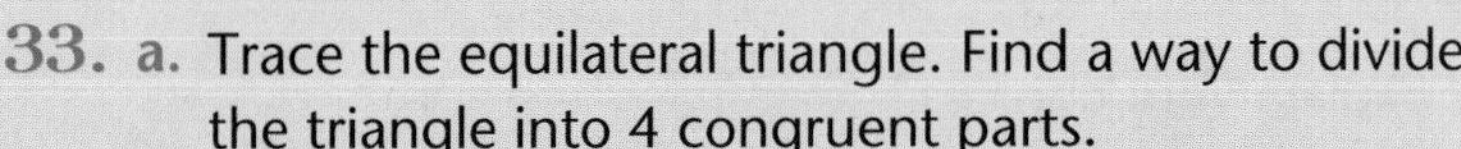

    b. Find a way to divide the triangle into 8 congruent parts.

34. Trace the equilateral triangle and find a way to divide it into 3 congruent parts.

Section 2
Extra Skill Practice

Tell whether each statement is *true* or *false*. If a statement is false, explain why.

1. 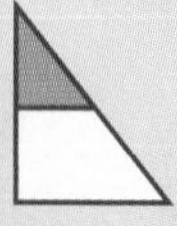

$\frac{1}{2}$ of the triangle is shaded.

2. 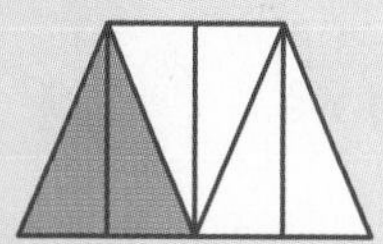

$\frac{2}{6}$ of the trapezoid is shaded.

3. 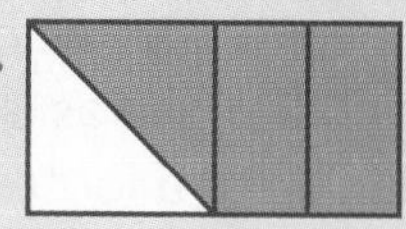

$\frac{3}{4}$ of the rectangle is shaded.

▇ represents the whole. Write each part to whole relationship as a fraction and as a mixed number.

4. 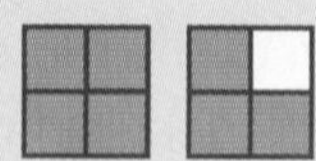

5. 

6. 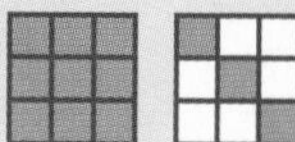

For each pair, explain why the shapes are or are not congruent.

7. 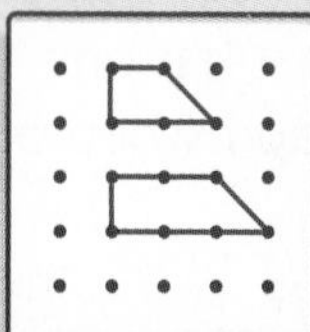

8. 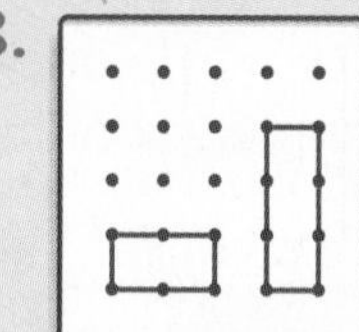

9. 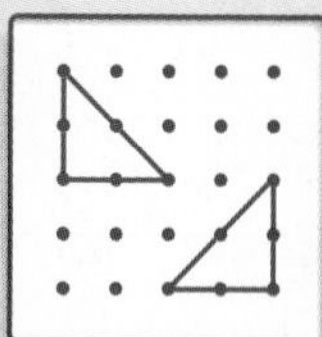

10. Jake has $\frac{1}{3}$ of the money he needs to buy a kite. If he has $1.50, how much does the kite cost?

Standardized Testing ▶ Free Response

1. Draw each figure. Then shade the part that represents the given fraction.

   (A) $\frac{4}{6}$ of a hexagon (B) $\frac{3}{4}$ of a square (C) $\frac{2}{8}$ of a circle

2. This house shape is formed by putting an equilateral triangle on top of a square.

   Which statements are true? Explain your choices.

   (A) All sides have the same length.
   (B) It is a pentagon.
   (C) The triangle is $\frac{1}{5}$ of the square.
   (D) It is a regular pentagon.

Section 3 Equivalent Fractions

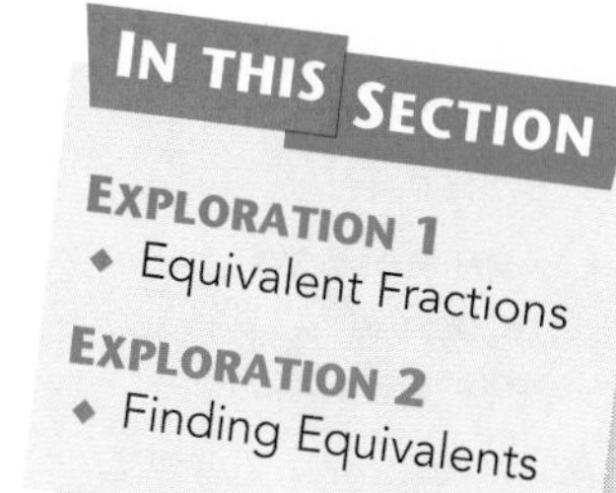

The Same or Different?

Setting the Stage

Although you may not notice them, many everyday objects show a variety of designs and patterns.

Designs for windows range from simple squares and rectangles to many-sided polygons to stained-glass works of art.

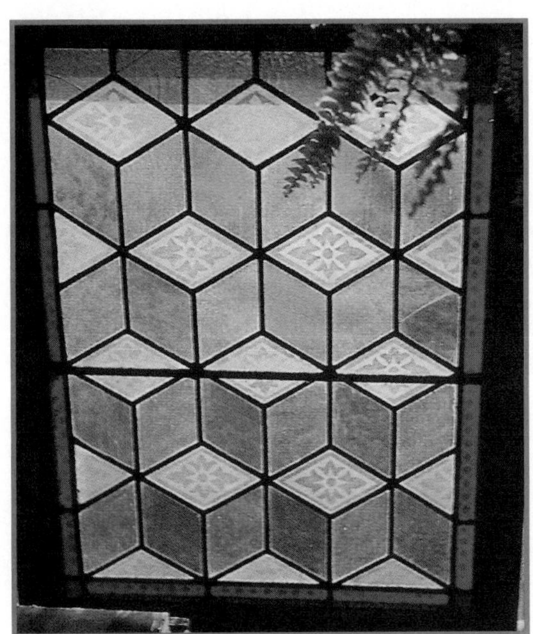

This "building block" window was created in the 1870s.

Think About It

1 Some of the pattern block shapes can be seen in the window. Which can you identify?

2 What other shapes and patterns do you notice in the window?

3 Use a fraction to describe a part of the window design.

▶ **Different fractions can name the same part of a whole design. In this section you'll find different ways to name parts of window designs.**

GOAL

LEARN HOW TO...
- recognize equivalent fractions

AS YOU...
- explore arrangements of window panes

KEY TERM
- equivalent fractions

Exploration 1

EQUIVALENT FRACTIONS $= \frac{2}{4} \; \frac{4}{8} \; \frac{6}{12}$

SET UP *You will need:* • *Labsheets 3A and 3B* • *pattern blocks*

Use the *Hexagon Section* on Labsheet 3A for Question 4.

4 **a.** Estimate the fraction of the hexagon covered by the star.

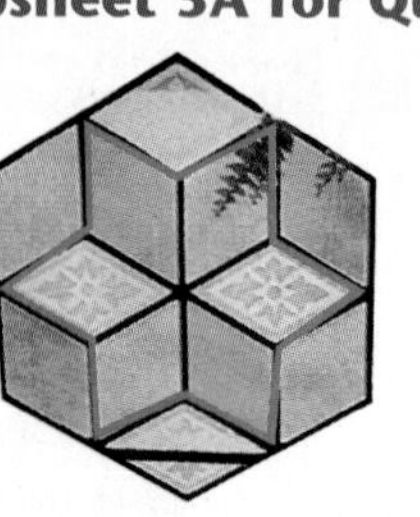

A hexagon-shaped section of the building block window.

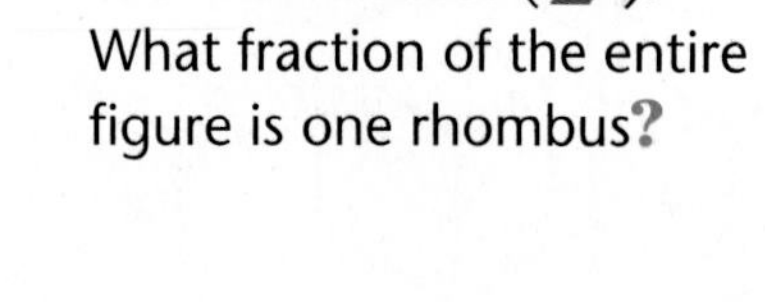

b. Cover the entire hexagon with **rhombuses** (▰). What fraction of the entire figure is one rhombus?

c. Cover just the star portion with **rhombuses** (▰). What fraction of the hexagon do these rhombuses represent?

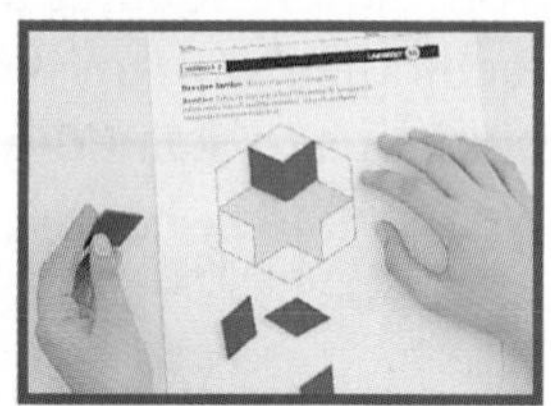

d. Now cover the entire hexagon with **triangles** (▲). What fraction of the hexagon does one triangle represent?

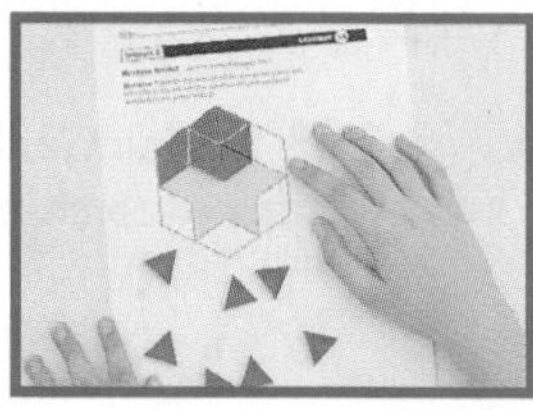

e. Cover just the star portion with **triangles** (▲). What fraction of the hexagon do these triangles represent?

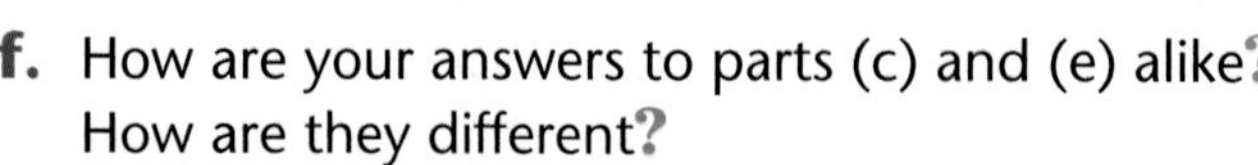

f. How are your answers to parts (c) and (e) alike? How are they different?

▶ **Fractions that name the same part of a whole are equivalent fractions. Question 4 shows that $\frac{6}{12}$ and $\frac{12}{24}$ are equivalent fractions.**

5 **Discussion** Name another fraction that is equivalent to $\frac{6}{12}$ and $\frac{12}{24}$. How do you know it is equivalent?

6 **Use Labsheet 3B.** Use the specified pattern blocks to make different *Divisions of Hexagon-Shaped Windows.*

7 **✓ CHECKPOINT** Pattern blocks covering part of a hexagon-shaped window ( ) are shown below.

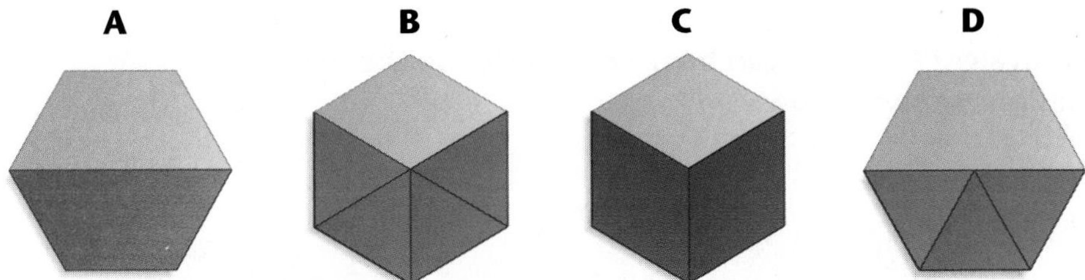

a. What fraction of each window is covered?

b. Which of the fractions in part (a) are equivalent?

8 The different window designs below are formed within the same outlined shape. Each design has a hexagon of clear glass in the center.

a. Complete the fractions that represent the part of each window that has colored panes.

b. Explain why the fractions in part (a) are equivalent.

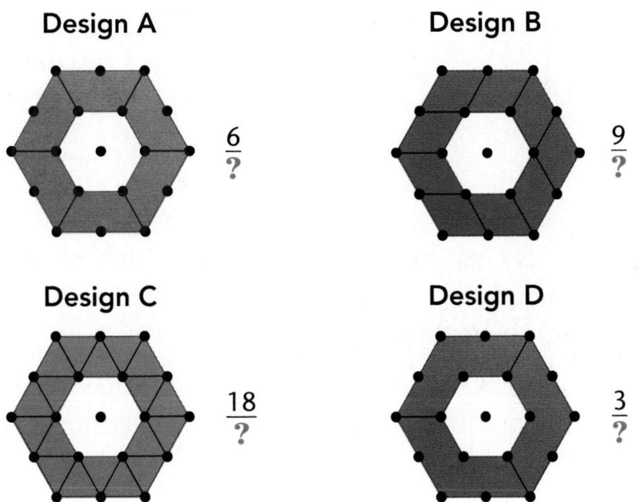

✓ QUESTION 7

...checks that you can recognize equivalent fractions.

HOMEWORK EXERCISES ▶ **See Exs. 1–9 on pp. 115–116.**

GOAL

LEARN HOW TO...
- find equivalent fractions
- write a fraction in lowest terms

AS YOU...
- use pattern blocks to make window designs

KEY TERM
- lowest terms

Exploration 2

FINDING = EQUIVALENTS

SET UP *You will need: • pattern blocks • fraction calculator (optional)*

▶ **Equivalent fractions can be used to describe the window designs shown below.**

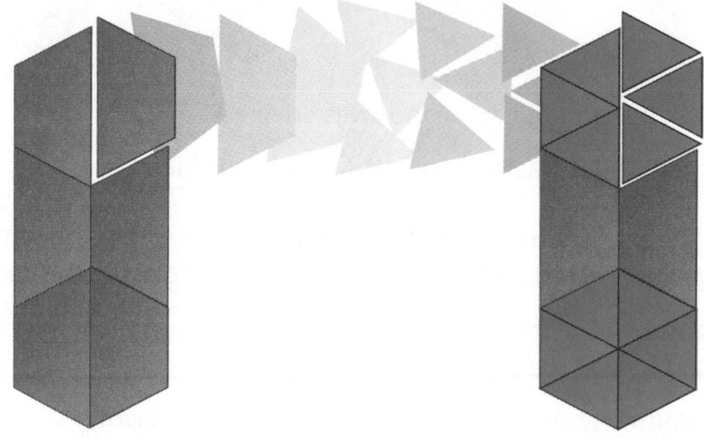

Original window design made with **6 trapezoids** (▲).

New window design is made by replacing **4 trapezoids** (▲) with **triangles** (▲).

9 **a.** Use **trapezoids** (▲) to create the original window. What fraction of the original window will be replaced with **triangles** (▲) to create the new window?

b. Without looking at the picture of the new window, how can you determine the number of triangles you will need to replace the 4 outside trapezoids?

c. If you were going to replace all of the trapezoids with triangles, how many triangles would you need?

d. What fraction of the new window is covered with triangles?

10 An equivalent fraction for the part of the new window that is covered by triangles can be found as follows.

You replaced 4 of the 6 **trapezoids** with triangles.

4 trapezoids became **12 triangles.**

$$\frac{4}{6} = \frac{4 \cdot ?}{6 \cdot ?} = \frac{12}{18}$$

You would need **18 triangles** (▲) to replace all 6 **trapezoids** (⏢).

a. What number must replace each question mark to make the equations true?

b. How are the products in the middle fraction related to your answers from Questions 9(b) and 9(c)?

FOR ▶ HELP with *number fact families*, see **TOOLBOX, p. 597**

11 Copy and complete the equivalent fractions. Be sure to include all the missing steps.

a. $\frac{1}{2} = \frac{1 \cdot 2}{2 \cdot 2} = \frac{2}{?}$ **b.** $\frac{1}{3} = \frac{1 \cdot 2}{3 \cdot 2} = \frac{2}{?}$ **c.** $\frac{2}{3} = \frac{2 \cdot ?}{3 \cdot ?} = \frac{?}{12}$

d. $\frac{3}{3} = \frac{3 \cdot ?}{3 \cdot ?} = \frac{?}{12}$ **e.** $\frac{3}{4} = \frac{3 \cdot ?}{4 \cdot ?} = \frac{?}{12}$ **f.** $\frac{8}{6} = \frac{? \cdot ?}{? \cdot ?} = \frac{?}{12}$

12 ✓ **CHECKPOINT** Complete each pair of equivalent fractions.

a. $\frac{3}{7} = \frac{?}{28}$ **b.** $\frac{5}{6} = \frac{45}{?}$ **c.** $\frac{2}{5} = \frac{?}{30}$

✓ **QUESTION 12**

...checks that you can use multiplication to find equivalent fractions.

13 Use your pattern blocks to show how $\frac{2}{5}$ is equivalent to $\frac{4}{10}$. Trace around the blocks you used.

▶ Equivalent fractions can also be used to describe these window designs.

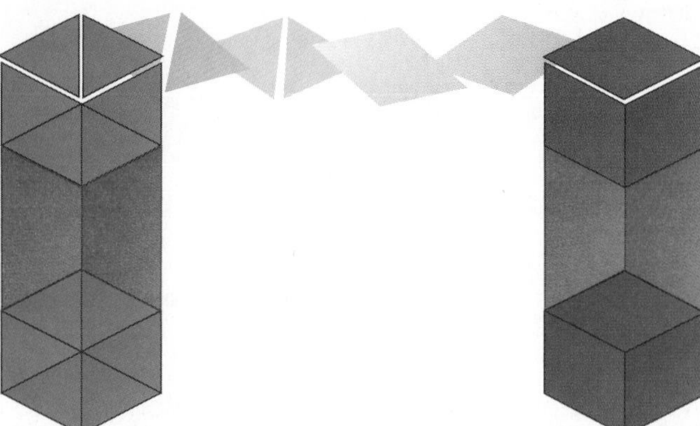

Original window design has $\frac{12}{18}$ of the design made from **triangles** (▲).

New window design made by replacing the triangles (▲) with **rhombuses** (▰).

14 An equation can be used to find an equivalent fraction representing the part of the new window that is covered by **rhombuses** (▰).

$$\mathbf{\frac{12}{18} = \frac{12 \div ?}{18 \div ?} = \frac{6}{9}}$$

a. Use pattern blocks to create the original window.

b. How many **triangles** (▲) can be covered with one **rhombus** (▰)? How can you use this information to find how many rhombuses you need to replace all of the triangles?

c. Create the new window. Is $\frac{6}{9}$ of the new window covered with rhombuses? Explain.

d. Why was division used in the equation? What number must replace each question mark?

15 Copy and complete the equivalent fractions.

a. $\frac{9}{12} = \frac{9 \div 3}{12 \div 3} = \frac{3}{?}$ **b.** $\frac{4}{6} = \frac{4 \div 2}{6 \div 2} = \frac{?}{3}$ **c.** $\frac{8}{16} = \frac{? \div ?}{16 \div 8} = \frac{?}{?}$

d. $\frac{64}{72} = \frac{64 \div 8}{? \div ?} = \frac{?}{9}$ **e.** $\frac{25}{30} = \frac{? \div ?}{? \div ?} = \frac{5}{?}$ **f.** $\frac{30}{36} = \frac{? \div ?}{? \div ?} = \frac{?}{12}$

✓ QUESTION 16

...checks that you can use division to find equivalent fractions.

16 ✓ CHECKPOINT Complete each pair of equivalent fractions.

a. $\frac{40}{64} = \frac{?}{8}$ **b.** $\frac{36}{108} = \frac{4}{?}$ **c.** $\frac{21}{33} = \frac{?}{11}$

▶ **Fractions like $\frac{2}{3}$ and $\frac{3}{4}$ are said to be in lowest terms since 1 is the greatest whole number that will divide both the numerator and denominator of the fraction evenly.**

17 Tell whether or not each fraction is in lowest terms. Explain how you know.

a. $\frac{3}{6}$ **b.** $\frac{21}{29}$ **c.** $\frac{5}{8}$ **d.** $\frac{11}{66}$

18 ✓ **CHECKPOINT** For each fraction, write an equivalent fraction in lowest terms.

a. $\frac{7}{14}$ **b.** $\frac{10}{30}$ **c.** $\frac{6}{48}$ **d.** $\frac{25}{125}$

✓ **QUESTION 18**

...checks that you can write fractions in lowest terms.

▶ **Calculating Equivalents A fraction calculator can be used to find equivalent fractions, in particular equivalent fractions in lowest terms.**

19 Fraction Calculator Enter the key sequence [1] [8] [/] [2] [4] on your calculator.

a. What number appears on the display?

b. Now press [SIMP] [=]. What number appears on the display? What did the calculator do to get that number?

c. Press [SIMP] [=] again. What number appears on the display? What did the calculator do?

d. What happens if you press [SIMP] [=] again? Why do you think this happens?

20 **a.** Enter the fraction $\frac{16}{28}$ on your calculator.

b. Press [SIMP] [=] repeatedly to find an equivalent fraction in lowest terms.

21 Use your calculator to tell if each pair of fractions is equivalent.

a. $\frac{27}{45}, \frac{5}{7}$ **b.** $\frac{85}{272}, \frac{20}{64}$ **c.** $\frac{14}{49}, \frac{2}{7}$

HOMEWORK EXERCISES ▶ See Exs. 10–28 on pp. 116–117.

Section 3 Key Concepts

Key Terms

equivalent fractions

Equivalent Fractions (pp. 109, 111, 112)

Fractions that name the same part of a whole are equivalent.

Examples

$\frac{1}{2}$, $\frac{2}{4}$, and $\frac{3}{6}$, are equivalent fractions since

$\frac{1}{2}$ = [1 of 2 parts shaded], $\frac{2}{4}$ = [2 of 4 parts shaded], and $\frac{3}{6}$ = [3 of 6 parts shaded].

When given a fraction, you can find an equivalent fraction by multiplying or dividing the numerator and denominator by the same whole number other than 0.

Examples

$\frac{5}{6} = \frac{5 \cdot 3}{6 \cdot 3} = \frac{15}{18}$, so $\frac{5}{6}$ is equivalent to $\frac{15}{18}$.

$\frac{24}{28} = \frac{24 \div 4}{28 \div 4} = \frac{6}{7}$, so $\frac{24}{28}$ is equivalent to $\frac{6}{7}$.

lowest terms

Lowest Terms (p. 113)

In the example above, $\frac{6}{7}$ is in the lowest terms because 1 is the only whole number that will divide both 6 and 7 evenly.

Key Concepts Questions

22 Divide the numerator and denominator of $\frac{18}{30}$ by 2. Is the result in lowest terms? If not, how can you find an equivalent fraction in lowest terms?

23 Make a shaded drawing for the fractions in each pair. Use your drawing to explain whether or not each pair is equivalent.

a. $\frac{1}{3}, \frac{3}{9}$ **b.** $\frac{3}{8}, \frac{1}{4}$ **c.** $\frac{2}{5}, \frac{4}{10}$

Section 3
Practice & Application Exercises

YOU WILL NEED

For Ex. 8:
- Labsheet 3B

1. The windows in the photograph below are identical except that the one on the right is partly open.

   a. What fraction of the window on the right is open?

   b. The photograph shows that another fraction is equivalent to the one in part (a). What is the other fraction?

Write two equivalent fractions that tell what part of each figure is shaded.

2. 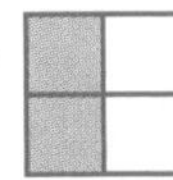

3. 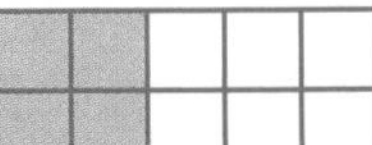

4. 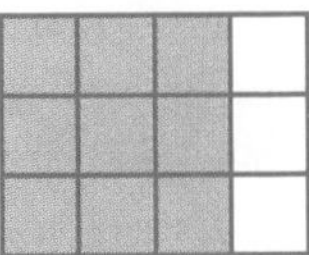

5. 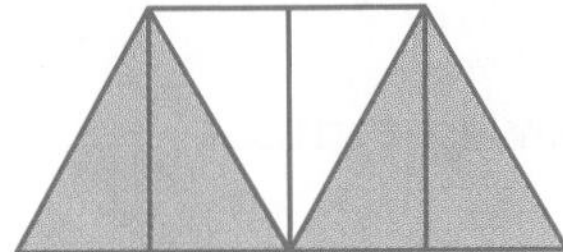

6. 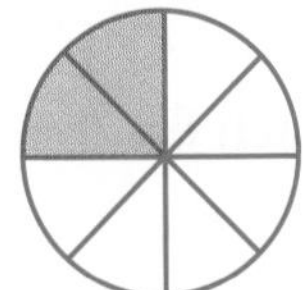

7. 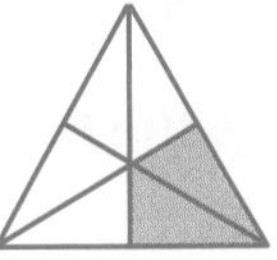

8. **Use Labsheet 3B.**

   a. Use your *Divisions of Hexagon-Shaped Windows* to complete the table on *Fractions Describing Hexagon-Shaped Windows.*

   b. What do all the fractions in the table have in common?

   c. What whole number does each fraction represent and what object does that number describe?

9. When special stamps are printed, several related designs may be arranged on a sheet.

a. Write three equivalent fractions to represent the part of the stamps showing the tallest vase.

Two rows from a sheet of 13¢ stamps recognizing Pueblo art.

b. What is the value in cents of the two rows of stamps?

c. Write a fraction different from the ones in part (a) that compares the value in cents of the stamps showing the tallest vase with the total value in cents of the two rows of stamps. How is this fraction related to the fractions you found in part (a)? Explain.

Complete each pair of equivalent fractions.

10. $\frac{3}{8} = \frac{?}{16}$ 11. $\frac{4}{7} = \frac{12}{?}$ 12. $\frac{2}{9} = \frac{?}{27}$

13. $\frac{12}{18} = \frac{?}{3}$ 14. $\frac{32}{40} = \frac{?}{5}$ 15. $\frac{12}{27} = \frac{4}{?}$

Find the next three terms in each sequence.

16. $\frac{1}{2}, \frac{2}{4}, \frac{3}{6}, \frac{4}{8}, \ldots$ 17. $\frac{2}{3}, \frac{4}{6}, \frac{6}{9}, \frac{8}{12}, \ldots$ 18. $\frac{1}{5}, \frac{3}{15}, \frac{9}{45}, \frac{27}{135}, \ldots$

Choose the fractions in each list that are in lowest terms.

19. $\frac{5}{20}, \frac{4}{20}, \frac{3}{20}$ 20. $\frac{8}{6}, \frac{9}{12}, \frac{5}{8}$ 21. $\frac{4}{8}, \frac{4}{9}, \frac{4}{10}$

Write each fraction in lowest terms.

22. $\frac{12}{20}$ 23. $\frac{24}{36}$ 24. $\frac{13}{52}$ 25. $\frac{5}{60}$

26. **Challenge** Find two pairs of equivalent fractions in the list below. Explain how you know each pair is equivalent.

$\frac{12}{9}$ $\frac{5}{4}$ $1\frac{3}{4}$ $1\frac{2}{6}$ $\frac{6}{9}$ $1\frac{21}{28}$

Reflecting on the Section

Be prepared to discuss your responses to Exercises 27 and 28 in class.

United States coins represent fractions of a dollar. For example, the value of a *quarter* is 25¢ or $\frac{25}{100}$ of a dollar.

27. **a.** What is $\frac{25}{100}$ in lowest terms?

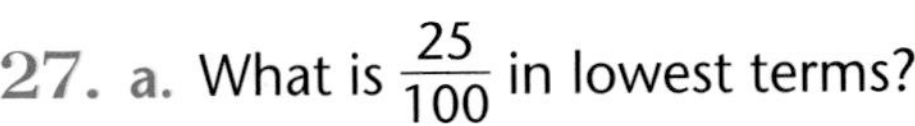

b. Why do you think a quarter is called a quarter?

28. Give two equivalent fractions that tell what part a dime is of a dollar. Are any of your answers in lowest terms? Explain.

Discussion

Exercises 27 and 28 check that you understand equivalent fractions.

Spiral Review

29. The picture at the right shows the stained glass dome of the Grand Hall on the third floor of the National Portrait Gallery in Washington, D.C.

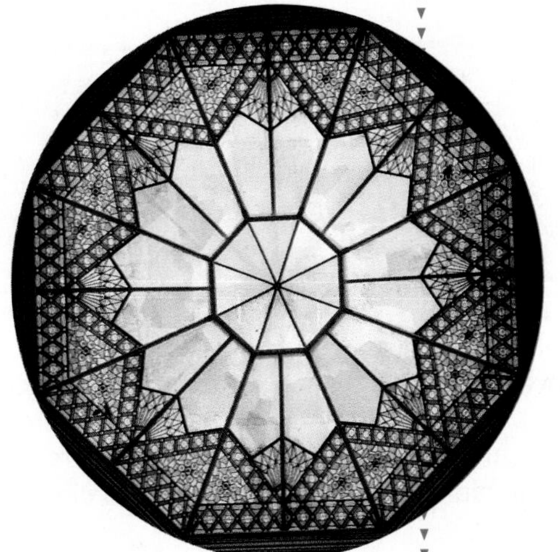

a. What polygons do you see in the figure? **(Module 2, p. 87)**

b. What fractions do you see in the figure? **(Module 2, p. 114)**

30. Is $\frac{1}{4}$ of the circle shaded? Explain why or why not. **(Module 2, p. 101)**

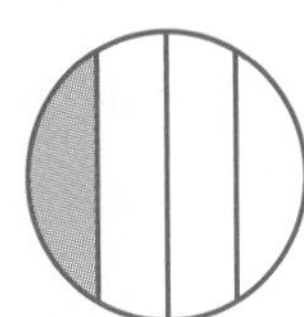

Subtract without using a calculator. **(Toolbox, p. 594)**

31. $\begin{array}{r} 291 \\ -\ 156 \\ \hline \end{array}$

32. $\begin{array}{r} 9431 \\ -\ 934 \\ \hline \end{array}$

33. $\begin{array}{r} 3101 \\ -\ 1808 \\ \hline \end{array}$

Sketch an irregular polygon with the symmetry described.
(Module 2, p. 87)

34. 2 lines of symmetry

35. no lines of symmetry

Pop-Up Art

SET UP *You will need:*
- *compass*
- *ruler*
- *scissors*
- *construction paper*

Showing Fractions Follow the steps below to make a fraction window.

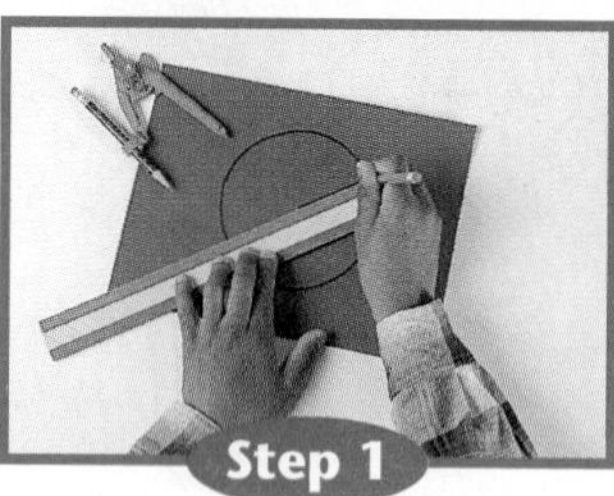

Draw a circle on dark colored paper. Draw a segment from the center of the circle to a point on the circle.

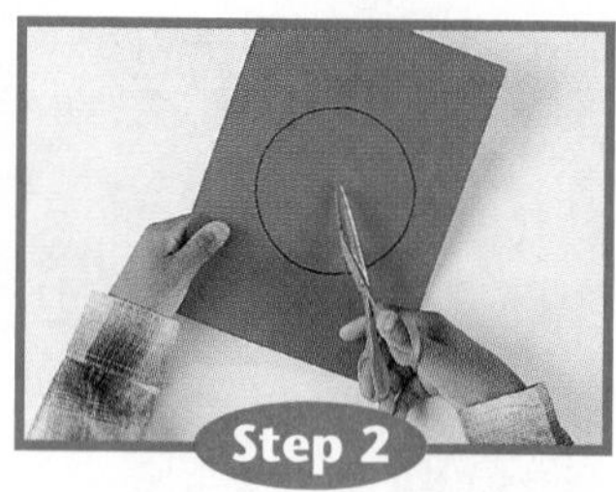

Cut along the segment. (Do not cut out the circle!) This is called a *radius* of the circle.

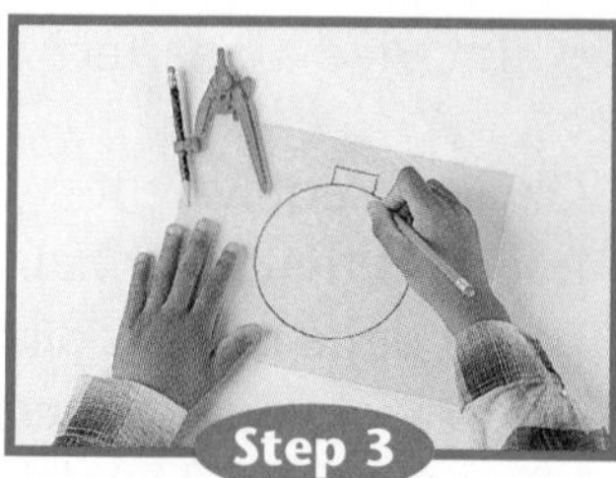

On light colored paper, draw another circle the same size as the first. Draw a tab at the top of the circle.

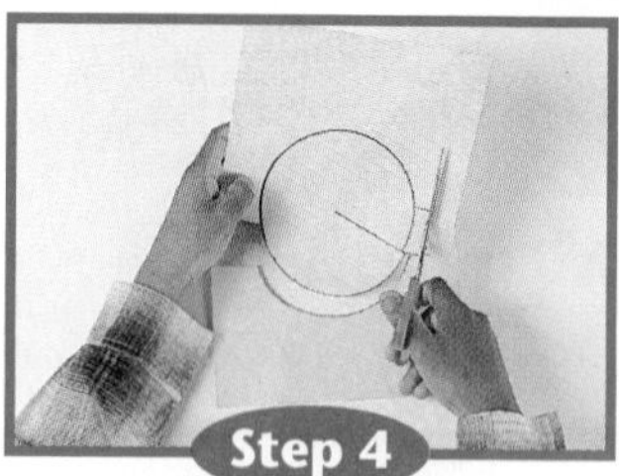

Beginning at the right of the tab, draw a radius of the circle. Cut out the circle and tab, and make a cut along the radius.

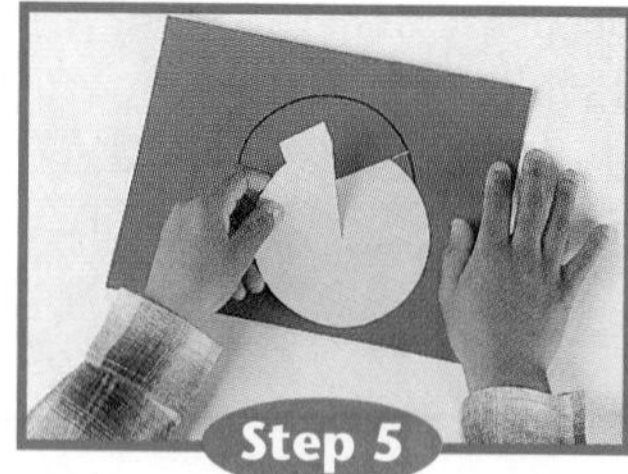

Slide the circle with the tab into the slit cut on the dark colored circle. Line up the centers and edges of the two circles.

Open and close the window by carefully moving the tab around the edge of the dark colored circle.

3 Rotate the tab to show these fractions of the dark colored circle: $\frac{1}{4}$, $\frac{1}{3}$, $\frac{1}{2}$, $\frac{2}{3}$, $\frac{3}{4}$. Sketch your results.

Finding Equivalent Fractions You can also use your fraction window to find equivalent fractions.

4 Rotate the tab to show $\frac{1}{8}$ of the dark colored circle. Now continue rotating the tab. Stop and look at the result each time another $\frac{1}{8}$ of the circle is uncovered. Use the window openings to complete these equivalent fractions.

a. $\frac{2}{8} = \frac{1}{?}$ b. $\frac{4}{8} = \frac{2}{?} = \frac{1}{?}$ c. $\frac{6}{8} = \frac{?}{?}$

Section 3 Extra Skill Practice

Write two equivalent fractions that tell what part of each figure is shaded.

1\.

2\. 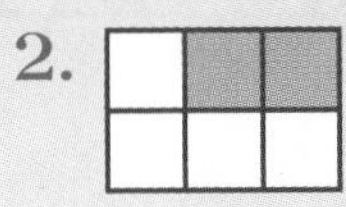

3\.

4\. 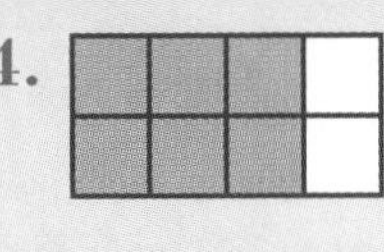

For each fraction, write three equivalent fractions.

5\. $\frac{2}{5}$ 6. $\frac{4}{9}$ 7. $\frac{4}{16}$ 8. $\frac{3}{8}$ 9. $\frac{8}{24}$

10\. $\frac{1}{6}$ 11. $\frac{2}{7}$ 12. $\frac{4}{32}$ 13. $\frac{1}{5}$ 14. $\frac{2}{18}$

15\. $\frac{6}{15}$ 16. $\frac{5}{8}$ 17. $\frac{3}{7}$ 18. $\frac{1}{13}$ 19. $\frac{8}{10}$

Complete each pair of equivalent fractions.

20\. $\frac{1}{2} = \frac{?}{12}$ 21. $\frac{6}{9} = \frac{?}{54}$ 22. $\frac{3}{7} = \frac{18}{?}$ 23. $\frac{8}{9} = \frac{?}{27}$

24\. $\frac{6}{8} = \frac{?}{4}$ 25. $\frac{3}{12} = \frac{?}{48}$ 26. $\frac{18}{27} = \frac{2}{?}$ 27. $\frac{17}{51} = \frac{?}{3}$

28\. $\frac{24}{40} = \frac{?}{10}$ 29. $\frac{72}{99} = \frac{8}{?}$ 30. $\frac{100}{?} = \frac{5}{6}$ 31. $\frac{?}{25} = \frac{12}{75}$

Write each fraction in lowest terms.

32\. $\frac{6}{9}$ 33. $\frac{5}{30}$ 34. $\frac{12}{20}$ 35. $\frac{8}{40}$ 36. $\frac{18}{30}$

37\. $\frac{21}{48}$ 38. $\frac{12}{24}$ 39. $\frac{4}{15}$ 40. $\frac{30}{100}$ 41. $\frac{9}{24}$

Standardized Testing ▶ Multiple Choice

1\. Which fraction is equivalent to $\frac{28}{36}$?

Ⓐ $\frac{12}{18}$ Ⓑ $\frac{70}{90}$ Ⓒ $\frac{84}{106}$ Ⓓ $\frac{128}{136}$

2\. Which fraction is in lowest terms?

Ⓐ $\frac{7}{84}$ Ⓑ $\frac{9}{43}$ Ⓒ $\frac{27}{72}$ Ⓓ $\frac{18}{100}$

Section 4 Transformations

IN THIS SECTION

EXPLORATION 1
- Translations, Rotations, and Reflections

EXPLORATION 2
- Transformations in Quilting

PATCH WORK QUILTS

Setting the Stage

Patchwork quilts are made from scraps of material or old clothing that are cut into shapes and sewn together into a pattern. Ideas for patterns and their names come from people's everyday experiences — the tools they use, the plants or animals they see, and the events or people that are important to them. Patchwork was especially important in colonial times, because fabric was scarce and expensive.

In the 1800s, quilting became so popular that an entire family would often work together to make a quilt.

A B E D C F

◀ This design, called Eight Hands Round, is named for a movement in square dancing.

▶ **A quilter can experiment with how to place pieces of material by sewing a copy of part of a design and moving it to different positions.**

Think About It

1 Give directions for *sliding, flipping,* or *turning* the outlined quilt patches on page 120 to make each move.

a. Move the triangle labeled A onto the triangle labeled B.

b. Move the group of patches labeled C to D.

c. Move the group of patches labeled E to F.

2 Can any of the moves in Question 1 be done in more than one way? Discuss your ideas.

Exploration 1

Translations, Rotations, and Reflections

GOAL

LEARN HOW TO...
- perform a translation, a rotation, and a reflection

AS YOU...
- create quilt patch designs

KEY TERMS
- translation
- rotation
- reflection
- transformation

SET UP *You will need:* • *Labsheets 4A and 4B* • *tracing paper* • *index card or cardboard* • *scissors* • *ruler*

3 Follow the steps below to make an isosceles right triangle. Later you will use your triangle to make quilt patch designs.

First

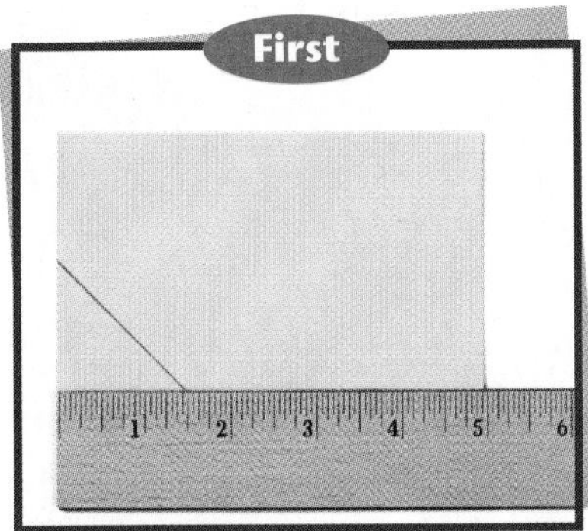

Draw an isosceles right triangle on an index card. The sides forming the right angle should each be $1\frac{1}{2}$ in. long.

Then

Cut out the triangle and label the sides as shown.

FOR HELP with *classifying triangles*, see **MODULE 1, p. 22**

▶ **A translation (slide) moves a figure by sliding it. Every point moves the same distance in the same direction along a flat surface.**

EXAMPLE

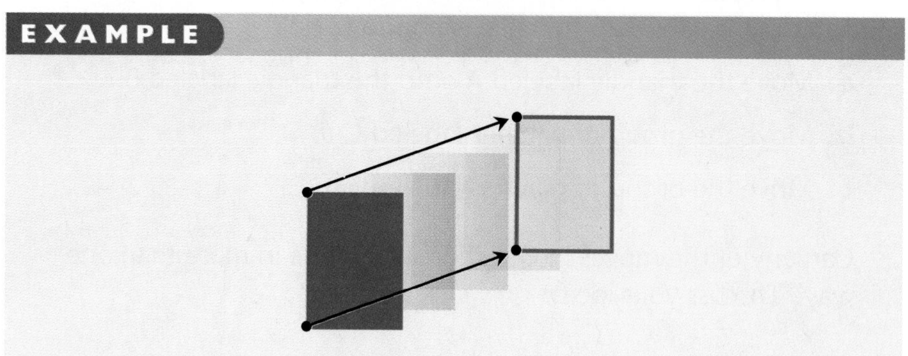

4 **a.** Place tracing paper over the Example above and trace the shaded rectangle. Slide your tracing along the arrows until it covers the unshaded rectangle.

b. Did you have to flip or turn the rectangle in part (a)?

c. What do the arrows tell you about the translation?

5 **Use Labsheet 4A.** Follow the directions on the labsheet and use your triangle to create a *Translation Patch.*

▶ **A rotation (turn) moves a figure by turning it either clockwise or counterclockwise around a fixed point.**

EXAMPLE

The **point of rotation** can be any fixed point outside, inside, or on the figure.

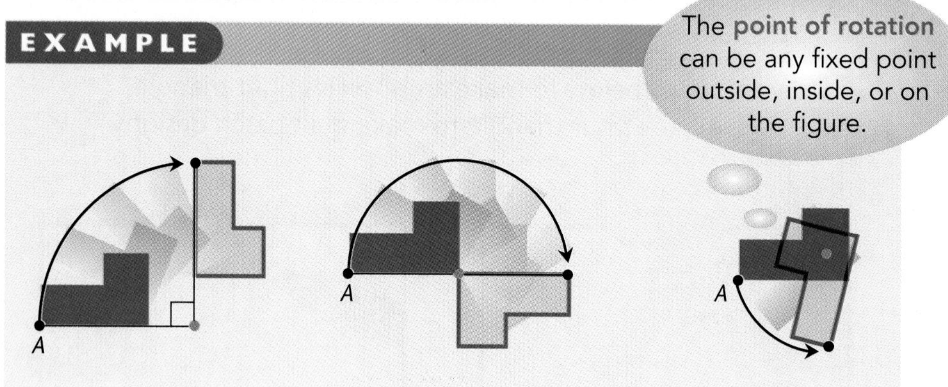

6 **a.** Place tracing paper over a rotation above. Trace the shaded figure. Put your pencil tip on the point of rotation. Rotate the tracing until it covers the unshaded figure, by moving point *A* along the arrow.

b. What does the arrow tell you about the rotation?

c. Could you get the same result by translating the figure?

7 **Use Labsheet 4A.** Follow the directions on the labsheet and use your triangle to create a *Rotation Patch.*

▶ **A reflection (flip) moves a figure by flipping it across a line.**

EXAMPLE

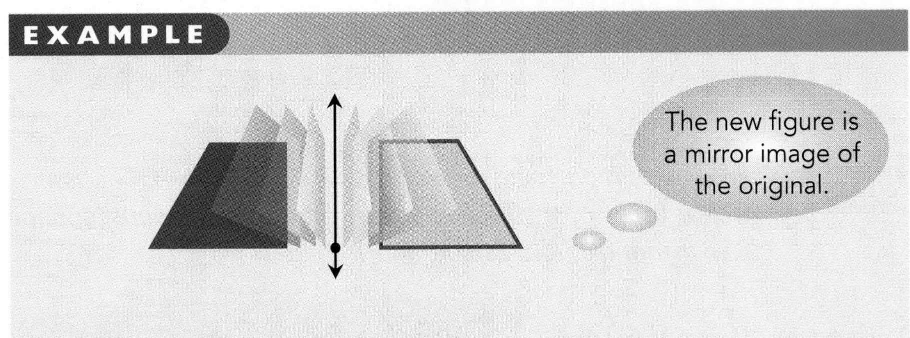

8 **a.** Place tracing paper over the shaded trapezoid in the Example. Trace the shaded figure, the line, and the point on the line. Flip your paper over so that the tracing covers the unshaded figure.

b. How did the line and the point on the line help you to flip the figure?

c. Could you get the same result by translating or rotating the trapezoid?

9 **Use Labsheet 4B.** Follow the directions on the labsheet and use your triangle to create a *Reflection Patch.*

▶ **A transformation is a change made to a figure or its position. Translations, rotations, and reflections are transformations that change the position of a figure but not its size or shape.**

10 **✓ CHECKPOINT** Name the transformation that will move each shaded trapezoid onto the unshaded trapezoid.

a.

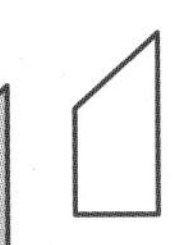

b.
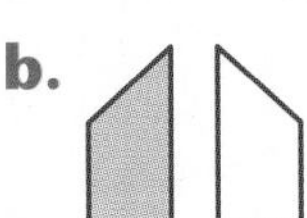

c.
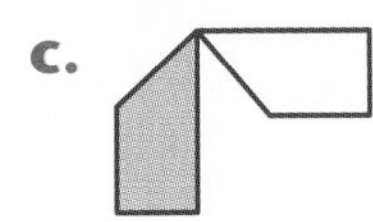

✓ QUESTION 10

...checks that you can recognize translations, rotations, and reflections.

11 **Use Labsheet 4B.** Follow the directions on the labsheet and use your triangle to *Create Your Own Patch.*

HOMEWORK EXERCISES ▶ **See Exs. 1–10 on pp. 128–129.**

GOAL

LEARN HOW TO...
- use transformations to make designs

AS YOU...
- create a zigzag quilt

Exploration 2

Transformations in QUILTING

SET UP *Work with a partner. You will need: • Labsheet 4C • scissors • clear tape • construction paper • drawing software (optional) • your triangle from Exploration 1*

▶ **This zigzag design is made entirely from isosceles right triangles, using two colors of material.**

You will make the section of the design outlined on the quilt.

12 Follow the steps below to make triangles for a zigzag quilt.

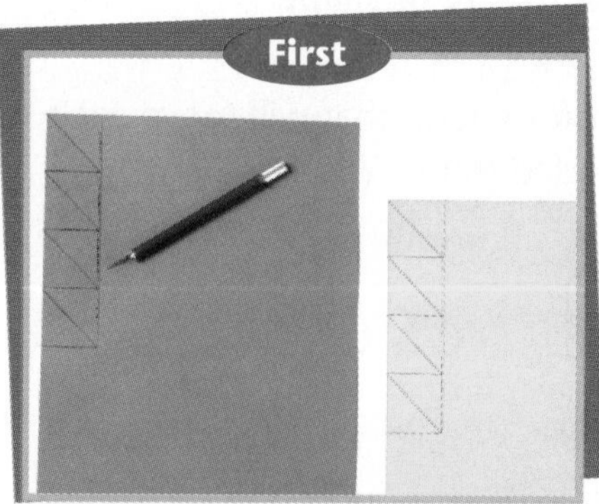

Choose one light and one dark color of construction paper. Use your triangle from Exploration 1 to trace 8 triangles of each color.

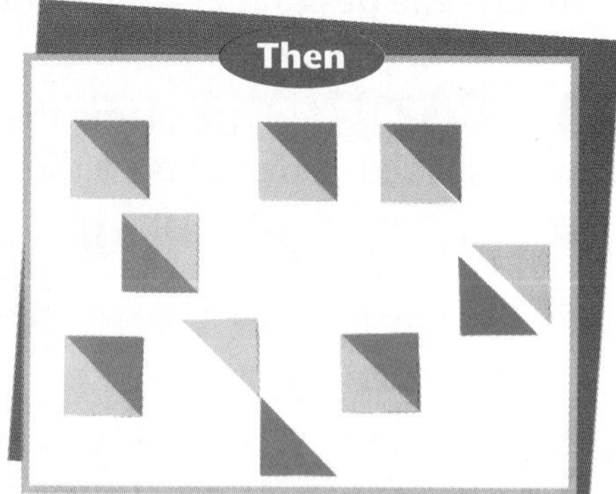

Cut out the triangles. Tape one triangle of each color together to make a square. Make 8 squares.

Use Labsheet 4C for Questions 13–17.

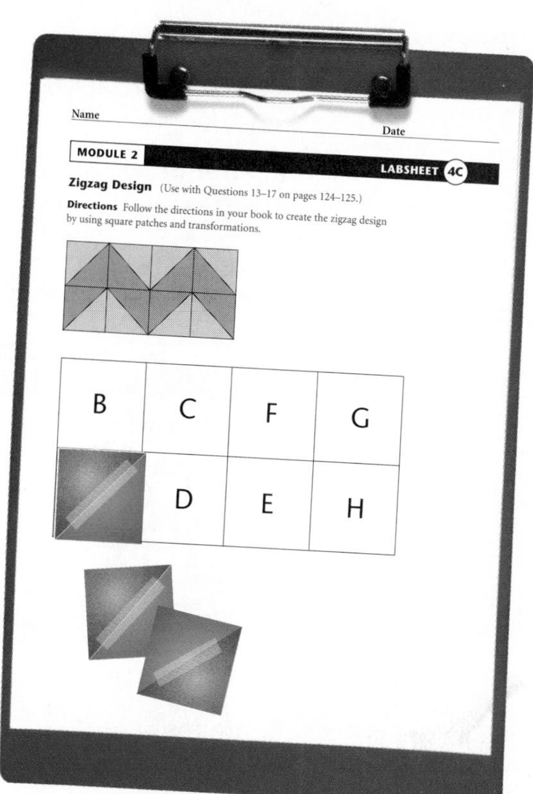

13 **a.** Place a square patch on the square labeled A on the *Zigzag Design*. Match the triangles and the light and dark colors. Tape the patch in place.

b. Place another patch on top of the patch taped over A, matching the triangles and colors. Use a transformation, or a series of transformations to move the top patch to square B so that it follows the zigzag pattern shown. Tape the patch in place.

c. Describe the transformation or transformations you used in part (b).

14 **Discussion** Compare answers for Question 13(c). Did everyone use the same transformations? If not, is one way better than another? Why?

15 ✔ **CHECKPOINT**

a. Place another patch on top of the patch taped over B on the *Zigzag Design*. Match the triangles and colors.

b. Find two different transformations that will move the top patch to C in just one move and continue the zigzag pattern. Tape the patch in place and describe the transformations.

✔ **QUESTION 15**

...checks that you can identify and describe transformations.

16 **a.** Place a patch on top of the patch taped over C.

b. Use a transformation, or a series of transformations to move the top patch to D so that it follows the zigzag pattern. Tape the patch in place. What transformation or series of transformations did you use?

17 **a.** Tape the four remaining patches together to make a separate copy of the large square formed by the patches on A, B, C, and D.

b. Place the copy over the large square so that the patterns match. Use a transformation to move the copy to cover squares E, F, G, and H, and continue the zigzag pattern. Describe the transformation you used.

HOMEWORK EXERCISES See Exs. 11–20 on pp. 129–130.

Using Computer Drawing Software

You can use computer drawing software to construct the quilt design. Your software may have the features shown below.

Step 1 Use the polygon tool to draw a triangle or other shapes.

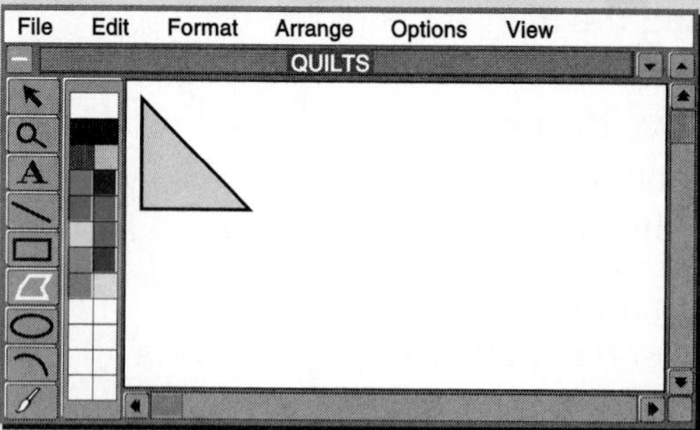

Step 2 Duplicate the shape you made. Experiment with your shapes by moving and filling them.

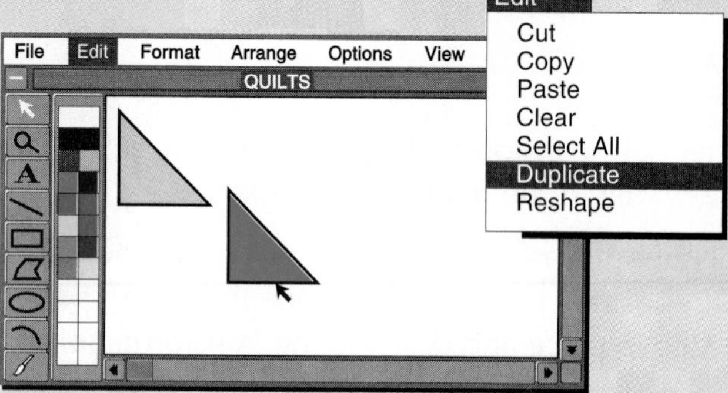

Step 3 You can rotate, flip, and move the shapes again to get what you want. Group them together so they can be copied and moved as one piece to make a quilt design.

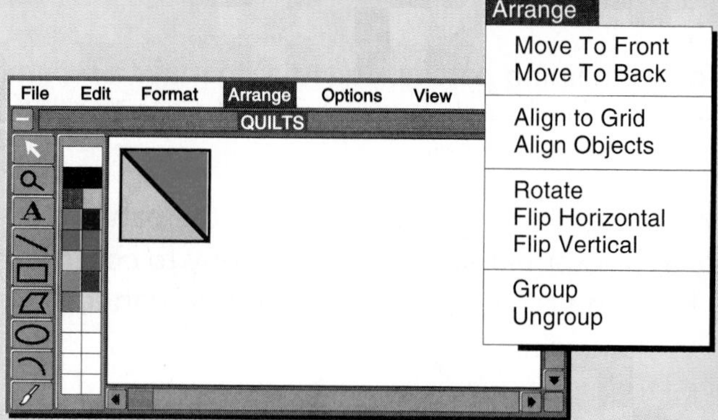

Section 4 Key Concepts

Transformations (pp. 122–123)

A transformation is a change made to a figure or its position. Translations, rotations, and reflections are transformations that change the position of a figure but not the size or the shape of the figure.

Examples

Translation (slide)

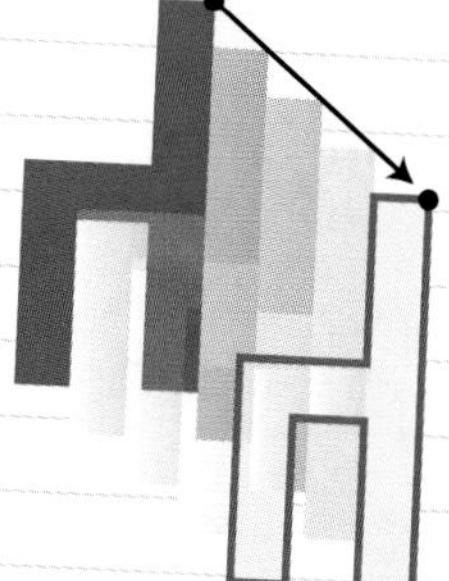

A translation moves every point the same distance in the same direction on a flat surface.

Rotation (turn)

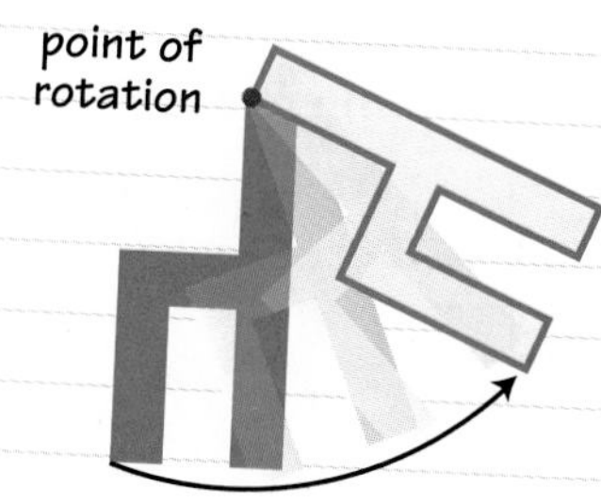

A rotation turns a figure around a fixed point.

Reflection (flip)

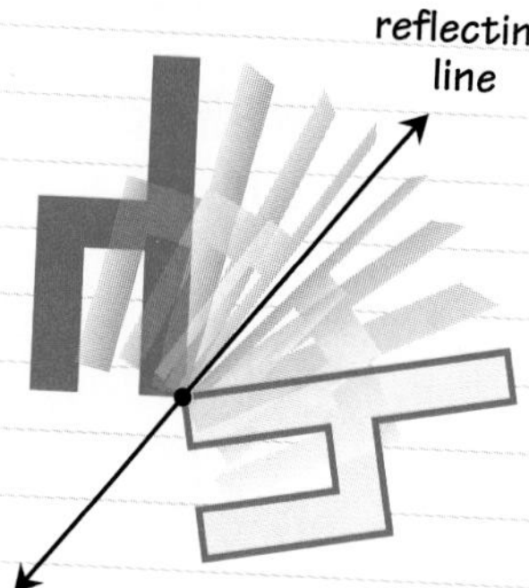

A reflection flips a figure across a line. The new figure is a mirror image of the original.

Key Terms

transformation

translation

rotation

reflection

Key Concepts Questions

18 Use transformations to describe how the figure on the screen changes from view to view.

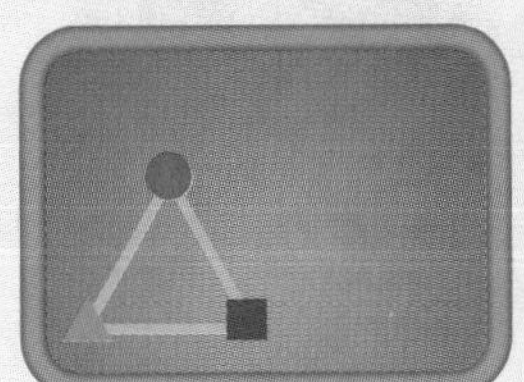
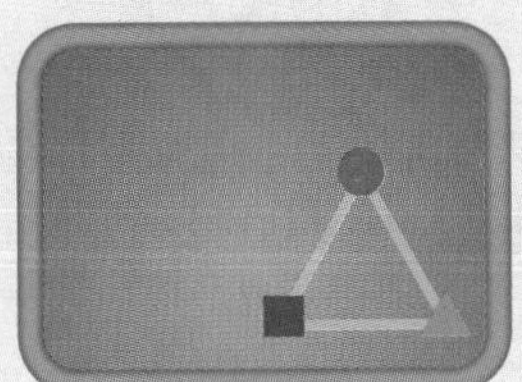
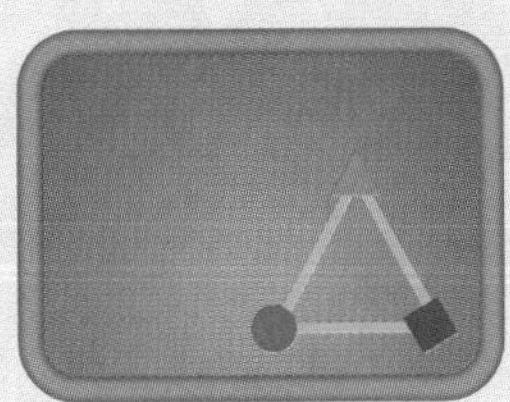

19 Make a simple drawing of an object. Now draw a translation, a rotation, and a reflection of the object. Label each drawing with the transformation you used.

Section 4

Practice & Application Exercises

YOU WILL NEED

For Exs. 11 and 19:
- Labsheet 4D

For Exs. 15 and 18:
- scissors
- glue
- decorative paper
- ruler
- drawing software (optional)

Name the transformation shown in each photo.

1. 

2. 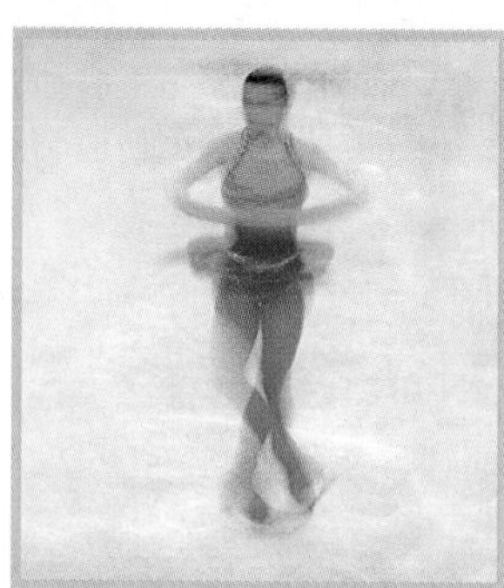

Name the transformation that will move each shaded figure onto the unshaded figure.

3. 

4. 

5. 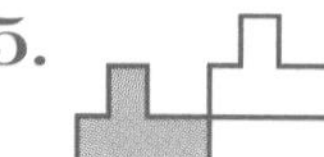

6.  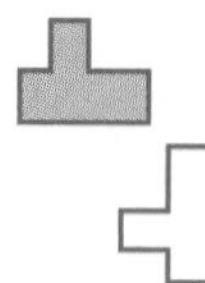

7.  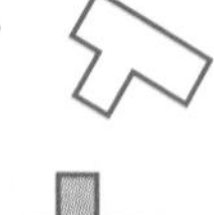

8.  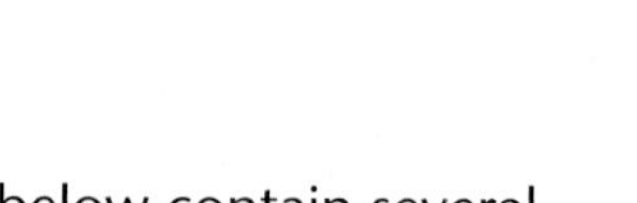

▲ Hex signs are painted on barns in Pennsylvania. Each color and shape used is said to have a different meaning.

9. **Arts** The Pennsylvania Dutch hex signs below contain several transformations. Dividing the signs into quarters makes it easier to see the transformations.

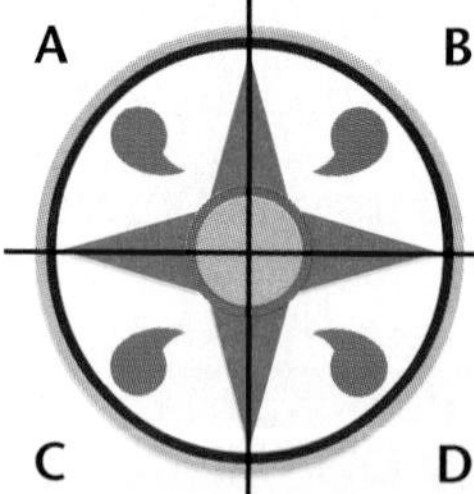

Sun, Star, and Rain Hex

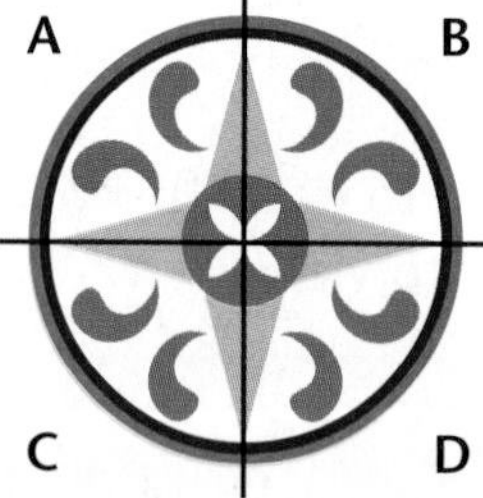

Double Rain Hex and Luck Symbol

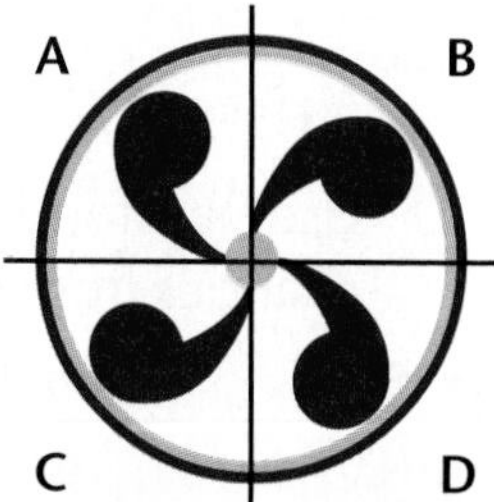

Hex Sign for Rain

a. For each hex sign, name the transformation needed to move quarter A to quarter B.

b. For one of the hex signs, you can move quarter A to quarter B in two ways. Name the hex sign and describe the two transformations.

10. Use transformations to describe how the position of the airplane changes from view to view.

11. **Use Labsheet 4D.** Follow the directions on the labsheet to sketch transformations on the *Grid for Transformations.*

Visual Thinking Sketch the next three terms in each sequence.

12. , , , , __?__, __?__, __?__, ...

13. , , , , __?__, __?__, __?__, ...

14. , , , , __?__, __?__, __?__, ...

15. a. **Create Your Own** Make design that is 40 cm by 40 cm using a combination of at least two transformations. Your original shape or shapes can be no larger than 10 cm by 10 cm. You may cut your shapes from construction paper, wrapping paper, or wallpaper; or you can use computer drawing software.

b. Describe the transformations used. Show a drawing of your original shape or shapes and any other diagrams that would help someone understand what you did.

In Exercises 16 and 17, A changes to B in the same way that C changes to what figure? Sketch each answer.

16. 17.

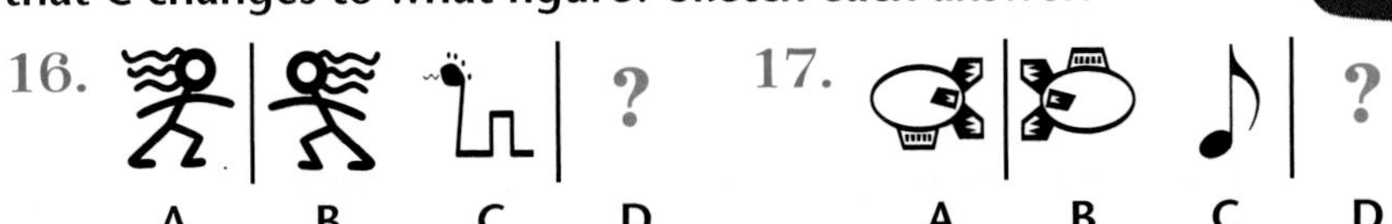

18. **Home Involvement** Many families have treasured quilts that represent their family history and heritage. You can create your own quilt square that displays something about your family's history.

a. To get ideas for your quilt square, discuss the following with your family:

- where your family originally came from
- people or places that have been important to your family
- objects or patterns that are associated with your family or culture

b. Make a sketch of a design for your square.

c. Create your quilt square. Use convenient materials such as colored paper, pieces of fabric, or white paper and fabric crayons.

d. Share your quilt square with your class. Explain how your design relates to your family's heritage.

19. **Challenge** Use the *Double Reflection Grid* on Labsheet 4D.

a. Follow the directions on the labsheet to draw two reflections of a trapezoid.

b. What single transformation has the same result as reflecting the trapezoid across line *AB* and then reflecting it across line *AC*?

RESEARCH

Exercise 20 checks that you can recognize translations, rotations, and reflections.

Reflecting on the Section

20. Look for examples of company or product logos that use translations, rotations, or reflections. Sketch or copy the designs and describe the transformations.

Logo of the Sarajevo Winter Olympics (1984)

Recycling Logo

Spiral Review

Write each fraction in lowest terms. **(Module 2, p. 114)**

21. $\frac{6}{18}$ 22. $\frac{24}{30}$ 23. $\frac{15}{25}$ 24. $\frac{9}{27}$

25. a. Use at least two of these shapes to make a sequence. **(Module 1, p. 8)**

b. Write a rule to describe your sequence. **(Module 1, p. 8)**

Compare each pair of whole numbers. Use <, >, or =. **(Toolbox, p. 590)**

26. 34 __?__ 43 27. 723 __?__ 689 28. 127 __?__ 1256

29. 658 __?__ 658 30. 3678 __?__ 985 31. 5924 __?__ 5687

Pop-Up Art

SET UP

You will need:
- *scissors*
- *ruler*
- *construction paper*

Translations Pop-up cards sometimes have pull tabs to slide, or translate, a picture.

 5 Follow the steps below to create a translation pop-up.

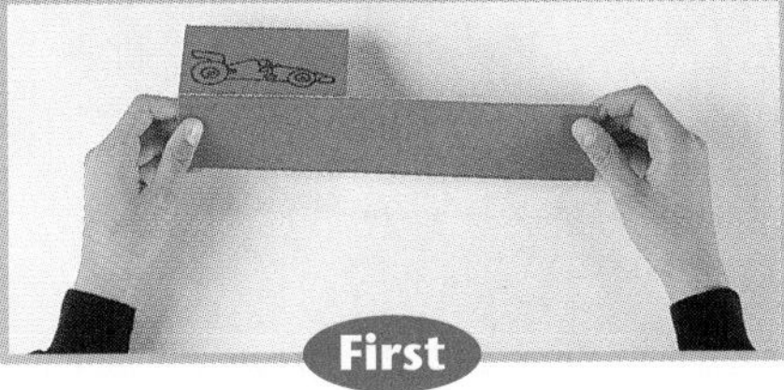

Cut and fold a piece of construction paper as shown. Draw a picture on the end of the pull tab above the fold.

Cut two slits on another piece of paper. Make sure the slits do not touch. Insert your picture and pull tab.

6 Pull the tab of your pop-up to translate your picture. About how far does your picture slide?

Section 4 Extra Skill Practice

Name the transformation or transformations that will move each shaded figure onto the unshaded figure.

1.

2.

3.

4.

5. 

6. 

7. 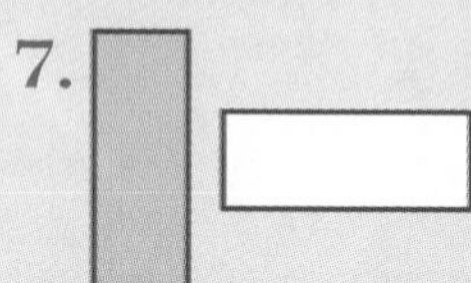

8. 

9. 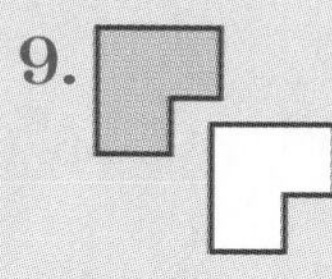

Match each situation with the transformation that best describes it. Choices may be used more than once.

A. rotation
B. reflection
C. translation

10. Opening a sliding glass door.

11. Closing a bureau drawer.

12. Flipping a page in a book.

13. Turning the minute hand of a clock to adjust the time.

Standardized Testing ▶ Open-ended

Which farmer really "rotates" the crops? Describe how the other farmers "transform" their fields.

A

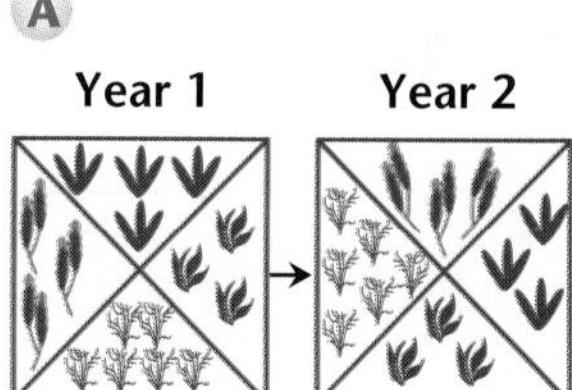

B

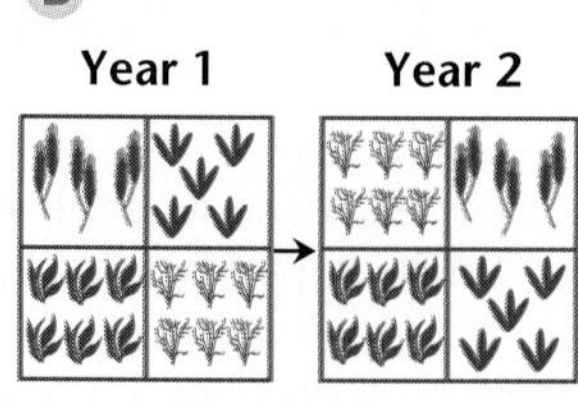

C

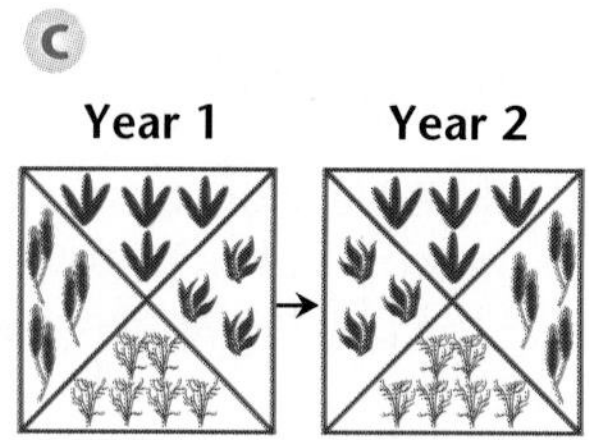

Section 5 Understanding Decimals

In This Section

Exploration 1
- Decimal Place Value

Exploration 2
- Comparing Decimals

Quite a Collection

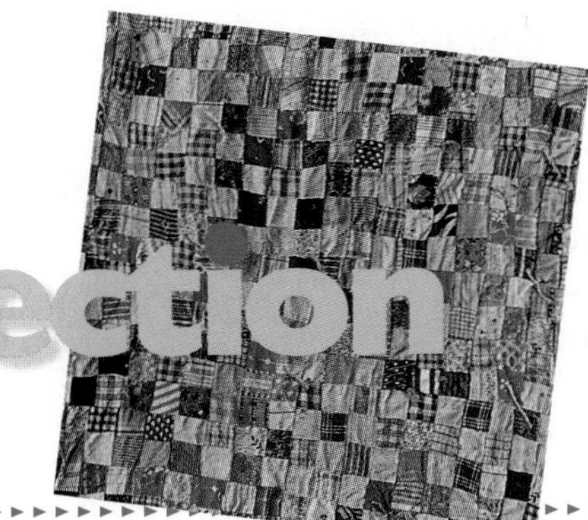

Setting the Stage

Set Up *Work in a group. You will need:* • *base-ten blocks* • *1 die*

Postage Stamp Quilts are made from small squares of material. Much skill is needed to sew together the tiny bits of material into strips and to join the strips together to form a quilt block. These quilts were popular during the Depression in the 1930s.

In the following game, base-ten blocks model the process of collecting scraps to make part of a Postage Stamp Quilt.

1 Follow the steps at the right to play the *Postage Stamp Quilt* game.

Game Rules Players alternate turns. On each turn follow the steps below. The first person with two quilt blocks is the winner.

First	Next	Then
Roll a die. Take the number of squares shown on the die.	Trade in squares for a strip whenever possible.	Trade in strips for a quilt block whenever possible.

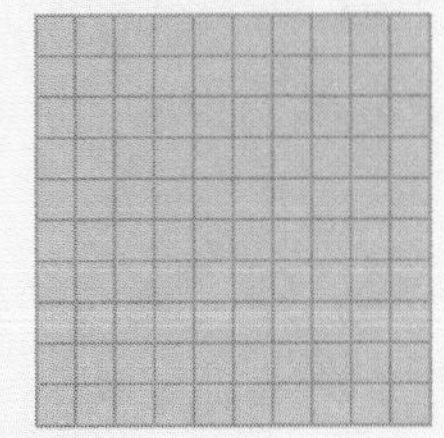

Think About It

2 One square is what fraction of a strip? One strip is what fraction of a quilt block? One square is what fraction of a quilt block?

3 **a.** How many small squares would make $\frac{17}{100}$ of a quilt block?

b. After making as many strips as possible, how many full strips would you have? How many squares would be left?

4 How can you represent each fraction of a quilt block using the least number of squares, strips, and quilt blocks?

a. $\frac{3}{10}$ **b.** $\frac{28}{100}$ **c.** $\frac{1}{2}$ **d.** $\frac{299}{100}$

GOAL

LEARN HOW TO...
- read and write decimals

AS YOU...
- discover patterns using base-ten blocks

KEY TERMS
- decimal system
- place value

Exploration 1

Decimal Place Value

SET UP *You will need:* • *Labsheets 5A and 5B* • *base-ten blocks*

▶ **The parts of the quilt block used in the game were based on ones, tens, and hundreds. This makes the 10 × 10 block, the strips, and the squares good models for the decimal system.**

5 Copy the place-value chart and fill in the **place values** to the left of the decimal point.

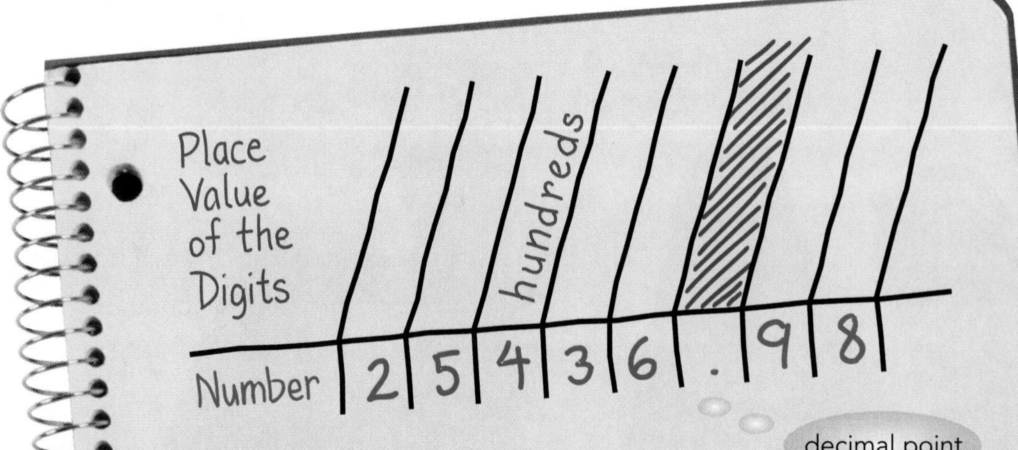

6 Use your place-value chart for 25,436.98.

a. Start in the ones place. Each time you move left one place, the place value is multiplied by what number?

b. Now start in the ten-thousands place. Each time you move right one place, the place value is __?__ by __?__.

7 **Try This as a Class** The pattern you found in Question 6 continues to the right of the decimal point. Think of the quilt block as one whole or 1.

a. To find the place value of the digit to the right of the ones place imagine dividing the quilt block by 10. Which base-ten block models this place value? This block is what fraction of the quilt block?

b. Which base-ten block would you use to model the place value of the next digit to the right? This block is what fraction of the quilt block?

8 Fill in the place values of the 9 and the 8 in your chart. What would be the place value of a digit to the right of the 8?

▶ **Place values to the right of the decimal point can be written using words, fractions, or decimals. Knowing the different forms for one tenth and one hundredth can help you write numbers in all three ways.**

Words	Fractions	Decimals	Models
one tenth	$\frac{1}{10}$	0.1	strip
one hundredth	$\frac{1}{100}$	0.01	square

The quilt block models one whole.

9 **Use Labsheet 5A.** Use the *Missing Values Table* on the labsheet.

a. Fill in the missing words, fractions, or decimals for the values of the 9 and the 8 in 25,436.98.

b. Why do you think there is a 0 between the decimal point and the 8 in the decimal form for eight hundredths?

10 **Use Labsheet 5A.** Follow the directions on the labsheet to shade the *Quilt Block*.

✓ QUESTION 11

...checks that you can write a number using words, a fraction, or a decimal.

11 **✓ CHECKPOINT** **Use Labsheet 5B.** Use the *Words to Fractions to Decimals Table.*

a. Use as few base-ten blocks as possible to represent each number. Then complete the missing information.

b. The word *and* was used in the word names of two of the numbers in the table. Why? What does it stand for?

HOMEWORK EXERCISES ▶ **See Exs. 1–18 on p. 139.**

GOAL

LEARN HOW TO...
- compare and order decimals

AS YOU...
- work with Postage Stamp Quilts and base-ten blocks

KEY TERM
- equivalent decimals

Exploration 2

Comparing Decimals

SET UP *You will need:* • *base-ten blocks* • *graph paper* • *colored pencils or markers*

The quilt block designs below have different parts **blue**.

0.6 blue

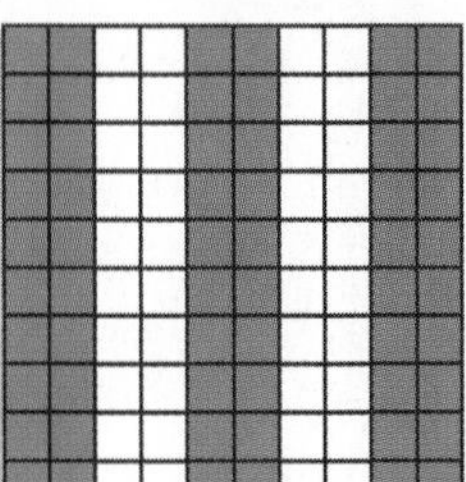

0.36 blue

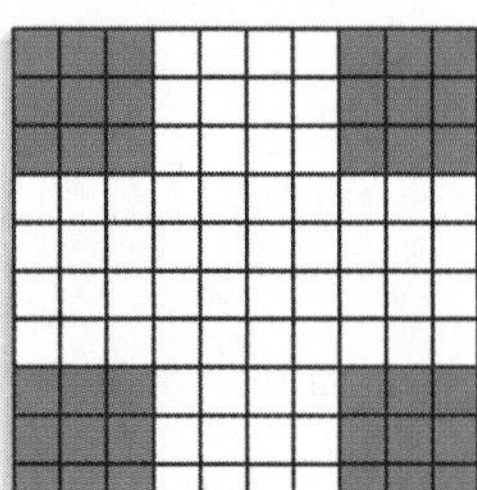

12 Which quilt block appears to have more blue?

▶ **You can also use decimals to make a comparison.**

13 **a.** Which is greater, 0.6 or 0.36? How do you know?

b. Show how you could use base-ten blocks to determine which is greater, 1.12 or 1.21.

14 **Try This as a Class** Quilt blocks could also be made using thousandth pieces, but that would take a lot of patience.

a. How many thousandths would it take to make a hundredth?

b. Discuss how, without using base-ten blocks, you can determine which decimal is greater, 1.068 or 1.07.

▲ George Yarrall made this Postage Stamp Quilt using 66,153 pieces and ten colors. It is believed that he started quilting to keep his hands flexible for his job as a jewelry engraver.

▶ **Equivalent Decimals** **You have compared decimals that represent different amounts. If two decimals represent the same amount, they are equivalent.**

15 **a.** Write the decimal for each picture below.

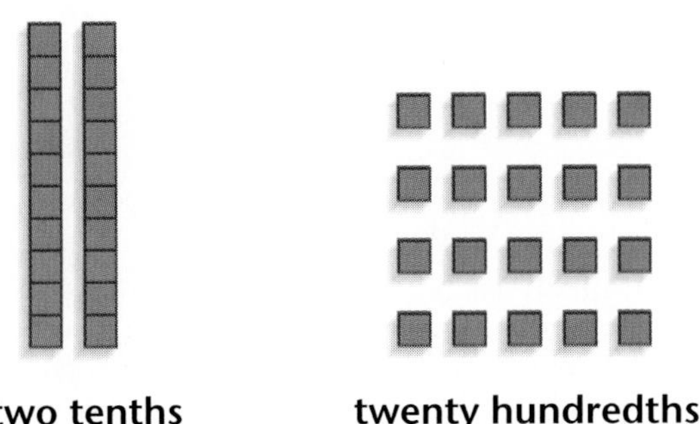

b. Are the decimals in part (a) equivalent? Explain.

c. Use the pictures in part (a) to explain why 0.2 > 0.19.

16 ✓ **CHECKPOINT** Compare each pair of decimals. Use <, >, or =.

a. 0.4 __?__ 0.39 **b.** 0.31 __?__ 1.2

c. 4.06 __?__ 4.0600 **d.** 1.061 __?__ 1.008

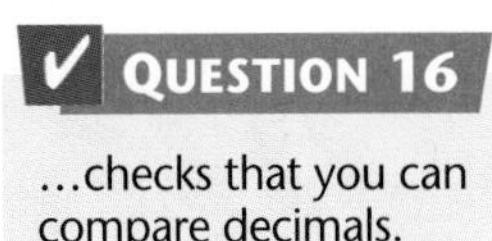

✓ **QUESTION 16**

...checks that you can compare decimals.

17 **Create Your Own** Use graph paper to design a Postage Stamp Quilt block that uses the following color combinations. Order the decimals from least to greatest.

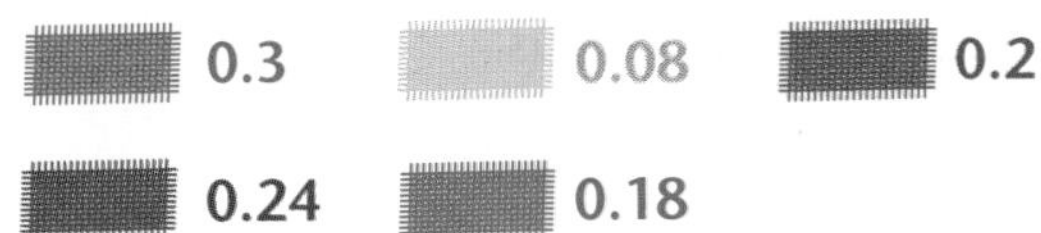

HOMEWORK EXERCISES ▶ See Exs. 19–29 on pp. 139–140.

Section 5 Key Concepts

Key Terms

decimal system

place value

equivalent decimals

Decimal System (pp. 134–137)

The decimal system is based on tens.

As you move **left** one place, the place value is **multiplied** by 10.

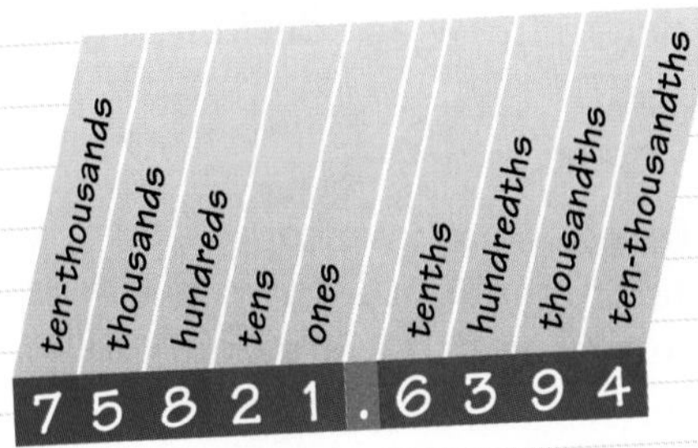

As you move **right** one place, the place value is **divided** by 10.

A number can be written in different ways.

Example

Words	Fraction	Decimal
Five and three thousandths	$5\frac{3}{1000}$	5.003

Comparing Decimals (pp. 136–137)

Decimals that represent the same amount are equivalent.

Example $0.3 > 0.27$ since $0.30 > 0.27$

0.3 and 0.30 are equivalent.

Key Concepts Questions

18 Write each number as a fraction and as a decimal.

a. forty-five and thirty-one hundredths

b. six hundred and ten thousandths

c. seven thousand two and three tenths

19 Why are there two zeros in the decimal 5.003?

20 Explain why $0.13 < 0.5$ even though $13 > 5$.

Section 5 Practice & Application Exercises

Science **It takes the planet Saturn 29.458 years to revolve around the sun. In the number 29.458, give the place value of each digit.**

1. 2
2. 9
3. 4
4. 5
5. 8

Write each decimal in words and as a fraction or mixed number.

6. 0.62
7. 8.3
8. 345.04
9. 1.002

Write each number as a decimal.

10. $\frac{29}{100}$
11. $\frac{3}{100}$
12. six and seven tenths
13. $\frac{205}{10,000}$
14. ninety-nine and nine thousandths

15.  represents one whole. Which coin represents one tenth? one hundredth?

16. Using only pennies, dimes, and one-dollar bills, how can you represent four and sixteen hundredths?

17. How can you use United States money to show that $0.40 = 0.4$?

18. **Challenge** You have used the quilt block to model one whole. Now think of a quilt made of 10 blocks as one whole. What fraction would one quilt block represent? one strip? one square?

Arts **Many cultures make designs by piecing together sections of fabric. These cloths from Ghana were made by sewing together long, narrow strips.**

19. In the photo at the bottom right, what part of the entire cloth does each strip represent?

20. If each strip in the cloth at the top right is used to model one tenth, write the decimal that represents the entire cloth.

1 strip

The fabrics on this page are examples of Men's Weave Ashante cloth from Ghana.

Suppose Postage Stamp Quilts are designed with the following color combinations. For each pattern, order the decimals from least to greatest.

21. 0.3 0.03 0.51 0.16

22. 0.24 0.4 0.08 0.28

23. 0.717 0.17 0.105 0.008

Compare each pair of decimals. Use <, >, or =.

24. 16.12 __?__ 16.125

25. 98.099 __?__ 98.901

26. 2.65 __?__ 2.650

27. 11 __?__ 10.989

28. Calculator Yvette's calculator is broken. Only these keys work: 0 1 + . .
How can Yvette get 27.063 to appear on the screen?

Journal

Exercise 29 checks that you understand decimal place value.

Reflecting on the Section

Write your response to Exercise 29 in your journal.

29. Suppose you are teaching a younger student about decimals and place value. Explain how you can tell which is greater, 0.6 or 0.58.

Spiral Review

Tell whether the shaded figure is a *reflection*, a *rotation* or a *translation* of the unshaded figure. (Module 2, p. 127)

30. 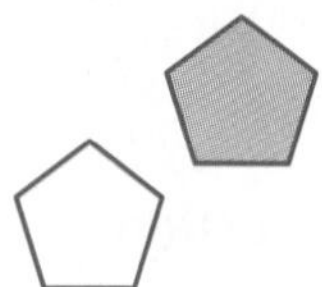

31. 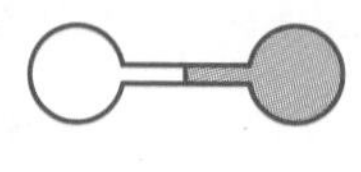

32. 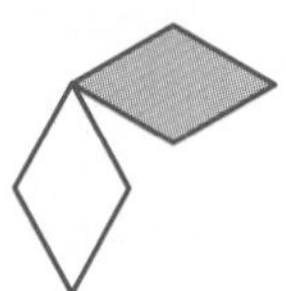

Estimate each sum or difference. (Module 1, p. 50)

33. $13.67 + 5.89

34. $158.23 − 34.67

35. $7.39 + 1.87

Explain how you could use mental math to find each sum. (Toolbox, p. 593 and Module 1, p. 46)

36. $21.41 + 6.29

37. $1.66 7.07 + 2.33

38. $11.50 + 3.75

Section 5

Extra Skill Practice

Write the value of each underlined digit.

1. $0.00\underline{5}$
2. $356\underline{4}.22$
3. $90.\underline{2}86$
4. $116.9\underline{8}$
5. $1\underline{2}.35$
6. $0.0\underline{1}8$
7. $159.\underline{5}34$
8. $5.102\underline{6}$

Write each number as a decimal and as a fraction or a mixed number.

9. two tenths
10. five-hundred thousandths
11. three hundred fifty-six and forty hundredths
12. four thousand and six tenths
13. one and twenty-five hundredths

Write each decimal in words.

14. 4.2
15. 0.026
16. 531.08
17. 10.205
18. 3.25
19. 1.004
20. 0.01
21. 11.100

Compare each pair of decimals. Use <, >, or =.

22. 6.13 __?__ 6.125
23. 75.001 __?__ 75.0009
24. 3.60 __?__ 3.600
25. 1.999 __?__ 1.9009
26. 0.520 __?__ 0.52
27. 73.04 __?__ 73.401

Order each list of numbers from least to greatest.

28. 6, 6.04, 6.008, 66.002
29. 123.1, 124, 12.3, 1.233, 0.123
30. 1.9, 1.99, 1.099, 1.909
31. 75.24, 7.0652, 7.526, 75.024

Standardized Testing ▸ Multiple Choice

Choose the decimal that represents each number.

1. Three thousand fifty-nine and one tenth

   A 0.10359 B 359.1 C 3000.69 D 3059.1

2. Four hundred and three thousandths.

   A 0.4003 B 400.003 C 0.403 D 403,000

Decimal Addition and Subtraction

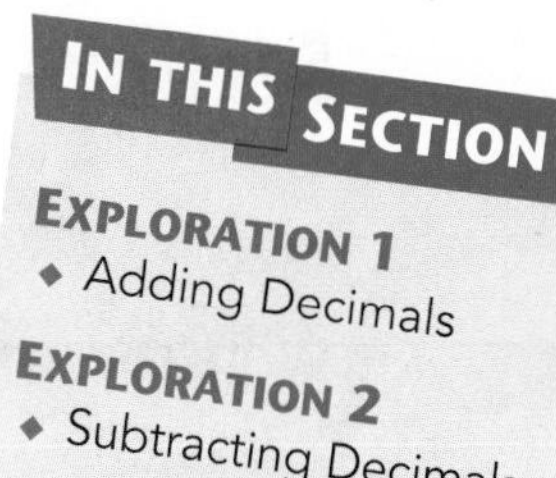

Designing Sports Cars

Setting the Stage

When engineers design cars, they consider such things as strength, speed, style, and safety. The pictures below show how the design of the Corvette, a popular American sports car, changed from 1956 to 1997.

1956

51 in.

168 in.

102 in.

1978

48 in.

44.8 in. 98 in. 42.4 in.

1997

47.7 in.

35.7 in. 104.5 in. 38.8 in.

Think About It

1 *Wheel base* refers to the distance between the center of the front wheel and the center of the rear wheel.

a. What is the wheel base of the 1956 model?

b. Which model has the shortest wheel base?

c. How has the wheel base of the Corvette changed over time?

2 What design features of a car do you think are related to safety? to speed? to style?

3 Estimate the total length of the 1978 model.

Exploration 1

Adding DECIMALS

GOAL

LEARN HOW TO...
- add decimals

AS YOU...
- model with base-ten blocks

SET UP *You will need base-ten blocks.*

▶ **To find the actual length of the 1978 model, you need to add decimals. You can use base-ten blocks to look at a simpler problem first.**

4 The base-ten blocks below represent the sum 1 + 0.1 + 0.01. Write this sum as a decimal.

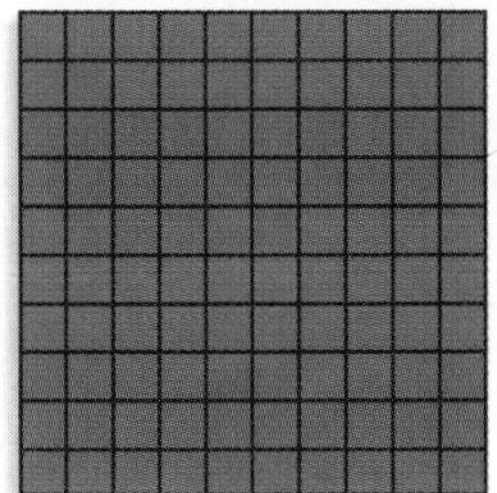

Flat		Rod		Small Cube		
1	+	0.1	+	0.01	=	?

EXAMPLE

Find the sum 1.64 + 0.49 using base-ten blocks.

1. Represent each decimal using base-ten blocks. **1.64** **0.49**

2. Add the small cubes together. Then trade for a rod, if possible.

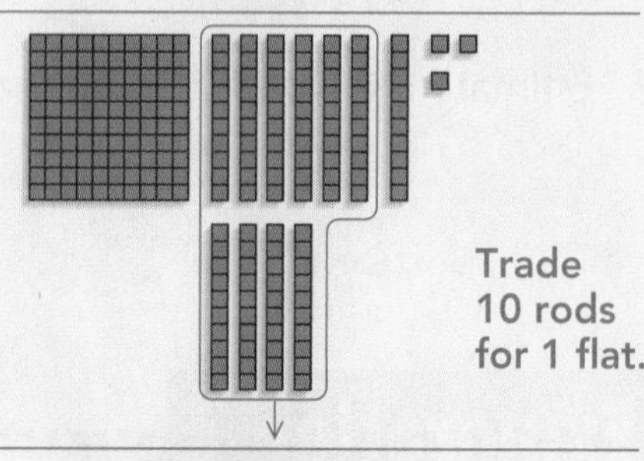

3. Next add the rods together. Then trade for a flat, if possible.

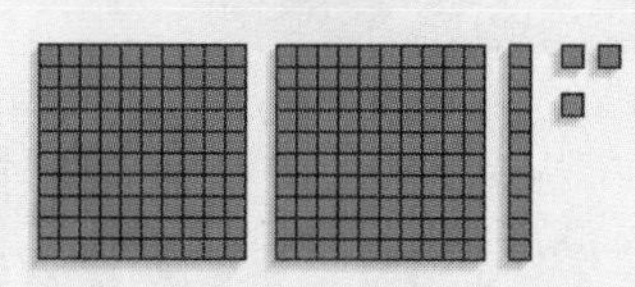

4. Since no more trading is possible, 2 flats, 1 rod, and 3 small cubes represent the sum **2.13**.

5 Use base-ten blocks to find each sum.

a. 3.14 + 1.75 **b.** 0.67 + 1.9 **c.** 1.65 + 0.06 + 0.3

6 **Discussion** How can you add decimals without using base-ten blocks? Record a method.

7 Leigha wrote the number sentence: 1.5 + 0.11 = 2.6

a. How can you use estimation to determine that Leigha's answer must be wrong?

b. What mistake do you think Leigha made?

✓ QUESTION 8

...checks that you can add decimals.

8 **✓ CHECKPOINT** Find each sum.

a. $\begin{array}{r} 0.25 \\ +\,1.79 \\ \hline \end{array}$ **b.** $\begin{array}{r} 52.03 \\ +\;\,0.785 \\ \hline \end{array}$ **c.** 0.009 + 0.999

d. 1.26 + 0.032 **e.** 3.706 + 0.954 **f.** 10.006 + 11.2 + 0.07

HOMEWORK EXERCISES ▶ See Exs. 1–17 on pp. 147–148.

Exploration 2

Subtracting DECIMALS

GOAL

LEARN HOW TO...
- subtract decimals

AS YOU...
- compare car designs

SET UP *You will need base-ten blocks.*

9 What would you have to do to find the difference between the Corvette's 1997 and 1978 heights?

EXAMPLE

Find the difference 1.43 – 0.58 using base-ten blocks.

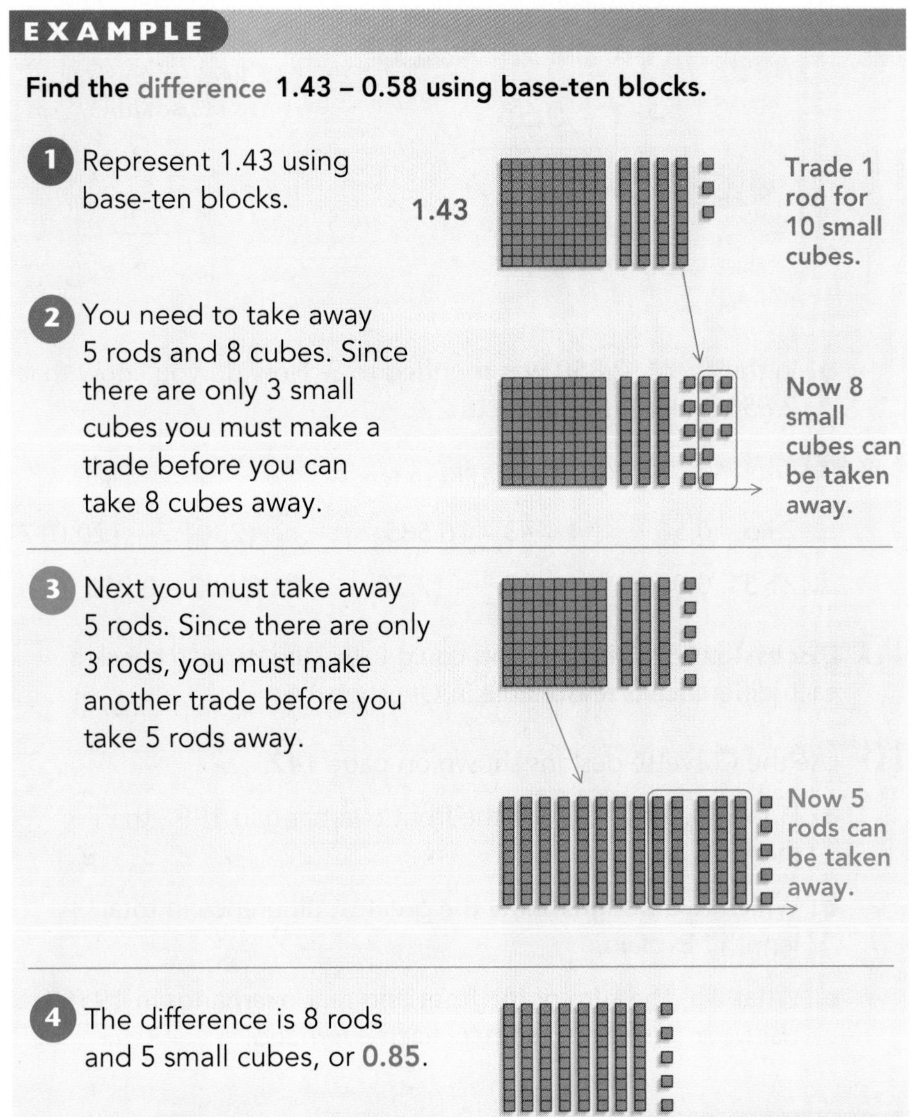

FOR ▶ HELP with *whole number subtraction*, see **TOOLBOX, p. 594**

10 Use base-ten blocks to find each difference.

a. 1.62 – 0.8 **b.** 1.62 – 0.80 **c.** 1.62 – 0.08

11 In Question 10, is subtracting 0.8 the same as subtracting 0.80 or 0.08?

12 **Discussion** How is subtraction of decimals like subtraction of whole numbers?

13 **Try This as a Class** The subtraction 2.85 – 1.063 is shown below.

a. Explain what is being done in each step.

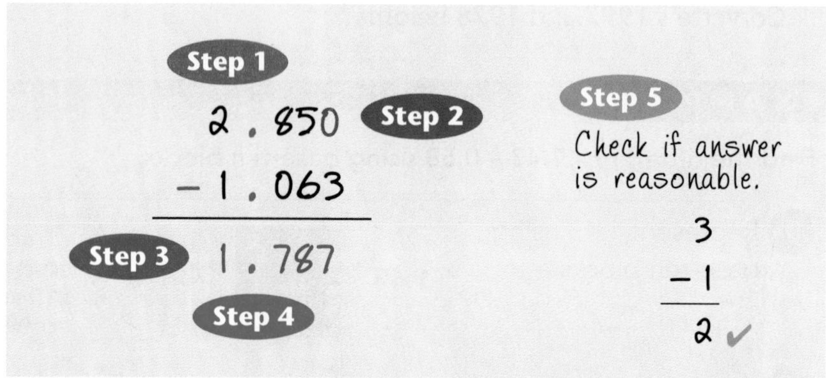

b. In the check, 2.850 was rounded to 3. How do you know that 2.850 is closer to 3 than to 2?

✓ QUESTION 14 ...checks that you can subtract decimals.

14 **✓ CHECKPOINT** Find each difference.

a. 2.45 – 0.56 **b.** 43 – 16.535 **c.** 12001.7 – 120.017

d. 21.5 – 0.009 **e.** 17.3 – 17.30 **f.** 0.082 – 0.015

15 **Discussion** Explain how you could use estimation to check if each difference is reasonable in Question 14.

16 Use the Corvette designs shown on page 142.

a. How much shorter was the front overhang in 1997 than in 1978?

b. Which two designs show the greatest difference in total length? Explain.

c. What was the sum of the front and rear overhangs in 1956? Use your answer to estimate each overhang.

HOMEWORK EXERCISES ▶ See Exs. 18–38 on pp. 149–150.

Section 6

Key Concepts

Adding and Subtracting Decimals (pp. 143–146)

To find the sum or difference of two decimal numbers:

Example

Step	Addition	Subtraction
1 Line up the decimals.	4.57 + 3.9	4.57 − 3.9
2 Write zeros so that both numbers have the same number of decimal places.	4.57 + 3.90	4.57 − 3.90
3 Add or subtract as with whole numbers.	4.57 + 3.90 8 47	4.57 − 3.90 67
4 Place the decimal point in the final answer. Place a zero in the ones place when there are no ones.	4.57 + 3.90 8.47	4.57 − 3.90 0.67

17 **Key Concepts Question** Explain how you can use estimation to check that the sum and the difference above are reasonable.

Section 6

Practice & Application Exercises

YOU WILL NEED

For Ex. 17:
- calculator

Find each sum without using a calculator.

1. 3.241 + 10.6

2. 14.606 + 8.217 + 0.888

3. 6.32 + 72.59

4. 4.76 + 20.005

5. 4.102 + 5.6 + 10.99

Lucita pays for a 49¢ item with a ten-dollar bill. After the numbers are entered, 0.51 shows up on the cash register display. The cashier hands Lucita 51¢ in change.

6. Explain the cashier's mistake.

7. What is Lucita's correct change?

8. **Estimation** Suppose you have exactly $20. Without finding the exact sum, decide whether you have enough money to buy the three items with the prices shown. (There is no tax on these items.) Explain how you know.

Find the next three terms in each sequence.

9. 0.3, 0.41, 0.52, 0.63,...

10. 6.3, 6.4, 6.6, 6.9, 7.3,...

FOR ▶ HELP with *mental addition*, see **TOOLBOX, p. 593**

Mental Math Explain how to use mental math to find each sum. It may help to think about money.

11. 2.75 + 3.25

12. 6.7 + 13.3

13. 5.35 + 2.8 + 1.65

14. 21.6 + 3.8

15. 0.045 + 0.036

16. 77.3 + 9.9

17. Calculator Use your calculator to find the sum 4.562 + 3.138.

a. What sum does the calculator display?

b. How many decimal places are there in the calculator display? Why does this happen?

Find each difference without using a calculator.

18. 10 – 4.5 19. 124.4 – 95.13 20. 0.567 – 0.49

21. 3.1 – 0.9 22. 76 – 54.87 23. 0.008 – 0.0034

Follow the order of operations to evaluate each expression.

24. 4.07 + 2 • 5 25. 26 ÷ (2.13 + 10.87)

Each answer is wrong. Find and explain each error and give the correct answer.

26. 4.6 + 0.42 = 0.88 27. 10.3 – 6.041 = 4.341

28. 12.30 – 0.03 = 12 29. 116.89 – 0.689 = 11.00

30. James had $126.59 in his bank account. Then he withdrew $27.50 and deposited $48.65. What is his new balance?

31. The subtraction 15 – 8 = 7 can be checked by making sure that 8 + 7 = 15. Find 16.29 – 2.85. Explain how you could use addition to check your answer.

Machine Parts **Machine parts are made with careful measurements. However, the actual size of a part is allowed to be a certain amount smaller or bigger than the size wanted. This allowed difference is called the *tolerance.* Explain whether or not each part can be used.**

4.5 – 4.38 = 0.12
0.12 in. is greater than the tolerance of **0.05** in., so the part is rejected.

	Part	Size wanted	Actual size	Tolerance
	Part example	4.5 in.	4.38 in.	0.05 in.
32.	Part 1	1.355 in.	1.372 in.	0.005 in.
33.	Part 2	1.280 in.	1.099 in.	0.025 in.
34.	Part 3	4.45 in.	4.671 in.	0.205 in.
35.	Part 4	2.010 in.	2.008 in.	0.010 in.

Challenge **Find the next three terms in each sequence.**

36. 7.1, 6.9, 7.2, 7.0, 7.3,... 37. 74, 75.1, 77.3, 80.6, 85,...

Oral Report

Exercise 38 checks that you understand decimal addition and subtraction.

Reflecting on the Section

Be prepared to report on the following topic in class.

38. Prepare a report that explains how the design of the Corvette has changed from 1956 to 1997. Use decimal addition and subtraction in your discussion.

Spiral Review

Write each number in words. (Module 2, p. 138)

39. 1.12 40. 0.803 41. 3.4 42. 50.28

43. Find the numbers that fit all three clues. (Module 1, p. 69)

Clue 1	Clue 2	Clue 3
The number is odd.	The sum of its digits is 15.	The number is less than 100.

Mental Math **Use mental math to evaluate.** (Toolbox, p. 598)

44. 28 • 100 45. 149 • 10 46. 386 • 1000

47. 2800 ÷ 100 48. 7290 ÷ 10 49. 72,000 ÷ 100

Extension 

Extending Decimal Place Value

Use the following list of decimals to answer Exercises 50–53.
0.00009, 0.0008, 1.00002, 0.00001, 0.00015

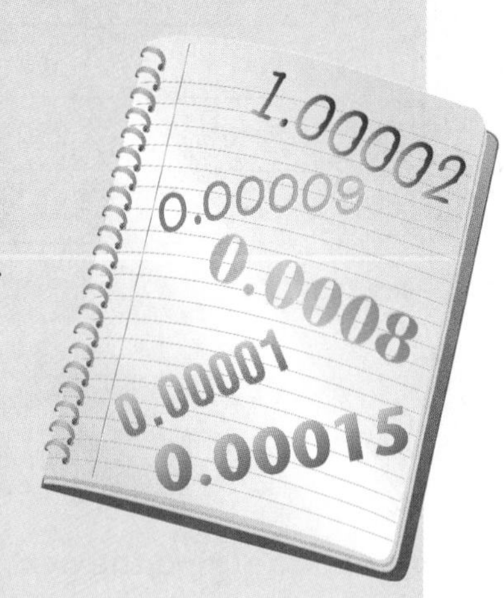

50. Write each decimal using words. (You may want to first extend your place-value table and fill in the missing place-value names. Then write the decimal in the table.)

51. Write the decimals in order from least to greatest.

52. Find the difference between 1.00002 and 0.00009.

53. Which two decimals have a sum of one ten-thousandth?

Find each sum.

1. $\begin{array}{r} 12.06 \\ +\ 9.4 \\ \hline \end{array}$

2. $\begin{array}{r} 1.599 \\ +\ 70.6 \\ \hline \end{array}$

3. $\begin{array}{r} 41.75 \\ +\ 9.673 \\ \hline \end{array}$

4. $\begin{array}{r} 6.61 \\ 21.85 \\ +\ 4.3 \\ \hline \end{array}$

5. 14.9 + 231.07
6. 16.08 + 0.37 + 5.9
7. 27 + 4.6 + 0.017
8. 1.25 + 12.75
9. 0.049 + 0.026
10. 98.2 + 4.7
11. 21.209 + 15.098
12. 33.55 + 0.55
13. 0.007 + 0.763

Find each difference.

14. $\begin{array}{r} 4.5 \\ -\ 1.7 \\ \hline \end{array}$

15. $\begin{array}{r} 70.42 \\ -\ 35.7 \\ \hline \end{array}$

16. $\begin{array}{r} 28.4 \\ -\ 5.162 \\ \hline \end{array}$

17. $\begin{array}{r} 86.005 \\ -\ 14.32 \\ \hline \end{array}$

18. 6.4 – 2.367
19. 147.61 – 5.724
20. 349 – 51.06
21. 12 – 3.5
22. 0.09 – 0.045
23. 132.42 – 61.34
24. 1.089 – 0.6
25. 34.2 – 0.004
26. 13 – 6.347

27. Jana had $20.50. She earns $6.75 baby-sitting one morning, but then spends $4.15 on lunch. Now how much money does Jana have?

Find the next three terms in each sequence.

28. 0.4, 0.54, 0.68, 0.82,...
29. 5.4, 5.5, 5.7, 6.0,...
30. 2.5, 2.7, 3.1, 3.7,...
31. 1.02, 1.12, 1.22, 1.32,...

Standardized Testing ▶ Performance Task

Jim receives $.10 from his father for mowing the lawn. His father promises that next time Jim mows he will get $.20, then $.40 for the third time, and so on.

Jim races to his calculator, does a few calculations, and exclaims, "The tenth time I mow I'll get $51.20!" "No, Jim," says Jim's dad, who takes the calculator and does his own calculations, "the tenth time you mow you'll get $4.60. You are $46.60 too high."

Given the promise, how can both Jim and his dad be right? Show your work.

Pop-Up Art

Summarizing In this module you have explored paper pop-up techniques and the mathematics related to them. To complete the module project you'll design and create your own pop-up. Your pop-up should include several of the techniques you have learned and can use more than one piece of paper. Here are two more pop-up techniques that may help.

SET UP

You will need:

- *construction paper*
- *scissors*
- *grid paper*

Pop-Up Staircases

Step 1 Use the double-slit method (from page 91) to construct a pop-up like the one shown.

Step 2 Fold the paper back down along its central fold.

Make another double slit across the two new folds.

Fold back the two loose sections between the cuts.

Open the card. Pull the loose sections toward you and recrease.

new folds

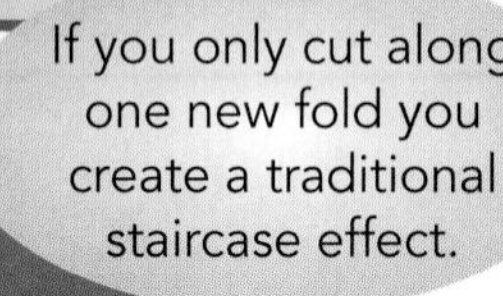

Step 3 Repeating the double-slit method on some or all of the new folds creates a pop-up staircase.

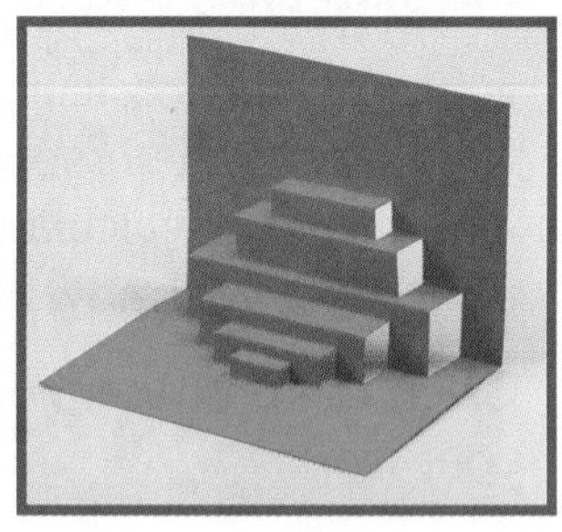

Polygon Buildings

Step 1 Make a pattern for a building like the one shown at the right on grid paper. Each square on the pattern is a wall of the building. Cut out the pattern. Make sure you cut around the tabs.

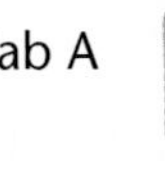

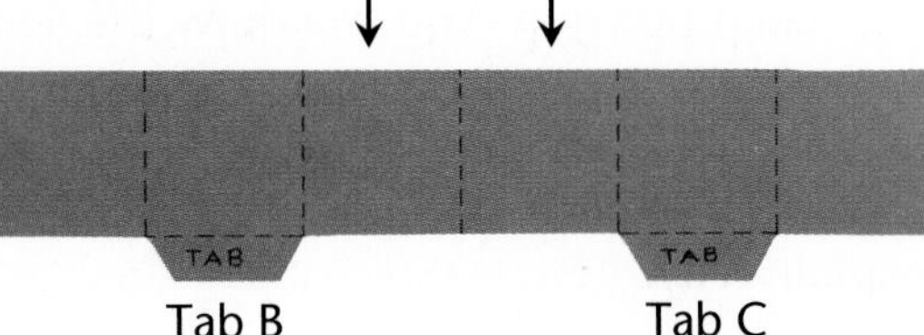

Step 2 Fold the pattern on the segments between walls. Make all the folds in the same direction. Tape Tab A to the outer wall on the opposite end of the pattern to form a hexagonal-shaped building.

Tab

Tab

Central Fold

Step 3 Place your building on a piece of paper with a central fold. Line up two of the folds of the building with the central fold. Tape Tab B and Tab C to the paper as shown.

You can experiment with patterns to make buildings in the shape of other polygons.

7 Plan the design of your pop-up. Make a drawing or sketch if necessary. Make sure your design includes the following features.

- an object that has line symmetry
- parallel lines
- two different types of quadrilaterals
- a reflection, a rotation, or a translation

8 Gather the materials you will need and create your pop-up.

9 Describe how you used each of the mathematical ideas from Question 7 to create your pop-up. If you also used fractions or decimals, explain how.

MODULE 2

Review and Assessment

You will need: • *Review and Assessment Labsheet* (Exs. 1, 2, and 19)

Use the Review and Assessment Labsheet for Exercises 1 and 2.

1. Follow the directions for *Identifying Quadrilaterals.* (Sec. 1, Explor. 1)

2. Follow the directions for naming and marking the *Polygons.* Identify each polygon. You will draw the lines of symmetry and mark a pair of parallel segments in each polygon. (Sec. 1, Explor. 1 and 2)

Tell whether each statement is *true* or *false*. If a statement is false, explain why. (Sec. 2, Explor. 1)

3. $\frac{1}{2}$ of the square is shaded.

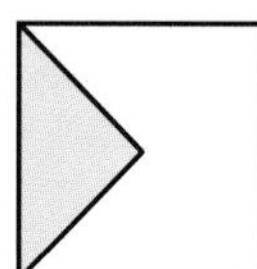

4. $\frac{3}{8}$ of the rectangle is shaded.

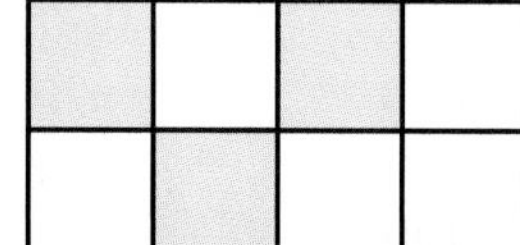

5. $\frac{1}{4}$ of the circle is shaded.

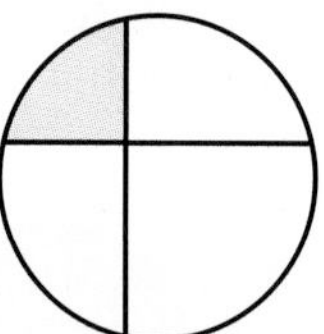

Each shape below is a fractional part of a whole. Copy each shape and make a possible drawing of the whole. (Sec. 2, Explor. 2)

6. $\frac{1}{3}$ of the whole

7. $\frac{1}{2}$ of the whole

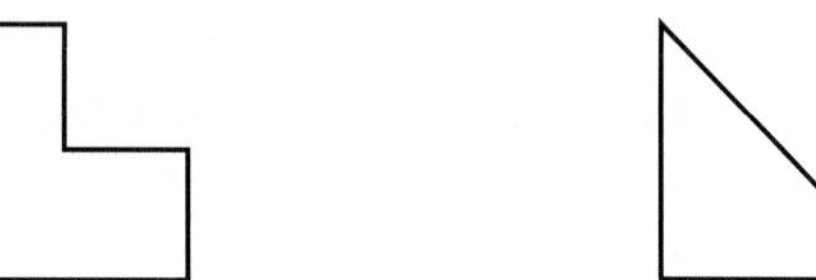

8. $\frac{3}{8}$ of the whole

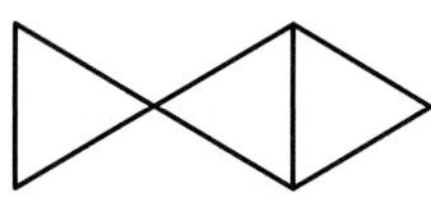

9. Which methods below will give a fraction equivalent to $\frac{2}{4}$? Explain. (Sec. 3, Explor. 2)

   a. $\frac{2+2}{4+2}$ b. $\frac{2 \cdot 2}{4 \cdot 2}$ c. $\frac{2 \div 2}{4 \div 2}$ d. $\frac{2-2}{4-2}$

10. Use the window section shown at the right to answer parts (a)–(b).

   a. Red lights are showing in what fraction of the windows? Write your answer using three equivalent fractions. (Sec. 3, Explor. 1)

   b. Write the fraction of windows showing red lights as a decimal. (Sec. 5, Explor. 1)

Write each fraction in lowest terms. (Sec. 3, Explor. 2)

11. $\frac{6}{24}$
12. $\frac{9}{12}$
13. $\frac{25}{30}$
14. $\frac{7}{14}$
15. $\frac{3}{8}$
16. $\frac{75}{100}$
17. $\frac{42}{48}$
18. $\frac{27}{99}$

19. **Use the Review and Assessment Labsheet.** Transformations can be seen in nature. For each of the *Flower Sketches*, show how one part of the flower is a reflection or a rotation of another part. (Sec. 4, Explor. 1)

Write each decimal in words. (Sec. 5, Explor. 1)

20. 6.56
21. 0.007
22. 1208.3
23. 35.1
24. 0.123
25. 25,001.05
26. 521.63
27. 1.022
28. 600.07

Compare each pair of decimals. Use $<$, $>$, or $=$. (Sec. 5, Explor. 2)

29. 3.1456 __?__ 3.1465
30. 0.17 __?__ 0.1701
31. 475.12 __?__ 475.120
32. 28.883 __?__ 28.8829
33. sixteen hundredths __?__ four tenths
34. fourteen and seven hundredths __?__ fourteen and seventy thousandths

Find each sum or difference without using a calculator.
(Sec. 6, Explor. 1 and 2)

35. 7.147 + 0.9 + 1.03
36. 18.25 – 3.08
37. 0.45 + 2.60 + 3.05
38. 4.93 – 2.718
39. 500 + 0.92
40. 9.253 + 1.747

41. Max spent $3.85 on his pop-up card. Rachel spent $2.34 less than Max. Alisha spent $1.47 more than Rachel. (Sec. 6, Explor. 1 and 2)
    a. Find how much each student spent.
    b. What was the total amount spent by the three students?

Reflecting on the Module

42. Write a letter to an adult member of your family describing the math you learned in this module and what you liked most and least about the module.

MODULE 3 STATISTICAL SAFARI

CONNECTING MATHEMATICS & The Theme

MODULE 3

SECTION OVERVIEW

1 Sets and Metric Measurement

As you study animal facts:

- Sort data using a Venn diagram
- Estimate metric length and mass
- Convert between metric units

2 Fractions and Percents

As you predict animal populations:

- Find fractions of whole numbers
- Write percents

3 Bar Graphs and Line Plots

As you learn about some unusual animals:

- Create and interpret bar graphs
- Create and interpret line plots

4 Mean, Median, Mode

As you think about the average number of children for families:

- Calculate mean, median, and mode
- Choose appropriate averages
- Use a calculator to change a fraction to a decimal
- Round decimal quotients

5 Dividing Decimals, Estimation, and Mental Math

As you learn about popular pets:

- Divide a decimal by a whole number
- Use estimation and mental math techniques

6 Stem-and-Leaf Plots and Dividing by a Decimal

As you study dinosaurs:

- Make and interpret stem-and-leaf plots
- Divide by a decimal

The Module Project

Be a Reporter

Extra, Extra! Read all about it!

"Study shows that there are over a million pet snakes in the United States."

As a reporter you will collect data about pets or another topic that interests you. The mathematics you learn in this module will help you organize, interpret, and present your results in a newspaper article.

More on the Module Project

See pp. 180, 192, 216, and 229.

INTERNET

To learn more about the theme:
http://www.mlmath.com

Sets and Metric Measurement

EXPLORATION 1
- Sorting Data

EXPLORATION 2
- Metric Length and Mass

EXPLORATION 3
- Converting Metric Units

Setting the Stage

In his book, *Savage Paradise,* wildlife photographer and writer Hugo van Lawick tells what happened when a herd of gazelles stopped to drink from a waterhole in Tanzania, East Africa.

> ... a lioness emerged from a bush forty yards away and swiftly ran to the waterhole. As she got closer, she increased her speed, but she was still ten yards short of the slope when the first gazelles appeared...on the way back to the plain.
>
> She hit out at a female gazelle which managed to jump sideways out of her reach. Then I saw a male gazelle run straight towards the lioness. When it reached her it hesitated a split second, then jumped straight over her. The lioness, however, had seen the gazelle and, rearing up on her hind legs, swiped at it with both paws in an embracing movement. The gazelle streaked through the embrace, with only millimeters to spare between the outstretched claws on either side of it.

Think About It

1 The lioness stood on her hind legs to catch the male gazelle. About how high do you think the lioness reached up?

2 The lioness missed the gazelle by millimeters. About how large or small do you think a millimeter is?

▶ **In this module you'll learn about the measurements and habits of different animals. You'll also describe and compare animal data using graphs and averages.**

Exploration 1

S·o·r·t·i·n·g Data

GOAL

LEARN HOW TO...
- sort data using a Venn diagram

AS YOU...
- explore the characteristics of animals

KEY TERMS
- set
- empty set
- Venn diagram

SET UP *Work in a group. You will need: • 10 animal cards from Labsheets 1A–1D • 10 index cards • 2 pieces of string, each 3 ft long*

3 Follow the steps below to sort your animal cards.

You may want to tie the ends of each piece of string together.

First

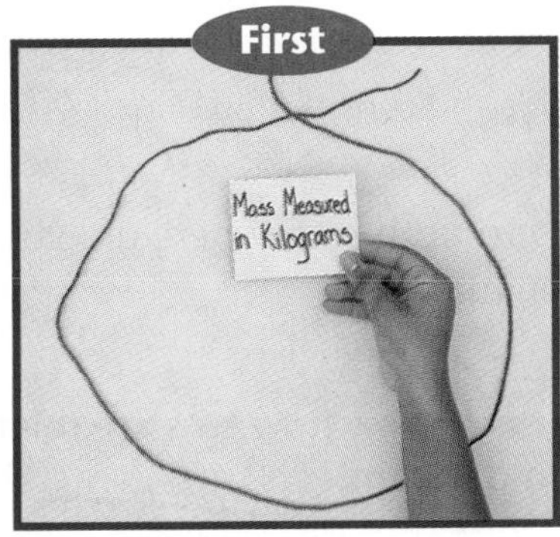

Place a loop of string on a desk. Write *Mass Measured in Kilograms* on an index card.

Then

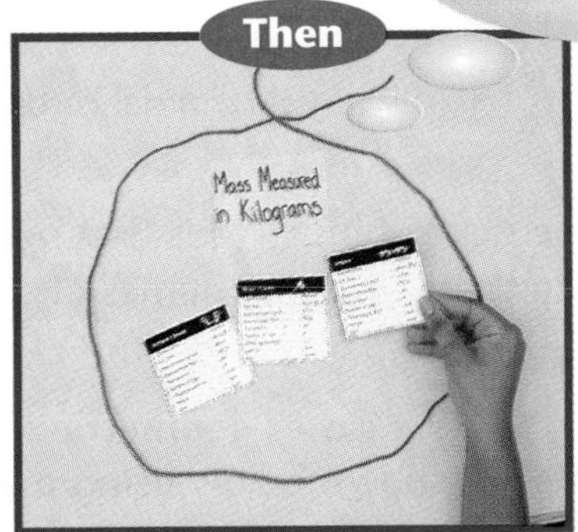

Place all the cards of animals with mass measured in kilograms inside the loop.

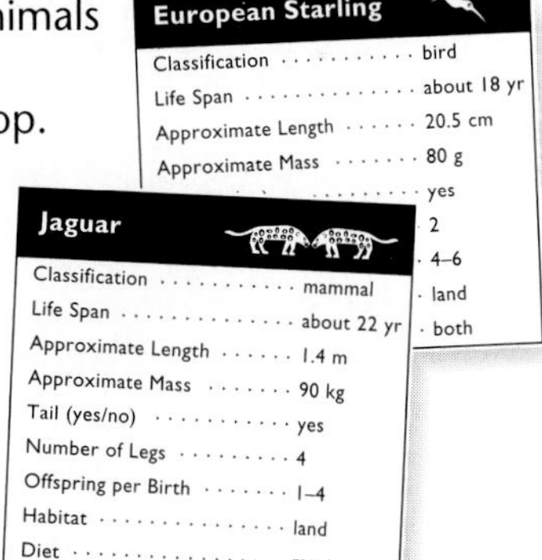

4 **a.** List the animals that you placed inside the loop.

b. How would you describe the size of an animal whose mass is measured in kilograms?

5 Clear the loop and repeat Questions 3 and 4 for each characteristic given below.

a. mass measured in grams

b. length measured in meters

c. length measured in centimeters

▶ **The animals you placed in the loop in Question 3 are a *set* of animals whose mass is measured in kilograms. A set is any collection of objects.**

6 Describe a set that would not have any of your group's animal cards in it. This set is called an **empty set**.

▶ **Looking at Two Sets** **Objects in one set sometimes share characteristics with objects in another set.**

7 Follow the steps below to sort your animal cards.

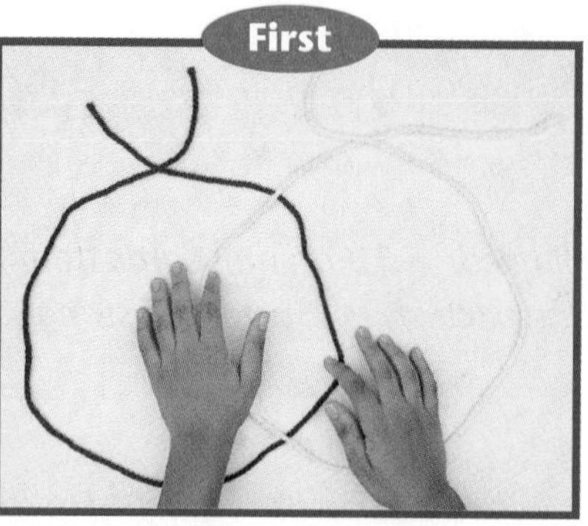

Place two overlapping loops on your work space.

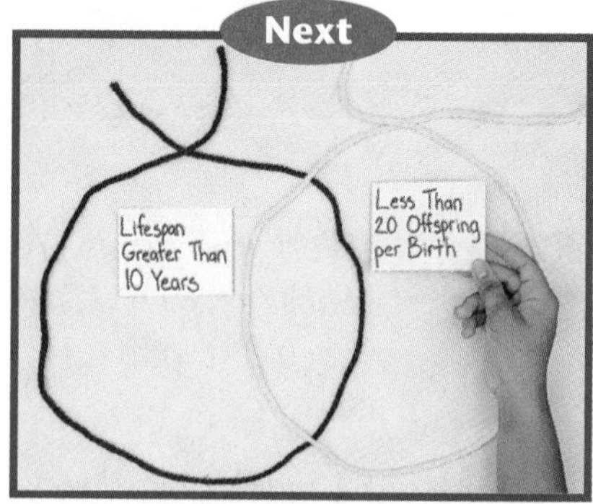

Label two index cards as shown and place one inside each loop.

Then Place your animal cards inside the correct loop.

8 If there are animal cards that belong to both sets, where did you place them? List the names of the animals.

▶ **A Venn diagram uses geometric shapes to show how sets are related. Two sets are shown below using a Venn diagram.**

...checks that you can sort data using a Venn diagram.

9 **CHECKPOINT** Use your animal cards and string to form sets to match each description. Then sketch and label a Venn diagram.

a. two sets that do not contain any of the same animals

b. two sets that contain some of the same animals

HOMEWORK EXERCISES ▶ **See Exs. 1–8 on pp. 166–167.**

Exploration 2

Metric Length and Mass

SET UP *Work in a group. You will need: • gram scale • meter stick or metric ruler*

GOAL

LEARN HOW TO...
- estimate length and mass in metric units

AS YOU...
- measure everyday objects

KEY TERMS
- meter (m)
- centimeter (cm)
- millimeter (mm)
- benchmark
- gram (g)
- milligram (mg)
- kilogram (kg)
- metric ton

10 Think back to your animal cards. Were small animals measured in meters or centimeters? in kilograms or grams?

▶ **Metric Length The metric system is used in most countries today. Metric units of length are based on the meter.**

The distance between little tick marks is a millimeter.

If you continue the ruler up to 100 centimeters, you get a meter.

cm 1 2 3 4 5 6 7 8 9 10

Ten millimeters is a centimeter.

▶ **You can use something whose measure you know as a benchmark to estimate lengths in metric units. For example, if you know your height in centimeters, you can use it as a benchmark to estimate the height of a doorway.**

11 Copy and complete the table. Use a meter stick to find a benchmark for each unit of length.

Length	Benchmark
1 millimeter (mm)	length of ?
1 centimeter (cm)	length of ?
1 meter (m)	length of ?

12 ✓ **CHECKPOINT** Use your benchmarks from Question 11 to estimate the length of each object.

a. a chalkboard (in meters)

b. a pencil (in centimeters)

c. an eraser on a pencil (in millimeters)

...checks that you can estimate length in metric units.

▶ **When you measure to find actual lengths, it can be helpful to use decimals to record your measurements.**

EXAMPLE

Find the length of the caterpillar in centimeters.

SAMPLE RESPONSE

The caterpillar measures 6 cm 4 mm. There are 10 tick marks in 1 cm, so 4 of these marks are $\frac{4}{10}$ of a centimeter, or 0.4 cm.

This means that 6 cm 4 mm = 6.4 cm.

13 Explain why 5 m 35 cm can be written as 5.35 m.

✓ QUESTION 14

...checks that you can use a ruler to measure length in metric units.

14 **✓ CHECKPOINT** Check your estimates in Question 12 by finding the actual length for each object in the given unit.

▶ **Metric Mass** **Metric units of mass are based on the gram. The table below gives benchmarks for some common units of mass.**

Mass	Benchmark
1 milligram (mg)	mass of a dash of salt
1 gram (g)	mass of a paper clip
1 kilogram (kg)	mass of a pair of sneakers
1 metric ton	mass of a compact car

15 Choose the appropriate metric unit (*metric ton, kilogram, gram,* or *milligram*) for measuring the mass of each animal.

a. a pony **b.** a frog **c.** a flea **d.** a whale

✓ QUESTION 16

...checks that you can estimate mass in metric units.

16 **✓ CHECKPOINT** Estimate the mass of each object using the given unit. Then use a scale to find the actual mass.

a. a pencil (g) **b.** a textbook (kg) **c.** a shoe (kg)

HOMEWORK EXERCISES See Exs. 9–19 on p. 167.

Exploration 3

Converting Metric Units

GOAL

LEARN HOW TO...
- convert between metric units

AS YOU...
- relate metric prefixes to place values

SET UP *You will need Labsheets 1E and 1F.*

Use the Student Resource below to answer Questions 17–19.

17 **a.** What does the prefix *kilo-* mean? A kilogram is how many times as large as a gram?

b. Name an animal whose mass is measured in kilograms.

18 **a.** What does the prefix *milli-* mean? A millimeter is what fractional part of a meter?

b. Name an animal whose length you would measure in millimeters.

19 A centimeter is one hundredth of a meter and a millimeter is one thousandth of a meter. How many millimeters are in one centimeter? How do you know?

Metric Prefixes

Student Resource

You can look at the prefixes of metric units of measure to see the relationships between the units. The most commonly used prefixes are in the shaded areas.

The prefixes are like place values, becoming ten times as great each time you move to the left in the table.

Centi- means "hundredth," so 1 **centi**meter is $\frac{1}{100}$ of a meter, and 100 centimeters is 1 meter.

Prefix	kilo-	hecto-	deka-	basic unit meter gram	deci-	centi-	milli-
Meaning	1000	100	10	1	0.1 or $\frac{1}{10}$	0.01 or $\frac{1}{100}$	0.001 or $\frac{1}{1000}$

A decimeter is 10 times as long as a centimeter.

A centimeter is 10 times as long as a millimeter.

So a decimeter is 10 • 10, or 100, times as long as a millimeter.

▶ **Metric Conversions You may need to convert from one unit to another to compare measurements.**

100 centimeters are in 1 meter so 500 centimeters are in 5 meters.

20 Which reptile is longer? By how many centimeters?

21 You can also compare the lengths of the reptiles in meters.

$$1 \text{ cm} = 0.01 \text{ m}$$
$$25 \text{ cm} = 25 \cdot 0.01 \text{ m}$$

Use your calculator to find $25 \cdot 0.01$. The crocodile is how many meters longer than the chameleon?

▶ **To convert between metric units, it is helpful to know how to multiply by the special multipliers 0.001, 0.01, 0.1, 10, 100, and 1000.**

22 **Use Labsheet 1E.** Use your calculator to complete the *Special Multipliers Multiplication Table.*

23 **Use Labsheet 1F.** Use the table of prefix meanings to fill in the missing information for the *Metric Conversions.*

EXAMPLE

Convert 453 mm to meters.

SAMPLE RESPONSE

$$1 \text{ mm} = 0.001 \text{ m}$$
$$\text{so } 453 \text{ mm} = 453 \cdot 0.001 \text{ m} = 0.453 \text{ m}$$

24 **Discussion** How can you check that the answer, 0.453 m, in the Example is reasonable?

✓ **QUESTION 25**

...checks that you can convert between metric units.

25 ✓ **CHECKPOINT** Replace each ? with the number that makes the statement true.

a. 1 g = ? mg
5 g = ? mg

b. 1 m = ? km
37 m = ? km

c. 1 metric ton = ? kg
4.2 metric tons = ? kg

HOMEWORK EXERCISES See Exs. 20–40 on p. 168.

Section 1 Key Concepts

Key Terms

Sets and Venn diagrams (pp. 159–160)

A set is any collection of objects. The empty set is a set with no objects in it. A Venn diagram uses geometric shapes to show how sets are related.

set

empty set

Venn diagram

Example

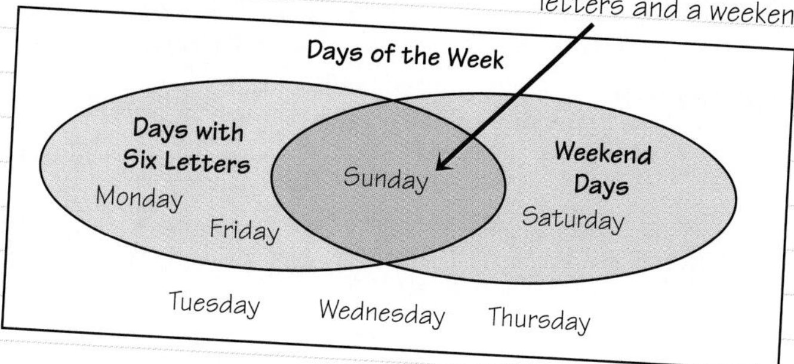

Metric System (pp. 161–164)

The tables below show the relationships among some commonly used metric units.

meter (m)

centimeter (cm)

millimeter (mm)

Units of length are based on the meter. A benchmark for 1 m is the length of an outstretched arm.

benchmark

kilometer (km)	meter (m)	centimeter (cm)	millimeter (mm)
1 km = 1000 m	1 m = 1000 mm	1 cm = 10 mm	1 mm = 0.1 cm
	1 m = 100 cm	1 cm = 0.01 m	1 mm = 0.001 m

gram (g)

milligram (mg)

kilogram (kg)

metric ton

Units of mass are based on the gram. A benchmark for 1 g is the mass of a paper clip.

metric ton	kilogram (kg)	gram (g)	milligram (mg)
1 metric ton = 1000 kg	1 kg = 1000 g	1 g = 1000 mg	1 mg = 0.001 g
1 metric ton = 1,000,000 g	1 kg = 0.001 metric ton	1 g = 0.001 kg	

Key Concepts Questions

26 What does the Venn diagram above tell you about Tuesday, Wednesday, and Thursday?

27 The mass of a giraffe is 0.8 metric tons and the mass of a four-eyed opossum is 800 g. The mass of the giraffe is how many times as great as the mass of the four-eyed opossum?

Section 1
Practice & Application Exercises

Use the Venn diagram below for Exercises 1–5.

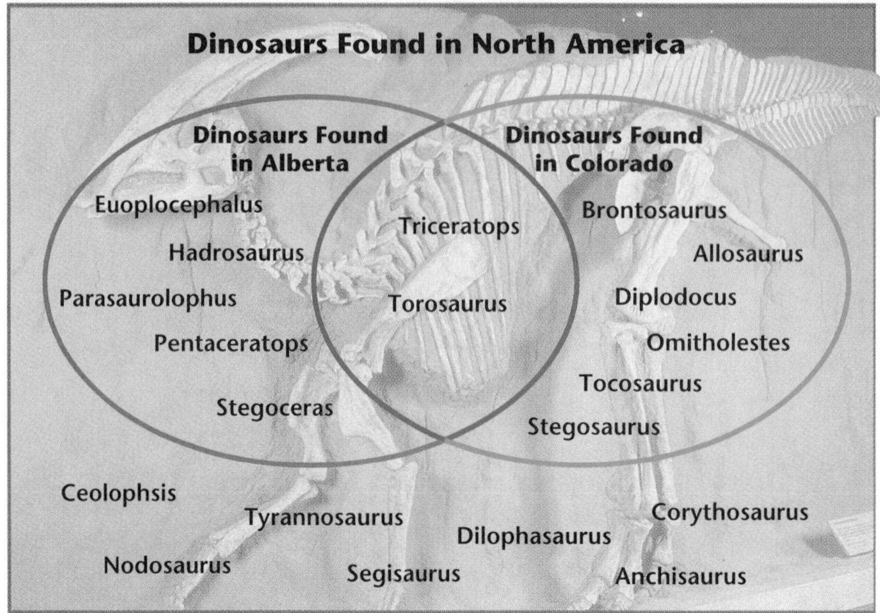

1. How many types of dinosaurs were found in Colorado? in Alberta?

2. How many types of dinosaurs were found in North America but not in Alberta or Colorado?

3. How many types of dinosaurs found in North America have been found outside of Colorado?

4. What does the Venn diagram tell you about *Triceratops* and *Torosaurus*?

5. According to the diagram, how many dinosaur types were found in North America?

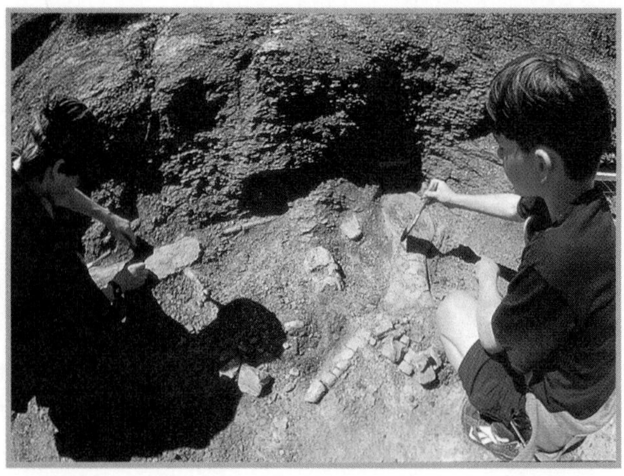

▶ Visitors can help dig up dinosaur fossils at the Royal Tyrrell Museum's Day Digs site in Alberta, Canada.

6. **Geometry Connection** Tell where each shape should be placed in the Venn diagram.

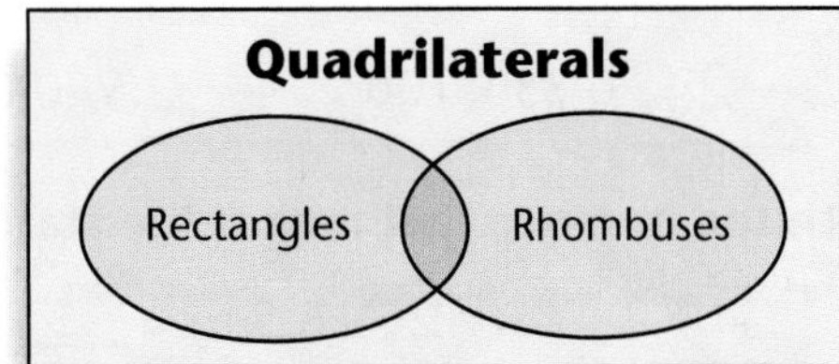

a. 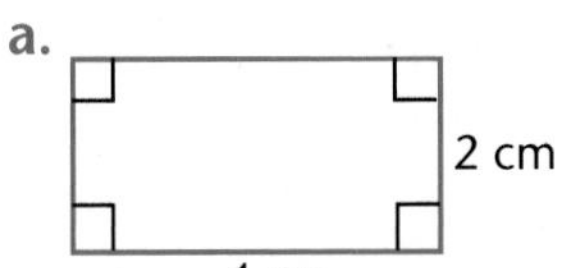

b. 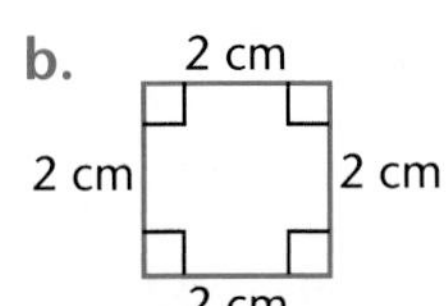

c. 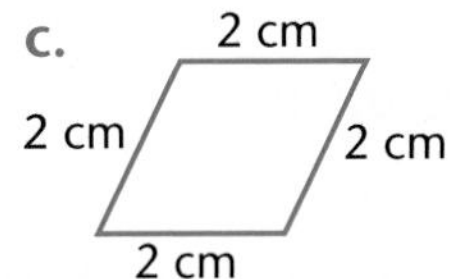

7. **Open-ended** Sketch a quadrilateral. Where would you place it in the Venn diagram for Exercise 6? Why?

8. **Challenge** For each diagram on the right, give an example of two sets that have the relationship shown.

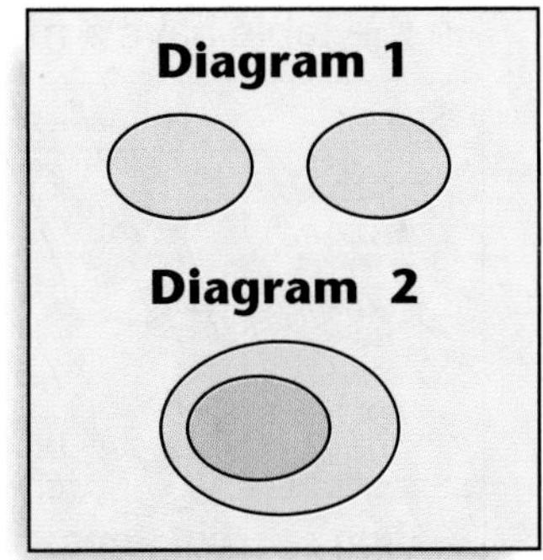

9. Suppose a table needs to be moved into a classroom. You want to know whether the table will fit through the doorway. Should you measure to the nearest *meter* or *centimeter*? Explain.

10. Suppose you are cutting shelf paper to line a drawer. Should you measure to the nearest *centimeter* or *millimeter*? Explain.

Choose the best estimate for each measurement.

11. the width of your classroom	*1 m*	*7 m*	*30 m*
12. the height of a soda can	*1.2 m*	*3.5 cm*	*120 mm*
13. the thickness of a quarter	*8 mm*	*1 cm*	*1 mm*

Decide which metric unit to use (*milligram, gram, kilogram,* or *metric ton*) for the mass of each object.

14. a vitamin pill 15. a baseball bat 16. an airplane

Choose the best estimate for the mass of each object.

17. a bicycle	*15 kg*	*150 g*	*0.5 metric tons*
18. a loaf of bread	*5 g*	*500 g*	*5 kg*
19. a piece of paper	*0.5 kg*	*0.5 g*	*5 kg*

Find each product.

20. 2 • 0.01
21. 3.4 • 0.001
22. 0.4 • 0.01
23. 0.007 • 10
24. 0.35 • 100
25. 0.001 • 0.1

Replace each _?_ with the number that makes the statement true.

26. 5 km = _?_ m
27. 6.5 m = _?_ cm
28. 584 m = _?_ km
29. 2540 mm = _?_ m
30. 0.6 m = _?_ mm
31. 72 cm = _?_ mm

Use the table to answer Exercises 32 and 33.

32. List the animals in order from least to greatest mass.

33. **Research** A kilogram is a little more than 2 pounds. Which animals in the table have a mass similar to that of a human baby at birth?

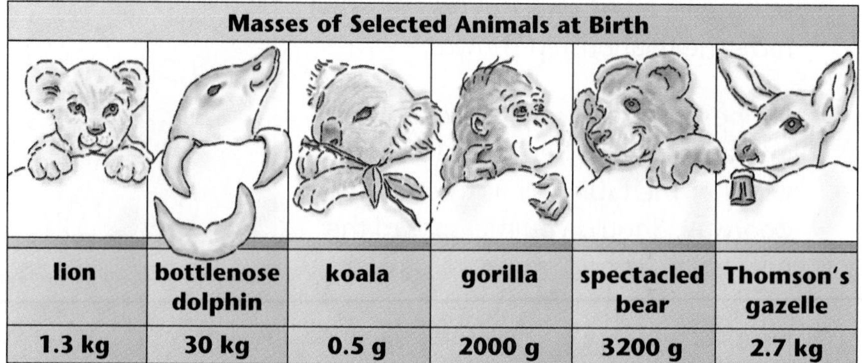

Masses of Selected Animals at Birth

lion	bottlenose dolphin	koala	gorilla	spectacled bear	Thomson's gazelle
1.3 kg	30 kg	0.5 g	2000 g	3200 g	2.7 kg

Replace each _?_ with <, >, or = .

34. 75 mg _?_ 7.5 g
35. 6 metric tons _?_ 600 kg
36. 5.3 kg _?_ 5380 g
37. 1500 kg _?_ 0.75 metric tons
38. 3000 mg _?_ 3 g
39. 490 g _?_ 4.9 kg

Journal

Exercise 40 checks that you understand set relationships.

Reflecting on the Section

Write your response to Exercise 40 in your journal.

40. DaQui had the following six animal cards: octopus, kangaroo, lobster, sea otter, cheetah, and giant clam. He correctly placed his cards in the set *Animals with a Mass Greater Than 20 kg* and in the set *Animals That Live in Water*. He found that he had four animals in each set. How can this be, since he had only six cards?

Spiral Review

Find each sum or difference. (Module 2, p. 147)

41. 5.621 – 3.109 42. 3.5 + 7.63 43. 2.004 – 0.007

44. Beth, Karen, and Steve are pen pals. Each lives in either Australia, Brazil, or France and owns either an iguana, a Chihuahua, or a rabbit. Use the clues to tell where each person lives and what pet he or she owns. (Module 1, p. 35)

- Karen sent a letter to France.
- Steve read about a pet Chihuahua in a letter from Australia.
- Beth owns a rabbit.
- The Brazilian owns an iguana.

Replace each ? with the number that makes the statement true.
(Module 2, p. 114)

45. $\frac{3}{8} = \frac{?}{32}$ 46. $\frac{3}{4} = \frac{?}{100}$ 47. $\frac{2}{?} = \frac{40}{100}$

Extension 

Venn Diagrams

This Venn diagram shows the number of sixth graders who take music, art, or drama at a school.

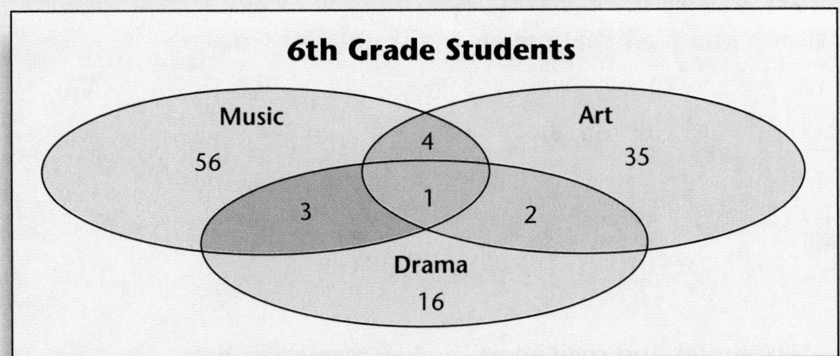

How many students take each of the following subjects?

48. music 49. art 50. drama

51. both music and art 52. both music and drama 53. both art and drama

54. all three subjects 55. music and art, but not drama 56. at least one of the three subjects

Section 1 Extra Skill Practice

For Exercises 1–3, use the Venn diagram below.

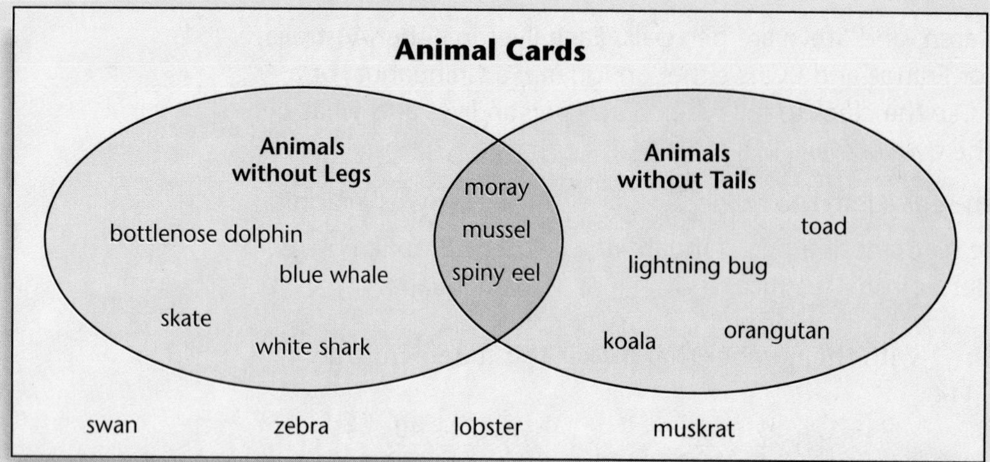

1. How many animals have no tails?
2. List the animals that are contained in both sets.
3. What does this diagram tell you about a lobster?

Find each product.

4. $3 \cdot 0.01$
5. $2.5 \cdot 0.001$
6. $0.2 \cdot 0.1$
7. $0.0003 \cdot 10$
8. $0.04 \cdot 0.01$
9. $0.348 \cdot 100$

Replace each __?__ with the number that makes the statement true.

10. 8 km = __?__ m
11. 2.5 m = __?__ cm
12. 300 m = __?__ km
13. 2930 mg = __?__ g
14. 280 kg = __?__ g
15. 0.4 metric tons = __?__ kg

Study Skills ▸ Preparing to do Homework

Looking back at examples and reviewing the key terms can help you prepare to do your homework.

1. Look at an Example in Section 1. What does it show you how to do?
2. What are the key terms in Section 1? Use one of the key terms in a sentence that shows the meaning of the term.

Section 2 Fractions and Percents

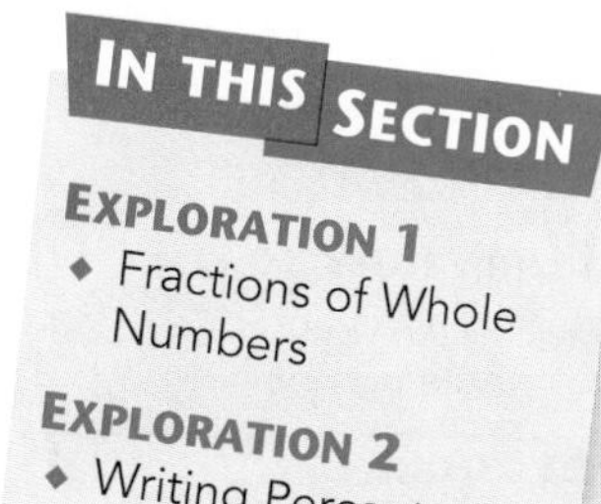

Something Fishy

Setting the Stage

SET UP *Work as a class. You will need:* • *Labsheet 2A* • *paper bag*

Wildlife researcher Kathleen Matthews equips trout with radio transmitters to study their movements in a river. Since it is impossible for her to catch all of the fish in a river, she only looks at some of the fish. By studying a *sample* of the fish, Kathleen can make predictions about the entire *population.*

▶ **With your class, you'll take samples from a bag containing 20 paper fish and predict what kinds of fish are in the bag.**

First follow Steps 1–4 for a sample of 1 fish. Repeat the steps for a sample of 4 fish and then for a sample of 10 fish.

STEP 1 Shake the bag to make sure the fish are well mixed. Then have one student draw the sample from the bag.

STEP 2 Predict what types of fish are in the bag.

STEP 3 Predict how many of each type of fish are in the bag. Why do you think so?

STEP 4 Put the fish back in the bag.

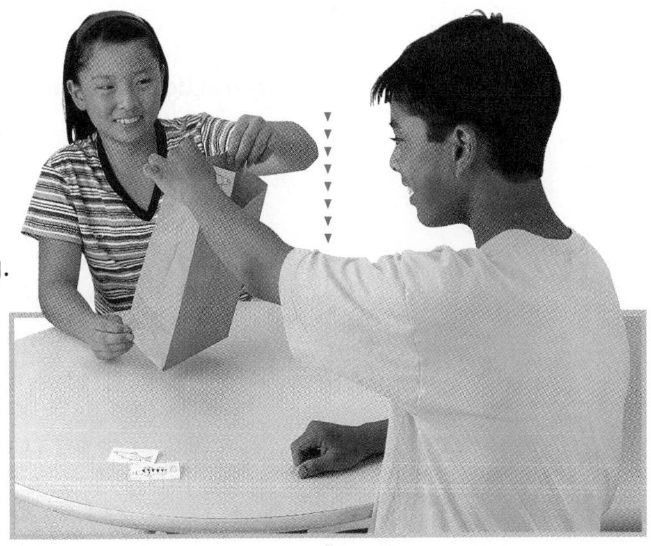

Think About It

1 **a.** Did your predictions in Steps 2 and 3 change as the size of the sample increased? Why?

b. Which sample size do you think best represents the population of 20 fish? Explain.

GOAL

LEARN HOW TO...

- find a fraction of a whole number

AS YOU...

- make predictions from a sample of animal cards

KEY TERMS

- sample
- population

Exploration 1

Fractions of Whole Numbers

SET UP *Work in a group. You will need:* • *Labsheet 2B* • *10 animal cards*

▶ **Fractions can be used to make predictions from a sample, which is part of a whole set of objects being studied. Your group has a sample of all the animal cards being used. The whole set of cards is the population.**

2 What fraction of your group's cards are mammals?

3 **a. Discussion** Predict what fraction of the cards in use by the class are mammals. How can you use your answer to Question 2 to help you make your prediction?

b. How many of the 50 cards being used by the class do you think are mammals? How can you use your answer to part (a) to help you find out?

▶ **Use Labsheet 2B. For Questions 4 and 5 you'll use dot paper to find fractions of whole numbers.**

4 Follow the directions for *Dot Grid 1* to find out how many cards are mammals if $\frac{2}{3}$ of 36 cards are mammals.

5 Follow the directions for *Dot Grid 2* to find out how many cards are reptiles if $\frac{3}{4}$ of 24 cards are reptiles.

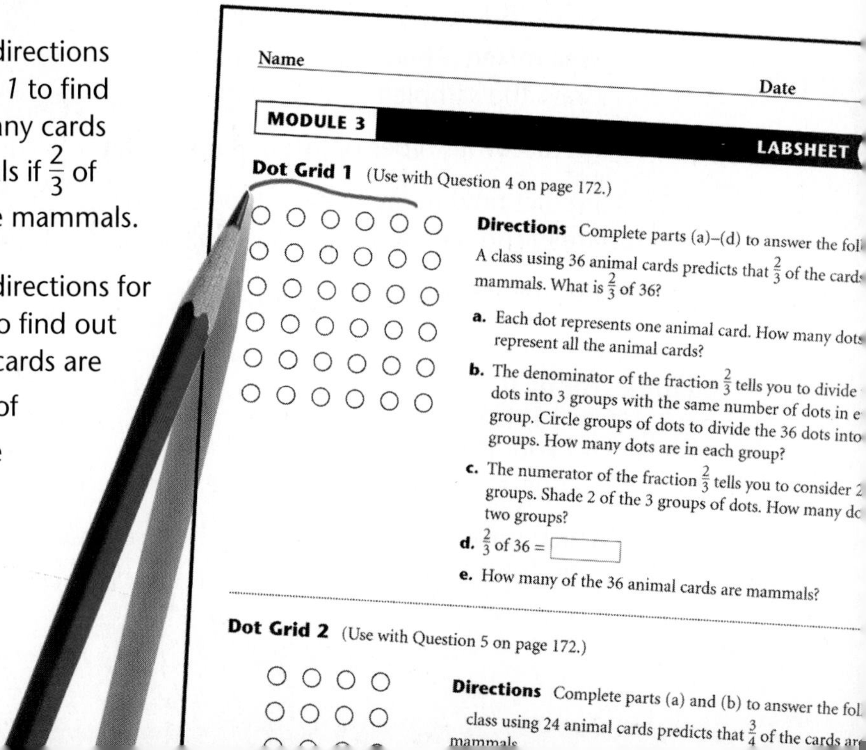

Name

Date

MODULE 3 LABSHEET

Dot Grid 1 (Use with Question 4 on page 172.)

Directions Complete parts (a)–(d) to answer the fol

A class using 36 animal cards predicts that $\frac{2}{3}$ of the card mammals. What is $\frac{2}{3}$ of 36?

a. Each dot represents one animal card. How many dots represent all the animal cards?

b. The denominator of the fraction $\frac{2}{3}$ tells you to divide dots into 3 groups with the same number of dots in e group. Circle groups of dots to divide the 36 dots into groups. How many dots are in each group?

c. The numerator of the fraction $\frac{2}{3}$ tells you to consider 2 groups. Shade 2 of the 3 groups of dots. How many dc two groups?

d. $\frac{2}{3}$ of 36 = ☐

e. How many of the 36 animal cards are mammals?

Dot Grid 2 (Use with Question 5 on page 172.)

Directions Complete parts (a) and (b) to answer the fol

class using 24 animal cards predicts that $\frac{3}{4}$ of the cards ar

▶ **You can also find a fraction of a whole number by using mental math.**

6 A class predicts that $\frac{3}{8}$ of their 48 animal cards are reptiles.

a. To find $\frac{3}{8}$ of 48 cards, you can first think about dividing the 48 cards into how many equal parts?

b. How many cards will be in each equal part?

c. How many of those equal parts should you take?

d. What is $\frac{3}{8}$ of 48?

e. How many of the 48 cards do you predict are reptiles?

7 ✓ **CHECKPOINT** Use mental math to find each value.

a. $\frac{4}{5}$ of 30 **b.** $\frac{5}{6}$ of 18 **c.** $\frac{2}{3}$ of 12 **d.** $\frac{3}{7}$ of 21

✓ **QUESTION 7**

...checks that you can use mental math to find a fraction of a whole number.

8 **Discussion** Think about the mental math method you used in Questions 6 and 7. Would you use this method to find $\frac{2}{5}$ of 12? Explain why or why not.

9 **a.** Combine your animal cards with those of another group or groups. What fraction of the combined cards are mammals?

b. Use your answer to part (a) to predict what fraction of the cards being used by the class are mammals.

c. How many of the cards being used by the class do you think are mammals?

10 **Try This as a Class** Count how many cards there are in the class that are mammals.

a. Was your prediction from Question 3(b) close?

b. What fraction of the class's cards are mammals?

11 **Try This as a Class** Suppose you combined your class's animal cards with the 50 animal cards of another class.

a. Predict how many of the combined cards are mammals.

b. Did you use your answer to Question 2 or to Question 10(b) to make your prediction? Why?

HOMEWORK EXERCISES See Exs. 1–17 on p. 177.

GOAL

LEARN HOW TO...
- write a percent
- relate fractions, decimals, and percents

AS YOU...
- compare samples that have different sizes

KEY TERM
- percent

Exploration 2

Writing Percen%s

SET UP *You will need Labsheets 2C and 2D.*

▶ **Describing with Percent** **If you predicted that 62 out of the 100 cards are mammals at the end of Exploration 1, then you predicted that 62 *percent* of the cards are mammals. Percent means "per hundred" or "out of 100."**

You can write your prediction as:

$\frac{62}{100}$ of the cards are mammals,

0.62 of the cards are mammals, or

62% of the cards are mammals.

% is the symbol for percent.

62% can also be represented by shading **62** squares on a 100-square grid.

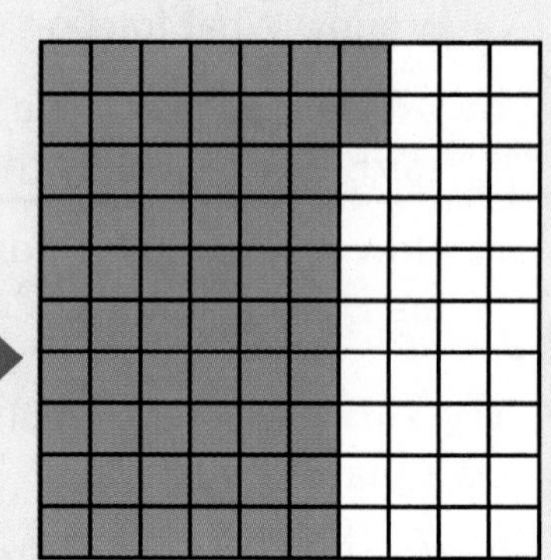

12 **a.** Write the number of unshaded squares in the grid above as a percent.

b. If you combine the shaded and unshaded squares in the grid above, what percent of the grid do you have?

c. Write the percent you found in part (b) as a fraction and as a decimal.

13 ✓ **CHECKPOINT** **Use Labsheet 2C.** Follow the directions on the labsheet for *Relating Fractions, Decimals, and Percents.*

✓ **QUESTION 13**

...checks that you can write a percent as a decimal and as a fraction.

14 **Discussion** Why is it hard to tell which sample has a greater fraction of trout?

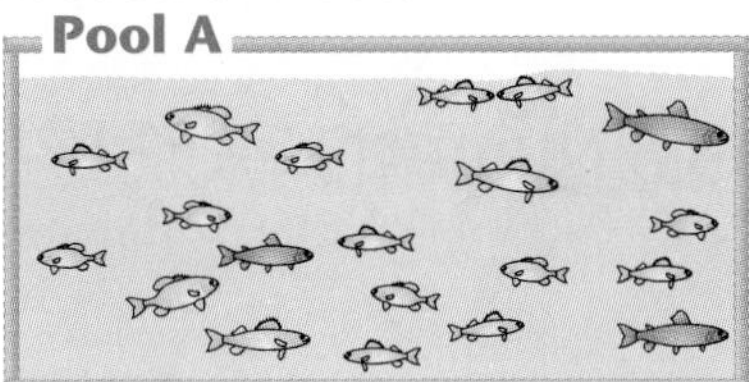

3 out of the 20 fish are trout.

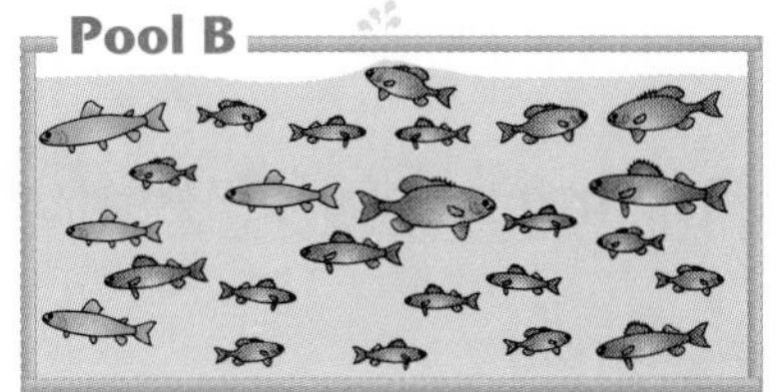

4 out of the 25 fish are trout.

Kathleen Matthews radio tracking trout in the north fork of the American River.

▶ **Using percents or decimals can help you compare two fractions.**

EXAMPLE

Write the fraction of trout in Pool A as a percent and as a decimal.

SAMPLE RESPONSE

You can write a fraction as a percent or as a decimal by writing an equivalent fraction in hundredths.

$\frac{3}{20} = \frac{3 \cdot 5}{20 \cdot 5} = \frac{15}{100}$ 15 hundredths is 15% or 0.15.

15 **a.** What is the fraction of trout in Pool B?

b. Which pool has the greater fraction of trout? Explain how you compared the fractions.

FOR ◀HELP with *finding equivalent fractions*, see **MODULE 2, p. 114**

16 **a.** Write 0.4 as a fraction: $0.4 = \frac{?}{10}$.

b. Write 0.4 as a percent: 0.4 = __?__ %.

17 Replace each __?__ with >, <, or = .

a. $\frac{13}{50}$ __?__ $\frac{1}{4}$ **b.** 0.7 __?__ $\frac{3}{4}$

18 ✔ **CHECKPOINT** Write each fraction or decimal as a percent.

a. $\frac{4}{5}$ **b.** 0.18 **c.** $\frac{1}{50}$ **d.** 0.9

✔ **QUESTION 18** ...checks that you can write decimals and fractions as percents.

▶ **Recognizing Percents and Decimals It is helpful to learn the percent and decimal forms for some simple fractions.**

19 **Use Labsheet 2D.** Follow the directions to find some *Common Fraction, Decimal, and Percent Equivalents.*

HOMEWORK EXERCISES ▶ **See Exs. 18–52 on pp. 178–179.**

Section 2 Key Concepts

Key Terms

sample

population

percent

Finding a Fraction of a Whole Number (pp. 172–173)

Example

$\frac{2}{3}$ of a sample of 15 fish are tuna. Use mental math to find $\frac{2}{3}$ of 15.

Think: Divide 15 into 3 equal-sized groups. There are 5 in each group. There are 10 in two groups, so $\frac{2}{3}$ of 15 = 10.

Understanding Percent (pp. 174–175)

Fraction Form: $\frac{25}{100}$ or $\frac{1}{4}$

Decimal Form: 0.25

Percent Form: 25%

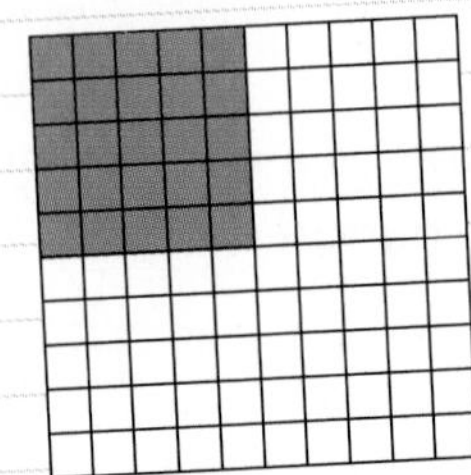

Percent means "per hundred" or "out of 100."

Using Percents or Decimals to Compare (p. 175)

Example Which is greater, $\frac{14}{25}$ or $\frac{120}{200}$?

When the denominator is greater than 100 you can divide to find an equivalent fraction out of 100.

Find equivalent fractions with denominators of 100.

$\frac{14}{25} = \frac{14 \cdot 4}{25 \cdot 4} = \frac{56}{100} = 0.56 = 56\%$ $\quad$ $\frac{120}{200} = \frac{120 \div 2}{200 \div 2} = \frac{60}{100} = 0.60 = 60\%$

So $\frac{120}{200}$ is greater than $\frac{14}{25}$.

Key Concepts Questions

20 **a.** Which is greater, $\frac{3}{4}$ of 24 or $\frac{3}{10}$ of 70?

b. Which is greater, $\frac{3}{4}$ or $\frac{3}{10}$?

21 Besides 100, is there another denominator you could use to write $\frac{120}{200}$ and $\frac{14}{25}$ as decimals? Explain.

Section 2

Practice & Application Exercises

YOU WILL NEED

For Ex. 18:
- Labsheet 2C
- base-ten blocks or pennies (optional)

Mental Math **Use mental math to find each value.**

1. $\frac{2}{3}$ of 12
2. $\frac{5}{6}$ of 18
3. $\frac{2}{5}$ of 20
4. $\frac{3}{4}$ of 12
5. $\frac{2}{9}$ of 27
6. $\frac{3}{16}$ of 32
7. $\frac{5}{8}$ of 24
8. $\frac{5}{10}$ of 30
9. If $\frac{2}{3}$ of 6 animal cards are sea animals, how many are sea animals?
10. If $\frac{4}{5}$ of 10 animal cards are birds, how many are birds?
11. How many mammals are there in a set of 14 animal cards that is $\frac{4}{7}$ mammals?

Plant Pollen **A pollen expert counted the pollen grains in a sample of a pollen deposit to make predictions about the deposit. Use the table of results for Exercises 12 and 13.**

Type of pollen	Number of grains in sample
pine	48
grass	36
oak	30
cactus	6
total	**120**

12. What fraction of the sample is each type of pollen? Write each fraction in lowest terms.
    a. pine
    b. grass
    c. oak
    d. cactus
13. Suppose the pollen expert estimates that 540 grains are in the deposit. Use your answers to Exercise 12 to estimate the number of grains of each type of pollen in the deposit.

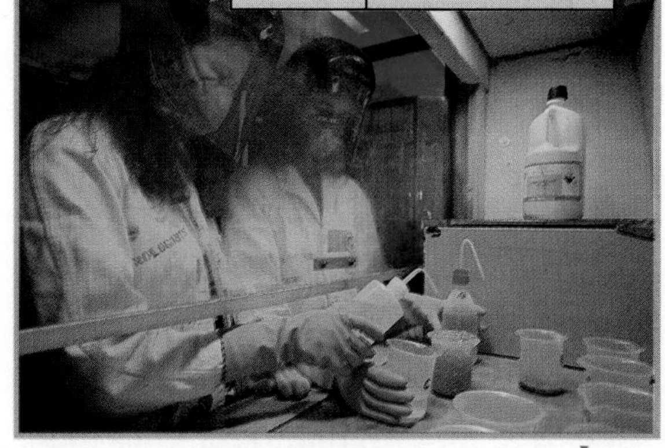

◀ Scientists study plant pollen that has been preserved in the ground to help learn how plants were used by ancient people.

For Exercises 14–16, use compatible numbers to estimate.

Example: $\frac{5}{6}$ of 31 is close to $\frac{5}{6}$ of 30, or about 25.

14. $\frac{2}{3}$ of 34
15. $\frac{1}{5}$ of 19
16. $\frac{3}{4}$ of 15
17. Five of Group A's animal cards were mammals. When they combined their animal cards with those of Group B, they had a total of 16 cards. When combined, $\frac{3}{4}$ of the cards were mammals. How many of Group B's cards were mammals?

FOR ◀HELP with *compatible numbers*, see **MODULE 1, p. 50**

18. **Use Labsheet 2C.** Follow the directions for *Shading Percents.* (First you may want to model the percents with base-ten blocks or pennies). Then write a fraction and a decimal for each shaded part.

Write each percent as a fraction and as a decimal.

19. 30%　　20. 54%　　21. 72%　　22. 99%

23. **Writing** In a raffle, Tanisha buys 4 out of 200 total tickets. In another raffle, her friend Dustin buys 6 out of 300 total tickets. Who is more likely to win? Why?

Write each decimal as a fraction and as a percent.

24. 0.37　　25. 0.4　　26. 0.59　　27. 0.02

28. 0.45　　29. 0.3　　30. 0.12　　31. 0.01

Write each fraction as a decimal and as a percent.

32. $\frac{3}{100}$　　33. $\frac{9}{25}$　　34. $\frac{170}{200}$　　35. $\frac{4}{5}$

36. $\frac{16}{25}$　　37. $\frac{17}{20}$　　38. $\frac{8}{10}$　　39. $\frac{69}{300}$

For Exercises 40–42, use the table showing world music sales.

40. Write a fraction and a percent for the number of CDs sold in 1987 out of the total music sales.

41. **Estimation** Estimate the percent of music sales that CDs were for each year. Explain how you made your estimate.

a. 1988
b. 1989
c. 1990

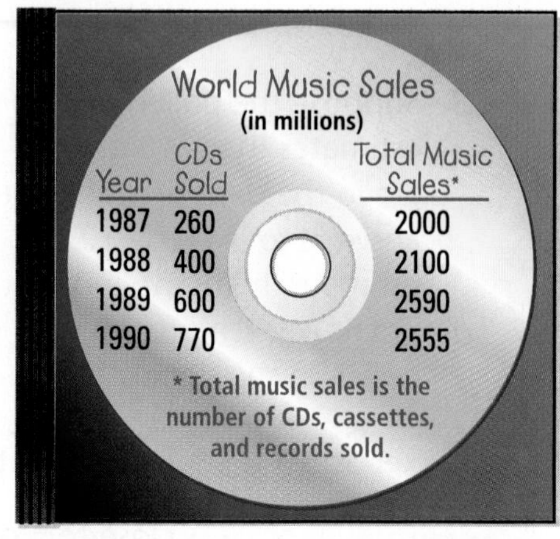

World Music Sales
(in millions)

Year	CDs Sold	Total Music Sales*
1987	260	2000
1988	400	2100
1989	600	2590
1990	770	2555

* Total music sales is the number of CDs, cassettes, and records sold.

42. **Interpreting Data** Total music sales included sales of records and cassettes. What do you think happened to the percent of record and cassette sales from 1987–1990? Why?

Replace each _?_ with >, <, or =.

43. $\frac{2}{5}$ _?_ 0.45　　44. 0.245 _?_ 23%　　45. 56% _?_ 0.28

46. 72% _?_ $\frac{3}{4}$　　47. 0.9 _?_ 9%　　48. $\frac{2}{8}$ _?_ 0.18

49. **Visual Thinking** Replace each ? with the number that makes the statement true.

A is __?__ % of the square.

B is __?__ % of the square.

C is __?__ % of the square.

D is __?__ % of the square.

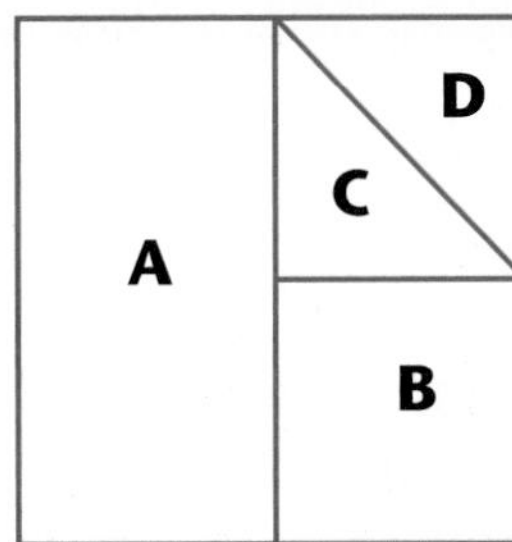

50. Explain how you can use thousandths to compare $\frac{16}{250}$ and $\frac{13}{200}$.

51. **Challenge** A researcher catches 45 fish, tags them, and puts them back in a pond. Later, a sample is taken from the pond and tags are found on $\frac{3}{5}$ of the fish. Estimate how many fish live in the pond. Explain how you made your estimate.

Reflecting on the Section

Be prepared to report on the following topic in class.

52. Suppose that 75% of the students in a class have brown eyes and 25% have red hair. Does this mean that every student in the class has either brown eyes or red hair? Explain your answer.

Oral Report

Exercise 52 checks that you understand the meaning of percent.

Spiral Review

Replace each ? with the number that makes the statement true. **(Module 3, p. 165)**

53. 700 cm = __?__ m

54. 9 kg = __?__ g

55. 30 mm = __?__ cm

56. 20 cm = __?__ mm

57. 500 g = __?__ kg

58. 8000 m = __?__ km

Use the table to answer Exercises 59 and 60. **(Module 1, p. 8)**

Term number	1	2	3	4	5
Term	7	14	21	28	35

59. Describe the relationship between the term and the term number.

60. What is the 60th term in the sequence?

Be a Reporter

SET UP

You will need:

- *Project Labsheet A*

Choosing a Topic How do reporters find answers to questions like "How many pet snakes are in the United States?" Using mathematics, of course! Your project is to collect and interpret data about a topic. At the end of the module you'll write a newspaper article about your results.

 **1** With your group, decide on a topic to investigate and what you want to find out about that topic. You may choose one of the topics below or come up with your own idea.

- junk food
- computers
- TV viewing
- shopping
- phone use
- reading
- sports
- music

Designing a Survey Over the next few days, you'll design a *survey* to collect information about your topic. A survey is a set of questions that you ask a group of people.

 **2** Decide what population, or group of people, you are interested in (for example, just sixth graders or just teachers).

 **3** **Use Project Labsheet A.** Follow the steps on the *Survey Worksheet* to write the questions for your survey.

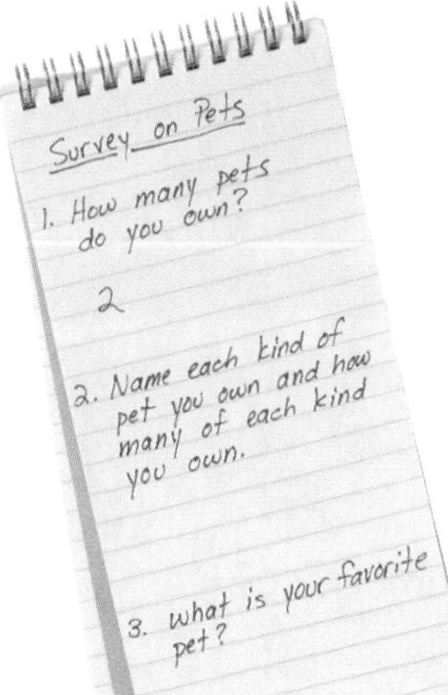

Collecting Your Data Over the next week, you'll probably only be able to survey a sample of your population. Usually, the larger the sample, the more accurate your results will be.

 **4** What do you think your sample size should be in order for your results to be accurate?

 **5** Now collect your data.

Section 2 Extra Skill Practice

Mental Math **Use mental math to find each of the following.**

1. $\frac{1}{2}$ of 16
2. $\frac{3}{5}$ of 20
3. $\frac{1}{3}$ of 27
4. $\frac{2}{7}$ of 21
5. $\frac{7}{8}$ of 56
6. $\frac{4}{9}$ of 54
7. $\frac{3}{4}$ of 124
8. $\frac{1}{6}$ of 90

Write each decimal as a percent and as a fraction.

9. 0.35
10. 0.14
11. 0.28
12. 0.55
13. 0.6
14. 0.01
15. 0.05
16. 0.17

Write each fraction as a decimal and as a percent.

17. $\frac{7}{100}$
18. $\frac{11}{20}$
19. $\frac{8}{25}$
20. $\frac{3}{5}$
21. $\frac{9}{10}$
22. $\frac{3}{25}$
23. $\frac{1}{20}$
24. $\frac{2}{5}$

Replace each __?__ with >, <, or =.

25. 9% __?__ $\frac{9}{10}$
26. 0.5 __?__ 52%
27. 70% __?__ 0.07
28. $\frac{1}{4}$ __?__ 0.3
29. 1.1 __?__ 100%
30. 30% __?__ $\frac{35}{100}$
31. 0.75 __?__ $\frac{3}{4}$
32. 20% __?__ $\frac{1}{10}$

Standardized Testing ▶ Free Response

1. Based on the Venn diagram, what percent of the X's are in Group A? in Group B? in both Group A and Group B?

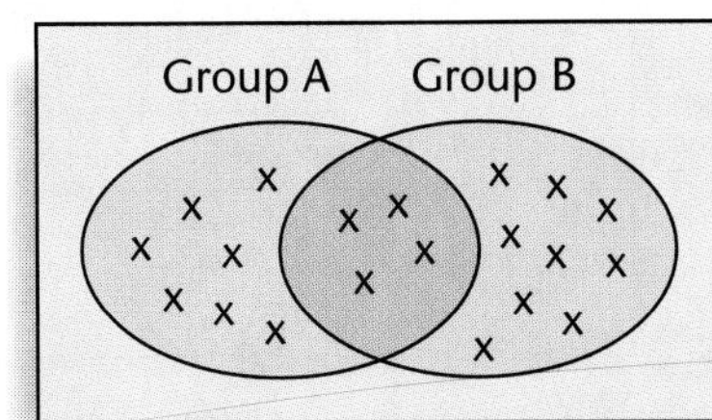

2. Draw a Venn diagram for 24 X's. Place $\frac{1}{2}$ of the X's in Group C, $\frac{2}{3}$ of the X's in Group D, and $\frac{1}{6}$ of the X's in both Group C and Group D.

Bar Graphs and Line Plots

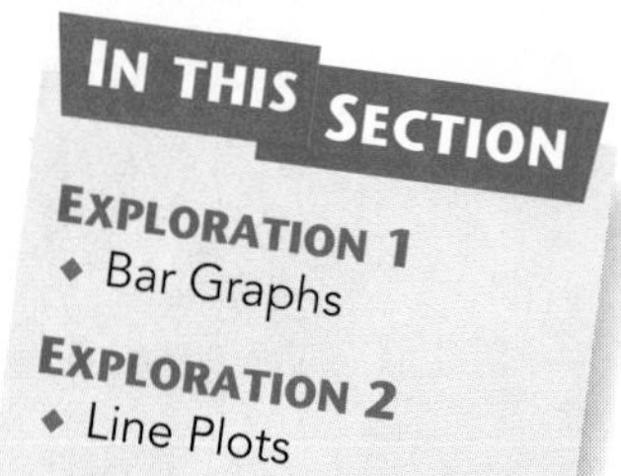

Amazing Animals

Setting the Stage

Studying data on how animals vary can help you discover more about them. One way to study data is to organize it in a visual display.

▶ **Data about animal speeds are displayed here in three different ways. One way may be more useful than another, depending on what you want to know about the data.**

Table

Maximum Speeds of Selected African Animals	
Animal	**Speed (miles per hour)**
giraffe	32
cheetah	70
elephant	25
lion	50
wildebeest	50
hyena	40
gazelle	50
zebra	40
jackal	35

Bar Graph

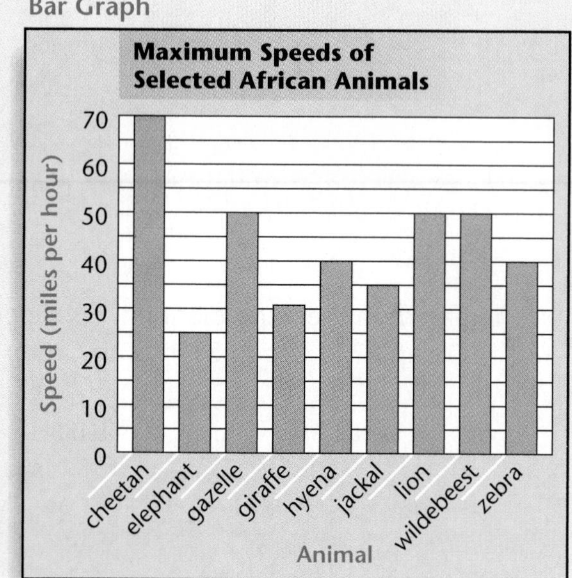

Line Plot

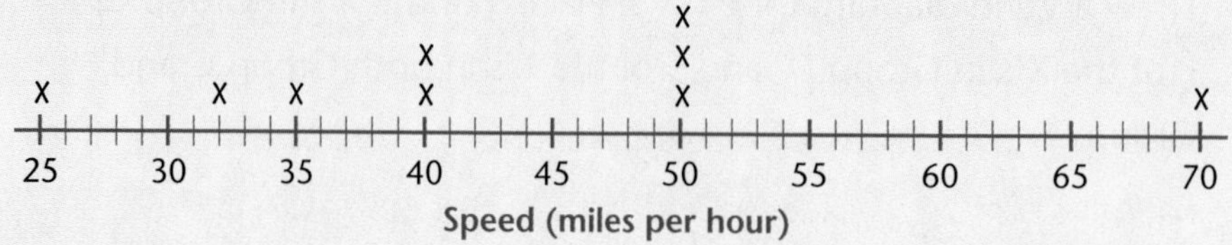

Think About It

1 Which animal is the fastest? Did you use the *table*, the *bar graph*, or the *line plot* to answer? Explain.

2 What is the most common speed? Which of the three ways of displaying the data makes it easiest to find that speed?

Exploration 1

BAR GRAPHS

SET UP *Work in a group. You will need 10 animal cards.*

GOAL

LEARN HOW TO...
- find the range of a set of data
- draw and interpret a bar graph

AS YOU...
- work with animal data

KEY TERMS
- bar graph
- range

▶ **In a bar graph you compare data by comparing the lengths of bars. A bar graph should always be clear enough that anyone can interpret it without an explanation.**

- Always include a **title**.
- The **numerical scale** can be placed at the bottom or at the side.
- The **scale numbers** should increase in equal-sized steps.

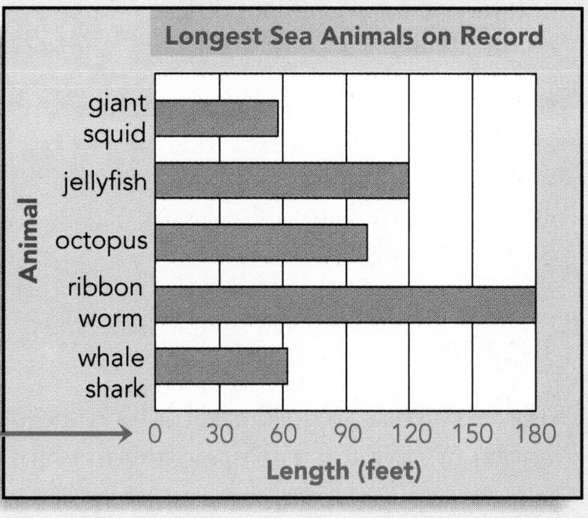

3 **Discussion** Use the bar graph above.

a. Suppose the numerical scale started with 30 instead of 0. How would the appearance of the bar graph change? Do you think this graph would be misleading? Explain.

b. Suppose the numerical scale on the bar graph used steps of 50 ft. How would this affect your ability to compare the data?

▶ **The range of a set of numerical data is the difference between the greatest and the least values.**

EXAMPLE

Find the range of the numbers 120, 180, 61, 57, and 100.

SAMPLE RESPONSE

Range = **greatest value** – **least value**
= **180** – **57**
= 123

4 How can the range of the data help you decide what size steps to use on the numerical scale of a bar graph?

✓ QUESTION 5

...checks that you can find the range of a set of data.

5 **✓ CHECKPOINT** Find the range of each set of numbers.

a. 7, 5, 1, 11, 9

b. 5.6, 12.8, 9, 25.4, 6

6 **Create Your Own** Follow the steps to make a bar graph.

Step 1 Choose five of your animal cards that use the same unit for measuring mass or the same unit for measuring length. Make a table and record the mass data or the length data.

Step 2 Write a title for your graph and label the two scales. Write the names of your animals on one scale and decide what size steps to use for the numerical scale.

Step 3 Draw the bars for your bar graph.

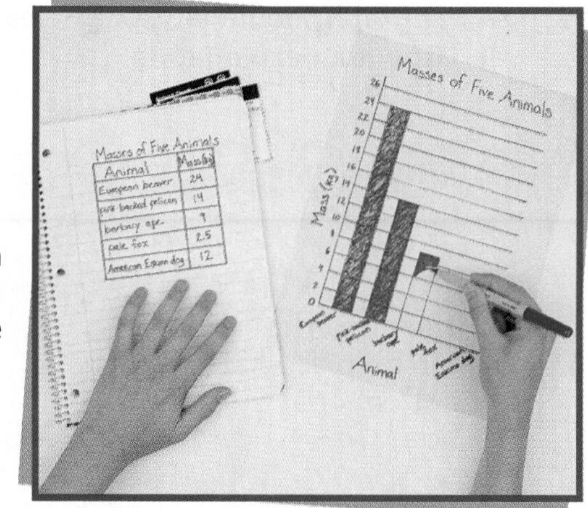

7 **Discussion** A *Stegosaurus* had a mass of about 4500 kg and a length of about 6 m. Suppose you want to add a *Stegosaurus* to your bar graph. What changes do you have to make to the setup of your graph?

✓ QUESTION 8

...checks that you can interpret a bar graph.

8 **✓ CHECKPOINT** What information does your table give you that your bar graph does not? What kinds of questions would be easier to answer by looking at your bar graph than by using your table? Explain.

HOMEWORK EXERCISES ▶ **See Exs. 1–13 on pp. 189–190.**

TECHNOLOGY Using Spreadsheet Software to Make Graphs

You can also use spreadsheet software to create your bar graph from Question 6.

Step 1 Enter the data for the graph into the spreadsheet. The data to be shown along the horizontal scale should be entered in column A and the data to be shown along the vertical scale should be entered in column B.

File Edit Format Calculate Options View

MASSES OF FIVE ANIMALS

B6 ×√ 12

	A	B	C	D	E
1	ANIMAL	MASS (KG)			
2	Beaver	24			
3	Pelican	14			
4	Ape	9			
5	Fox	2.5			
6	Eskimo dog	12			

Step 2 To create a graph, highlight the data you entered and select the option that makes a chart. Then select the type of graph you want to make.

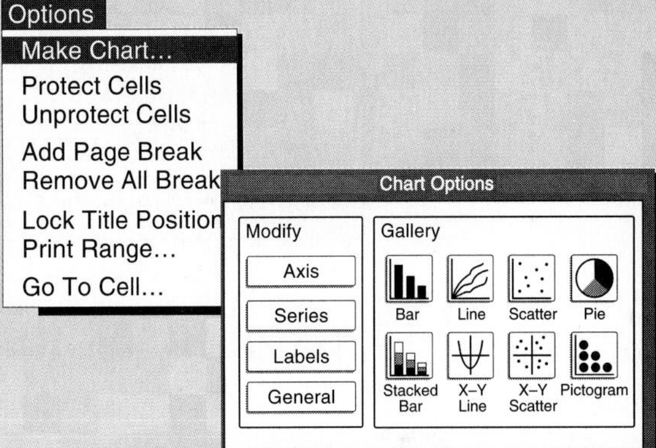

Step 3 Experiment with the labels, grid lines, and scale until the graph appears the way you want it to. Be sure to include a title.

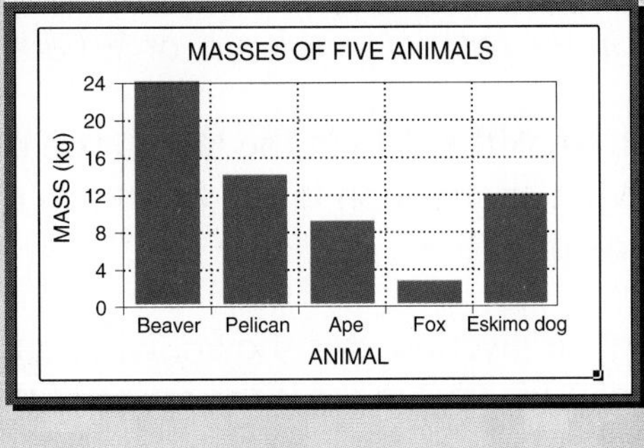

GOAL

LEARN HOW TO...
- draw and interpret a line plot

AS YOU...
- work with animal data

KEY TERM
- line plot

Exploration 2

Line Plots

▶ ***Invertebrates* are animals without backbones. They are often very small. The table and the line plot below show the lengths of five giants of the invertebrate world.**

Five Giant Invertebrates	
Animal	Length (cm)
bird-eating spider	25
African giant snail	39
tropical stick insect	33
atlas moth	28
Andaman Island centipede	33

bird-eating spider

Five Giant Invertebrates

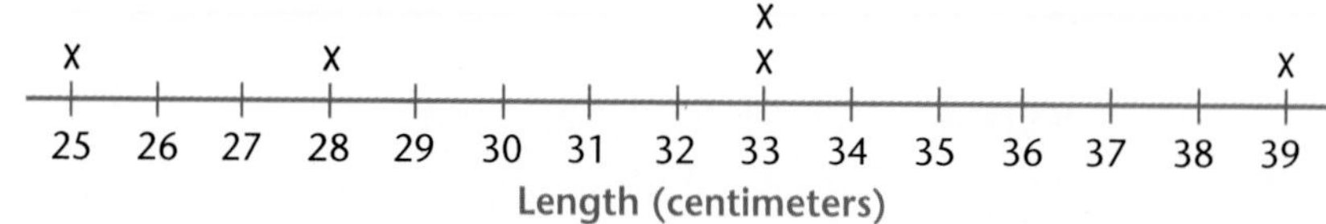

9 Suppose you pick up a bird-eating spider. Will it fit *on the tip of your finger, in the palm of your hand,* or *in both hands*?

10 How do you think the data in the table were used to draw the line plot? What information is lost when you transfer data from a table to a line plot?

11 **a.** For the giant invertebrates shown, what is the longest length? the shortest length? What is the range of the lengths?

b. Did you use the table or the line plot to find the longest and shortest lengths? Why?

12 At what numbers does the scale on the line plot above start and end? Why do you think these numbers were chosen?

▶ **Setting Up a Scale** A **line plot** displays data using a line marked with a scale. The scale must include the greatest and least values of the data.

If you make a line plot before having all your data, you may want to include some extra numbers to the left and right in case the data includes some surprisingly small or large values.

13 ✓ CHECKPOINT Use the table below.

a. Find the range of the data.

b. Make a line plot for the data.

c. What do you notice about how the data are distributed in the line plot? (*Hint:* Look for clusters of data and gaps in the data.)

Sleeping Habits of Selected Animals

Animal	Hours spent sleeping each day*
elephant	4
giraffe	4
hyena	18*
jaguar	11
lion	20*
mouse	13
okapi	5
rabbit	10
raccoon	10
squirrel	14

*Includes hours spent resting.

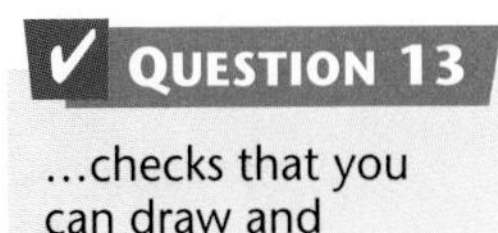

✓ QUESTION 13

...checks that you can draw and interpret a line plot.

14 Try This as a Class Use the table and your line plot to help you estimate how many hours a day each animal below sleeps. (*Hint:* Look at the clusters of animals in your line plot. Think about what each animal eats and where it sleeps.)

a. cheetah b. antelope c. beaver

HOMEWORK EXERCISES ▶ **See Exs. 14–22 on pp. 191–192.**

Section 3 Key Concepts

Key Terms

bar graph

Bar Graphs (pp. 183–185)

- A graph must include a title.
- The numerical scale must use the same size steps.
- Non-numerical information is sometimes arranged alphabetically.
- The bars can be horizontal or vertical.
- You can estimate the heights of bars that are between grid lines.

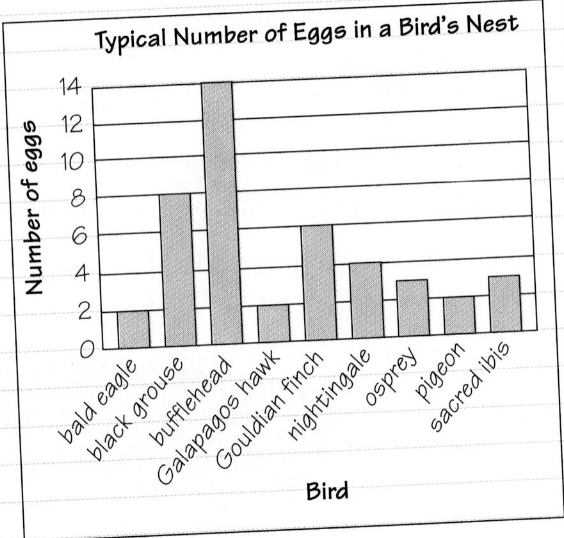

range

Range (p. 184)

The range of a collection of numerical data is the difference between the greatest and the least values.

line plot

Line Plots (pp. 186–187)

The scale must include the greatest and least values.

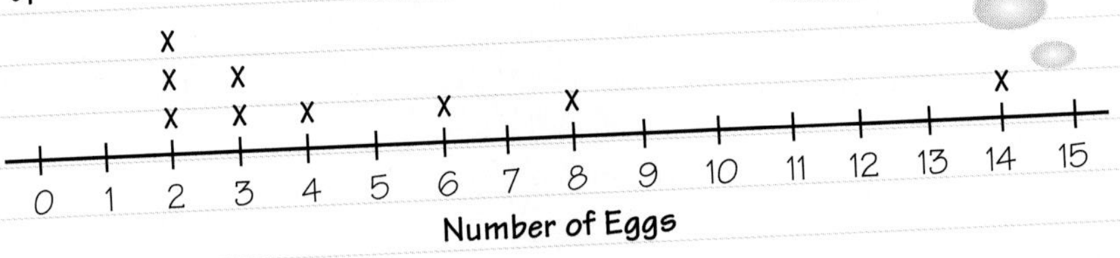

15 Key Concepts Question

a. What is the range of the typical numbers of eggs?

b. Which graph makes it easier for you to find the range? Can you find the range using the other graph? Explain.

Section 3
Practice & Application Exercises

1. Find the range of the weights shown in the table below. Then draw a bar graph to display the weight data.

Weights of Four Members of the Cat Family				
Type of cat	bobcat	ocelot	cheetah	mountain lion
Weight (pounds)	25	30	115	170

A *double bar graph* compares two related sets of data. Use the double bar graph below for Exercises 2–7.

The key shows what the two types of bars represent.

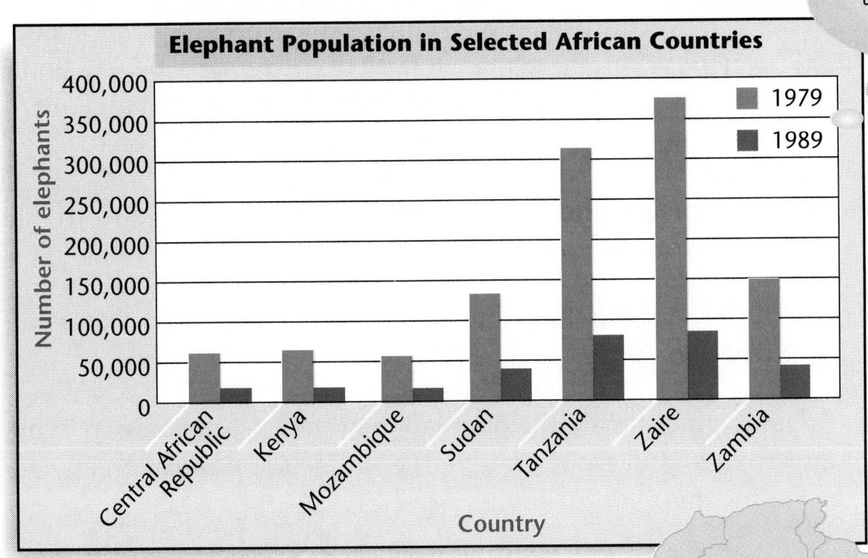

2. About how many elephants were there in Tanzania in 1979? in 1989?

3. The number of elephants in Tanzania in 1989 was about what percent of the number in 1979?

4. Which country had the most elephants in 1979?

5. Which countries had the fewest elephants in 1989?

6. Which country shows the greatest change in elephant population between 1979 and 1989? the smallest change?

7. **Interpreting Data** What story does the graph tell? How does a double bar graph help to tell this story?

SUDAN
CENTRAL AFRICAN REPUBLIC
KENYA
ZAIRE
TANZANIA
ZAMBIA
MOZAMBIQUE

Social Studies Use the table below for Exercises 8–12.

Regional Population in the United States (to the nearest thousand)				
Year	**West**	**Midwest**	**South**	**Northeast**
1950	20,190,000	44,461,000	47,197,000	39,478,000
1990	52,786,000	59,669,000	85,446,000	50,809,000

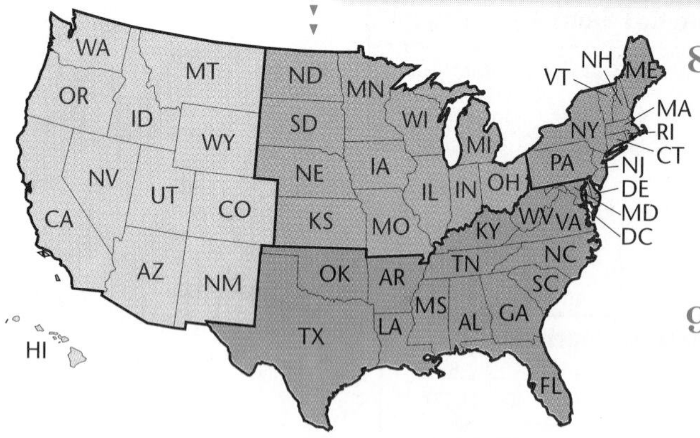

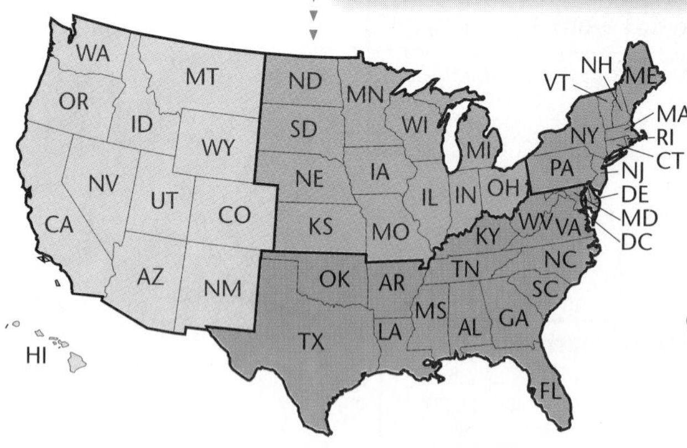

8. a. Was the population in the West in 1990 closer to 50 million or 55 million? Explain.

   b. Round each population to the nearest million.

9. Draw a double bar graph showing the population in each of the regions in 1950 and in 1990. Make each interval on the numerical scale represent 10 million people.

10. Which region had the greatest number of people in 1950? in 1990? Did you use your graph or the table to answer? Why?

11. Which region more than doubled its population during the period from 1950 to 1990?

FOR ▶ HELP with *rounding whole numbers*, see **TOOLBOX, p. 591**

12. **Estimation** Estimate the population of the United States in 1950 and in 1990. Is it easier for you to estimate the population by using the graph or the table? Why?

13. a. A ranger is responsible for keeping the populations of deer, antelope, and bison approximately equal at a wildlife reservation. Which of the graphs do you recommend the ranger put in the yearly report to the reservation directors? Why?

    b. Explain why the graphs seem to give different messages.

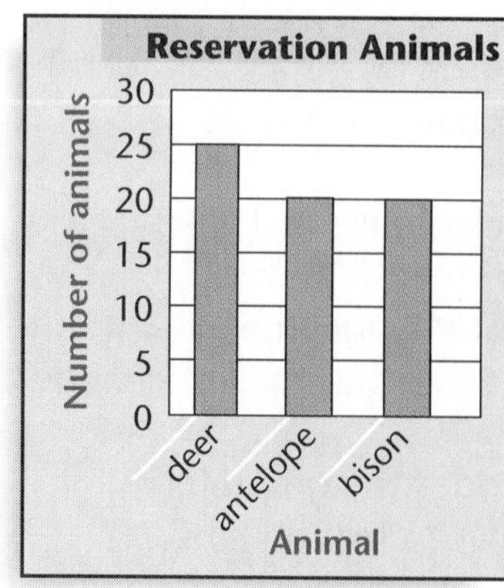

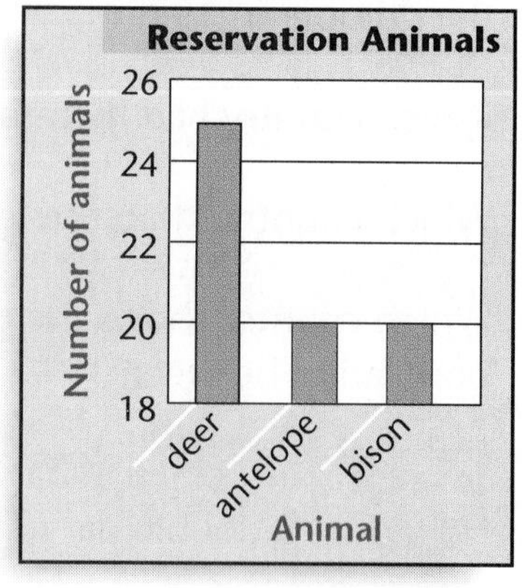

Use the line plot for Exercises 14–16.

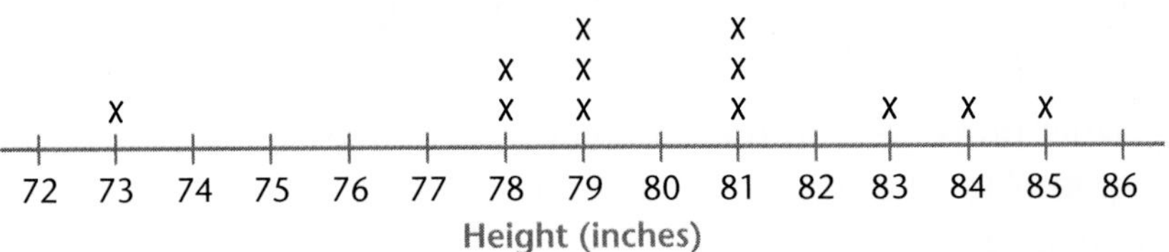

14. What is the range of the heights of the players?

15. How many players are over 78 in. tall?

16. What can you conclude about the heights of the players?

▲ The 1992 United States men's Olympic basketball team won the gold medal in Barcelona, Spain.

17. A pet store owner kept track of how long it took to sell a shipment of tropical fish. She recorded how many weeks each fish was kept before it was sold. The results were 1, 2, 3, 1, 1, 3, 5, 1, 1, 1, 2, 1, 1, 2, 6.

a. Find the range of the data.

b. Make a line plot for the data.

Use the table below to answer Exercises 18–21.

Average Life Spans									
Animal	cat	dog	goat	guinea pig	horse	pig	rabbit	sheep	white mouse
Life span (years)	12	12	8	4	20	10	5	12	3

18. Make a line plot for the data.

19. Is there an age on your line plot that has more X's than any other? If so, which age?

20. Is there an age on your line plot that has the same total number of X's to the right of it as there are to the left of it? Explain.

21. What can you conclude about the life spans of the animals?

RESEARCH

Exercise 22 checks that you can compare a bar graph with a line plot.

Reflecting on the Section

22. Look back at the graphs on page 182.

a. What type of information shows up clearly in each graph? What type of information is not shown or is difficult to see?

b. What do you see as the advantages and disadvantages of each graph? In what type of situation might each graph be most effective?

Spiral Review

Write each percent as a fraction in lowest terms. (Module 3, p. 176)

23. 50% 24. 90% 25. 75% 26. 40%

Find the value of each expression. (Module 1, p. 51)

27. $2 + 16 \div 2$ 28. $5 \cdot (12 - 7)$ 29. $27 - 10 \cdot 2$

Round each number to the given place. (Toolbox, p. 591)

30. 758 (hundreds) 31. 5405 (tens) 32. 949 (thousands)

Be a Reporter

Displaying Your Data After you collect your data, you need to show how people answered your survey questions. Visual displays can quickly help readers understand your results.

6 For each of your survey questions, decide whether a bar graph, a double bar graph, or a line plot will best represent the data you are collecting. Consider whether one type of display provides information that another does not.

7 Create your displays. Make sure that anyone looking at them can understand the results of your survey.

For Exercises 1–3, use the bar graph below.

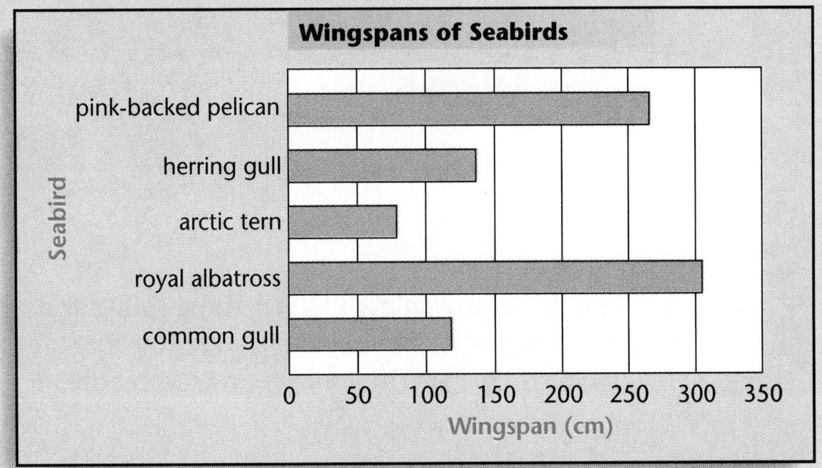

1. Which bird has the widest wingspan? the narrowest?

2. Estimate the difference between the wingspans of the gulls.

3. Estimate the range of the seabird wingspans.

For Exercises 4–5, use the line plot shown.

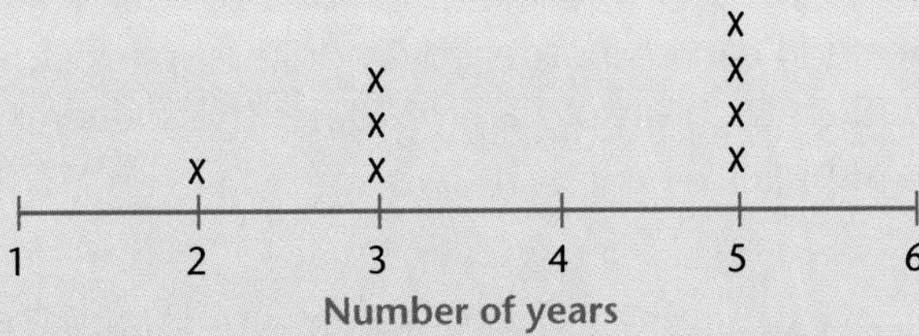

4. How many of the types of frogs live more than 3 years?

5. How many of the types of frogs live at least 2 years?

Standardized Testing ▸ Open-ended

Would you choose a line plot or a bar graph to display the daily temperatures for a month? Explain your reasoning.

FOR ASSESSMENT AND PORTFOLIOS

What a Zoo!

The Situation

It is time to order toy animals to sell in the souvenir shop at the zoo. You have been asked to help decide what toy animals to buy and how many of each to order. The table below summarizes the data on sales last year.

Animal	Numbered ordered	Number sold
lion	60	51
iguana	15	1
panda bear	80	62
tiger	15	15
seal	30	19
total	**200**	**148**

The shop can also order toy monkeys, parrots, and giraffes from the supplier. Each unsold animal costs the souvenir shop $1.00 to return to the supplier.

The Problem

Decide which toy animals the shop should sell and how many of each to order.

Something to Think About

- Based on last year's sales, are there any toy animals you should order more of? less of?
- Are there questions you would like to ask those who run the zoo that would affect what toy animals you would order?

Present Your Results

Prepare a report for the souvenir shop manager that clearly states your recommendations. Be sure to explain the mathematics and the reasoning that helped you decide.

Section 4 Mean, Median, Mode

EXPLORATION 1
- Finding Mean, Median, and Mode

EXPLORATION 2
- Appropriate Averages

Setting the Stage

In *The Phantom Tollbooth*, by Norton Juster, Milo is surprised to see what seems to be half of a child.

> "Pardon me for staring," said Milo, after he had been staring for some time, "but I've never seen half a child before."
>
> "It's .58 to be precise," replied the child from the left side of his mouth (which happened to be the only side of his mouth).
>
> "I beg your pardon?" said Milo.
>
> "It's .58," he repeated; "it's a little bit *more* than a half."
>
> "Have you always been that way?" asked Milo impatiently, for he felt that that was a needlessly fine distinction.
>
> "My goodness, no," the child assured him. "A few years ago I was just .42 and, believe me, that was terribly inconvenient."
>
> "What is the rest of your family like?" said Milo, this time a bit more sympathetically.
>
> "Oh, we're just the average family," he said thoughtfully; "mother, father, and 2.58 children—and, as I explained, I'm the .58."

Think About It

1 **a.** What do you think the word *average* means?

b. How do you think the average 2.58 was found?

2 Do you think the average number of children for families in your class is 2.58? Why or why not?

GOAL

LEARN HOW TO...
- use averages to describe data

AS YOU...
- use chips to model sheep populations

KEY TERMS
- average
- mean
- median
- mode

Exploration 1

FINDING Mean, Median, AND Mode

SET UP *Work in a group. You will need 40 chips.*

▶ **The average number of children in human families affects the population size. This is also true for animal families. When an animal population gets too large, wildlife biologists sometimes move animals to places where there is more food and space.**

Mountain region	Mount Baldy	Mount Edith	Spanish Peaks	Granite Peaks	Fog Horn Peak	Immigrant Peak	Lone Mountain	Twin Peaks	Trapper Peak	Scapegoat Mountain
Sheep population	11	6	4	13	6	8	13	17	19	13

3 **a.** Each region can support about the same number of bighorn sheep. Follow the steps below to find where a wildlife biologist should move the sheep to balance the first five populations.

First

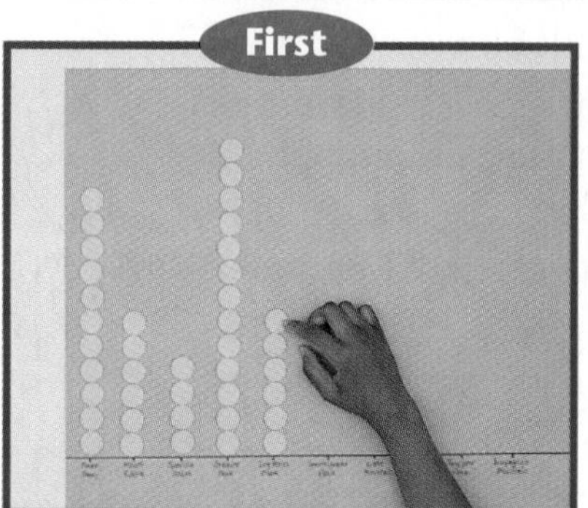

Use chips on a piece of paper to make a graph similar to a line plot of the first five sheep populations. Let each chip represent one sheep.

Then

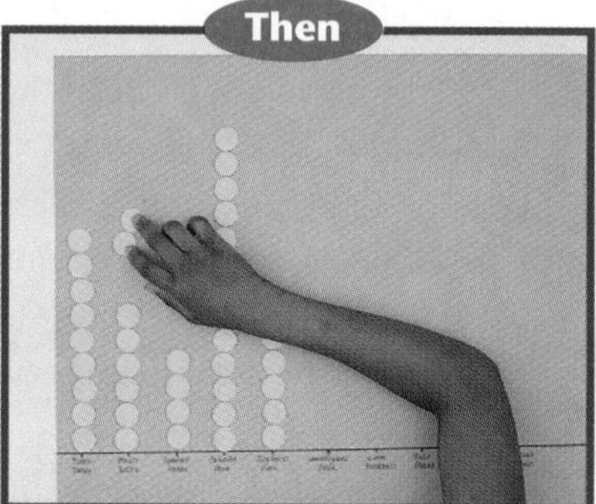

Move the chips so that each mountain region has as close to the same number of sheep as possible.

b. How many bighorn sheep will be in each region after the move?

▶ **The average you found in Question 3(b) is the mean. In this case, the mean tells you how many sheep will be in each region when the total sheep population is divided as evenly as possible among the regions.**

4 **Discussion** Suppose you want to move the sheep so that each of the ten regions has the same number of sheep.

a. How can you find the mean number of bighorn sheep without using chips?

b. What is the average number of sheep for all ten regions?

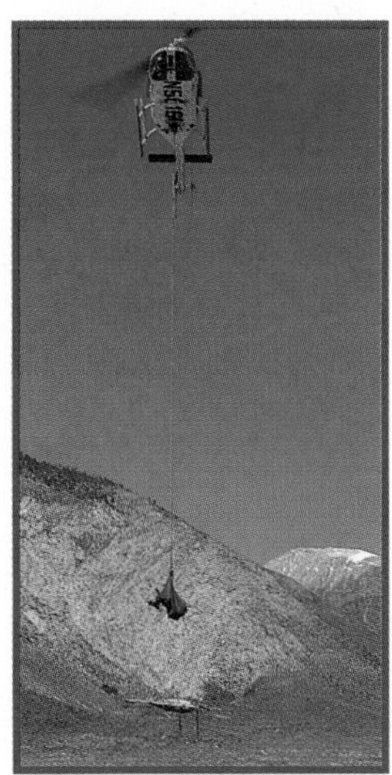

▲ Bighorn sheep are moved hanging upside down to prevent injury. It is the most humane way of moving them.

▶ **Using Other Averages The mean may not be the best number of sheep for each mountain region. A wildlife biologist may want to look at other kinds of averages.**

5 To find the best number of sheep for each region, a biologist might study the data and find the most common number of sheep in each region. According to the data in the table on page 196, what number of sheep occurs most often?

▶ **The data item or items that occur most often in a set of data is the mode. One way to find the mode is to make a line plot.**

6 **a.** Make a line plot of all ten bighorn sheep populations using X's instead of chips. Use the same size X's for each mark.

b. Using your line plot, how can you determine the mode?

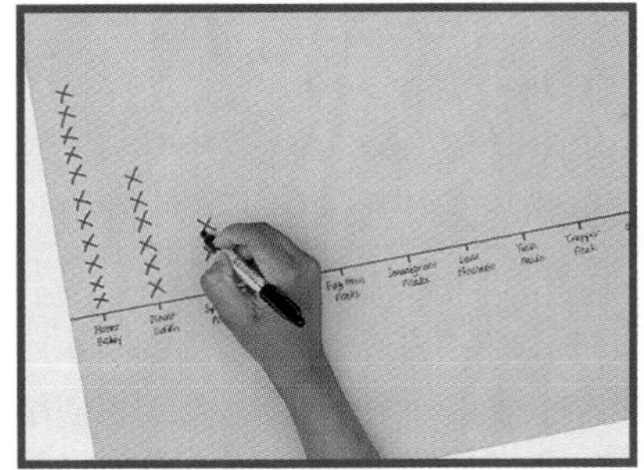

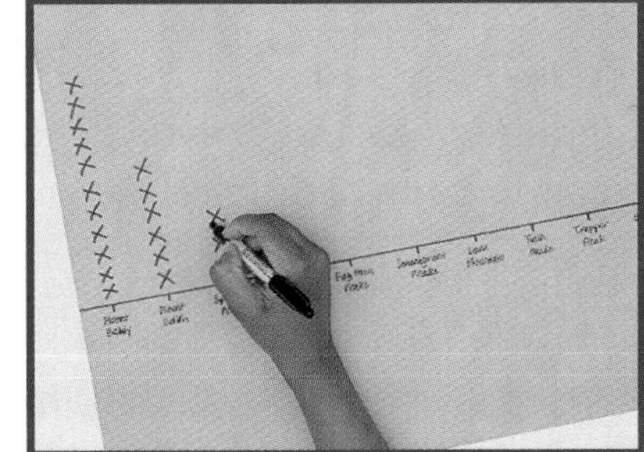

▶ **Another way to represent the sheep population data with a single number is to choose the population that is in the middle when the data are listed in numerical order.**

7 **a.** List the sheep populations from least to greatest.

b. Using your list from part (a), cross out data items two at a time so that each time you cross out the least and greatest remaining items. Describe what happens.

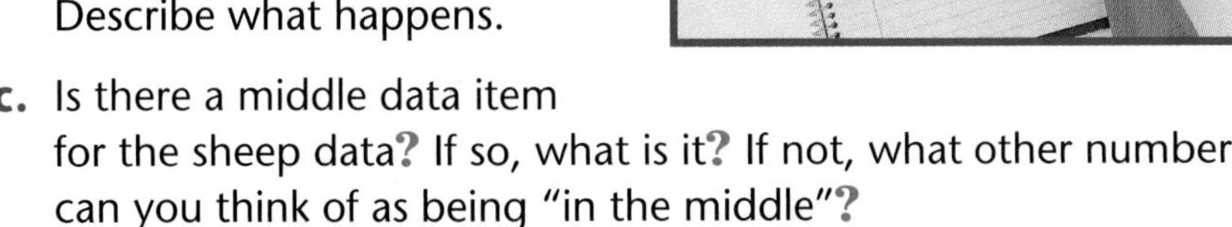

c. Is there a middle data item for the sheep data? If so, what is it? If not, what other number can you think of as being "in the middle"?

▶ **The middle item in a set of data listed in numerical order is the median. If there is no single middle item, the median is the number halfway between the two data items closest to the middle.**

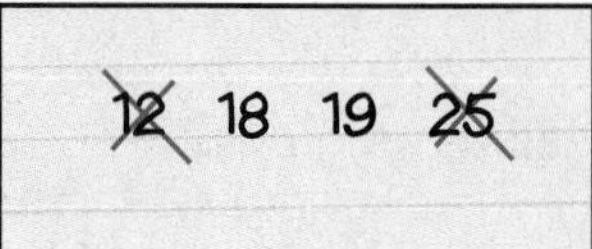

If the middle two numbers are 18 and 19, then the median is 18.5 because it is halfway between 18 and 19.

8 What is the median for the sheep data you listed in numerical order for Question 7?

EXAMPLE

Find the mean, the median, and the mode for the following data: 11, 22, 31, 22, 14.

SAMPLE RESPONSE

To find the **mean**, add the data items and then divide by the number of items.	11 + 22 + 31 + 22 + 14 = 100 100 ÷ 5 = **20**
To find the **median**, order the data from least to greatest and then find the middle value.	11, 14, **22**, 22, 31
To find the **mode**, look for the data item that appears most frequently. The mode is 22 since it appears twice and every other data item appears only once.	11, 14, **22**, **22**, 31

...checks that you can find the mean, the median, and the mode of a set of data.

9 **✓ CHECKPOINT** Most elephants live in herds that consist of many adults and their young. The number of young elephants in eight different herds is listed below. Find the mean, the median, and the mode.

27, 16, 31, 27, 11, 51, 40, 93

▲ Some herds of African elephants may have up to 1,000 members, while herds of Asiatic elephants have only 5 to 60 members.

10 **Discussion** If the average number of children in a family is 2.58, could this average be a mean? a median? a mode? Explain.

HOMEWORK EXERCISES ▶ **See Exs. 1–8 on p. 203.**

Exploration 2

Appropriate Averages

GOAL

LEARN HOW TO...
- write a fraction as a decimal using a calculator
- choose appropriate averages
- round decimal quotients

AS YOU...
- find the average number of children for different families

SET UP *You will need:* • *11 chips* • *calculator*

▶ **Since families have whole numbers of children, it may seem strange for the mean number of children to be a decimal. To see how this can happen, you'll explore the mean number of children for four families.**

Family A	Family B	Family C	Family D
2 children	0 children	1 child	0 children

11 **a.** Find the median and the mode for the data in the table.

b. What division would you have to do to find the mean?

12 Make a graph similar to a line plot using chips for the data. Can you move the chips so that each family has the same number of chips? Explain.

13 Suppose you can divide each of the three chips into four equal parts. If you move the parts so that each family has the same number, how many parts does each family get? What fraction of a whole chip does each family get?

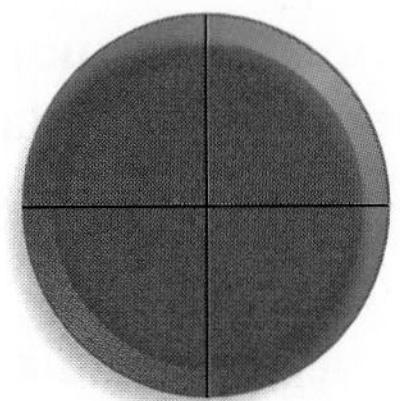

14 **Discussion** Look at your answers to Question 11(b) and Question 13.

a. What fraction does 3 ÷ 4 equal? What decimal?

b. What is the mean number of children for the families?

c. Do you think the *mean*, the *median*, or the *mode* best describes the number of children for the four families? Explain.

▶ **A fraction represents a division. In Question 13 you found that 3 chips divided by 4 equals $\frac{3}{4}$ of a chip. You can use division to write any fraction as a decimal.**

EXAMPLE

Use division to write $\frac{3}{8}$ as a decimal.

SAMPLE RESPONSE

$\frac{3}{8} = 3 \div 8.$ Use a calculator:    0.375

15 **a.** Add a Family E with 8 children to the line plot you made in Question 12.

b. Calculator If you move the chips so that each family has as close to the same number of chips as possible, how many chips are left over? What fraction of a chip should each family get? Use division to write this as a decimal.

c. Find the mean, the median, and the mode for the five families.

d. Compare the averages you found in part (c) with the averages you found in Question 11(a) and Question 14(b). Which changed the least? the most?

e. **Discussion** Which average do you think best describes the number of children for the five families?

16 Calculator Use division to write $\frac{4}{7}$ as a decimal.

▶ **Rounding** **Some quotients, like the one you found in Question 16, have many decimal places. You can round a decimal to a specific place value to make it easier to work with.**

▼ Baboons live in groups called *troops*.

17 **a.** Calculator Use a calculator to find the mean number of offspring for the three baboon troops in the table.

Baboon troop	Number of adults	Number of offspring
A	30	34
B	14	16
C	35	39

b. Is the mean closer to 29.6 or 29.7? Explain.

c. What place value was the mean in part (b) rounded to?

EXAMPLE

To the nearest hundredth, find the mean number of adults in the three troops of baboons from Question 17.

SAMPLE RESPONSE

Find the mean of 30, 14, and 35.

(30 + 14 + 35) ÷ 3 = 79 ÷ 3

You round decimals in the same way as you round whole numbers.

Look at the digit to the right of the hundredths place.

3 is less than 5, so 26.333333 is closer to 26.33 than to 26.34.

18 **Discussion** Use the Example above.

a. Why is the 3 in the thousandths place compared with 5?

b. Explain how to round 26.333333 to the nearest thousandth.

19 Round 9.84753 to the nearest thousandth.

20 ✓ **CHECKPOINT** Calculator Write each fraction as a decimal. Round your answers to the nearest hundredth.

a. $\frac{2}{3}$ **b.** $\frac{5}{9}$ **c.** $\frac{1}{7}$ **d.** $\frac{8}{5}$

✓ **QUESTION 20**

...checks that you can write fractions as decimals and can round decimals.

21 **a.** Calculator Find the mean, the median, and the modes of the data in the table. If necessary, round to the nearest hundredth.

b. Which average or averages do you think best describe the number of children in the TV families? Explain.

TV family	Number of children
Brady Bunch	6
Dr. Quinn, Medicine Woman	4
Home Improvement	3
Full House	3
Family Matters	2
Cosby Show	5
Step by Step	6

HOMEWORK EXERCISES See Exs. 9–29 on pp. 203–205.

Section 4 Key Concepts

Key Terms

average

mean

median

mode

Averages (pp. 196–198)

The mean, the median, and the mode are types of averages.

Example Data: 6, 3, 2, 4, 6, 3

Sum of data = 24
Number of items = 6
mean = 24 ÷ 6 = 4

Ordered data:
2, 3, 3, 4, 6, 6
median = (3 + 4) ÷ 2
= 3.5

2, 3, 3, 4, 6, 6
3 and 6 are the modes.

For some situations, and depending on the data, some averages may be more appropriate to use than others.

Writing a Fraction as a Decimal (pp. 199–200)

You can use division to write every fraction as a decimal.

Example $\frac{3}{7} = 3 \div 7$ which is about 0.4285714286

Rounding Decimals (pp. 200–201)

It is often helpful to round a decimal to a particular place.

Example Round 0.4285714286 to the nearest thousandth.

thousandths place

0.4285714286
↑
5 ≥ 5

0.429 ←Round the 8 up to 9.

Key Concepts Questions

22 Find five whole numbers that have a mean of 4, a median of 3, and a mode of 2.

23 Calculator Write $\frac{6}{7}$ as a decimal. Round to the nearest thousandth.

Section 4

Practice & Application Exercises

Find the mean, the median, and the mode of each data set.

1. masses of 8 butterflies (mg):
   12, 18, 15, 8, 11, 17, 18, 13

2. weights of 7 kittens (ounces):
   5, 8, 12, 4, 12, 3, 5

3. litter sizes of 10 coyotes:
   4, 6, 4, 8, 7, 6, 7, 9, 5, 4

4. lengths of 5 babies (in.):
   19, 22, 21, 20, 18

5. **Football** Ronney Jenkins rushed for 619 yd and scored 7 touchdowns in a single game. His touchdowns came on runs of 93, 84, 26, 79, 43, 87, and 15 yards. What are the mean, the median, and the mode of his touchdown runs?

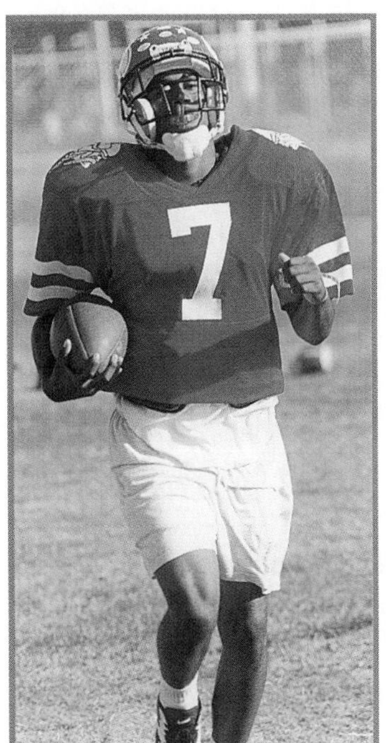

◀ In 1995, Ronney Jenkins set a new national high school football rushing record in Oxnard, California.

6. **Writing** The average depth of a local lake is reported to be 2 ft. Do you think you can wade across this lake? What information might be hidden when reporting this average?

7. **Open-ended** Find a set of six whole numbers that have a mean, a median, and a mode of 50. The numbers cannot all be the same.

8. **Challenge** The mean of nine test scores is 61.
   a. What is the sum of the scores?
   b. If a score of 100 is added to the group of scores, what is the new mean?

9. The grade book below shows Thom's scores on his quizzes. He told his mom he had an average of 92 for his quiz scores. Which average is he using? Is this an appropriate average in this case? Why?

YOU WILL NEED

For Exs. 10–17, and Ex. 26(b):
- calculator

Subject . . . STEM 6
Section . . . 3

Students	Quiz 1 (Sept. 14)	Quiz 2 (Sept. 16)	Quiz 3 (Sept. 21)	Quiz 4 (Sept. 23)	Quiz 5 (Sept. 28)	Quiz 6 (Sept. 30)	Quiz 7 (Oct. 5)	Quiz 8 (Oct. 7)
1 Thom Wilson	92	85	78	92	71	77	80	
3 Kamala Pramar	98	79	84	90	90	89	75	
5 Sarah Adams	82	84	91	92	80	80	83	

Calculator **Write each fraction in Exercises 10–17 as a decimal rounded to the nearest hundredth.**

10. $\frac{5}{8}$ 11. $\frac{8}{11}$ 12. $\frac{1}{8}$ 13. $\frac{5}{6}$

14. $\frac{4}{3}$ 15. $\frac{9}{8}$ 16. $\frac{2}{5}$ 17. $\frac{7}{4}$

18. Look at your results from Exercises 10–17. How can you tell whether a fraction is greater than or less than 1 without doing any calculations?

19. Copy the number line and mark a point for each fraction from Exercises 10–17.

Round each decimal to the given place.

20. 0.3962 (tenths)

21. 0.3962 (thousandths)

22. 13.695 (hundredths)

23. 4.346 (tenths)

24. 56.6 (ones)

25. 102.342 (hundredths)

26. **Gymnastics** Six judges each score a gymnast from 1 through 10 points. The highest and lowest scores are not used. The mean of the remaining four scores is the final score. The table shows the top women's scores for the floor exercise in the 1996 Olympic Games in Atlanta, Georgia.

GYMNAST	JUDGES' SCORES					
Dominique Dawes, USA	9.85	9.80	9.80	9.85	9.85	9.85
Lilia Podkopayeva, UKR	9.90	9.90	9.85	9.85	9.90	9.90
Simona Amonar, ROM	9.85	9.80	9.80	9.90	9.90	9.85

a. Why do you think the highest and lowest scores are not used in finding the mean?

b. Calculator Use a calculator to find the posted score for each gymnast. Round to the nearest thousandth.

c. Who won the gold medal in the floor exercise?

27. **Choosing a Method** Suppose you want to mark off 8 equal sections on a 25-inch board. Which form of the quotient 25 ÷ 8 is easiest to work with? Why?

A. 3 R1 B. 3.125 C. $3\frac{1}{8}$

28. **Research** Find information on the typical temperature in a city for each month in a year.

a. Find the mean, the median, and the mode of your data.

b. Does one average describe the temperature of the city better than another? Do you think this same type of average would best describe the temperature for a city with a different climate? Explain.

Reflecting on the Section

Be prepared to discuss your response to Exercise 29 in class.

29. The masses of six animals in a zoo are listed as 5, 8, 24, 30, 32, and 1020 kg. The zookeeper reported the average mass to be 186.5 kg. Which average did the zookeeper use? Is this average appropriate? Explain.

Discussion

Exercise 29 checks that you understand the meaning of the mean, the median, and the mode.

Spiral Review

30. Draw a bar graph to display the data. (Module 3, p. 188)

31. Use your graph from Exercise 30 to estimate the range. (Module 3, p. 188)

Item	Cost
book	$3.80
gum	$.65
pen	$1.20
card	$2.25
soap	$1.75

32. How many thousandths are in one tenth? (Module 2, p. 138)

Find each sum. (Module 2, p. 147)

33. 0.24 + 3.88 34. 5.65 + 2.25 35. 1.007 + 0.009

Divide. (Toolbox, p. 596)

36. $3\overline{)774}$ 37. $29\overline{)13079}$ 38. 415 ÷ 61

Section 4 Extra Skill Practice

You will need: • *calculator* (Exs. 16–27)

Find the mean, the median, and the mode for each set of data.

1. 10, 12, 9, 8, 15, 12
2. 4, 4, 2, 3, 4, 6, 5
3. 21, 22, 24, 23, 22, 20
4. 16, 9, 13, 9, 12, 16, 9
5. 245, 601, 322, 212
6. 1, 0, 0, 4, 5, 9, 2
7. Look back at your answers to Exercises 1–6. For each set of data, tell which average or averages you think are most appropriate to use. Explain your choices.

Round each decimal to the given place.

8. 12.457 (hundredths)
9. 5.02841 (tenths)
10. 0.5548 (tenths)
11. 2.7847 (thousandths)
12. 45.23 (ones)
13. 678.999 (hundredths)
14. 773.0008 (thousandths)
15. 21.573 (ones)

Calculator **Use division to write each fraction as a decimal. Round your answers to the nearest hundredth.**

16. $\frac{9}{48}$
17. $\frac{8}{15}$
18. $\frac{2}{9}$
19. $\frac{4}{3}$
20. $\frac{14}{9}$
21. $\frac{17}{21}$
22. $\frac{3}{10}$
23. $\frac{4}{7}$
24. $\frac{11}{12}$
25. $\frac{8}{3}$
26. $\frac{5}{7}$
27. $\frac{9}{13}$

Standardized Testing ▶ Multiple Choice

Which stacks of pennies show the mean, the median, and the mode, of the pennies in stacks a–e?

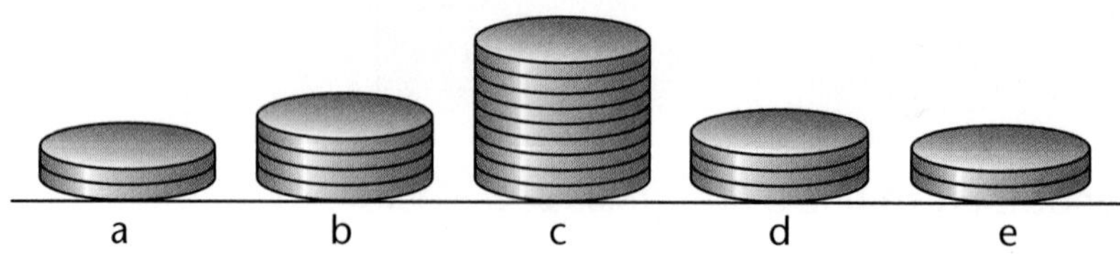

A. mean: b
median: c
mode: e

B. mean: a and e
median: d
mode: b

C. mean: b
median: d
mode: a and e

D. mean: a and e
median: c
mode: b

Dividing Decimals, Estimation, and Mental Math

IN THIS SECTION

EXPLORATION 1
- Dividing a Decimal

EXPLORATION 2
- Estimation and Mental Math

The Perfect Pet

Setting the Stage

Many famous people have had unusual animals as pets. Take the Pet Quiz below and try to match the pet to the famous person.

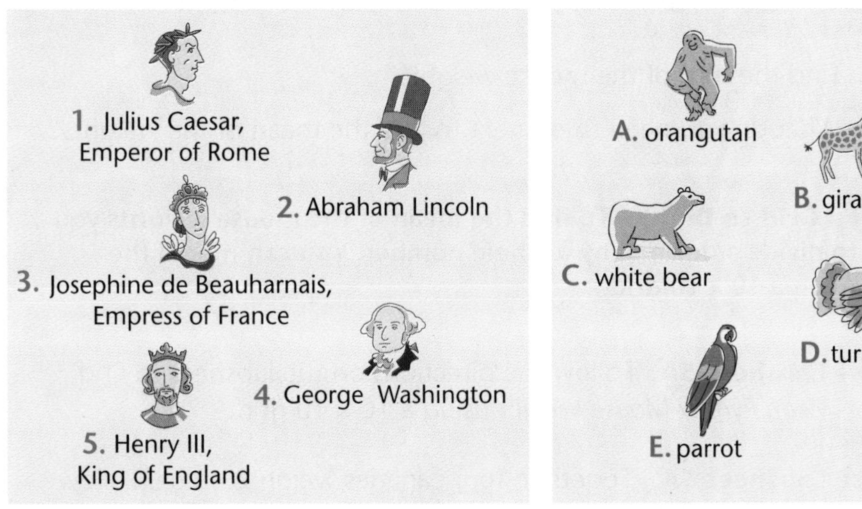

Think About It

1 How many of the five famous people did you match with the correct pet (answers are at bottom of page)? Write your answer as a percent.

2 There were about 53 million pet dogs in the United States in 1991 and 35 million households owned at least one dog. Use a calculator to find the mean number of dogs in a household. Round your answer to the nearest tenth.

▶ **Some of the most popular pets to own are dogs, cats, mice, hamsters, rabbits, snakes, lizards, fish, or birds.**

1B, 2D, 3A, 4E, 5C

GOAL

LEARN HOW TO...
- divide a decimal by a whole number

AS YOU...
- work with 10 × 10 grids

Exploration 1

Dividing).Decimals

SET UP *You will need Labsheets 5A and 5B.*

▶ **Small pets, such as mice, hamsters, or birds, can be easy to take care of and inexpensive to own. The smallest mouse is the northern pygmy mouse. The weights of three pygmy mice are shown below.**

oz is the symbol for ounce.

0.28 oz　　0.29 oz　　0.33 oz

3 **a.** Find the sum of the mouse weights.

b. What do you need to do next to find the mean of the weights?

▶ **Using a Grid to Divide** **To find the mean of the mouse weights you need to divide a decimal by a whole number. You can model the division on a 10 × 10 grid.**

4 **Use Labsheet 5A.** Follow the directions on the labsheet to find the *Mean Pygmy Mouse Weight* using a 10 × 10 grid.

5 **Use Labsheet 5A.** Together, four canaries weigh 2.40 oz. Follow the directions and use the grids on the labsheet to find the *Mean Canary Weight.*

✓ QUESTION 6

...checks that you can use grids to divide a decimal by a whole number.

6 **✓ CHECKPOINT** **Use Labsheet 5B.** Use the *Decimal Division Grids* to find the quotients 0.06 ÷ 3, 0.36 ÷ 9, and $2\overline{)1.30}$.

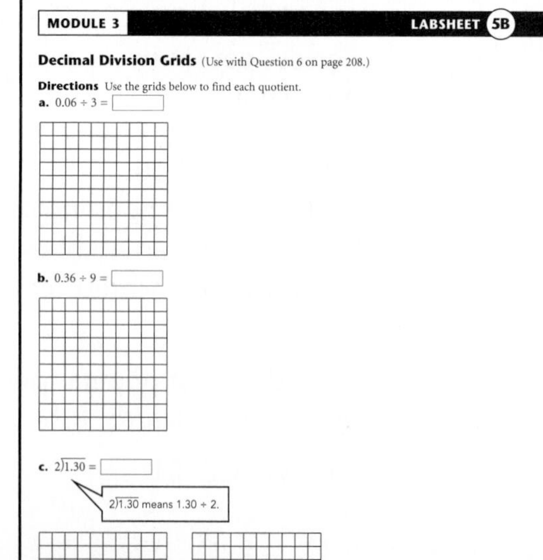
MODULE 3　　LABSHEET 5B

Decimal Division Grids (Use with Question 6 on page 208.)

Directions Use the grids below to find each quotient.

a. 0.06 ÷ 3 = ▭

b. 0.36 ÷ 9 = ▭

c. $2\overline{)1.30}$ = ▭

$2\overline{)1.30}$ means 1.30 ÷ 2.

▶ **Estimating a Quotient** **You can use compatible numbers to quickly check that a quotient seems reasonable.**

EXAMPLE

Five hamsters on a scale weigh 21.5 oz. Could the mean weight of the hamsters be 0.43 oz? Why or why not?

SAMPLE RESPONSE

Estimate 21.5 ÷ 5 to check that 0.43 is a reasonable answer.

21.5 ÷ 5 is about 20 ÷ 5.

20 ÷ 5 = 4, so the answer of 0.43 is *not* reasonable.

7 Discussion Copy each division at the right.

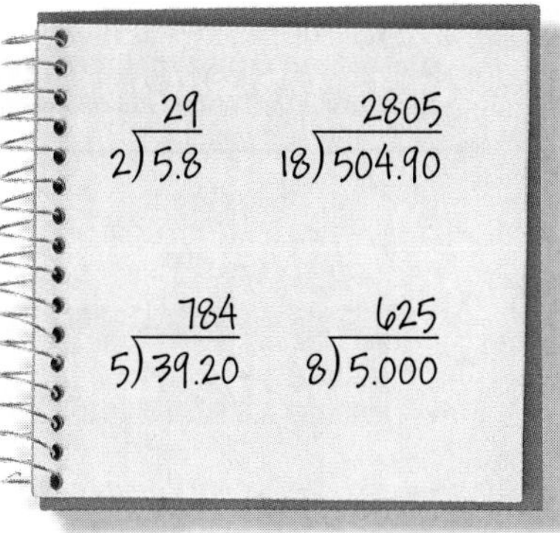

a. Use estimation to place the decimal point in the quotient. Explain your reasoning.

b. How do you think the numbers in each quotient in part (a) were determined?

c. Look at the position of the decimal points in each quotient and dividend you wrote in part (a). How can you place the decimal point without estimating?

8 ✓ CHECKPOINT Find each quotient. Estimate to check that each answer seems reasonable.

a. $3\overline{)106.23}$ **b.** 3.78 ÷ 14 **c.** $5\overline{)258.65}$

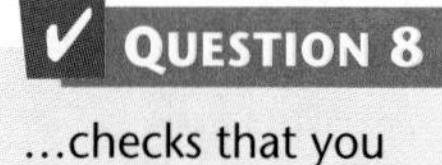

...checks that you can divide a decimal by a whole number.

▶ **Remainders Sometimes a division has a remainder. For these divisions, you have to write zeros to the right of the decimal point in the dividend to continue to divide.**

EXAMPLE

```
   2.5           2.52             2.525
8)20.2        8)20.20          8)20.200
 -16           -16              -16
   42            42               42
  -40           -40              -40
    2             20               20
(remainder)      -16              -16
                   4               40
                                  -40
                                    0
```

write a **zero**

write another **zero**

9 Try This as a Class

a. Divide 15 by 4.

b. How is 15 related to 15.0 and 15.00?

c. In part (a), how did you know when to write another zero and when to stop?

✓ QUESTION 10

...checks that you can write zeros in a dividend when finding a quotient.

10 ✓ CHECKPOINT Find each quotient. Use estimation to check that each quotient seems reasonable.

a. $29.2 \div 8$ b. $6\overline{)7.05}$ c. $4\overline{)21.25}$ d. $\frac{12}{5}$

HOMEWORK EXERCISES ▶ See Exs. 1–16 on pp. 214.

GOAL

LEARN HOW TO...
- use estimation and mental math strategies

AS YOU...
- find average weights for different pets

KEY TERMS
- front-end estimation
- trading off

Exploration 2

Estimation and Mental Math

▶ **Large and unusual animals were kept as pets by powerful and wealthy people long ago. Even though most pets today are cats and dogs, these pets can sometimes grow surprisingly large.**

Charlemagne, the emperor of France in the 8th and 9th centuries, had a pet named Abul Abba—a pet elephant!

11 Most domestic cats weigh between 6 lb and 15 lb. Find the mean of the four cat weights below.

6.69 lb 7.56 lb 8.50 lb 9.31 lb

▶ **Using Estimation** **Suppose you want to estimate the total weight of the four cats. One way to estimate a sum is to use *front-end estimation.* Front-end estimation focuses on the *front-end,* or left-most digits, since they have the greatest value.**

EXAMPLE

Use front-end estimation to estimate the sum of 2.56, 3.42, 7.78, and 5.30.

SAMPLE RESPONSE

First Add the front-end digits.

$$\begin{array}{r} 2.56 \\ 3.42 \\ 7.78 \\ +\ 5.30 \\ \hline \end{array}$$

$2 + 3 + 7 + 5 = 17$

The sum is more than 17.

Next Look at what is left.

$$\left.\begin{array}{r} .56 \\ .42 \end{array}\right\} \text{about } 1 \qquad \left.\begin{array}{r} .78 \\ +\ .30 \end{array}\right\} \text{about } 1$$

About 2 more.

Then Adjust your first estimate. $17 + 2 = 19$

The sum is about 19.

12 Use front-end estimation to estimate the sum of the weights of the four cats from Question 11. Use the sum to estimate the mean weight.

13 **Discussion** The world's fattest cat is owned by Paul Kragh of Denmark. Paul's cat weighs 38.58 lb!

a. How do you think adding the weight of a fifth cat, the world's fattest cat, would affect the mean weight in Question 12?

◀ The world's fattest cat maintains his figure by eating almost $4\frac{1}{2}$ lb of raw cod each day.

b. Use front-end estimation to estimate the mean of the five cat weights.

c. Do you think the mean is an appropriate average to use when you have one data value that is very different from the rest of the data? Why?

✔ QUESTION 14

... checks that you can use front-end estimation to estimate a sum.

14 ✔ CHECKPOINT Use front-end estimation to estimate each sum.

a. 543 + 29 + 634 + 997

b. 2.21 + 3.05 + 1.3

c. 24 + 72 + 66 + 13 + 5

d. 35.2 + 71.8 + 15.4

▶ **Using Mental Math** **One way to find a sum using mental math is by trading off.**

EXAMPLE

Use trading off to find the sum of the following Golden Retriever weights: 57 lb and 68 lb.

SAMPLE RESPONSE

Add 3 to 57 to make it a round 60.

$$\begin{array}{r} 57 \\ +\ 68 \\ \hline \end{array} \quad \begin{array}{c} \xrightarrow{+3} \\ \xrightarrow{-3} \end{array} \quad \begin{array}{r} 60 \\ +\ 65 \\ \hline 125 \end{array}$$

Subtract 3 to make up for adding 3.

15 One of the heaviest breeds of dogs is the St. Bernard. Use trading off to find the sum of the following St. Bernard weights.

166 lb   184 lb

✔ QUESTION 16

... checks that you can use trading off to find a sum.

16 ✔ CHECKPOINT Use trading off to find each sum.

a. $\begin{array}{r} 121 \\ +\ 99 \\ \hline \end{array}$

b. $\begin{array}{r} 4.76 \\ +\ 2.49 \\ \hline \end{array}$

c. $\begin{array}{r} 53 \\ 75 \\ +\ 97 \\ \hline \end{array}$

17 The Chihuahua is the smallest breed of dog. Without doing any written calculations, tell whether the *mean*, the *median*, or the *mode* is the best average to use to describe the Chihuahua weights below. Explain your choice.

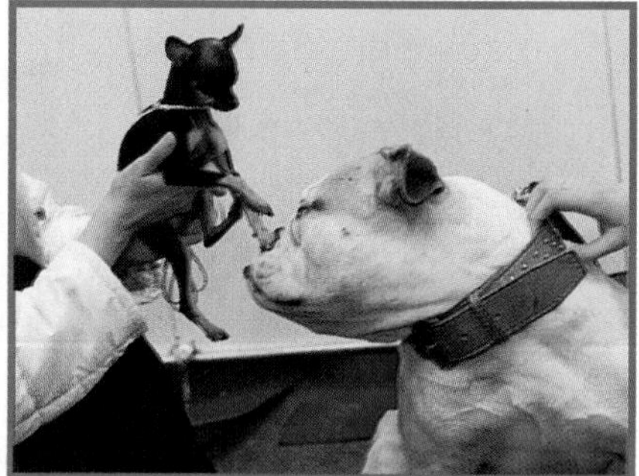

Weights of seven Chihuahuas:
1.9 lb, 2.0 lb, 2.1 lb, 2.4 lb, 5.1 lb, 6.0 lb, 6.0 lb

HOMEWORK EXERCISES ▶ See Exs. 17–33 on pp. 214–216.

Section 5

Key Concepts

Key Terms

Dividing a Decimal by a Whole Number (pp. 208–210)

Divide as though both numbers were whole numbers.

$4\overline{)0.6}$

Write the decimal point in the quotient directly above the decimal point in the dividend.

$$\begin{array}{r} 0.15 \\ 4\overline{)0.60} \\ \underline{4} \\ 20 \\ \underline{20} \\ 0 \end{array}$$

← Write a zero to the right of the dividend when the division does not come out evenly.

Front-end Estimation (pp. 211–212)

front-end estimation

Front-end estimation focuses on the left-most digits for a first estimate. The other digits help you adjust the estimate.

Example

The sum is greater than 300.

35 + 78 is about 100.

$$\begin{array}{r} 135 \\ +\ 278 \\ \hline \end{array}$$

So 135 + 278 is about 400.

Trading Off (p. 212)

trading off

One way to find a sum using mental math is by trading off.

Example Find 1.95 + 2.37.

$$\begin{array}{r} 1.95 \\ +\ 2.37 \\ \hline \end{array} \xrightarrow{+0.05} \begin{array}{r} 2.00 \\ 2.37 \\ \hline \end{array}$$

Add 0.05 to 1.95 to make it a round 2.00.

4.37 − 0.05 = 4.32 Subtract 0.05 to make up for what you added.

Key Concepts Question

18 **a.** Use front-end estimation to estimate the mean of 7.28, 8.4, and 8.2.

b. Use trading off to help find the exact mean of 7.28, 8.4, and 8.2. How close was your estimate in part (a)?

Section 5 Practice & Application Exercises

Estimation **Use compatible numbers to check the position of the decimal point in each quotient. If a quotient is incorrect, give the correct quotient.**

1. $4\overline{)783.2}$ with quotient 19.58
2. $20\overline{)41}$ with quotient 2.05
3. $7\overline{)21.14}$ with quotient 30.2

4. After traveling for 4 days, Brianna's odometer read 994.8 miles. What is the mean distance she drove each day?

Find each quotient. Use estimation to check that each quotient seems reasonable.

5. $6\overline{)0.48}$
6. $8\overline{)4.976}$
7. $13.08 \div 12$
8. $124.5 \div 6$
9. $37.3 \div 4$
10. $11\overline{)215.6}$

11. **Geometry Connection** The perimeter of a square is 5.23 cm. Find the length of one side.

12. The Pentagon Building is one of the largest office buildings in the world. Its outermost wall is in the shape of a regular pentagon with a perimeter of about 1.6 km. How many *meters* long is one side of the Pentagon?

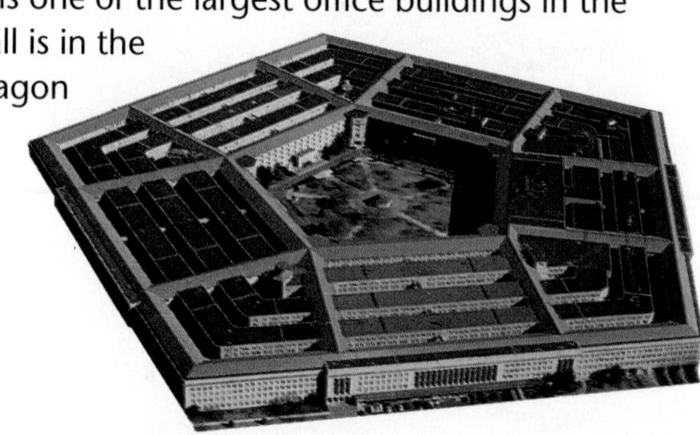

► The Pentagon Building, in Arlington, Virginia, is the headquarters for the Department of Defense of the United States government.

Choosing a Method **Use a calculator, pencil and paper, or mental math to write each fraction as a decimal.**

13. $\frac{7}{8}$
14. $\frac{12}{200}$
15. $\frac{9}{5}$
16. $\frac{756}{1000}$

Estimation **Use front-end estimation to estimate each sum.**

17. 1324 + 2235
18. 13.2 + 17.4 + 24.2
19. 312 + 560 + 125
20. 12 + 84 + 73 + 56

Mental Math **Use trading off to find each sum.**

21. 36 + 48
22. 0.24 + 0.31
23. 79 + 36
24. 3.4 + 5.8
25. 18 + 23 + 37
26. $1.26 + $2.69

Writing In a cricket-jumping contest, the cricket with the greatest mean for two jumps wins. Amber can enter only one cricket, so she conducted eight trial jumps with her two crickets. Use the results in the table to answer Exercises 27–29.

27. Which cricket do you think Amber should enter in the contest? Why do you think so?

28. Amber found out that one of her competitors has a cricket that almost always jumps 20 cm. Which of Amber's crickets may have a better chance of beating this competitor? Why?

29. If one of the competitors enters a cricket that almost always jumps 24 cm, which cricket should Amber enter? Why?

Cricket Jumps (cm)	
Cricket 1 (Dasher)	Cricket 2 (Mercury)
18.7	26.0
21	9.1
22.0	14.0
20.3	20.3
21.6	19.9
20.1	18.0
21.6	28.1
20.9	26.0

Estimation The male populations in the table all *cluster* around the value 1,800,000. You can estimate the sum of the populations by multiplying 1,800,000 by 3.

Population in the United States in 1991		
Age	Male	Female
11	1,875,000	1,786,000
12	1,783,000	1,701,000
13	1,746,000	1,668,000

30. Use clustering to estimate the total population of males 11–13 years old.

31. What number do the female populations (ages 11–13) cluster around? Estimate the total population of females 11–13 years old in the table. Explain how you made your estimate.

Survey of six people's favorite kind of nut:

almond, cashew
almond, walnut
pecan, almond

32. **Challenge** Would you use the *mean*, the *median*, or the *mode* to describe this set of data? Explain your choice.

Visual THINKING

Exercise 33 checks that you can divide a decimal by a whole number.

Reflecting on the Section

33. Travis used a 10×10 grid to show $0.17 \div 2$.

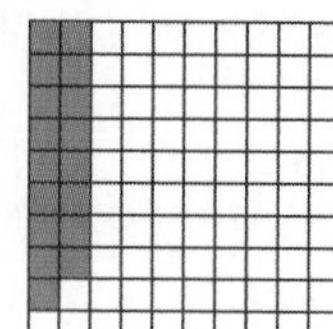

a. Divide: $2\overline{)0.17}$

b. What decimal represents one half of a grid square?

c. Explain how to use Travis's grid model to find $0.17 \div 2$.

Spiral Review

Round each decimal to the given place. (Module 3, p. 202)

34. 64.37 (ones)

35. 13.403 (hundredths)

36. 2.97 (tenths)

37. 0.3611 (thousandths)

Which combinations of side lengths can form a triangle? Explain your reasoning. (Module 1, p. 22)

38. 2 in., 6 in., 7 in.

39. 5 cm, 8 cm, 3 cm

40. 20 ft, 35 ft, 13 ft

41. 1 m, 0.7 m, 0.4 m

Find each value. (Module 3, p. 176)

42. $\frac{3}{5}$ of 35

43. $\frac{9}{10}$ of 80

44. $\frac{7}{8}$ of 24

Be a Reporter

Choosing an Average Sometimes a single number can give readers a good idea of what a set of data is like. Now you'll look closely at the information you have collected and choose one or more averages to summarize and describe your data.

Find the mean, the median, and the mode for the results of each of your survey questions.

Think about which average gives the clearest idea of your data for each of your survey questions. Write a paragraph describing your survey results. Be sure to include each of the averages you chose.

Section 5
Extra Skill Practice

Find each quotient. Use estimation to check that each quotient seems reasonable.

1. $5\overline{)0.45}$
2. $8\overline{)97.68}$
3. $12.46 \div 2$
4. $110.4 \div 6$
5. $9\overline{)31.086}$
6. $12\overline{)64.8}$
7. $3\overline{)12.045}$
8. $394.24 \div 4$
9. $124.607 \div 7$

Tell whether the quotient is correct in each division. If a quotient is not correct, give the correct quotient.

10. $\begin{array}{r} 20.685 \\ 2\overline{)53.7} \end{array}$
11. $\begin{array}{r} 72.2 \\ 3\overline{)21.66} \end{array}$
12. $\begin{array}{r} 57.25 \\ 8\overline{)458} \end{array}$
13. $\begin{array}{r} 52 \\ 11\overline{)57.2} \end{array}$
14. $\begin{array}{r} 149.3 \\ 6\overline{)895.8} \end{array}$
15. $\begin{array}{r} 57.96 \\ 14\overline{)825.44} \end{array}$

Estimation **Use front-end estimation to estimate each sum.**

16. 2130 + 1225 + 1410
17. 2.6 + 3.7 + 1.2 + 4.3
18. 12.42 + 10.53 + 7.08
19. 210 + 150 + 140 + 305
20. 5.7 + 2.3 + 3.2 + 0.2
21. 81 + 48 + 23 + 52 + 12

Mental Math **Use trading off to find each sum.**

22. 24 + 68
23. 0.72 + 0.31
24. 98 + 207
25. 3.6 + 2.3
26. 71 + 33 + 48
27. 1.4 + 1.7 + 3.6
28. 21.2 + 32.4 + 11.7
29. 86 + 42 + 58
30. 0.12 + 0.28 + 0.3

Standardized Testing ▶ Multiple Choice

1. Raymond buys 5 quarts of punch for his party for a total of $7.25. Including Raymond, there are 8 people at the party. How many quarts of punch are there for each person?

   A 1.45 B 0.625 C 0.906 D 1.6

2. Which division is *not* correct?

   A $\begin{array}{r} 1.79 \\ 3\overline{)5.37} \end{array}$ B $\begin{array}{r} 1.4 \\ 4\overline{)5.6} \end{array}$ C $\begin{array}{r} 20.25 \\ 4\overline{)81} \end{array}$ D $\begin{array}{r} 321.25 \\ 8\overline{)257} \end{array}$

Stem-and-Leaf Plots and Dividing by a Decimal

EXPLORATION 1
- Stem-and-Leaf Plots

EXPLORATION 2
- Dividing by a Decimal

DINOSAURS

Setting the Stage

Tyrannosaurus rex

predator (meat-eater)

A *Tyrannosaurus rex* could eat a lot at once and then not eat for days. An 8-ton *Tyrannosaurus rex* needed to eat a mean of 186 lb of meat per day and could eat about 2 tons of meat at a sitting!

length: 40 feet **weight:** 4–8 tons

Euoplocephalus

(you-op-loh-**SEF**-ah-lus)
plant-eater

A *Euoplocephalus* was one of the slowest dinosaurs. Its defense against predators was the bony armor along its back, head, and neck. It also had a huge club at the end of its tail.

length: 18 feet **weight:** 3 tons

Think About It

1 What animal living today do you think might be as long as a *Euoplocephalus*? What animal might be as heavy?

2 **Estimation** If an 8-ton *Tyrannosaurus rex* ate 2 tons of meat, in about how many days did it need to eat again? (1 ton = 2000 lb)

Exploration 1

Stem-and-Leaf Plots

GOAL

LEARN HOW TO...
- make and interpret a stem-and-leaf plot

AS YOU...
- compare dinosaur data

KEY TERM
- stem-and-leaf plot

SET UP *You will need Labsheet 6A.*

▶ **A *Euoplocephalus* seems large compared with animals alive today, but how did it compare with other plant-eating dinosaurs? Because the sizes of dinosaurs were spread over a wide range, an average size may not tell you much. Instead, it may be more useful to make a stem-and-leaf plot.**

Some Plant-Eating Dinosaurs	
Dinosaur	Length (feet)
Anatosaurus	40
Ankylosaurus	25
Centrosaurus	20
Chasmosaurus	16
Corythosaurus	33
Edmontonia	23
Edmontosaurus	43
Euoplocephalus	**18**
Hadrosaurus	33
Pachyrhinosaurus	20
Panoplosaurus	23
Parasaurolophus	33
Parksosaurus	7
Sauropelta	25
Styracosaurus	18
Tenontosaurus	24
Torosaurus	20
Triceratops	30

Title

Lengths of Some Plant-Eating Dinosaurs

```
0 | 7
1 | 6 8 8
2 | 0 0 0 3 3 4 5 5
3 | 0 3 3 3
4 | 0 3

  1 | 8 → means 18 ft
```

The stems are listed in order from least to greatest.

The leaf of each data value is written to the right of its stem.

This row contains the lengths 30 ft, 33 ft, 33 ft, and 33 ft.

A vertical line separates the stems from the leaves.

Key

3 **Discussion** Use the stem-and-leaf plot above.

a. Explain what "4|03" means.

b. How many of the plant-eating dinosaurs were 18 ft long?

c. Why do you think the numbers 0 through 4 were used as the stems in the stem-and-leaf plot?

d. Was the *Euoplocephalus* long or short compared with the other plant-eating dinosaurs in the table? Explain.

4 **a.** Were the answers to parts (b) and (d) of Question 3 easier to determine from the table or from the stem-and-leaf plot? Explain.

b. What information from the table do you lose by showing the data in a stem-and-leaf plot?

Use Labsheet 6A for Questions 5 and 6.

5 **Try This as a Class** Follow the directions on the labsheet to complete the stem-and-leaf plot for the *Weights of Plant-Eating Dinosaurs.*

6 Look at your stem-and-leaf plot from Question 5.

a. Why is there no leaf for the stem 1?

b. What are the modes of the plant-eating dinosaur weights? What is the median?

c. How did the weight of a *Euoplocephalus* compare with the weights of the other plant-eating dinosaurs in the table?

d. How are the stem-and-leaf plots for the weights and lengths of the plant-eating dinosaurs similar? How are they different?

▶ **A stem-and-leaf plot can also be used to compare the lengths of predatory dinosaurs with the lengths of the plant-eating dinosaurs they ate.**

✓ QUESTION 7

...checks that you can make and interpret a stem-and-leaf plot.

7 **✓ CHECKPOINT** Make a stem-and-leaf plot for the lengths of the predatory dinosaurs in the table.

a. How did an 18-foot-long *Euoplocephalus* compare in length with the predatory dinosaurs?

b. Use your stem-and-leaf plot and the one on page 219. How did the lengths of the plant-eating dinosaurs compare with the lengths of the predatory dinosaurs?

Some Predatory Dinosaurs

Dinosaur	Length (feet)
Albertosaurus	26
Allosaurus	35
Chirostenotes	7
Daspletosaurus	30
Deinonychus	13
Dromaeosaurus	6
Dromiceiomimus	11
Microvenator	4
Nanotyrannous	17
Ornithomimus	13
Struthiomimus	13
Troödon	8
Tyrannosaurus rex	40
Velociraptor	7

HOMEWORK EXERCISES ▶ See Exs. 1–12 on pp. 224–225.

Exploration 2

Dividing by a Decimal

GOAL

LEARN HOW TO...
- divide by a decimal

AS YOU...
- explore the feeding habits of predatory dinosaurs

SET UP *You will need Labsheet 6B.*

Some scientists believe that dinosaurs ate, slept, and moved more like birds than like lizards. Assuming that is true, scientists can calculate how much and how often dinosaurs ate.

▶ **A 6-kilogram *Microvenator* needed to eat about 0.4 kg of meat a day. Suppose the animals it hunted had a mass of about 0.05 kg each.**

8 What would you need to do to find out how many animals a *Microvenator* needed to catch each day?

Use Labsheet 6B for Questions 9 and 10.

9 Follow the directions on the labsheet to model the division 0.4 ÷ 0.05 on the *Animal Division Grid*.

10 ✓ **CHECKPOINT** Use the *Division Grids* to find 0.60 ÷ 0.15, 0.28 ÷ 0.04, and $0.9\overline{)0.45}$.

...checks that you can use a grid to divide by a decimal.

11 **Discussion** Look for a pattern in the divisions.

divisor — dividend

$6\overline{)12}$ $\quad$ $18\overline{)36}$ $\quad$ $60\overline{)120}$ $\quad$ $600\overline{)1200}$

a. How is the divisor of 6 in the first division related to each of the other divisors? How is the dividend of 12 related to each of the other dividends?

b. Write another division problem that has the same divisor and dividend relationship with the first division.

c. Find all five quotients. What do you notice about them?

d. What happens to a quotient when you multiply the dividend and the divisor by the same number?

▶ **In Section 5 you divided a decimal by a whole number. You can use this skill and the pattern you found in Question 11 to divide a decimal or a whole number by a decimal.**

12 A 68-kilogram *Deinonychus* needed to eat a mean of about 2.6 kg of meat per day. Suppose a *Deinonychus* ate 12.48 kg of a *Hadrosaurus* all at once. To find out in how many days it needed to eat again, you can do this division:

$$2.6\overline{)12.48}$$

a. What can 2.6 be multiplied by to make it a whole number?

b. If you multiply the divisor by the number you found in part (a), what must you do to the dividend to keep the quotient from changing?

c. Rewrite the division by performing the operations described in parts (a) and (b). Then find the quotient. In how many days did the *Deinonychus* need to eat again?

13 **Discussion** To find the quotient $0.25\overline{)28}$, Roland rewrote the division as $25\overline{)280}$. Is this correct? Explain.

✓ QUESTION 14

...checks that you can divide by a decimal.

14 **✓ CHECKPOINT** Find each quotient.

a. $0.9\overline{)0.072}$ **b.** $0.426 \div 0.12$ **c.** $2.4\overline{)9}$

15 A *Velociraptor* had a mass of about 70 kg and ate about one fourth of its own body weight of meat at one sitting.

a. How much would a *Velociraptor* eat at one sitting?

b. Suppose a pack of *Velociraptors* hunted a 448-kilogram *Tenontosaur*. About how many *Velociraptors* could the *Tenontosaur* feed?

HOMEWORK EXERCISES ▶ **See Exs. 13–26 on pp. 225–226.**

Section 6 Key Concepts

Key Term

stem-and-leaf plot

Stem-and-Leaf Plots (pp. 219–220)

One way to compare data is to make a stem-and-leaf plot.

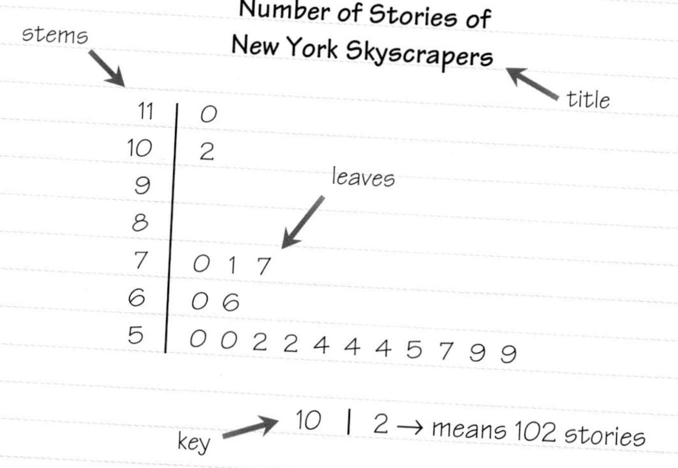

Dividing by a Decimal (pp. 221–222)

Example Find $0.8\overline{)0.052}$.

$0.8\overline{)0.052}$ ×10 ×10

Multiply both numbers by a number that makes the divisor a whole number.

$8\overline{)0.520}$ (write a zero)

Divide as you divide whole numbers.

$\begin{array}{r} 0.065 \\ 8\overline{)0.520} \end{array}$ (write 0 for $8\overline{)5}$)

Place the decimal point in the quotient directly above the decimal point in the dividend.

Key Concepts Questions

16 **a.** What is the range of the skyscraper data?

b. What is the median of the data? What is the mode?

17 Show the steps in the Example. How do you know when the division is complete?

Section 6

Practice & Application Exercises

For Exercises 1–3, use the stem-and-leaf plot showing the science quiz scores for one class.

1. What was the low score in the class? the high score?

2. How many students scored in the 70s?

3. Find the mean, the median, and the mode of the scores.

Science Quiz Scores

Stem	Leaves
6	2
7	2 3 5 8
8	2 6 6 6 9
9	4 6 8
10	0

8 | 2 represents a score of 82

Use the table and the partially completed stem-and-leaf plot to answer Exercises 4–8.

Small and Medium-Sized Predatory Dinosaurs		
Dinosaur	Mass (kg)	Meat consumption (kg per day)
Chirostenotes	50	2.1
Deinonychus	68	2.6
Dromaeosaurus	45	1.9
Dromiceiomimus	144	4.6
Microvenator	6	0.4
Ornithomimus	153	4.8
Struthiomimus	150	4.7
Troödon	50	2.1
Velociraptor	73	2.7

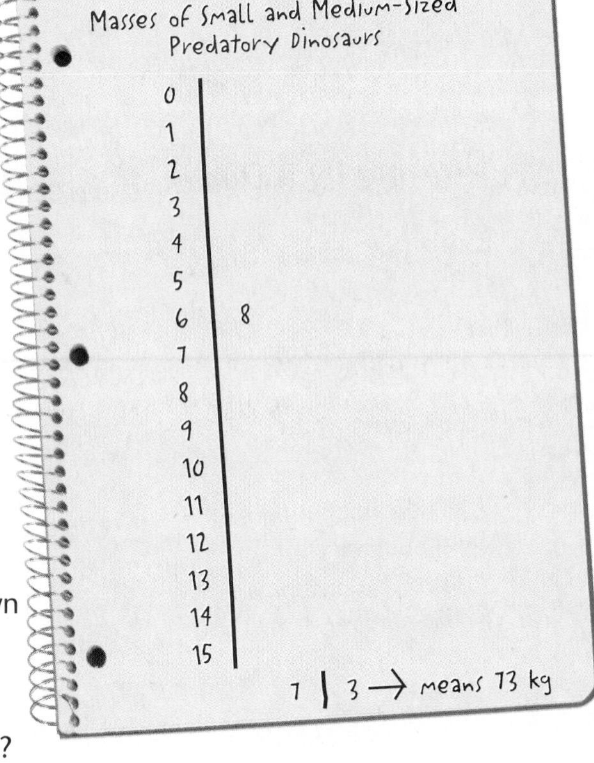

4. Which dinosaur's mass is shown in the stem-and-leaf plot?

5. Why were the numbers 0 through 15 used for the stems?

6. Copy and complete the stem-and-leaf plot.

7. Make a stem-and-leaf plot for the meat consumption of the dinosaurs.

8. **Writing** Compare your stem-and-leaf plots from Exercises 6 and 7. Do they have the same gaps or clusters of data? Explain why you think the plots are alike or different.

Choosing a Data Display **Use the stem-and-leaf plot or the bar graph to answer Exercises 9–12. For each question, tell which display you used and why.**

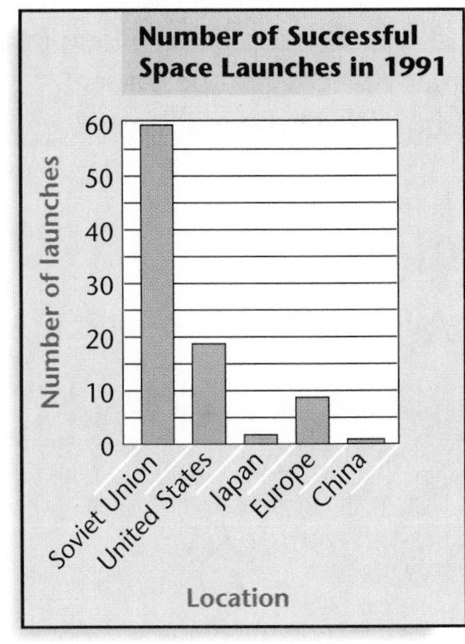

Number of Successful Space Launches in 1991

Stem	Leaf
0	1 2 8
1	8
2	
3	
4	
5	9

1 | 8 → means 18 launches

◄ The Chinese Long March 2 being launched to release a satellite.

9. Which location had 18 space launches in 1991?

10. What was the greatest number of launches for a location?

11. Which location had the least number of space launches?

12. What was the total number of space launches in 1991?

Find each quotient. Show your work.

13. $0.07\overline{)4.2}$
14. $3\overline{)0.06}$
15. $0.3\overline{)0.84}$
16. $0.5\overline{)0.356}$
17. $2.4\overline{)45}$
18. $0.8\overline{)4.9}$
19. $0.002\overline{)0.571}$
20. $7.5\overline{)16.2}$
21. $6.25\overline{)5.6375}$

22. Apples are on sale for \$.48 per pound. How many pounds of apples can you buy for \$3?

23. The height of a tree is 542.85 cm. In a photograph of the tree, the height is only 0.7 cm. The tree's actual height is how many times as large as its height in the photo?

24. **Running** In 1988, Belayneh Densimo of Ethiopia ran a marathon (26.2 mi) in Rotterdam in a record 126.8 min. Find his mean time for a mile. Round your answer to the nearest tenth.

25. **Challenge** A carpenter is cutting a board that is 3.75 m long into pieces that are 0.3 m long. How many pieces can the carpenter cut from the board? How long is the leftover piece of board?

Journal

Exercise 26 checks that you can interpret a stem-and-leaf plot and can divide by a decimal.

Reflecting on the Section

Write your response to Exercise 26 in your journal.

Weights of Selected Newborns

Stem	Leaves
6	3 4
7	2 2 4
8	0 3
9	2

7 | 2 → means 7.2 lb

Weights of Selected 1-Year-Olds

Stem	Leaves
1	7 8 8 8 9
2	3 5
3	0

2 | 3 → means 23 lb

26. Use the stem-and-leaf plots above.
   a. Find the mean weight for newborns and for 1-year-olds.
   b. A 1-year-old is about how many times as heavy as a newborn? (Use the mean weights from part (a).)
   c. Can you tell what the 1-year-old weight is for a 9.2 lb newborn? Explain.

Spiral Review

Estimation **Use front-end estimation to estimate each sum.** (Module 3, p. 213)

27. 1250 + 3782 28. 16.7 + 4.8 + 5.4 29. 820 + 345 + 521

Is each figure a polygon? If not, explain why not. (Module 2, p. 87)

30. 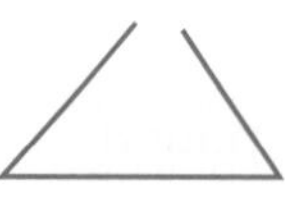
31. 
32. 
33. 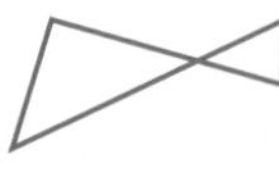

Write each fraction as a percent. (Module 3, p. 176)

34. $\frac{4}{5}$ 35. $\frac{6}{20}$ 36. $\frac{1}{4}$ 37. $\frac{3}{25}$

Extension 

Back-to-Back Stem-and-Leaf Plots

You can use a *back-to-back stem-and-leaf plot* to compare two related sets of data.

Olympic 100-Meter Dash Winning Times 1956–1992 (to the nearest tenth of a second)

Men		Women
9 9	9	
5 3 2 1 1 0 0 0	10	5 8
	11	0 0 0 1 1 1 4 5

means 10.0 seconds for men ← 0 | 10 | 5 → means 10.5 seconds for women

38. What is the fastest time for a man? for a woman?

39. Find the mean, the median, and the modes for each set of data.

40. What time did both a man and a woman get?

41. Why does a back-to-back stem-and-leaf plot make it easy to compare the data sets?

Career Connection

Publisher: Lizette Cruz-Watko

Newspaper publishers like Lizette Cruz-Watko use a unit called a *column inch* to measure the height and width of newspaper text. In Lizette's newspaper one column inch is 2.065 in. wide. Blank space is left between column inches.

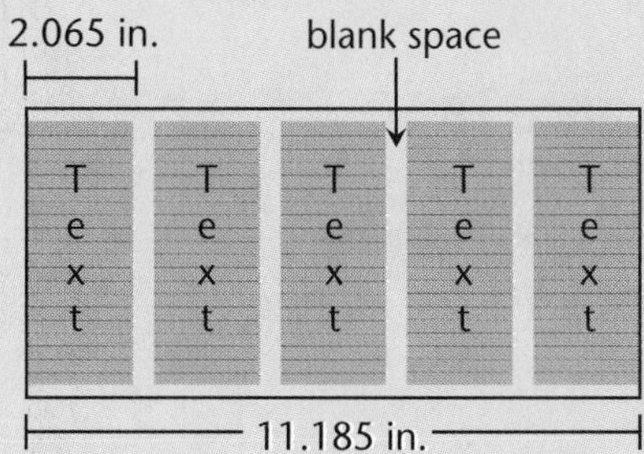

▲ Lizette Cruz-Watko launched North Carolina's first Spanish-language newspaper, *La Voz de Carolina.*

42. Lizette's newspaper is 11.185 in. wide and 5 column inches across as shown above. How many inches are left for the blank space between the columns of text?

43. Use your answer to Exercise 42 to find how many inches apart the columns of text are in the newspaper.

Section 6
Extra Skill Practice

For Exercises 1–4, use the stem-and-leaf plot below.

Mark's Social Studies Test Scores

Stem	Leaves
7	7 9 9
8	0 0 3 3 3 7 7 8 9
9	2 4 4 6
10	0

9 | 2 → means a score of 92

1. What is Mark's lowest score?

2. What is his highest score?

3. On how many tests did Mark score an 80?

4. Find the mean, the median, and the mode of Mark's scores.

Find each quotient.

5. $0.2\overline{)3.4}$
6. $0.05\overline{)11.25}$
7. $1.8\overline{)6.12}$
8. $0.3\overline{)1.29}$
9. $0.009\overline{)0.108}$
10. $7.5\overline{)70.125}$
11. $1.6\overline{)7.68}$
12. $6.12\overline{)34.884}$
13. $0.021\overline{)0.1953}$
14. $0.08\overline{)5.6}$
15. $3.4\overline{)153.68}$
16. $2.75\overline{)8.9375}$

Standardized Testing ▶ Performance Task

Explain why the quotient is always greater than the dividend when the divisor is between 0 and 1. Include at least one example in your explanation.

Quotient is greater than dividend.

Divisor is between 0 and 1.) Dividend is positive.

Be a Reporter

Summarizing Your Results Besides gathering data, a newspaper reporter must also present data to readers. Newspaper articles often have visual displays as well as a written summary of the results of a survey.

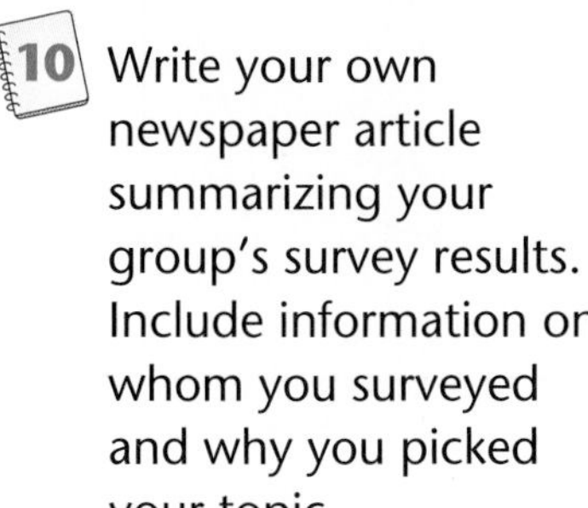

10 Write your own newspaper article summarizing your group's survey results. Include information on whom you surveyed and why you picked your topic.

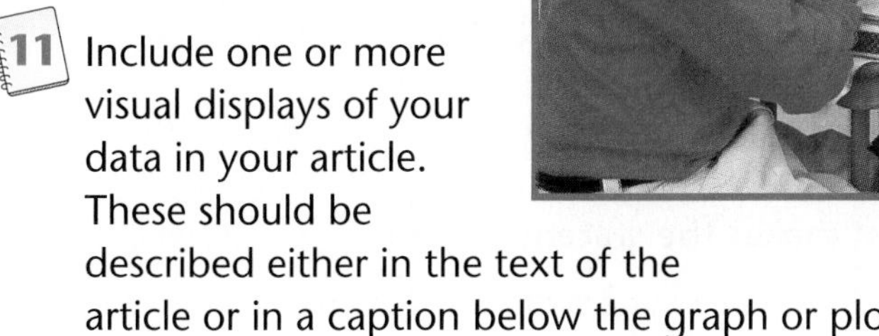

11 Include one or more visual displays of your data in your article. These should be described either in the text of the article or in a caption below the graph or plot.

12 Write a headline for your article. It should catch your readers' interest and describe what the article is about.

13 Read your entire newspaper article. Make sure it is clear and accurately represents the data you collected.

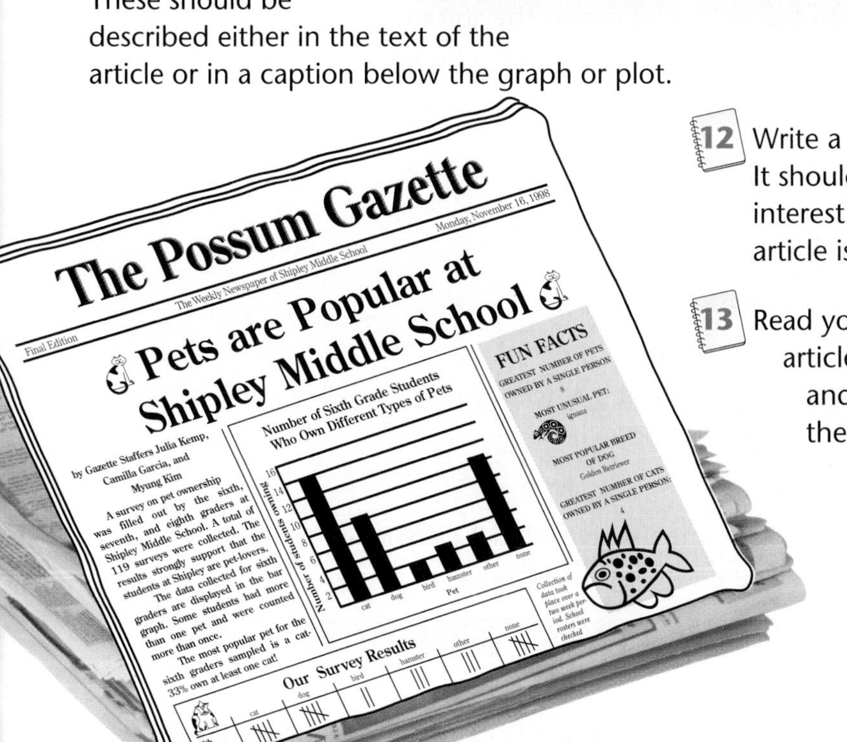

The Possum Gazette

The Weekly Newspaper of Shipley Middle School

Final Edition — Monday, November 16, 1998

Pets are Popular at Shipley Middle School

by Gazette Staffers Julia Kemp, Camilla Garcia, and Myung Kim

A survey on pet ownership was filled out by the sixth, seventh, and eighth graders at Shipley Middle School. A total of 119 surveys were collected. The results strongly support that the students at Shipley are pet-lovers.

The data collected for sixth graders are displayed in the bar graph. Some students had more than one pet and were counted more than once.

The most popular pet for the sixth graders sampled is a cat-33% own at least one cat!

FUN FACTS

GREATEST NUMBER OF PETS OWNED BY A SINGLE PERSON: 8

MOST UNUSUAL PET: iguana

MOST POPULAR BREED OF DOG: Golden Retriever

GREATEST NUMBER OF CATS OWNED BY A SINGLE PERSON: 4

Our Survey Results

	cat	dog	bird	hamster	other	none
6th graders	𝍸	𝍸	II	III	III	𝍸

Collection of data took place over a two week period. School rosters were checked

MODULE 3 Review and Assessment

Use the Venn diagram to answer Exercises 1–3. (Sec. 1, Explor. 1)

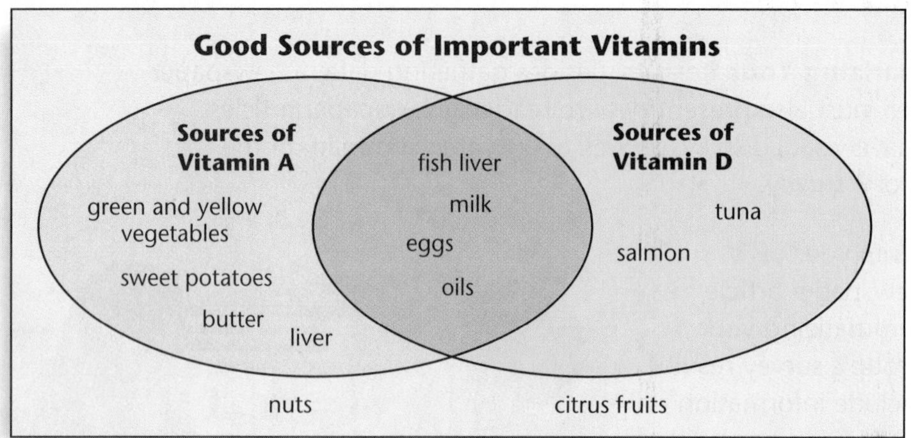

1. Which foods are good sources of vitamin A?

2. How many foods are good sources of vitamins A and D?

3. Why are nuts and citrus fruits outside of the sets?

Replace each ? with the value that makes the statement true. (Sec. 1, Explor. 3)

4. 8 km = ___?___ m

5. 2.3 cm = ___?___ mm

6. 1300 mg = ___?___ g

7. 4 metric tons = ___?___ kg

8. 5 m = ___?___ cm

9. 2.3 kg = ___?___ g

Find each value. (Sec. 2, Explor. 1)

10. $\frac{3}{7}$ of 21

11. $\frac{5}{6}$ of 24

12. $\frac{2}{5}$ of 125

13. $\frac{7}{9}$ of 63

Write each fraction as a decimal and as a percent. (Sec. 2, Explor. 2)

14. $\frac{3}{5}$

15. $\frac{64}{200}$

16. $\frac{9}{20}$

17. $\frac{207}{300}$

18. Make a bar graph and a line plot for the data in the table. Which display includes more information? Explain. (Sec. 3, Explor. 1 and 2)

Typical Monthly Rainfall in Seattle, WA (rounded to the nearest inch)												
Month	Jan.	Feb.	Mar.	Apr.	May	June	July	Aug.	Sept.	Oct.	Nov.	Dec.
Inches of rain	6	4	4	2	2	1	1	1	2	3	6	6

19. Find the mean, the median, and the mode for the rainfall data on page 230. Round your answers to the nearest tenth if necessary. (Sec. 4, Explor. 1 and 2)

Find each quotient. (Sec. 5, Explor. 1)

20. $6\overline{)21.03}$
21. $8\overline{)156.2}$
22. $18\overline{)354.69}$
23. $\frac{5}{8}$
24. $\frac{15}{4}$
25. $\frac{8}{22}$

Estimation Use front-end estimation to estimate each sum. (Sec. 5, Explor. 2)

26. 146 + 609 + 234
27. \$15.13 + \$24.49
28. 3.3 + 8.15 + 6.65

Mental Math Use trading off to find each sum. (Sec. 5, Explor. 2)

29. 23 + 79
30. 1.06 + 4.98
31. 0.75 + 0.24 + 0.86

Use the stem-and-leaf plot below to answer Exercises 32–34. (Sec. 6, Explor. 1)

Copperhead Snake Lengths

Stem	Leaves
6	1 5 5
7	2 7 7 7 9
8	0 1 6 6 6
9	0 0 1

7 | 2 → means 72 cm

32. What is the length of the longest copperhead snake in the stem-and-leaf plot?

33. What is the range of the snake lengths?

34. Find the median and the mode of the snake lengths.

Find each quotient. (Sec. 6, Explor. 2)

35. $25.4\overline{)1653.54}$
36. $7.6\overline{)48.944}$
37. $2.55\overline{)3.06}$

Reflecting on the Module

38. **Choosing a Method** In this module you have used estimation, mental math, paper and pencil, and a calculator to solve problems. For what types of situations would you use mental math? estimation? When might you want to use paper and pencil instead of a calculator? Explain.

MODULE 4

MIND GAMES

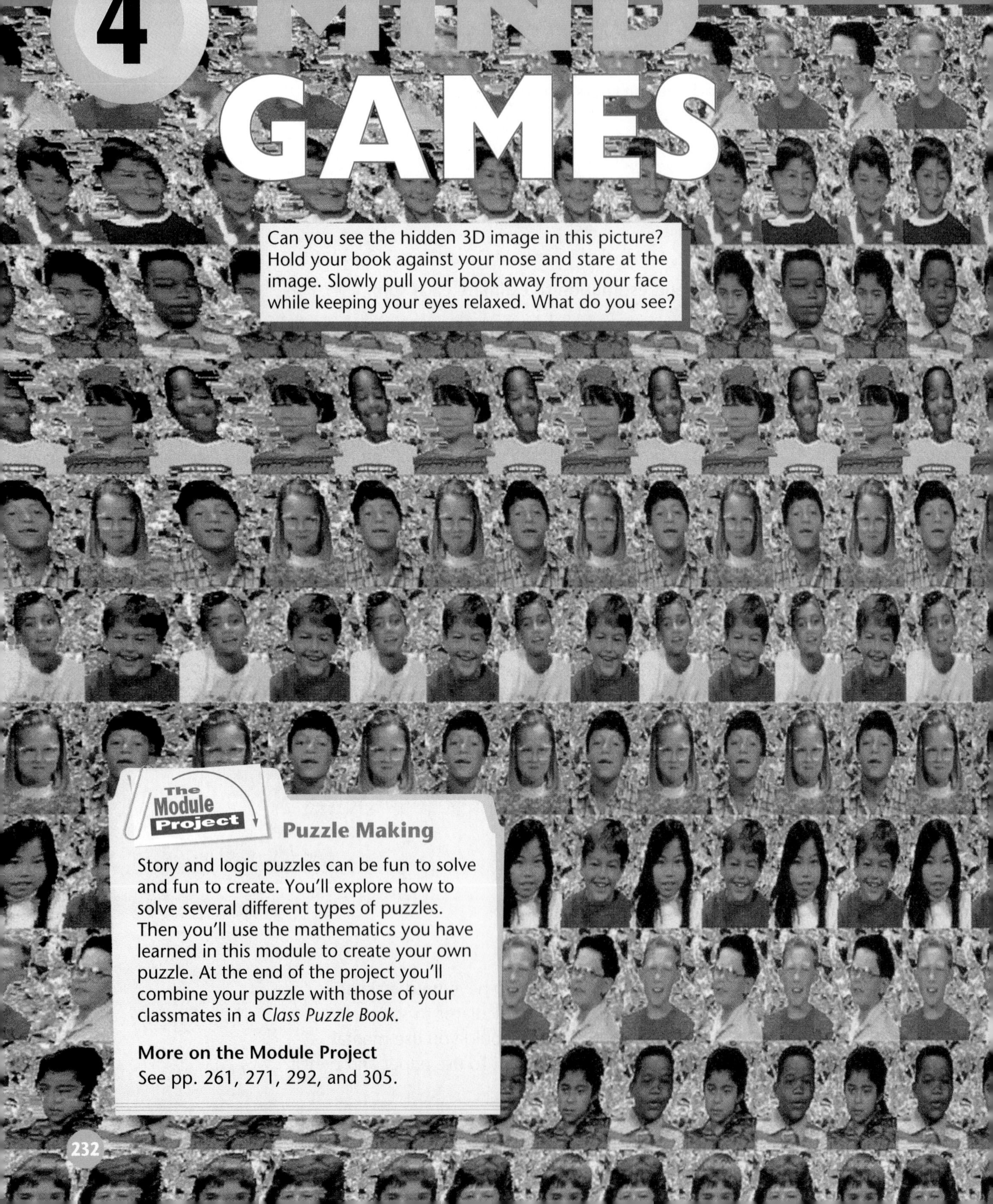

Can you see the hidden 3D image in this picture? Hold your book against your nose and stare at the image. Slowly pull your book away from your face while keeping your eyes relaxed. What do you see?

The Module Project

Puzzle Making

Story and logic puzzles can be fun to solve and fun to create. You'll explore how to solve several different types of puzzles. Then you'll use the mathematics you have learned in this module to create your own puzzle. At the end of the project you'll combine your puzzle with those of your classmates in a *Class Puzzle Book*.

More on the Module Project

See pp. 261, 271, 292, and 305.

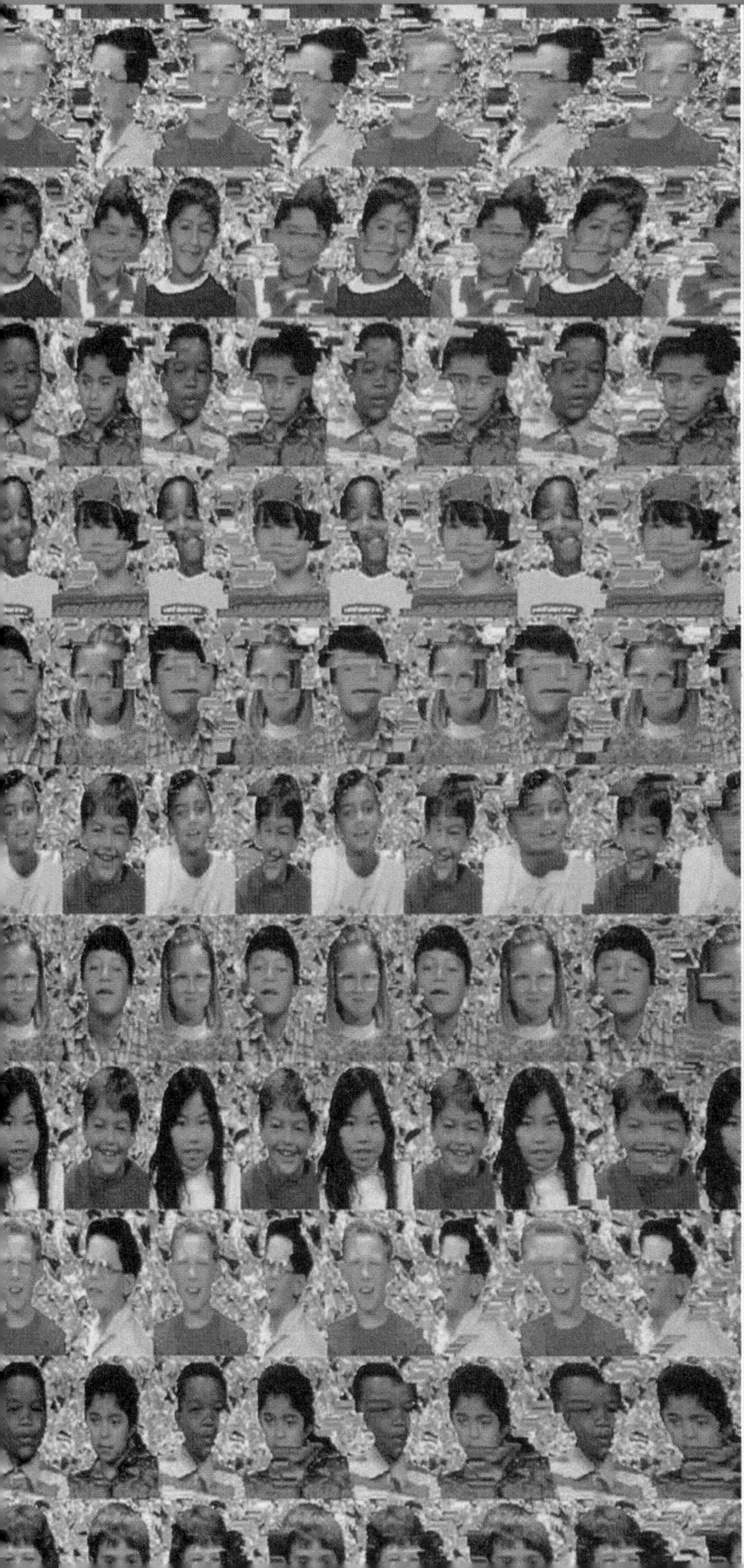

CONNECTING
MATHEMATICS & The Theme

MODULE 4

SECTION OVERVIEW

1 Probability

As you perform coin tosses and play a game with a die:

- Find experimental and theoretical probabilities
- Write probabilities as decimals and as percents

2 Factors and Divisibility

As you develop game strategies:

- Use divisibility tests
- Find greatest common factors
- Find prime factorizations
- Explore powers of a number

3 Fraction Multiplication

As you solve a story puzzle:

- Fold paper to multiply fractions
- Use common factors to write fractions in lowest terms

4 Decimal Multiplication

As you play target number games:

- Multiply decimals
- Estimate decimal products

5 Equations and Graphs

As you play Guess My Rule *and solve a geography puzzle:*

- Graph coordinates on a grid
- Write and evaluate expressions
- Write equations
- Relate area and perimeter

6 Multiples and Mixed Numbers

As you explore patterns in games:

- See patterns in multiples
- Write mixed numbers as fractions and vice versa
- Find mixed-number quotients

INTERNET
To learn more about the theme:
http://www.mlmath.com

Section 1 Probability

IN THIS SECTION

EXPLORATION 1
- Experimental Probability

EXPLORATION 2
- Theoretical Probability

Outcomes in Games

Setting the Stage

In this module you'll discover mathematical ideas as you develop strategies for games and puzzles. First you will explore chance and how it can affect a game. One way chance affects games is in choosing which team gets to start.

In football a coin toss is used to decide which team gets to choose whether to kick off or receive the ball on the first play of the game.

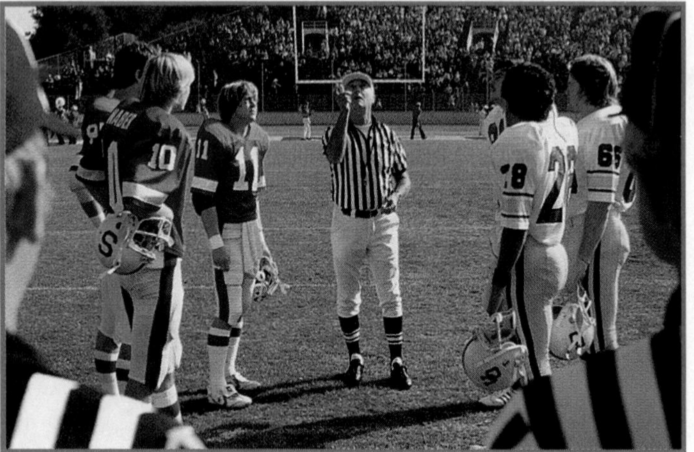

The Romans used coin flipping for decision making. The face of the emperor Caesar was on one side of every Roman coin. If Caesar's head came up on a coin toss, it was taken to mean that he approved of the decision.

Think About It

1 Do you think a coin toss is a fair way to decide which team gets the choice of kicking off or receiving the ball first? Why?

2 Suppose your teacher tosses a coin each day. If a head appears, you'll have a math quiz. About how many math quizzes do you think you'll have each week? Explain.

Exploration 1

Experimental Probability

GOAL

LEARN HOW TO...
- find experimental probabilities
- write probabilities as decimals and as percents

AS YOU...
- perform coin toss experiments

KEY TERMS
- experiment
- outcome
- probability
- experimental probability
- equally likely

SET UP *Work with a partner. You will need a coin.*

▶ **A single toss of a coin is an example of an experiment. The result of the toss, a head or a tail, is an outcome.**

3 With your partner, toss a coin 20 times. Make a tally table and tally the outcomes of your 20 tosses.

4 **a.** Which outcome occurred more often in your 20 flips?

b. What fraction of the tosses were heads?

c. What fraction of the tosses were tails?

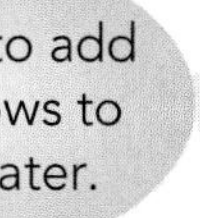

5 **Discussion** How can you use the fraction from Question 4(b) to describe the chance of getting a head when you toss a coin?

▶ A **probability** is a number that tells you how likely it is for something to happen. The fractions you found in Question 4 are probabilities.

You can find an experimental probability by repeating an experiment a number of times and observing the results, as you did with coin tosses.

$$\text{Experimental probability of an outcome} = \frac{\text{number of times the outcome happened}}{\text{number of times the experiment was repeated}}$$

EXAMPLE

Suppose heads occurred on 23 out of 40 tosses of a coin. What is the experimental probability of heads?

SAMPLE RESPONSE

$$\text{Experimental probability of heads} = \frac{\text{number of times heads occurred}}{\text{number of times the coin was tossed}} = \frac{23}{40}$$

6 Find out the number of heads and tails tossed by four other pairs of students. Extend your table to include their data.

✓ **QUESTION 7**

...checks that you understand experimental probability.

7 ✓ **CHECKPOINT** Use your table of data from Question 6.

a. Find the experimental probability of heads for each pair of students. Are the probabilities the same?

b. Suppose you toss the coin again 20 times. What do you expect the experimental probability of heads to be? Why?

8 Your table now has data for 100 tosses. Find the experimental probability of heads and of tails for the 100 tosses.

FOR ◀ HELP

with *relating fractions, decimals, and percents*, see

MODULE 3, p. 176

▶ **Decimal and Percent Forms** **When you compare probabilities, it is often easier to look at the decimal or percent form.**

9 **a.** Write the experimental probabilities you found for your 20 tosses and for all 100 tosses as decimals and as percents.

b. **Discussion** How do the experimental probabilities you found for 20 tosses compare with those you found for 100 tosses?

▶ **In Question 11 you will find probabilities using data from the whole class. To write these probabilities as decimals or as percents you may need to round.**

10 In one class the probability of heads was $\frac{117}{240}$. To estimate the probability to the nearest whole percent, two students began by finding a decimal.

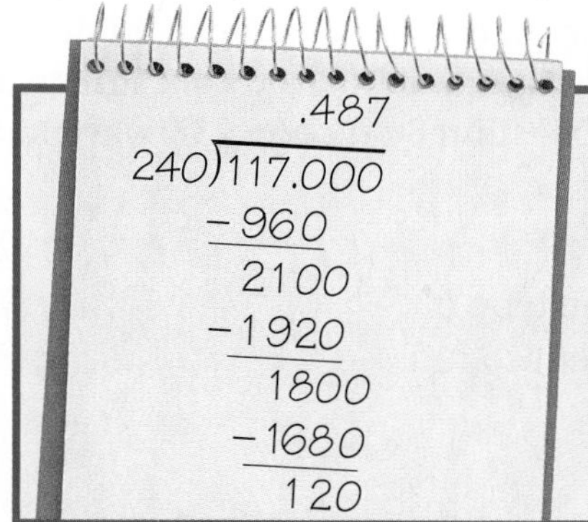

a. To which place should Mina round the calculator display?

b. Why did Keith carry out the division to the thousandths place?

11 **Try This as a Class** Collect the coin toss data from the experiments for the whole class.

a. How many times was the outcome heads? tails?

b. What is the experimental probability of heads? of tails? Write each answer as a fraction, a decimal, and a whole percent.

12 **Discussion** Compare the experimental probabilities for *your 20 tosses*, for *the 100 tosses recorded in your table*, and for *the class's total tosses*. Which gives you the best idea of the chances of getting heads?

13 **a.** Suppose you flip a coin 1000 times. About how many times do you expect the result to be heads? tails?

b. Use your answers from part (a). About what percent of the 1000 tosses would you expect to be heads? tails?

▶ **Outcomes are equally likely if they have the same chance of occurring.**

14 **a.** When you toss a coin, are the chances of getting heads and of getting tails equally likely?

b. Look back at Question 1 on page 234. Based on what you have learned, do you think the toss of a coin is a fair way to make choices? Explain.

HOMEWORK EXERCISES ▶ **See Exs. 1–4 on p. 243.**

TECHNOLOGY Using Probability Software To Run An Experiment

You can use probability software to conduct experiments, such as tossing a coin, rolling a die, or spinning a spinner. The steps below show you how to gather data for 100 coin tosses. You can use the results to answer Question 8 on page 236 without ever tossing a coin.

Step 1 Select the type of experiment to run.

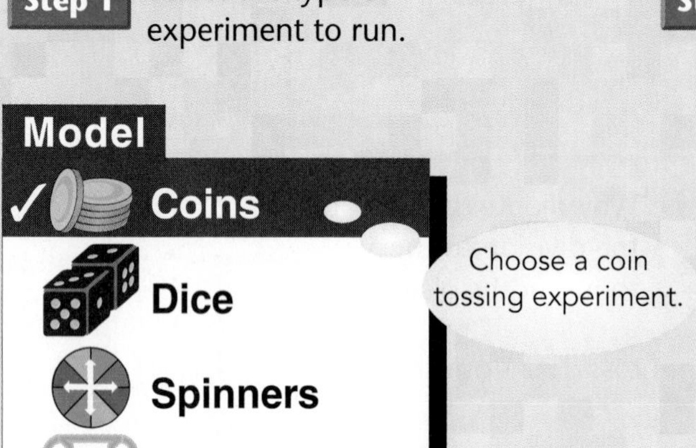

Step 2 Enter how many times to conduct the experiment. Then select how you would like to display the results.

100
0 Tries

Enter 100 tosses.

Choose a table display.

Step 3 Run the experiment.

Frequency is the number of times the outcome occurred.

Values	A	B
	Freq.	Rel. Freq.
H	52	52.0%
T	48	48.0%
Sum:	100	100%

Experimental probability is also called *relative frequency*. It can be shown as a fraction, a decimal, or a percent.

Your table will show you data for 100 coin tosses. You can choose to have it record the number of times each outcome occurred, the experimental probability of each outcome, or both.

Exploration 2

Theoretical Probability

GOAL

LEARN HOW TO...
- find theoretical probabilities
- identify impossible and certain events
- plot probabilities on a number line

AS YOU...
- play the game *Never a Six*

KEY TERMS
- event
- theoretical probability
- impossible event
- certain event

SET UP *Work with a partner. You will need:* • *Labsheet 1A* • *die or numbered cube*

The object of the game *Never a Six* is to be the first player to score a total of 50 or more points.

Never a Six

- Players alternate turns.
- On your turn, roll the die. If the result is not a 6, record the number rolled. This is your point score for that roll.
- If you roll a 6, your turn is over. Any points rolled during the turn cannot be added to your total score.
- You may continue to roll the die and record points until you decide to stop or until you roll a 6.
- If you decide to stop, total the points you rolled during your turn and add them to your total score.

Use Labsheet 1A for Questions 15 and 16.

15 With a partner, play one game of *Never a Six*. Record in the table your rolls and the resulting score for each turn.

16 **a.** List all the possible outcomes for a single roll of a die.

b. Look at the numbers you rolled during the game of *Never a Six*. Do all the numbers seem to have an equal chance of occurring? Explain.

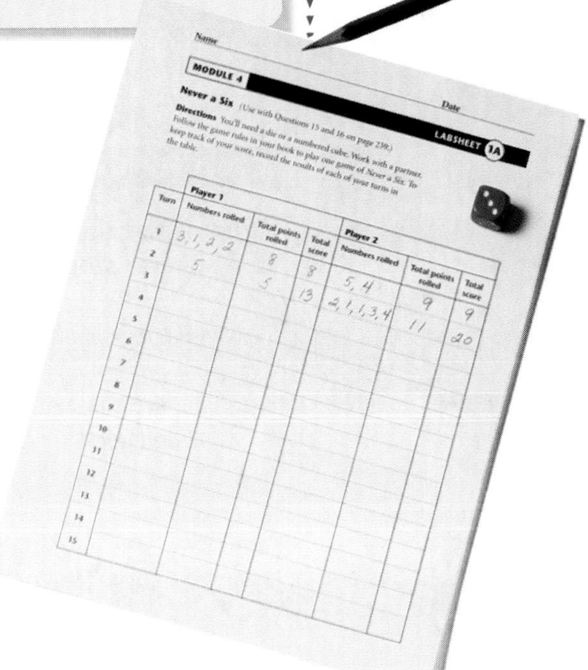

▶ **An event is a set of outcomes for a particular experiment. For example, in *Never a Six* the outcomes a roll of 4 and a roll of 5 make up the event scoring more than 3 points on a single roll.**

Event	=	set of outcomes
scoring more than 3 points on a roll in *Never a Six*		 

17 List the outcomes of a single roll of a die that make up each event in the game *Never a Six*.

a. scoring less than 3 points

b. scoring an odd number of points

c. scoring 0, 1, 2, 3, 4, or 5 points

d. scoring 0 points

e. scoring 6 points

You need to count the number of times the outcome was either 4 or 5.

18 **Use Labsheet 1A.** Find the experimental probability of the event *scoring more than 3 points on the first roll of a turn.*

▶ **When you find the probability of an event without doing an experiment, it is called a theoretical probability. You can find theoretical probability when the outcomes are equally likely, such as when you are using a spinner with equal-sized parts.**

$$\text{Theoretical probability of an event} = \frac{\text{number of outcomes in the event}}{\text{total number of possible outcomes}}$$

EXAMPLE

What is the theoretical probability that the spinner stops on an odd number?

SAMPLE RESPONSE

odd outcomes: 1, 3

$$\text{Theoretical probability of an odd number} = \frac{\text{number of odd outcomes}}{\text{total number of possible outcomes}} = \frac{2}{4}$$

all possible outcomes: 1, 2, 3, or 4

19 ✓ **CHECKPOINT** Determine the theoretical probability of each event in Question 17.

✓ **QUESTION 19**

...checks that you can find the theoretical probability of an event.

▶ **Impossible and Certain Events** **If an event cannot happen, it is an impossible event, and it has a probability of 0. If an event must happen, it is a certain event, and it has a probability of 1.**

20 Were any of the events in Question 17 impossible? certain? If so, which ones?

21 **Discussion** Are there any events where the probability could be greater than 1 or less than 0? Explain.

▶ **You can plot probabilities on a number line by dividing the part of the number line between 0 and 1 into equal parts.**

EXAMPLE

Plot the probability that the spinner in the Example on page 240 lands on an odd number.

- Sketch a number line. Label 0 and 1.
- Mark off and label four equal parts between 0 and 1.
- Plot the point $\frac{2}{4}$.

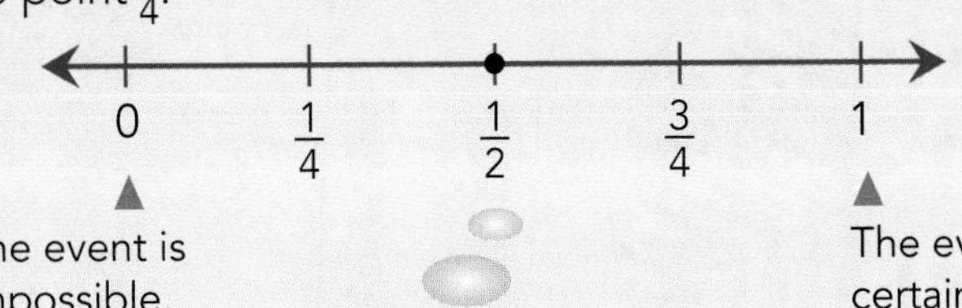

22 **Try This as a Class** Look back at the theoretical probabilities you found in Question 19.

a. Including the 0 and 1 marks, how many marks are needed to make 6 sections on the number line?

b. Draw and label a number line. Plot and label each probability on your number line.

HOMEWORK EXERCISES See Exs. 5–11 on pp. 244–245.

Section 1 Key Concepts

Key Terms

experiment

outcome

probability

equally likely

experimental probability

theoretical probability

event

impossible event

certain event

Outcomes of an Experiment (p. 235)

An experiment is an activity whose results can be observed and recorded. The result of an experiment is an outcome.

Probability

A probability is a number from 0 through 1 that tells you how likely something is to happen. Probabilities can be written as fractions, decimals, or percents. When each outcome in an experiment has the same probability, the outcomes are equally likely. **(pp. 235–237)**

An experimental probability is found by repeating an experiment and observing the outcomes. **(pp. 235–236)**

A theoretical probability is found without doing an experiment. **(pp. 239–241)**

Example For the outcome *red*, the theoretical probability is $\frac{1}{3}$ and the experimental probability is $\frac{29}{80}$ (about 0.36, or 36%).

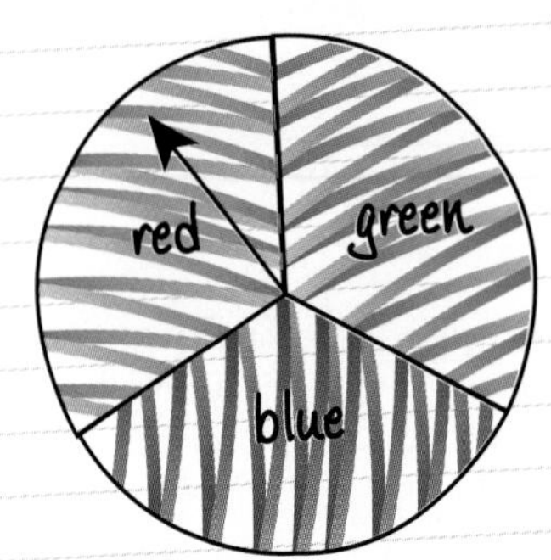

Outcome	Number of spins
red	29
blue	24
green	27
total	80

Percent means "per hundred." Round to the nearest hundredth.

Events (p. 240)

An event is a set of outcomes. For the spinner above, landing on yellow or white is an impossible event and landing on red, blue, or green is a certain event.

23 **Key Concepts Question** For the spinner above, find the experimental and theoretical probabilities of the event *the spinner stops on blue or green*. Write your answers as whole percents.

Section 1
Practice & Application Exercises

1. a. What are the possible outcomes when you draw one marble from the bag? When you draw two marbles at once?

   b. For each experiment in part (a), are the outcomes for that experiment equally likely?

2. a. Explain how the numbers in the *Experimental probability of heads* column were calculated.

John Kerrich's Data for 10,000 Tosses of a Coin		
Number of tosses	Number of heads	Experimental probability of heads
10	4	0.400
100	44	0.440
1,000	502	0.502
10,000	5,067	0.507

   b. Kerrich got 5,067 heads in 10,000 tosses. How many tails did he get? What was the experimental probability of tails?

3. What is the experimental probability that the spinner stops on B? Write your answer as a fraction and as a whole percent.

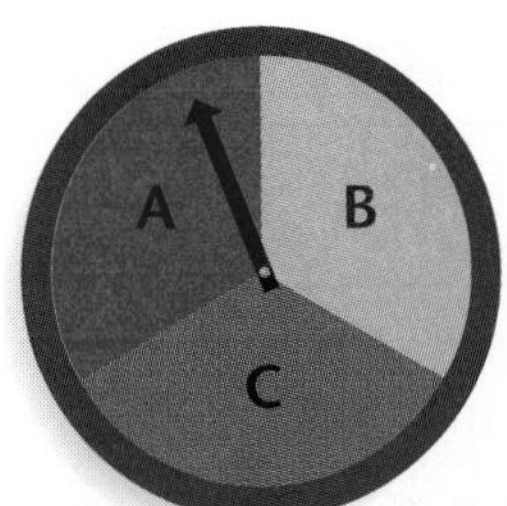

Outcome	Total
A	17
B	25
C	18

4. a. A die was rolled 25 times. On 8 of the rolls, the outcome was ⚄. What is the experimental probability of rolling ⚄? Write your answer as a fraction, a decimal, and a percent.

   b. On how many rolls was the outcome *not* ⚄? What is the experimental probability of *not* rolling ⚄? Write your answer as a fraction, a decimal, and a percent.

   c. Suppose the die is thrown 100 times. Based on the experimental probabilities you found, about how many times do you expect to roll a ⚄? *not* roll a ⚄?

YOU WILL NEED

For Ex. 19:
- bag
- 10 pennies, some shiny, some dull

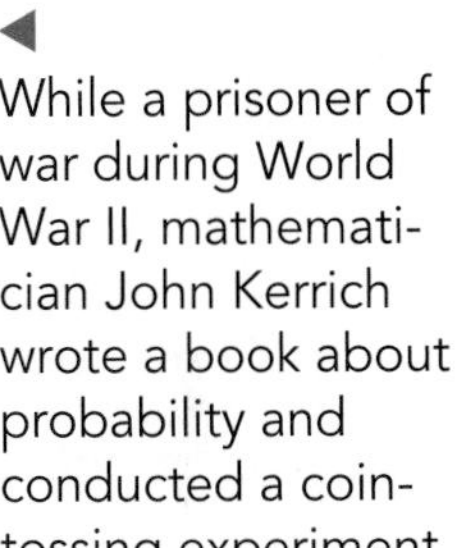

◀ While a prisoner of war during World War II, mathematician John Kerrich wrote a book about probability and conducted a coin-tossing experiment.

Find the theoretical probability of each event.

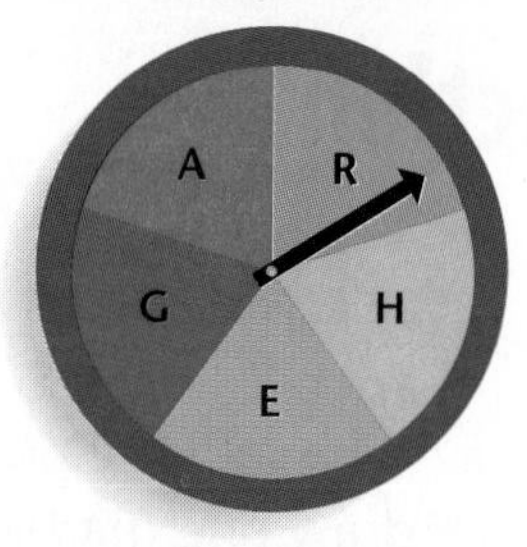

5. The spinner stops on A.

6. The spinner stops on a vowel.

For Exercises 7 and 8, suppose you pick a card, without looking, from the thirteen heart cards in a standard deck.

Hearts(♥):          

7. Are all the outcomes for picking one card equally likely? Explain why or why not.

8. a. List the possible outcomes for picking a numbered card.
   b. What is the theoretical probability of picking a numbered card?
   c. What is the theoretical probability of picking an even-numbered card? an odd-numbered card?
   d. Plot your answers from parts (b) and (c) on a number line.

9. **Open-ended** Give an example of a certain event and of an impossible event in everyday life.

10. **Basketball** Each season the National Basketball Association (NBA) holds a lottery to decide the order in which its teams will pick new players. Until 1993, each team that did not make the playoffs was assigned from 1 to 11 balls marked with the team's logo. The first ball drawn in the lottery determined the team that would get first pick.

Rank of eleven non–playoff teams	Number of balls
11th-place team	11
10th-place team	10
9th-place team	9
⋮	⋮
1st-place team	1

   a. What was the theoretical probability that the 11th-place team got the first pick? the 5th-place team? the 1st-place team? Write each as a fraction, a decimal, and a whole percent.
   b. **Writing** Did the best team stand a good chance of getting one of the top new players for next season? Does this seem fair? Explain your thinking.

Reflecting on the Section

Write your response to Exercise 11 in your journal.

11. Develop a strategy for playing the game *Never a Six*. Explain why your strategy helps. Play the game again to test your strategy. How does probability relate to your strategy?

Journal

Exercise 11 checks that you can apply probability.

Spiral Review

Find the mean, the median, and the mode for each set of data. **(Module 3, pp. 202 and 213)**

12. 48, 52, 76, 49, 81, 42

13. 2, 12.12, 7.1, 15, 5.16, 11

Replace each __?__ with the number that makes the statement true. **(Module 3, p. 165)**

14. 2 m = __?__ mm

15. 65 mg = __?__ g

16. 34 km = __?__ m

Find the missing terms in each sequence. **(Module 1, p. 8)**

17. 4, 16, 64, __?__, __?__, 4096

18. 6.6, __?__, __?__, 5.7, 5.4, 5.1

Extension 

Applying Experimental Probability

19. Have a friend or relative put 10 pennies into a bag—some shiny and the rest dull. Do not look at how many of each are put into the bag!

    a. Take one penny from the bag. Record whether it is shiny or dull in a tally table. Put the coin back in the bag.

    b. Repeat part (a) 29 more times.

    c. Use the data in your table to find the experimental probability of drawing each kind of penny.

    d. Predict how many shiny pennies and how many dull pennies are in the bag. Then check your prediction.

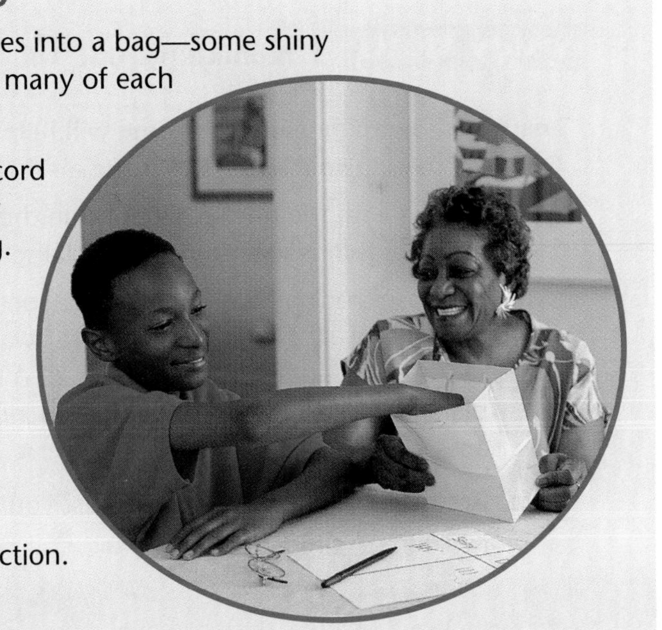

Section 1
Extra Skill Practice

Suppose a die was rolled 80 times with the results shown.

Outcome	Total
⚅	16
⚄	14
⚃	13
⚂	15
⚁	12
⚀	10

1. What is the experimental probability of rolling a 3? Write your answer as a fraction.
2. What is the experimental probability of rolling an even number? Write your answer as a decimal.
3. What is the experimental probability of rolling a number less than 5? Write your answer as a percent.
4. What is the experimental probability of rolling an odd number? Write your answer as a fraction.

Find the theoretical probability of each event. Write each probability as a fraction.

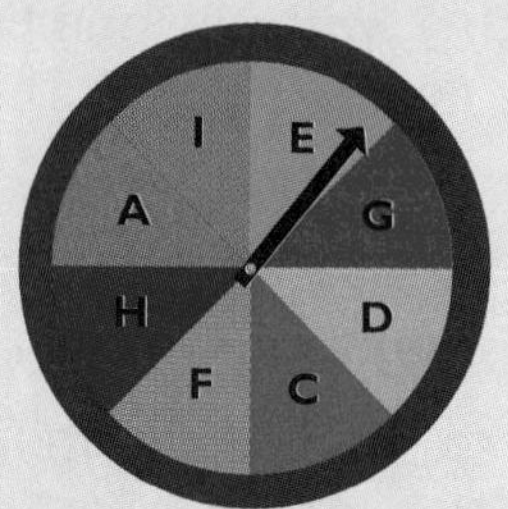

5. The spinner stops on A.
6. The spinner stops on B.
7. The spinner stops on C or F.
8. The spinner stops on a vowel.
9. Were any of the events in Exercises 5–8 impossible? certain? If so, which ones?
10. Plot each probability you found in Exercises 5–8 on a number line. Label your number line and each point you plot.

Study Skills ▸ Managing your Time

Learning how to manage your time will help you achieve your goals. One way to plan your time is to make a schedule.

1. Beginning with the time you get up in the morning, write a schedule of things you do on a normal school day.
2. a. Suppose that one day you need to spend an hour working on a school project. Neighbors who are away have also asked you to spend 30 minutes cat-sitting and 20 minutes watering their plants. Now adjust your schedule to include time for these activities.

   b. Are there any other ways to adjust your schedule to include the activities from part (a)? Explain.

Section 2 Factors and Divisibility

IN THIS SECTION

EXPLORATION 1
- Testing for Divisibility

EXPLORATION 2
- Prime Factors

EXPLORATION 3
- Powers of Numbers

Paper Clip Products

Setting the Stage

SET UP *Work with a partner. You will need: • Labsheet 2A • 2 paper clips • 10 each of two different-colored chips*

Paper Clip Products is a strategy game involving multiplication.

Paper Clip Products

- Player 1 starts. Place your two paper clips on numbers in the factor list. They may be on the same factor. Multiply the numbers and place a chip on the product on the game board. (Player 2 will use a different chip color.)
- Player 1 and Player 2 alternate turns. On a turn, leave one paper clip where it is, and move the other clip to any factor. Cover the new product with a chip.
- A turn ends when a player covers a product or if a product is not on the game board or is already covered.
- A player wins by covering three adjacent products horizontally, vertically, or diagonally.

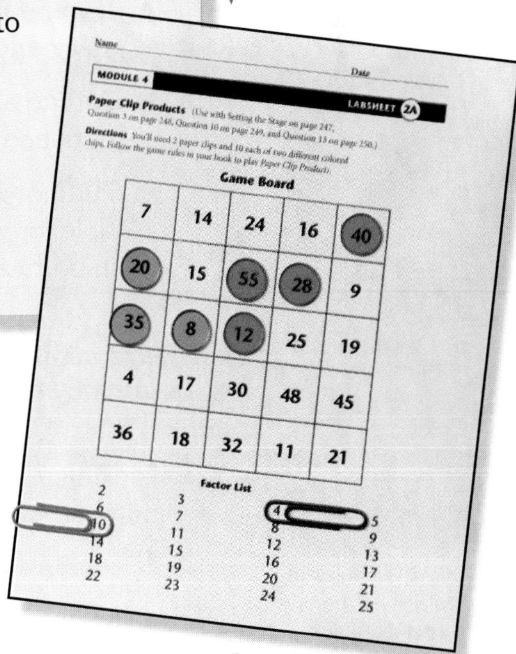

Name

Date

MODULE 4 LABSHEET 2A

Paper Clip Products (Use with Setting the Stage on page 247, Question 3 on page 248, Question 10 on page 249, and Question 13 on page 250.)

Directions You'll need 2 paper clips and 10 each of two different colored chips. Follow the game rules in your book to play *Paper Clip Products*.

Game Board

7	14	24	16	40
20	15	55	28	9
35	8	12	25	19
4	17	30	48	45
36	18	32	11	21

Factor List

2	3	4	5
6	7	8	9
10	11	12	13
14	15	16	17
18	19	20	21
22	23	24	25

Use Labsheet 2A. **Play the *Paper Clip Products* game twice.**

Think About It

1 When you were Player 1, how did you decide where to place the first two paper clips?

2 What kind of moves did you avoid? Why?

GOAL

LEARN HOW TO...
- use divisibility tests
- find factors
- find the greatest common factor

AS YOU...
- develop a strategy for playing *Paper Clip Products*

KEY TERMS
- divisible
- factor
- greatest common factor (GCF)

Exploration 1

Testing for Divisibility

SET UP *You will need Labsheets 2A and 2B.*

▶ **To develop a strategy for playing *Paper Clip Products*, you can use a Venn diagram to sort the numbers on the game board.**

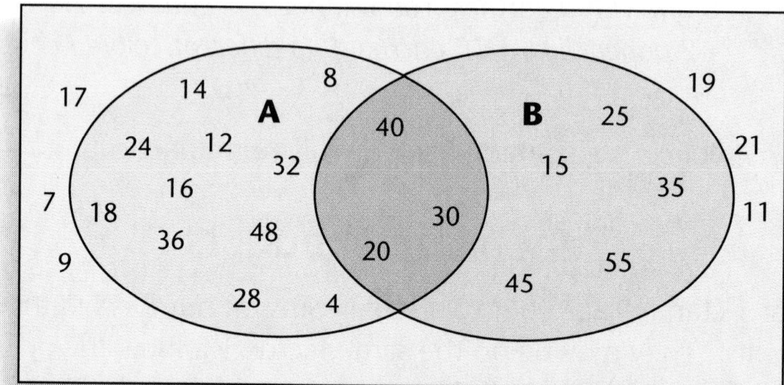

3 **Use Labsheet 2A.**

a. If you put a paper clip on 2, your opponent will be able to cover any number in set A above. Explain why.

b. Putting a paper clip on what factor makes it possible for your opponent to cover any number in set B?

c. Putting your paper clip on what factor or factors makes it possible for your opponent to cover 20, 30, and 40, the numbers in both set A and set B?

▶ **When a number can be divided evenly by another number, it is divisible by that number.**

4 Look back at your answers to Question 3. Just by looking at a number, how can you tell if it is divisible by 2? by 5? by 10?

✓ QUESTION 5

...checks that you can determine whether a number is divisible by 2, by 5, or by 10.

5 ✓ CHECKPOINT Without dividing, tell whether each number is divisible by 2, by 5, or by 10.

a. 125   b. 326   c. 270   d. 681

▶ **In Questions 6–9, you'll discover ways to test for divisibility by 3 and by 9.**

6 The number 351 is divisible by 3. Tell whether each rearrangement of the digits of 351 is still divisible by 3.

a. 135 **b.** 153 **c.** 315

d. 351 **e.** 513 **f.** 531

7 **Use Labsheet 2B.** Follow the directions to discover a *Divisibility Test for 3.*

8 **Discussion** Use the questions to explore divisibility by 9.

a. If a number is divisible by 9, is it divisible by 3? Explain.

b. If a number is divisible by 3, is it divisible by 9? Explain.

c. The test for divisibility by 9 is similar to the one for 3. Find a divisibility test for 9. Try your divisibility test on the numbers 18, 54, 117, 243, and 5409 to be sure it works.

9 ✓ **CHECKPOINT** Test each number for divisibility by 3 and by 9.

a. 96 **b.** 288 **c.** 502 **d.** 68,913

...checks that you can determine whether a number is divisible by 3 or by 9.

▶ **Finding Factors When a whole number is divisible by a second whole number, the second number is a factor of the first. To find a complete list of factors, it is helpful to begin with 1 and check in order for pairs of factors.**

EXAMPLE

To find the factors of 12:

$1 \cdot 12 = 12$

$2 \cdot 6 = 12$

$3 \cdot 4 = 12$

1, 2, 3, 4, 6, 12

factors of 12

To find the factors of 4:

$1 \cdot 4 = 4$

$2 \cdot 2 = 4$

1, 2, 4

factors of 4

The factor 2 pairs with itself. $2 \cdot 2 = 4$

10 **Use Labsheet 2A.** Find all the numbers on the game board that cannot be covered. What do you notice about the factors of these numbers?

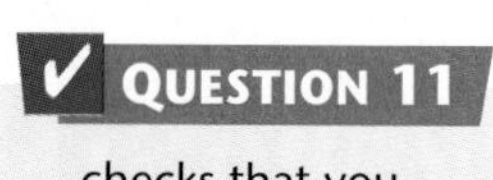

...checks that you can find factors of a number.

11 ✓ **CHECKPOINT** List all the factors of each number.

a. 24 **b.** 13 **c.** 32 **d.** 18

▶ **Common Factors** **Developing a strategy for playing *Paper Clip Products* involves finding factors that numbers have in common.**

12 Use your lists of factors from Question 11. Find the common factors of each pair of numbers.

a. 18 and 32 **b.** 18 and 24 **c.** 13 and 18

13 **Use Labsheet 2A.** Suppose the paper clips are on 2 and 3.

a. Name two different moves you could use to cover 18.

b. Which move from part (a) should you avoid if you do not want your opponent to cover 32 on the next turn?

▶ **The greatest common factor (GCF) of two or more numbers is the greatest number that is a factor of each number. Finding the GCF will be useful when you simplify fractions.**

EXAMPLE

Find the greatest common factor of 16 and 20.

SAMPLE RESPONSE

List the factors of each number.

Circle the common factors.

Factors of 16: (1), (2), (4), 8, 16

Factors of 20: (1), (2), (4), 5, 10, 20

Common factors: 1, 2, 4

The GCF of 16 and 20 is 4.

...checks that you can find the greatest common factor of a set of numbers.

14 ✓ **CHECKPOINT** Use the common factors you listed in Questions 11–12. Find the greatest common factor of each set of numbers.

a. 18 and 32 **b.** 18, 24, and 32 **c.** 13 and 18

HOMEWORK EXERCISES ▶ See Exs. 1–19 on p. 258.

Exploration 2

Prime Factors

SET UP *Work with a partner. You will need: • Labsheet 2C • paper clips • 15 each of two different-colored chips*

GOAL

LEARN HOW TO...
- recognize primes and composites
- use a factor tree to find prime factors

AS YOU...
- develop a strategy for playing *Prime Time*

KEY TERMS
- prime
- composite
- prime factorization
- factor tree

Prime Time is another strategy game involving factors.

Prime Time

- To begin, the first player places two paper clips on factors below the game board. He or she then covers the product of the factors on the game board with a colored chip.
- Players alternate turns. On a turn, a player has a choice of three ways to cover a new product.

  Move one paper clip to another factor.
  OR Place another paper clip on any factor.
  OR Take a paper clip off any factor.
- A turn ends when a player covers a product. A turn also ends if a product is not on the game board or is already covered.
- A player wins by covering three adjacent numbers horizontally, vertically, or diagonally.

15 **Use Labsheet 2C.** With your partner, play three games of *Prime Time.*

▶ **All whole numbers greater than 1 are either *prime* or *composite*. A prime number has exactly two factors, 1 and the number itself. A composite number has more than two factors.**

16 Explain why 1 is neither prime nor composite.

17 **Use Labsheet 2C.** Are the factors below the game board prime or composite? the numbers on the game board? Explain.

✓ **QUESTION 18**

...checks that you can determine whether a number is prime or composite.

18 ✓ **CHECKPOINT** Tell whether each number is prime or composite. Explain your reasoning.

a. 13 **b.** 305 **c.** 71 **d.** 243

19 **a.** **Use Labsheet 2C.** Suppose a player covers 20 on the game board. What factors are the paper clips on and how many paper clips are on each factor?

b. Besides the factors covered in part (a), are there any other prime numbers that can be used to get a product of 20? Explain.

▶ **Every composite number can be written as the product of prime factors. This product is the prime factorization of the number. A factor tree helps you find the prime factorization.**

EXAMPLE

Use a factor tree to find the prime factorization of 12.

SAMPLE RESPONSE

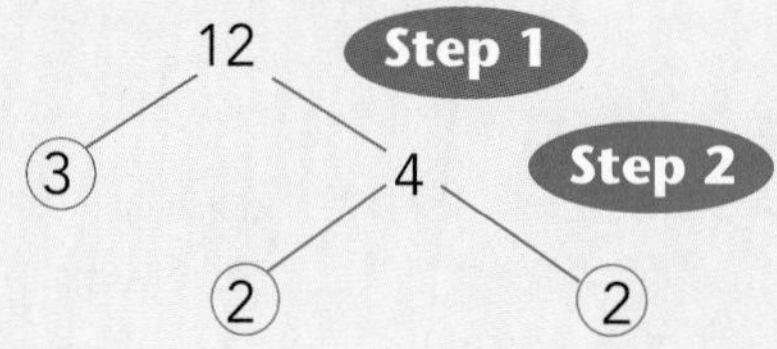

The prime factorization of 12 is 2 • 2 • 3.

20 **Try This as a Class** Use the Example above.

a. What is done in Step 1? Why is the 3 circled but not the 4?

b. What is done in Step 2? Why does the factor tree end?

c. What parts of the tree are used to write the prime factorization?

21 **a.** Sketch a factor tree for 12 using 2 and 6 for factors in the first step.

b. Why do you think your tree ends with the same circled numbers as the tree in the Example on page 252?

c. Why do you not want to use the factors 1 and 12 for factors in the first step of the tree?

22 **a.** Copy and complete the factor tree for 48 shown below.

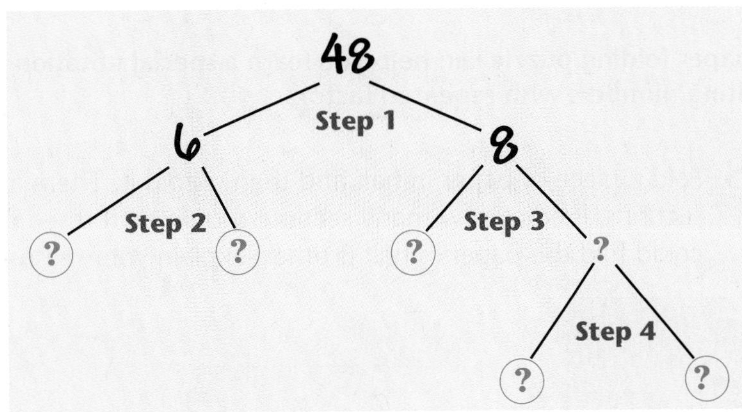

b. Why are more branches necessary to make this tree than to make the factor tree for 12?

c. What is the prime factorization of 48?

23 **Discussion** What happens when you try to make a factor tree for 47? What do you think is the prime factorization of 47?

24 **✓ CHECKPOINT** Use a factor tree to find the prime factorization of 36.

...checks that you can use a factor tree to find the prime factorization of a number.

25 **Try This as a Class** Compare your factor tree for 36 with those of your classmates. Did everyone use the same pair of factors in the first branch? Did the same prime factors always show up at the ends of the branches? Why?

26 **Discussion** Explain how prime factorization is used in the game *Prime Time*.

27 Think about making another *Prime Time* game board using the factors 2, 3, 5, and 7. What are two composite numbers you can put on your game board that cannot be covered?

HOMEWORK EXERCISES See Exs. 20–33 on p. 259.

GOAL

EXPLORE...
- powers of a number

AS YOU...
- investigate a paper folding puzzle

KEY TERMS
- power
- exponent
- base
- standard form
- exponential form

Exploration 3

Powers of Numbers

SET UP *You will need:* • *paper for folding* • *calculator*

▶ **A paper folding puzzle can help you learn a special notation for writing numbers with repeated factors.**

28 Fold a piece of paper in half and then unfold it. There are two sections. Predict how many sections would be formed if you could fold the paper in half 8 times. Explain your reasoning.

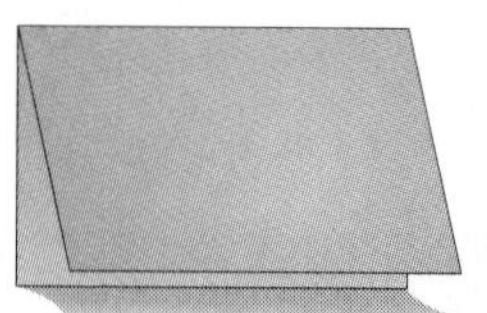

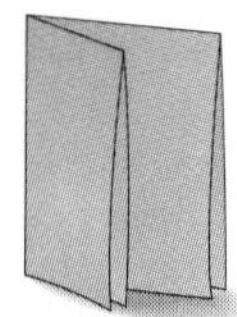

▶ **One strategy to solve Question 28 is to look for a pattern.**

29 **a.** Make a table like the one below.

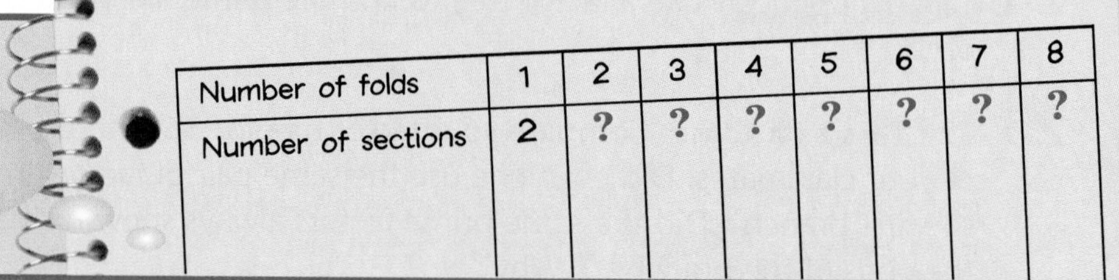

Number of folds	1	2	3	4	5	6	7	8
Number of sections	2	?	?	?	?	?	?	?

Leave space to add two more rows to your table later.

b. Record the number of sections formed by 1 fold. Continue folding the paper in half as many times as possible. After each fold, record the number of sections.

c. Look at your table. Each time you make a new fold, how does the number of sections change? Use the pattern to complete the table.

30 How does your prediction in Question 28 compare with the results for 8 folds in Question 29(c)?

31 You can use the pattern you discovered in Question 29(c) to rewrite the number of sections. Label and fill in the third row of your table as shown.

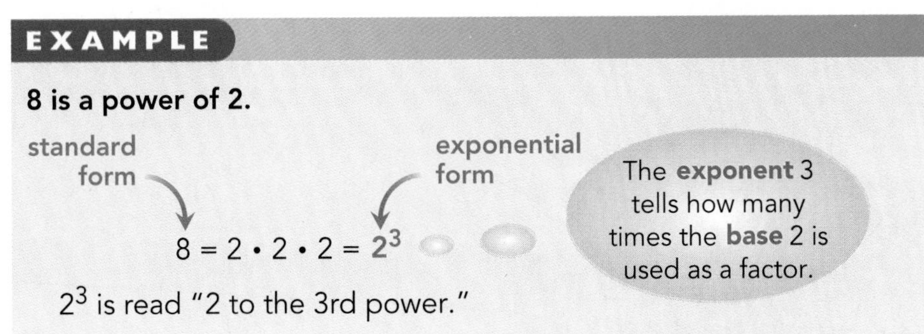

Number of folds	1	2	3
Number of sections	2	4	8
Rewritten form	2	2 • 2	2 • 2 • 2

▶ **Using Exponents There is a short way to write a product like 2 • 2 • 2. A number that can be written using an *exponent* and a *base* is a power of the base.**

EXAMPLE

8 is a power of 2.

standard form → exponential form

$8 = 2 \cdot 2 \cdot 2 = 2^3$

The **exponent** 3 tells how many times the **base** 2 is used as a factor.

2^3 is read "2 to the 3rd power."

32 **a.** In your table, label the fourth row *Powers of 2*. Fill it in by rewriting the numbers of sections using exponents.

b. Discussion How did you write 2 in exponential form? Why?

33 How do you read 3^4?

34 ✓ **CHECKPOINT** Find the value of each expression.

a. 3^4 **b.** 4^3 **c.** 10^2 **d.** 7^1

...checks that you can find the value of a number written using an exponent.

35 Calculator Scientific calculators have a power key y^x. Follow the steps below to find the value of 2^8.

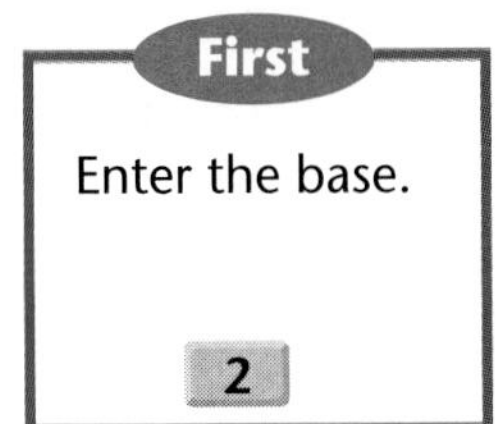

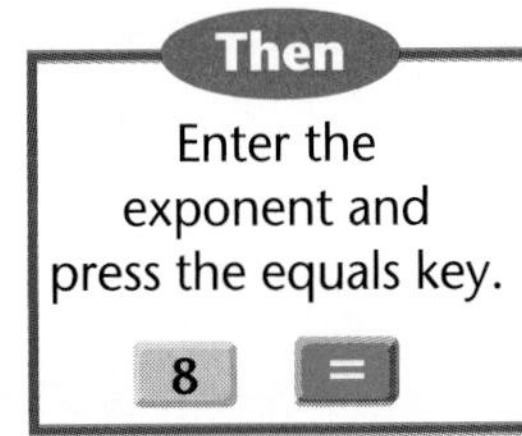

36 **a.** How many sections would be formed if you could fold a piece of paper in half 12 times? Write your answer using an exponent.

b. Use a calculator to find the standard form of your answer in part (a).

You can also write the 3 as 3^1

▶ **You can use exponents to write prime factorizations.** **For example, the prime factorization of 75 is $3 \cdot 5 \cdot 5$, or $3 \cdot 5^2$. The prime factorization of 29 is 29, or 29^1, because 29 is already prime.**

37 Write each prime factorization using exponents.

a. 40 **b.** 81 **c.** 23

HOMEWORK EXERCISES ▶ **See Exs. 34–49 on pp. 259–260.**

Section 2 Key Concepts

Key Terms

divisible

Divisibility Rules (pp. 248–249)

You can tell whether a number is divisible by 2, 5, or 10 by looking at the ones digit.

Divisibility test	Ones digit
2	0, 2, 4, 6, or 8
5	0 or 5
10	0

A number is divisible by 3 if the sum of its digits is divisible by 3.

A number is divisible by 9 if the sum of its digits is divisible by 9.

factor

greatest common factor (GCF)

Factors and Common Factors (pp. 249–250)

To find the greatest common factor, find all the factors the numbers have in common. Then, pick the greatest of these common factors.

Example The common factors of 30 and 45 are 1, 3, 5, and 15. The greatest common factor of 30 and 45 is 15.

Section 2 Key Concepts

Key Terms

Prime and Composite Numbers (pp. 252–253)

prime

composite

Every composite number can be written as the product of prime factors. Use factor trees to find prime factorizations.

Example Find the prime factorization of 24.

prime factorization

factor tree

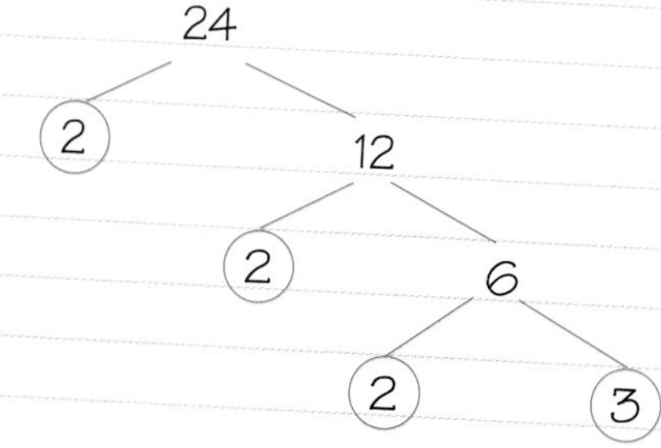

The prime factorization of 24 is $2 \cdot 2 \cdot 2 \cdot 3$.

Powers (p. 254–256)

power
- **exponent**
- **base**

When a number can be written using an exponent and a base, the number is a power of the base. The example shows that 64 is 4 to the 3rd power.

standard form

exponential form

Example

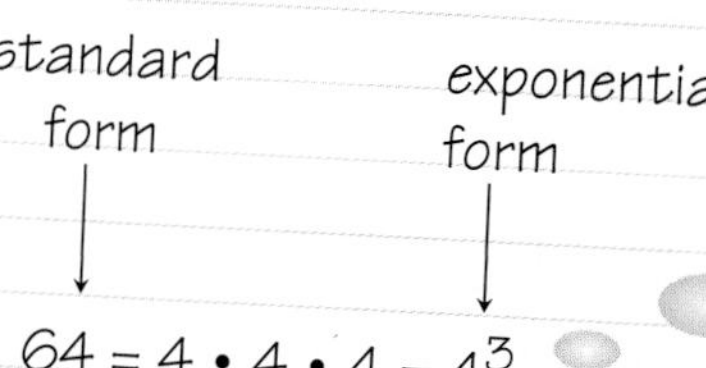

$64 = 4 \cdot 4 \cdot 4 = 4^3$

The exponent 3 tells how many times the base 4 is used as a factor.

You can use exponents to write prime factorizations.

Example The prime factorization of 24, shown at the top of the page, can be written as $2^3 \cdot 3^1$, or $2^3 \cdot 3$.

38 Key Concepts Question

a. How can divisibility rules help you to find the prime factorization of 261?

b. Write the prime factorization of 261 using exponents.

Section 2
Practice & Application Exercises

Test each number for divisibility by 2, 3, 5, 9, and 10.

1. 168 2. 53 3. 499 4. 66,780

5. 4326 6. 75 7. 1011 8. 50,436

List all the factors of each number. Then find the greatest common factor of each set of numbers.

9. 14 and 28 10. 11 and 17 11. 21 and 51

12. 43 and 69 13. 54, 36, and 72 14. 22, 64, and 80

Mental Math **Show how to find each product using mental math. Use what you know about factors and compatible numbers.**

Example: $36 \cdot 25 = 9 \cdot 4 \cdot 25 = 9 \cdot 100 = 900$

15. $25 \cdot 48$ 16. $12 \cdot 75$ 17. $16 \cdot 125$

18. **Displaying Data** You are going to make a pictograph of this data using ❀ as the symbol for a number of species.

Approximately 60,000 of the world's 90,000 known plant species are endangered. In Namibia, a country of southwest Africa, a Welwitchia Mirabilis shows its flowers.

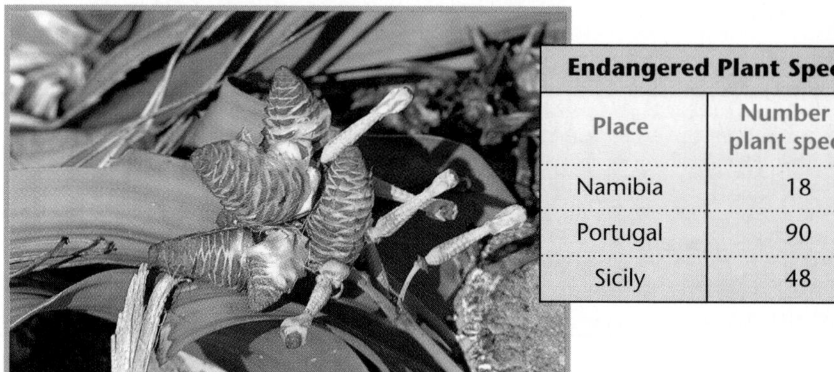

Endangered Plant Species	
Place	Number of plant species
Namibia	18
Portugal	90
Sicily	48

a. You must decide what number of species each ❀ symbol will represent. What numbers will let you represent the data with only whole symbols?

b. Use your answer from part (a) to make a pictograph that contains as few symbols as possible. Be sure to tell how many species each ❀ represents.

FOR ▶ HELP with *making a pictograph*, see **TOOLBOX, p. 603**

19. **Challenge** A *perfect number* equals the sum of all its factors, not including the number itself. The first *perfect number* is 6 because 6 = 1 + 2 + 3. Find the next *perfect number*.

Tell whether each number is *prime* or *composite*.

20. 25 21. 37 22. 135

23. 51 24. 306 25. 91

Write the prime factorization of each number.

26. 42 27. 144 28. 53

29. 280 30. 484 31. 840

32. This diagram organizes the prime factors of 20 and 36.

20	36
5 · 2 · 2 · 3 · 3	

a. Describe how the prime factorizations of 20 and 36 were used to make the diagram above.

b. How are the numbers in the overlapping region in the diagram above related to the GCF of 20 and 36?

c. Create a similar diagram for the prime factors of 24 and 30 and use it to find the GCF of 24 and 30.

33. **Challenge** The prime factorization of 60 has four prime factors since $60 = 2 \cdot 2 \cdot 3 \cdot 5$. Which two-digit numbers have the most factors in their prime factorizations?

Find the value of each expression.

34. 7^4 35. 5^2 36. 6^3 37. 3^5

38. Write the prime factorization of 1800 using exponents.

Write each number in exponential form with either 2 or 3 as the exponent.

39. 36 40. 8 41. 100 42. 125

43. **Computers** The smallest pieces of information stored in computer memory are called *bits*. One *byte* of memory is made up of 2^3 bits. One *kilobyte* of memory is 2^{10} bytes.

a. In standard form, how many bits are in a byte? how many bytes are in a kilobyte?

b. A computer with 512 kilobytes can store how many bytes of information? how many bits of information?

YOU WILL NEED

For Exs. 44–46:
- calculator

 Calculator **Predict which number will be greater. Then check your prediction with a calculator.**

44. 2^{15} or 3^{15} 45. 10^3 or 3^{10} 46. 4^4 or 16^2

47. a. **Writing** Write each power of ten from 10^1 to 10^9 in exponential and standard form. How does the exponent of each power relate to the number of zeros in the standard form?

b. A *googol* is 10^{100}. Written in standard form, a googol is 1 followed by how many zeros?

48. **Visual Thinking** The number 9 is a *square number* because you can make a square from 9 square tiles.

a. Use drawings to find three other square numbers.

b. Rewrite 9 and each square number from part (a) in exponential form with 2 as the exponent. Can every square number be written this way? Explain.

Oral Report

Exercise 49 checks that you can apply your understanding of divisibility and prime factorization.

Reflecting on the Section

Be prepared to discuss your answer to Exercise 49 in class.

49. **a.** Write the prime factorization of each number in the table. What do you notice about the prime factors of the numbers that are divisible by 6?

b. Use your results from part (a) and the divisibility tests you know. Write a divisibility test for 6.

Divisible by 6	Not divisible by 6
72	44
30	39
114	175
24	63
138	70

Spiral Review

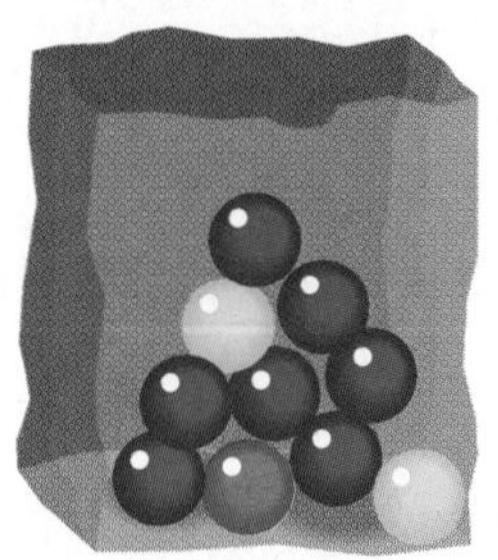

50. What is the theoretical probability of drawing a red marble from the bag shown? a green marble? **(Module 4, p. 242)**

51. If possible, sketch a triangle that is both obtuse and scalene. **(Module 1, p. 22)**

Write each fraction in lowest terms. **(Module 2, p. 114)**

52. $\frac{3}{12}$ 53. $\frac{10}{30}$ 54. $\frac{4}{16}$ 55. $\frac{6}{9}$

Extension ▶▶

Numbers to the Zero Power

$2^5 = 32$

$2^4 = 16$

$2^3 = 8$

$2^2 = 4$

$2^1 = 2$

56. a. What mathematical operation is used to go from 32 to 16? from 16 to 8? Does this pattern continue throughout the sequence 32, 16, 8, 4, 2?

    b. Based on the pattern, what is the value of 2^0?

    c. How does this compare with the number of sections after 0 folds in the paper-folding pattern in Exploration 3 on page 254? Explain.

Puzzle Making

Over the next few weeks, you'll explore several different types of puzzles as you help create a *Class Puzzle Book*. The completed project will include an original puzzle from each member of your class.

The number puzzle at the right includes clues that involve divisibility.

What's the Number?

- It has two digits.
- It is divisible by 5.
- It is divisible by 3.
- It is an odd number.
- It is greater than 70.

1 **a.** Solve the puzzle. Is there more than one possible answer?

b. How can you combine the two divisibility clues?

c. Suppose the fourth clue had been, "It is an even number." What would the solution be?

2 Write a number puzzle that has five clues. At least one clue must involve divisibility.

Section 2 Extra Skill Practice

Test each number for divisibility by 2, 3, 5, 9, and 10.

1. 26 2. 19 3. 42 4. 135 5. 141

Find the GCF of each set of numbers.

6. 12 and 24
7. 8 and 15
8. 30 and 100
9. 45 and 63
10. 14, 49, and 98
11. 24, 40, and 88

Tell whether each number is *prime* or *composite*.

12. 49 13. 57 14. 11 15. 132 16. 79

Write the prime factorization of each number.

17. 18 18. 32 19. 27 20. 49 21. 100

Find the value of each expression.

22. 8^2 23. 7^3 24. 2^5 25. 4^4 26. 12^2

Replace each __?__ with >, <, or =. Explain your choice.

27. 2^3 __?__ 3^2
28. 2^4 __?__ $2 \cdot 2 \cdot 2 \cdot 2$
29. 3^4 __?__ $4 \cdot 4 \cdot 4$

Write the prime factorization of each number using exponents.

30. 126 31. 300 32. 54 33. 256 34. 98

Write each number in exponential form. Use 2 or 3 as the exponent.

35. 25 36. 49 37. 1000 38. 64 39. 121

Standardized Testing ▶ Performance Task

1. a. List ten numbers that have 20 as a factor.
   b. Look for patterns in your list from part (a). Then write a divisibility test for 20.

2. a. Use a factor tree to find the prime factorization of each of these powers of ten: 10^1, 10^2, 10^3.
   b. Use your results from part (a) to find the prime factorization of 10^8 without sketching a factor tree.

FOR ASSESSMENT AND PORTFOLIOS

EXTENDED E2 EXPLORATION

THE CLEANING CREW

The Situation

A group of middle school students decided to spend the summer cleaning parks. In their area, there are 25 city and county parks they can clean. The students were given a choice of payment methods.

payment method A

$100 per park

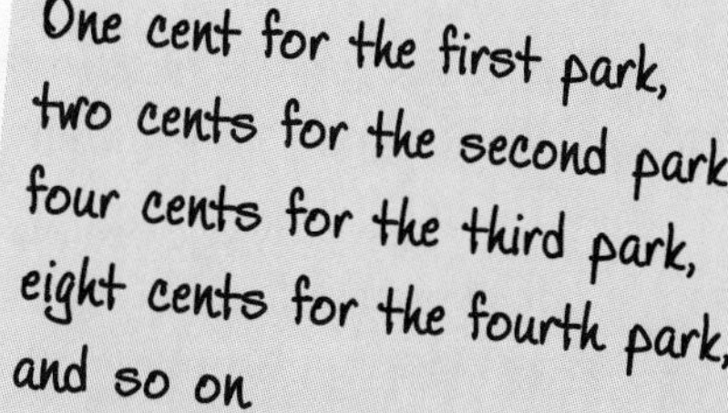

The Problem

Decide which payment method you would advise the students to choose.

Something to Think About

- Which problem solving strategies seem helpful for this problem?
- Do you see any connections to other problems you have solved?

Present Your Results

Write a summary that clearly explains why you chose the method of payment you did. Include any drawings, diagrams, charts, or tables you used to solve the problem.

Fraction Multiplication

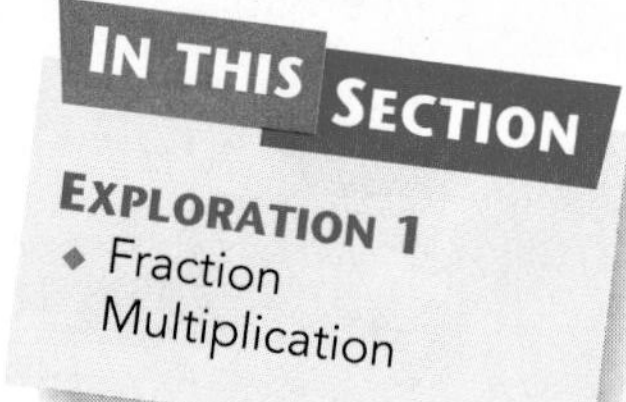

A Fair Share

Setting the Stage

Since ancient times, mathematics problems have been used as puzzles. The story below is an example of such a puzzle.

Three brave, but not very bright, treasure hunters recovered a small box of priceless Spanish doubloons aboard a sunken ship. They took the coins back to their campsite. Since it was late, they decided to go to sleep and divide the treasure the next day.

One of the treasure hunters, fearing that the others did not understand mathematics well enough to give out fair shares, took $\frac{1}{3}$ of the coins in the middle of the night and fled into the darkness.

Later that night, another treasure hunter awoke and saw that some of the coins were missing. That treasure hunter took $\frac{1}{3}$ of the remaining coins and also fled into the night.

The third treasure hunter awoke and was surprised to see the others gone and many of the coins missing. Trusting that the others left a fair share, the third treasure hunter took the remaining coins and walked away whistling happily.

Which of the treasure hunters ended up with the greatest share of the doubloons?

Think About It

1 Do you think any of the treasure hunters ended up with more than a fair share of doubloons? If so, which ones? Explain.

2 Do you need to know how many doubloons were in the box to answer the question? Explain.

Exploration 1

Fraction Multiplication

SET UP *You will need:* • *paper for folding* • *colored pencils*

GOAL

LEARN HOW TO...
- multiply fractions
- use common factors to write fractions in lowest terms

AS YOU...
- use paper folding to solve the treasure puzzle

3 a. The first treasure hunter took $\frac{1}{3}$ of the treasure. What fraction of the treasure was left for the others?

b. The second treasure hunter took $\frac{1}{3}$ of the part that was left behind. Copy and complete the phrase below.

2nd treasure hunter's share $= \frac{1}{3}$ of __?__ (part left behind by the 1st hunter)

▶ **Finding a Part of a Part When you find a fractional part of a part, you are multiplying fractions. You can model this with paper folding.**

4 Let a sheet of paper represent the whole treasure. Then work through Steps 1–4 to model $\frac{1}{3}$ of $\frac{2}{3}$, or $\frac{1}{3} \cdot \frac{2}{3}$.

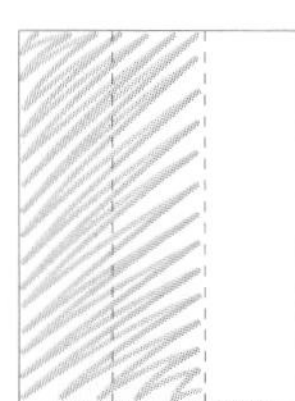

Step 1 Fold the paper into thirds with vertical folds. Shade two of the columns to represent the remaining coins.

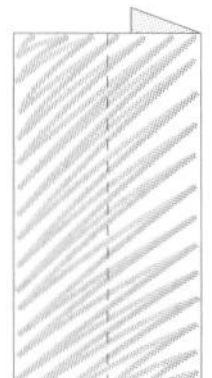

Step 2 Refold the paper so only the shaded part is showing.

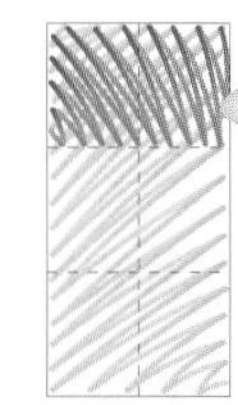

Step 3 Fold the paper into thirds with horizontal folds. Shade one of the rows using a different color.

Step 4 Unfold your paper and examine your results.

5 Use your unfolded paper to answer parts (a)–(c).

The first hunter took $\frac{1}{3}$ of the whole treasure.

The second hunter took $\frac{1}{3}$ of the $\frac{2}{3}$ left behind by the first hunter.

a. How many small regions is the whole paper divided into?

b. What fraction of the whole paper is double-shaded?

c. What fraction of the whole treasure did the second treasure hunter take?

6 **a.** Write a fraction multiplication problem that represents the part of the whole treasure that was left for the third treasure hunter.

b. What fraction of the whole treasure was left for the third treasure hunter?

7 **Discussion** Which treasure hunter got the greatest share of the treasure? What fraction of the remaining coins should the second treasure hunter have taken so that everyone got a fair share? Explain.

Remember, this means $\frac{1}{3}$ of $\frac{1}{2}$.

8 Use paper folding to find $\frac{1}{3} \cdot \frac{1}{2}$.

a. Use vertical folds and shading to model $\frac{1}{2}$ with paper folding.

b. Use your model from part (a) to find $\frac{1}{3} \cdot \frac{1}{2}$. Remember to use horizontal folds and shade with a different color.

c. What fraction of the whole paper is double-shaded?

9 **Discussion** A student folded paper as shown to find $\frac{2}{3} \cdot \frac{4}{5}$. Use the sketch to find the product.

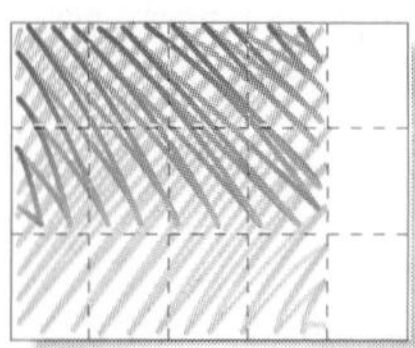

▶ **A Pattern for Multiplication** **By looking back at the results of your paper-folding, you can discover a method for multiplying fractions without using a visual model.**

10 **Try This as a Class** Make a table of the products you found.

a. How is the numerator of each product related to the numerators in the problem?

b. How is the denominator of each product related to the denominators in the problem?

c. Explain how you can multiply two fractions without using paper folding or a sketch.

Question	Multiplication problem	Product
5c	$\frac{1}{3} \cdot \frac{2}{3}$	$\frac{2}{9}$
6	$\frac{2}{3} \cdot \frac{2}{3}$	?
8	$\frac{1}{3} \cdot \frac{1}{2}$	?
9	$\frac{2}{3} \cdot \frac{4}{5}$	?

d. Use your method from part (c) to find $\frac{3}{4} \cdot \frac{4}{5}$.

11 **CHECKPOINT** Find each product without paper folding.

a. $\frac{3}{7} \cdot \frac{1}{2}$ b. $\frac{2}{3} \cdot \frac{3}{5}$ c. $\frac{2}{5} \cdot \frac{10}{12}$ d. $\frac{3}{8} \cdot \frac{4}{9}$

...checks that you can multiply fractions.

▶ **Lowest Terms** **Some products you found were not in lowest terms. You learned to write fractions in lowest terms by dividing the numerator and the denominator by the same whole number.**

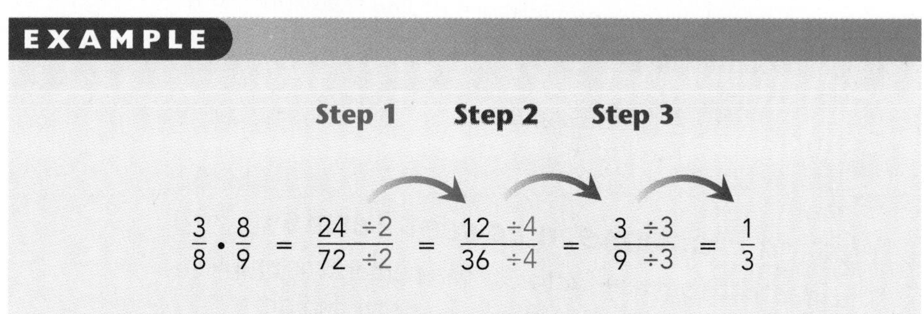

$$\frac{3}{8} \cdot \frac{8}{9} = \frac{24 \div 2}{72 \div 2} = \frac{12 \div 4}{36 \div 4} = \frac{3 \div 3}{9 \div 3} = \frac{1}{3}$$

FOR ◀HELP with *writing fractions in lowest terms*, see **MODULE 2, p. 114**

12 a. The number you divide by has to be a common factor of both the numerator and the denominator. Why?

b. Divide by a different common factor in Step 1 of the Example. Show the steps to find the fraction in lowest terms.

c. How can you write $\frac{24}{72}$ in lowest terms in fewer than three steps?

13 **Discussion** Think about what you learned about common factors in Section 2. How can you write $\frac{24}{72}$ in lowest terms in one step?

...checks that you can write a fraction in lowest terms.

14 ✓ **CHECKPOINT** Write each product in lowest terms.

a. $\frac{2}{3} \cdot \frac{3}{5}$ b. $\frac{2}{5} \cdot \frac{10}{12}$ c. $\frac{3}{8} \cdot \frac{4}{9}$

15 In the story, each treasure hunter took a whole number of coins. What do you know about the original number of coins in the box?

HOMEWORK EXERCISES ▶ See Exs. 1–17 on pp. 269–270.

Section 3 Key Concepts

Multiplying Fractions (pp. 265–267)

Step 1 Multiply the numerators of the fractions to find the numerator of the product.

Step 2 Multiply the denominators of the fractions to find the denominator of the product.

Example $\frac{3}{4} \cdot \frac{8}{15} = \frac{3 \cdot 8}{4 \cdot 15} = \frac{24}{60}$

Writing Fractions in Lowest Terms (p. 267)

The greatest common factor of the numerator and the denominator of a fraction can be used to find an equivalent fraction in lowest terms in one step.

Example $\frac{24}{60} = \frac{24 \div 12}{60 \div 12} = \frac{2}{5}$

The GCF of 24 and 60 is 12.

16 **Key Concepts Question** When you multiply two whole numbers other than 0, the product is always greater than or equal to either number. Is this true when you multiply two fractions? Give an example.

Section 3

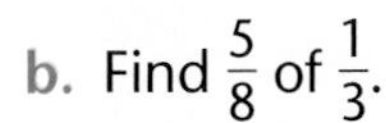

Practice & Application Exercises

1\. a. Find $\frac{1}{3}$ of $\frac{5}{8}$.

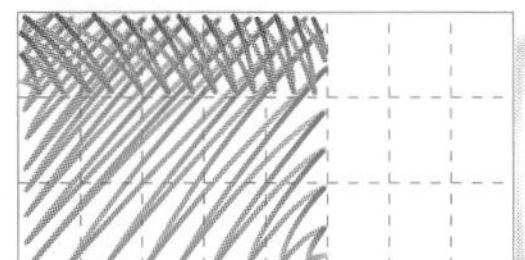

b. Find $\frac{5}{8}$ of $\frac{1}{3}$.

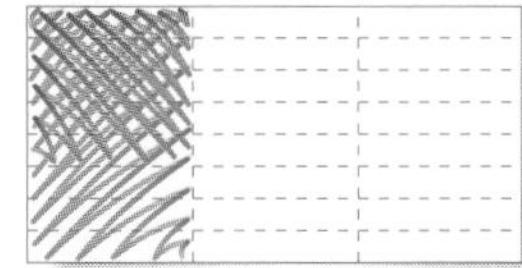

c. How do the products in parts (a) and (b) compare?

Use common factors to write each fraction in lowest terms.

2\. $\frac{12}{18}$

3\. $\frac{25}{40}$

4\. $\frac{32}{48}$

5\. $\frac{28}{70}$

Find each product. Write your answer in lowest terms.

6\. $\frac{3}{5} \cdot \frac{1}{2}$

7\. $\frac{4}{9} \cdot \frac{5}{6}$

8\. $\frac{7}{10} \cdot \frac{2}{3}$

9\. $\frac{1}{12} \cdot \frac{1}{12}$

10\. $\frac{1}{2} \cdot \frac{4}{5}$

11\. $\frac{9}{16} \cdot \frac{2}{3}$

12\. $\frac{10}{20} \cdot \frac{14}{30}$

13\. $\frac{16}{21} \cdot \frac{3}{4}$

14\. Three fifths of a group of students surveyed said they would like to visit the National Zoo. If $\frac{5}{6}$ of those $\frac{3}{5}$ also said they would like to visit the Air and Space Museum, what fraction of the students surveyed said they would like to visit both attractions?

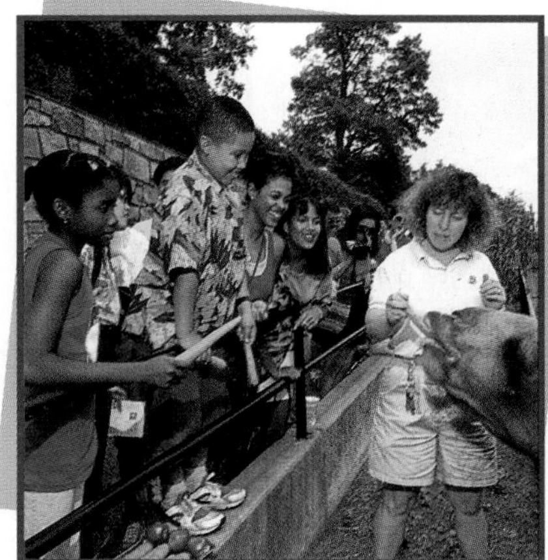

15\. One fifth of a farmer's corn crop is destroyed by hail. Later that summer, $\frac{1}{3}$ of the remaining crop is eaten by insects. To file an insurance claim, the farmer needs to find the part of the total original crop eaten by insects. The farmer says it is $\frac{1}{15}$. Is this correct? Explain.

16. **Challenge** Read the story puzzle below. How many brownies did the original recipe make?

Don decided to make $\frac{1}{2}$ the number of brownies from a recipe. He changed the recipe by cutting the amount of each ingredient in half.

Later he gave his reduced recipe to his sister Sylvie. She changed it to make only $\frac{1}{4}$ of Don's recipe.

Sylvie gave her recipe to Julio, who made $\frac{2}{3}$ of the amount in Sylvie's recipe. Julio made 30 brownies.

Visual THINKING

Exercise 17 checks that you understand fraction multiplication.

Reflecting on the Section

17. a. The model below was used to multiply two fractions. The double-shaded part shows the product. What are the fractions, and what is their product?

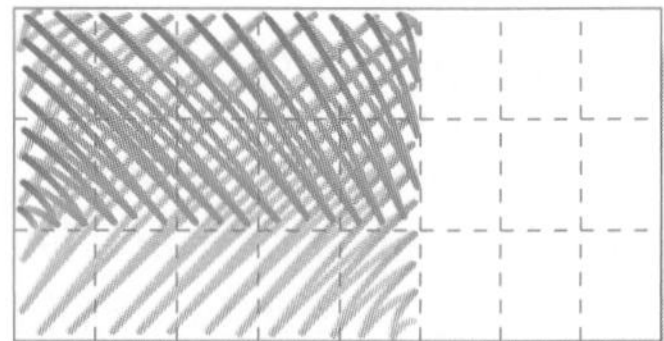

b. Use your rule for multiplying fractions to check your answer to part (a).

c. Express the product of the fractions in lowest terms.

Spiral Review

Write the prime factorization of each number using exponents. (Module 4, p. 257)

18. 44 19. 125 20. 56 21. 117

For each pair, explain why the shapes *are* or *are not* congruent. (Module 2, p. 87, pp. 98–100)

22.

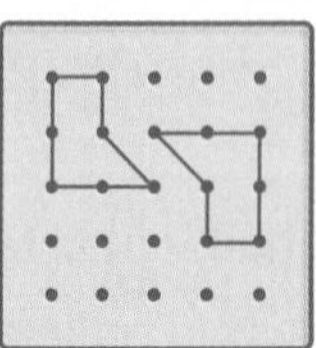

23.

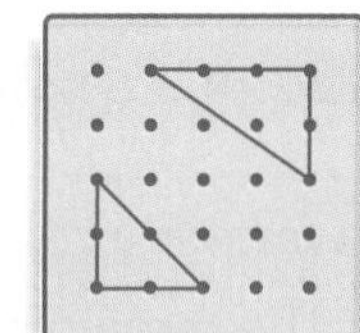

Find each product without a calculator. (Toolbox, p. 595)

24. 15 • 26 25. 24 • 382 26. 32 • 505

Extension 

Products in Lowest Terms

Here is another way to find a product like $\frac{3}{20} \cdot \frac{4}{5}$ in lowest terms. Divide a numerator and a denominator by the common factor 4 *before* you multiply.

divide by 4 → 1

divide by 4 → 5

$$\frac{3}{\cancel{20}_5} \cdot \frac{\cancel{4}^1}{5} = \frac{3}{25}$$

3 • 1 = 3

5 • 5 = 25

27. Find $\frac{5}{12} \cdot \frac{4}{15}$ in lowest terms as shown above and as shown on page 267. Which method is easier for you? Why?

Puzzle Making

Using Fractions Here is a way to create a story puzzle.

Step 1: Start with a number that has many factors. Choose some operations to carry out.

Step 2: Use the numbers from Step 1 to write the clues.

Step 3: Think of a theme. Then create a story using the clues.

Puzzle answer = 120		**Puzzle clues**
$\frac{1}{2}$ of 120 = 60	→	• Person A took $\frac{1}{2}$.
120 – 60 = 60 $\frac{1}{3}$ of 60 = 20	→	• Person B took $\frac{1}{3}$ of what was left.
60 – 20 = 40 40 – 40 = 0	→	• Person C took the 40 that were left.

Camp Cookies Puzzle When Janell went to camp, her mom sent along a box of cookies. Janell gave half of the cookies to her roommate. She then gave one third of the remaining cookies to her camp counselor. Janell hid the 40 cookies that were left. How many cookies did Janell's mom send?

3 **Create Your Own** Follow Steps 1–3 to write your own fraction story puzzle that has an answer of 270.

Section 3 Extra Skill Practice

Write each fraction in lowest terms.

1. $\frac{6}{12}$
2. $\frac{5}{20}$
3. $\frac{11}{99}$
4. $\frac{14}{35}$
5. $\frac{18}{24}$
6. $\frac{26}{39}$
7. $\frac{30}{45}$
8. $\frac{15}{24}$
9. $\frac{27}{36}$
10. $\frac{22}{36}$
11. $\frac{16}{40}$
12. $\frac{42}{54}$

Find each product. Write each answer in lowest terms.

13. $\frac{1}{2} \cdot \frac{2}{3}$
14. $\frac{3}{16} \cdot \frac{4}{9}$
15. $\frac{5}{12} \cdot \frac{6}{25}$
16. $\frac{1}{2} \cdot \frac{1}{2}$
17. $\frac{27}{32} \cdot \frac{2}{9}$
18. $\frac{10}{39} \cdot \frac{13}{20}$
19. $\frac{11}{25} \cdot \frac{15}{22}$
20. $\frac{42}{63} \cdot \frac{24}{35}$
21. $\frac{7}{9} \cdot \frac{12}{20}$
22. $\frac{14}{24} \cdot \frac{2}{3}$
23. $\frac{5}{12} \cdot \frac{16}{30}$
24. $\frac{18}{45} \cdot \frac{15}{36}$
25. The string section makes up about $\frac{2}{3}$ of a symphony orchestra.
    a. Cellos make up about $\frac{1}{5}$ of the string section. About what part of a symphony orchestra are cellos?
    b. Violins make up about $\frac{3}{5}$ of the string section. About what part of a symphony orchestra are violins?

Standardized Testing ▶ Free Response

Write each fractional answer in lowest terms.

1. Half the marbles in a bag are black and half are white. Each marble is either shiny or dull. One-sixth of the black marbles are shiny, and six-sevenths of the white marbles are dull. What fraction of the marbles in the bag are of each type?
   a. shiny black b. dull white c. shiny white
2. Another bag contains the following marbles: 8 shiny black marbles, 7 dull black marbles, and 9 red marbles. Find the theoretical probability of picking each type of marble.
   a. red b. black c. white d. black or red

Section 4 Decimal Multiplication

IN THIS SECTION

EXPLORATION 1
- Multiplying Decimals

EXPLORATION 2
- Estimating Decimal Products

Target Games

Setting the Stage

SET UP *Work with a partner. You will need:* • *Labsheet 4A* • *calculator*

Games like darts test your ability to hit a target. The goal of *Target Number* is to find a product close to the target number.

Use mental math and estimation.

Target Number

- Player 1 chooses a number to multiply by the constant factor, trying to come as close to the target number as possible. The player then uses a calculator to find the product.
- Players take turns challenging each other's product. A player can win a game in two ways—If his or her product is not challenged, or if it is closer to the target number than the challenger's product.

Sample Game 1 Target Number = 226	Constant Factor = 13
Perry multiplies the constant factor by 15.	13 • 15 = 195
Mary challenges by multiplying by 18.	13 • 18 = 234
Perry challenges by multiplying by 16.	13 • 16 = 208 Mary wins!

Mary wins since 234 is closer to the target number than Perry's 208.

Use Labsheet 4A. Play at least three games of *Target Number*.

Think About It

1 In Game 1, is there a way that Perry could have successfully challenged Mary? Explain.

GOAL

LEARN HOW TO...
- multiply decimals
- estimate decimal products

AS YOU...
- model decimal products on grids

Exploration 1

Multiplying Decimals

SET UP *You will need Labsheet 4B.*

Mary and Perry played Game 2 of *Target Number* as shown.

Sample Game 2 Target Number = 408	Constant Factor = 7
Mary multiplies the constant factor by 59.	7 • 59 = 413
Perry challenges by multiplying by 58.	7 • 58 = 406
Mary decides not to challenge Perry.	Perry wins!

2 Think about using a decimal to challenge Perry in Game 2. Should the decimal be greater than or less than 58.5? Why?

▶ **To successfully challenge another player in *Target Number*, it may be necessary to multiply by a decimal. Decimal products, like fraction products, can be modeled by shading a part of a part.**

EXAMPLE

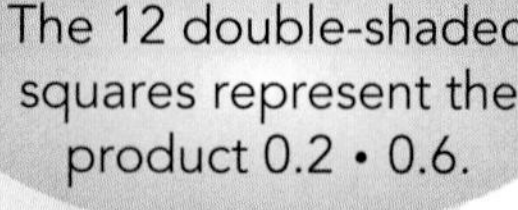

Model the product 0.2 • 0.6 using a 10 x 10 grid to represent 1 whole.

Step 1 Lightly shade 0.6.

Step 2 Double-shade 0.2 of the part shaded in Step 1.

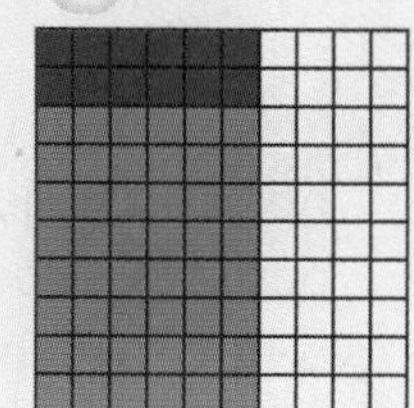

3 Discussion

a. What part of the whole grid is each small square? Write your answer as a fraction and as a decimal.

b. What part of the whole grid is double-shaded? What does 0.2 • 0.6 equal? Write your answer as a decimal.

c. Find $\frac{2}{10}$ of $\frac{6}{10}$ in fraction form. Why is this the same as 0.2 • 0.6?

Use Labsheet 4B for Questions 4–6.

4 Use the *Decimal Multiplication Grids* to model the decimal products 0.5 • 0.4 and 0.3 • 0.3.

5 Follow the directions for *Decimal and Fraction Products* to compute decimal products using fraction multiplication.

6 **Try This as a Class** Look back at your completed *Decimal and Fraction Products* table.

a. How are the digits in the decimal factors in the first column used to find the digits in the decimal product?

b. How is the number of decimal places in the decimal product related to the number of decimal places in the factors?

c. To find the product 0.25 • 0.3, you need to write a zero as a placeholder after you multiply the digits. Which is correct, *0.075* or *0.750*? Why?

7 Find 0.5 • 0.4 and 0.3 • 0.3 without using grids or fractions. Compare the products with those in Question 4.

8 ✓ **CHECKPOINT** Find each decimal product.

a. 0.8 • 0.09 **b.** 0.3 • 1.5 **c.** 2.5 • 4

d. 0.02 • 0.003 **e.** 22.6 • 3.1 **f.** 2.004 • 0.5

... checks that you can find decimal products.

▶ **Estimating Products** **Estimation can help you place the decimal point in a product or check that your answer is reasonable.**

EXAMPLE

Estimate:
The product is about 800 • 5, or 4000.

Place the decimal point here since 3787.2 is about 4000.

789 • 4.8 = 3787.2

9 **Try This as a Class** Estimate to find the correct place for the decimal point in each product. Explain your thinking.

a. 0.9 • 0.7 = 63 **b.** 416 • 0.23 = 9568

c. 0.04 • 0.27 = 108 **d.** 3.05 • 0.13 = 3965

HOMEWORK EXERCISES ▶ See Exs. 1–12 on pp. 278–279.

GOAL

LEARN HOW TO...
- improve your estimating skills

AS YOU...
- play *Target Number Plus or Minus 1*

Exploration 2

Estimating Decimal Products

SET UP *Work with a partner. You will need one calculator.*

In a new game, *Target Number Plus or Minus 1*, the goal is to find a product that is within 1 of the target number. To play the game, follow the flowchart below. You must use estimation and mental math to decide what numbers to enter in the calculator.

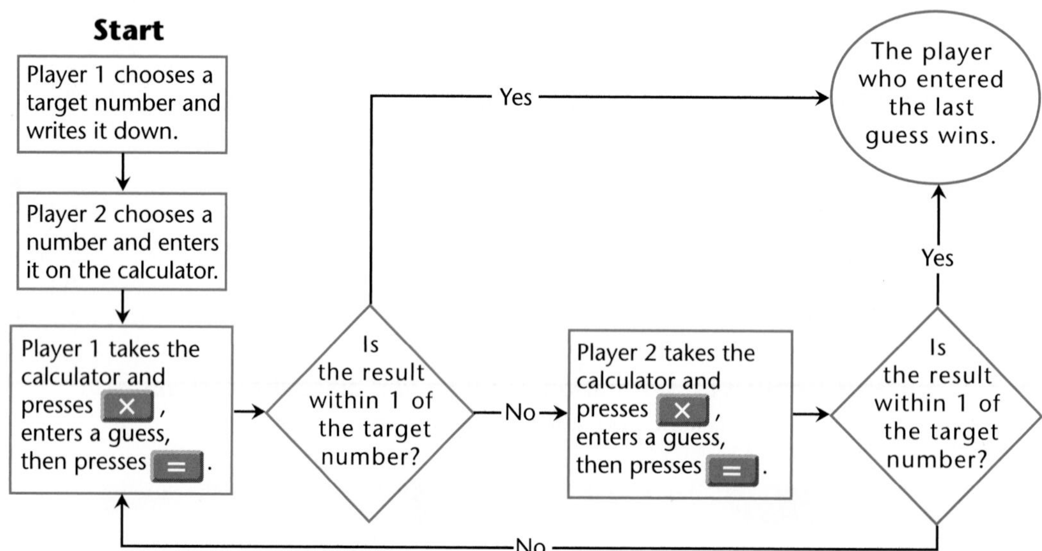

Sample Game

Player 1 chose 196 for the target number.
Player 2 chose the number 7.

Player	Keys pressed	Display
2	7	7.
1	× 2 5 =	175.
2	× 1 . 1 =	192.5
1	× 1 . 0 2 =	196.35

Since 196.35 is within 1 of 196, Player 1 wins!

10 Play *Target Number Plus or Minus 1* at least 5 times. Each time you play, record the target number, the keys pressed during each player's turn, and the products that are displayed.

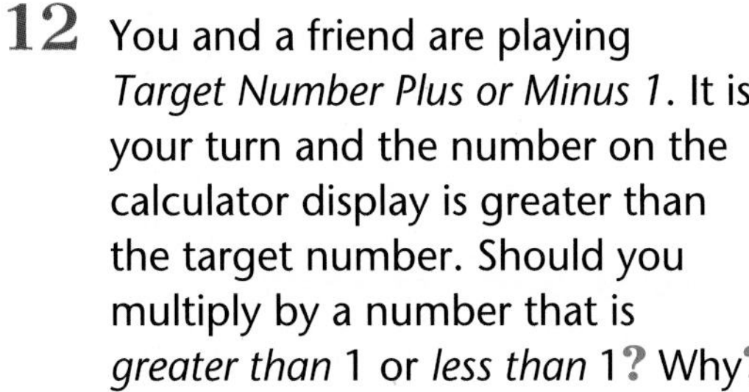

11 Lian and Elena are playing *Target Number Plus or Minus 1.* The target number is 54. After Lian completes her turn, the calculator display shows 55.05. "I've won!," Lian shouts. "55 is within one of 54!" Elena disagrees. She says the game is not over yet. Who is right? Why?

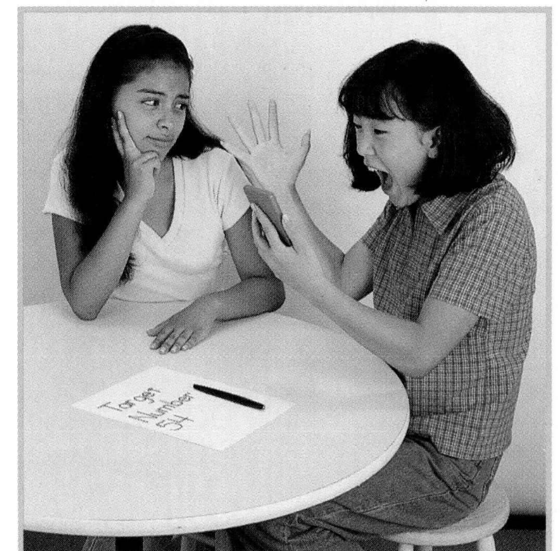

12 You and a friend are playing *Target Number Plus or Minus 1*. It is your turn and the number on the calculator display is greater than the target number. Should you multiply by a number that is *greater than* 1 or *less than* 1? Why?

13 **Mental Math** Use mental math to find each product.

a. 545 • 0.1 **b.** 72 • 0.01 **c.** 23.8 • 0.01

14 **Try This as a Class** In parts (a)–(d), use your estimation skills to choose the decimal that will give a product within 1 of the target number when multiplied by the number on the calculator. Explain each choice.

a. Target Number = 50 Calculator displays [7.]

Choices: 7.1 7.5 7.7 7.9

b. Target Number = 75 Calculator displays [11.]

Choices: 7.05 6.17 6.45 6.82

c. Target Number = 88 Calculator displays [160.]

Choices: 1.90 1.82 0.75 0.55

d. Target Number = 50 Calculator displays [545.]

Choices: 0.09 0.20 2.00 10.9

HOMEWORK EXERCISES ▶ See Exs. 13–25 on pp. 279–280.

Section 4 Key Concepts

Decimal Multiplication (pp. 274–275)

Example Find $6.17 \cdot 5.3$.

Step 1 Multiply the numbers as whole numbers.

$617 \cdot 53 = 32701$

2 decimal places

$2 + 1 = 3$
3 decimal places

Step 2 Use the sum of the number of decimal places in the factors to place the decimal point in the product.

$6.17 \cdot 5.3 = 32.701$

1 decimal place

Step 3 Use estimation to check that your answer is reasonable.

$6.17 \cdot 5.3$ is about $6 \cdot 5$ or 30. The answer of 32.701 is reasonable.

15 Key Concepts Question Your goal is to multiply 9 by a decimal to get a product within 1 of 93. Use estimation to find such a decimal. Explain your thinking. Multiply to check your estimate.

Section 4 Practice & Application Exercises

Copy each problem. Then correctly place the decimal point in each product.

1. $255 \cdot 0.21 = 5355$
2. $3.2 \cdot 8.8 = 2816$
3. $0.98 \cdot 1.05 = 1029$
4. $0.05 \cdot 9.8 = 49$

Find each product without a calculator. Then use estimation to check that your answer is reasonable.

5. $0.3 \cdot 0.12$
6. $4.8 \cdot 5.9$
7. $7.8 \cdot 0.6$
8. $0.09 \cdot 0.01$
9. $24.8 \cdot 0.36$
10. $1.98 \cdot 0.67$

11. **Writing** Without multiplying, would you expect 2.8 • 0.52 to be *greater than* or *less than* 1.4? Why?

12. A recycling company recycles aluminum to a manufacturer for $1.13 per pound. If the recycling company has 329.7 pounds to recycle, how much money will the recycling company receive?

Mental Math Use mental math to find each product.

13. 67 • 0.01 14. 0.01 • 84.7 15. 263.5 • 0.01

16. **Energy** A color TV uses 0.23 kilowatts of power. Suppose the electric company charges $0.14 per kilowatt for every hour of use. Choose the best estimate of the cost to watch one hour of TV.

a. $0.32 b. $0.03

c. $3.22

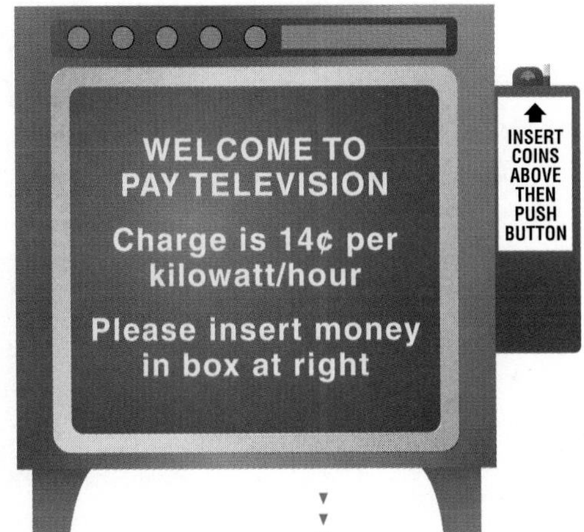

17. By age 18, a child in the United States will have watched an average of about 17,000 hours of television. Use your answer from Exercise 16 to estimate the cost of watching 17,000 hours of television.

18. This week, Julie Elliot worked her regular 40 hours plus 5.75 hours overtime. For every hour she works overtime, she is paid for 1.5 hours. Her hourly wage is $6.34.

a. Estimate Julie's total wages this week.

b. Find the exact amount Julie earned this week.

Predict whether each product will be *greater than, less than,* or *equal to* the number in pink. Explain how you know.

19. **7.8** • 0.87 20. **0.013** • 1 21. **0.16** • 1.5

22. Tamika has a certificate of deposit that earns 4% interest annually. At the end of one year the bank will pay her 4% of the $235.73 she deposited. Estimate 0.04 • $235.73 to choose the correct amount she will receive after one year.

a. 94¢ b. $9.43 c. $94.29 d. $942.92

23. **Open-ended** Use estimation to find a decimal that will give a product within 1 of 164 when multiplied by 80.

24. Challenge Find the least and the greatest possible products for each expression using any of the digits 1–9. A digit may be used only once to find each product.

a. ?.? × ?

b. ?.? × ?.?

Reflecting on the Section

Visual THINKING

Exercise 25 checks that you understand decimal multiplication.

25. a. Explain how you can use the product 3 • 21 to find 0.3 • 0.21.

b. Part of a 10 × 100 grid used to model 0.3 • 0.21 is shown. If the whole grid were shown, how many small squares would there be?

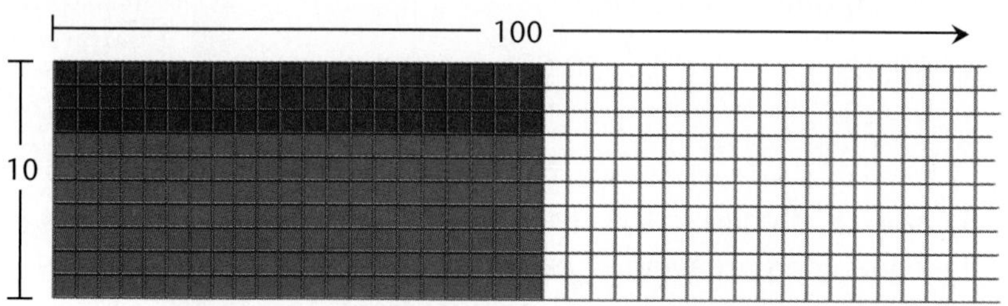

c. Does the shading on the grid show the same result as you found in part (a)? Explain.

Spiral Review

Write each product in lowest terms. (Module 4, p. 268)

26. $\frac{1}{4} \cdot \frac{3}{8}$ **27.** $\frac{2}{9} \cdot \frac{3}{5}$ **28.** $\frac{4}{9} \cdot \frac{3}{4}$

Find the perimeter of each figure. (Toolbox , p. 599)

29.

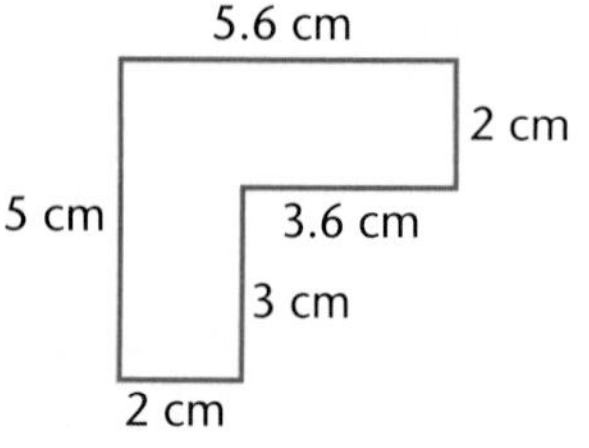

30.

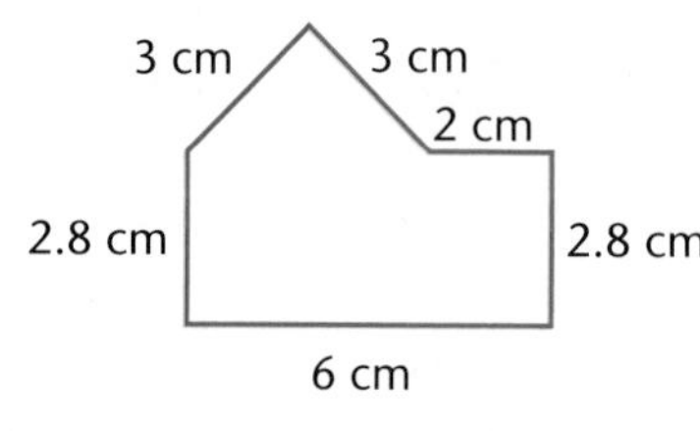

Evaluate each expression. (Module 1, p. 51)

31. 34 – 6 • 3 **32.** (7 + 16) • 4 **33.** 35 – 12 + 9

Section 4 Extra Skill Practice

Copy each problem. Then place the decimal point in each product.

1. 5.23 • 38 = 19874
2. 652 • 0.24 = 15648
3. 0.002 • 46 = 92
4. 0.4 • 9.01 = 3604

Mental Math **Use mental math to find each product.**

5. 0.1 • 27.6
6. 3.05 • 0.01
7. 534.9 • 0.01

Find each product without using a calculator. Then use estimation to check that your answer is reasonable.

8. 0.6 • 0.42
9. 2.7 • 3.1
10. 9.4 • 0.8
11. 4.35 • 0.54
12. 216 • 1.49
13. 5.6 • 0.009
14. 0.24 • 16.2
15. 37.5 • 0.02
16. 9.8 • 2.08

Use estimation to find the decimal that will give a product within 1 of each target number when multiplied by the constant factor. Explain your choice.

17. Target Number = 35 Constant Factor = 101
    Choices: 0.25 0.35 2.9
18. Target Number = 80 Constant Factor = 55
    Choices: 0.75 1.45 1.65
19. Target Number = 176 Constant Factor = 28
    Choices: 5.89 6.31 7.17

Standardized Testing ▶ Open-ended

1. Write a word problem that can be solved using the number sentence 8.99 • 2.5 = __?__.
2. Find a number you can multiply 7.6 by to get a product which is greater than 3.8, but less than 7.6.
3. Write an example to show that the product of two numbers can sometimes be less than either of the factors.

Section 5 Equations and Graphs

IN THIS SECTION

EXPLORATION 1
- Graphing on a Coordinate Grid

EXPLORATION 2
- Expressions and Equations

Guess My Rule

Setting the Stage

SET UP *Work with a partner. You will need Labsheet 5A.*

In the TV game *Name That Tune*, contestants tried to name a song by listening to just a few of its notes. In *Guess My Rule* you'll try to name a rule by knowing just a few pairs of numbers.

Guess My Rule

Players alternate turns. On your turn:

- Your partner takes a rule card without showing it to you.
- You try to guess the hidden rule by giving *input* values (numbers) one at a time. Your partner will apply the rule on the card to the input and tell you the result, or the *output*.
- You can give at most ten input values, and you can try guessing the rule after any of them. Your turn ends when you correctly guess the rule, or when you have made three incorrect guesses.

The player who correctly guesses the most rules wins.

Multiply the input by 2.

Sample Turn

Input	Output	Guess	Response
2	4	Add 2 to the input.	Incorrect
0	0	(no guess made)	
3	6	Multiply input by 2.	Correct

Use Labsheet 5A. **Play *Guess My Rule* using the eight rule cards.**

Think About It

1 Did you use a special strategy for choosing the input values when you were guessing a rule? If so, describe your strategy.

2 Write a rule that can produce the following table.

Input	1	2	5	12
Output	10	20	50	120

3 Use the rule from Question 2 to find the output for each input.

a. 3 **b.** 0 **c.** 1000 **d.** 2.5

Exploration 1

Graphing on a Coordinate Grid

GOAL

LEARN HOW TO...
- graph pairs of values on a coordinate grid

AS YOU...
- build on the game *Guess My Rule*

KEY TERMS
- ordered pair
- coordinate grid
- axes
- origin

SET UP *You will need Labsheet 5B.*

▶ **Each input and output value in *Guess My Rule* can be written as an ordered pair. An example is shown in the table below.**

4 **Use Labsheet 5B.** For each input value, apply the rule to find the output value. Then write each input and its output as an ordered pair. Record your results in the *Rule Table.*

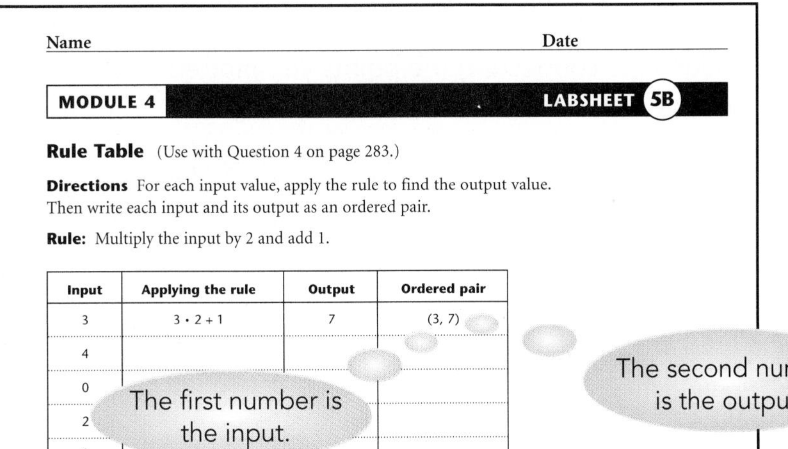
Name Date

MODULE 4 LABSHEET 5B

Rule Table (Use with Question 4 on page 283.)

Directions For each input value, apply the rule to find the output value. Then write each input and its output as an ordered pair.

Rule: Multiply the input by 2 and add 1.

Input	Applying the rule	Output	Ordered pair
3	3 • 2 + 1	7	(3, 7)
4			
0			
2			
1			

Student Resource

Graphing on a Coordinate Grid

Ordered pairs can be graphed as points on a **coordinate grid**. The grid is formed using two number lines as *axes*.

The **axes** intersect at the point (0, 0), called the **origin**.

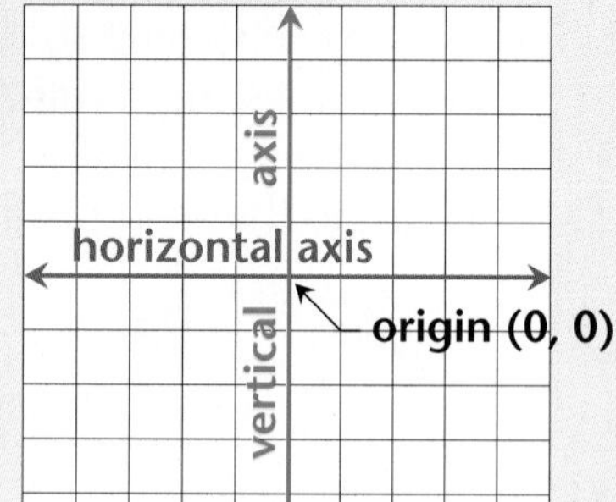

To graph the ordered pair (2, 3) on a coordinate grid, follow these steps.

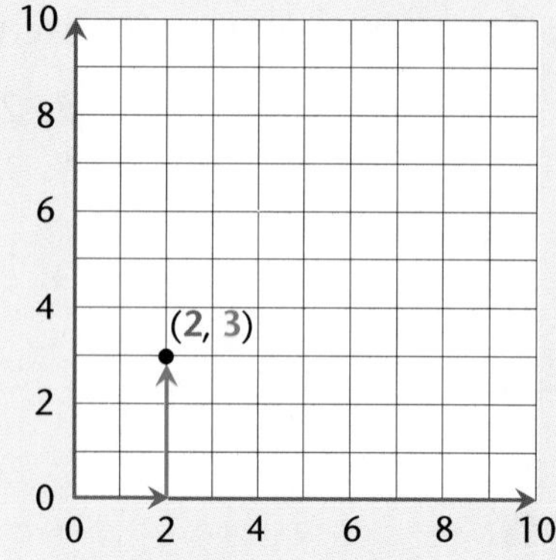

Step 1 Number a scale on each axis.

Step 2 Start at the origin. The first coordinate, 2, tells you how far to move across.

Step 3 The second coordinate, 3, tells you how far to move up.

Step 4 Mark the point. This is the graph of (2, 3).

5 Read the Student Resource above. Describe the steps you need to take to graph each ordered pair.

a. (1, 4) **b.** $(2\frac{1}{2}, 3)$

Use Labsheet 5B for Questions 6–9.

6 Write the ordered pair for each point *A–D* on the *Coordinate Grid* on your labsheet.

...checks that you can graph ordered pairs.

7 ✓ **CHECKPOINT** On the *Empty Coordinate Grid*, graph the ordered pairs you listed in the *Rule Table*.

8 **a.** Draw segments connecting the points you plotted on the *Empty Coordinate Grid* in order from left to right.

b. What do you notice about the points on the graph?

9 Use your graph from Question 8 to predict the missing value.

a. input 3.5, output = ___?___ **b.** output 11, input = ___?___

HOMEWORK EXERCISES ▶ See Exs. 1–16 on pp. 289–290.

Exploration 2

Expressions and Equations

SET UP *You will need centimeter graph paper.*

GOAL

LEARN HOW TO...
- write and evaluate expressions
- write equations
- relate area and perimeter

AS YOU...
- solve a geography puzzle

KEY TERMS
- variable
- evaluate an expression
- equation

▶ **Much of the Earth's surface is covered by three oceans. The clues to the puzzle *What's My Size?* compare their sizes.**

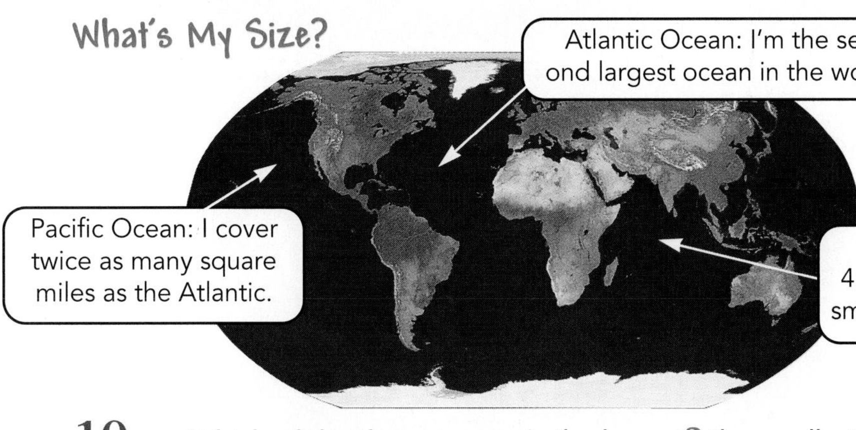

10 **a.** Which of the three oceans is the largest? the smallest?

b. If you knew the area of one of these oceans, could you find the area of the others?

▶ **Variables and Expressions** **You can write mathematical expressions for the clues to show the relationships between the ocean sizes.**

Let n represent the number of square miles covered by the Atlantic.

Size of Each Ocean

Atlantic: n

Pacific: $2 \cdot n$

Indian:

"twice n" is $2 \cdot n$

You learned in Module 1 that an expression can contain numbers and operations. Expressions can also contain variables. Variables are letters or symbols that represent quantities that are unknown or that can change.

FOR HELP with *expressions*, see **MODULE 1, p. 51**

11 Let the variable n represent the number of square miles covered by the Atlantic. Use the clues on page 285 to write an expression for the size of the Indian Ocean.

12 **a.** You can choose any letter for a variable. Choose a variable to represent an input value for the rule: *Multiply the input by 7.*

b. Use the variable you chose to write an expression for the output value of the rule in part (a).

FOR ◀HELP with *order of operations*, see **MODULE 1, p. 51**

▶ **To evaluate an expression with one or more variables, you substitute a number for each variable. Then carry out any operations in the expression.**

EXAMPLE

Evaluate the expression $3 + 2 \cdot x$ when $x = 7$ and when $x = 3.4$.

SAMPLE RESPONSE

When $x = 7$

Substitute **7** for x.

$3 + 2 \cdot x = 3 + 2 \cdot \mathbf{7}$

$= 3 + 14$

$= 17$

When $x = 3.4$

Substitute **3.4** for x.

$3 + 2 \cdot x = 3 + 2 \cdot \mathbf{3.4}$

$= 3 + 6.8$

$= 9.8$

✓ QUESTION 13

...checks that you can evaluate an expression.

13 **✓ CHECKPOINT** Evaluate $4 \cdot k + m$ for the given values of k and m.

a. $k = 3$, $m = 7$

b. $k = 2.5$, $m = 4$

c. $k = \frac{1}{5}$, $m = 3$

d. $k = 6.2$, $m = 3.4$

14 The Atlantic Ocean covers about 32,000,000 square miles. You can use this fact to to solve the puzzle *What's My Size?*

a. What is the size of the Pacific Ocean?

b. Use the expression you wrote in Question 11 to find the area of the Indian Ocean.

▶ **Writing Equations** You can show that two expressions have the same value by writing the symbol "=" between them. The mathematical sentence that results is an **equation**.

Examples of equations

$3 - 1 = 5 - 3$ $\quad$ $2 \bullet n = 64{,}000{,}000$ $\quad$ $a = b + 5$

In Questions 15–17, you'll develop equations for finding the area and perimeter of a rectangle. Remember, the area of a figure is the number of square units of surface it covers.

FOR ▶ HELP with *area*, see **TOOLBOX, p. 600**

15 **a.** Use the grid lines to draw four different rectangles with an area of 24 cm^2 on graph paper.

Each small square has an area of 1 cm by 1 cm, or 1 square centimeter (1 cm^2).

b. Copy and complete the table for the rectangles you drew in part (a).

Length (cm)	Width (cm)	Area (cm^2)
6	4	24

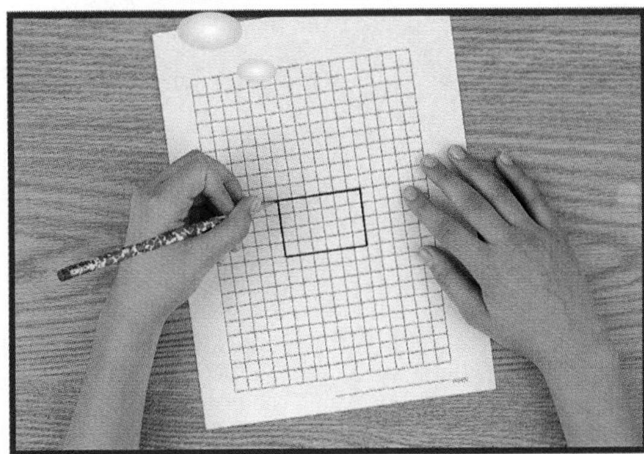

16 **Try This as a Class** Look at your table.

a. How are length and width related to area?

b. Choose variables for length, width, and area. Write a rule in the form of an equation for finding the area of a rectangle.

17 ✓ **CHECKPOINT** Use your table from Question 15.

a. Add another column to your table. Find and record the perimeter of each rectangle.

b. How are the length and width of each rectangle related to the perimeter?

c. Choose variables for length, width, and perimeter. Write a rule in the form of an equation for finding the perimeter of a rectangle.

d. Draw a rectangle with length 6 cm and width 3 cm. Use it to check your rule for finding the perimeter.

✓ **QUESTION 17**

...checks that you can write an equation using variables.

HOMEWORK EXERCISES ▶ See Exs. 17–37 on pp. 290–291.

Section 5 Key Concepts

Key Terms

ordered pair

coordinate grid

origin

axes

variable

evaluate an expression

equation

Coordinate Grid (pp. 283–284)

The numbers in an ordered pair give the location of a point on a coordinate grid.

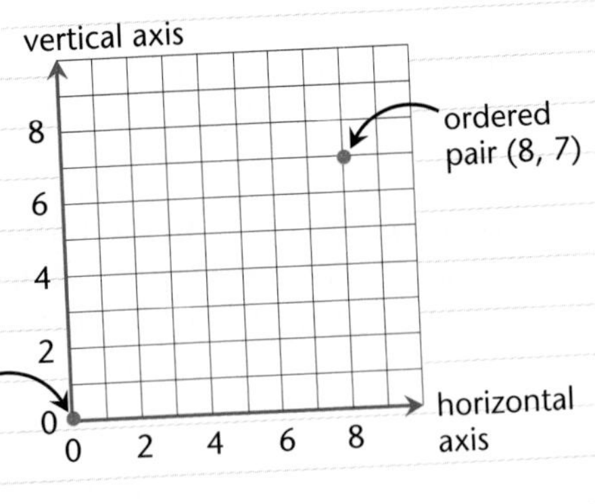

Variables and Expressions (pp. 285–286)

An expression can contain numbers, variables, and operations.

Example Evaluate the expression $24 - 3 \cdot n$ when $n = 5$.

$$24 - 3 \cdot n = 24 - 3 \cdot 5$$
$$= 24 - 15$$
$$= 9$$

Substitute 5 for the variable n to evaluate the expression.

Equations (p. 287)

The rules you wrote for finding the area and the perimeter of a rectangle are equations.

Example

Amount of surface the rectangle covers

Distance around the rectangle

$A = l \cdot w$
$= 3 \cdot 2$
$= 6$
Area is 6 cm^2.

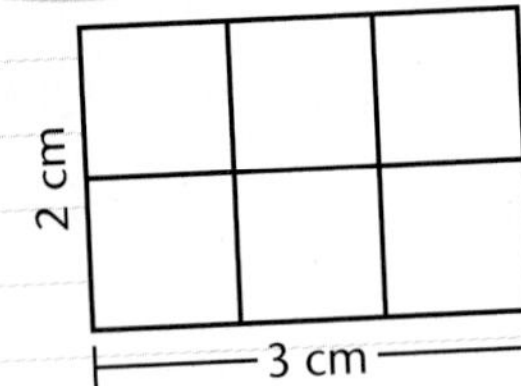

$P = 2 \cdot l + 2 \cdot w$
$= 2 \cdot 3 + 2 \cdot 2$
$= 6 + 4$
$= 10$
Perimeter is 10 cm.

18 **Key Concepts Question** Write an expression to represent the sum of a number and seven. Evaluate your expression when the number is 22.

Section 5 Practice & Application Exercises

YOU WILL NEED

For Exs. 5–13, 15, and 36:
- graph paper

Apply the rule "multiply by 3 and then add 2" to each input. Write each input and output as an ordered pair.

1. 1
2. 5
3. 8
4. 22

Copy the coordinate grid on graph paper. Graph each ordered pair on your coordinate grid. Label each point.

5. (4, 1)
6. (2, 6)
7. (0, 5)
8. (1, 3)
9. (2, 0)
10. $(\frac{1}{2}, \frac{1}{2})$
11. (6, 4)
12. (0, 0)

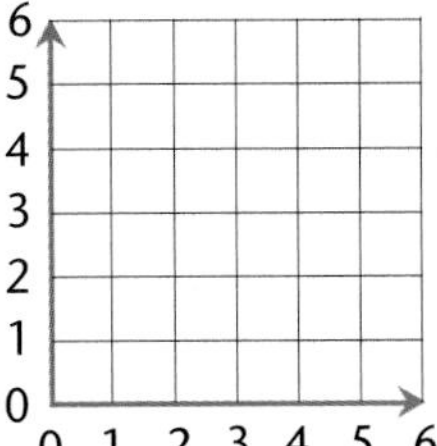

13. a. Graph the ordered pairs in the table on a new coordinate grid.

Input	2	7	5	8
Output	2	12	8	14

b. Draw segments to connect the points you graphed in order from left to right.

c. Use your graph to predict the missing values.
input $4\frac{1}{2}$, output = __?__ output 10, input = __?__

d. List the pairs of inputs and outputs from least to greatest. How can you use patterns to check your answers in part (c)?

14. The table shows how many minutes of parking time (output) drivers get when they put quarters (input) into a parking meter.

Number of quarters (input)	8	7	6	5	4	3	2	1
Minutes of parking time (output)	120	105	90	?	60	45	?	?

a. Write a rule for the output based on the input.

b. Use your rule to find the missing values in the table.

15. **Geometry Connection** Use a new coordinate grid.

a. Graph the ordered pairs (2, 2), (5, 2), (5, 5), and (2, 5).

b. Draw segments to connect the points in the order listed in part (a). Then connect the last point to the first point.

c. Name the polygon you formed in part (b). Be as specific as possible.

16. **Challenge** Transform the polygon you graphed in Exercise 15 by sliding it 2 units to the right and 2 units up. What are the new coordinates of the vertices of the polygon?

Write an expression for each word phrase.

17. the product of six and ten

18. eleven less than nineteen

19. a number divided by five

20. a number multiplied by six

Let v represent an input value. Choose the letter of the expression that represents the output value for each rule.

A. $v - 3$	B. $3 \cdot v$	C. $v + 3$
D. $3 \div v$	E. $v \div 3$	F. $3 - v$

21. Add 3 to the input.

22. Subtract the input from 3.

23. Multiply the input by 3.

24. Divide the input by 3.

Evaluate each expression when $x = 4$ and $y = 10$.

25. $5 \cdot x$

26. $y + 3$

27. $x + 6.3$

28. $y \div 2$

29. $y - x$

30. $3 \cdot x - 2$

Find the area and the perimeter of each rectangle.

31.

5 ft

12 ft

32.

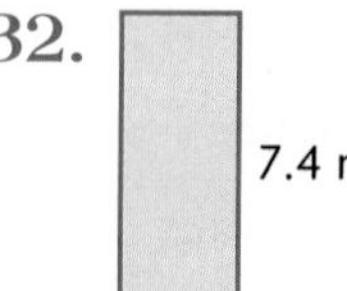

33. **Open-ended** Write a word problem that can be solved by evaluating the expression $24 \cdot n$ when $n = 2$.

34. The *Twins Days Festival* in Twinsburg, Ohio, is the largest annual gathering of twins, triplets, and quadruplets in the world. Write an expression for each number in parts (a)–(d). Use t for the number of sets of twins, p for the number of sets of triplets, and q for the number of sets of quadruplets.

a. the number of people at the festival who are twins

b. the number of people at the festival who are triplets

c. the number of people at the festival who are quadruplets

d. the total number of people who are twins, triplets, or quadruplets at the festival

▲ The Twins Days Festival attracts people from every state of the United States and many other countries.

35. At the 1995 *Twins Days Festival* there were 2798 registered sets of twins, 26 sets of triplets, and 2 sets of quadruplets. Evaluate each expression you wrote in Exercise 34.

36. a. Draw four squares of different sizes on graph paper. Record the area and perimeter of each in a table.

b. Write a rule in the form of an equation to find the area of a square if you know the length of its sides.

c. Write a rule to find the perimeter of a square.

Reflecting on the Section

Write your response to Exercise 37 in your journal.

37. The rule on a *Guess My Rule Card* was applied to the input values 0.5, 1.5, and 2. The pairs of input and output values are shown on the graph.

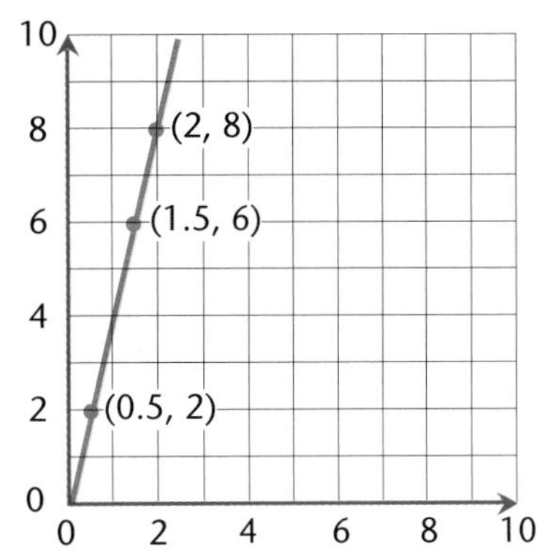

a. Use the graph to predict the output if the input is 1.

b. Guess the rule.

c. Let x represent an input value and let y represent an output value. Write your rule in the form of an equation: $y =$ ___?___.

Journal

Exercise 37 checks that you can connect an equation with a graph.

Spiral Review

Find each product. (Module 4, p. 278)

38. 1.5 • 0.06 39. 5.23 • 1.008 40. 0.9 • 10.47

41. Margo has $1.15 in coins. She wants to buy a note pad that costs $1.00. She does not have exact change. What coins can Margo have? (Module 1, p. 35)

42. One rectangle represents a whole. Write a fraction and a mixed number to describe the entire shaded amount. (Module 2, p. 101)

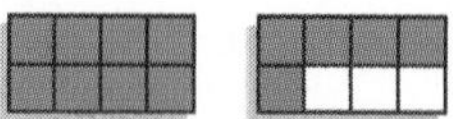

Puzzle Making

Locations on a Grid A grid can help you visualize clues about locations to solve some logic puzzles.

Who lives closest to the school?

Jamyce, Reneé, D.J., Guy, and Tyler all live within 5 blocks of their school. They live directly east, west, north, or south of school.

D.J. lives 1 block from Guy and 4 blocks from school.

To get to Jamyce's house, Reneé walks 3 blocks east to the school, and then 5 blocks north.

Tyler lives 2 blocks from school.

Only Guy and D.J. walk in the same direction after school.

Reneé lives as far as Guy from school but in the opposite direction.

4 Solve the puzzle. Use a grid to help picture the locations. Start by drawing a point to mark the location of the school.

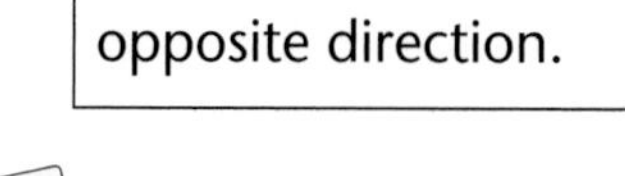

5 Create a logic puzzle that can be solved by using a grid. Your puzzle should have at least four clues.

Section 5

Extra Skill Practice

Name the point that is the graph of each ordered pair.

1. (7, 3) 2. $(4, 3\frac{1}{2})$ 3. (0, 5)

Write the coordinates of each point.

4. *B* 5. *D* 6. *F*

10
8
6
4
2
0
0 2 4 6 8 10
E *F* *A* *C* *G* *B* *D*

Write an expression for each statement.

7. five less than a number
8. a number divided by seven
9. a number plus twelve
10. the product of six and a number

Evaluate each expression when $a = 3$ and $b = 5$.

11. $a \cdot 8$ 12. $10 - b$ 13. $a + b$ 14. $4 \cdot b + a$

Find the area and the perimeter of each rectangle.

15.
5 cm
8 cm

16.
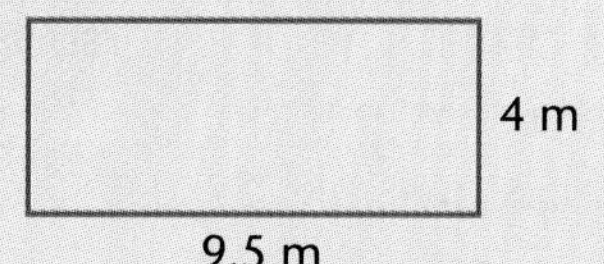

17.
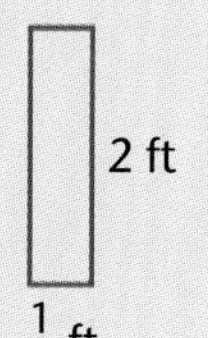

Standardized Testing ▸ Multiple Choice

1. Which set of three points lies on the line shown?

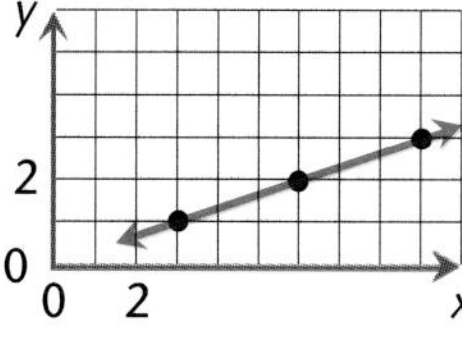

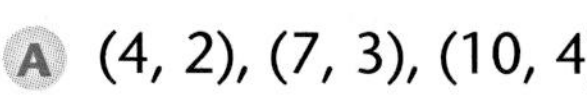

Ⓐ (4, 2), (7, 3), (10, 4)

Ⓑ (1, 3), (2, 6), (3, 9)

Ⓒ (3, 1), (6, 2), (9, 3)

2. Which equation shows the relationship between the first value (*f*) and the second value (*s*) shown in the table?

f	1	2	3	4	5
s	2	4	6	8	10

Ⓐ $f = s$ Ⓑ $2 \cdot f = s$ Ⓒ $f = 3 \cdot s$ Ⓓ $\frac{1}{2} \cdot f = s$

Section 6 Multiples and Mixed Numbers

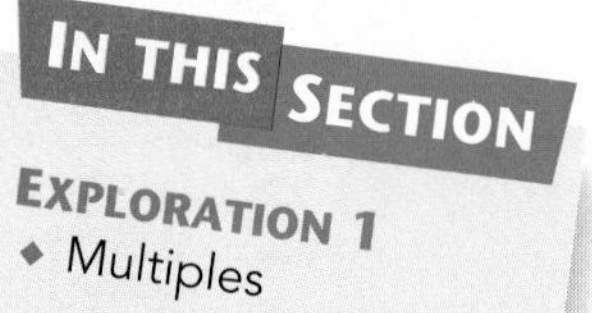

Pattern Play

Setting the Stage

SET UP *Work in a group.*

▶ ***Pattern Tick-Tock* is a game that tests your ability to see number patterns. Play the game with your group.**

Pattern Tick-Tock

- Sit in a circle. The first person begins the counting with "one." Then the next person says "two," and so on **except** when a number is divisible by:

  4—the person says **tick** instead of the number

  6—the person says **tock** instead of the number

  4 and **6**—the person says **tick-tock** instead of the number

- If a mistake is made, the counting starts over. Continue until 50.

Think About It

1 List the numbers that each word replaced.

a. tick **b.** tock **c.** tick-tock

2 Which word was said most often: *tick*, *tock*, or *tick-tock*? Why was it said most often?

Three

Tock

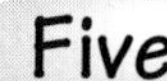

Exploration 1

Multiples

SET UP *You will need Labsheet 6A.*

GOAL

LEARN HOW TO...
- find multiples and least common multiples

AS YOU...
- analyze the game *Pattern Tick-Tock*

KEY TERMS
- multiple
- least common multiple (LCM)

▶ **In *Pattern Tick-Tock*, it is important to be able to recognize *multiples*. A multiple of a whole number is the product of that number and any nonzero whole number.**

For example, 12 is a multiple of 6 since $6 \cdot 2 = 12$.

3 When you played *Pattern Tick-Tock*, "tick" replaced the multiples of what number?

▶ **The multiples of a number form a sequence. Study the sequence for the multiples of 4 shown below.**

Term number	1	2	3	4	5	6	...
Term	4	8	12	16	20	24	...

4 **a.** How is each term in the sequence above related to its term number?

b. What is the 100th term in the sequence?

5 What sequence of multiples appeared in your answer to part (c) of Question 1?

6 ✓ **CHECKPOINT** **Use Labsheet 6A.** Follow the directions on the labsheet to complete the *Sequence Tables for Multiples*. For each sequence, you'll also write a general rule and use it to extend the sequence.

...checks that you can write and extend lists of multiples.

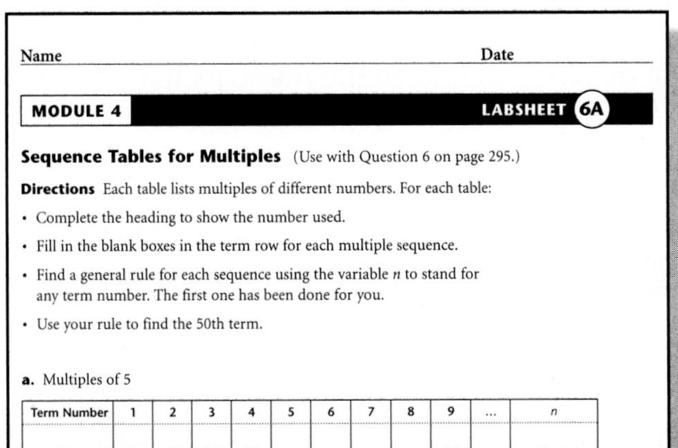
Name Date

MODULE 4 LABSHEET 6A

Sequence Tables for Multiples (Use with Question 6 on page 295.)

Directions Each table lists multiples of different numbers. For each table:
- Complete the heading to show the number used.
- Fill in the blank boxes in the term row for each multiple sequence.
- Find a general rule for each sequence using the variable *n* to stand for any term number. The first one has been done for you.
- Use your rule to find the 50th term.

a. Multiples of 5

Term Number	1	2	3	4	5	6	7	8	9	...	*n*
Term	5	10	15	20					45	...	$5 \cdot n$

You'll use what you know about multiples to answer Question 7.

7 Maya met Jim at the mall. They really liked each other but were too shy to say how they felt. Hoping to see Maya, Jim returns to the mall every 5 days. Hoping to see Jim, Maya returns to the mall every 6 days.

a. List the first seven multiples of 5 to represent the days Jim returns to the mall.

b. List the first seven multiples of 6 to represent the days Maya returns to the mall.

c. Look at the two lists of multiples. In how many days will Maya and Jim be at the mall on the same day?

▶ **The least common multiple (LCM) of two or more numbers is the least number that is a multiple of all the numbers. The answer to Question 7(c) is the least common multiple of 5 and 6.**

EXAMPLE

Find the least common multiple of 8 and 6.

SAMPLE RESPONSE

List the multiples of each number. Then circle the common multiples.

Multiples of 8: 8, 16, (24), 32, 40, (48), ...

Multiples of 6: 6, 12, 18, (24), 30, 36, 42, (48), ...

Common multiples: 24, 48, ...

The LCM of 8 and 6 is 24.

✔ QUESTION 8

...checks that you can find the LCM of two numbers.

8 ✔ CHECKPOINT Find the least common multiple of each pair of numbers.

a. 3 and 9 b. 12 and 9 c. 25 and 15

9 Use lists of multiples to find all the numbers that "tick-tock" will replace in a game of *Pattern Tick-Tock* if you count to 100 and use "tick" for 8 and "tock" for 12.

HOMEWORK EXERCISES See Exs. 1–12 on p. 301.

Exploration 2

Mixed Numbers

SET UP *Work in a group. You will need:* • *pattern blocks* • *die or numbered cube*

GOAL

LEARN HOW TO...
- write a fraction greater than 1 as a mixed number and vice versa

AS YOU...
- trade pattern blocks in the game *Flex Your Hex*

10 Play the game *Flex Your Hex* with your group.

FLEX YOUR HEX

- Place about 30 triangles and about 15 hexagons in a pile.
- On your turn, roll the die and take the number of triangles shown on the die from the pile. Trade for a hexagon if you have enough triangles.
- The winner is the first player to collect five hexagons.

Your 1st roll: 

You take 5 triangles.

You cannot trade.

Your 2nd roll: 

You add to

You can trade.

You now have

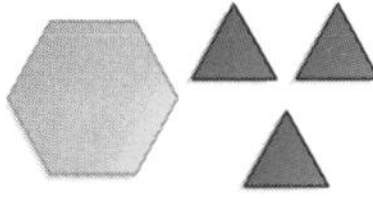

11 If you have 4 triangles, what is the probability that your next roll will give you enough triangles to trade for a hexagon?

12 **Discussion**

a. What part of a hexagon is one triangle?

b. How does this fraction equation represent a roll of 2 on your first turn and a roll of 3 on your next turn?

$$\frac{2}{6} + \frac{3}{6} = \frac{5}{6}$$

c. What fraction equation can you use to represent a first roll of 6 and a second roll of 5?

d. Will the denominator always be 6 when you add up your rolls? Explain.

13 **Try This as a Class** Suppose your first two rolls add up to $\frac{8}{6}$.

a. How many triangles do you have?

b. After trading, how many hexagons and triangles will you have? How can you use division to find out?

c. What fractional part of a hexagon are the remaining triangles in part (b)? Use this fraction to write the number of hexagons as a mixed number.

FOR HELP with *mixed numbers*, see **MODULE 2, p. 101**

▶ **Fractions to Mixed Numbers You can write fractions greater than 1 as mixed numbers by using division. Pattern block trades can show this process.**

EXAMPLE

Write the fraction $\frac{10}{6}$ as a mixed number.

SAMPLE RESPONSE

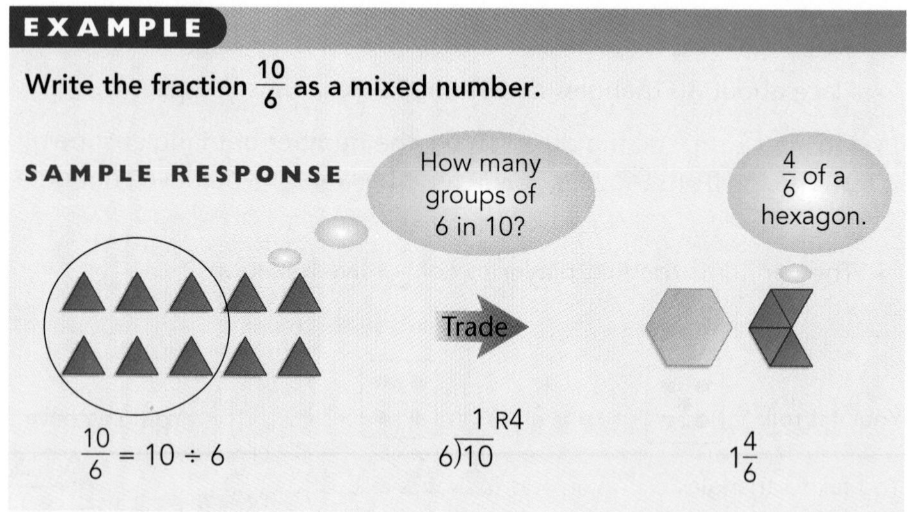

14 **Discussion** Three blue **rhombuses** (▰) make a yellow **hexagon** (⬢).

a. Explain why seven blue rhombuses make $\frac{7}{3}$ yellow hexagons.

b. Explain how to write $\frac{7}{3}$ as a mixed number.

✓ QUESTION 15

...checks that you can write a fraction as a mixed number.

15 **✓ CHECKPOINT** Write each fraction as a mixed number if possible. If it is not possible, explain why not.

a. $\frac{27}{8}$ **b.** $\frac{3}{4}$ **c.** $\frac{32}{5}$ **d.** $\frac{3}{3}$

▶ **You can also write mixed numbers as answers to whole number divisions. The Example above shows that $10 \div 6 = 1\frac{4}{6}$.**

16 **Try This as a Class** Use the division 17 ÷ 3.

a. Draw a picture to find the quotient as a mixed number.

b. Explain how you can tell what fraction to use in the mixed number without drawing a picture.

c. Think about the problem:

A bowling league has 3-member teams.
How many teams can be formed from 17 people?

Do you think the mixed number in part (a) is an appropriate answer? If not, how would you answer the question? Explain.

▶ **Mixed Numbers to Fractions** **You have learned how to write fractions greater than one as mixed numbers. You can also write mixed numbers as fractions greater than one.**

EXAMPLE

Write the mixed number $2\frac{1}{3}$ as a fraction.

SAMPLE RESPONSE

$2\frac{1}{3} \quad = \quad 2 + \frac{1}{3} \quad = \quad \frac{6}{3} + \frac{1}{3} = \frac{7}{3}$

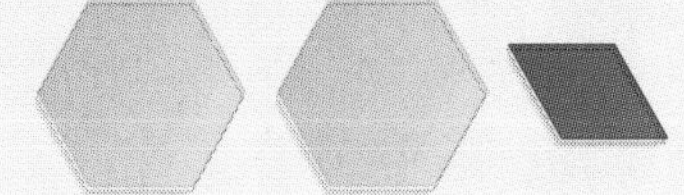

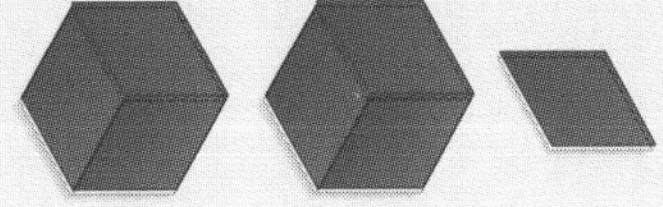

17 **Discussion** Look at the Example.

a. Why was 2 written as $\frac{6}{3}$?

b. Explain how to write $4\frac{2}{3}$ as a fraction.

18 Explain how to write $2\frac{1}{4}$ as a fraction.

19 ✓ **CHECKPOINT** Write each mixed number as a fraction.

a. $1\frac{3}{4}$ **b.** $2\frac{1}{2}$ **c.** $10\frac{2}{3}$ **d.** $3\frac{5}{6}$

✓ **QUESTION 19**

...checks that you can write a mixed number as a fraction.

HOMEWORK EXERCISES ▶ **See Exs. 13–34 on pp. 301–302.**

Section 6 Key Concepts

Key Terms

multiple

least common multiple

Multiples (pp. 295–296)

You can find the least common multiple (LCM) of two or more numbers by listing multiples of each number in order. You can stop when you find a multiple that is common to all the numbers.

Example

multiples of 4: 4, 8, (12), 16, 20, (24), ...
multiples of 6: 6, (12), ...
The least common multiple of 4 and 6 is 12.

You can stop at 12.

Fractions Greater Than 1 (pp. 298–299)

- A mixed number can be written as a fraction by rewriting the whole number as a fraction and then combining it with the fractional part already there.
- Fractions greater than 1 can be written as mixed numbers by using division.

Quotients as Mixed Numbers (pp. 298–299)

The remainder in a division problem can be written over the divisor to form a fraction.

Example

$17 \div 5 = 3\frac{2}{5}$

Remember that you may not always want mixed number answers in every situation.

Key Concepts Questions

20 Find the LCM of 9 and 15.

21 Write $\frac{37}{12}$ as a mixed number. Write your mixed number as a fraction to check your work.

22 Describe a division situation where a mixed number is an appropriate answer and one where it is not appropriate.

Section 6

Practice & Application Exercises

List the first seven multiples of each number.

1. 7
2. 25
3. 99
4. 106

5. Suppose you can withdraw only multiples of $20.00 from a bank teller machine. Which amounts can you withdraw?

   a. $40.00 b. $250.00 c. $160.00 d. $220.00

Find the least common multiple of each set of numbers.

6. 3 and 7
7. 6, 9, and 12
8. 14 and 10
9. 16 and 20
10. 48 and 12
11. 15 and 35

12. The fountains at Disney's EPCOT Center in Florida contain special-effect devices called *shooters.* They shoot columns of water at different time intervals.

    a. Suppose a fountain has one shooter that shoots water every 8 seconds and another that goes off every 12 seconds. How long after the fountain is turned on will both shooters go off at the same time?

    b. A third shooter shoots water every 6 seconds. Suppose all three shooters just went off together. How many seconds will pass before all three go off again at the same time?

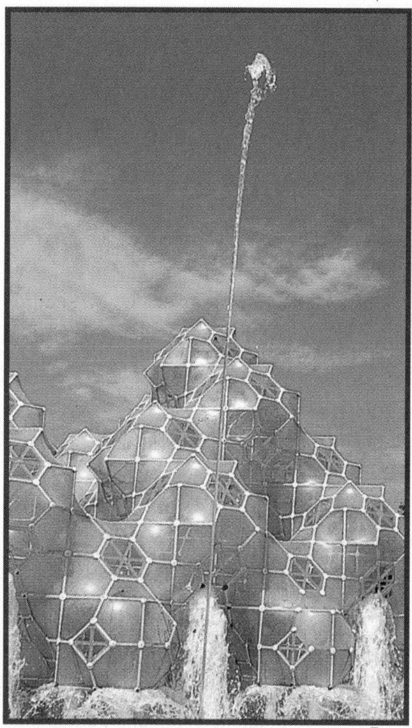

Write each fraction as a mixed number.

13. $\frac{21}{4}$
14. $\frac{15}{8}$
15. $\frac{41}{6}$
16. $\frac{14}{3}$

Write each mixed number as a fraction.

17. $4\frac{1}{5}$
18. $1\frac{7}{12}$
19. $11\frac{1}{2}$
20. $2\frac{2}{3}$
21. $7\frac{4}{5}$
22. $3\frac{1}{8}$
23. $6\frac{5}{7}$
24. $9\frac{9}{11}$

Visual Thinking **Copy the number line. Mark and label a point on the line where each fraction or mixed number would lie.**

25. $\frac{14}{6}$ 26. $\frac{9}{6}$ 27. $2\frac{1}{6}$ 28. $1\frac{2}{3}$

Write each quotient as a mixed number.

29. $26 \div 5$ 30. $52 \div 7$ 31. $98 \div 10$

32. Suppose you roll a 3 on your first five turns of *Flex Your Hex*. The sequence represents the hexagons or part of a hexagon you had after each turn.

$$\frac{3}{6}, \frac{6}{6}, \frac{9}{6}, \frac{12}{6}, \frac{15}{6}$$

   a. Write a rule for finding any term in the sequence from its term number.

   b. If possible, write each term in the sequence as a mixed number to show the results after trading.

   c. Suppose you keep rolling a 3 on every turn. In how many turns will you collect 5 hexagons?

33. Suppose you are sharing 6 dollars among 4 people. Which form of $6 \div 4$ would you use to describe each share? Explain your choice.

   a. 1 R2 b. 1.50 c. $1\frac{1}{2}$

Discussion

Exercise 34 checks that you understand mixed numbers.

Reflecting on the Section

Be prepared to discuss your response to Exercise 34 in class.

Here is a shortcut for changing a mixed number to a fraction.

- **Multiply** the whole number and the denominator. **Add** the numerator. $2 \times 3 + 1 = 7$
- Write the result over the **original denominator, 3.**

$$2\frac{1}{3} = \frac{7}{3}$$

34. Look back at the Example on page 299. Use the idea of trading pattern blocks to explain each step in the shortcut.

Spiral Review

35. Find the area and the perimeter of a rectangle with a width of 7 cm and a length of 13.5 cm. (Module 4, p. 288)

Use mental math, paper and pencil, or a calculator to write each fraction as a percent. Round to the nearest whole percent. Explain your method. (Module 3, p. 176; Module 4, p. 237)

36. $\frac{3}{5}$ 37. $\frac{5}{6}$ 38. $\frac{130}{200}$ 39. $\frac{21}{59}$

Find the missing numerator or denominator in each pair of equivalent fractions. (Module 2, p. 114)

40. $\frac{3}{8} = \frac{15}{?}$ 41. $\frac{25}{100} = \frac{?}{4}$ 42. $\frac{?}{3} = \frac{24}{36}$

Career Connection

Choreographer and Dancer: Emiko Tokunaga

Choreographers like Emiko Tokunaga create the steps dancers perform. Emiko designs combinations of dance steps to fit a piece of music. A piece of music can be broken into *measures*, which are groups of beats.

43. Emiko would like two dancers to each perform a different combination of steps, repeating the combination as needed so each reaches the final pose at the end of a piece of music.
    a. One dancer is to perform a combination of steps that is 4 measures long while the other is to perform a combination that is 12 measures long. How many measures long must the piece of music be?
    b. Suppose Emiko adds a third dancer. This dancer performs a combination of steps that is 8 measures long. Can the same piece of music be used? Explain.

Emiko Tokunaga is the Radcliffe College Dance Coordinator. ▲ With her sister Yasuko, she started the Tokunaga Dance Ko. (TDK), which has performed around the world. TDK was the first company selected by the Japan-United States Friendship Commission for their cultural exchange program.

Extra Skill Practice

List the first seven multiples of each number.

1. 4
2. 12
3. 33
4. 110

Find the least common multiple of each set of numbers.

5. 2, 4 and 9
6. 9 and 27
7. 30 and 50
8. 15 and 45
9. 20, 40, and 60
10. 140 and 210

Write each fraction as a mixed number.

11. $\frac{10}{3}$
12. $\frac{14}{9}$
13. $\frac{17}{4}$
14. $\frac{5}{3}$
15. $\frac{21}{2}$

Write each mixed number as a fraction.

16. $1\frac{1}{2}$
17. $5\frac{4}{9}$
18. $2\frac{1}{8}$
19. $3\frac{3}{7}$
20. $9\frac{4}{5}$

Write each quotient as a mixed number.

21. $11 \div 5$
22. $35 \div 3$
23. $18 \div 4$
24. $19 \div 2$

Standardized Testing ▶ Multiple Choice

For Exercises 1–3, choose the word which makes the statement true.

1. The product of two numbers is __?__ a common multiple of the two numbers.

   A sometimes B always C never

2. The least common multiple of two numbers is __?__ one of the numbers.

   A sometimes B always C never

3. The least common multiple of two numbers is __?__ smaller than both numbers.

   A sometimes B always C never

4. Which terms are missing from the sequence?

   $\frac{8}{9}$, __?__, $1\frac{7}{9}$, $2\frac{2}{9}$, __?__, __?__, $3\frac{5}{9}$, 4, __?__

   A $1\frac{4}{9}$, $2\frac{4}{9}$, 3, $4\frac{5}{9}$ B 1, $2\frac{4}{9}$, 3, $4\frac{4}{9}$ C $1\frac{1}{3}$, $2\frac{2}{3}$, $3\frac{1}{9}$, $4\frac{4}{9}$

Puzzle Making

Choosing a Puzzle In this module you have created a number puzzle, a story puzzle, and a logic puzzle. Now you'll decide on a puzzle to include in a class puzzle book.

6 Choose the best puzzle you have created, or write a new one. Your puzzle should include at least one idea from this module:

- probability
- common factors
- fraction multiplication
- coordinate grid
- mixed numbers as fractions
- decimal multiplication
- powers of a number
- divisibility
- multiples

7 Look back over your puzzle. Are the directions and the information clear? Try out your puzzle on a friend or a family member. Then make any necessary revisions.

8 a. Write your puzzle neatly on a sheet of paper that can be three-hole punched to fit in a class notebook. You can attach an envelope to include any clue cards or other materials needed to solve the puzzle.

b. Label your puzzle sheet with the title of the puzzle and your name as the puzzle maker. You may decorate or illustrate your puzzle sheet if you wish.

9 On a separate sheet of paper write the answer to your puzzle and show how it can be solved. Label your answer sheet the same way as your puzzle sheet.

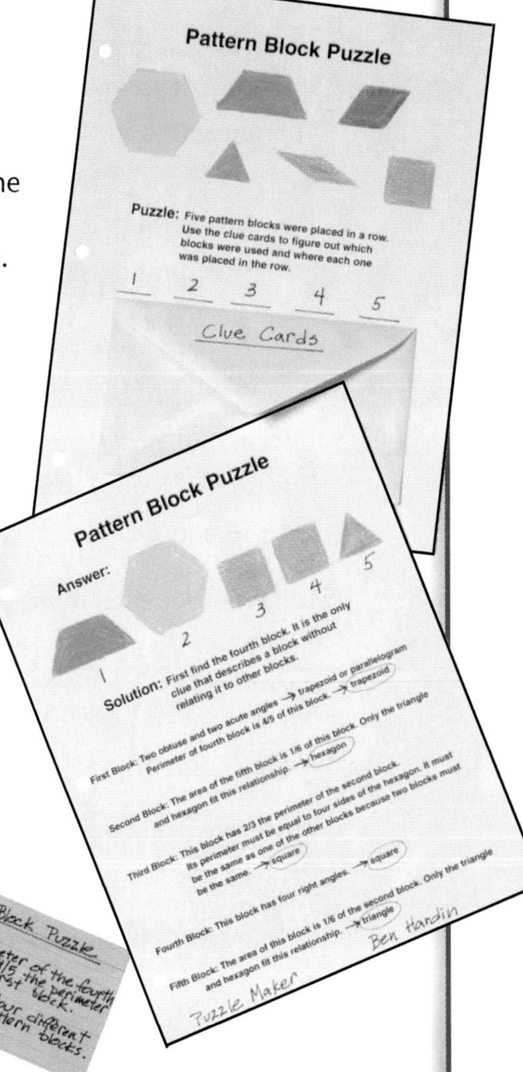

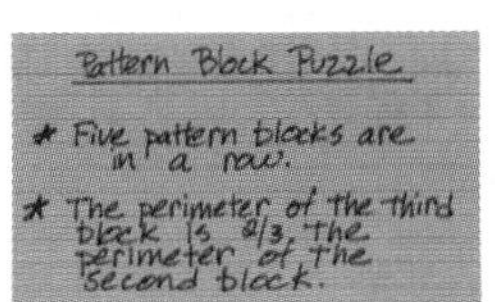

Pattern Block Puzzle
* The fourth block has four right angles.
* The first block has two obtuse angles and two acute angles.

Pattern Block Puzzle
* The area of the fifth block is 1/3 the area of the first block, but 1/6 the area of the second block.
* Two of the blocks are the same type.

Pattern Block Puzzle
* The perimeter of the fourth block is 4/5 the perimeter of the first block.
* There are four different types of pattern blocks.

MODULE 4

Review and Assessment

You will need: • *graph paper* (Ex. 31)

A four-sided die with sides numbered 1 to 4 was rolled 75 times with the results shown. For Exercises 1–3 find the experimental probability of each event. Write each answer as a whole percent. (Sec. 1, Explor. 1)

Outcome	Total
1	16
2	18
3	22
4	19

1. rolling the number 2
2. rolling an even number
3. rolling a number greater than 4
4. Find the theoretical probability of each event in Exercises 1–3. Write each probability as a fraction and as a percent. (Sec. 1, Explor. 2)

For Exercises 5–8 list every digit from 0 through 9 that will complete the number to make each statement true. (Sec. 2, Explor. 1)

The ones digit in the number below is missing.

721,638,51?

5. The number is divisible by 2.
6. The number is divisible by 5.
7. The number is divisible by 3.
8. The number is divisible by 9.

9. **Writing** Jim listed 1, 2, 3, 4, 9, 12, 27, 36, 54, and 108 as the factors of 108. Is his list complete? How did you check? (Sec. 2, Explor. 1)

Find the GCF of each set of numbers. (Sec. 2, Explor. 1)

10. 36 and 48
11. 15, 20, and 32
12. 26 and 52

Tell whether each number is *prime* or *composite*. (Sec. 2, Explor. 2)

13. 22
14. 51
15. 47
16. 111,111

Replace each ? with >, <, or =. Explain your choice. (Sec. 2, Explor. 3)

17. 2^5 ? 5^2
18. 4^3 ? 2^6
19. 3^3 ? $3 \cdot 3 \cdot 3 \cdot 3$

Write the prime factorization of each number using exponents. (Sec. 2, Explor. 3)

20. 32
21. 97
22. 300
23. 231

Find each product. Write each answer in lowest terms. (Sec. 3, Explor. 1)

24. $\frac{3}{8} \cdot \frac{4}{15}$
25. $\frac{5}{7} \cdot \frac{2}{3}$
26. $\frac{5}{16} \cdot \frac{8}{9}$
27. $\frac{3}{5} \cdot \frac{15}{24}$

Find each product without using a calculator. Then, use estimation to check that your answer is reasonable. (Sec. 4, Explor. 1 and Explor. 2)

28. $0.4 \cdot 0.32$

29. $36.3 \cdot 51$

30. $4.7 \cdot 0.006$

31. a. Graph the ordered pairs in the table on a coordinate grid. (Sec. 5, Explor. 1)

Input	3	7	4	8
Output	7	15	9	17

b. Draw segments to connect the points you graphed in order from left to right.

c. Use your graph to predict the missing values.

input $5\frac{1}{2}$, output = ___?___

output = 10, input = ___?___

32. Let *w* represent the width of a rectangle that is twice as long as it is wide. Write an expression for each. (Sec. 5, Explor. 2)

a. length of the rectangle

b. area of the rectangle

33. Evaluate each expression in Exercise 32 when $w = 3.6$. (Sec. 5, Explor. 2)

34. Mark has swim practice every other day. His brother swims every third day. If they both practice on Monday, what is the next day both Mark and his brother will have practice? (Sec. 6, Explor. 1)

Find the missing digit. (Sec. 6, Explor. 2)

35. $6\frac{3}{5} = \frac{?}{5}$

36. $\frac{34}{9} = ?\frac{7}{9}$

37. $4\frac{2}{7} = \frac{30}{?}$

38. $\frac{31}{8} = 3\frac{?}{8}$

Reflecting on the Module

39. **Writing** Choose four key terms from the list on either page 242 or page 288. Use the key terms correctly in a paragraph that describes what you have learned about the concepts outlined on the same page.

MODULE 5

CREATING THINGS

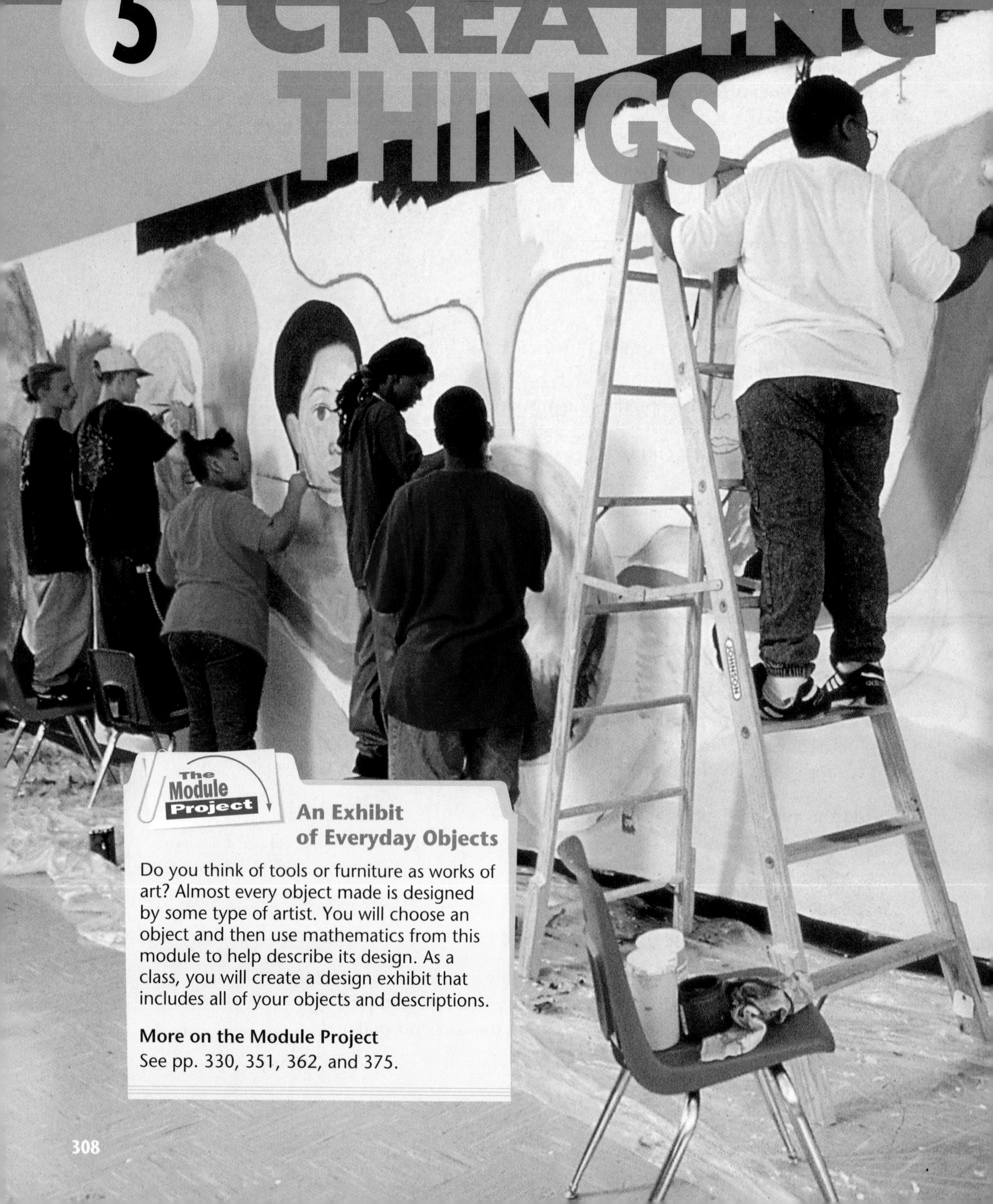

The Module Project

An Exhibit of Everyday Objects

Do you think of tools or furniture as works of art? Almost every object made is designed by some type of artist. You will choose an object and then use mathematics from this module to help describe its design. As a class, you will create a design exhibit that includes all of your objects and descriptions.

More on the Module Project

See pp. 330, 351, 362, and 375.

CONNECTING MATHEMATICS & The Theme

MODULE 5 SECTION OVERVIEW

1 Comparing Fractions
As you use paper folding:
- Use number sense
- Use common denominators to write equivalent fractions
- Use decimals
- Choose a method to compare fractions

2 Customary Units of Length
As you investigate the Great Wall of China:
- Estimate and measure lengths
- Measure in fractions of an inch
- Convert, add, and subtract customary units of length

3 Addition and Subtraction of Fractions
As you learn about weaving:
- Add and subtract fractions

4 Addition and Subtraction of Mixed Numbers
As you look at masks and relief art from different cultures:
- Add mixed numbers
- Subtract mixed numbers

5 Capacity and Mixed Number Multiplication
As you work with recipes:
- Use and convert customary units of capacity
- Use the distributive property
- Multiply mixed numbers

6 Division with Fractions
As you explore geometric puzzles:
- Divide by fractions and mixed numbers

INTERNET
To learn more about the theme:
http://www.mlmath.com

Section 1 Comparing Fractions

IN THIS SECTION

EXPLORATION 1
- Fraction Number Sense

EXPLORATION 2
- Common Denominators

Paper Folding

Setting the Stage

SET UP *You will need:* • *Labsheet 1A* • *scissors*

Sadako and the Thousand Paper Cranes
by Eleanor Coerr with paintings by Ronald Himler

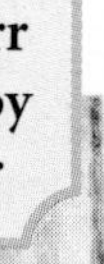

This story takes place in Japan. In the excerpt below, Chizuko visits her friend, Sadako, who is very ill and in the hospital.

Chizuko was pleased with herself. "I've figured out a way for you to get well," she said proudly. "Watch!" She cut a piece of gold paper into a large square. In a short time she had folded it over and over into a beautiful crane.

Sadako was puzzled. "But how can that paper bird make me well?"

"Don't you remember that old story about the crane?" Chizuko asked. "It's supposed to live for a thousand years. If a sick person folds one thousand paper cranes, the gods will grant her wish and make her healthy again." She handed the crane to Sadako. "Here's your first one."

Think About It

1 As the story continues, Sadako folds 644 paper cranes and her classmates fold the rest. Together they fold 1000 cranes.

  a. What fraction of the cranes does Sadako fold?

  b. What fraction do her classmates, including Chizuko, fold?

2 a. **Use Labsheet 1A.** Cranes are challenging to make. Follow the directions on your labsheet to fold a simpler shape—a penguin.

  b. How many parts did you divide your square into by folding? Are any of the parts the same size?

▶ **When you think of using mathematics to create things, you may imagine spaceships, skyscrapers, robots, and other examples of modern technology. But, even the designs of simple things involve mathematics. In this module you'll see how mathematics is used to create things.**

Exploration 1

Fraction $\frac{\text{Number}}{\text{Sense}}$

GOAL

LEARN HOW TO...
- use number sense to compare fractions

AS YOU...
- fold fraction strips

KEY TERM
- inequality

SET UP *You will need:* • *Labsheet 1B* • *scissors*

▶ **The Japanese art of creating things by folding paper is called *origami*. In this Exploration, you'll fold paper to make fraction strips. An example of a completed strip is shown below.**

The dotted lines show where the paper is folded to form three equal-sized pieces.

$\frac{1}{3}$	$\frac{1}{3}$	$\frac{1}{3}$

Each piece is labeled as $\frac{1}{3}$ of a strip.

Use Labsheet 1B for Questions 3 and 4.

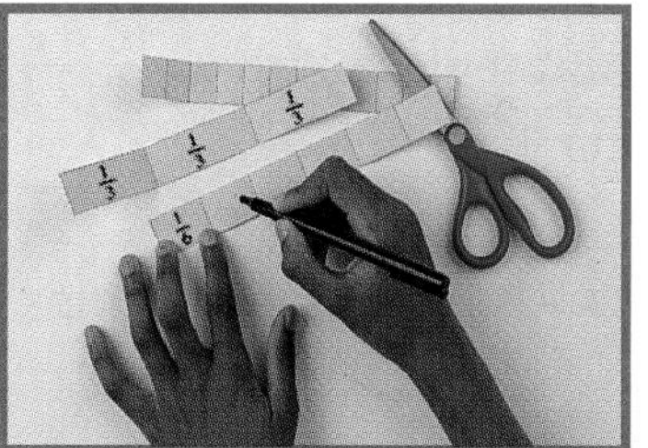

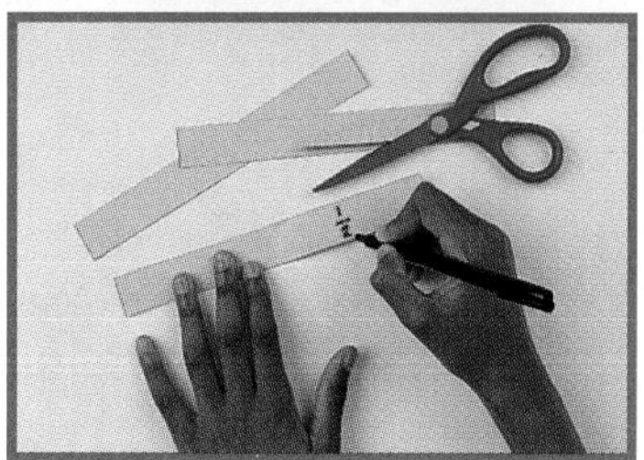

3 Cut out the *Fraction Strips* for thirds, sixths, and twelfths. Fold each strip along the dotted lines and label each part with the fraction name. (The strip for thirds is already labeled.)

4 Cut out the blank strips and fold them so that one strip is folded into halves, one is folded into fourths, and one is folded into eighths. Label each part with the fraction name.

5 Explain how you folded a strip into eighths.

▶ **You can use your strips to compare fractions and to develop your number sense about fractions.**

EXAMPLE

Use fraction strips to compare $\frac{2}{3}$ and $\frac{10}{12}$.

SAMPLE RESPONSE

The original strips are the same length, so you are comparing parts of the same whole.

$\frac{1}{12}$	$\frac{1}{12}$	$\frac{1}{12}$	$\frac{1}{12}$	$\frac{1}{12}$	$\frac{1}{12}$	$\frac{1}{12}$	$\frac{1}{12}$	$\frac{1}{12}$	$\frac{1}{12}$	$\frac{1}{12}$	$\frac{1}{12}$

$\frac{1}{3}$	$\frac{1}{3}$	$\frac{1}{3}$

First Fold the strip for thirds to show $\frac{2}{3}$.

Then Fold the strip for twelfths to show $\frac{10}{12}$ and place it directly above the $\frac{2}{3}$ strip.

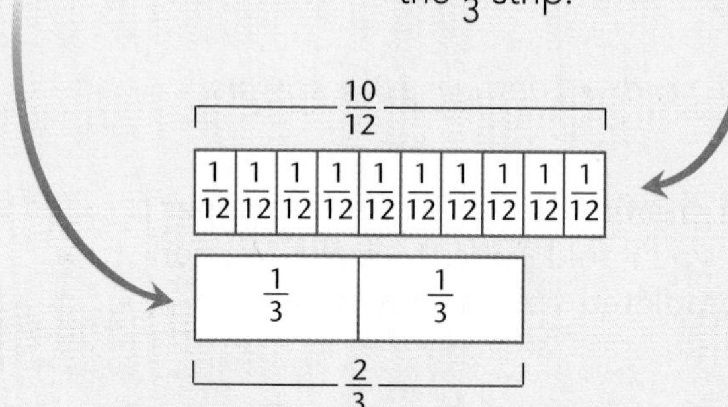

You can see that $\frac{10}{12}$ of a strip is longer than $\frac{2}{3}$ of a strip, so $\frac{10}{12} > \frac{2}{3}$.

▶ **A statement such as $\frac{10}{12} > \frac{2}{3}$ that uses the symbol $>$ or $<$ to compare two numbers is an inequality.**

6 Use your fraction strips to compare each fraction with $\frac{1}{2}$. Replace each __?__ with $>$, $<$, or $=$.

a. $\frac{4}{8}$ __?__ $\frac{1}{2}$ **b.** $\frac{5}{12}$ __?__ $\frac{1}{2}$ **c.** $\frac{7}{8}$ __?__ $\frac{1}{2}$

d. $\frac{2}{3}$ __?__ $\frac{1}{2}$ **e.** $\frac{1}{4}$ __?__ $\frac{1}{2}$ **f.** $\frac{2}{6}$ __?__ $\frac{1}{2}$

7 **Discussion** Look at your results in Question 6. Just by looking at its numerator and denominator, how can you tell whether a fraction is equal to $\frac{1}{2}$? greater than $\frac{1}{2}$? less than $\frac{1}{2}$?

8 Explain how you can use your answers to Question 6, parts (c) and (f), to compare $\frac{7}{8}$ and $\frac{2}{6}$. Then write an inequality that compares $\frac{7}{8}$ and $\frac{2}{6}$.

9 **✓ CHECKPOINT** Use mental math to compare each fraction with $\frac{1}{2}$. Then replace each __?__ with >, <, or = .

a. $\frac{2}{9}$ __?__ $\frac{13}{15}$ b. $\frac{5}{10}$ __?__ $\frac{1}{12}$ c. $\frac{5}{12}$ __?__ $\frac{8}{14}$

✓ QUESTION 9

...checks that you can compare fractions by comparing with $\frac{1}{2}$.

▶ **Other Patterns** **There are other relationships between numerators and denominators that will help you compare fractions.**

10 **a.** On each of your fraction strips, fold one part over so that the rest of the parts are face down. Arrange the parts facing up in order from shortest to longest and record the fractions in that order.

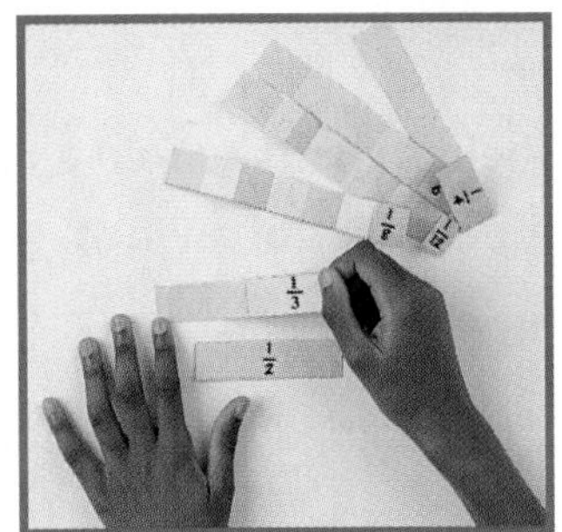

b. The numerators of the fractions showing on your fraction strips are all 1. What do you notice about the order of the denominators?

c. Which fraction is greater, $\frac{1}{9}$ or $\frac{1}{4}$? Explain how you decided.

d. Explain how to order $\frac{2}{6}$, $\frac{2}{4}$, $\frac{2}{3}$, $\frac{2}{2}$, and $\frac{2}{8}$ from least to greatest.

11 **a.** Turn each fraction strip over so that the one section you folded is underneath. For each strip, write the fraction that names the part of the strip you can see.

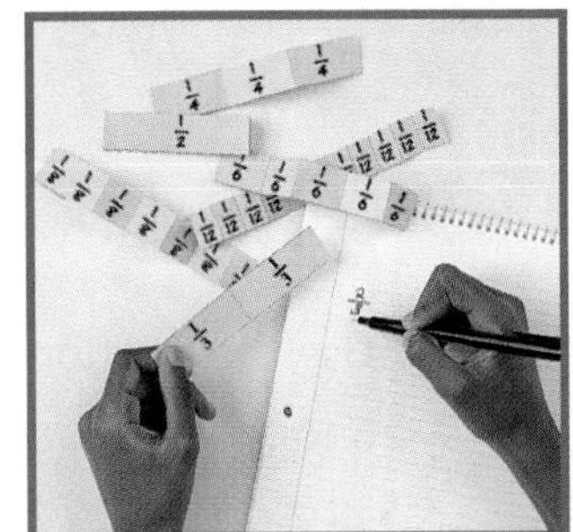

b. What relationship do you notice between the numerator and the denominator of each fraction?

c. Arrange the folded strips so the parts you can see are in order from shortest to longest and record the fractions in that order.

d. Which fraction is greater, $\frac{6}{7}$ or $\frac{10}{11}$? Explain how you decided.

e. Order $\frac{100}{101}$, $\frac{150}{151}$, $\frac{1000}{1001}$, and $\frac{50}{51}$ from least to greatest.

12 **✓ CHECKPOINT** Replace each __?__ with >, <, or =.

a. $\frac{3}{15}$ __?__ $\frac{3}{10}$ b. $\frac{1}{9}$ __?__ $\frac{1}{11}$ c. $\frac{8}{9}$ __?__ $\frac{10}{11}$

✓ QUESTION 12

...checks that you can use number sense to compare fractions.

HOMEWORK EXERCISES ▶ See Exs. 1–15 on pp. 317.

GOAL

LEARN HOW TO...
- use common denominators to write equivalent fractions
- use decimals to compare fractions

AS YOU...
- choose a method to compare fractions

KEY TERMS
- common denominator
- least common denominator

Exploration 2

Common Denominators

SET UP *You will need a fraction calculator (optional).*

▶ **Thelma wants to fold a one-inch strip into thirds. Her ruler does not show thirds of an inch. She thinks $\frac{1}{3}$ is a little less than $\frac{3}{8}$.**

13 **Discussion** Can you use one of the number sense methods you learned in Exploration 1 to compare $\frac{1}{3}$ and $\frac{3}{8}$? Explain.

▶ **Using Equivalent Fractions to Compare** **One way to compare fractions with different denominators is to find equivalent fractions that are easy to compare.**

14 **a.** Copy and complete each list of equivalent fractions.

$$\frac{1}{3} = \frac{?}{6} = \frac{?}{9} = \frac{?}{12} = \frac{?}{15} = \frac{?}{18} = \frac{?}{21} = \frac{?}{24} = \frac{?}{27}$$

$$\frac{3}{8} = \frac{?}{16} = \frac{?}{24} = \frac{?}{32} = \frac{?}{40}$$

b. Use the fractions with 24 as the denominator to compare $\frac{1}{3}$ and $\frac{3}{8}$. Was Thelma correct?

c. Suppose you continue to list equivalent fractions for $\frac{1}{3}$ and $\frac{3}{8}$. What is the next denominator common to both lists?

FOR HELP with *least common multiples*, see **MODULE 4, p. 300**

▶ **The least common denominator of two fractions is the least common multiple (LCM) of their denominators. The least common denominator of $\frac{1}{3}$ and $\frac{3}{8}$ is 24, which is the LCM of 3 and 8.**

15 **Try This as a Class**

a. Find the least common denominator of $\frac{5}{8}$ and $\frac{7}{10}$.

b. What else must you do to compare the two fractions in part (a)?

c. Is $\frac{5}{8}$ greater than or less than $\frac{7}{10}$?

EXAMPLE

Use a common denominator to compare $\frac{5}{6}$ and $\frac{7}{9}$.

SAMPLE RESPONSE

First Find a common multiple of the denominators.

multiples of 6: 6, 12, 18, ...
multiples of 9: 9, 18, ...

The least common denominator of 6 and 9 is 18.

Then Write equivalent fractions using a common denominator.

$\frac{5}{6} = \frac{15}{18}$ $\frac{7}{9} = \frac{14}{18}$

$\frac{15}{18} > \frac{14}{18}$, so $\frac{5}{6} > \frac{7}{9}$.

16 **Discussion** Suppose you use 54 as the common denominator to write equivalent fractions in the Example. What will the new numerators be? Will the final answer be the same? Explain.

17 ✓ **CHECKPOINT** Replace each ? with >, <, or =.

a. $\frac{5}{7}$? $\frac{3}{4}$ **b.** $\frac{13}{15}$? $\frac{4}{5}$ **c.** $\frac{17}{20}$? $\frac{21}{25}$

✓ **QUESTION 17**

...checks that you can compare fractions using a common denominator.

▶ **Using Decimals to Compare** **When the least common denominator is difficult to find, you may choose to compare fractions by changing the fractions to decimals.**

18 Write $\frac{22}{100}$ and $\frac{9}{44}$ as decimals. Use the decimals to compare the fractions.

FOR ◀ HELP

with *writing fractions as decimals*, see

MODULE 3, p. 202.

19 Fraction Calculator Enter 9 / 4 4 and press F⊂D. What do you think F⊂D does?

20 Write each fraction as a decimal rounded to the nearest hundredth. Then replace each ? with >, <, or =.

a. $\frac{5}{13}$? $\frac{4}{11}$ **b.** $\frac{17}{26}$? $\frac{55}{101}$ **c.** $\frac{21}{250}$? $\frac{16}{189}$

21 Would you choose *mental math, paper and pencil,* or a *calculator* to compare $\frac{10}{11}$ and $\frac{120}{121}$? Explain.

HOMEWORK EXERCISES ▶ See Exs. 16–38 on pp. 317–319.

Section 1 Key Concepts

Key Terms

Using Number Sense to Compare Fractions (pp. 311–313)

- See if the numerators or the denominators are the same.

Examples $\frac{1}{2} > \frac{1}{3}$, since halves are greater than thirds.

$\frac{2}{5} < \frac{3}{5}$, since $2 < 3$.

inequality

- See if one fraction is greater than $\frac{1}{2}$ and the other is less than $\frac{1}{2}$.

Example $\frac{3}{4} > \frac{1}{2}$ and $\frac{2}{9} < \frac{1}{2}$, so $\frac{3}{4} > \frac{2}{9}$.

- See if both fractions are one part less than a whole.

Example $\frac{7}{8} > \frac{6}{7}$, since $\frac{7}{8}$ is closer to a whole.

Using a Common Denominator to Compare Fractions (pp. 314–315)

common denominator

least common denominator

You can write equivalent fractions to compare any two fractions.

Example $\frac{2}{3} > \frac{5}{8}$, since $\frac{16}{24} > \frac{15}{24}$.

24 is a common denominator.

Using Decimals to Compare Fractions (p. 315)

You can use decimals to compare any two fractions.

Example

$\frac{3}{10} = 0.3$ and 4 [÷] 11 results in [0.3636364],

so $\frac{3}{10} < \frac{4}{11}$.

22 **Key Concepts Question** What method would you use to compare each pair of fractions? Explain.

a. $\frac{7}{15}$ and $\frac{3}{5}$ **b.** $\frac{6}{9}$ and $\frac{8}{9}$ **c.** $\frac{5}{13}$ and $\frac{12}{19}$

Section 1 Practice & Application Exercises

YOU WILL NEED

For Exs. 29 and 30:
- paper for folding
- hole punch
- scissors

1. **Visual Thinking** Is the fraction strip folded into fifths? Explain.

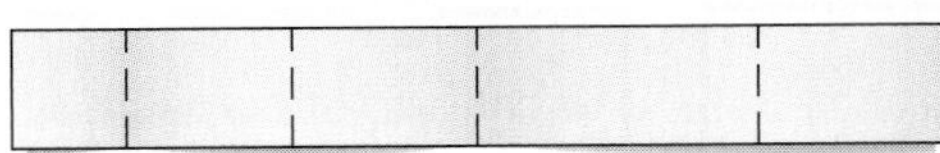

Write an inequality that compares each fraction with $\frac{1}{2}$.

2. $\frac{5}{8}$ 3. $\frac{2}{4}$ 4. $\frac{2}{3}$ 5. $\frac{5}{12}$

Write the fractions in order from least to greatest.

6. $\frac{5}{7}, \frac{5}{10}, \frac{5}{6}, \frac{5}{100}, \frac{5}{3}$

7. $\frac{9}{10}, \frac{99}{100}, \frac{2}{3}, \frac{49}{50}$

Mental Math Use number sense to compare the fractions. Replace each ? with >, <, or =.

8. $\frac{7}{15}$ ___?___ $\frac{7}{12}$ 9. $\frac{59}{60}$ ___?___ $\frac{58}{59}$ 10. $\frac{47}{100}$ ___?___ $\frac{24}{36}$

11. $\frac{19}{20}$ ___?___ $\frac{5}{6}$ 12. $\frac{15}{22}$ ___?___ $\frac{15}{23}$ 13. $\frac{11}{18}$ ___?___ $\frac{9}{20}$

14. **Algebra Connection** The inequality $x < \frac{3}{4}$ means that x represents any number less than $\frac{3}{4}$. Give two values for x that are fractions and that make the inequality a true statement.

15. **Writing** Kyra and Chloe each ate half of a pizza. Explain how it is possible that Kyra ate more pizza than Chloe did.

Use a common denominator to compare the fractions. Replace each ? with >, <, or =.

16. $\frac{7}{12}$ ___?___ $\frac{3}{4}$ 17. $\frac{3}{5}$ ___?___ $\frac{5}{8}$ 18. $\frac{7}{20}$ ___?___ $\frac{3}{8}$

19. $\frac{5}{6}$ ___?___ $\frac{4}{7}$ 20. $\frac{17}{30}$ ___?___ $\frac{8}{15}$ 21. $\frac{6}{12}$ ___?___ $\frac{15}{30}$

Use decimals to compare. Replace each ? with >, <, or =.

22. $\frac{93}{126}$ ___?___ $\frac{321}{400}$ 23. $\frac{65}{121}$ ___?___ $\frac{15}{29}$ 24. $\frac{225}{276}$ ___?___ $\frac{24}{25}$

Replace each ? with >, <, or =.

25. 30% ___?___ $\frac{2}{5}$ 26. $\frac{4}{5}$ ___?___ 79% 27. 76% ___?___ $\frac{3}{4}$

FOR HELP with *percent*, see **MODULE 3, p. 176**

28. Visual Thinking A rectangular sheet of paper is folded twice. Then it is cut and punched through all the layers as shown below. Without folding or cutting, sketch what you think the unfolded paper will look like. Explain the method you used.

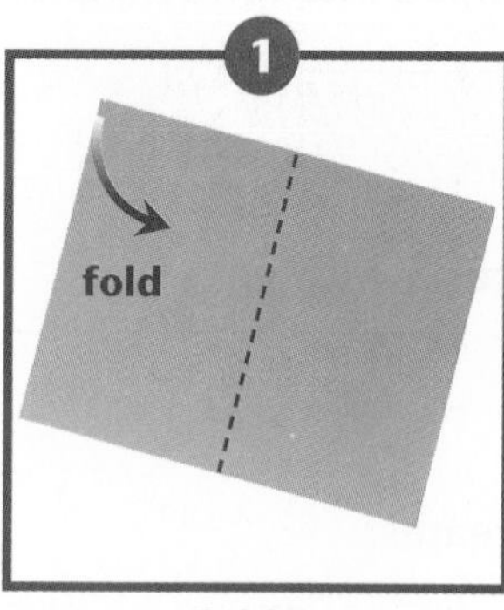

fold 1

fold 2

cut and punch

29. Check your prediction in Exercise 28 by folding and cutting as shown above. Then unfold the paper to see the results.

a. How many sections were formed by the folds?

b. How many circles were formed by each punched hole?

c. How many lines of symmetry does the unfolded paper design have?

30. Create Your Own Try a different pattern of folds, punches, and cuts. Before unfolding the paper, make a sketch to predict the results.

Choosing a Method **Use mental math, paper and pencil, or a calculator to compare the fractions. Replace each ? with >, <, or =.**

31. $\frac{11}{17}$? $\frac{51}{82}$ **32.** $\frac{45}{160}$? $\frac{101}{200}$ **33.** $\frac{22}{25}$? $\frac{4}{5}$

34. If you could only use the calculator for one comparison in Exercises 31–33, which one would it be? Why?

35. Probability Connection Trinja bought 50 of the 540 raffle tickets sold by a sports booster club. Nathan bought 42 of the 490 raffle tickets sold by another booster club. Who is more likely to win a prize?

36. Industrial Technology A mechanic needs a socket wrench to remove a bolt. A $\frac{1}{4}$-inch socket is too small. A $\frac{3}{8}$-inch socket is too large. Choose the letter of the size the mechanic should try next. Explain your choice.

A. $\frac{7}{32}$ in. B. $\frac{13}{32}$ in. C. $\frac{5}{16}$ in. D. $\frac{3}{16}$ in.

37. **Challenge** The seven colored shapes shown are used in the Chinese puzzle game tangram. Copies of the red triangle can be put together to form each of the other pieces.

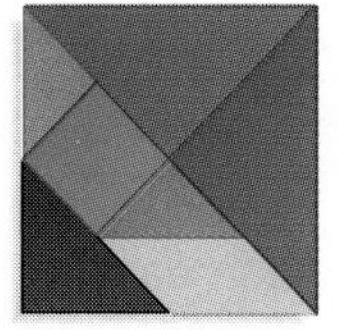

a. Write a fraction that describes what part of the whole square each group of pieces represents.

b. Which group represents the greatest fraction? the least?

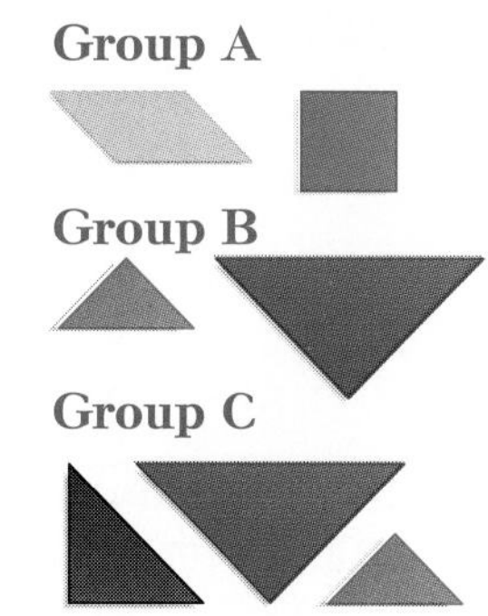

Reflecting on the Section

Write your response to Exercise 38 in your journal.

38. What types of fractions would you compare using each method? Give an example for each method.

- number sense
- a calculator
- a common denominator

Journal

Exercise 38 checks that you can choose an appropriate method to compare fractions.

Spiral Review

Write each fraction as a mixed number. (Module 4, p. 300)

39. $\frac{11}{2}$ 40. $\frac{27}{12}$ 41. $\frac{31}{7}$ 42. $\frac{13}{3}$

43. Make a stem and leaf plot of these daily high temperatures in degrees Fahrenheit for a city in the Midwest during July: 78, 82, 64, 61, 69, 56, 59, 77, 72, 78, 89, 87, 85, 91, 90, 84, 82, 68, 72, 78, 77, 98, 85, 87, 101, 80, 78, 82, 69, 71, 91. (Module 3, p. 223)

Draw a figure that has the given number of lines of symmetry. (Module 2, p. 87)

44. 1 line of symmetry 45. 2 lines of symmetry

Extension 

Combining Inequalities

Read as "$\frac{1}{25}$ is less than $\frac{1}{20}$ and $\frac{1}{20}$ is less than $\frac{1}{10}$."

Two inequalities can be combined in one math statement. For example, $\frac{1}{25} < \frac{1}{20}$ and $\frac{1}{20} < \frac{1}{10}$ can be written as $\frac{1}{25} < \frac{1}{20} < \frac{1}{10}$. Find a fraction that can be used to replace each __?__.

46. $\frac{1}{4} <$ __?__ $< \frac{1}{2}$ 47. $\frac{3}{8} <$ __?__ $< \frac{3}{4}$ 48. $\frac{4}{7} <$ __?__ $< \frac{3}{4}$ 49. $\frac{3}{7} <$ __?__ $< \frac{5}{6}$

Compare the fractions. Replace each ? with >, <, or =.

1. $\frac{5}{6}$? $\frac{5}{8}$
2. $\frac{15}{16}$? $\frac{30}{32}$
3. $\frac{7}{12}$? $\frac{1}{4}$
4. $\frac{3}{8}$? $\frac{3}{14}$

Use a common denominator to compare the fractions. Replace each ? with >, <, or =.

5. $\frac{5}{8}$? $\frac{3}{10}$
6. $\frac{11}{8}$? $\frac{4}{9}$
7. $\frac{3}{5}$? $\frac{1}{3}$
8. $\frac{6}{7}$? $\frac{10}{11}$

Use decimals to compare the fractions. Replace each ? with >, <, or =.

9. $\frac{13}{51}$? $\frac{19}{40}$
10. $\frac{67}{92}$? $\frac{17}{23}$
11. $\frac{32}{73}$? $\frac{27}{65}$
12. $\frac{89}{117}$? $\frac{107}{205}$
13. $\frac{12}{133}$? $\frac{23}{197}$
14. $\frac{6}{35}$? $\frac{9}{75}$

Use mental math, paper and pencil, or a calculator to compare the fractions. Replace each ? with >, <, or =.

15. $\frac{5}{12}$? $\frac{1}{6}$
16. $\frac{19}{101}$? $\frac{71}{111}$
17. $\frac{19}{30}$? $\frac{3}{4}$
18. $\frac{1}{12}$? $\frac{1}{14}$
19. $\frac{25}{26}$? $\frac{33}{34}$
20. $\frac{2}{111}$? $\frac{4}{222}$
21. $\frac{1}{8}$? $\frac{2}{9}$
22. $\frac{3}{14}$? $\frac{1}{16}$

Study Skills ▶ Reviewing for Assessment

One way to review for assessment is to read or make a summary of what you have learned. The important ideas are summarized on the Key Concepts page at the end of the section.

1. Find the Key Concepts page for this section. If you want to know more about using a common denominator to compare fractions, what other page can you turn to?

Another way to review is to *pair-share* by sharing ideas with a partner before and after exploring a new topic.

2. Before you begin the next section, read the Exploration titles on pp. 322 and 324. Pair up and share with your partner everything you already know about the listed topics. Plan to get together with your partner to share what you have learned after you have completed the section.

Section 2 Customary Units of Length

IN THIS SECTION

EXPLORATION 1
- Investigating Benchmarks

EXPLORATION 2
- Converting Customary Units of Length

Building the Great Wall

Setting the Stage

The Great Wall of China was built more than 2000 years ago. It stretches all the way across northern China and is the longest wall ever built.

"I shall fix the old walls," replied the emperor. "I shall build a new and mightier wall and shall join all the walls together. I shall have one long wall across the top of China. It will stretch from Liaodong in the east to Lintao in the west. It will be six horses wide at the top, eight at the bottom, and five men high. I shall build it at the edge of our steepest mountains. No...barbarian will be able to go around it, over it, under it, or through it. It will be the Great Wall!"

From *The Great Wall of China* by Leonard Everett Fisher

Think About It

1 **a.** What unit of measure did the emperor use for the height of the Great Wall? Why do you think he chose this unit?

b. Estimate the height of the Great Wall in feet. Explain your reasoning.

2 **a.** The emperor used "horses" to describe the width of the Great Wall. In most places the Great Wall is about 24 ft wide at the bottom. Use this fact to find the measure of one "horse" in feet.

b. Do you think the emperor was using the *length*, the *width*, or the *height* of one horse as a unit of measure? Explain.

GOAL

LEARN HOW TO...
- develop benchmarks for inch, foot, and yard
- find fractional measures on a ruler

AS YOU...
- find the lengths of everyday objects

Exploration 1

Investigating Benchmarks

SET UP *You will need:* • *ruler* • *yardstick*

The Chinese emperor who built the Great Wall used a person's height to describe the height of the wall.

Our customary system of measurement uses the units inch (in.), foot (ft), yard (yd), and mile (mi) to measure lengths. Some of these units were based on the lengths of parts of the body.

FOR◀HELP with *benchmarks*, see **MODULE 3, p. 161**

3 Which body lengths below make good benchmarks for the units listed? Which do not? Why?

a. inch: distance from the tip of your thumb to your thumb's first joint

b. foot: distance from your heel to the tip of your big toe

c. yard: distance from your nose to your middle fingertip with your arm stretched out straight to the side

4 **a.** Find everyday objects that can be used as benchmarks for an inch, a foot, and a yard.

b. Use your benchmarks to estimate each measurement.
- the length of your textbook in inches
- the height of the classroom doorway in feet
- the length of your classroom in yards.

Reading a Ruler **To get more accurate measurements of the objects in Question 4(b), you can use a ruler. It is important to understand the markings on a ruler so that you can read it correctly.**

5 **Try This as a Class** Use your ruler.

a. Find the markings for inches, half-inches, quarter-inches, and eighth-inches. Explain how you found them.

b. Find the marking for each measurement and give another name for it: $\frac{2}{8}$ in., $\frac{2}{4}$ in., $\frac{4}{8}$ in., $\frac{4}{4}$ in.

c. Draw a segment that is $1\frac{7}{8}$ in. long. Is this segment closer to 2 in. or $1\frac{1}{2}$ in.?

6 What is the length of the pencil shown on page 322 to the nearest $\frac{1}{2}$ in.? to the nearest $\frac{1}{4}$ in.? to the nearest $\frac{1}{8}$ in.?

7 **Discussion** Think about your answers to Question 6.

a. When is measuring to the nearest $\frac{1}{8}$ in. better than measuring to the nearest $\frac{1}{4}$ in.? Why?

b. No measurement, no matter how good, is ever exact. Why do you think this is so?

▶ **Sometimes it is helpful to write a measurement using a combination of units, such as feet and inches.**

Unit Relationships
1 ft = 12 in.
1 yd = 3 ft = 36 in.
1 mi = 1760 yd = 5280 ft

8 A person who is 4 ft 10 in. tall is between 4 ft tall and 5 ft tall. Is the person's height closer to 4 ft or to 5 ft?

9 ✓ **CHECKPOINT** Use a ruler or a yardstick.

...checks that you can measure length in customary units.

a. Measure each object named in Question 4(b):

- length of your textbook (to nearest $\frac{1}{8}$ in.)
- height of the classroom doorway (in feet and inches)
- length of your classroom (in yards, feet, and inches)

b. Are the estimates you gave in Question 4(b) close to the actual measurements you just found?

10 If you could measure the length of the Great Wall of China, what customary unit of length would you use? Why?

HOMEWORK EXERCISES See Exs. 1–13 on p. 328.

GOAL

LEARN HOW TO...
- convert between customary units of length
- add and subtract lengths

AS YOU...
- explore the dimensions of various landmarks

Exploration 2

Converting Customary UNITS of Length

▶ **The Great Wall of China is about 6 yd thick at the top and 8 yd thick at the bottom. Sometimes a measurement is easier to understand if it is converted to a unit used for a familiar measurement.**

For example, the thickness of the Great Wall may be easier to imagine if you convert 6 yd to feet, since your height is measured in feet.

11 Do you expect 6 yd to be greater or less than 6 ft? Explain.

▶ **You can use multiplication to convert a measurement from a larger unit to a smaller unit.**

EXAMPLE

Convert 6 yd to feet.

SAMPLE RESPONSE

6 yd = __?__ ft

6 yd = 18 ft
× 3

Multiply by 3 to convert from yards to feet.
1 yd = 3 ft
× 3

12 Ur was an ancient walled city in Southwest Asia (located in modern day Iraq). Its walls were over 29 yd thick.

a. How many feet thick were the walls at Ur?

b. Suppose you and your classmates stand shoulder to shoulder across the top of one of the walls at Ur. About how many students are needed to reach from one side of the wall to the other?

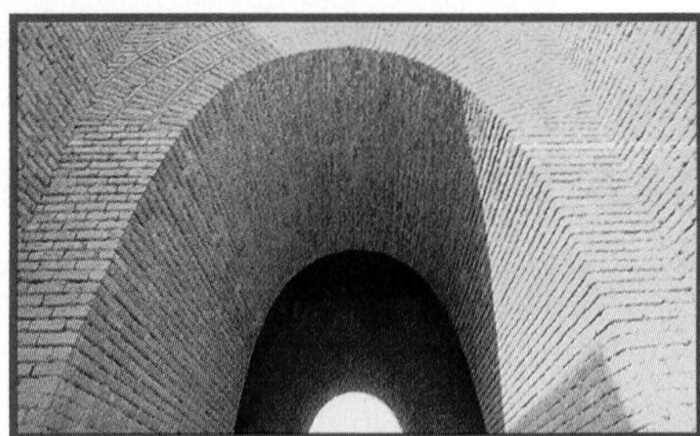

The walls of Ur were destroyed by attackers in 2006 BC. Shown here is the Arch of Al-Masqua Gate, part of an ancient wall still standing in the city of Ninevah, also in modern day Iraq.

c. How many inches thick were the city walls at Ur?

13 How many inches is 2 yd? $\frac{1}{2}$ yd? $2\frac{1}{2}$ yd?

▶ **Converting to Larger Units** **The Great Wall of China is about 4 million yards long. Since it is difficult to imagine 4 million yards, it may be helpful to convert to miles.**

14 There are 1760 yd in a mile. Estimate the length of the Great Wall in miles. Explain your method.

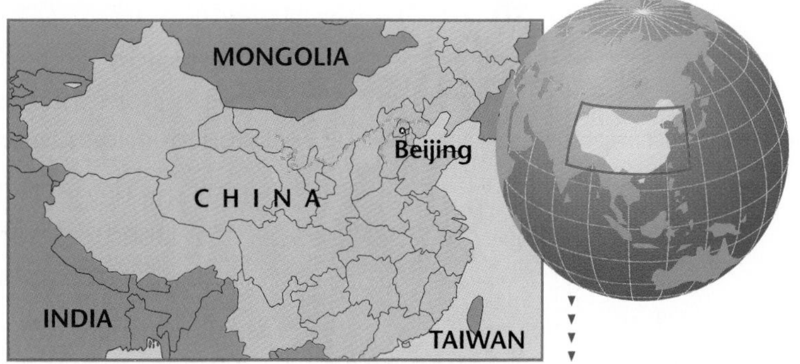

▶ **You can use division to convert a measurement from a smaller unit to a larger unit.**

EXAMPLE

Convert 63 in. to yards.

SAMPLE RESPONSE

63 in. = __?__ yd

63 in. = $1\frac{3}{4}$ yd

÷ 36

Divide by 36 to convert from inches to yards.
36 in. = 1 yd
÷ 36

15 Explain why $1\frac{3}{4}$ yd can also be written as 1 yd 2 ft 3 in.

16 The length of the Great Wall is actually 3,784,000 yd.

a. Find the length of the Great Wall in miles.

b. Compare your answer in part (a) with your estimate in Question 14.

c. The distance from California to New York is about 3000 mi. How does this distance compare with the length of the Great Wall of China?

17 ✓ **CHECKPOINT** Replace each __?__ with the number that makes the statement true.

a. 3 yd = __?__ in. **b.** 90 in. = __?__ yd **c.** 3 mi = __?__ ft

d. 0.5 mi = __?__ yd **e.** 16 ft = __?__ yd **f.** $2\frac{1}{2}$ ft = __?__ in.

✓ **QUESTION 17**

...checks that you can convert between customary units of measure.

▶ **Adding and Subtracting Measurements** **You may need to convert between units when you add or subtract measurements.**

18 **Discussion** To find the height of the Statue of Liberty from the base to the tip of the torch, a student added the measurements of its parts.

a. Is the height of the Statue of Liberty closer to 150 ft or 151 ft? Explain.

b. To simplify the measurement, the student wrote 150 ft 13 in. as 151 ft 1 in. What do you think *simplify* means in this case?

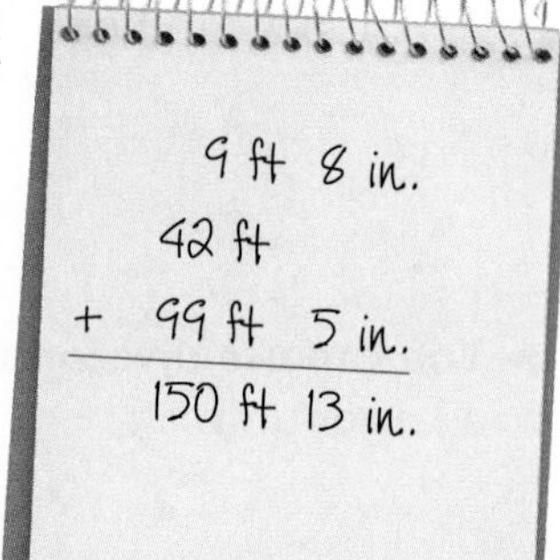

▶ **When you subtract measurements, you may need to regroup first.**

EXAMPLE

You can not subtract 9 in. from 5 in. You must regroup.

```
  3 ft 5 in.
– 2 ft 9 in.
```

Do not forget to decrease the number of feet!

There are 12 in. in a foot.
5 in. + 12 in. = 17 in.

```
  2     17
  3 ft  5 in.
– 2 ft  9 in.
        8 in.
```

19 In a subtraction problem, a student correctly converted 4 yd 1 ft to 3 yd 4 ft. Why are these measurements equal?

✓ QUESTION 20

...checks that you know how to add and subtract customary measurements.

20 **✓ CHECKPOINT** Add or subtract. Simplify answers when possible.

a. 8 in. + 10 in.

b. 7 ft 8 in. – 5 ft 9 in.

c. 6 mi 1280 yd + 2 mi 927 yd

d. 4 yd 2 ft + 2 yd 1 ft

e. 6 yd – 2 yd 2 ft

f. 5 mi 963 yd – 2 mi 1258 yd

HOMEWORK EXERCISES ▶ See Exs. 14–33 on pp. 328–329.

Section 2 Key Concepts

Measuring Length in Customary Units (pp. 322–323)

Length is measured in inches, feet, yards, or miles. You can use benchmarks to estimate lengths. To find more accurate measurements, you can use a ruler.

Example Measure the length of the paper clip.

To the nearest inch: 2 in.

To the nearest $\frac{1}{2}$ in.: 2 in.

To the nearest $\frac{1}{4}$ in.: $1\frac{3}{4}$ in.

You can use combinations of units to write a measurement. For example, nine-time All-Star basketball player Robert Parish is 7 ft 1 in. tall.

Converting Customary Units of Length (pp. 324–325)

To convert between customary units of length you need to choose an appropriate relationship.

1 ft = 12 in. 1 yd = 3 ft = 36 in. 1 mi = 1760 yd = 5280 ft

You can multiply to convert from a larger unit to a smaller one. You can divide to convert from a smaller unit to a larger one.

Adding and Subtracting Lengths in Customary Units (p. 326)

You may need to regroup. **Example**

$$\begin{array}{r} 2 \text{ ft } 10 \text{ in.} \\ -\ 1 \text{ ft } 11 \text{ in.} \\ \hline \end{array} \qquad \begin{array}{r} \overset{1}{\cancel{2}} \text{ ft } \overset{22}{\cancel{10}} \text{ in.} \\ -\ 1 \text{ ft } 11 \text{ in.} \\ \hline 11 \text{ in.} \end{array}$$

21 Key Concepts Question Your windows are 72 in. long. To make curtains, you need fabric the length of the window plus 9 in. How many yards of fabric is that?

Section 2
Practice & Application Exercises

YOU WILL NEED

For Exs. 4, 33:
- ruler or tape measure

Use your benchmarks to estimate each measurement.

1. width of a dinner fork, to the nearest inch
2. height of the room you sleep in, to the nearest yard
3. distance from your shoulder to the tip of your middle finger with your arm outstretched, to the nearest foot
4. Use a ruler or a tape measure to find actual measurements for Exercises 1–3. Were your estimates close to the actual measurements?

Name something that is about as long as each measurement.

5. 8 in.
6. 4 ft
7. 15 ft
8. 25 yd

For each situation in Exercises 9–11, name an appropriate customary unit or combination of units for measuring.

9. checking that the height of a basketball hoop meets NBA regulations
10. finding the length of a route when planning a car trip
11. measuring a city's monthly rainfall for a weather report
12. **Social Studies** The Egyptian *cubit* was a unit of length in ancient Egypt.
    a. Use inches to measure your cubit.
    b. The standard Egyptian cubit was about $18\frac{1}{4}$ in. long. Is this *longer* or *shorter* than your cubit?

1 cubit

13. What is the length of the bandage to the nearest $\frac{1}{2}$ in.? the nearest $\frac{1}{4}$ in.? the nearest $\frac{1}{8}$ in.?

Replace each ? with the number that makes the statement true.

14. 6 yd = __?__ ft
15. 12,320 yd = __?__ mi
16. $5\frac{1}{2}$ yd = __?__ in.
17. 54 in. = __?__ ft
18. 11 ft = __?__ yd
19. $8\frac{1}{4}$ ft = __?__ in.

Write each measurement as a fraction of a yard.

20. 15 in. 21. 2 ft 22. 5 ft 23. 1 ft 6 in.

24. **Writing** Four students' measurements of the length of a table are 66 in., $5\frac{1}{2}$ ft, 5 ft 6 in., and 1yd 2 ft 6 in. Explain how they can all be correct.

25. **Airport Runways** The diagram shows the runway layers at the Denver International Airport. Find the total thickness of a runway.

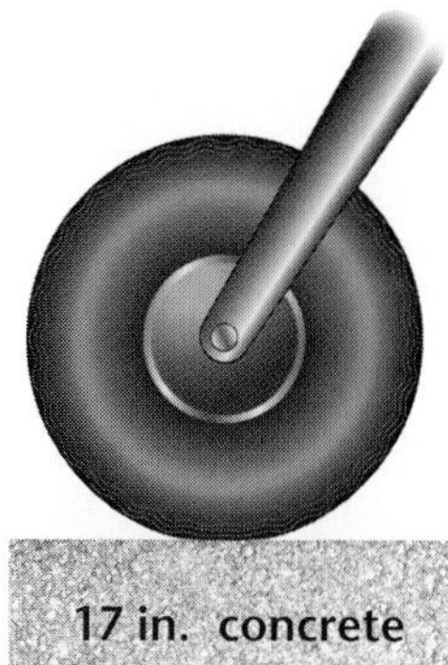

17 in. concrete

8 in. cement

12 ft soil with lime

6 ft packed soil

(not drawn to scale)

Find each sum or difference. Simplify answers when possible.

26. 3 yd 2 ft + 7 yd 1 ft

27. 1382 yd + 1576 yd

28. 3 yd 1 ft − 2 yd 2 ft

29. 8 ft 9 in. − 3 ft 11 in.

30. 6 ft 9 in. + 3 ft 5 in.

31. 9 yd − 1 yd 2 ft

32. **Challenge** For the ship shown to pass through the locks safely, the gate between Locks 1 and 2 must be opened so water flows from Lock 1 to Lock 2. When the water levels in the two locks are equal, how much has the water level in Lock 1 dropped?

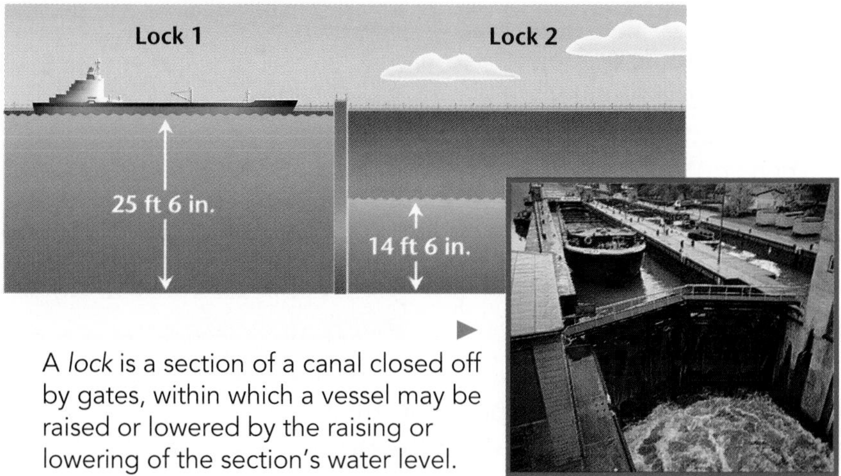

A *lock* is a section of a canal closed off by gates, within which a vessel may be raised or lowered by the raising or lowering of the section's water level.

Reflecting on the Section

33. a. Measure the length of your step in inches. Measure from the heel of one foot to the heel of the other foot.

b. Use your step length from part (a) as a benchmark. Estimate the number of steps it would take you to walk 3,784,000 yd, the length of the Great Wall.

RESEARCH

Exercise 33 checks that you understand how to use benchmarks.

Spiral Review

Replace each ? with >, <, or =. (Module 5, p. 316)

34. $\frac{2}{5}$? $\frac{7}{15}$

35. $\frac{1}{6}$? $\frac{3}{8}$

36. $\frac{5}{7}$? $\frac{9}{13}$

37. In how many different ways can you make change for a half-dollar coin using only nickels, dimes, and quarters? (Module 1, p. 35)

An Exhibit of Everyday Objects

When you hear the phrase "work of art," do you think of things like helmets and toasters? If not, you may be surprised to know that items like these can be found in the Architecture and Design collection at the Museum of Modern Art in New York City.

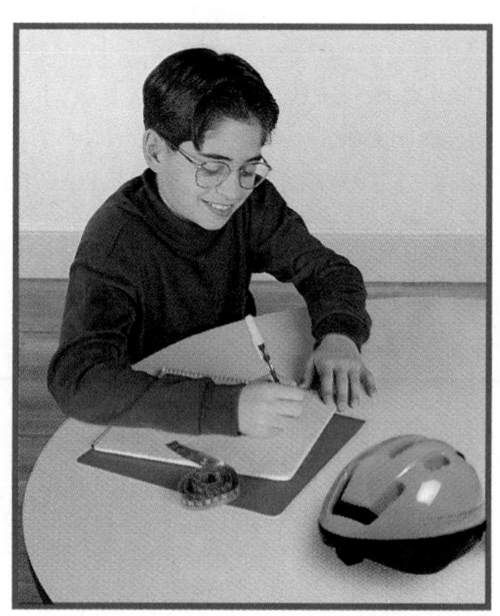

Over the next few weeks, you'll choose an object that you think could be added to the Architecture and Design collection. You'll investigate its dimensions and design. Then you'll prepare a description of your object for an exhibit card and you'll write a section of a catalog for the exhibit. Finally, you'll display your object in your classroom along with the objects chosen by your classmates.

Measuring Length in Customary Units Suppose you are asked by a museum to select an item to include in an exhibit like the Architecture and Design collection.

SET UP

You will need:

- *a customary ruler*

1 Find an everyday object you think would be an interesting addition to the collection. If the object is too large to bring into your classroom, try to find a photo.

2 Make a sketch of your object. Measure the height, the length, the width, or other dimensions of your object in customary units. Record the information on your drawing.

Section 2 Extra Skill Practice

You will need: • *ruler* (Exs. 1–4)

Measure the length of the needle as directed.

1. to the nearest inch
2. to the nearest $\frac{1}{2}$ in.
3. to the nearest $\frac{1}{4}$ in.
4. to the nearest $\frac{1}{8}$ in.

Replace each ? with the number that makes the statement true.

5. $2\frac{1}{4}$ ft = ? in.
6. 3.1 mi = ? yd
7. $12\frac{1}{2}$ ft = ? yd
8. 3900 ft = ? mi
9. 18 in. = ? yd
10. 42 in. = ? ft
11. $3\frac{3}{4}$ yd = ? ft
12. 3080 yd = ? mi
13. 5 yd = ? in.
14. 4 mi = ? ft
15. 8 in. = ? ft
16. 46 in. = ? yd

Find each sum or difference. Simplify answers when possible.

17. 6 ft 3 in. + 10 ft 4 in.
18. 3 yd 4 ft + 12 ft
19. 8 yd 1 ft − 7 yd 2 ft
20. 9 ft 8 in. + 2 ft 4 in.
21. 13 yd 2 ft − 6 ft
22. 11 yd − 1 yd 2 ft
23. 1122 yd + 709 yd
24. 6 ft 1 in. − 5 ft 9 in.
25. 4 ft 9 in. + 16 in.

Standardized Testing ▶ Performance Task

You are given three strips of paper. One is 2 ft 9 in., the second is 3 ft 4 in., and the third is 3 ft 2 in. Without cutting the strips, describe how to attach the three strips of paper together to create a single strip exactly 3 yd long.

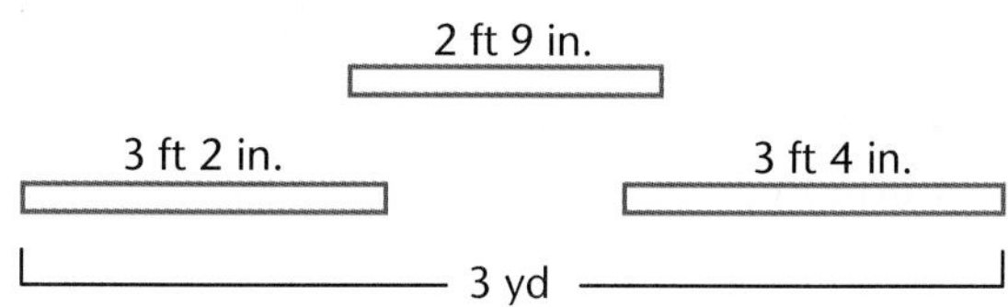

Addition and Subtraction of Fractions

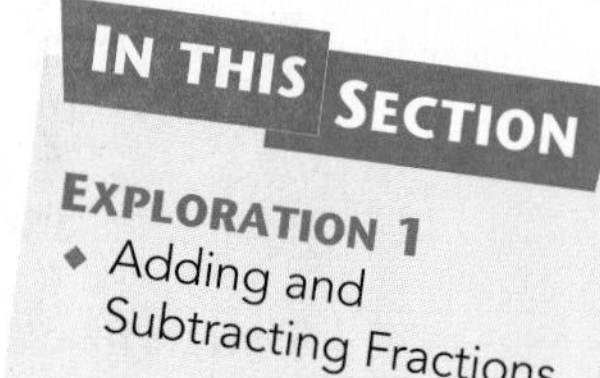

Over and UNDER

Setting the Stage

The craft of weaving began long ago. Pieces of woven cloth over 8000 years old have been found in Turkey and in Peru. Many cultures are known for their fine weaving. Some familiar examples are Irish tweeds, Native American baskets, Persian carpets, and Guatemalan cloth.

The Pomo Indians of northern California are among the world's most skillful basketmakers. They are famous for the beauty and delicacy of their work and the variety of their designs.

Pomo basketweaver Laura Somersol uses roots to weave her baskets, then adds beads and feathers as part of the decoration.

Think About It

1 Brainstorm for one minute about things that may not have been created if people had not learned how to weave.

2 The Pomo Indians often made baskets with as many as sixty stitches in one inch.

a. About how long is one stitch?

b. Do you think you can mark 60 dots along an inch without overlapping the dots? Explain.

Exploration 1

Adding and Subtracting Fractions

GOAL

LEARN HOW TO...
- add and subtract fractions

AS YOU...
- explore measurements of ribbons in a weaving pattern

SET UP *You will need your fraction strips from Section 1.*

▶ **Paper ribbons can be woven over and under one another to create this bookmark. You can find the width of two rows by adding $\frac{1}{4} + \frac{1}{4}$.**

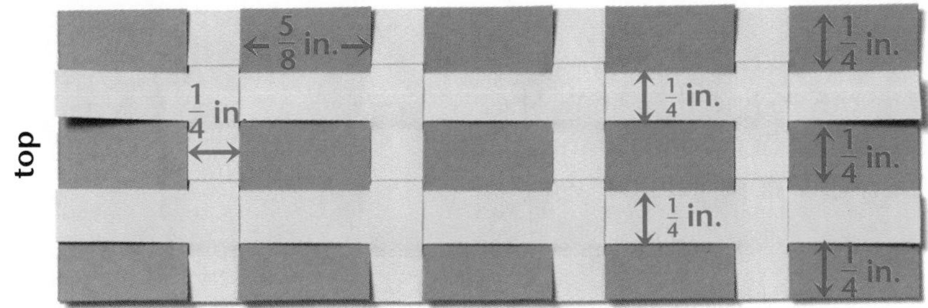

3 Use your fraction strips to find each sum.

a. $\frac{1}{4} + \frac{1}{4}$ **b.** $\frac{1}{4} + \frac{3}{4}$ **c.** $\frac{1}{8} + \frac{3}{8}$

4 **Discussion** Describe a way to add fractions with the same denominator without using fraction strips. Then show that you get the same answer for $\frac{5}{12} + \frac{2}{12}$ using your method or using strips.

▶ **To find the length of the side of the bookmark, you need to add fractions with different denominators.**

EXAMPLE

Show $\frac{5}{8} + \frac{1}{4}$ using fraction strips.

First Fold an eighths strip to show $\frac{5}{8}$ and a fourths strip to show $\frac{1}{4}$. Place the folded strips end to end.

Then Fold another eighths strip to match the length of the sum.

$\frac{1}{8}$	$\frac{1}{8}$	$\frac{1}{8}$	$\frac{1}{8}$	$\frac{1}{8}$	$\frac{1}{4}$	
$\frac{1}{8}$	$\frac{1}{8}$	$\frac{1}{8}$	$\frac{1}{8}$	$\frac{1}{8}$	$\frac{1}{8}$	$\frac{1}{8}$

$$\frac{5}{8} + \frac{1}{4} = \frac{7}{8}$$

5 **Try This as a Class** Use the Example on page 333.

a. To find the sum of $\frac{5}{8}$ and $\frac{1}{4}$, a strip of eighths was used. How many eighths matched the length of $\frac{1}{4}$?

b. If you had a sixteenths strip could you use it to find $\frac{5}{8} + \frac{1}{4}$? a twelfths strip? Explain using words and pictures.

6 Which fraction strip can you use to find each sum?

a. $\frac{1}{2} + \frac{3}{4}$ **b.** $\frac{1}{12} + \frac{5}{6}$ **c.** $\frac{2}{6} + \frac{1}{4}$ **d.** $\frac{2}{3} + \frac{1}{4}$

7 Rewrite each expression in Question 6 so that the fractions have common denominators. Then find each sum. Write each answer in lowest terms.

8 Joan needed to rename two fractions to find their sum. She organized her work like this. Copy and complete her work.

✓ QUESTION 9

...checks that you can add fractions.

9 **✓ CHECKPOINT** Find each sum. Write each answer in lowest terms.

a. $\frac{1}{10} + \frac{7}{10}$ **b.** $\frac{2}{9} + \frac{2}{3}$ **c.** $\frac{2}{3} + \frac{6}{7}$ **d.** $\frac{5}{8} + \frac{1}{12}$

10 Without measuring, find the lengths of the top and the side of the bookmark shown on page 333.

▶ **Subtracting Fractions** **You can make two narrow paper ribbons from one wide ribbon. Suppose you cut a strip of ribbon $\frac{1}{4}$ in. wide from a strip of ribbon $\frac{3}{4}$ in. wide. To find the width of the ribbon left after cutting off $\frac{1}{4}$ in., you can subtract: $\frac{3}{4} - \frac{1}{4} = \frac{2}{4}$.**

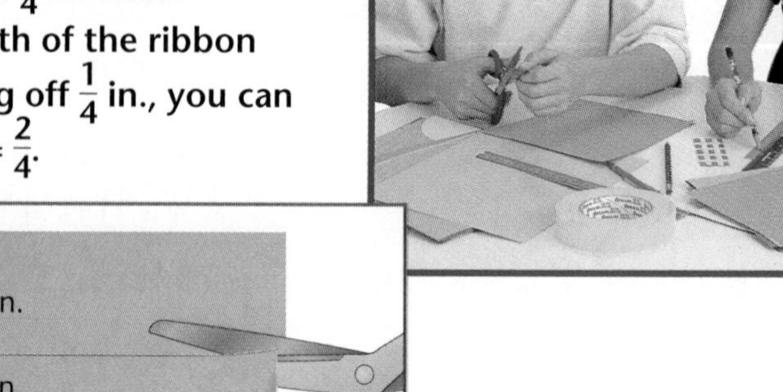

11 **Discussion** When you subtract two fractions that have the same denominator, how do you find the numerator of the difference? What is the denominator of the difference?

▶ **Suppose you cut a strip of ribbon $\frac{1}{4}$ in. wide from a strip of ribbon $\frac{5}{6}$ in. wide. You can find the width of the left-over strip of ribbon by subtracting. Fraction strips can help you think about how to subtract fractions with different denominators.**

EXAMPLE

Show $\frac{5}{6} - \frac{1}{4}$ using fraction strips.

First Fold sixths and fourths strips to show $\frac{5}{6}$ and $\frac{1}{4}$. Place the shorter strip over the longer one. Align the strips on the right.

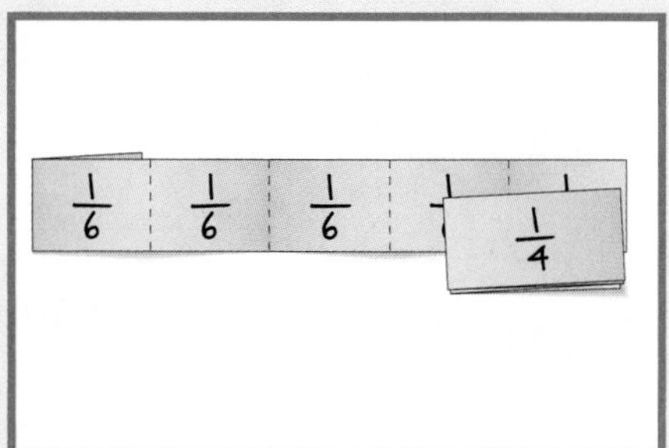

Then Fold another strip to match the length of the part of the $\frac{5}{6}$ strip that is not covered. This part is the difference between $\frac{5}{6}$ and $\frac{1}{4}$.

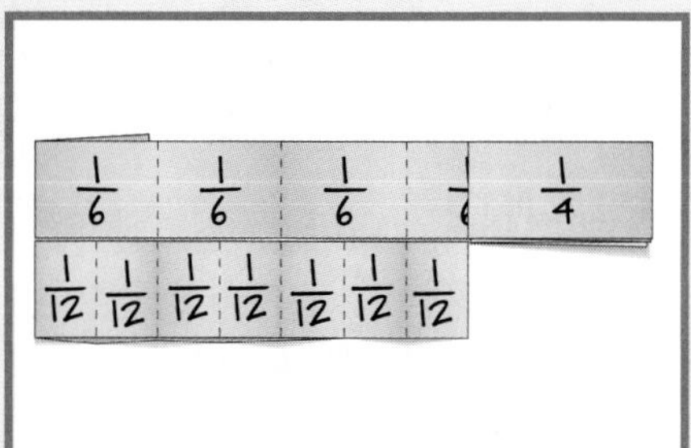

$$\frac{5}{6} - \frac{1}{4} = \frac{7}{12}$$

12 How can you subtract $\frac{1}{4}$ from $\frac{5}{6}$ without using fraction strips?

13 ✓ **CHECKPOINT** Use a common denominator to find each difference. Write each answer in lowest terms.

a. $\frac{5}{6} - \frac{7}{10}$ **b.** $\frac{2}{3} - \frac{1}{2}$ **c.** $\frac{4}{7} - \frac{3}{14}$

...checks that you can subtract fractions.

HOMEWORK EXERCISES ▶ **See Exs. 1–17 on pp. 337–338.**

Section 3 Key Concepts

Adding Fractions (pp. 333–334)

To add fractions

- first write the fractions with a common denominator,
- next add the numerators,
- then write the sum of the numerators over the common denominator.

Example

Find $\frac{3}{8} + \frac{1}{3}$.

$\frac{9}{24} + \frac{8}{24} = \frac{17}{24}$

You can use **24** as a common denominator.

Add the numerators. $9 + 8 = 17$

Subtracting Fractions (pp. 334–335)

To subtract fractions

- first write the fractions with a common denominator,
- next subtract the numerators,
- then write the difference of the numerators over the common denominator.

Example

Find $\frac{2}{3} - \frac{1}{2}$.

$\frac{4}{6} - \frac{3}{6} = \frac{1}{6}$

You can use **6** as a common denominator.

Subtract the numerators. $4 - 3 = 1$

Key Concepts Questions

14 Find each sum. Write each answer in lowest terms.

a. $\frac{3}{20} + \frac{7}{10}$ **b.** $\frac{6}{11} + \frac{5}{44}$ **c.** $\frac{1}{15} + \frac{6}{20}$ **d.** $\frac{3}{4} + \frac{4}{7}$

15 **a.** Explain the steps you would take to subtract $\frac{1}{3}$ from $\frac{3}{7}$.

b. Use your steps from part (a) to find $\frac{3}{7} - \frac{1}{3}$.

Section 3 Practice & Application Exercises

YOU WILL NEED

For Ex. 13:
- scissors
- tape
- colored paper
- ruler

Find each sum. Write each answer in lowest terms.

1. $\frac{1}{3}+\frac{4}{9}$
2. $\frac{3}{10}+\frac{3}{5}$
3. $\frac{1}{4}+\frac{4}{5}$
4. $\frac{5}{6}+\frac{3}{10}$
5. $\frac{4}{9}+\frac{2}{9}+\frac{1}{9}$
6. $\frac{1}{2}+\frac{1}{4}+\frac{3}{8}$

Find each difference. Write each answer in lowest terms.

7. $\frac{6}{7}-\frac{2}{7}$
8. $\frac{5}{6}-\frac{1}{6}$
9. $\frac{3}{4}-\frac{5}{8}$
10. $\frac{2}{3}-\frac{1}{6}$
11. $\frac{5}{9}-\frac{2}{5}$
12. $\frac{7}{12}-\frac{1}{10}$

13. **Create Your Own** Weave strips of paper $\frac{1}{2}$ in. wide and $\frac{1}{4}$ in. wide over and under each other to make a paper mat. Use tape to hold the pieces in place. Give the final dimensions of your mat.

14. **Music** In written music, the shape of a note shows how long the note should be held. A dot to the right of a note tells you to add on half the value of the note to make it last longer. Use the chart to help you find the value of each note or combination of notes.

A whole note is held four times as long as a quarter note.

a. b. c. d. e. f.

Displaying Data **The circle graph shows the approximate results of a survey about the ages of World Wide Web users.**

15. a. About what fraction of World Wide Web users were over 20 years old?
    b. A circle graph shows the division of a whole into parts. Write a fraction for the part that is labeled *5–20*.
    c. What does the fraction you wrote in part (b) tell you about the World Wide Web users surveyed?

Ages of World Wide Web Users (April 1996)

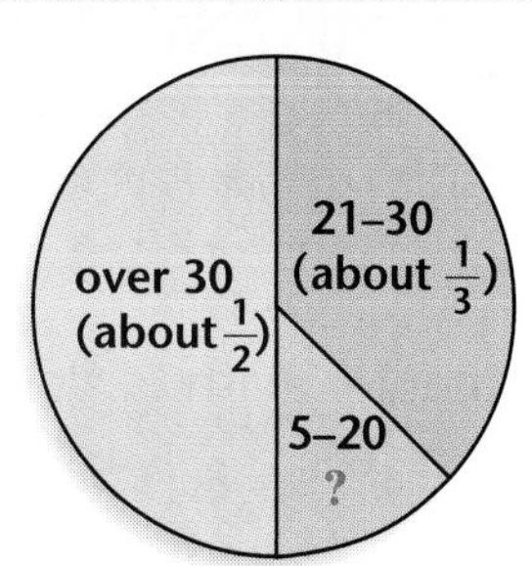

16. **Challenge** On the map, $\frac{1}{4}$ in. represents about 100 mi. A student measures $\frac{3}{8}$ in. between Medellín and Bogotá, $\frac{1}{2}$ in. between Bogotá and Cali, and $\frac{1}{2}$ in. between Cali and Medellín. What is the total mileage of a trip beginning and ending in Medellín with stops in Bogotá and Cali as shown?

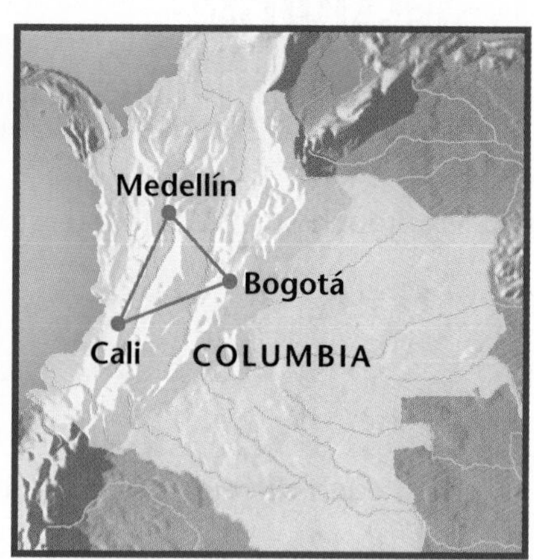

Oral Report

Exercise 17 checks that you understand addition and subtraction of fractions.

Reflecting on the Section

Be prepared to report on the following topic in class.

17. Find another situation where addition or subtraction of fractions is used to create something. Give an example of how mathematics is used in the situation.

Spiral Review

Replace each __?__ with the number that makes the statement true. **(Module 5, p. 327)**

18. 21 in. = __?__ ft 19. 2 mi = __?__ yd 20. 16 ft = __?__ yd

Use the Venn diagram. **(Module 3, p. 165)**

21. How many of the cities listed are capitals? seaports? capitals and seaports? capitals or seaports? neither a capital nor a seaport?

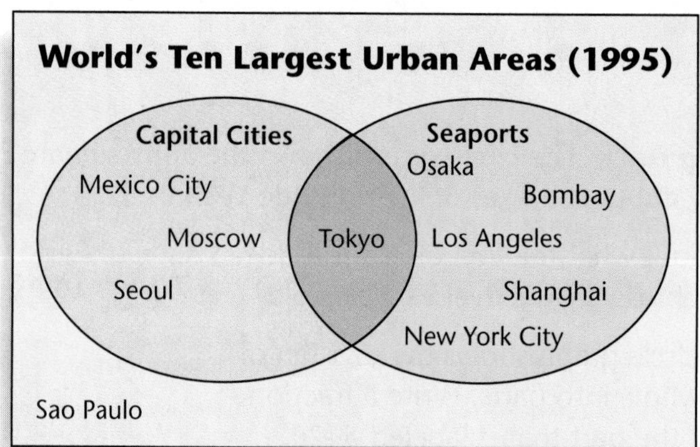

Use mental math to find each sum. **(Module 1, p. 50)**

22. 12 + 15 + 8 23. 45 + 7 + 33 24. 16 + 10 + 14 + 9

Section 3 Extra Skill Practice

Find each sum. Write each answer in lowest terms.

1. $\frac{1}{6}+\frac{3}{10}$
2. $\frac{1}{8}+\frac{3}{8}$
3. $\frac{2}{3}+\frac{5}{18}$
4. $\frac{7}{12}+\frac{5}{18}$
5. $\frac{8}{11}+\frac{1}{3}$
6. $\frac{7}{15}+\frac{7}{15}$
7. $\frac{5}{12}+\frac{1}{5}$
8. $\frac{3}{5}+\frac{3}{8}$
9. $\frac{3}{16}+\frac{9}{10}$

Find each difference. Write each answer in lowest terms.

10. $\frac{12}{13}-\frac{1}{13}$
11. $\frac{7}{8}-\frac{11}{20}$
12. $\frac{9}{10}-\frac{1}{2}$
13. $\frac{7}{8}-\frac{2}{16}$
14. $\frac{3}{4}-\frac{3}{7}$
15. $\frac{11}{12}-\frac{1}{10}$
16. $\frac{5}{9}-\frac{1}{3}$
17. $\frac{12}{15}-\frac{3}{10}$
18. $\frac{5}{8}-\frac{5}{9}$

Find each sum or difference. Write each answer in lowest terms.

19. $\frac{1}{3}+\frac{9}{10}$
20. $\frac{4}{7}-\frac{3}{14}$
21. $\frac{3}{4}+\frac{1}{6}$
22. $\frac{2}{3}-\frac{9}{16}$
23. $\frac{7}{24}+\frac{7}{8}$
24. $\frac{4}{5}-\frac{1}{2}$
25. $\frac{5}{6}+\frac{8}{15}$
26. $\frac{2}{9}-\frac{1}{11}$
27. $\frac{11}{12}+\frac{23}{36}$

Find the value of each expression. Write each answer in lowest terms.

28. $\frac{7}{10}-\frac{3}{20}+\frac{4}{5}$
29. $\frac{5}{8}+\frac{5}{36}-\frac{1}{4}$
30. $\frac{8}{9}-\frac{2}{7}+\frac{1}{2}$
31. $\frac{5}{7}-\frac{1}{28}+\frac{3}{4}$
32. $\frac{2}{9}+\frac{1}{5}+\frac{7}{30}$
33. $\frac{5}{6}+\frac{1}{8}-\frac{1}{12}$

Standardized Testing ▶ Open-ended

1. Use each number listed as a common denominator. For each one write an example that shows adding or subtracting fractions with different denominators.
   - A. common denominator: 16
   - B. common denominator: 24
   - C. common denominator: 10
   - D. common denominator: 15
2. Pick one of your examples from Question 1. Write a word problem that can be solved using the addition or subtraction you showed.

FOR ASSESSMENT AND PORTFOLIOS

A Weighty Question

The Situation

An old balance scale is on sale at a rummage sale. Only the four weights shown are being sold with the scale. The person selling the balance claims that you can use those weights to find any mass that is in whole kilograms from 1 kg through 40 kg.

The Problem

Prove that the seller's claim is true by showing how to measure each mass from 1 kg through 40 kg.

Something to Think About

- How can you organize your work to make sure you do not skip any values?
- Which problem solving strategies seem helpful for this problem?

Present Your Results

Describe what you did to solve the problem. Include any tables, pictures, or charts you made to organize your data. Describe any patterns you noticed while solving the problem.

Section 4 Addition and Subtraction of Mixed Numbers

IN THIS SECTION

EXPLORATION 1
- Adding Mixed Numbers

EXPLORATION 2
- Subtracting Mixed Numbers

Setting the Stage

SET UP *You will need Labsheet 4A.*

Throughout history masks have been used in many different cultural celebrations. On the first and second of November, soon after Halloween, many Mexican-Americans celebrate *Día de Muertos*, the Day of the Dead. This holiday honors relatives and friends who have died during the year. It is traditional to make and display papier-mâché masks like the one shown.

Special masks, called *calaveras*, are made by the entire family.

Think About It

1 About what size would a mask have to be to cover your face?

2 **Use Labsheet 4A.** Name two types of polygons used in the *Mask* pattern.

GOAL

LEARN HOW TO...
- add mixed numbers

AS YOU...
- determine the amount of string needed for a mask

Exploration 1

Adding Mixed Numbers

SET UP *Work with a partner. You will need:* • *Labsheet 4A* • *ruler*

A relief mask has a design that is raised from a flat background. You can glue string, yarn, cotton balls, or even sea shells on a cardboard mask to create a raised design.

▶ **To estimate how much material is needed for a mask, you may need to estimate a sum of mixed numbers.**

3 The length of string, in inches, needed to outline the jaw on the mask is $1\frac{5}{8} + 1\frac{3}{4} + 1\frac{5}{8}$.

a. Round each measurement to the nearest whole number and find the sum to estimate the length of string.

b. Is your estimate *less than*, *equal to*, or *greater than* the sum? Why?

▶ **Using a Ruler To find the actual amount of string needed to outline the jaw, you can use a ruler to add the measurements.**

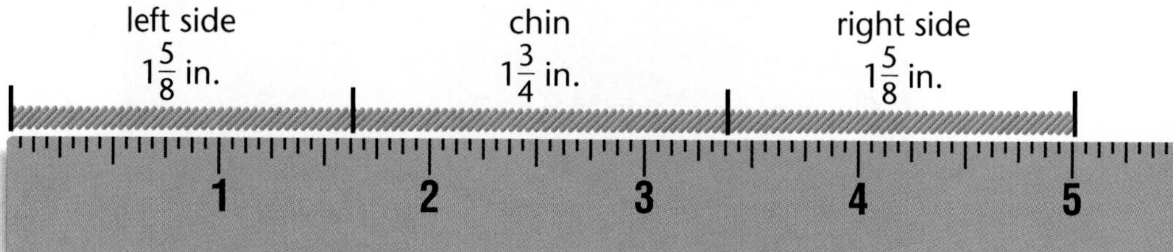

4 **a.** Use the ruler to find $1\frac{5}{8} + 1\frac{3}{4} + 1\frac{5}{8}$. Compare your answer with your estimate in Question 3.

b. Another way to find the sum is to measure off 3 in. and then measure off lengths for $\frac{5}{8}$ in., $\frac{3}{4}$ in., and $\frac{5}{8}$ in. Why does this method work?

5 Why is it difficult to find the sum $2\frac{2}{3} + 3\frac{3}{4}$ on a ruler?

▶ **Using Paper and Pencil** You can find the sum of mixed numbers by adding the whole numbers and the fractions separately.

EXAMPLE

Find $2\frac{2}{3} + 3\frac{3}{4}$.

SAMPLE RESPONSE

Add the whole numbers.

Add the fractions.

$$\begin{array}{rcr} 2\frac{2}{3} & = & 2\frac{8}{12} \\ +\ 3\frac{3}{4} & = & +\ 3\frac{9}{12} \\ \hline & & 5\frac{17}{12} = 6\frac{5}{12} \end{array}$$

6 **Discussion** In the Example, why were $\frac{2}{3}$ and $\frac{3}{4}$ written as $\frac{8}{12}$ and $\frac{9}{12}$? Why do you think $5\frac{17}{12}$ was written as $6\frac{5}{12}$?

7 Find $4\frac{3}{4} + 1\frac{5}{8}$ without a ruler. Check your answer on a ruler.

8 **a.** Explain the steps Paulo used.

b. Do you prefer Paulo's method or the one in the Example? Why?

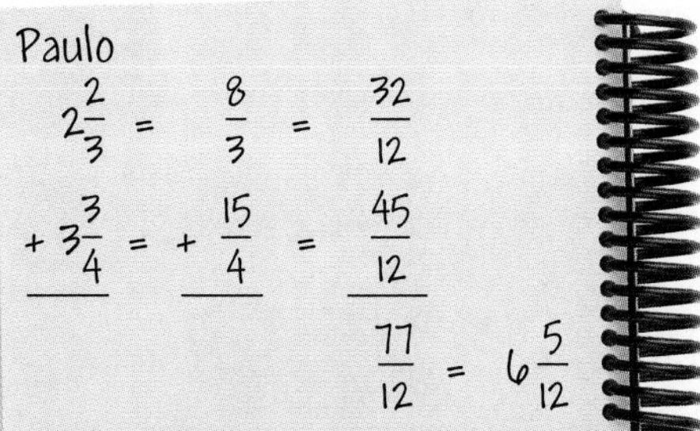

9 Use Paulo's method to find $1\frac{4}{5} + 6\frac{2}{3}$.

10 ✓ **CHECKPOINT** Find each sum. Then write each sum in lowest terms.

a. $10\frac{1}{4} + 2\frac{5}{6}$ **b.** $\frac{3}{5} + 4\frac{3}{8}$ **c.** $6\frac{1}{4} + 5\frac{3}{8} + 3\frac{3}{4}$

✓ **QUESTION 10**

...checks that you can add mixed numbers.

11 **Use Labsheet 4A.** Is 20 in. of string enough to outline the jaw, the mouth, and each pair of rectangles that make the eyes on the *Mask*? Did you use *paper and pencil* or *estimation* to find your answer? Explain.

HOMEWORK EXERCISES See Exs. 1–14 on p. 348.

GOAL

LEARN HOW TO...
- subtract mixed numbers

AS YOU...
- design a pin

Exploration 2

Subtracting Mixed Numbers

SET UP *Work with a partner. You will need a ruler.*

Artists are often inspired by patterns found in nature or in the arts and crafts of other cultures. Suppose you use the pattern on this Native American blanket to make a raised design for a pin.

12 Describe how to use mental math to determine that 5 in. of string is needed to outline this rectangular pin.

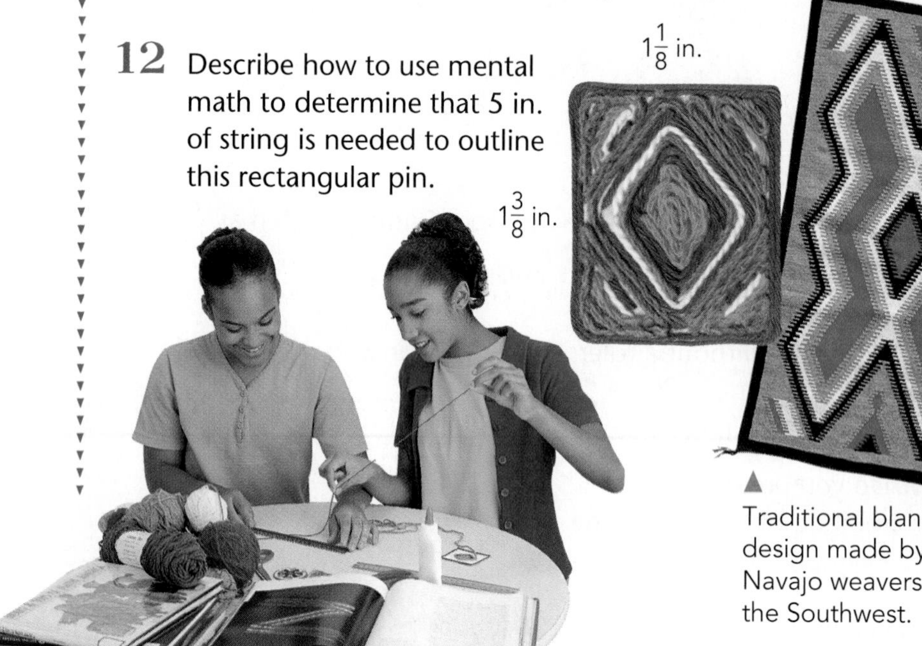

Traditional blanket design made by Navajo weavers of the Southwest.

▶ **Using a Ruler Suppose you have $6\frac{3}{4}$ in. of string. You can use the ruler to see how much string is left after the pin is outlined.**

1. Start with $6\frac{3}{4}$ in. of string.
2. Take away 5 in. of string.
3. This much is left.

1 2 3 4 5 6 7

13 **a.** Write a subtraction problem to represent the situation shown in the ruler diagram on page 344.

b. Find the answer. How can you do this without the ruler?

14 Use a ruler or draw a picture to find $4\frac{1}{2} - 3\frac{1}{4}$.

▶ **Using Pencil and Paper** **To subtract mixed numbers without a ruler, you can find a common denominator as you did to add mixed numbers.**

15 **a.** Copy the subtraction problem. Then write the fractions with a common denominator.

b. Find the difference. Explain how you subtracted.

c. Compare your answer with the one from Question 14.

$$\begin{array}{rcr} 4\frac{1}{2} & = & 4\frac{?}{?} \\ -\ 3\frac{1}{4} & = & -\ 3\frac{?}{?} \\ \hline \end{array}$$

16 Gwen has $14\frac{3}{4}$ in. of string and uses $5\frac{3}{8}$ in. to outline a feature on a mask. How much string does she have left?

17 **Try This as a Class** Use the problem shown.

$$\begin{array}{rcrcr} 3\frac{3}{8} & = & 3\frac{3}{8} & = & 2\frac{11}{8} \\ -\ 1\frac{1}{2} & = & -\ 1\frac{4}{8} & = & -\ 1\frac{4}{8} \\ \hline \end{array}$$

a. Why was $1\frac{1}{2}$ rewritten as $1\frac{4}{8}$?

b. Can you subtract $\frac{4}{8}$ from $\frac{3}{8}$? Explain why or why not.

c. Show that $3\frac{3}{8} = 2\frac{11}{8}$. (*Hint:* $3\frac{3}{8} = 2 + 1 + \frac{3}{8}$.)

d. Write the answer to the problem.

18 Claire's method is the same as the method shown in Question 17, but she uses a shortcut to write her steps. Describe what she did in her work.

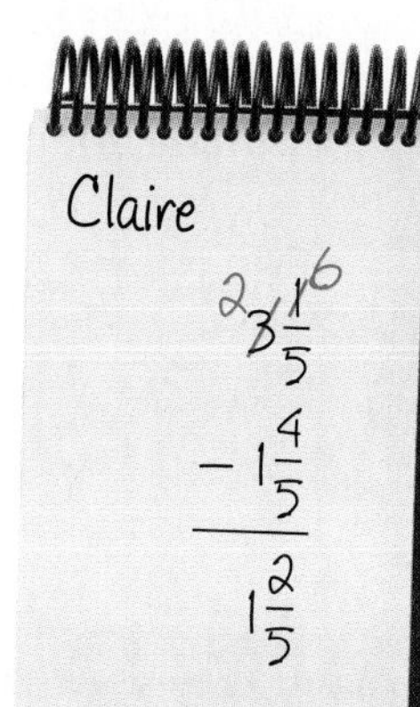

19 Find $4\frac{1}{2} - 3\frac{2}{3}$.

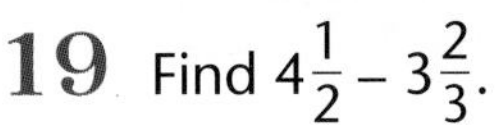

20 Show how you can find $2\frac{1}{5} - 1\frac{7}{10}$ by changing the mixed numbers to fractions.

21 **Try This as a Class** Use the problem $6 - 2\frac{1}{4}$.

a. Explain why you can write 6 as $5\frac{4}{4}$.

b. Why would you want to write 6 as $5\frac{4}{4}$ to find the difference?

c. Find the difference.

22 If you have 9 yd of yarn and use $3\frac{3}{4}$ yd in a craft project, how much is left for your next craft project?

▶ **Using Mental Math** **Addition and mental math can be used to solve subtraction problems when one number is a mixed number and the other is a whole number.**

23 Explain how you can find the difference $4 - 2\frac{1}{3}$ by thinking about what number to add to $2\frac{1}{3}$ to get 4:

$$2\frac{1}{3} + \underline{\ ?\ } = 4$$

24 Use mental math to find each difference.

a. $10 - 7\frac{3}{8}$ **b.** $8\frac{3}{4} - 5$ **c.** $11 - 6\frac{2}{3}$

✓ QUESTION 25

...checks that you can subtract mixed numbers.

25 **✓ CHECKPOINT** Find each difference. Write each answer in lowest terms.

a. $5\frac{3}{7} - 2\frac{1}{2}$ **b.** $4\frac{3}{8} - 2$ **c.** $10\frac{2}{3} - 3\frac{2}{5}$

d. $6 - 3\frac{1}{9}$ **e.** $3\frac{5}{8} - 1\frac{3}{4}$ **f.** $5\frac{1}{4} - 4\frac{5}{6}$

26 **a.** Sketch your own design for a pin the size of the rectangle shown.

b. Suppose you have 6 in. of red yarn. Measure to see how much will be left after you use it to outline your pin.

Create a design for a pin this size

HOMEWORK EXERCISES ▶ See Exs. 15–31 on pp. 348–350.

Section 4

Key Concepts

Adding Mixed Numbers (pp. 342–343)

- **Estimating** One way to estimate a sum or difference of mixed numbers is to round to the nearest whole number.

- **Using paper and pencil** Add the whole numbers and the fractions separately.

Example

$$\begin{array}{rcl} 2\frac{1}{2} & = & 2\frac{3}{6} \\ +\,3\frac{2}{3} & = & +\,3\frac{4}{6} \\ \hline & & 5\frac{7}{6} = 6\frac{1}{6} \end{array}$$

Write fractions with a **common denominator.**

Simplify so that the fraction is less than 1 and in lowest terms.

Subtracting Mixed Numbers (pp. 344–346)

- **Using paper and pencil** First subtract the fractions. Then subtract the whole numbers. You may need to regroup a whole.

Example

Regroup 4 as $3\frac{6}{6}$.

$$\begin{array}{rcrcr} 4\frac{1}{3} & = & 4\frac{2}{6} & = & 3\frac{8}{6} \\ -\,1\frac{5}{6} & = & -\,1\frac{5}{6} & = & -\,1\frac{5}{6} \\ \hline & & & & 2\frac{3}{6} = 2\frac{1}{2} \end{array}$$

Write in lowest terms.

- **Using mental math** Think of a related addition sentence when subtracting from a whole number.

Example To find $8 - 3\frac{5}{6}$, think $3\frac{5}{6} + \underline{\ ?\ } = 8$.

If you add $\frac{1}{6}$, you get 4. So you need to add $4\frac{1}{6}$, to get 8.

27 Key Concepts Question Find each sum or difference. Use estimation to check that each answer is reasonable.

a. $7\frac{5}{6} + 2\frac{3}{4}$ **b.** $7 - 1\frac{4}{5}$ **c.** $10\frac{1}{4} - 6\frac{5}{8}$

Section 4

Practice & Application Exercises

YOU WILL NEED

For Ex. 26:
- fraction calculator (optional)

Estimate each sum by first rounding each mixed number to the nearest whole number and then adding.

1. $5\frac{3}{5} + 4\frac{1}{8}$
2. $7\frac{2}{7} + 2\frac{6}{7}$
3. $2\frac{1}{3} + 3\frac{1}{8}$

Find each sum. Write each answer in lowest terms.

4. $2\frac{1}{8} + 1\frac{3}{4}$
5. $4\frac{2}{3} + 5\frac{1}{2}$
6. $1\frac{2}{3} + 4\frac{4}{5}$
7. $2\frac{1}{3} + 6\frac{5}{8}$
8. $\frac{5}{7} + 1\frac{5}{14}$
9. $1\frac{8}{9} + 3\frac{5}{6}$

FOR ◀ HELP
with *compatible numbers*, see
MODULE 1, p. 50

Mental Math **Show how to use compatible numbers to find each sum. (*Hint:* To add three or more mixed numbers, see if any have fraction parts with a sum of 1.)**

10. $4\frac{1}{3} + 18\frac{1}{2} + 5\frac{2}{3}$
11. $8\frac{4}{5} + 6\frac{1}{3} + 4\frac{3}{8} + 1\frac{1}{5} + 2\frac{5}{8}$

12. Sonya is making costumes for a play. She needs $1\frac{1}{2}$ yd of ribbon for one costume, $3\frac{2}{3}$ yd of ribbon for another costume, and $2\frac{1}{4}$ yd of ribbon for a third costume. What is the total amount of ribbon she needs?

13. **Estimation** Another way to estimate is to first round to the nearest half.

about 5

$$\begin{array}{r} 4\frac{4}{5} \\ +\ 3\frac{3}{8} \\ \hline \text{about } 8\frac{1}{2} \end{array}$$

about $3\frac{1}{2}$

   a. Explain why $3\frac{3}{8}$ was rounded to $3\frac{1}{2}$ instead of 3.

   b. Do you think $8\frac{1}{2}$ is a *low* or a *high* estimate? Explain.

   c. Find the exact sum and compare it with the estimate.

14. Estimate $11\frac{2}{7} + 4\frac{3}{5}$ by first rounding to the nearest half.

Find each difference. Write each answer in lowest terms.

15. $3\frac{2}{5} - 2\frac{1}{4}$
16. $4\frac{2}{3} - 2\frac{8}{9}$
17. $2\frac{1}{8} - 1\frac{3}{4}$
18. $23\frac{1}{2} - 5\frac{6}{7}$
19. $17 - 9\frac{5}{11}$
20. $4\frac{5}{12} - 3\frac{13}{36}$

Use mental math to find each difference. Explain what you did.

21. $7 - 3\frac{1}{3}$ 22. $5\frac{3}{5} - 2$ 23. $3 - 1\frac{1}{4}$

24. **Photography** The image on an instant photograph is $3\frac{5}{8}$ in. long and $2\frac{7}{8}$ in. wide. What are the dimensions of a piece of cardboard you would need to make a mat with a $\frac{3}{4}$ in. border around the top and sides, and 1 in. along the bottom?

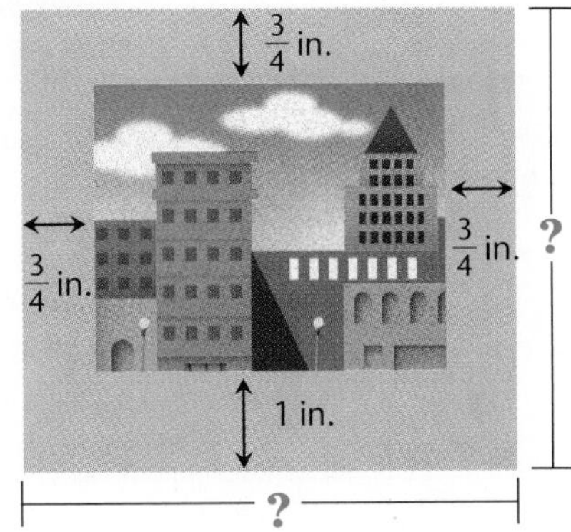

25. Kele is $2\frac{7}{8}$ in. taller than Sharon. Rosa is $2\frac{1}{2}$ in. shorter than Kele, but $\frac{5}{8}$ in. taller than Gary.

a. Who is taller, Sharon or Gary? By how much?

b. Find the difference between Kele's height and Gary's height.

26. Fraction Calculator Another way to add and subtract mixed numbers is by using a calculator.

a. To find the sum $3\frac{7}{8} + 1\frac{3}{4}$, enter

b. Press Ab/c . What did this do?

c. Estimate $3\frac{7}{8} + 1\frac{3}{4}$ to check that the answer displayed is reasonable.

d. Use a calculator to find $6\frac{1}{2} - 1\frac{4}{5}$. Estimate to check that the answer displayed is reasonable.

27. **Woodworking** Nails are sometimes referred to in units called "pennies." A 2-penny nail is 1 in. long. Each increase of a penny means an increase of $\frac{1}{4}$ in. in length up to 3 in.

a. What is the length of a 4-penny nail?

b. A carpenter hammers a 4-penny nail through a board that is $\frac{3}{4}$ in. thick. If the nail is hammered in straight, how far will the nail stick out of the board?

28. A plumber needs to replace the middle pipe in the diagram. Find the length of the middle pipe.

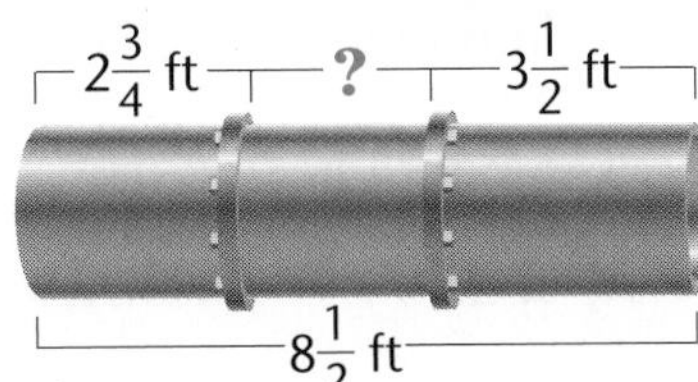

Interpreting Data Use the table to answer Exercises 29 and 30.

Records for the Olympic High Jump from 1980–1996			
Competitor	**Country**	**Distance**	**Year**
Charles Austin	United States	7 ft $10\frac{1}{4}$ in.	1996
Guennadi Avdeenko	former U.S.S.R.	7 ft $9\frac{1}{2}$ in.	1988
Gerd Wessig	East Germany	7 ft $8\frac{3}{4}$ in.	1980

▲ Charles Austin's 1996 gold medal winning jump.

29. How much farther did Austin jump than Guennadi Avdeenko?

30. How much farther did Guennadi Avdeenko jump than Gerd Wessig?

Reflecting on the Section

Journal

Exercise 31 checks that you understand mixed number subtraction.

Write your response to Exercise 31 in your journal.

31. Mary and Russ each tried to find $4\frac{3}{15} - 1\frac{10}{15}$. Explain what is wrong with each student's work.

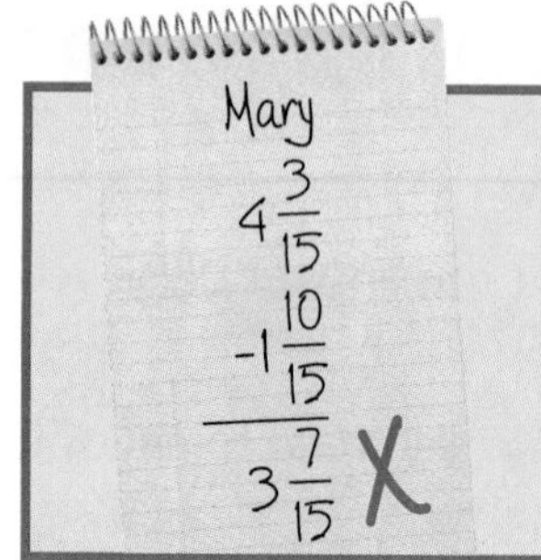

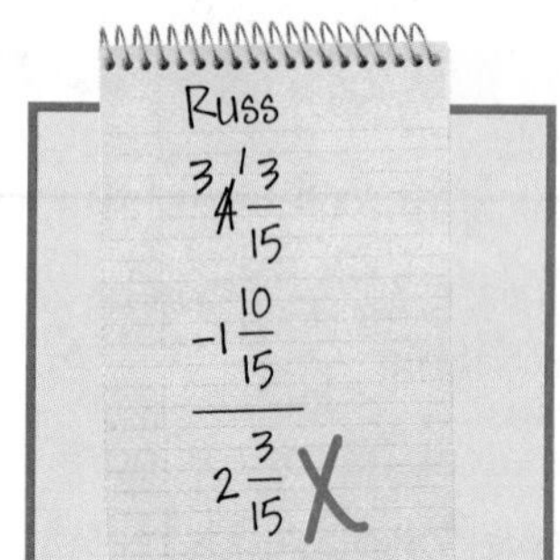

Spiral Review

Find each sum or difference in lowest terms. (Module 5, p. 336)

32. $\frac{1}{5} + \frac{4}{25}$

33. $\frac{5}{6} - \frac{3}{4}$

34. $\frac{7}{10} + \frac{2}{3}$

Tell whether each event is *certain, impossible,* or *neither* when you roll a single die. (Module 4, p. 242)

35. odd number

36. number less than 7

37. multiple of 8

Use mental math to find each value. (Module 3, p. 176)

38. $\frac{1}{3}$ of 27

39. $\frac{2}{5}$ of 15

40. $\frac{5}{6}$ of 48

Extension 

Making Connections about Regrouping

41. a. A flight leaves at 1:37 PM and arrives at 4:16 PM. Show how to use subtraction with regrouping to find the elapsed time.

    b. How is the regrouping you use when you add and subtract time measurements like the regrouping you use when you add and subtract mixed numbers? How is it different?

FOR ▶ HELP with *elapsed time*, see **TOOLBOX, p. 601**

42. Make a list of different types of numbers or measurements that you know how to add and subtract. Describe similarities and differences in how regrouping is used for the items on your list.

43. Make up a money or measurement system of your own. It can be totally imaginary (for example, using zings and zangs) or it can use real objects as units. Explain how the units in your system are related. Then show how to use regrouping to add and subtract.

An Exhibit of Everyday Objects

Adding and Subtracting Fractions Before a new object is added to the Architecture and Design collection of the Museum of Modern Art, a committee looks at its design and how it is related to the object's use.

Answer these questions to investigate the design of your object.

 3 Use the sketch you made of your object. Choose one of its dimensions.

a. Add $\frac{1}{2}$ in. to the dimension

b. Subtract $\frac{1}{2}$ in. from the dimension.

c. Suppose the person or machine that made the object had been inaccurate by $\frac{1}{2}$ in. Would a difference of $\frac{1}{2}$ in. in the dimension you investigated affect how your object serves its purpose? Explain.

 4 What material is used in your object's construction? Why do you think this material was chosen? Explain.

Section 4
Extra Skill Practice

Find each sum. Write each answer in lowest terms.

1. $1\frac{1}{2} + 6\frac{3}{4}$
2. $5\frac{5}{16} + 3\frac{7}{8}$
3. $2\frac{3}{5} + 7\frac{1}{2}$
4. $4\frac{3}{4} + 3\frac{1}{6}$
5. $2\frac{7}{12} + 1\frac{8}{15}$
6. $6\frac{2}{3} + 5\frac{4}{7}$

Find each difference. Write each answer in lowest terms.

7. $4\frac{5}{9} - 2\frac{1}{2}$
8. $36\frac{2}{3} - 4\frac{1}{6}$
9. $18\frac{3}{4} - 14\frac{1}{7}$
10. $12\frac{7}{8} - 10\frac{3}{4}$
11. $16\frac{4}{9} - 7\frac{5}{6}$
12. $7\frac{2}{7} - 3\frac{5}{14}$

Use mental math to find each difference.

13. $8\frac{3}{4} - 5\frac{1}{2}$
14. $6\frac{5}{8} - 2$
15. $12 - 9\frac{11}{16}$
16. $21 - 6\frac{7}{10}$
17. $32\frac{1}{2} - 14$
18. $7\frac{1}{3} - 4\frac{2}{3}$

Find each sum or difference. Write each answer in lowest terms.

19. $33\frac{1}{3} - 16\frac{1}{2}$
20. $2\frac{1}{3} + 3\frac{8}{9}$
21. $7\frac{3}{5} - 6\frac{3}{4}$
22. $1\frac{7}{32} + 2\frac{3}{8}$
23. $4\frac{5}{9} - 1\frac{3}{5}$
24. $11\frac{3}{4} + 16\frac{5}{6}$
25. $8\frac{5}{6} - 5\frac{3}{7}$
26. $132\frac{1}{2} - 71\frac{3}{4}$
27. $5\frac{3}{7} + 8\frac{4}{5}$

Standardized Testing ▶ Multiple Choice

1. Mrs. Quant buys a beef roast that weighs $5\frac{1}{4}$ lb and a ham that weighs $8\frac{1}{2}$ lb. How many pounds of meat does she buy?

   (A) $3\frac{1}{4}$ lb (B) $13\frac{1}{3}$ lb (C) $13\frac{3}{8}$ lb (D) $13\frac{3}{4}$ lb (E) None of these

2. After being cooked the $8\frac{1}{2}$-pound ham loses $\frac{5}{8}$ of a pound. Mrs. Quant slices $4\frac{1}{3}$ lb for sandwiches and serves the rest for dinner. How much ham is served for dinner?

   (A) $3\frac{1}{2}$ lb (B) $3\frac{7}{12}$ lb (C) $3\frac{11}{24}$ lb (D) $12\frac{5}{24}$ lb (E) None of these

Section 5 Capacity and Mixed Number Multiplication

IN THIS SECTION

EXPLORATION 1
- Customary Units of Capacity

EXPLORATION 2
- Multiplying Mixed Numbers

RECIPE for SUCCESS

Setting the Stage

SET UP *You will need $\frac{1}{2}$ pint, pint, quart, and gallon milk containers.*

In South Africa and in the United Kingdom, Red Nose Day is a day of fun to raise funds for children's programs. Each year a different kind of red nose is sold. One year it was one that changed color in hot water. Some cars even have red noses tied to their radiator grills!

On Red Nose Day there are thousands of fund-raising events. In the past, people have knitted the longest scarf in history, baked the world's largest pancake, and created the world's largest milkshake. The recipe for the giant milkshake used about 1900 gallons of milk!

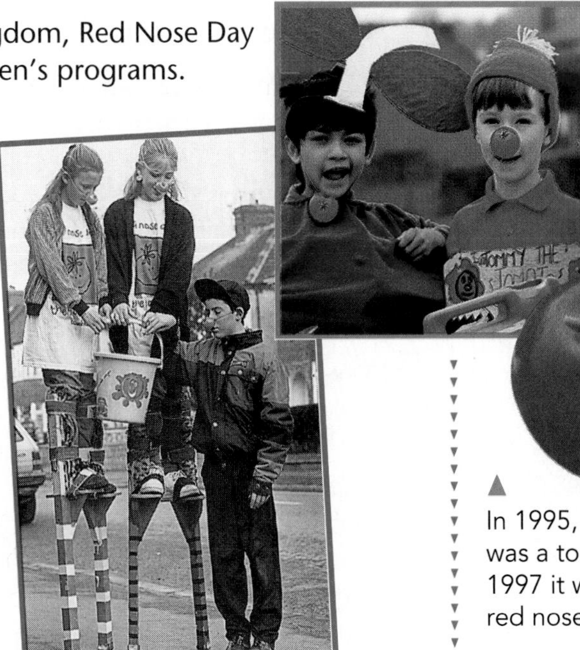

▲ In 1995, the red nose was a tomato and in 1997 it was a shaggy red nose.

Think About It

1 Look at the milk containers to help you estimate. The largest container is a one-gallon container. Do you think you could store 1900 of them in your classroom? Explain.

2 About how many people do you think the 1900-gallon milkshake served? Explain your thinking.

GOAL

LEARN HOW TO...
- use benchmarks for customary units of capacity
- convert between customary units of capacity

AS YOU...
- estimate the capacities of containers

KEY TERMS
- capacity
- fluid ounce (fl oz)
- cup (c)
- pint (pt)
- quart (qt)
- gallon (gal)

Exploration 1

Customary Units of Capacity

SET UP *You will need containers of various sizes.*

▶ **Milk containers are good benchmarks for estimating *capacity*. The capacity of a container is the amount it can hold. In the customary system, capacity is measured in gallons (gal), quarts (qt), pints (pt), cups (c), or fluid ounces (fl oz).**

3 Think about the milk containers to decide whether each statement is reasonable. If not, explain why not.

a. Some tea kettles can hold about $1\frac{1}{2}$ quarts of water.

b. I have to fill a cup four times to make $\frac{1}{2}$ pint.

c. The maximum capacity of a car's fuel tank is 15 cups.

4 **Estimation** Estimate the capacity of each container your teacher shows you. Your teacher will then tell you the actual capacities.

5 **Try This as a Class** Explain how the G, Q, P, C, and 8 in the diagram show the relationships among customary units of capacity. (*Hint:* 8 fl oz = 1 c)

6 A recipe needs 2 c of tomato sauce. Will a 12 fl oz can of tomato sauce be enough? Explain.

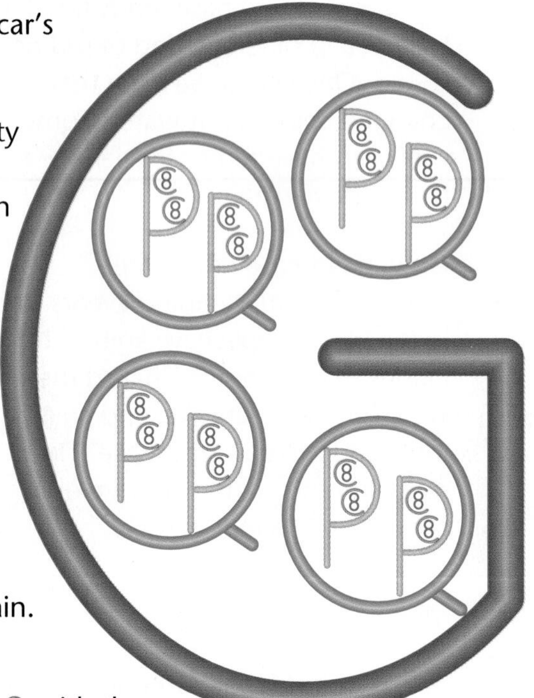

✓ QUESTION 7

...checks that you understand the relationships between customary units of capacity.

7 **✓ CHECKPOINT** Replace each ? with the number that makes the statement true. Use the diagram above.

a. __?__ pt = $\frac{1}{2}$ qt **b.** 1 qt = __?__ gal **c.** __?__ pt = 1 c

d. __?__ pt = $\frac{1}{4}$ gal **e.** 16 fl oz = __?__ c **f.** $\frac{1}{8}$ qt = __?__ c

8 **Discussion** Suppose you need about 100 cups of juice for a party. The juice is sold in half-gallon bottles.

a. How many cups are in a half gallon?

b. Should you multiply or divide to change 100 cups to half gallons? Why? 100 c = __?__ half gallons.

c. How many half-gallon bottles should you buy?

FOR HELP with *converting units*, see **MODULE 5, p. 327**

9 ✓ **CHECKPOINT** Replace each __?__ with the number that makes the statement true.

a. 15 qt = __?__ pt **b.** 26 fl oz = __?__ c **c.** 22 qt __?__ gal

10 About how many people can a 1900-gallon milkshake serve? Assume one person will drink 1 pt during Red Nose Day.

✓ **QUESTION 9**

...checks that you can convert between customary units of capacity.

HOMEWORK EXERCISES See Exs. 1–12 on p. 359.

Exploration 2

Multiplying Mixed Numbers

SET UP *Work in a group. You will need pattern blocks.*

GOAL

LEARN HOW TO...
- use the distributive property
- multiply mixed numbers

AS YOU...
- increase a recipe

KEY TERMS
- distributive property
- reciprocals

▶ **Whether you are creating a giant milkshake for a special event like Red Nose Day, or just slightly increasing a recipe, you can multiply the amounts needed for a recipe to serve more people.**

11 For four cakes, a baker needs $1\frac{1}{3}$ cups of almonds 4 times.

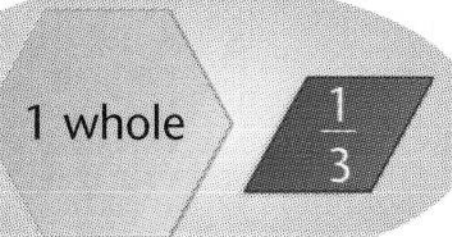

a. Use pattern blocks to show $4 \cdot 1\frac{1}{3}$.

b. Group together any rhombuses that can form hexagons, and trade them for hexagons. Record the total number of hexagons and rhombuses you have after the trade.

c. How many cups of almonds are needed for four cakes?

12 Use pattern blocks to find the amounts of flour and raspberries for four Surprise Layer Cakes.

▶ **To multiply an amount by 4, you can add the same amount four times. You can also use the distributive property as shown in the Example.**

EXAMPLE

Find $4 \cdot \left(1\frac{1}{3}\right)$.

Think of $1\frac{1}{3}$ as $1 + \frac{1}{3}$.

SAMPLE RESPONSE

$$4 \cdot \left(1 + \frac{1}{3}\right) = (4 \cdot 1) + \left(4 \cdot \frac{1}{3}\right)$$

four **whole** cups; four $\frac{1}{3}$ cups

$$= 4 + \frac{4}{3}$$

$\frac{1}{3}$ taken 4 times is $\frac{4}{3}$.

$$= 4 + 1\frac{1}{3}$$

$$= 5\frac{1}{3}$$

13 **Discussion** Explain how to find $2\frac{1}{2} \cdot 3$ using the distributive property.

✓ **QUESTION 14**

...checks that you can use the distributive property to multiply a whole number and a mixed number.

14 ✓ **CHECKPOINT** Find each product. Show your steps.

a. $6 \cdot 4\frac{1}{2}$ **b.** $2 \cdot 2\frac{1}{6}$ **c.** $3\frac{1}{4} \cdot 3$

15 **Try This as a Class** Explain each step of Karina's method for finding $4 \cdot 2\frac{1}{3}$.

Karina

Raspberries for 4 cakes

$$4 \cdot 2\frac{1}{3} = \frac{4}{1} \cdot \frac{7}{3}$$

$$= \frac{28}{3}$$

$$= 9\frac{1}{3}$$

$9\frac{1}{3}$ cups of raspberries

16 Use Karina's method to find each product.

a. $3 \cdot \frac{2}{5}$

b. $6 \cdot 1\frac{5}{8}$

c. $4 \cdot 6\frac{1}{2}$

▶ **Multiplying Mixed Numbers** **You have learned to multiply fractions and to write a mixed number as a fraction. You can combine these two skills to multiply mixed numbers.**

17 Find the product $5\frac{1}{2} \cdot 3\frac{1}{2}$ by first writing the mixed numbers as fractions. Write your answer as a mixed number in lowest terms.

18 ✔ **CHECKPOINT** Below are three multiplication expressions.

A. $6 \cdot 3\frac{1}{2}$ **B.** $\frac{3}{4} \cdot 1\frac{3}{8}$ **C.** $2\frac{1}{6} \cdot 12\frac{1}{2}$

a. Explain how they are different.

b. Find each product in lowest terms.

c. Did you use the same method to find each product? Explain.

✔ **QUESTION 18**

...checks that you can multiply mixed numbers.

19 One batch of trail mix requires $\frac{2}{3}$ c raisins. How many cups of raisins does Jim need for $1\frac{1}{2}$ batches?

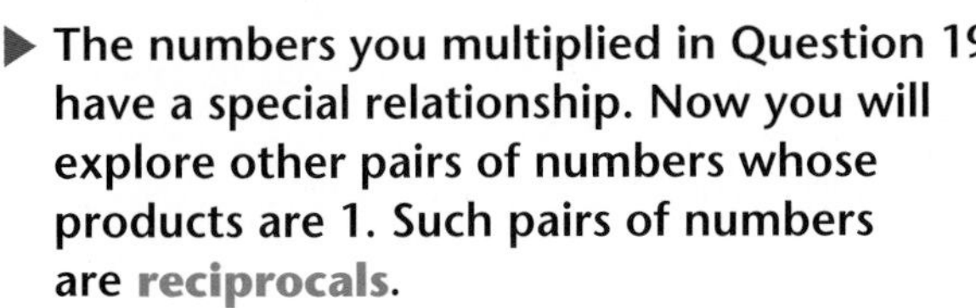

▶ **The numbers you multiplied in Question 19 have a special relationship. Now you will explore other pairs of numbers whose products are 1. Such pairs of numbers are reciprocals.**

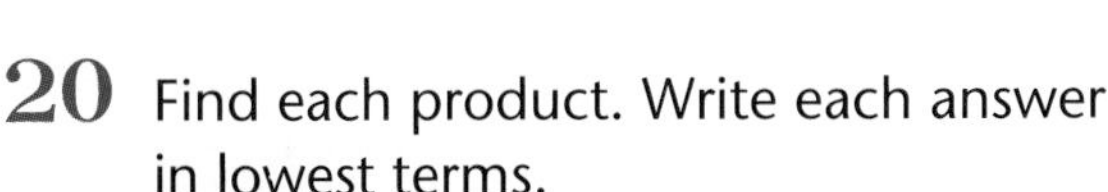

20 Find each product. Write each answer in lowest terms.

a. $\frac{11}{8} \cdot \frac{8}{11}$ **b.** $2 \cdot \frac{1}{2}$ **c.** $\frac{4}{9} \cdot 2\frac{1}{4}$

21 How are the two numbers in each problem in Question 20 related?

22 By what number can you multiply $\frac{4}{7}$ to get a product of 1? What is the reciprocal of $\frac{4}{7}$?

23 **Discussion** Are $2\frac{3}{4}$ and $2\frac{4}{3}$ reciprocals? Explain.

24 ✔ **CHECKPOINT** Write the reciprocal of each number.

a. $\frac{8}{9}$ **b.** 3 **c.** $\frac{1}{5}$ **d.** $1\frac{4}{5}$

✔ **QUESTION 24**

...checks that you can find the reciprocal of a number.

HOMEWORK EXERCISES ▶ **See Exs. 13–40 on pp. 359–361.**

Section 5 Key Concepts

Key Terms

capacity

fluid ounce (fl oz)

cup (c)

pint (pt)

quart (qt)

gallon (gal)

distributive property

reciprocals

Capacity (pp. 354–355)

You can use customary units of capacity to measure how much a container can hold.

1 cup = 8 fluid ounces
1 pint = 2 cups
1 quart = 2 pints
1 gallon = 4 quarts

Example

$2\frac{1}{2}$ qt = __?__ c $2\frac{1}{2}$ qt = 10 c (× 4)

Multiply to convert to a smaller unit. 1 qt = 4 c

Multiplying Mixed Numbers (pp. 355–357)

One way to multiply a mixed number by a whole number is to use the distributive property. (p. 356)

You can always write mixed numbers as fractions to multiply.

Example

$1\frac{1}{2} \cdot 3\frac{2}{5} = \frac{3}{2} \cdot \frac{17}{5} = \frac{51}{10}$, or $5\frac{1}{10}$

Reciprocals (p. 357)

Reciprocals are two numbers whose product is equal to 1. One way to find the reciprocal of a number is to write it as a fraction and then interchange the numerator and the denominator.

Example

$4\frac{1}{2}$ and $\frac{2}{9}$ are reciprocals, since $\frac{9}{2} \cdot \frac{2}{9} = 1$.

$4\frac{1}{2} = \frac{9}{2}$

25 Key Concepts Question A recipe calls for $3\frac{1}{4}$ c of water.

a. How many fluid ounces is this?

b. How many cups of water do you need to make 6 times as much as the original recipe?

Section 5
Practice & Application Exercises

Choose the letter of the most reasonable measurement for the capacity of each object.

1. 
2. 
3. 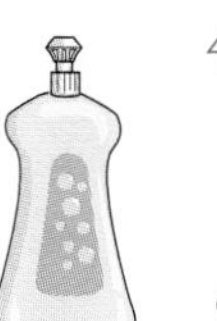
4. 
5. 

A. 4 gal B. 1 fl oz C. $1\frac{1}{2}$ pt D. 10 fl oz E. 3 qt

Replace each ? with the number that makes the statement true.

6. 6 pt = __?__ qt
7. $5\frac{1}{2}$ gal = __?__ qt
8. 5 c = __?__ qt
9. $2\frac{1}{2}$ pt = __?__ c
10. 20 fl oz = __?__ c
11. 6 c = __?__ pt

12. **Writing** Below are the ingredients for making paper-sculpture figures. You have only a one-cup measuring cup. Explain how you can measure the correct amount for each ingredient.

3 qt pulp (old newspaper and warm water)
1 pt paste
2 c plaster of Paris

Mental Math Use the distributive property and mental math to find each product. Write each answer in lowest terms.

13. $3 \cdot 5\frac{1}{4}$
14. $2\frac{1}{3} \cdot 3$
15. $10 \cdot 3\frac{1}{5}$
16. $4 \cdot 2\frac{1}{2}$
17. $5\frac{1}{6} \cdot 5$
18. $6\frac{1}{8} \cdot 8$

Find each product. Write each answer in lowest terms.

19. $2\frac{1}{3} \cdot 3\frac{1}{5}$
20. $6\frac{1}{2} \cdot \frac{2}{3}$
21. $\frac{3}{5} \cdot 2\frac{1}{4}$
22. $1\frac{1}{3} \cdot 2\frac{1}{5}$
23. $7\frac{1}{6} \cdot 1\frac{1}{2}$
24. $1\frac{5}{8} \cdot \frac{3}{13}$

25. Show two methods for finding $3\frac{2}{3} \cdot 5$.

26. **Language Arts** In Mildred Pitts Walter's novel *Justin and the Best Biscuits in the World*, ten-year-old Justin Ward learns about much more than biscuits on a visit to his grandfather's ranch. Justin learns that past generations of Wards were among the many African-American cowhands who helped build the American West.

As he prepares a lunch of homemade biscuits, stewed raisins, and smoked pork, Justin's grandfather remembers:

"When I was a boy about your age, I used to go with my father on short runs with cattle. We'd bring them down from the high country onto the plains."

"Did you stay out all night?" [Justin asks.]

"Sometimes. That was the time I liked most. The cook often made for supper what I am going to make for lunch."

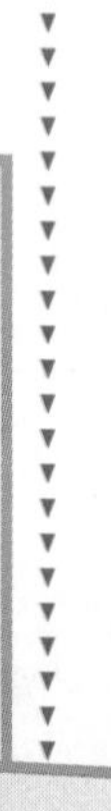

▲ Before becoming an award-winning author, Mildred Pitts Walter was a teacher in Louisiana.

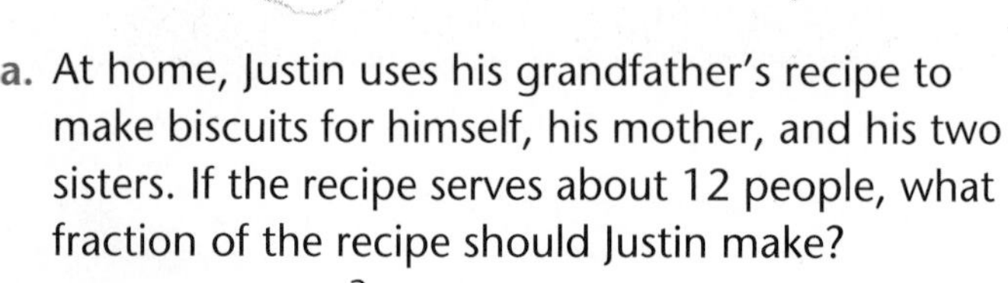

Illustrator ▶ Catherine Stock was born in Sweden and has lived in many countries including the United States.

a. At home, Justin uses his grandfather's recipe to make biscuits for himself, his mother, and his two sisters. If the recipe serves about 12 people, what fraction of the recipe should Justin make?

b. If the biscuit recipe calls for $1\frac{3}{4}$ c of all-purpose flour, how much flour should Justin use?

c. How much flour is needed if the recipe is increased to serve 30 people?

Write the reciprocal of each number.

27. 10 28. $7\frac{1}{2}$ 29. $\frac{2}{3}$ 30. $\frac{8}{5}$

Mental Math Use mental math to find each product by first multiplying pairs of reciprocals.

31. $3 \cdot \frac{5}{8} \cdot \frac{8}{5}$ 32. $2 \cdot \frac{5}{9} \cdot \frac{1}{2} \cdot \frac{8}{11} \cdot \frac{9}{5}$

Predict whether each product will be *greater than* or *less than* $4\frac{4}{5}$. Explain your reasoning. Then multiply to check your prediction.

33. $\frac{2}{3} \cdot 4\frac{4}{5}$ 34. $1\frac{1}{12} \cdot 4\frac{4}{5}$ 35. $\frac{9}{8} \cdot 4\frac{4}{5}$ 36. $4\frac{4}{5} \cdot \frac{2}{5}$

Science Rocks contain small amounts of radioactive elements that decrease over time. Scientists measure the age of rocks using half lives, the time it takes for a rock to lose half of its radioactive material.

Example: A rock that has $\frac{1}{4}$ of its radioactive elements is **2 half lives** old since $\frac{1}{4} = \frac{1}{2} \cdot \frac{1}{2}$.

Amount of radioactive elements remaining	Number of half lives
1	0
$\frac{1}{2}$	1
$\frac{1}{4}$	2

37. How many half lives old is a rock that has $\frac{1}{16}$ of its original radioactive elements?

38. What fraction of its original radioactive elements does a rock have that is 6 half lives old?

39. Suppose you multiply two fractions that are between 0 and 1. Is the product *between 0 and 1* or *greater than 1*? Give some examples to support your answer.

Reflecting on the Section

Be prepared to discuss your response to Exercise 40 in class.

40. Choose a different method to find each product. Show your work and explain why you chose each method.

a. $6\frac{1}{8} \cdot \frac{1}{3}$ b. $10\frac{2}{5} \cdot \frac{1}{3}$

Discussion

Exercise 40 checks that you can choose a method to multiply mixed numbers.

Spiral Review

Find each sum or difference in lowest terms. (Module 5, p. 347)

41. $6\frac{1}{2} + 4\frac{1}{3}$ 42. $5\frac{3}{10} - 4\frac{4}{5}$ 43. $8 + 7\frac{7}{8}$

Estimate each answer. (Module 1, p. 50)

44. \$82 • \$51 45. \$178 – \$59 46. \$34.69 + \$17.14

Write each quotient as a mixed number. (Module 4, p. 300)

47. $6\overline{)13}$ 48. $11\overline{)62}$ 49. $9\overline{)75}$

Career Connection

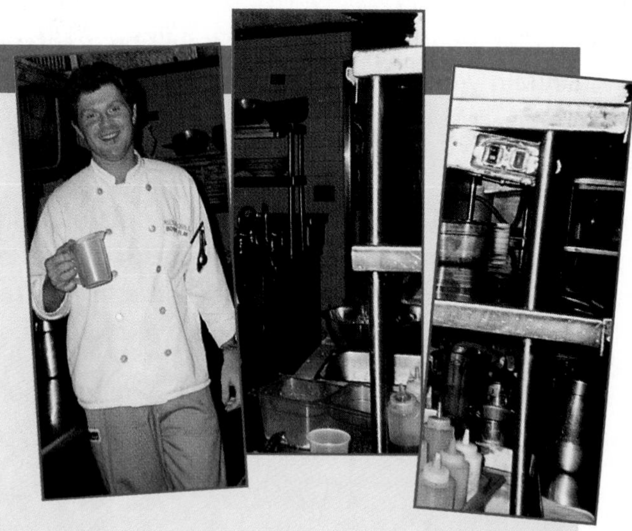

Chef: Bobby Flay

Bobby Flay became interested in cooking as a teenager. He impressed his first employers so much that they paid for him to study at the French Culinary Institute in New York City.

Chefs learn to test recipes in small batches, adjust them to taste, and then prepare large amounts.

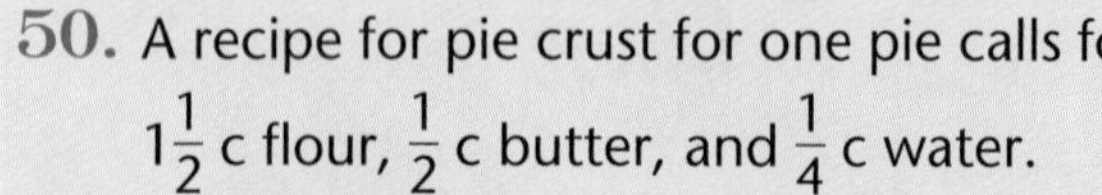

50. A recipe for pie crust for one pie calls for $1\frac{1}{2}$ c flour, $\frac{1}{2}$ c butter, and $\frac{1}{4}$ c water.

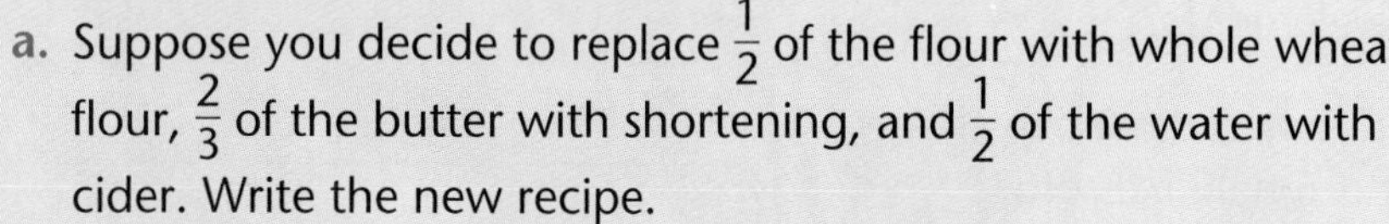

a. Suppose you decide to replace $\frac{1}{2}$ of the flour with whole wheat flour, $\frac{2}{3}$ of the butter with shortening, and $\frac{1}{2}$ of the water with cider. Write the new recipe.

b. If you buy a half gallon of cider, how much will be left after making 6 pies?

An Exhibit of Everyday Objects

Multiplying Mixed Numbers Moving an art treasure to a gallery or a museum requires careful handling. One factor to consider when packing an object is its size.

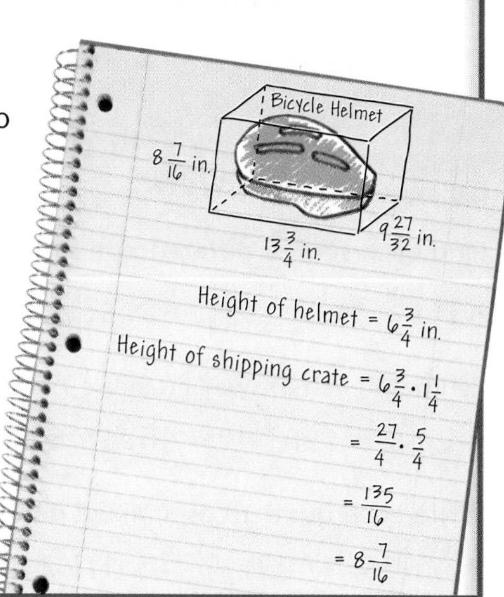

5 Suppose you have a shipping crate whose length, width, and height are all one and a quarter times as large as the length, width, and height of your object.

a. What are the dimensions of the shipping crate?

b. Do you think this crate would be a reasonable size for shipping your object? Explain.

Section 5 Extra Skill Practice

Replace each ? with the number that makes the statement true.

1. ___?___ pt = 2 gal
2. 1 gal = ___?___ fl oz
3. ___?___ qt = 2 c
4. ___?___ qt = 96 fl oz
5. ___?___ qt = 7 pt
6. $1\frac{1}{2}$ c = ___?___ fl oz
7. 28 fl oz = ___?___ pt
8. $\frac{1}{2}$ gal = ___?___ c
9. 16 c = ___?___ pt

Find each product. Write each answer in lowest terms.

10. $5 \cdot 4\frac{1}{8}$
11. $2 \cdot 6\frac{2}{5}$
12. $3\frac{5}{6} \cdot 4$
13. $1\frac{1}{8} \cdot 6\frac{1}{4}$
14. $\frac{3}{10} \cdot \frac{10}{3}$
15. $2\frac{1}{2} \cdot \frac{3}{8}$
16. $\frac{7}{12} \cdot 1\frac{5}{7}$
17. $3\frac{1}{5} \cdot 1\frac{3}{4}$
18. $2\frac{2}{9} \cdot 5\frac{1}{3}$

Write the reciprocal of each number.

19. $\frac{1}{6}$
20. $3\frac{7}{8}$
21. 32
22. $\frac{4}{3}$

Use mental math to find each product by first multiplying pairs of reciprocals.

23. $4 \cdot \frac{3}{5} \cdot \frac{1}{2} \cdot \frac{5}{3} \cdot 3$
24. $5 \cdot \frac{9}{7} \cdot \frac{1}{2} \cdot \frac{2}{3} \cdot \frac{3}{2} \cdot \frac{7}{9} \cdot \frac{1}{5}$

Standardized Testing ▶ Free Response

How many cups of apple juice do you need to make 1 gal of fruit smoothie?

Beverages

1 pint of Fruit Smoothie

Blend together:

$\frac{1}{3}$ c frozen strawberry puree

$\frac{1}{4}$ c frozen banana puree

1 c white grape juice

Then add apple juice until you have 1 pint.

Section 6 Division with Fractions

IN THIS SECTION

EXPLORATION 1
- Dividing by a Fraction

EXPLORATION 2
- Dividing Fractions and Mixed Numbers

Dividing the Puzzle

Setting the Stage

SET UP *Work in a group. You will need:* • *Labsheet 6A* • *scissors*

Have you ever tried to put together a tangram or a geometric puzzle? The puzzle pieces may form a square, a star, or some other geometric shape. You can draw a shape and then cut it apart to create a geometric puzzle.

Think About It

Use the *Geometric Puzzle* on Labsheet 6A.

1 Try to visualize how the pieces might fit together to form a square. Then follow the directions to cut and arrange the puzzle pieces.

2 **a.** What types of polygons are the puzzle pieces? Are any pieces regular polygons? If so, which ones?

b. Which puzzle pieces are congruent?

3 What strategies did you use to solve the puzzle?

Exploration 1

Dividing by a Fraction

GOAL

LEARN HOW TO...
- divide a whole number by a fraction

AS YOU...
- investigate geometric puzzle pieces

SET UP *Work in a group. You will need:* • *Labsheet 6B* • *ruler* • *tape* • *trapezoid-shaped puzzle pieces*

▶ **Suppose your class is making puzzles out of tagboard for a math carnival. Your group decides to make a more challenging version of the puzzle on Labsheet 6A. You can do this by replacing the square puzzle piece with four smaller squares.**

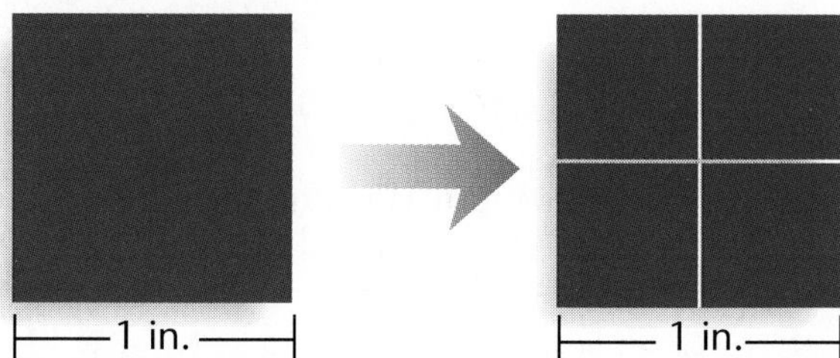

4 In parts (a) and (b), you'll find out how many squares you can cut from a strip of tagboard that is $\frac{1}{2}$ in. wide and 5 in. long.

a. The squares are $\frac{1}{2}$ in. long, so you must find how many $\frac{1}{2}$ in. lengths are in 5 in. This is the same as finding $5 \div \frac{1}{2}$. One way to do this is with a ruler. How many times does $\frac{1}{2}$ in. fit into 5 in.? What is $5 \div \frac{1}{2}$?

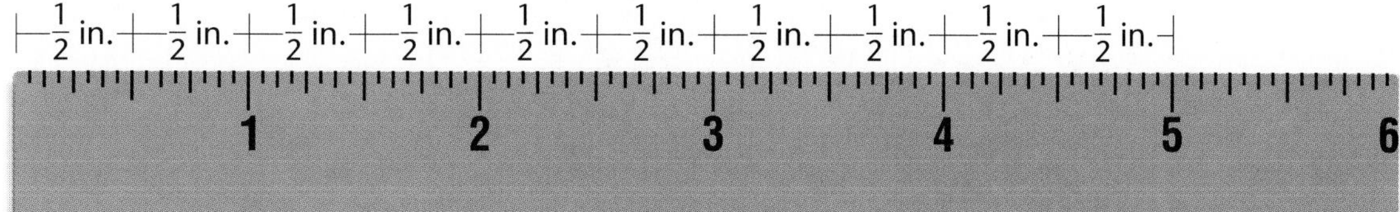

b. Instead of marking off each $\frac{1}{2}$ in., think about the number of halves in 1. How many are there? How you can use this number to find the number of halves in 5?

Use Labsheet 6B for Questions 5 and 6.

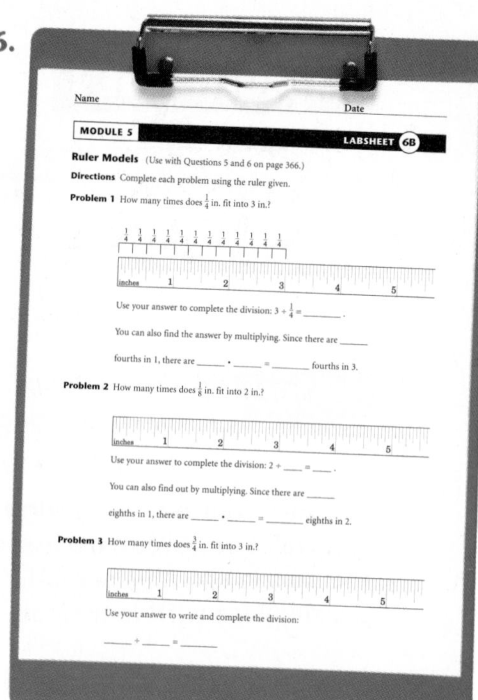

Name ______ Date ______

MODULE 5 — LABSHEET 6B

Ruler Models (Use with Questions 5 and 6 on page 366.)

Directions Complete each problem using the ruler given.

Problem 1 How many times does $\frac{1}{4}$ in. fit into 3 in.?

Use your answer to complete the division: $3 \div \frac{1}{4} =$ ______.

You can also find the answer by multiplying. Since there are ______ fourths in 1, there are ______ • ______ = ______ fourths in 3.

Problem 2 How many times does $\frac{1}{8}$ in. fit into 2 in.?

Use your answer to complete the division: $2 \div$ ____ = ____.

You can also find out by multiplying. Since there are ______ eighths in 1, there are ______ • ______ = ______ eighths in 2.

Problem 3 How many times does $\frac{3}{4}$ in. fit into 3 in.?

Use your answer to write and complete the division:

______ ÷ ______ = ______

5 The *Ruler Models* and questions on the labsheet will help you explore division of a whole number by a fraction. Complete the labsheet.

▶ **In Question 4 you saw that $5 \div \frac{1}{2}$ can be found by multiplying 5 by 2. Notice that $\frac{1}{2}$ and 2 (also written $\frac{2}{1}$) are reciprocals.**

6 **a.** Explain how reciprocals and multiplication were used in Problems 1 and 2 on Labsheet 6B.

b. Use your method from part (a) to find $3 \div \frac{3}{4}$. Compare your answer with the one you gave for Problem 3 on Labsheet 6B.

▶ **You can use a reciprocal and multiplication to divide a whole number by any fraction.**

EXAMPLE

Find $6 \div \frac{2}{3}$. Write the quotient in lowest terms.

SAMPLE RESPONSE

$$6 \div \frac{2}{3} = 6 \cdot \frac{3}{2} = \frac{6}{1} \cdot \frac{3}{2} = \frac{18}{2} = 9$$

To divide by $\frac{2}{3}$, **multiply** by the reciprocal, $\frac{3}{2}$.

✓ QUESTION 7

...checks that you can divide a whole number by a fraction.

7 **✓ CHECKPOINT** Find each quotient. Write the answer in lowest terms.

a. $7 \div \frac{1}{7}$ **b.** $10 \div \frac{1}{5}$ **c.** $3 \div \frac{3}{8}$ **d.** $8 \div \frac{2}{5}$

▶ **Looking at Remainders** **In Question 8 you'll see that sometimes the quotient is not a whole number.**

8 One method for making copies of the two trapezoid-shaped puzzle pieces is to cut out rectangles and then cut them in half to form the trapezoids.

a. To find out how large the rectangles should be, tape your two trapezoid-shaped puzzle pieces together to form a rectangle. What are the dimensions of the rectangle?

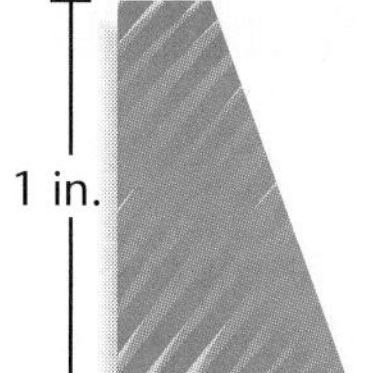

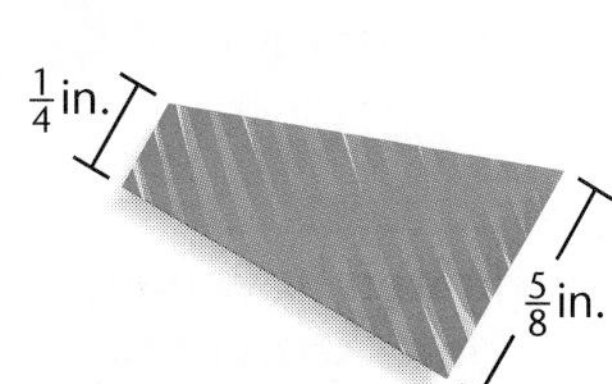

b. Use your taped rectangle and a ruler to find the greatest number of complete rectangles that can be cut from a strip of tagboard that is 1 in. wide by 5 in. long.

c. About what fraction of a rectangle can be made from the leftover tagboard?

1 2 3 4 5 6

9 **Try This as a Class** You'll use your results from Question 8.

a. How does the expression $5 \div \frac{7}{8}$ represent the number of rectangles you can cut from the strip?

b. When you use $5 \cdot \frac{8}{7}$ to find $5 \div \frac{7}{8}$, you get the answer $5\frac{5}{7}$. What does the fraction part $\frac{5}{7}$ mean?

c. Compare $5\frac{5}{7}$ with your answers in Question 8.

10 **a.** **Discussion** Describe a situation represented by $9 \div \frac{3}{4}$.

b. Use multiplication by a reciprocal to find $9 \div \frac{3}{4}$.

c. What does the remainder represent in your situation?

11 ✓ **CHECKPOINT** Find each quotient.

a. $5 \div \frac{5}{8}$ **b.** $8 \div \frac{7}{10}$ **c.** $2 \div \frac{7}{3}$

✓ **QUESTION 11**

...checks that you can divide a whole number by a fraction.

HOMEWORK EXERCISES See Exs. 1–11 on p. 371.

GOAL

LEARN HOW TO...
- divide by fractions and mixed numbers

AS YOU...
- think about lengths on a ruler

Exploration 2

DIVIDING Fractions and Mixed Numbers

▶ **In Exploration 1, you investigated how many puzzle pieces less than an inch long could be cut from a strip of tagboard several inches long. To find out, you divided a whole number by a fraction. Now you'll investigate dividing a fraction by a fraction.**

12 **a.** Which is longer, $\frac{3}{4}$ in. or $\frac{3}{8}$ in.?

b. Use the ruler shown to find $\frac{3}{4} \div \frac{3}{8}$.

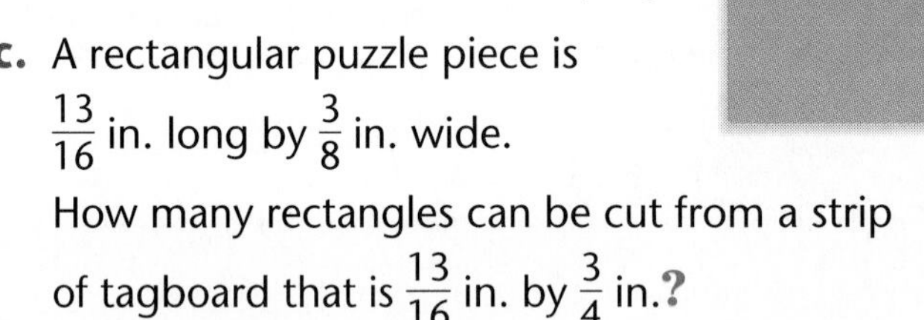

c. A rectangular puzzle piece is $\frac{13}{16}$ in. long by $\frac{3}{8}$ in. wide. How many rectangles can be cut from a strip of tagboard that is $\frac{13}{16}$ in. by $\frac{3}{4}$ in.?

13 **Discussion** Use the ruler to think about how many $\frac{7}{8}$ in. lengths are in $\frac{3}{4}$ in. Do you think $\frac{3}{4} \div \frac{7}{8}$ is a *whole number*, a *fraction*, or a *mixed number*? Why?

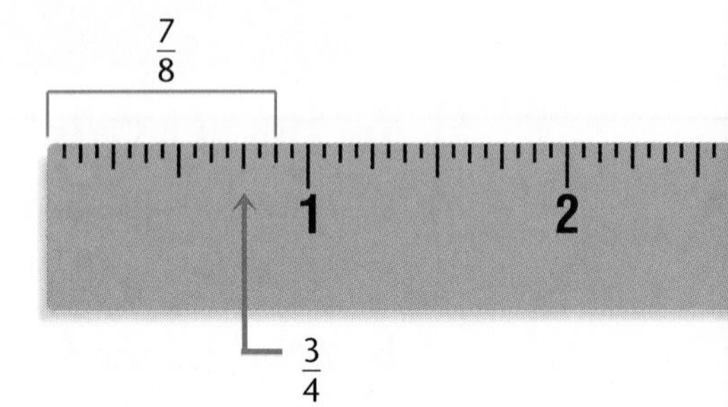

14 **Try This as a Class** When you divide a number by a greater number, is the quotient *less than 1*, *equal to 1*, or *greater than 1*? How does the quotient compare with 1 when you divide by a smaller number? when you divide by an equal number?

▶ **Using Reciprocals** **You have used a reciprocal to divide a whole number by a fraction. You can use the same method to divide a fraction by a fraction.**

15 **a.** Use the reciprocal of $\frac{3}{8}$ to rewrite $\frac{3}{4} \div \frac{3}{8}$ as a related multiplication. Find the product and write your answer in lowest terms.

b. Compare your answers in part (a) and Question 12(b).

16 **✓ CHECKPOINT** First decide whether each quotient will be *greater than 1* or *less than 1*. Then find each quotient. Write each answer in lowest terms.

a. $\frac{1}{4} \div \frac{1}{9}$ **b.** $\frac{7}{16} \div \frac{3}{4}$ **c.** $\frac{11}{12} \div \frac{6}{7}$

✓ QUESTION 16

...checks that you can divide a fraction by a fraction.

17 **Discussion** Suppose a group is making a puzzle with pieces large enough for young children.

a. About how many $2\frac{1}{4}$ in. by $2\frac{1}{4}$ in. squares can be cut from a $2\frac{1}{4}$ in. by $7\frac{1}{2}$ in. tagboard strip? Explain your reasoning.

b. About what fraction of a square will be left?

▶ **Dividing with Mixed Numbers** **One way to find the number of squares in Question 17 is to divide mixed numbers.**

18 **a.** Explain each step Ana used to divide two mixed numbers.

b. Is it reasonable that Ana's answer is less than 1? Why?

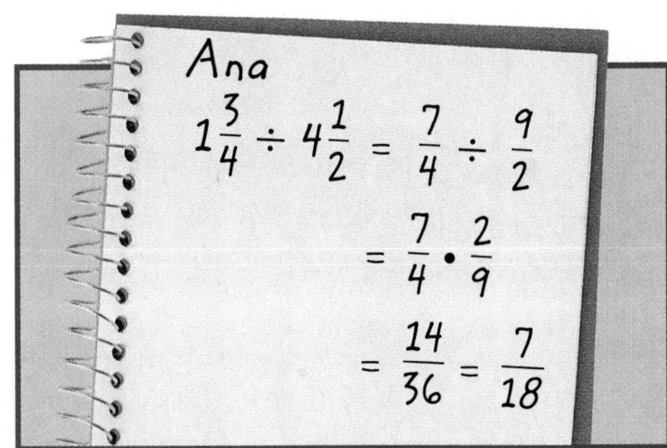

19 Use Ana's method to find $7\frac{1}{2} \div 2\frac{1}{4}$. Compare your answer with your estimates from Question 17.

20 **✓ CHECKPOINT** Find each quotient. Write each answer in lowest terms.

a. $2\frac{1}{3} \div 5$ **b.** $4\frac{1}{2} \div 1\frac{3}{4}$ **c.** $2\frac{5}{6} \div \frac{1}{2}$

d. $3\frac{3}{4} \div 7\frac{1}{2}$ **e.** $\frac{7}{12} \div 1\frac{17}{24}$ **f.** $13 \div 4\frac{5}{13}$

✓ QUESTION 20

...checks that you can divide fractions and mixed numbers.

HOMEWORK EXERCISES ▶ **See Exs. 12–24 on pp. 371–373.**

Section 6 Key Concepts

Dividing by a Fraction (pp. 365–367)

To divide by a fraction, you can multiply by its reciprocal.

Using Number Sense in Division (pp. 368–369)

When you divide a number by a smaller number, the quotient is greater than 1. When you divide a number by a greater number, the quotient is less than 1.

Example

Find $\frac{3}{10} \div \frac{3}{4}$. Write the answer in lowest terms.

Multiply by the reciprocal of the divisor.

$$\frac{3}{10} \div \frac{3}{4} = \frac{3}{10} \cdot \frac{4}{3} = \frac{12}{30} = \frac{2}{5}$$

The quotient is less than 1 since $\frac{3}{4} > \frac{3}{10}$.

Dividing by a Mixed Number (p. 369)

To divide by a mixed number, you can write the mixed numbers as fractions and then multiply by the reciprocal of the divisor.

Example

Find $1\frac{1}{2} \div 4\frac{3}{8}$. Write the answer in lowest terms.

Write mixed numbers as fractions.

$$1\frac{1}{2} \div 4\frac{3}{8} = \frac{3}{2} \div \frac{35}{8}$$

$$= \frac{3}{2} \cdot \frac{8}{35} = \frac{24}{70} = \frac{12}{35}$$

21 **Key Concepts Question** Suppose a package of strawberry dessert mix makes $5\frac{1}{2}$ cups. How many $\frac{2}{3}$ cup servings does the package make?

Section 6
Practice & Application Exercises

YOU WILL NEED

For Ex. 22:
- ruler
- scissors

Find each quotient. Write each answer in lowest terms.

1. $1 \div \frac{1}{2}$
2. $3 \div \frac{1}{3}$
3. $8 \div \frac{3}{4}$
4. $6 \div \frac{3}{4}$
5. $1 \div \frac{2}{5}$
6. $4 \div \frac{4}{9}$
7. $12 \div \frac{4}{3}$
8. $10 \div \frac{3}{5}$

9. Noreen has a 10 ft long piece of lumber. She needs to cut $\frac{3}{4}$ ft pieces from it for a class project. How many $\frac{3}{4}$ ft pieces can be cut from the board? Will there be wood left over? If so, how much?

10. A supermarket sells Italian seasoning in small jars that contain $2\frac{3}{8}$ oz. A wholesale club sells the same Italian seasoning in a large economy-size jar that contains 13 oz. How many times as much Italian seasoning is in the large jar as in the small jar?

11. a. How are the expressions $8 \div 5$ and $8 \cdot \frac{1}{5}$ related? Are $2.5 \div 10$ and $2.5 \cdot 0.1$ related in the same way? Explain.
    b. Based on part (a), describe a shortcut for finding a quotient when a decimal is divided by 10, 100, 1000, and so on.

Find each quotient. Write each answer in lowest terms.

12. $\frac{2}{9} \div \frac{1}{10}$
13. $3\frac{3}{4} \div 2\frac{1}{3}$
14. $4\frac{1}{3} \div 2$
15. $2\frac{3}{4} \div 6$
16. $\frac{5}{6} \div \frac{2}{3}$
17. $2\frac{4}{5} \div \frac{8}{9}$

18. **Stock Market** Newspapers report stock values by listing the cost per share for each company and the daily rise or fall in cost. The stock values shown here are recorded in fractions of a dollar. By the year 2001, the stock market is scheduled to use decimals.
    a. What is the net change in price for MathCo on Tuesday?
    b. How many whole shares of MathCo's stock can an investor buy with \$1000 at the closing price on Monday? on Tuesday?

What the price for one share of stock is at the end of the day. (Close)

Change in closing price from the previous day. (Net Chg)

Monday	Hi	Lo	Close	Net Chg
MapLtd	$15\frac{3}{4}$	$15\frac{1}{16}$	$15\frac{3}{16}$	$+\frac{1}{8}$
MathCo	$10\frac{5}{8}$	$10\frac{1}{4}$	$10\frac{3}{8}$	$+\frac{1}{16}$
MiniMkt	$33\frac{7}{8}$	$33\frac{1}{2}$	$33\frac{1}{2}$	$-\frac{3}{16}$

Tuesday	Hi	Lo	Close	Net Chg
MapLtd	$15\frac{1}{2}$	$14\frac{15}{16}$	$15\frac{1}{8}$	$-\frac{1}{16}$
MathCo	$10\frac{3}{8}$	$9\frac{5}{16}$	$9\frac{7}{16}$	
MiniMkt	$34\frac{3}{16}$	$33\frac{1}{8}$	$33\frac{7}{8}$	

$+\frac{1}{16}$ means that today's closing price is $\frac{1}{16}$ of a dollar higher than yesterday's.

19. Clarence has $1\frac{1}{2}$ c of milk. How many times can he pour out $\frac{1}{3}$ c? Will he have any milk left over?

20. Ali has $13\frac{1}{2}$ gal of paint. He needs about $3\frac{1}{2}$ gal of paint for each room in his house. He plans to paint as many rooms as he can.

a. How many rooms can he paint?

b. About how much paint will he use?

c. About how much paint will be left over?

21. **Bird-watching** Sandpipers are long-legged wading birds. One of the smallest is the semipalmated sandpiper, which usually is no longer than $6\frac{3}{4}$ in. One of the largest is the upland sandpiper, which can be as long as $12\frac{1}{2}$ in.

a. **Estimation** Without dividing, tell whether the upland sandpiper is *more than* or *less than* twice as long as the semipalmated sandpiper. Explain your thinking.

b. Find $12\frac{1}{2} \div 6\frac{3}{4}$ to check your answer in part (a).

upland sandpiper

semipalmated sandpiper

22. a. **Create Your Own** Design a geometric puzzle that can be cut from a 2 in. by 6 in. strip of paper. It should have 5 to 7 pieces shaped like three or more types of polygons.

b. Make a drawing that shows how all the pieces can be cut from a 2 in. by 6 in. strip.

c. **Geometry Connection** Trace your puzzle pieces to make a drawing that shows how they fit together to form a polygon. What kind of polygon is it? Label each puzzle piece with the name of its shape.

23. **Challenge** You learned to use the distributive property and mental math to find the product $6 \cdot 2\frac{1}{3}$.

$$6 \cdot \left(2 + \frac{1}{3}\right) = (6 \cdot 2) + \left(6 \cdot \frac{1}{3}\right)$$

Do you think there is a distributive property of division? Explain your thinking. (*Hint*: Does $6 \div 2\frac{1}{3}$ equal $(6 \div 2) + \left(6 \div \frac{1}{3}\right)$?)

Reflecting on the Section

24. The puzzle pieces shown fit together to form a square. Suppose you have a strip of tagboard that measures $8\frac{1}{2}$ in. by 3 in. Can you cut out three copies of the puzzle? Why or why not?

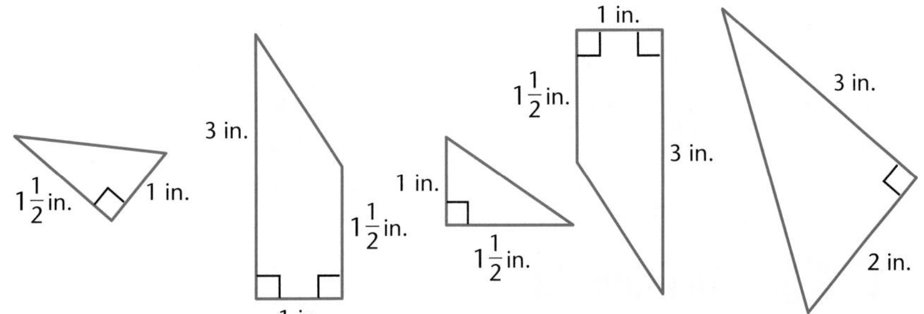

Visual THINKING

Exercise 24 checks that you can apply mixed number skills.

Spiral Review

Use the distributive property to find each product. Write each answer in lowest terms. **(Module 5, p. 358)**

25. $9 \cdot 2\frac{1}{3}$ 26. $7\frac{1}{5} \cdot 6$ 27. $12 \cdot 1\frac{3}{4}$

Write the ordered pair for each point on the coordinate grid. **(Module 4, p. 288)**

28. *A* 29. *B* 30. *C*

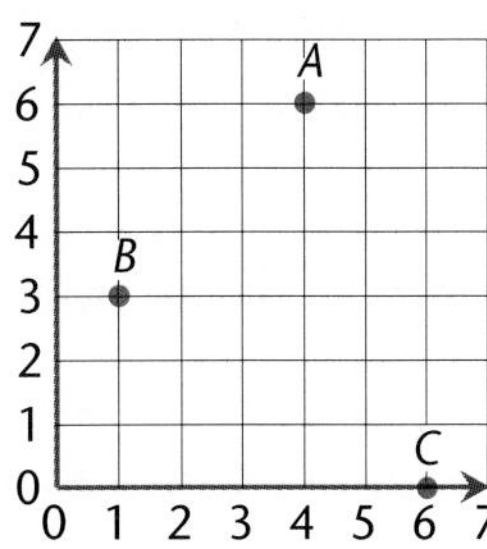

Complete each pair of equivalent fractions. **(Module 2, p. 114)**

31. $\frac{7}{8} = \frac{?}{16}$ 32. $\frac{4}{5} = \frac{12}{?}$ 33. $\frac{9}{45} = \frac{1}{?}$

Section 6 Extra Skill Practice

Find each quotient. Write each answer in lowest terms.

1. $1 \div \frac{1}{8}$
2. $6 \div \frac{2}{3}$
3. $12 \div \frac{3}{5}$
4. $5 \div \frac{1}{2}$

Find each quotient. Write each answer in lowest terms.

5. $3 \div \frac{7}{8}$
6. $1 \div \frac{3}{4}$
7. $2 \div \frac{5}{9}$
8. $7 \div \frac{2}{3}$
9. $14 \div \frac{6}{11}$
10. $6 \div \frac{5}{4}$
11. $1 \div \frac{4}{7}$
12. $4 \div \frac{5}{3}$

Find each quotient. Write each answer in lowest terms.

13. $\frac{3}{5} \div \frac{1}{6}$
14. $\frac{1}{6} \div \frac{2}{5}$
15. $\frac{9}{16} \div \frac{3}{8}$
16. $3\frac{1}{8} \div \frac{1}{8}$
17. $4\frac{2}{3} \div \frac{1}{2}$
18. $4\frac{2}{5} \div 2\frac{1}{4}$
19. $6\frac{3}{4} \div 3$
20. $2\frac{1}{2} \div 1\frac{3}{4}$
21. $3 \div 5\frac{3}{4}$
22. $5\frac{1}{3} \div 1\frac{3}{5}$
23. $\frac{9}{10} \div 18$
24. $3\frac{3}{8} \div 2\frac{1}{4}$

Standardized Testing ▶ Multiple Choice

1. When dividing a fraction by a smaller fraction, the quotient will be __?__.

   (A) less than 1 (B) equal to 1 (C) greater than 1 (D) Not enough information

2. Which statement tells a correct way to divide a number by a mixed number?

   (A) Change the mixed number to a fraction, then multiply.

   (B) Change the mixed number to a fraction, then divide by the reciprocal of the fraction.

   (C) Multiply by the reciprocal of the fractional part of the mixed number.

   (D) Change the mixed number to a fraction, then multiply by the reciprocal of the fraction.

   (E) None of these is correct.

An Exhibit of Everyday Objects

Creating Your Design You have been studying your object's design. Now you'll use the information you gathered to prepare a classroom exhibit of everyday objects as works of art.

6 When art is displayed, information about the piece is usually displayed as well. This information typically includes the name of the artist or designer, the dimensions, the name of the piece, and the material used to construct the piece. Prepare a card describing your object that includes this information.

7 Decide with your class how you will put together an exhibit catalog so that you can gather the materials you would like to include.

8 Write a brief summary for the catalog that describes why you chose your object. Include the sketch you made with its dimensions labeled. You should also explain how its design relates to its function. Include at least one of the calculations you did with fractions in your explanation.

9 With your classmates, set up your cards and objects for viewing in your "Everyday Objects as Works of Art" exhibit.

10 View all of the objects in the exhibit. Do you think that visitors to your exhibit might look at everyday objects differently after seeing it? Explain.

MODULE 5 Review and Assessment

You will need: • *ruler and nickel* **(Exs. 12–14)**

Write the fractions in order from least to greatest. **(Sec. 1, Explor. 1 and 2)**

1. $\frac{4}{7}, \frac{2}{3}, \frac{5}{3}, \frac{3}{100}$
2. $\frac{9}{10}, \frac{4}{5}, \frac{99}{100}, \frac{19}{20}$
3. $\frac{7}{8}, \frac{4}{5}, \frac{1}{7}, \frac{1}{4}$
4. $\frac{5}{6}, \frac{2}{3}, \frac{1}{4}, \frac{1}{2}$

Use a common demoninator to compare the fractions. Replace each __?__ with >, <, or =. **(Sec.1, Explor. 2)**

5. $\frac{5}{8}$ __?__ $\frac{7}{12}$
6. $\frac{4}{9}$ __?__ $\frac{6}{15}$
7. $\frac{11}{16}$ __?__ $\frac{3}{4}$
8. $\frac{8}{13}$ __?__ $\frac{2}{3}$

Write each fraction as a decimal rounded to the nearest hundredth. Then replace each __?__ with >, <, or =. **(Sec. 1, Explor. 2)**

9. $\frac{8}{11}$ __?__ $\frac{9}{13}$
10. $\frac{15}{27}$ __?__ $\frac{68}{103}$
11. $\frac{39}{83}$ __?__ $\frac{3}{7}$

Measure the width of a nickel as described. **(Sec. 2, Explor. 1)**

12. to the nearest $\frac{1}{2}$ in.
13. to the nearest $\frac{1}{4}$ in.
14. to the nearest $\frac{1}{8}$ in.

Replace each __?__ with the number that makes the statement true. **(Sec. 2, Explor. 2)**

15. $3\frac{1}{2}$ yd = __?__ in.
16. 34 in. = __?__ ft
17. $5\frac{1}{4}$ ft = __?__ in.
18. 26 ft = __?__ yd
19. 1 mi 250 yd = __?__ ft
20. 6000 ft = __?__ mi

Find each sum. Write each sum in lowest terms. **(Sec. 3, Explor. 1; Sec. 4, Explor. 1)**

21. $\frac{5}{8} + \frac{7}{8}$
22. $\frac{4}{7} + \frac{1}{3}$
23. $\frac{21}{8} + \frac{13}{4}$
24. $3\frac{3}{10} + \frac{1}{6}$
25. $4\frac{5}{6} + 1\frac{5}{6}$
26. $5\frac{1}{6} + \frac{1}{8}$
27. $8\frac{1}{5} + \frac{15}{8}$
28. $\frac{26}{5} + \frac{13}{10}$
29. A truck driver drove from Albuquerque to Los Angeles in $15\frac{1}{2}$ h and from Los Angeles to San Francisco in $7\frac{2}{3}$ h. How long did the entire trip take? **(Sec. 4, Explor. 1)**

Use mental math or paper and pencil to find each sum or difference. **(Sec. 4, Explors. 1 and 2)**

30. $2\frac{1}{2} + 1\frac{1}{2} + 4\frac{1}{2}$
31. $9 - 2\frac{3}{4}$
32. $\frac{1}{8} + \frac{1}{2} + \frac{3}{8} + \frac{1}{4}$
33. $10 - 4\frac{1}{16}$
34. It is $4\frac{1}{2}$ mi to school from Andy's house and $3\frac{1}{3}$ mi to school from Marguerite's house. How much farther does Andy live from school than Marguerite does? **(Sec. 4, Explor.2)**

Find each difference. Write each difference in lowest terms.
(Sec. 3, Explor. 1; Sec. 4, Explor. 2)

35. $\frac{5}{8} - \frac{1}{4}$ 36. $8\frac{2}{3} - 2\frac{3}{5}$ 37. $7\frac{2}{7} - \frac{3}{7}$ 38. $3 - \frac{2}{5}$

39. $5\frac{1}{10} - 3\frac{3}{10}$ 40. $\frac{7}{8} - \frac{1}{3}$ 41. $8\frac{3}{4} - 6\frac{2}{3}$ 42. $2\frac{3}{5} - 1\frac{5}{8}$

43. A recipe calls for $\frac{1}{2}$ c of cooking oil. Choose the letter of each amount that will supply enough oil for the recipe. (Sec. 5, Explor. 1)

A. $\frac{1}{4}$ pt B. $\frac{1}{3}$ c C. 5 fl oz D. $\frac{1}{16}$ gal

44. To make 1 chicken loaf you need $1\frac{3}{4}$ c of chicken broth. Suppose you want to make 7 loaves to freeze. How may cups of broth do you need? How many pints? How many fluid ounces?
(Sec. 5, Explors. 1 and 2)

Find each product. Write each product in lowest terms. (Sec. 5, Explor. 2)

45. $6\frac{3}{4} \cdot 1\frac{2}{3}$ 46. $3\frac{1}{3} \cdot 2\frac{1}{2}$ 47. $1\frac{5}{8} \cdot \frac{1}{3}$ 48. $\frac{3}{5} \cdot 4\frac{5}{6}$

Use the distributive property and mental math to find each product. Write each answer in lowest terms. (Sec. 5, Explor. 2)

49. $4 \cdot 1\frac{3}{4}$ 50. $2\frac{5}{6} \cdot 12$ 51. $5 \cdot 3\frac{1}{5}$ 52. $2\frac{3}{5} \cdot 10$

53. If Adela buys a board that is 8 ft long and 2 ft wide, will she have enough to cut 10 pieces that are $\frac{3}{4}$ ft by 2 ft? Explain.
(Sec. 6, Explor.1)

Find each quotient. Write each quotient in lowest terms.
(Sec. 6, Explor. 1 and 2)

54. $2\frac{1}{3} \div 1\frac{1}{2}$ 55. $8 \div \frac{1}{3}$ 56. $\frac{3}{5} \div \frac{3}{7}$ 57. $3\frac{1}{6} \div 4$

58. $3\frac{3}{8} \div 3$ 59. $\frac{1}{4} \div \frac{9}{16}$ 60. $1\frac{3}{18} \div \frac{7}{9}$ 61. $6\frac{1}{2} \div 12$

Reflecting on the Module

62. Write a letter to a family member or friend describing what you have done in this module. Discuss how fractions are used to create things.

MODULE 6 COMPARISONS and PREDICTIONS

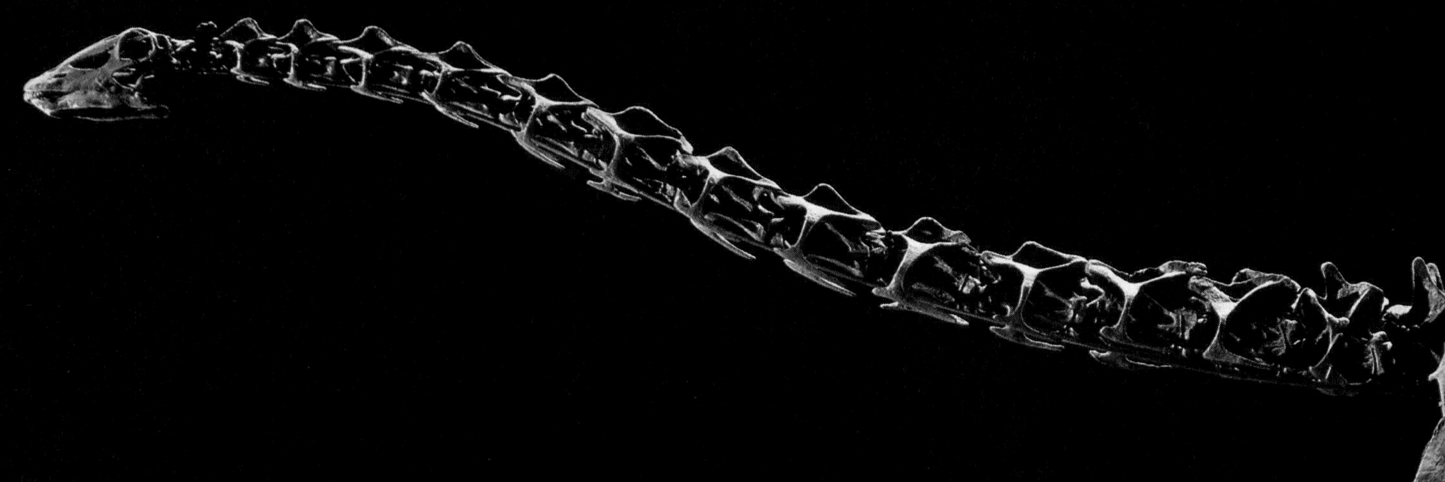

Mystery Tracks

Scientists study the clues left behind by dinosaurs, like bones and footprints, to figure out how they looked and moved. You can tell a lot about who made a set of footprints by taking measurements and calculating ratios. In this project you'll gather data about your own "tracks" and make predictions about a set of mystery tracks.

More on the Module Project

See pp. 387, 410, 436, and 449.

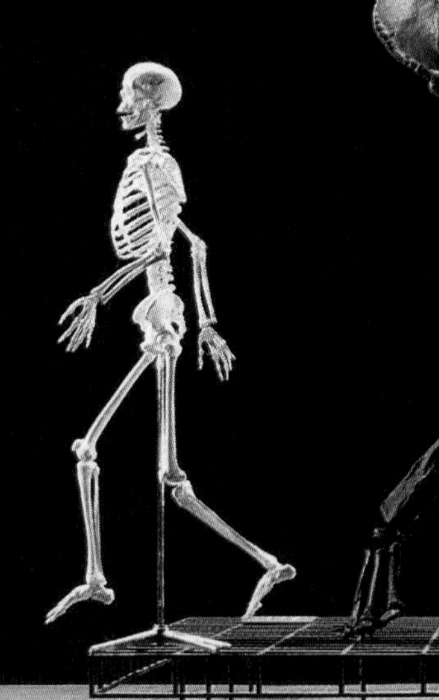

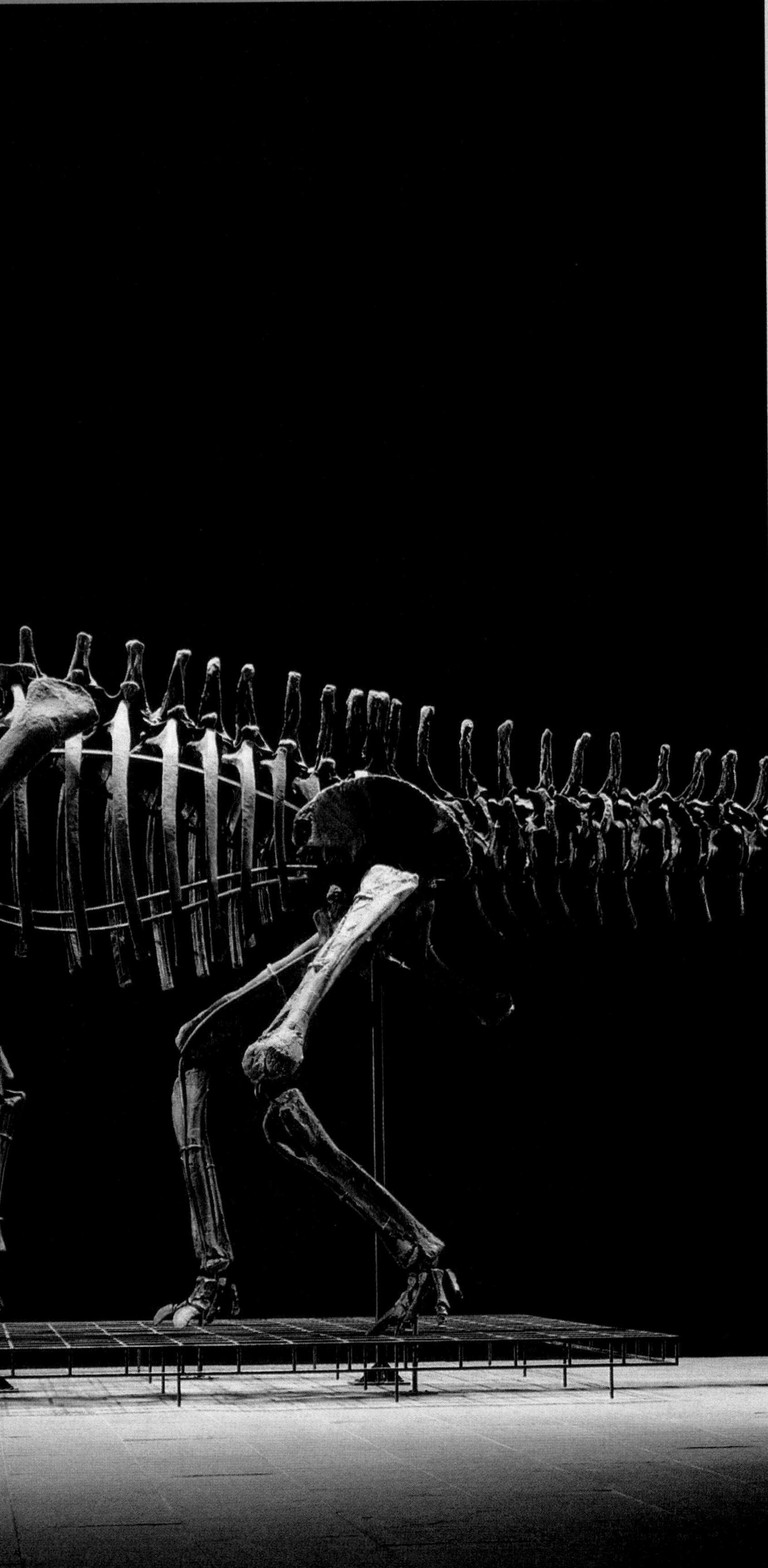

CONNECTING
MATHEMATICS & The Theme

MODULE 6 SECTION OVERVIEW

1 Exploring Ratios
As you explore the heights of Mr. Short and Mr. Tall:
- Make comparisons using ratios
- Write equivalent ratios

2 Rates
As you simulate a sandbag brigade:
- Use rates to make predictions
- Find unit rates

3 Using Ratios
As you find body ratios:
- Write a ratio as a decimal
- Use ratios and scatterplots to make predictions

4 Proportions
As you compare the jumping abilities of humans and animals:
- Use cross products to find equivalent ratios
- Write and use a proportion to solve a problem

5 Geometry and Proportions
As you look at how artists use models and scale drawings:
- Identify similar and congruent figures
- Use proportions to find missing side lengths
- Measure and draw angles

6 Percents and Probability
As you examine Olympic softball data:
- Use a fraction to estimate and to find a percent of a number
- Make a tree diagram to find probabilities

INTERNET
To learn more about the theme:
http://www.mlmath.com

Exploring Ratios

Mr. Short and Mr. Tall

Setting the Stage

Comparing things and making predictions based on those comparisons is an important use of mathematics. In the poem, Shel Silverstein makes comparisons to describe what the world would be like if you were only one inch tall.

From
Where the Sidewalk Ends
by Shel Silverstein

ONE INCH TALL

If you were only one inch tall, you'd ride a worm to school.
The teardrop of a crying ant would be your swimming pool.
A crumb of cake would be a feast
And last you seven days at least,
A flea would be a frightening beast
If you were one inch tall.

If you were only one inch tall, you'd walk beneath the door,
And it would take about a month to get down to the store.
A bit of fluff would be your bed,
You'd swing upon a spider's thread,
And wear a thimble on your head
If you were one inch tall.

You'd surf across the kitchen sink upon a stick of gum.
You couldn't hug your mama, you'd just have to hug her thumb.
You'd run from people's feet in fright,
To move a pen would take all night,
(This poem took fourteen years to write—
'Cause I'm just one inch tall).

Think About It

1 If the author spent the same amount of time writing each verse of the poem, about how many years did he take to write one verse?

2 Pretend you are only one inch tall and you are standing in the doorway of your classroom looking in. Compare your view of the room with the view you see in real life.

Exploration 1

COMPARING MEASURES

SET UP *Work with a partner. You will need:*
- *pennies*
- *one-inch squares*

GOAL

LEARN HOW TO...
- make comparisons using ratios
- recognize and write equivalent ratios

AS YOU...
- explore the heights of Mr. Short and Mr. Tall

KEY TERMS
- ratio
- equivalent ratios

▶ **You'll explore ways to compare the heights of Mr. Short and Mr. Tall and to predict one height from the other.**

3 **a.** How many pennies tall is Mr. Short?

b. How many squares tall is Mr. Short?

4 **Discussion** Mr. Tall looks exactly like Mr. Short except that he is 12 pennies tall.

a. How can you compare Mr. Short's height and Mr. Tall's height in pennies?

b. *Without measuring*, predict Mr. Tall's height in squares. Explain your thinking.

c. Describe a way you can use pennies and squares to check your prediction in part (b).

d. How many squares tall is Mr. Tall? How does this compare with your prediction?

e. How does Mr. Short's height in squares compare with Mr. Tall's height in squares?

▶ **To find Mr. Tall's height in squares, it can be helpful to use a special type of comparison called a *ratio*. The comparison below using pennies is an example of a ratio.**

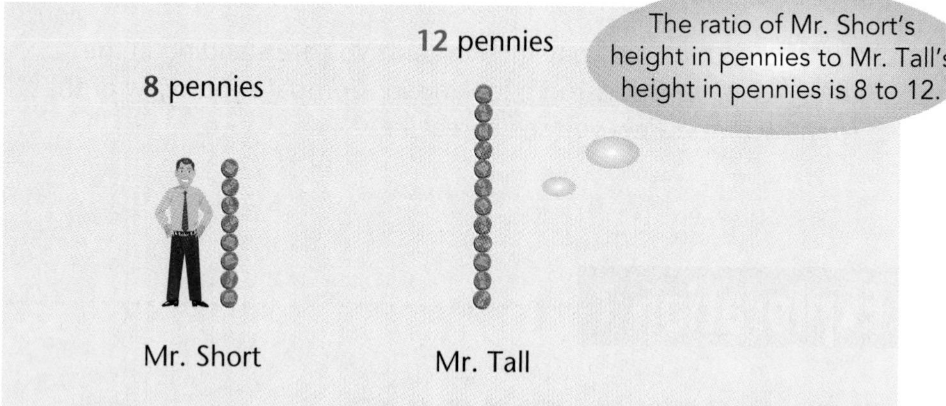

▶ **The ratio of two numbers or measures can be written several ways:**

using the word "to"	with a colon	as a fraction
8 to 12	8 : 12	$\frac{8}{12}$

✓ QUESTION 5

...checks that you can write a ratio to compare two quantities.

5 **✓ CHECKPOINT** Write the ratio of the number of boys in your classroom to the number of girls in your classroom in three ways.

6 **Discussion** Do you get the same ratio as in Question 5 if you compare the number of girls to the number of boys? Explain.

▶ **You can write other ratios that compare Mr. Short's height in pennies with Mr. Tall's height in pennies.**

7 **a.** Suppose you compare half of Mr. Short's height with half of Mr. Tall's height. What do you think the ratio will be?

b. Separate the number of pennies in Mr. Short's height into two equal-sized groups. Then separate the number of pennies in Mr. Tall's height into two equal-sized groups.

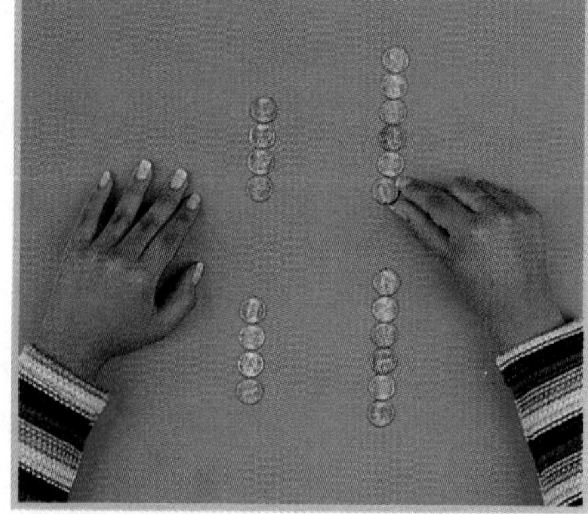

c. Write the ratio that compares half of Mr. Short's height in pennies with half of Mr. Tall's height in pennies. Was your prediction from part (a) correct?

8 **a.** Find another way to separate the pennies in Mr. Short's height into equal-sized groups.

b. Separate Mr. Tall's height in pennies into the same number of groups as in part (a).

c. Draw a sketch of your answers to parts (a) and (b). Then write a new ratio that compares Mr. Short's height in pennies with Mr. Tall's height in pennies.

9 Use your results from Question 4(e).

a. Find a way to separate the squares in Mr. Short's height into equal-sized groups so that the squares in Mr. Tall's height can also be separated into the same number of groups. Sketch your answer.

b. Write a new ratio that compares Mr. Short's height with Mr. Tall's height in squares.

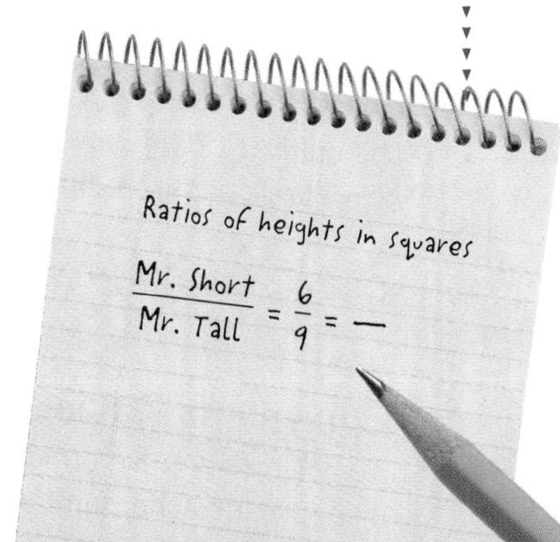

10 **a.** List all the ratios you found that compare Mr. Short's height with Mr. Tall's height. Write each ratio as a fraction.

b. How are these fractions related?

▶ **Equivalent Ratios** **Two ratios are equivalent if they can be written as equivalent fractions.**

FOR HELP with *equivalent fractions*, see **MODULE 2, p. 114**

11 **a.** Write the ratios 9 : 12 and 6 : 8 as fractions.

b. **Discussion** Explain how you can show that the ratios in part (a) are equivalent.

12 ✓ **CHECKPOINT** Tell whether each ratio is equivalent to the ratio 8 to 12 that compares Mr. Short's height with Mr. Tall's height.

a. $\frac{18}{24}$ **b.** 24 : 16 **c.** $\frac{12}{18}$ **d.** 54 to 81

e. 6 : 10 **f.** $\frac{108}{112}$ **g.** 72 to 108 **h.** 40 : 60

✓ **QUESTION 12**

...checks that you can recognize equivalent ratios.

HOMEWORK EXERCISES ▶ **See Exs. 1–13 on pp. 385–386.**

Section 1 Key Concepts

Key Terms

ratio

Ratios (p. 382)

A ratio is a special type of comparison of two numbers or measures. Ratios can be written in different ways. The order of the numbers in a ratio makes a difference.

Example You can write the ratio of the number of cashews to the number of pretzels in three different ways.

10 to 4   10 : 4 $\frac{10}{4}$

The snack mix has 10 cashews for every 4 pretzels.

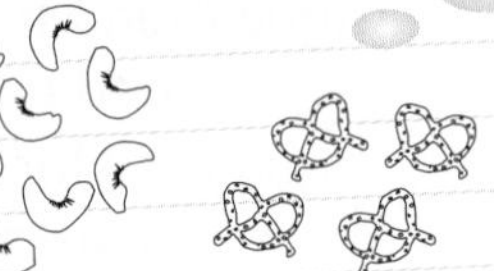

equivalent ratios

Equivalent Ratios (p. 382–383)

Sometimes a ratio can be shown another way by separating each measure into the same number of groups.

Example

You can compare half the number of cashews with half the number of pretzels.

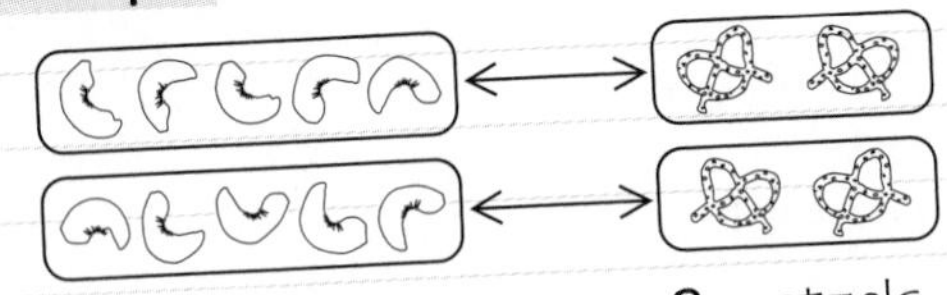

5 cashews to **2** pretzels

Equivalent ratios can be written as equivalent fractions.

Example 10 : 4 is equivalent to 5 : 2 because $\frac{10}{4}$ and $\frac{5}{2}$ are equivalent fractions.

13 **Key Concepts Question** Suppose that in a can of mixed nuts there are 12 peanuts for every 9 cashews.

a. Write the ratio of the number of cashews to the number of peanuts in each of the three forms.

b. Find a ratio that is equivalent to the one in part (a).

c. Is the ratio of the number of peanuts to the number of cashews equivalent to the ratio in part (a)? Explain.

Section 1

Practice & Application Exercises

1. Write the ratio of the number of dogs to the number of paws in each picture.

   a. 

   b.

   c. Are the ratios you found in parts (a) and (b) equivalent? If so, explain why.

2. **Gliders** The flight performance of a glider, an aircraft with no engine, can be measured with a glide ratio. A glide ratio compares the gliding distance with the height dropped.

height 500 m

gliding distance 9000 m

▲ Otto Lilienthal built the first controllable glider in the late 1800s.

   a. Write the glide ratio for the glider above in three ways.

   b. Suppose the glider starts at half the height and travels half as far. Write this ratio in three ways.

   c. Are the ratios you found in parts (a) and (b) equivalent? If so, explain why.

   d. Find another ratio equivalent to the ones you wrote in parts (a) and (b). Explain how you found the ratio.

Tell whether the ratios are equivalent.

3. $\frac{3}{5}$ and $\frac{9}{15}$

4. $\frac{5}{12}$ and $\frac{10}{8}$

5. $\frac{4}{3}$ and $\frac{16}{9}$

6. 1 : 6 and 5 : 30

7. 9 : 2 and 32 : 8

8. 12 : 6 and 8 : 4

9. a. For every three steps Mr. Short takes, Mr. Tall takes one step. Write this comparison as a ratio in three ways.

   b. Suppose Mr. Tall takes nine steps. How many steps will Mr. Short take?

   c. Suppose Mr. Short takes twelve steps. How many steps will Mr. Tall take?

10. **Volleyball** Before serving in the game of volleyball, players often announce the ratio of their score to the opposing team's score. Suppose Team A has 4 points and Team B has 6 points. The score ratio 6 to 4 is announced. Which team is serving the ball?

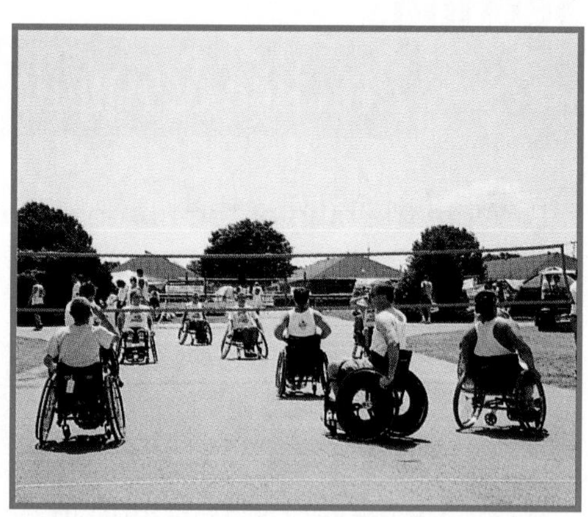

11. **Language Arts** Think of some things you would or would not be able to do if you were one inch tall. Then write another verse for the poem *One Inch Tall.*

12. **Challenge** The poem *One Inch Tall* says, "If you were only one inch tall, you'd walk beneath the door, and it would take about a month to get down to the store." Imagine that you are one inch tall. Estimate the distance to the store in the poem. Explain how you found your answer.

RESEARCH

Exercise 13 checks that you can use ratios to compare.

Reflecting on the Section

13. Pick an object such as a pencil or a book to use as a measuring tool. Use the object as a unit of length to measure the heights of several other objects. Make sketches that compare the objects you measured and write the ratios that can be formed from the sketches.

Spiral Review

Find each quotient. (Module 5, p. 370)

14. $8 \div \frac{5}{6}$ 15. $\frac{7}{9} \div \frac{2}{3}$ 16. $14\frac{3}{4} \div \frac{5}{8}$

Choosing a Method **Use mental math or paper and pencil to find each answer.** (Module 3, pp. 168 and 223; Module 4, p. 278)

17. $0.48 \div 0.6$ 18. $5.24 \cdot 0.01$ 19. $43.6 \div 0.5$

20. $27 \cdot 0.001$ 21. $3.6 \div 0.4$ 22. $0.76 \cdot 0.8$

Complete each pair of equivalent fractions. (Module 2, p. 114)

23. $\frac{9}{12} = \frac{?}{4}$ 24. $\frac{20}{4} = \frac{?}{1}$ 25. $\frac{8}{10} = \frac{?}{25}$

Mystery Tracks

Imagine searching for evidence of dinosaurs that lived millions of years ago. Do you picture finding a large bone, or even a whole skeleton? Surprisingly, some dinosaurs and other extinct animals are known only from the tracks they left behind. Footprints can provide several clues about an animal such as height, weight, age, and running speed.

Since dinosaur tracks are rare, you'll study your own "tracks" and learn how mathematics can be used to make predictions from them. Be sure to save the data you gather over the next few weeks. To complete the project, you'll try to discover who made a set of mystery tracks.

SET UP

You will need:

- *metric ruler*
- *chalk or large newsprint and marker*

Measuring and Comparing Lengths Scientists measure dinosaur tracks in several ways. Some ways of measuring the tracks of dinosaurs that walked on two legs are shown.

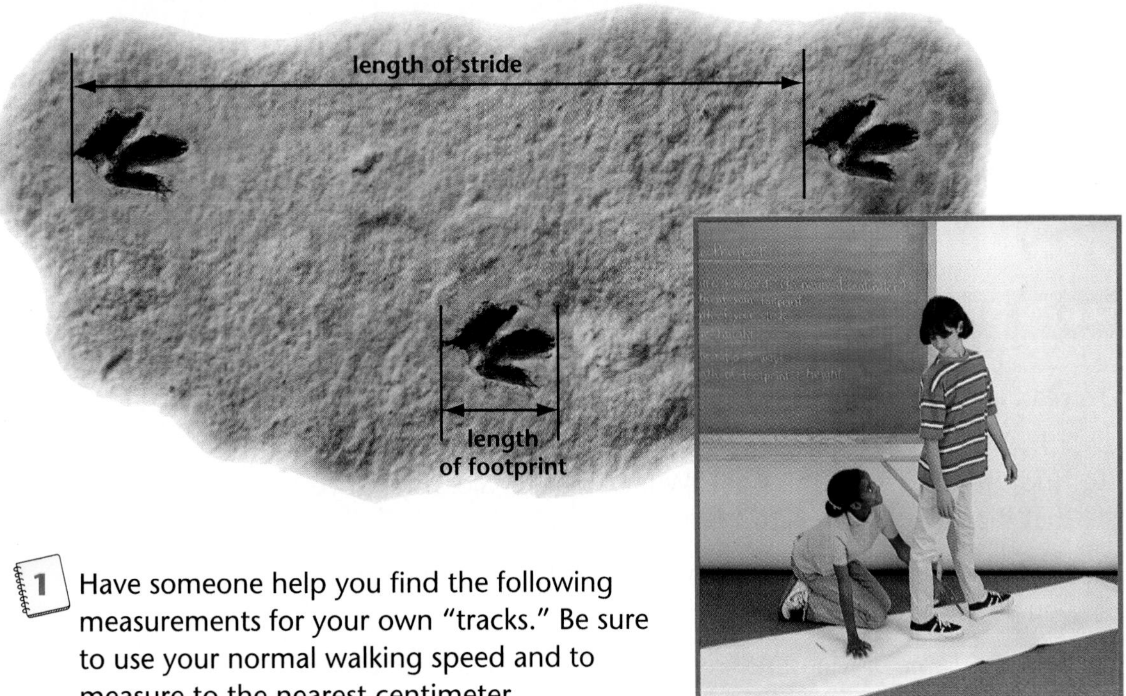

1 Have someone help you find the following measurements for your own "tracks." Be sure to use your normal walking speed and to measure to the nearest centimeter.

- the length of your footprint
- the length of your stride
- your height

2 Write the ratio of the length of your footprint to your height in three ways.

Section 1 Extra Skill Practice

Write each ratio in three ways.

1. number of pencils to number of pens
2. number of erasers to number of pencils
3. number of notebooks to number of folders
4. number of folders to number of book covers

School Store Inventory Supply	
pencils	256
pens	120
erasers	60
notebooks	32
folders	37
book covers	183

Draw a picture to show each ratio.

5. Number of stars to number of squares is five to three.
6. Number of forks to number of spoons is 4 : 8.
7. Number of apples to number of pears is $\frac{5}{6}$.
8. Number of cars to number of tires is $\frac{1}{4}$.

Tell whether the ratios are equivalent.

9. 6 : 5 and 24 : 20
10. 7 : 12 and 21 : 32
11. 21 : 8 and 8 : 21
12. $\frac{8}{24}$ and $\frac{2}{3}$
13. $\frac{25}{3}$ and $\frac{75}{9}$
14. $\frac{6}{8}$ and $\frac{9}{12}$
15. 13 to 5 and 10 to 26
16. 4 to 7 and 14 to 17
17. 3 to 11 and 33 to 121

Study Skills Using Mathematical Language

To read and to talk about mathematics, you need to understand the language. When you need help, use your book as a resource.

1. Find the Glossary in this book. What does the Glossary tell you that the word *ratio* means?
2. Find the Table of Symbols in this book. What does the table tell you about the symbol 8 : 12?
3. Find the Table of Measures in this book. What information does the table give you about the length of 1 meter?
4. Find the index in this book. Look up *measurement*. What ideas about measurement does this book include?

Section 2 Rates

In This Section

Exploration 1
- Using Rates and Unit Rates

The SANDBAG BRIGADE

Setting the Stage

SET UP *Work as a class. You will need: • object to represent a sandbag • watch or clock to time seconds • tape measure*

In the summer of 1993, flooding caused billions of dollars worth of damage to homes and property in the Midwest. Many young volunteers helped fight the flood waters.

Muddy water lapped at his shoulders, and the sky threatened rain. But Jesse Blaise, 12, stood his soggy ground. He was working hard to protect the North Lee County Historic Center in Fort Madison, Iowa, from the great Mississippi River flood of 1993. Shawn Pulis, 14, worked nearby. "Volunteers brought us boatloads of sandbags," he says. "We stacked them around the building."

The volunteers worked around the clock for 13 days. It paid off. The water receded to the riverbed. The building stood. "I was so tired," says Shawn, "but I felt really good."

[**"Great Flood," National Geographic World, October, 1993**]

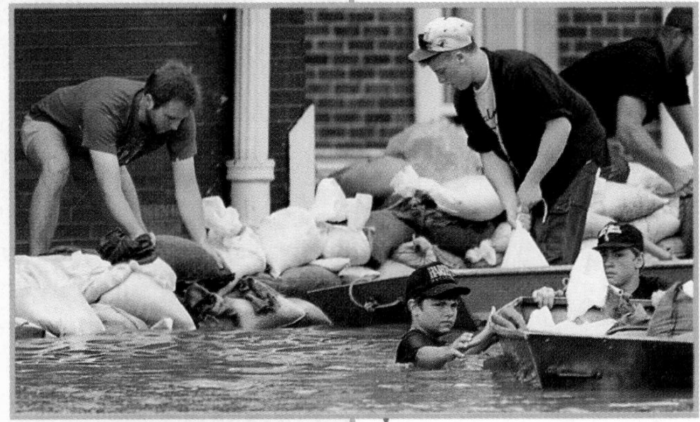

Follow the steps to simulate a sandbag brigade.

Step 1 **Line ten students up side by side. Hand an object representing a sandbag from one end of the line to the other.**

Step 2 **Record how far the object is passed and how long it takes.**

Think About It

1 Suppose your class's brigade is 100 ft long. About how long will it take to pass a sandbag from one end to the other?

2 Suppose it takes one minute to pass a sandbag from one end of a brigade to the other. About how long do you expect the brigade to be?

GOAL

LEARN HOW TO...
- use rates to make predictions
- find unit rates

AS YOU...
- analyze data from your class's sandbag brigade

KEY TERMS
- rate
- unit rate

Exploration 1

Using RATES and UNIT RATES

▶ **You can use ratios and the data from your class's sandbag brigade to make predictions.**

3 **a.** What unit was used to measure the distance the sandbag was passed in your class?

b. What unit was used to measure the time it took?

c. Write a ratio that compares the distance the sandbag was passed with the time it took. Label the units of measure.

▶ **Ratios like the one you wrote in Question 3(c) that compare two quantities measured in different units are rates. Rates can be used to describe how one measure depends on another measure.**

EXAMPLE

30 miles per gallon (mi/gal) is a rate that describes how far a car can travel on one gallon of gas.

30.48 cm for every 12 in. is a rate used to convert measurements from inches to centimeters and vice versa.

4 In Section 1, you found that the ratio of Mr. Short's height to Mr. Tall's height was 8 pennies to 12 pennies. Is this a ratio? a rate? Explain.

5 **Try This as a Class** Explain how you can use the rates in the Example on page 390 to answer each question. Discuss which of the four answers are easy to find and why.

a. How many gallons of gas does the car need to travel 60 mi? to travel 80 mi?

b. How many centimeters are in 30 in.? in 36 in.?

▶ **Using a Table One way to answer questions involving rates is to make a table.**

6 Suppose a brigade of students passes a sandbag 15 ft in 5 seconds.

a. Make a table that predicts how far the sandbag can be passed in 5, 10, 15, 20, 25, and 30 seconds.

Distance passed (feet)	15	?	?	?	?	?
Time (seconds)	5	10	15	20	25	30

b. Explain how you predicted the distance the sandbag can be passed in 30 seconds.

c. Explain two ways to predict how far the sandbag can be passed in 60 seconds.

7 ✓ **CHECKPOINT** Use the rate in Question 6. Predict how long it will take to pass a sandbag 150 ft.

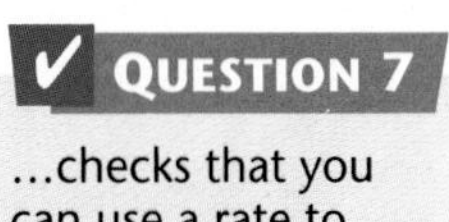

...checks that you can use a rate to make a prediction.

The data in the table you created in Question 6(a) represent equivalent ratios.

$$\frac{15 \text{ feet}}{5 \text{ seconds}} \text{ is equivalent to } \frac{30 \text{ feet}}{10 \text{ seconds}}.$$

8 Show that $\frac{15}{5}$ and $\frac{30}{10}$ are equivalent ratios.

9 **Discussion** Suppose a sandbag can be passed 15 feet in 5 seconds. How can you use equivalent ratios to predict how far the sandbag can be passed in 8 seconds?

▶ **To answer Question 9, it is helpful to find a *unit rate*. A unit rate gives an amount per one unit. For example, 30 mi/gal is a unit rate because it gives the distance a car can travel on one gallon of gas.**

EXAMPLE

To find a unit rate for the sandbag brigade in Question 6, you need to find an equivalent ratio with a denominator of one second.

First Write the given rate as a fraction.

Then Set up a rate for the number of feet per one second.

$$\frac{15 \text{ feet}}{5 \text{ seconds}} = \frac{x \text{ feet}}{1 \text{ second}}$$

10 **a.** What value of x will make the ratios equivalent in the Example? How did you find this value?

b. Use the value of x to write the unit rate in the form: A sandbag can be passed _?_ feet per second.

c. Show how the unit rate can be used to find the distance a sandbag can be passed in 12 seconds.

11 **Try This as a Class** You can also find a unit rate that shows how long it will take to pass a sandbag one foot.

a. Find a value for y so that the ratios below are equivalent. Explain how you found the value.

$$\frac{5 \text{ seconds}}{15 \text{ feet}} = \frac{y \text{ seconds}}{1 \text{ foot}}$$

Notice that the order in the ratios has been changed to seconds : feet.

b. Use the value of y to write the unit rate in the form: It takes _?_ seconds to pass a sandbag one foot.

c. Show how the unit rate can be used to find how long it will take the brigade to pass a sandbag 175 ft.

✓ **QUESTION 12**

...checks that you can find a unit rate.

12 ✓ **CHECKPOINT** Find the unit rate for each rate.

a. 250 mi in 5 h

b. 56 marbles in 4 bags

c. $4.00 for 5 pens

d. 800 turns per 60 seconds

HOMEWORK EXERCISES ▶ **See Exs. 1–21 on pp. 393–395.**

Section 2 Key Concepts

Key Terms

Rates (pp. 390–391)

A rate is a ratio that compares two quantities measured in different units.

rate

Example $2 for 5 limes is a rate.

Rates may be equivalent ratios.

The pairs of numbers in the table form equivalent ratios. $\frac{\$2}{5 \text{ limes}} = \frac{\$4}{10 \text{ limes}}$

Example

Price (dollars)	2	4	6	8
Number of limes	5	10	15	20

Unit Rates (p. 392)

A unit rate gives an amount per one unit.

unit rate

Example Find an equivalent ratio with a denominator of 1.

$\frac{\$2}{5 \text{ limes}} = \frac{x}{1 \text{ lime}} = \frac{\$.40}{1 \text{lime}}$, or $.40 per lime

$2 \div 5 = 0.40$

13 **Key Concepts Question** Use the rate from the Examples. What is the cost of 25 limes? 12 limes? Explain your methods.

Section 2 Practice & Application Exercises

YOU WILL NEED

For Ex. 18:
- Labsheet 2A
- your class's brigade data
- ruler

For Exs. 23–26:
- calculator

For Ex. 29:
- graph paper

Tell whether the rates are equivalent ratios.

1. $\frac{4.2 \text{ m}}{2 \text{ jumps}}, \frac{10.5 \text{ m}}{5 \text{ jumps}}$
2. $\frac{48 \text{ breaths}}{3 \text{ min}}, \frac{95 \text{ breaths}}{5 \text{ min}}$
3. $15 for 6 lb, $20 for 8 lb
4. $2 for 5 pens, $8 for 20 pens
5. 12 laps in 3 h, 3 laps in 1 h
6. 35 mi in 2 h, 145 mi in 4 h
7. $\frac{65 \text{ words}}{1 \text{ min}}, \frac{195 \text{ words}}{3 \text{ min}}$
8. $\frac{3 \text{ measures}}{12 \text{ beats}}, \frac{7 \text{ measures}}{21 \text{ beats}}$

Find a unit rate for each rate.

9. $54 for 18 h

10. 700 mi on 20 gal

11. 150 ft in 100 steps

12. 500 turns in 8 min

13. 17 pages in 5 min

14. $3 for 5 oranges

15. Suppose pens are packaged in two ways: $2.64 for 6 pens or $3.80 for 10 pens. Which package is the better buy? Explain.

16. **Research** Go to the grocery store. Find and record the prices for different quantities of the same item. Compare unit rates to determine which quantity is the better buy.

17. **Science** Mars travels around the sun at a rate of about 15 mi in one second. How far does Mars travel in one minute? in one hour?

FOR◄HELP with *graphing on a coordinate grid*, see MODULE 4, p. 288

18. **Use Labsheet 2A. You will need your class's brigade data.**

a. Complete the table of *Sandbag Brigade Data.*

b. Graph the data in the table. Draw segments to connect the points you graphed in order from left to right.

c. Use your graph to predict how far a sandbag can be passed in 18 seconds.

d. Use a ruler to extend the line of your graph to predict how long it will take to pass a sandbag 100 ft.

e. Use a unit rate to make the predictions in parts (c) and (d). Then compare the predictions you made using a unit rate with those you made using the graph.

19. While visiting Italy, an American student found a CD that cost 36,960 lira. At that time, five United States dollars were worth 6160 Italian lira. How much was the CD in United States dollars?

20. **Writing** Gloria Jones drives 15 mi to work in about half an hour. Write her rate of travel in miles per hour. Why do you think this rate is called her "average" speed?

Reflecting on the Section

Write your response to Exercise 21 in your journal.

21. At top speed, a zebra can run 176 ft in 3 seconds, a roadrunner can run 220 ft in 10 seconds, and a cheetah can run 88 ft in one second. Which animal is the fastest? Which is the slowest? Explain.

Journal

Exercise 21 checks that you understand how to use rates to make comparisons.

Spiral Review

22. The ratio of triangles to squares is 6 to 10. Make a sketch to find an equivalent ratio. (Module 6, p. 384)

Calculator **Write each fraction as a decimal rounded to the nearest hundredth.** (Module 3, p. 202)

23. $\frac{5}{6}$ 24. $\frac{12}{23}$ 25. $\frac{45}{62}$ 26. $\frac{84}{116}$

Find the mean for each set of data. (Module 3, p. 202)

27. 75, 86, 73, 80, 86, 80 28. 48, 52, 75, 47, 83, 48

Extension

A Doubling Rate

29. Suppose you put $100 in a bank account where your money doubles every ten years. The table shows how it will grow.

Number of years	0	10	20	30	40
Money in account	$100	$200	$400	$800	$1600

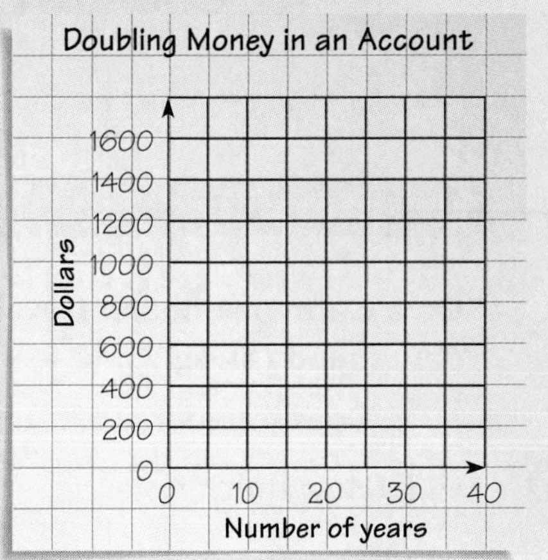

a. Copy the coordinate grid and plot the data shown in the table. Connect the points in order from left to right.

b. How is the rate of growth for money in the account different from other rates in the section? (*Hint:* Are the ratios of years to money in the account equivalent?)

Section 2 Extra Skill Practice

Tell whether each ratio is a rate.

1. 5 lb to 50 lb
2. 27 m in 2 seconds
3. 3 gal per minute
4. 2 steps in 1 second
5. 4 mi for every 9 mi
6. 5 hits in 8 times at bat

Tell whether the rates are equivalent ratios.

7. $\frac{150 \text{ words}}{3 \text{ min}}, \frac{450 \text{ words}}{9 \text{ min}}$
8. \$7 for 5 lb, \$16.20 for 9 lb
9. 204 mi on 6 gal, 68 mi on 2 gal
10. $\frac{212 \text{ heartbeats}}{4 \text{ min}}, \frac{343 \text{ heartbeats}}{7 \text{ min}}$

Find a unit rate for each rate.

11. 24 km in 3 h
12. 1500 m in 5 min
13. \$45 for 6 books
14. 7 pages in 4 min
15. 84 mi on 3 gal
16. 250 ft in 200 steps

Tell which is a better buy.

17. \$4.20 for 8 oranges or \$5.76 for 12 oranges
18. \$2.24 for 16 oz of apple juice or \$3.36 for 24 oz of apple juice
19. Saturn travels around the sun at a rate of about 6 mi in one second.
    a. How far does Saturn travel in one minute?
    b. How far does Saturn travel in one hour?
20. Copy and complete the table.

Number of pages	5	10	15	20	?
Time (minutes)	8	?	?	?	40

Standardized Testing ▶ Performance Task

On a warm day, sound travels 13,224 feet in 12 seconds. On a cool day, sound travels 7,140 feet in 7 seconds.

1. a. Does sound travel faster through warm air or through cool air?
   b. How much faster?
2. On a warm day, how far does sound travel in 15 seconds?

Section 3 Using Ratios

IN THIS SECTION

EXPLORATION 1
- Comparing Ratios

EXPLORATION 2
- Estimating Ratios

EXPLORATION 3
- Predicting with a Graph

BODY RATIOS

Setting the Stage

In the Jonathan Swift classic *Gulliver's Travels*, Lemuel Gulliver is shipwrecked and swims to the island of Lilliput, where the people have an average height of slightly less than six inches. Since Gulliver's only clothes were those he was wearing, the Lilliputians had to make new clothing for him.

GULLIVER'S TRAVELS *by Jonathan Swift*

The seamstresses took my measure as I lay on the ground, one standing at my neck, and another at my mid-leg, with a strong cord extended, that each held by the end, while the third measured the length of the cord with a rule of an inch long. Then they measured my right thumb, and desired no more; for by a mathematical computation, that twice round the thumb is once round the wrist, and so on to the neck and the waist; and by the help of my old shirt, which I displayed on the ground before them for a pattern, they fitted me exactly.

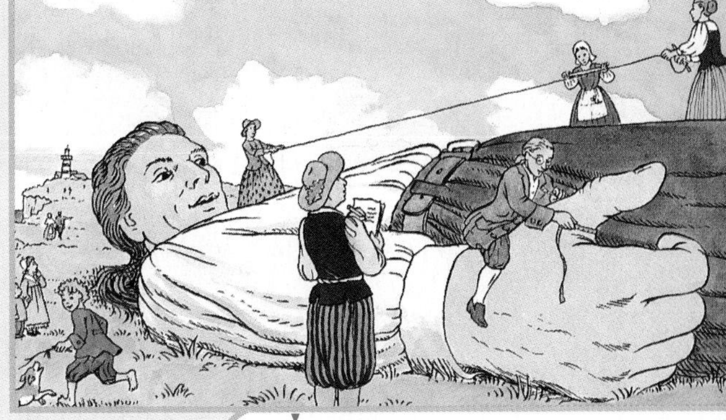

Think About It

1 The height of a Lilliputian is about what fraction of your height?

2 What two measurements did the Lilliputians take in order to make a shirt for Gulliver?

3 **a.** What do you think Gulliver meant by "twice round the thumb is once round the wrist"?

b. What do you think he meant by "and so on to the neck and the waist"?

GOAL

LEARN HOW TO...
- use measurements to decide whether a ratio is reasonable
- write a ratio as a decimal

AS YOU...
- compare your own body ratios with those in *Gulliver's Travels*

Exploration 1

Comparing RATIOS

SET UP *Work in a group. You will need: • scissors • string • metric ruler*

▶ **In this exploration, you'll test whether the ratios used by the Lilliputians can be used to accurately predict your body measurements.**

4 Have someone in your group help you measure as shown.

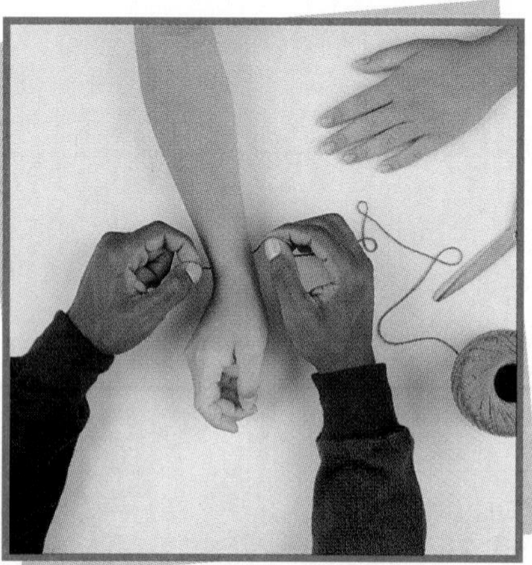

First

Cut a piece of string equal to the distance around your wrist.

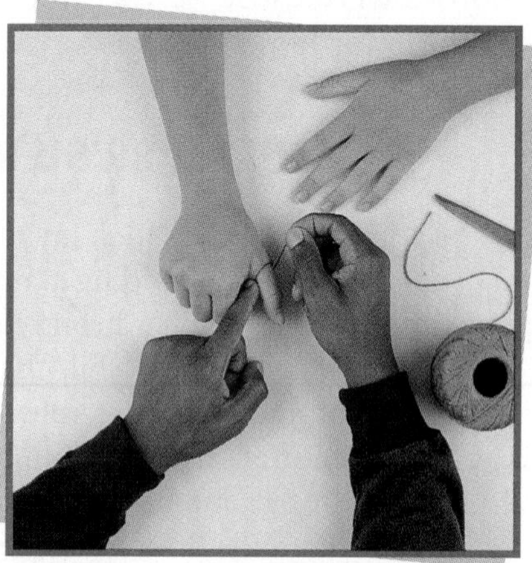

Then

Wrap this string around the base of your thumb.

5 **a.** About how many times did the string go around your thumb?

b. Did others in your group get about the same results?

c. Do you think the relationship between the distance around the wrist and the distance around the thumb will be about the same for most students in your grade? Explain.

d. How does the relationship you observed compare with Gulliver's claim that "twice around the thumb is once around the wrist"?

6 **a.** Suppose the distance around a classmate's thumb is 5 cm. What do you expect the distance around the wrist to be?

b. Write the measurements from part (a) as a ratio in two ways:

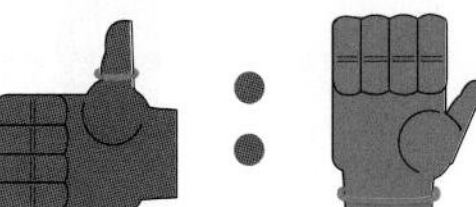

(distance around thumb : distance around wrist)

$\underline{\ ?\ } : \underline{\ ?\ } = \frac{?}{?}$

c. Write the fraction from part (b) as a decimal.

FOR ◀ HELP
with *writing a fraction as a decimal*, see
MODULE 3, p. 176

▶ **It is often useful to write a ratio as a single decimal number. For example, the ratio of 3 to 4 is 0.75, or 0.75 to 1.**

7 Copy and complete the table as you answer parts (a) and (b).

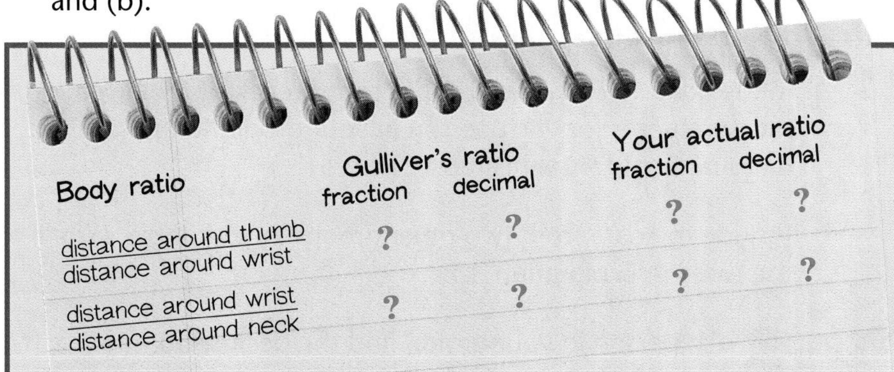

Body ratio	Gulliver's ratio fraction	Gulliver's ratio decimal	Your actual ratio fraction	Your actual ratio decimal
$\frac{\text{distance around thumb}}{\text{distance around wrist}}$	?	?	?	?
$\frac{\text{distance around wrist}}{\text{distance around neck}}$	?	?	?	?

a. Use the relationships described by Gulliver on page 397 to write each body ratio as a fraction and as a decimal.

b. Wrap string to find the ratios for your body. Measure the length of the string in millimeters. Write each ratio as a fraction and as a decimal to the nearest hundredth.

8 ✔ **CHECKPOINT** Look at your table from Question 7.

a. How do Gulliver's ratios compare with your ratios? Which form of the ratios did you use to compare? Explain your choice.

b. Do you think Gulliver's ratios are reasonable estimates? Explain.

...checks that you can decide whether a ratio is reasonable.

9 **Discussion** Suppose the distance around a person's thumb is 9 cm. Explain how you can use ratios to predict the distance around the person's neck.

HOMEWORK EXERCISES ▶ See Exs. 1–7 on pp. 406–407.

GOAL

LEARN HOW TO...
- find a ratio to describe data
- use a ratio to make predictions

AS YOU...
- look for other body ratios

KEY TERM
- "nice" fraction

Exploration 2

Estimating RATiOS

SET UP *Work in a group of four. Your group will need: • Labsheet 3A • scissors • string • metric ruler*

▶ **Now you'll explore whether other body ratios are about the same for most people. Use the Student Resource to help you measure.**

10 **Estimation** Do you think your reach is more or less than 1 m?

Use Labsheet 3A for Questions 11–14.

11 **a.** In the *Body Measurements Table*, record each of the given measurements for each person in your group. Round each measurement to the nearest 0.5 cm.

b. Include the data from two other groups in your table. (You'll use these in Exploration 3.)

12 **a.** For each person in your group, find the decimal form of each ratio in the *Body Ratios Table*. Round to the nearest hundredth. Record your results in the table.

b. Which columns of your table have ratios that are about the same for everyone?

c. Find and record the mean of the ratios in each column.

▶ **Ratios are often expressed as fractions. "Nice" fractions, such as $\frac{1}{3}$, $\frac{1}{4}$, and $\frac{2}{5}$, make it easier to do computations mentally.**

As you answer Questions 13–15, record in your *Body Ratios Table* the "nice" fractions you find to describe your data.

13 **a.** **Discussion** Which ratio below is closest to the mean of your group's tibia to height ratios? Explain how you know.

$\frac{1}{1}$ $\frac{1}{2}$ $\frac{1}{3}$ $\frac{1}{4}$ $\frac{1}{5}$ $\frac{1}{6}$

b. Use your ratio from part (a) to predict the tibia length of a person who is 150 cm tall.

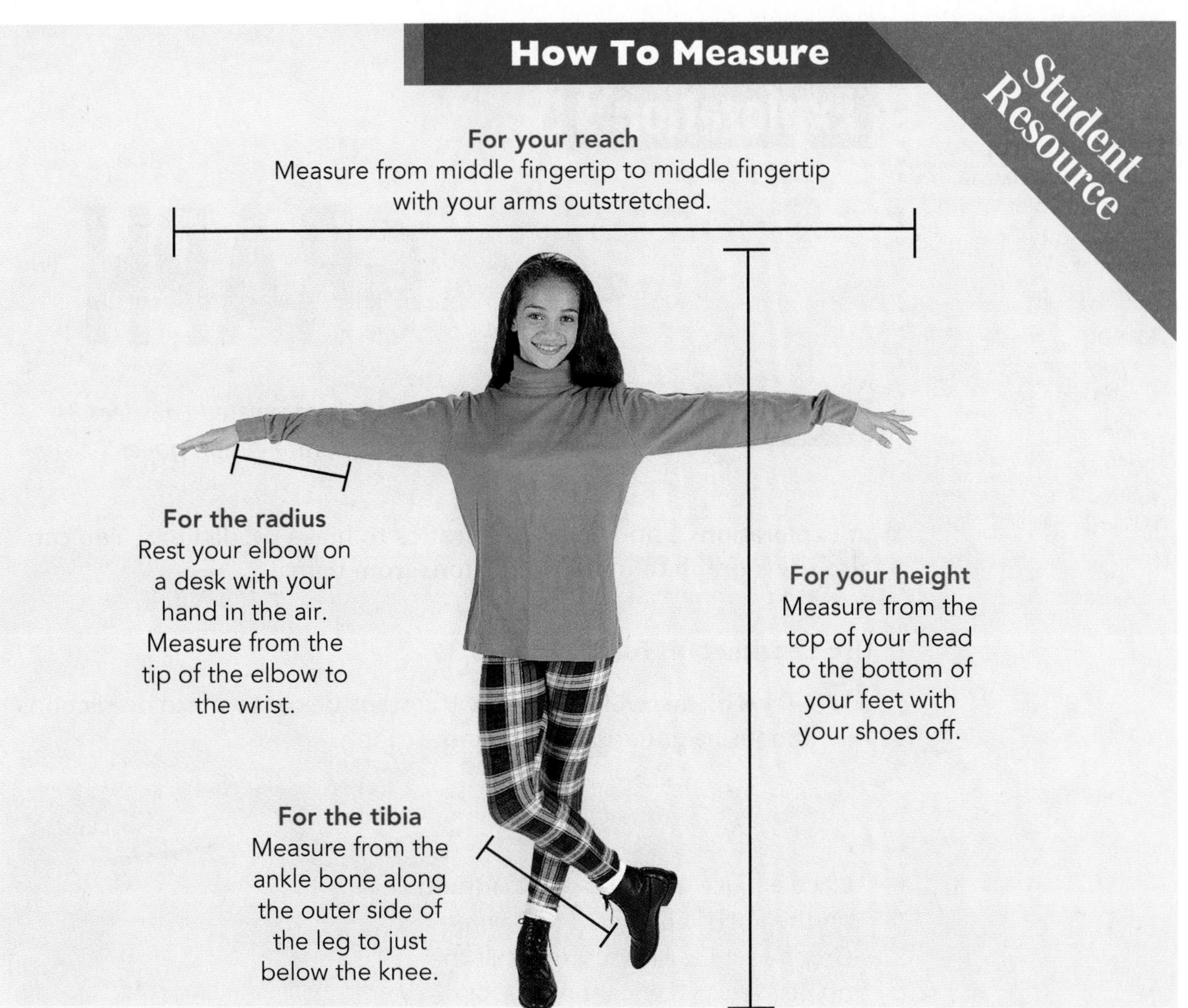

14 ✓ CHECKPOINT

a. What "nice" fraction is close to the mean of the radius to height ratios?

b. Suppose a person's radius is 18 cm long. About how tall do you expect the person to be?

✓ QUESTION 14

...checks that you can find and use a fraction to make a prediction.

15 **a.** Write a "nice" fraction that is close to the mean of the reach to height ratios.

b. Suppose a person is 180 cm tall. About how long do you think the person's reach is?

16 Use your results from Questions 13–15. Draw and label a sketch of a 6-inch tall Lilliputian that shows the reach, tibia, and radius.

HOMEWORK EXERCISES See Exs. 8–15 on pp. 407–408.

GOAL

LEARN HOW TO...
- fit a line to data in a scatter plot
- use a scatter plot to make predictions

AS YOU...
- analyze the body ratio data you collected

KEY TERMS
- fitted line
- scatter plot

Exploration 3

Predicting with a GRAPH

SET UP *Work in a group. You will need:* • *completed Labsheet 3A* • *Labsheet 3B* • *uncooked spaghetti* • *graph paper*

▶ **In Explorations 1 and 2 you used ratios to make predictions. You can also use a graph to make predictions from data.**

Use Labsheet 3B for Questions 17–21.

17 **Try This as a Class** Follow the steps below to make predictions about height and reach using a graph.

Step 1

Place a piece of uncooked spaghetti on the *Reach Compared to Height Graph* so it lies close to most of the points. Try to have about the same number of points on one side of the spaghetti as on the other side.

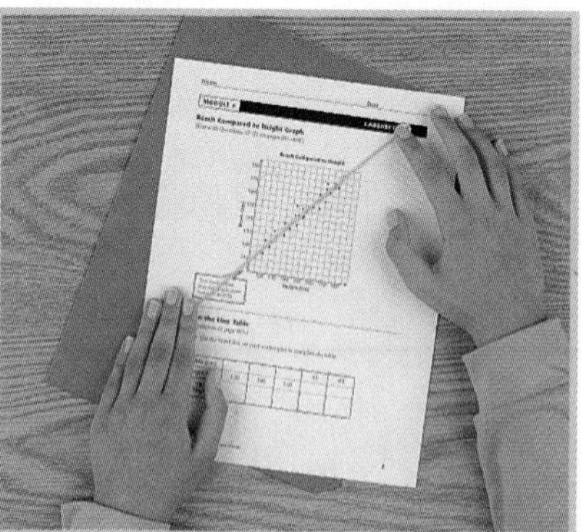

Step 2

Draw a line segment on the *Reach Compared to Height Graph* along the edge of your spaghetti. The segment you drew on the graph is a **fitted line**. It can be used to predict unknown measurements using known ones.

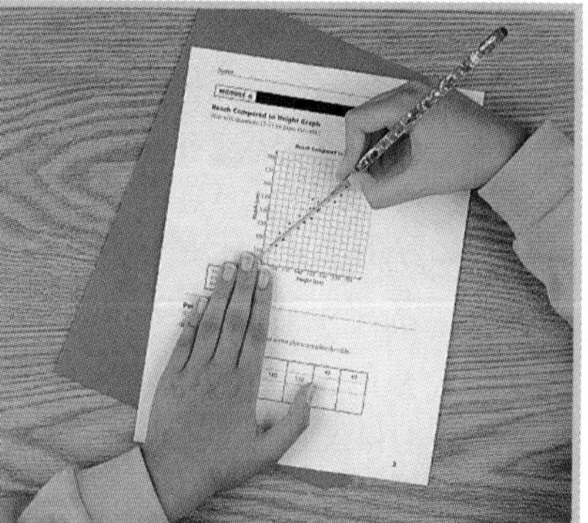

18 **a.** How can the fitted line help you predict a person's height if you know the person's reach is 135 cm?

b. What do you expect the reach of a person 152 cm tall to be?

19 **Discussion** Look at the scales used on the *Reach Compared to Height Graph*. Why do you think the labeling on the scales starts at a height of 120 cm and at a reach of 110 cm?

Use your data from Labsheet 3A for Questions 20 and 21.

20 Use the data on the heights and the lengths of the tibias from all three groups in your *Body Measurements Table*. You will make a graph similar to the *Reach Compared to Height Graph*.

FOR◀HELP with *plotting points*, see **MODULE 4, p. 296**

a. Look at the height and the length of the tibia data. What are the shortest and the tallest heights? What are the shortest and the longest lengths of the tibias?

b. Use your answers from part (a) to draw and label the scales for your graph. You do not have to start your labeling at (0,0).

c. Plot a point representing the height and the length of the tibia for each person.

Name ______ Date ______

MODULE 6 **LABSHEET 3A**

Body Measurements Table
(Use with Questions 11–12 on page 400, Question 20on page 403, Exercise 13 on page 407, and Exercise 17 on page 408.)

	Person number	Height (cm)	Tibia (cm)	Radius (cm)	Reach (cm)
Your group	1				
	2				
	3				
	4				
Two other groups	5				
	6				
	7				
	8				
	9				
	10				
	11				
	12				

Body Ratios Table
(Use with Questions 12–15 on pages 400–401 and Question 21 on page 403.)

Group member	$\frac{\text{Tibia}}{\text{Height}}$	$\frac{\text{Radius}}{\text{Height}}$	$\frac{\text{Reach}}{\text{Height}}$
1			
2			
3			
4			
Mean			
"Nice" fraction			

d. The type of graph you made is a **scatter plot**. What do you notice about the points in your scatter plot?

e. Follow the steps in Question 17 to draw a fitted line for your scatter plot.

21 ✓ **CHECKPOINT** Use your graph from Question 20.

...checks that you can use a scatter plot and a fitted line to make a prediction.

a. Suppose a person's tibia is 42 cm long. About how tall do you expect the person to be?

b. Use the fitted line on your scatter plot to complete the *Points on the Line Table* on Labsheet 3B.

c. How do the tibia and height ratios in the *Points on the Line Table* compare with the "nice" fraction you recorded on Labsheet 3A?

HOMEWORK EXERCISES ▶ See Exs. 16–20 on pp. 408–409.

TECHNOLOGY Using Technology to Make Scatter Plots

You can also use spreadsheet software or other graphing technology to make your scatter plot for Question 20 on page 403. This technology is helpful when you have a lot of data values to show.

Step 1 Enter the data for the graph into the spreadsheet. The data for the horizontal axis should be entered in column A. The corresponding data for the vertical axis should be entered in column B.

File Edit Format Calculate Options View

HEIGHT VS TIBIA

	A	B	C	D	E
1	Height (cm)	Tibia (cm)			
2	129	30			
3	135	32			

Step 2 To create a graph, highlight the data you entered and select the option that makes a chart. Then select the type of graph you want to make.

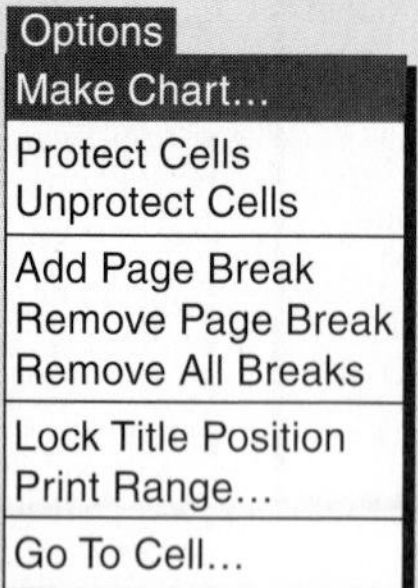

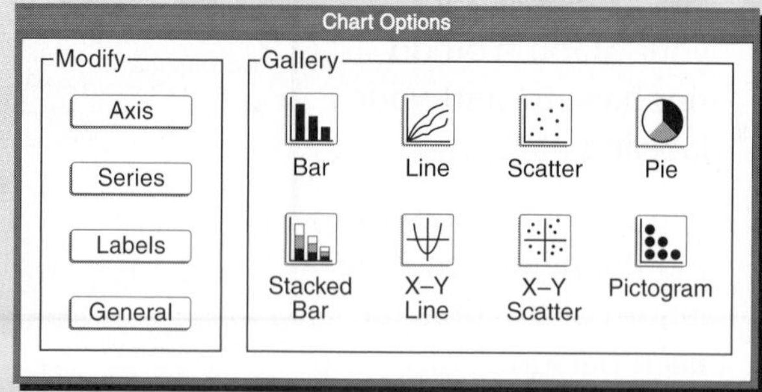

Step 3 Experiment with the labels, grid lines, and scale until the graph appears the way you want it to. Be sure to include a title.

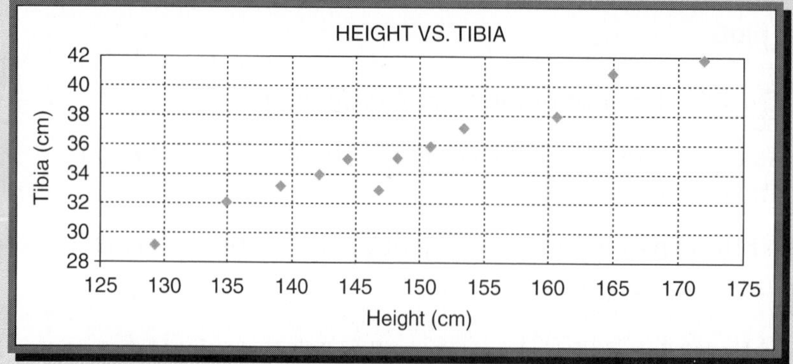

Step 4 You can print out the graph and draw a fitted line through your scatter plot as you did in Exploration 3. Some graphing technology will let you draw a fitted line, or it will draw one for you.

Section 3

Key Concepts

Key Terms

Using Ratios (pp. 399–401)

Different forms of ratios are more useful in different situations.

- Using the decimal form can help you to compare ratios. To find the decimal, first write the ratio as a fraction. Then divide the numerator by the denominator.

Example length of one step = 64 cm
height = 151 cm

The ratio is about 0.42 or 0.42 to 1.

$$\frac{\text{step length}}{\text{height}} = \frac{64}{151} \qquad 151\overline{)64.000} = 0.423$$

- "Nice" fractions, like $\frac{1}{2}$, $\frac{2}{3}$, or $\frac{3}{4}$, are often used to describe ratios in a simple way, making computation easier. Look to see if the decimal form is close to a "nice" fraction.

"nice" fraction

Example The ratio 0.42 is close to 0.4, which equals the "nice" fraction $\frac{4}{10}$, or $\frac{2}{5}$. This ratio can be used to estimate the height of a person whose step length is 60 cm.

$$\frac{\text{step length}}{\text{height}} = \frac{2}{5} = \frac{60}{?} \qquad \frac{2 \times 30}{5 \times 30} = \frac{60}{150}$$

The height of the person is probably about 150 cm.

Key Concepts Questions

22 Use the "nice" fraction in the second example to estimate the step length of a person 145 cm tall.

23 For every mile the blue car is driven, the red car is driven $2\frac{1}{2}$ miles.

a. Write the ratio of miles the blue car is driven to miles the red car is driven in decimal form.

b. Use your answer to part (a) to find how many miles the blue car is driven when the red car is driven 6 miles.

Continued on next page

Section 3

Key Concepts

Key Terms

scatter plot

fitted line

Using Scatter Plots (pp. 402–403)

(pp. 402–403)

A scatter plot is a graph that shows the relationship between two sets of data.

You can use a fitted line to make predictions from data when the points seem to lie on a line.

Length of Step Compared to Height

Length of step (cm): 30, 40, 50, 60, 70

Height (cm): 130, 140, 150, 160, 170

24 **Key Concepts Question** Use the scatter plot and fitted line to predict the step length of a person who is 145 cm tall.

Section 3

Practice & Application Exercises

YOU WILL NEED

For Exs. 13 and 17:
- completed Labsheet 3A

For Exs. 17 and 19:
- graph paper
- piece of uncooked spaghetti or a clear plastic ruler

1. Use the ratio 1 : 2 as an estimate for the body ratios *thumb to wrist, wrist to neck,* and *neck to waist.*

   a. Suppose the distance around Gulliver's wrist is 20 cm. Estimate his thumb, neck, and waist measurements.

   b. **Create Your Own** Make and label a sketch of Gulliver's shirt. Select reasonable measurements for the cuffs and neckline.

2. Each oval has a vertical height of 12 mm.

A	B	C	D
width: 15 mm	width: 6 mm	width: 12 mm	width: 4 mm

a. For each oval, write the ratio of the width to the height as a fraction and as a decimal.

b. What does the ratio of the width to the height tell you about the general shape of the ovals?

Write each ratio as a decimal to the nearest hundredth.

3. 7 : 9   4. 6 : 11   5. 2 : 7   6. 8 : 19

7. **Interpreting Data** Look at the graph.

a. From the bar graph, what can you conclude about the projected number of personal computers in Australia and in Japan in the year 2000?

b. In the year 2000, the projected population for Australia is 19 million people and for Japan is 127 million people. Estimate the ratio of the number of people to the number of personal computers for each country as a decimal.

c. Do the bar graph and the ratios in part (b) give the same message about the number of personal computers in Australia and Japan? Why?

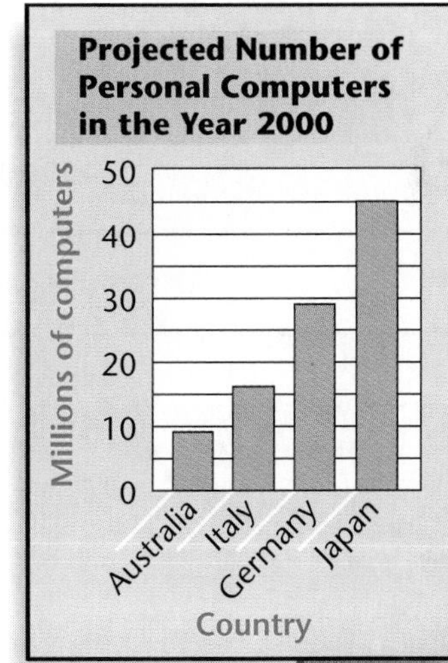

8. Solve the following problems to see how an archaeologist might be able to use body ratios.

a. A human radius 27 cm long was found. Estimate the person's height. (Use 1 : 6 as the ratio for *length of radius to height*.)

b. A human tibia 46 cm long was discovered at the same site as the radius in part (a). Estimate the person's height. (Use 1 : 4 as the ratio for *length of tibia to height*.)

c. Do you think both bones are from the same person? Explain.

Write a "nice" fraction for each ratio.

9. 5 : 26   10. 0.31   11. $\frac{12}{38}$ 12. 0.6 to 1

13. **Use the data from Labsheet 3A.** Write a "nice" fraction that compares the length of the tibia with the length of the radius.

14. Some students dropped a ball from different heights. They recorded how high it bounced for each drop height.

   a. The ratio of bounce height to drop height was about 0.81. Write a "nice" fraction close to 0.81.

   b. Predict how high their ball will bounce when they drop it from a height of 5 ft.

   c. On one drop the ball bounced to a height of 28 in. Estimate the drop height the students used.

15. **Home Involvement** Find at least two other people whose ages are different from yours. Record the body measurements shown on page 401 for them. Compare the ratios of these measurements with the "nice" fractions you found for your group. Prepare a presentation of your findings.

16. a. Which fitted line would you use to make predictions about the distance around a person's head or predictions about a person's height? Why?

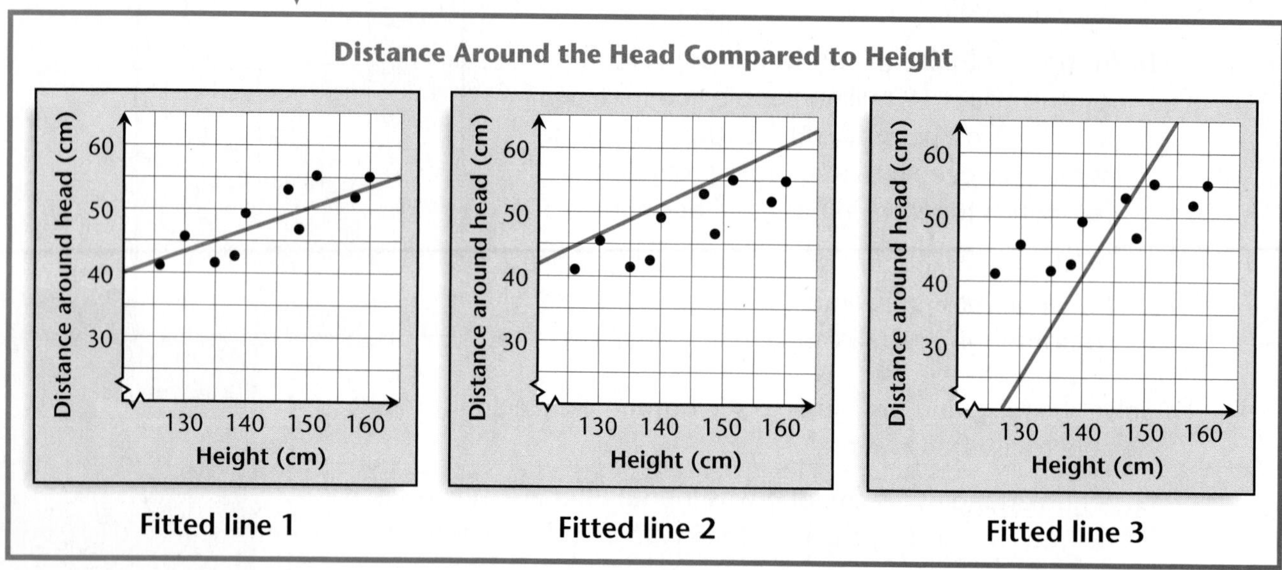

   b. Use your choice from part (a) to predict each measurement.

   - height for a distance around the head of 45 cm
   - the distance around your own head

Radius (cm)	Height (cm)
?	120
?	150
?	180
24	?
32	?

17. a. **Use the data from Labsheet 3A.** On graph paper, make a scatter plot that shows the relationship between the height and the length of the radius.

   b. Draw a fitted line on your scatter plot. Copy the table at the left. Then use your fitted line to complete it.

18. Nearly 8000 terra-cotta warriors that are $5\frac{1}{2}$ to 6 feet tall have been found near Lintong, China. These figures were found close to the burial site of Qin Shihuangdi, the first emperor of China. Some believe that this army was built to fight the emperor's battles after death.

a. Use your scatter plot from Exercise 17 to estimate the length of a 6-foot warrior's radius. (Remember: 1 ft is about 30.5 cm.)

◀ The warriors are made of terra-cotta, a type of ceramic clay.

b. **Writing** A 6-foot warrior is 6 in. taller than a $5\frac{1}{2}$-foot warrior. Does this mean that the tibia of a 6-foot warrior is 6 in. longer than the tibia of the $5\frac{1}{2}$-foot warrior? Explain.

19. a. When English is translated into Spanish it takes up a different amount of space. On graph paper, make a scatter plot with a fitted line that shows the relationship between the number of pages in English and the number of pages in Spanish.

b. Predict the number of pages of Spanish for an article that is 14 pages long in English.

c. Predict the number of pages of English for an article that is 30 pages long in Spanish.

Pages in English	Pages in Spanish
13	14
13	15
15	17
16	18
16	19
18	21
19	21
19	23
20	23
21	23
21	25
23	26
24	28

Reflecting on the Section

Write your response to Exercise 20 in your journal.

20. Think of some ratios you use in your daily life. Use sketches or descriptions to show what these ratios mean and how you could use them to find unknown values. Include different forms of ratios and explain why each form is used.

Journal

Exercise 20 checks that you understand how ratios are used.

Spiral Review

Find a unit rate for each rate. (Module 6, p. 393)

21. 99 mi on 3 gal

22. $17 for 6 lb

23. $\frac{265 \text{ heartbeats}}{5 \text{ min}}$

24. Suppose heads occurred on 14 out of 30 tosses of a coin. Find the experimental probability of heads. (Module 4, p. 242)

Find each missing number. (Toolbox, p. 597)

25. $45 \div \underline{\ ?\ } = 5$

26. $\underline{\ ?\ } \cdot 8 = 96$

27. $\underline{\ ?\ } - 12 = 25$

28. $\underline{\ ?\ } \div 9 = 17$

29. $12 \cdot \underline{\ ?\ } = 180$

30. $7 + \underline{\ ?\ } = 30$

Mystery Tracks

Making Predictions Now you'll use your "track" data and your classmates' data to predict height.

Write your *foot length to height* ratio as a decimal. Collect the following data from each of your classmates (including yourself): height, stride length, and the *foot length to height* ratio.

a. Make a scatter plot that compares stride length with height. If appropriate, fit a line to the data.

b. Use your graph to predict your height from your stride length. How close is the prediction to your actual height?

a. Find the mean of the *foot length to height* ratios. Then write a "nice" fraction that is close to the mean.

b. Use your results from part (a) to predict your height from your foot length. How close is the prediction to your actual height?

Why do you think scientists use foot length and stride length together to predict the heights of dinosaurs?

Section 3 Extra Skill Practice

You will need: • *graph paper* (Ex. 2)
• *piece of uncooked spaghetti or clear ruler* (Ex. 2)

For Exercises 1 and 2, use the data in the table.

Person	A	B	C	D	E	F	G	H
$\frac{\text{kneeling height (cm)}}{\text{Standing height (cm)}}$	$\frac{75}{102}$	$\frac{90}{122}$	$\frac{101}{137}$	$\frac{82}{108}$	$\frac{109}{145}$	$\frac{113}{152}$	$\frac{101}{135}$	$\frac{94}{128}$

1. a. Write each *kneeling height to standing height* ratio as a decimal. Round to the nearest hundredth.
   b. Find the mean of the *kneeling height to standing height* ratios.
   c. Write a "nice" fraction that is close to the mean.
   d. Use your "nice" fraction to estimate the missing entries in the table below.

Kneeling height (cm)	94	?	?	87
Standing height (cm)	?	132	140	?

2. a. Make a scatter plot that shows the relationship between the kneeling height and the standing height of each person in the table.
   b. Use a piece of uncooked spaghetti or a clear ruler to draw a fitted line on your scatter plot.
   c. Use your scatter plot to estimate the missing entries in the table in Exercise 1(d). How do your answers compare?

Standardized Testing ▶ Open-Ended

Write a word problem that involves using ratios to make a comparison or prediction.

Solve your word problem. What form of the ratio did you use? Explain why you chose that form.

FOR ASSESSMENT AND PORTFOLIOS

The IDEAL Chair

SET UP *You will need:* • *ruler* • *string*

The Situation

Sometimes it is hard to find a comfortable chair to sit in. The chairs in your classroom are different from the chairs in a primary classroom. The chairs in a restaurant are probably different from the chairs in your home.

The Problem

Design the ideal school chair for students in your grade level.

Something to Think About

- What things should be considered in designing the ideal school chair for students in your grade level?
- How might you find data for each of the things you will consider?
- What are some ways to keep your ideas and data organized?

Present Your Results

Describe your solution and the methods you used to find it. Show any charts, tables, sketches or models you prepared. Are there other possible solutions? Tell what you tried that worked, and what you tried that did not work. What did you do when you were stuck?

Section 4 Proportions

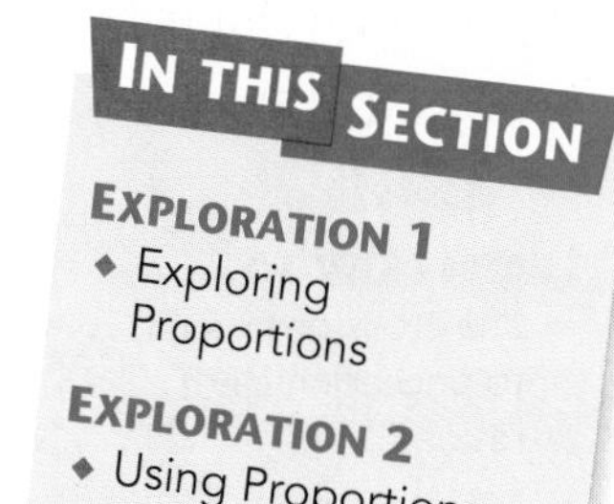

Jumping Ability

Setting the Stage

Look at the table and graph to see how the world-record long jump for a human compares to the records of several animals.

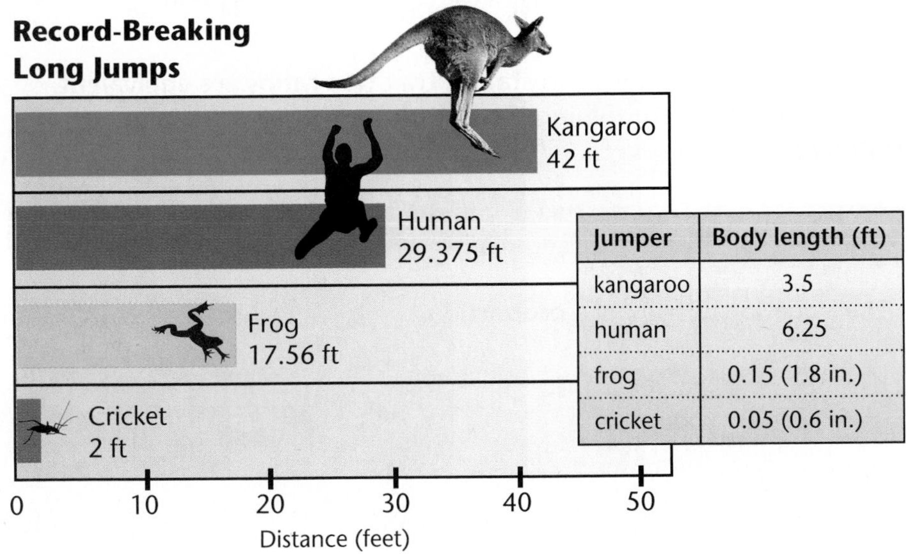

Jumper	Body length (ft)
kangaroo	3.5
human	6.25
frog	0.15 (1.8 in.)
cricket	0.05 (0.6 in.)

Think About It

1 **a.** Which of the four jumped the farthest?

b. Which of the four can jump more than 10 times its body length? more than 100 times?

c. Is it fair to compare jumping ability by examining just the distance jumped? Explain.

2 Describe how ratios written in decimal form can be used to identify which jumper traveled the farthest for its size.

GOAL

LEARN HOW TO...
- use cross products to find equivalent ratios
- find the missing term in a proportion

AS YOU...
- predict how far a jackrabbit can jump

KEY TERMS
- proportion
- cross products

Exploration 1

EXPLORING PROPORTIONS

▶ **When frightened, a black-tailed jackrabbit can jump about as far for its size as the record-breaking kangaroo. You can use this fact to estimate how far a jackrabbit 18 in. long can jump. To find out how, you'll explore some properties of equivalent ratios.**

3 **Discussion** Tell whether the ratios in each pair are equivalent. Explain how you know.

a. $\frac{10}{12}$ and $\frac{25}{30}$ **b.** $\frac{8}{24}$ and $\frac{4}{20}$ **c.** $\frac{10}{40}$ and $\frac{101}{400}$

d. $\frac{8}{6}$ and $\frac{2}{18}$ **e.** $\frac{12}{36}$ and $\frac{5}{15}$ **f.** $\frac{16}{24}$ and $\frac{27}{36}$

▶ **A proportion is an equation stating that two ratios are equivalent. One method for determining if two ratios are equivalent is to compare cross products.**

EXAMPLE

The equation $\frac{16}{10} = \frac{24}{15}$ is a proportion.

One cross product is 16 • 15.

The other cross product is 10 • 24.

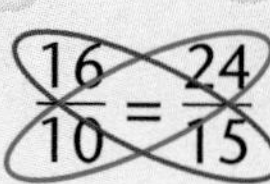

4 Find the products 16 • 15 and 10 • 24. What do you notice?

5 **a.** Find the cross products for each pair of equivalent ratios in Question 3. What do you notice about them?

b. Find the cross products for the pairs of ratios that are not equivalent in Question 3. What do you notice?

6 **Discussion** How do you think cross products can be used to tell whether two ratios are equivalent?

7 ✓ **CHECKPOINT** Use cross products to tell whether the ratios are equivalent.

a. $\frac{11}{4}$ and $\frac{15}{6}$ **b.** $\frac{8}{14}$ and $\frac{24}{32}$ **c.** $\frac{12}{30}$ and $\frac{30}{75}$

✓ **QUESTION 7**

...checks that you can use cross products to tell whether two ratios are equivalent.

8 **Try This as a Class** Cathy used cross products to help her find the missing term in the proportion $\frac{9}{12} = \frac{x}{20}$.

$\frac{9}{12} = \frac{x}{20}$

$12 \bullet x = 9 \bullet 20$ —— Step 1

$12 \bullet x = 180$ —— Step 2

$x = 180 \div 12$ —— Step 3

$x = 15$ —— Step 4

a. Explain what she did in each step.

b. How can you check whether 15 is the correct value?

c. Can you also use equivalent fractions to find the missing term in the proportion $\frac{9}{12} = \frac{x}{20}$? Explain.

9 **Calculator** Write a calculator key sequence to find the missing term in the proportion $\frac{12}{16} = \frac{18}{y}$.

10 ✓ **CHECKPOINT** Find the missing term in each proportion.

a. $\frac{15}{20} = \frac{9}{y}$ **b.** $\frac{18}{n} = \frac{12}{8}$ **c.** $\frac{5}{12} = \frac{12.5}{m}$

✓ **QUESTION 10**

...checks that you can find a missing term in a proportion.

11 Now you are ready to estimate how far a jackrabbit can jump.

a. **Discussion** You were told that "A black-tailed jackrabbit can jump about as far for its size as the record-breaking kangaroo." What do you think this means?

b. Use the table on page 413. Why can the proportion below be used to estimate how far a jackrabbit with a body 18 in. long can jump?

$$\frac{42}{3.5} = \frac{d}{1.5}$$

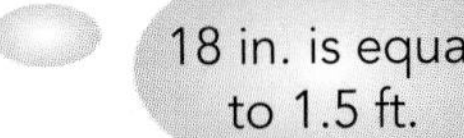

c. Find the missing term in the proportion in part (b).

d. Would you expect the jackrabbit to jump exactly the distance you found in part (c)? Explain.

HOMEWORK EXERCISES See Exs. 1–11 on p. 419.

GOAL

LEARN HOW TO...
- write a proportion to solve a problem
- use a proportion to make a prediction

AS YOU...
- explore the jumping ability of a frog

Exploration 2

Using PROPORTIONS

Frogs are much better jumpers than humans. To appreciate just how much better, you can use a proportion to explore how far someone with the jumping ability of a frog could jump.

EXAMPLE

Suppose a 6.25 foot (6 ft 3 in.) tall human has the jumping ability of the record-breaking frog that is 0.15 ft long and can jump 17.56 ft. Write a proportion to find how far this person can jump.

Step 1 Study the situation to find what measurements are being compared.

$$\frac{\text{jump distance (ft)}}{\text{body length (ft)}}$$

Jump distance is being compared to body length.

Step 2 Decide what ratios to show in the proportion.

Ratio for the frog		Ratio for the human
$\frac{\text{jump distance}}{\text{body length}}$	=	$\frac{\text{jump distance}}{\text{body length}}$

Step 3 Fill in the information you know to write the proportion. You know the jump distance and body length of the frog, and the body length of the human. Use variables for values you do not know.

$$\frac{17.56}{0.15} = \frac{d}{6.25}$$

You want to find the jump distance for the human.

12 **Discussion** Why was a variable used for the human jump distance?

13 Find the missing term in the proportion. How does the answer compare with the world record for humans given on page 413?

▶ **The super-jumper problem may be a bit unrealistic, but there are many real problem situations where using a proportion is a good method for making predictions.**

14 Suppose a school fundraiser makes \$1.75 profit for every 6 rolls of wrapping paper sold. One class of students sells 256 rolls.

a. What phrase tells you what measurements are being compared? What two words indicate a ratio is being used?

b. Write a proportion by filling in the values you know. Use a variable for the value you do not know.

Profit ratio for 6 rolls		**Profit ratio for 256 rolls**
$\frac{\text{profit}}{\text{number of rolls sold}}$	=	$\frac{\text{profit}}{\text{number of rolls sold}}$

c. What is the profit on 256 rolls?

15 ✓ **CHECKPOINT** Suppose a car travels 330 mi on 12 gal of gas. Use a proportion to predict how many gallons of gas it will take to travel 500 mi. Show your work.

✓ **QUESTION 15**

...checks that you can write a proportion and use it to make a prediction.

▶ **In some problem situations, writing a proportion to make a prediction is not appropriate.**

16 **Discussion** The height and the jump distances for the human world-record holder are given on page 413. Do you think it is appropriate to use these measures in a proportion to estimate how far a 5-foot tall person can jump? Explain.

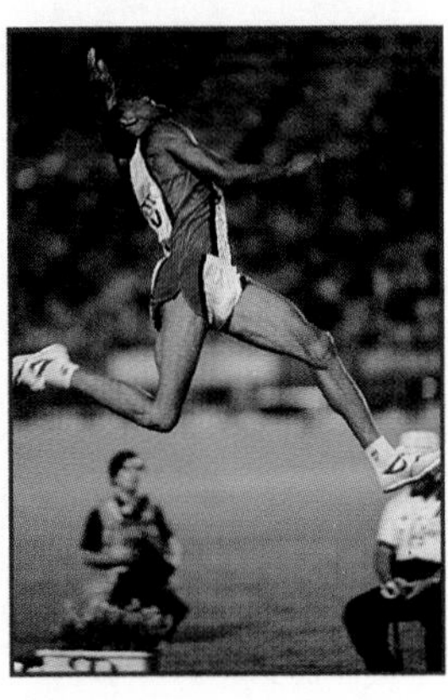

▲ On August 30, 1991, Mike Powell set a record jump of 29 ft $4\frac{1}{2}$ in.

17 **Try This as a Class** If appropriate, use a proportion to solve each problem. If it is not appropriate to use a proportion, explain why not.

a. While resting, Tani's heart beats 11 times in 10 seconds. How many times will his heart beat during a 2-minute rest?

b. The ratio of body weight to daily food intake for a bird is 10 to 4. How much will a 150-pound person eat in a day?

c. In 1996, Gail Devers ran 100 m in 11.11 seconds to win an Olympic gold medal. How long would it take her to run 1500 m?

HOMEWORK EXERCISES ▶ See Exs. 12–18 on pp. 420–421.

Section 4 Key Concepts

Key Terms

proportion

cross products

Recognizing Proportions (p. 414)

A proportion is an equation stating that two ratios are equivalent.

Example $\frac{4}{6} = \frac{12}{18}$ is a proportion because $\frac{4 \cdot 3}{6 \cdot 3} = \frac{12}{18}$.

The cross products in a proportion are equal.

Example

$\frac{4}{6} = \frac{12}{18}$

$4 \cdot 18 = 72$

$6 \cdot 12 = 72$

Finding a Missing Term in a Proportion (p. 415)

You can use cross products to find the missing term in a proportion.

Example Find the missing term in the proportion $\frac{10}{15} = \frac{x}{12}$.

Use cross products to write an equation.

$15 \cdot x = 10 \cdot 12$

$15 \cdot x = 120$

$x = 120 \div 15$

$x = 8$

Then use division to find the value of the variable.

You can check by substituting 8 for x and then checking that the ratios are equivalent.

Key Concepts Questions

18 Use cross products to tell whether the ratios are equivalent.

a. $\frac{5}{6}$ and $\frac{17}{20}$ **b.** $\frac{48}{36}$ and $\frac{220}{165}$ **c.** $\frac{21}{13}$ and $\frac{189}{117}$

19 Describe two ways to find the missing term in the proportion $\frac{45}{35} = \frac{18}{n}$. Then solve the proportion using both methods. Did you get the same result?

Section 4 Key Concepts

Writing a Proportion (pp. 416–417)

When you write a proportion to solve a problem, it is important to set up the proportion correctly.

Example Suppose Miguel's dog eats 2 lb of dog food every 3 days. How many pounds of food will the dog eat in 31 days?

Ratio for 3 days — Ratio for 31 days

$$\frac{2}{3} = \frac{x}{31}$$

pounds of dog food (numerators: 2 and x); number of days (denominators: 3 and 31)

Key Concepts Questions

20 Use the proportion in the Example to find how many pounds of food Miguel's dog will eat in 31 days. Would you get the same answer if you used the proportion $\frac{3}{2} = \frac{31}{x}$? Explain.

21 It is not always appropriate to use a proportion to solve a problem involving ratios. Give an example to illustrate this.

Section 4 Practice & Application Exercises

Find all the equivalent ratios in each list.

1. $\frac{15}{60}, \frac{24}{32}, \frac{75}{300}, \frac{21}{28}, \frac{3.5}{14}$

2. $\frac{6}{7}, \frac{10}{12.5}, \frac{30}{35}, \frac{16}{20}, \frac{40}{45}$

Find the missing term in each proportion.

3. $\frac{3}{12} = \frac{5}{n}$

4. $\frac{4}{24} = \frac{6}{x}$

5. $\frac{5}{15} = \frac{y}{24}$

6. $\frac{s}{7} = \frac{3.5}{1.4}$

7. $\frac{20}{8} = \frac{4.5}{d}$

8. $\frac{5}{m} = \frac{12.5}{40}$

9. $16 : 3 = 64 : r$

10. $p : 15 = 4 : 9$

11. $7 : w = 56 : 40$

12. Choose the proportions that have been set up correctly for solving the problem.

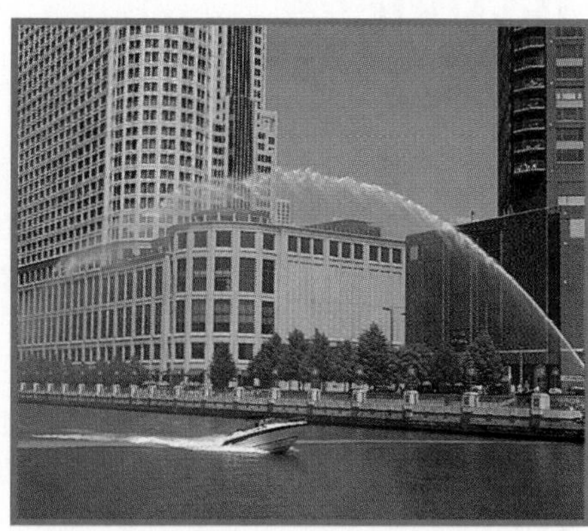

The *Water Arc* in Chicago, Illinois, shoots about 21,000 gal of water over the Chicago River during each 10-minute show. How many gallons of water does it shoot in four minutes?

A. $\frac{21,000}{10} = \frac{4}{x}$ B. $\frac{10}{21,000} = \frac{4}{x}$ C. $\frac{21,000}{10} = \frac{x}{4}$

13. In the movie *Honey, I Shrunk the Kids*, an inventor accidentally shrinks his children. They become so small that they are mistakenly thrown out with the trash and must make their way back to the house.

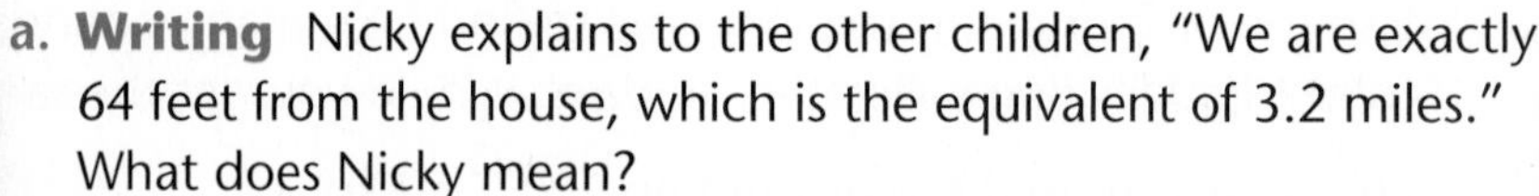

a. **Writing** Nicky explains to the other children, "We are exactly 64 feet from the house, which is the equivalent of 3.2 miles." What does Nicky mean?

b. Nicky can walk one mile in 20 min at his normal height. To predict how long it will take him to walk to the house at his new height, a proportion has been labeled. Fill in the values you know. Use a variable for the value you do not know.

Ratio for 1 mile		Ratio for 3.2 miles
$\frac{\text{distance}}{\text{time}}$	=	$\frac{\text{distance}}{\text{time}}$

c. Find the missing term in your proportion.

14. **Challenge** In Exercise 13 Nicky's height was roughly $\frac{1}{4}$ in. Estimate Nicky's normal height. (Remember that 1 mi = 5280 ft.)

15. **Probability Connection** A die lands on 2 in 5 out of 24 rolls. Find the experimental probability of landing on 2. Use your answer and a proportion to predict the number of times a die will land on 2 in 60 rolls.

If appropriate, use a proportion to solve each problem. If it is not appropriate to use a proportion, explain why not.

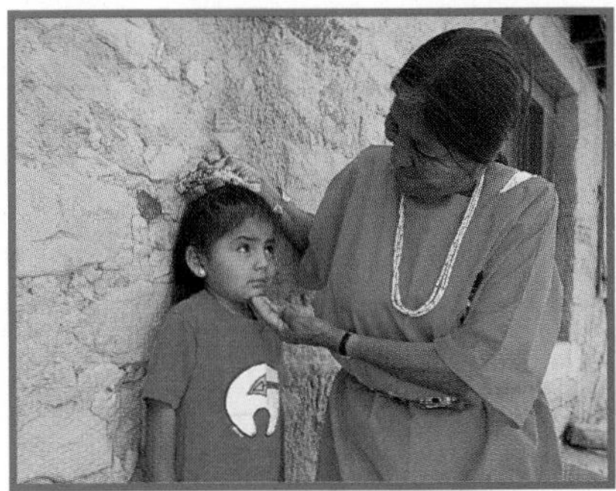

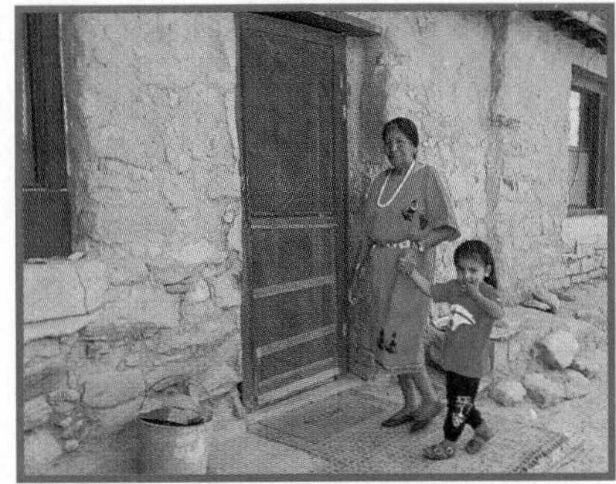

16. Three-year-old Mina is 32 in. tall. Mina grew 4 in. in one year. How tall will Mina be in 18 years?

17. For every 4 steps Mina takes, her grandmother takes 3 steps. How many steps will Mina walk if her grandmother walks 54 steps?

Reflecting on the Section

Be prepared to report on the following topic in class.

18. a. Write a problem about your everyday life that can be solved using a proportion. Be sure your problem is one in which it is appropriate to use a proportion.

    b. Solve the problem you wrote for part (a). Be sure to include an explanation of how you solved it.

Oral Report

Exercise 18 checks that you know how to write a proportion to solve a problem.

Spiral Review

19. a. The mean of the ratios for *distance around the thumb to distance around the neck* for some people is 0.26. Write a "nice" fraction that is close to the mean. **(Module 6, p. 405)**

    b. Predict the distance around the neck of a person whose thumb measurement is 3.75 in.

Draw an example of each type of angle. **(Module 1, p. 22)**

20. acute
21. obtuse
22. straight
23. right

24. Trace the figure. Then find three ways to divide the figure into eight congruent parts. **(Module 2, p. 103)**

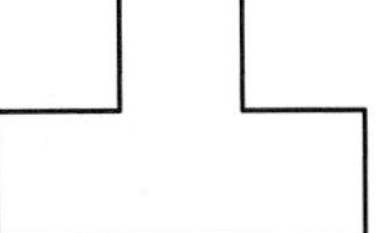

Section 4 Extra Skill Practice

Use cross products to tell whether the ratios are equivalent.

1. $\frac{12}{18}$ and $\frac{4}{6}$
2. $\frac{8}{10}$ and $\frac{12}{15}$
3. $\frac{3}{50}$ and $\frac{6}{75}$
4. $\frac{1.5}{3}$ and $\frac{10}{20}$

Find the missing term in each proportion.

5. $\frac{n}{8} = \frac{12}{2}$
6. $x : 5 = 27 : 45$
7. $\frac{9}{13} = \frac{27}{r}$
8. $\frac{8}{12} = \frac{12}{g}$
9. $\frac{d}{4} = \frac{13}{26}$
10. $\frac{2}{n} = \frac{3}{9}$
11. $3 : 8 = k : 20$
12. $\frac{2.5}{5} = \frac{c}{8}$

If appropriate, use a proportion to solve each problem. If it is not appropriate to use a proportion, explain why not.

13. Eight newspapers cost \$3.60. How much will six newspapers cost?
14. Five white cars drove past Mark's house from 6:00 to 9:00 A.M. How many will pass his house in twenty-four hours?
15. Janis used four yards of ribbon to make six bows. How many yards of ribbon will she need to make ten more bows?

Standardized Testing ▶ Multiple Choice

1. For which values of x and y will the proportion $\frac{x}{25} = \frac{15}{y}$ be correct?

   I. $x = 20$, $y = 20$ II. $x = 12.5$, $y = 30$ III. $x = 100$, $y = 5$ IV. $x = 5$, $y = 75$

   A I only B IV only C I and III D II and IV

2. For which problems is it appropriate and correct to find the solution using the proportion $\frac{x}{75} = \frac{10}{45}$?

   I. Darren read 10 pages of a book in 45 minutes. Predict how many pages he can read in 12 minutes.

   II. Sheri bought 10 tapes for the school music library for \$45. If the tapes all have the same price, how many can she buy for \$75?

   III. Elsa drank 10 oz of water after she finished a 45 min. exercise class. How much do you think she will drink after a 75 min class?

   A I only B II only C I and III D II and III

Section 5 Geometry and Proportions

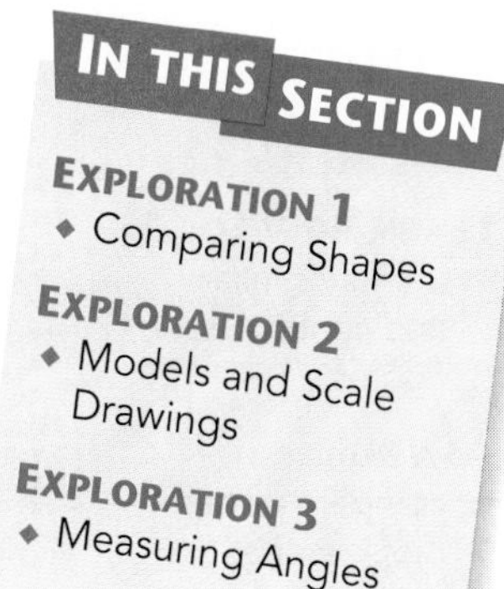

Setting the Stage

Some artists use mathematics to help them design their creations. In M.C. Escher's *Square Limit* below, the fish are arranged so that there are no gaps or overlapping pieces.

Think About It

1 How did Escher create the impression that the design goes on forever inside the square?

2 How are the fish in the middle of the design and the surrounding fish alike? How are they different?

GOAL

LEARN HOW TO...
- identify similar and congruent figures

AS YOU...
- compare pattern block shapes

KEY TERMS
- similar figures
- corresponding parts
- congruent figures

Exploration 1

COMPARING SHAPES

SET UP *Work with a partner. You will need: • Labsheet 5A • pattern blocks • metric ruler • tracing paper*

▶ **The drawing below shows how Escher used a pattern of squares and triangles to create *Square Limit.* The two outlined triangles on the drawing are *similar.* Similar figures have the same shape but not necessarily the same size.**

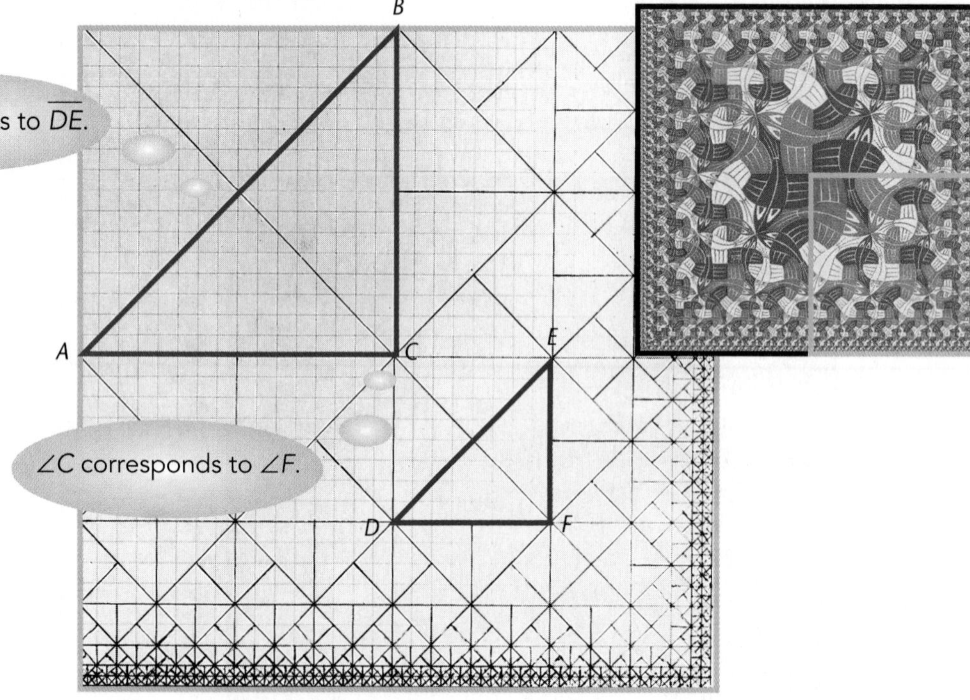

▶ **When two figures are similar, for each part of one figure there is a corresponding part on the other figure.**

3 **Discussion** Look at similar triangles *ABC* and *DEF*.

a. Name another pair of corresponding sides.

b. Name another pair of corresponding angles.

c. How many pairs of corresponding angles are there? How many pairs of corresponding sides?

▶ **Sometimes it is hard to tell whether two figures are similar just by looking at them. To help determine if two figures are similar, you'll use pattern blocks to create similar figures and explore relationships between their corresponding parts.**

4 **Try This as a Class** Trapezoid *ABCD* and trapezoid *EFGH* are similiar.

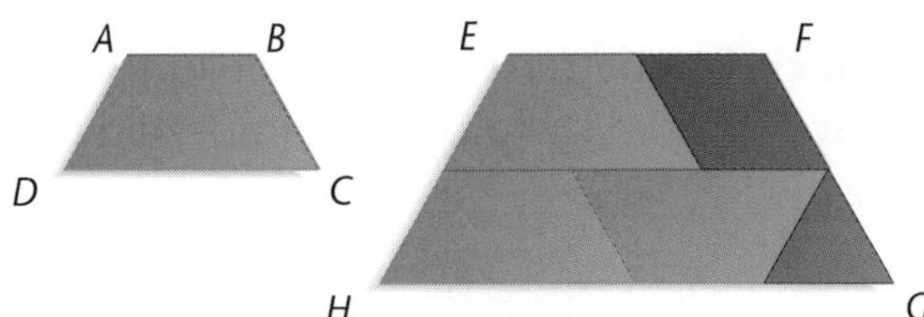

a. Use pattern blocks to build the two trapezoids. Trace around and label each trapezoid as shown.

b. Copy and complete the tables.

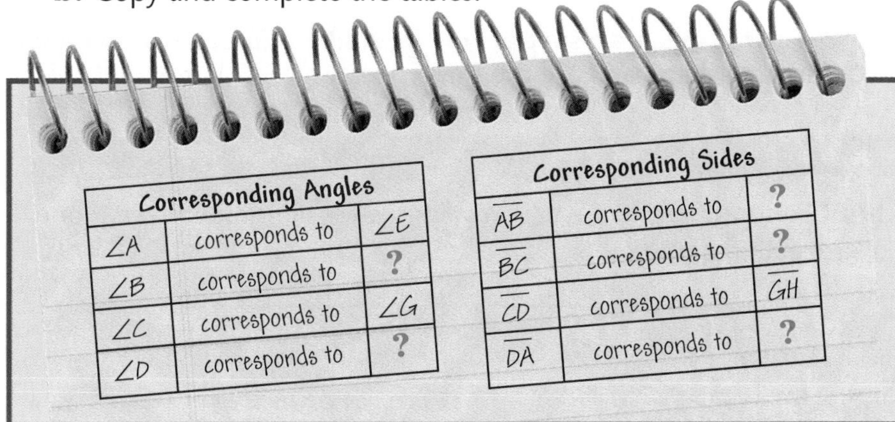

Corresponding Angles		
∠A	corresponds to	∠E
∠B	corresponds to	?
∠C	corresponds to	∠G
∠D	corresponds to	?

Corresponding Sides		
$\overline{AB}$	corresponds to	?
$\overline{BC}$	corresponds to	?
$\overline{CD}$	corresponds to	$\overline{GH}$
$\overline{DA}$	corresponds to	?

c. Place a red trapezoid pattern block on top of your tracing of trapezoid *EFGH*. Use it to compare each pair of corresponding angles. What do you notice?

5 Three sides of a red trapezoid are 1 unit long and one side is 2 units long.

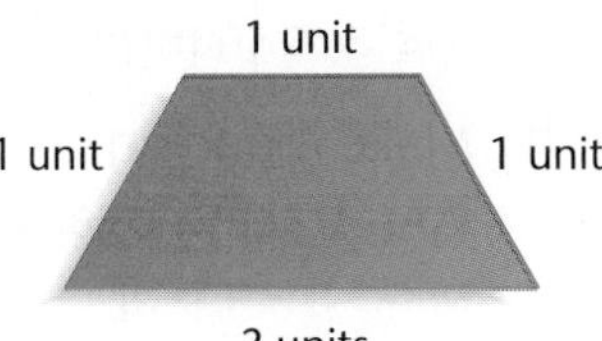

a. How many units long is each side of trapezoid *EFGH*?

b. Write the ratio of the length of $\overline{AB}$ to the length of $\overline{EF}$ as a fraction.

c. Copy and complete the ratios of the lengths of the other pairs of corresponding sides. Write each ratio as a fraction.

BC means the length of $\overline{BC}$.

$\frac{BC}{FG} = \frac{?}{?}$ $\frac{CD}{GH} = \frac{?}{?}$ $\frac{DA}{HE} = \frac{?}{?}$

d. What do you notice about the ratios in parts (b) and (c)?

6 **Discussion** Think about your results in Questions 4 and 5.

a. When two figures are similar, what do you think is true about their corresponding angles?

b. What do you think is true about the ratios of the lengths of their corresponding sides?

7 **Try This as a Class** Use pattern blocks to build the trapezoid below. Is this trapezoid similar to one red trapezoid pattern block? Why or why not?

▶ **Congruent figures are a special type of similar figures because they have the same shape and are the same size.**

EXAMPLE

$\triangle ABC$ is congruent to $\triangle XYZ$. Two figures are congruent even if one is a reflection of the other.

$\triangle ABC$ means triangle ABC.

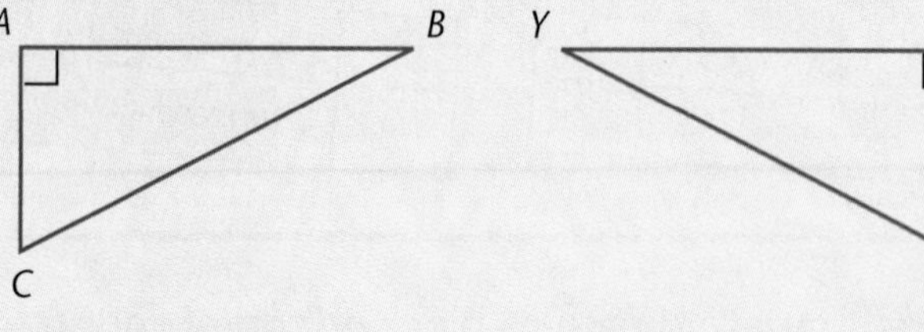

8 **a.** Identify the corresponding angles and corresponding sides of the two triangles in the Example.

b. Make a tracing of one of the two triangles in the Example. Place your tracing over the other triangle so that the corresponding parts match up.

c. What is the ratio of the lengths of the corresponding sides in two congruent figures? Explain.

✓ **QUESTION 9**

...checks that you can determine if two figures are similar or congruent.

9 ✓ **CHECKPOINT** **Use Labsheet 5A.** Follow the directions on the labsheet to determine which of the *Polygon Pairs* are similar and which are congruent.

HOMEWORK EXERCISES ▶ **See Exs. 1–9 on pp. 432–433.**

Exploration 2

Models and SCALE DRAWINGS

SET UP *You will need a ruler.*

GOAL

LEARN HOW TO...
- use proportions to find missing lengths

AS YOU...
- work with scale models and drawings

KEY TERM
- scale

In South Dakota, a model of the Sioux leader Chief Crazy Horse is being used to construct what may be the world's largest sculpture. When completed, the sculpture will measure 563 feet high by 641 feet long!

▶ **When creating a large piece of art, an artist often makes a model similar to what the completed artwork will be.**

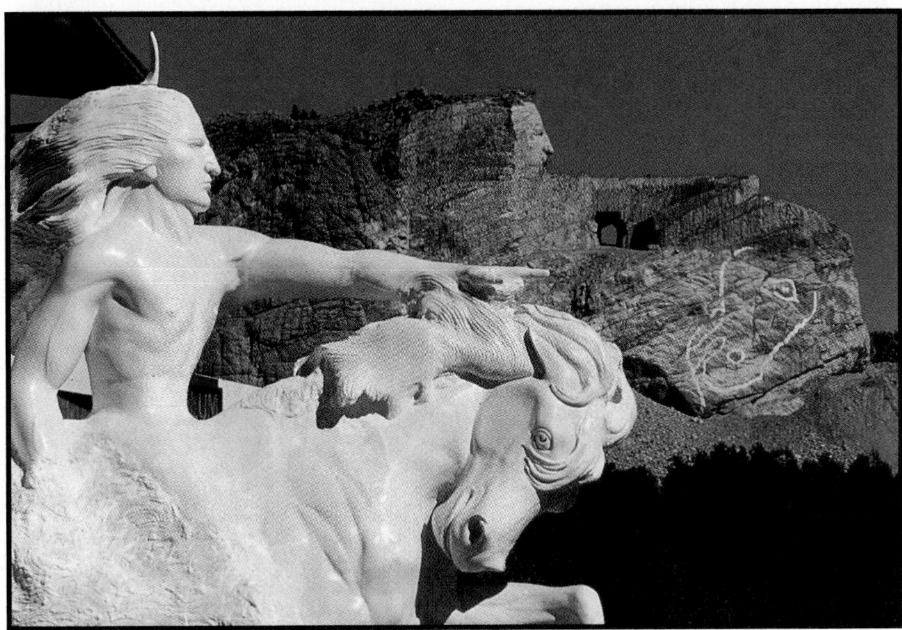

10 **a.** The Crazy Horse model is similar to the sculpture. What do you know about their corresponding measurements?

b. The height of the model is 16.56 ft. Write and solve a proportion to find the length of the model. Round your answer to the nearest hundredth.

11 **Try This as a Class** Did everyone get the same answer for Question 10(b)? Did everyone use the same proportion?

12 **Discussion** Explain how you can find the length of the arm on the sculpture when you know that the arm on the model is 7.74 ft long and the height of the model is 16.56 ft.

✓ **QUESTION 13**

...checks that you can use proportions to find missing lengths in similar figures.

13 ✓ **CHECKPOINT** Use a proportion to find the missing length in each pair of similar figures.

a.

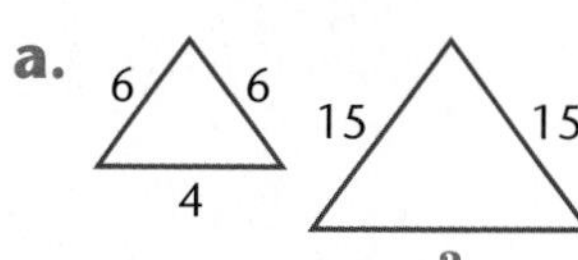

b.

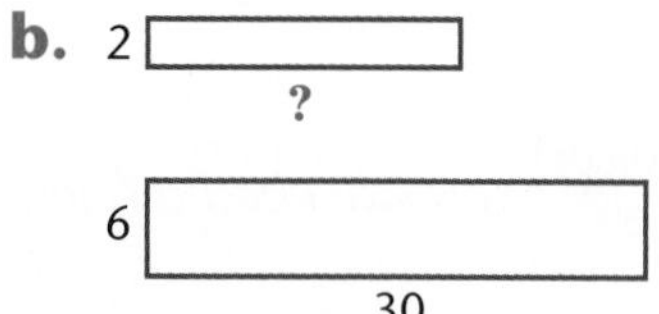

▶ **The ratio of a measurement on a model or a drawing to the corresponding measurement on the actual object is the scale. The Crazy Horse model uses the scale 1 ft : 34 ft.**

EXAMPLE

Use the scale to find the actual length of the living room.

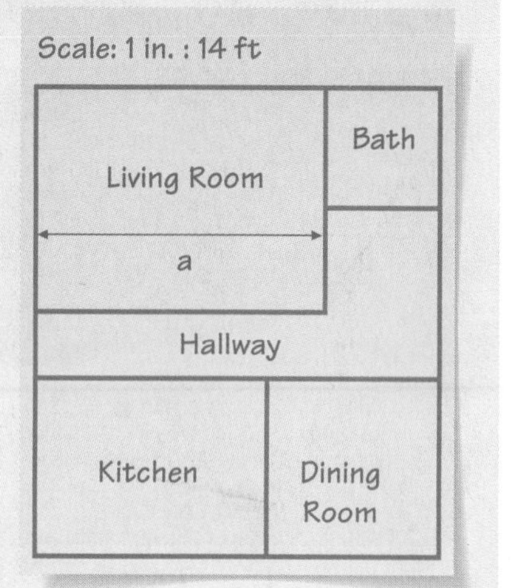

SAMPLE RESPONSE

$$\frac{\text{drawing (in.)}}{\text{actual (ft)}} \rightarrow \frac{1}{14} = \frac{1.25}{a}$$

$$a = 17.5$$

The actual living room is 17.5 ft long.

14 **Try This as a Class** Use the floor plan above.

a. Find the dimensions of the actual kitchen.

b. Find the dimensions of the actual bath.

✓ **QUESTION 15**

...checks that you can use a scale to find missing measurements in similar figures.

15 ✓ **CHECKPOINT**

a. In an architect's drawing a building is 2.5 ft tall. The actual building is 40 ft tall. What is the scale?

b. The height of the building's front door is 8 ft. What is the height of the door in the drawing of the building?

HOMEWORK EXERCISES ▶ See Exs. 10–20 on pp. 433–434.

Exploration 3

MEASURING Angles

SET UP *You will need:* • *Labsheet 5B* • *protractor*

16 The photo shows the angle made by the statue's arm. Is the angle *acute, right,* or *obtuse*?

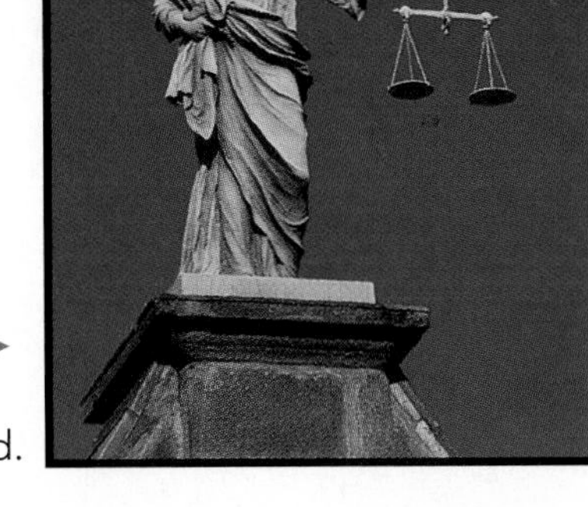

A statue representing justice at the Royal Palace in Dublin, Ireland.

GOAL

LEARN HOW TO...
- measure an angle using a protractor
- draw an angle using a protractor

AS YOU...
- examine angles used in art

KEY TERM
- protractor

FOR HELP with *classifying angles*, see **MODULE 1, p. 19**

▶ **Artists must be able to measure the size of angles, since even a small difference in the way an angle is drawn can make a model or scale drawing inaccurate. You can measure an angle using a protractor.**

Using a Protractor

Student Resource

The steps below show how to use a protractor to measure an angle.

First Place the center mark of the protractor on the vertex of the angle.

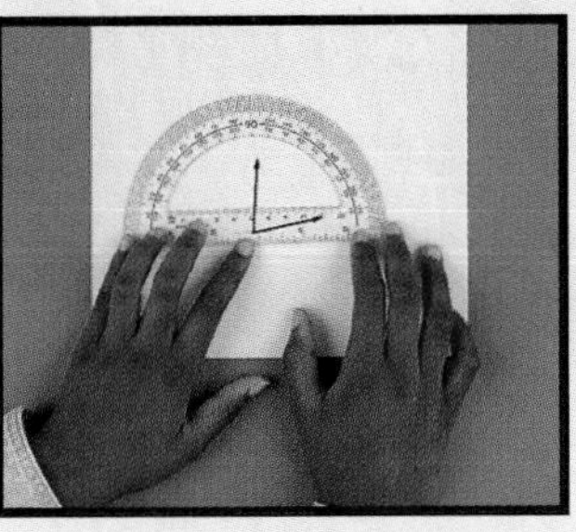

Next Place the 0° mark on one side of the angle. You may need to extend the sides of the angle.

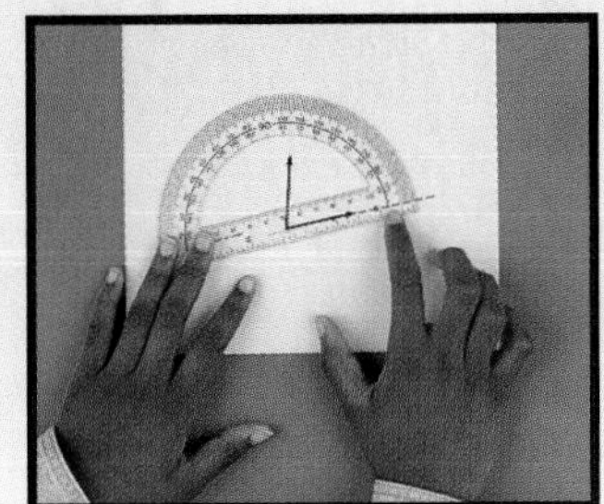

Then Read the number where the other side of the angle crosses the scale.

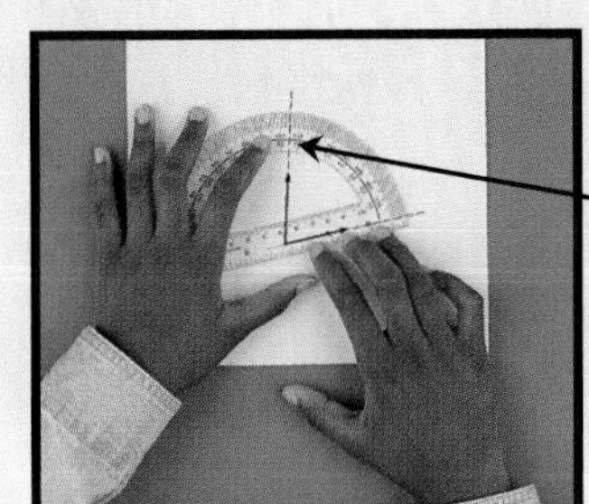

Read the number on the bottom scale since you used its 0° mark.

The measure of $\angle ABC$ is 75°.

17 **Try This as a Class** Estimate the measure of the angle shown in the statue photo on page 429. Then use a protractor to find the exact measure. How close was your estimate?

18 **Use Labsheet 5B.** Measure each of the *Angles* shown.

▶ **To create a model or scale drawing, an artist must also be able to draw an angle of a certain size.**

19 **Discussion** How can you use what you have learned about measuring angles with a protractor to draw a 62° angle?

✓ **QUESTION 20**

...checks that you can use a protractor.

20 ✓ **CHECKPOINT** Use a protractor to draw an angle with each measure. Classify each angle as *right*, *acute*, or *obtuse*.

a. 125° **b.** 38° **c.** 90°

HOMEWORK EXERCISES ▶ See Exs. 21–30 on pp. 434–435.

Section 5 Key Concepts

Key Terms

similar figures

congruent figures

corresponding parts

Similar and Congruent Figures (pp. 424–426)

Similar figures have the same shape, but not necessarily the same size. Congruent figures are similar figures that have the same shape and the same size.

Example Quadrilateral *ABCD* is congruent to *EFGH*.

$\overline{AB}$ corresponds to $\overline{EF}$.

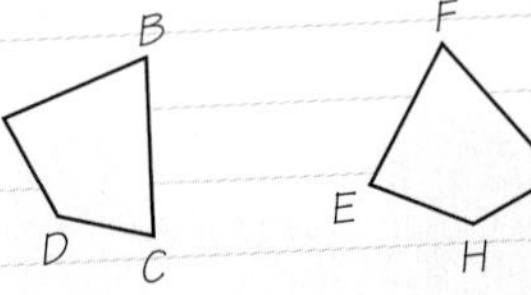

$\angle D$ corresponds to $\angle H$.

Section 5 Key Concepts

Key Terms

Properties of Similar Figures (pp. 424–426)

Example $\triangle ABC$ is similar to $\triangle DEF$.

The corresponding angles have the same measure.

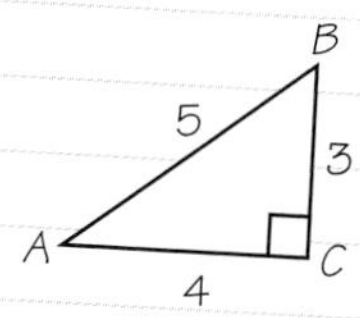

Angles equal in measure:
$\angle A$ and $\angle D$
$\angle B$ and $\angle E$
$\angle C$ and $\angle F$

The ratios of the lengths of corresponding sides are equivalent.

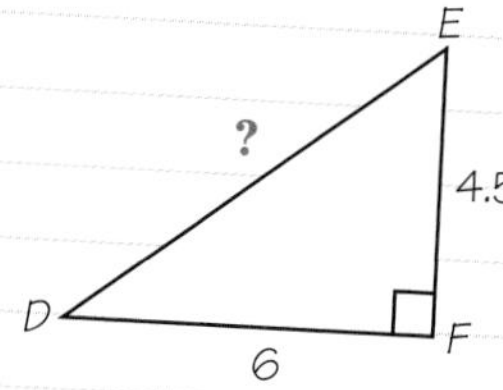

$$\frac{AB}{DE} = \frac{BC}{EF} = \frac{CA}{FD}$$

CA means the length of $\overline{CA}$.

Proportions and Scale (pp. 427–428)

scale

You can use proportions to find missing lengths in similar figures.
To find *DE* in $\triangle DEF$ solve: $\frac{4}{6} = \frac{5}{?}$
You can use the scale of a drawing or a model to write a proportion to find the measurements of an actual object.

Measuring Angles with a Protractor (pp. 429–430)

protractor

You can use the top scale to measure this angle.

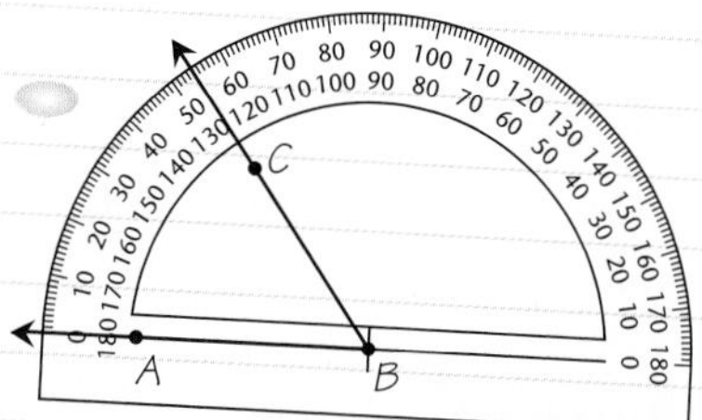

The measure of $\angle ABC$ is 54°.

Key Concepts Questions

21 **a.** Solve the proportion $\frac{4}{6} = \frac{5}{?}$ to find *DE* in the Example.

b. Write another proportion that you could use to find *DE*.

22 Suppose the scale used on a map is 1 in. to 2 mi. How long is a road that is 6 in. long on the map?

Section 5

Practice & Application Exercises

YOU WILL NEED

For Ex. 16–18 and 30:
- customary ruler

For Ex. 21–29:
- protractor

For Ex. 24:
- compass or round object

For Ex. 41:
- metric ruler

Pattern Block Side Lengths

1 unit, 1 unit, 1 unit (triangle)

1 unit, 1 unit, 1 unit, 1 unit (rhombus)

1 unit, 1 unit, 1 unit, 2 units (trapezoid)

The figures in each pair are similar. Make a table showing all the pairs of corresponding angles and corresponding sides.

1. 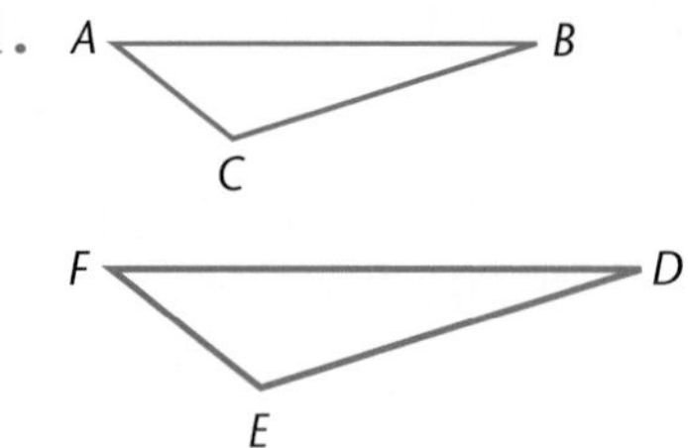

2. 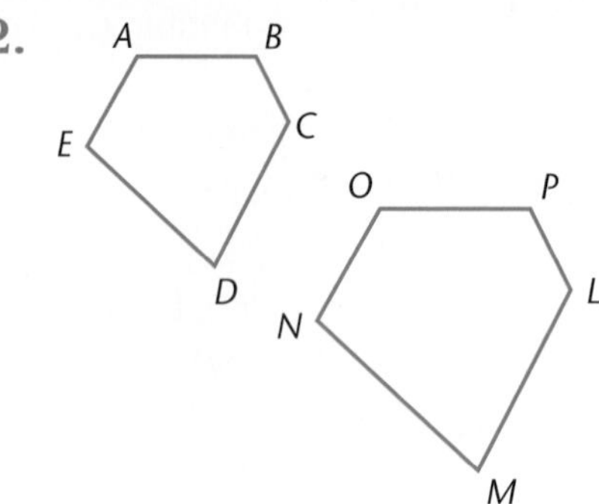

Tell whether the figures in each pair are similar or congruent. If they are not similar, explain how you know.

3. 

4. 

5. 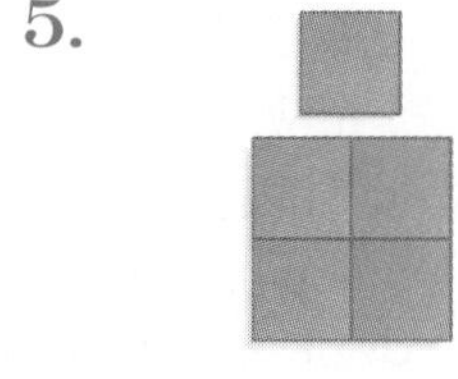

Use the rectangles for Exercises 6–8.

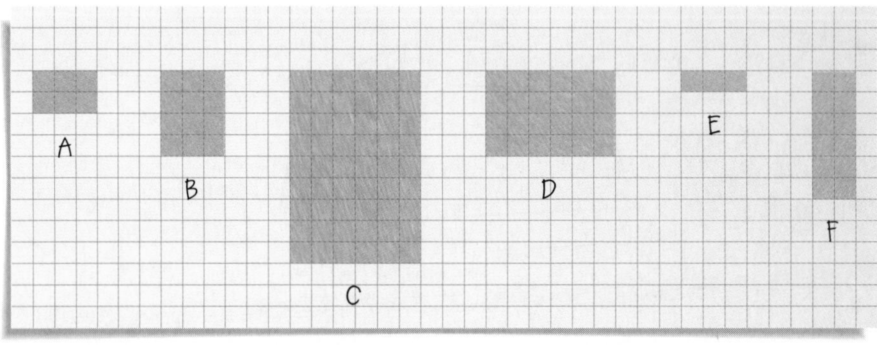

6. Name all the rectangles that are similar to rectangle A. What is the ratio of the lengths of the corresponding sides?

7. Name all the rectangles that are similar to rectangle E. What is the ratio of the lengths of the corresponding sides?

8. Make a sketch of a rectangle that is similar but not congruent to rectangle B. Label the length of each side.

9. Which two nails are similar? Explain.

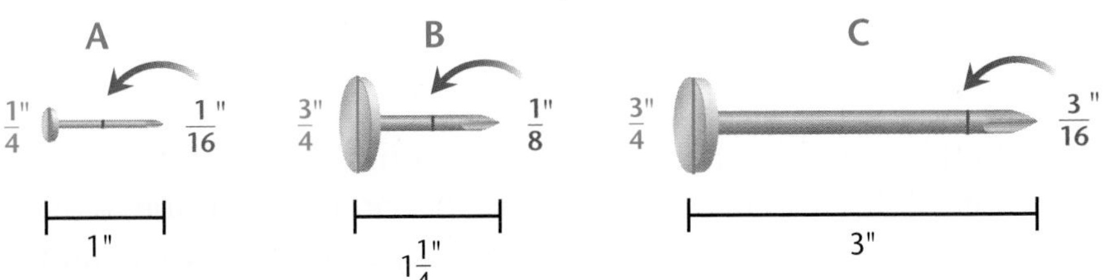

The figures in each pair are similar. Use proportions to find the missing lengths.

10.

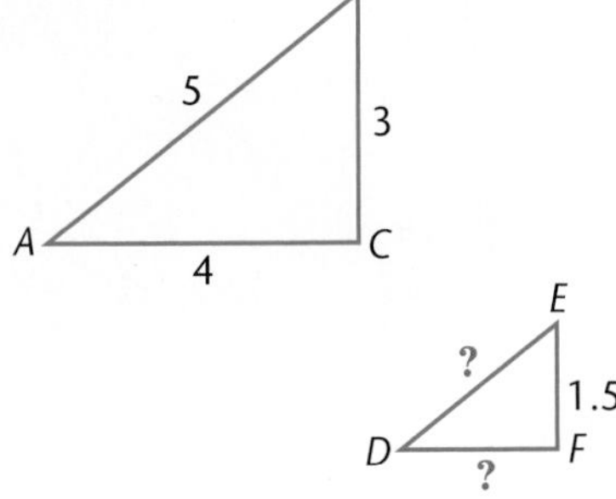

11.

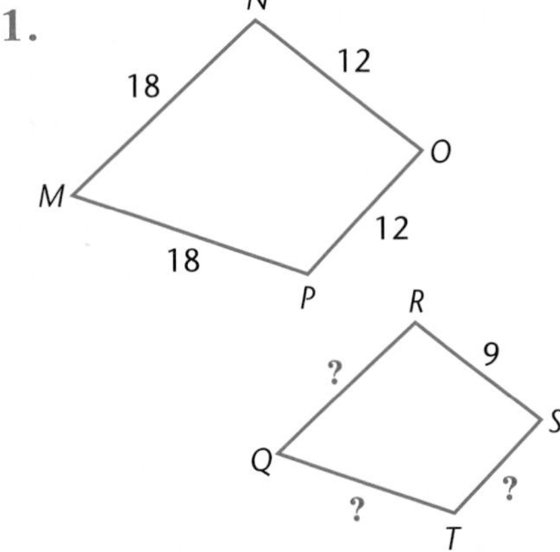

12. The Mount Rushmore sculpture of four United States presidents was built using a smaller model with a scale of 1 in. to 12 in. The model used was 5 ft tall. What is the height of the sculpture?

For each scale, find how long a measure of 3 in. on the drawing would be on the actual object.

13. 1 in. : 5 ft

14. 2 in. : 3 ft

15. $\frac{1}{2}$ in. : $2\frac{1}{2}$ ft

Social Studies **In Exercises 16–18, use the scale on the map to estimate the actual distance between each pair of cities.**

16. Lusaka and Harare

17. Tete and Ndola

18. Tete and Harare

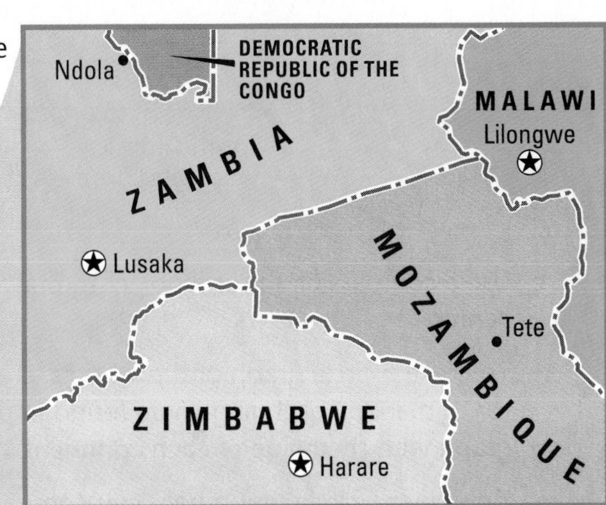

Scale: 1 in. = 160 mi

19. The makers of the movie *Earthquake* made a 54-foot-long miniature of the 880-foot-long Hollywood Dam.

   a. Find the scale used to build the miniature.

   b. In the movie, the dam breaks and washes away buildings. The miniature buildings were built on the same scale as the miniature dam. If an actual house is 60 ft long and 40 ft wide, find the dimensions of a miniature house.

20. **Challenge** One of the models of the Death Star in *Star Wars* was built using a scale of 1 ft to 2,400 ft. In the movie, the Death Star was made to look like a sphere one mile in diameter. What was the diameter of the model? (1 mi = 5,280 ft)

Trace each angle and extend the rays. Then find each angle's measure.

21. 

22. 

23. 

24. **Displaying Data** A *circle graph* can show the part to whole relationship between each continent and the total land area.

World Land Area	
Continent	**Percent of total land area***
Asia	30
Africa	20
North America	16
South America	12
Antarctica	10
Europe	7
Australia	5

*Approximate percents.

   a. Write each percent in the table as a fraction out of 100.

   b. In a circle graph the entire 360° circle represents 100%. Use a proportion to find the number of degrees for each continent.

South America

Angle is 43°

Round to the nearest whole degree.

Example

	Percent		Degrees
South America → Total land area →	$\frac{12}{100}$	=	$\frac{43.2}{360}$

   c. Use a compass or a round object to draw a circle and find its center.

   d. To make a circle graph of the world's land area, use a protractor to mark off each angle you found in part (b). Label your graph with the name of each continent and write a title.

   e. How does a circle graph help you compare data?

25. The femur is a bone in the thigh that runs from the hip to the knee in humans. The angle at the top of the femur changes as a person ages. Measure each angle.

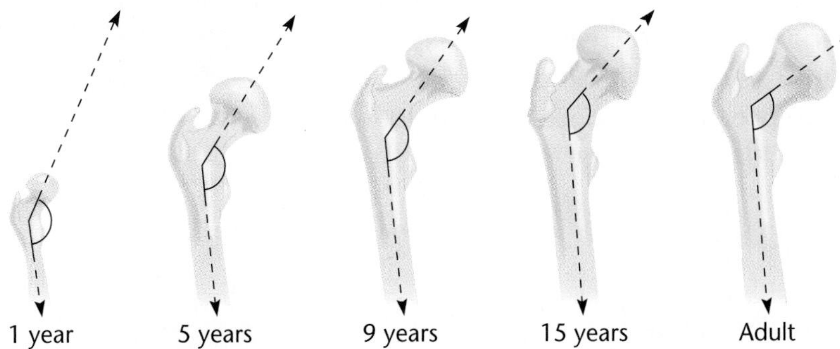

Use a protractor to draw an angle with each measure.

26. 56° 27. 123° 28. 17° 29. 79°

Reflecting on the Section

30. Many miniatures are built using a 1 in. to 12 in. scale. Measure the length, the width, and the height of your bed. Use the scale to find the measurements for a miniature of your bed. Then make a scale drawing of your bed.

▲ This miniature house is an exact copy of an 1865 home. The tiny oil lamps actually work!

RESEARCH

Exercise 30 checks that you can use scale and proportions.

Spiral Review

Use cross products to tell whether the ratios are equivalent. (Module 6, p. 418)

31. $\frac{4}{25}$ and $\frac{5}{30}$ 32. $\frac{21}{28}$ and $\frac{9}{12}$ 33. $\frac{3.5}{5}$ and $\frac{11.2}{16}$

Mental Math Use mental math to add or subtract. (Module 3, p. 213; Module 5, p. 347)

34. $6 - 2\frac{2}{5}$ 35. $3.97 + 5.23$ 36. $2\frac{1}{4} + 4\frac{5}{6} + 1\frac{3}{4}$

Write each fraction as a percent. (Module 3, p. 176)

37. $\frac{2}{5}$ 38. $\frac{3}{10}$ 39. $\frac{3}{4}$ 40. $\frac{4}{8}$

Career Connection

Oceanographer: Marcia McNutt

Marcia McNutt uses sonar and satellites to create scale maps of an ocean floor. These maps can be used to locate underwater volcanoes or to show an ocean floor's depth. This map shows the Southern Austral Islands, in the South Pacific Ocean.

41. a. The actual distance from the volcano at Marotiri to the one at Macdonald Seamount is about 264 km. Write a scale for the map.

    b. Use your scale to estimate the actual distance from the volcano at Rapa to the volcano at Marotiri.

42. Estimate the depth of the ocean at Marotiri.

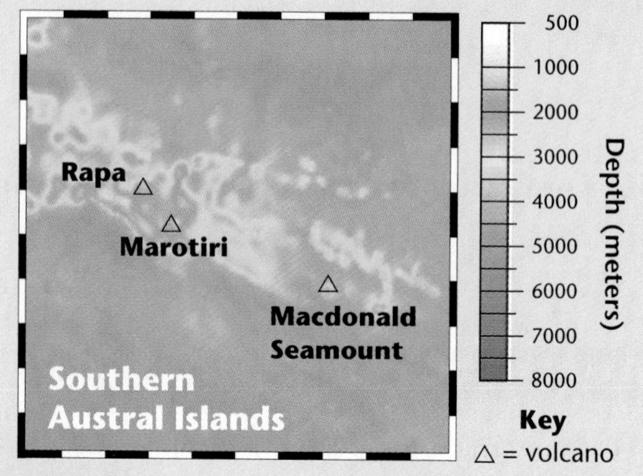

Mystery Tracks

SET UP

You will need
- *protractor*
- *ruler*

Using Angles Now you'll look for a method to tell whether a person was walking or running when making tracks.

 7 The diagram shows where to measure a person's step angle. Have someone help you measure your step angle to the nearest degree. Walk at your normal speed.

 8 How do you think your step angle changes when you run? Have someone help you measure your step angle for a running speed.

 9 How can you use the measure of the step angle to tell whether tracks were made by someone walking or running?

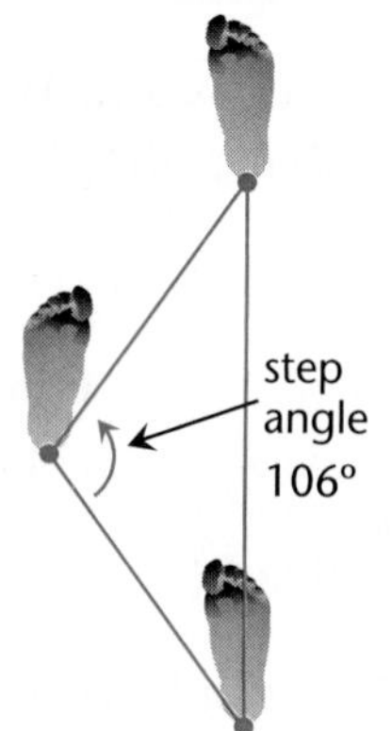

Section 5
Extra Skill Practice

You will need: • *protractor* (Exs. 8–11)

Tell whether the figures in each pair are similar or congruent. If they are not similar, explain how you know.

1.

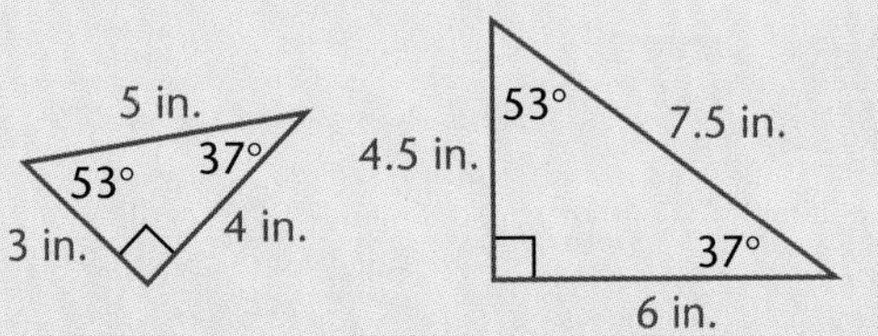

2.

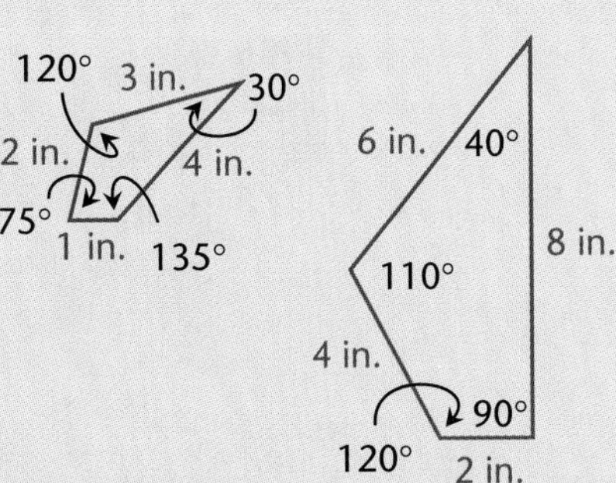

Use proportions to find the missing lengths in each pair of similar figures.

3. 6.3 cm, 2.1 cm; ?, 10.8 cm

4. 2 in., 2 in., 3 in., 3 in., 1 in.; ?, ?, ?, ?, $\frac{3}{4}$ in.

For each scale, find how long a measure of 4 inches on the drawing would be on the actual object.

5. 1 in. : 12 in.

6. 2 in. : 5 ft

7. $\frac{1}{2}$ in. : 10 ft

Use a protractor to draw an angle with each measure.

8. 81°

9. 177°

10. 21°

11. 110°

Standardized Testing ▶ Performance Task

You will need: • *tape measure* • *ruler*

Make a scale drawing of a room in your home. Include marks that show where windows and doors are in the room. Write the scale used on your drawing.

Section 6 Percents and Probability

IN THIS SECTION

EXPLORATION 1
- Using Fractions for Percents

EXPLORATION 2
- Tree Diagrams

Playing the Percentages

Setting the Stage

About 40 million people play softball in the United States. From this enormous group of athletes, 2000 women tried out for the 1996 U.S. Olympic Softball Team. Only 15 made the team. Can you imagine comparing 2000 players to select the best 15?

The youngest player, 18-year-old Christa Williams, attended classes at night and during the summer so she could graduate from high school on time and still practice with the Olympic team.

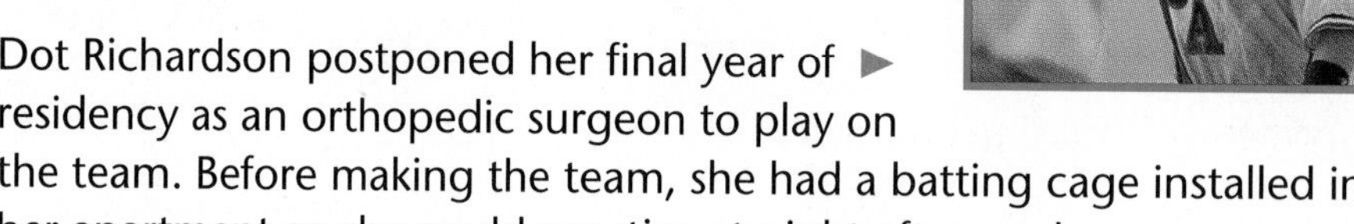

Dot Richardson postponed her final year of ▶ residency as an orthopedic surgeon to play on the team. Before making the team, she had a batting cage installed in her apartment so she could practice at night after work.

Think About It

1 Nine members of the Olympic softball team were from California. What percent of the team is this?

2 The population of the United States is about 250 million. About what percent of people in the United States play softball?

Exploration 1

USING Fractions for Percents

SET UP *You will need Labsheet 6A.*

GOAL

LEARN HOW TO...
- use a fraction to find a percent of a number
- use a fraction to estimate a percent of a number

AS YOU...
- examine data about the members of the U.S. Olympic softball team

▶ **When choosing players for a team, coaches often compare players' past performances. In this exploration you'll use percents to examine a variety of facts and figures about the players chosen for the 1996 Olympic softball team.**

3 Lisa Fernandez, a pitcher, set a college record by winning 93% of her games at UCLA. Lisa won 93 games. How many losses did she have?

4 Jennifer McFalls was an alternate for the Olympic team. She got a hit in 50% of the times she batted in the 1994 qualifier for the Pan American games.

a. What fraction in lowest terms is equivalent to 50%?

b. Jennifer batted 24 times in the 1994 qualifier. Show how to use the fraction you found in part (a) to find how many hits she got.

FOR◀HELP with *writing a percent as a fraction*, see **MODULE 3, p. 176**

5 Write each percent as a fraction in lowest terms.

a. 25% **b.** 10% **c.** 20%

6 Shelly Stokes, a catcher, got a hit in 25% of her 696 at-bats while at Fresno State University. Use the fraction you found in Question 5(a) to find the number of hits she had.

7 ✓ **CHECKPOINT** Another catcher, Gillian Boxx, got hits in 80% of her at-bats at the 1994 International Softball Federation Women's World Championship. She batted 5 times. Use a fraction in lowest terms to find how many hits she had.

...checks that you can use a fraction to find a percent of a number.

▶ **Estimating with Percents** **You can use a "nice" fraction to estimate a percent or a percent of a number.**

EXAMPLE

In her softball games at college, Jennifer McFalls stole 27 bases in 31 attempts. Use a "nice" fraction to estimate the percent of her attempts that were successful.

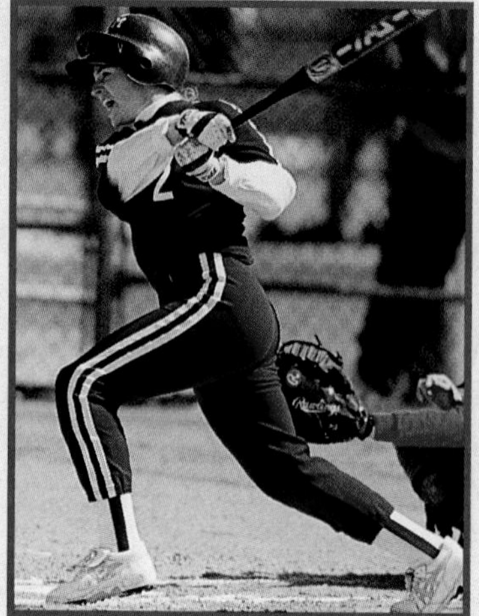

SAMPLE RESPONSE

$\frac{27}{31}$ is close to $\frac{27}{30}$.

$\frac{27}{30} = \frac{9}{10} = 90\%$

About 90% of her attempts were successful.

8 Michele Smith won 82 out of 102 games while pitching for Oklahoma State University. Use a "nice" fraction to estimate the percent of games that she won.

▶ **You know the percent equivalents for many "nice" fractions. In Question 9, you will learn the percent form for $\frac{1}{3}$ and $\frac{2}{3}$.**

9 **Use Labsheet 6A.** Use the *Grid for Thirds* to write $\frac{1}{3}$ and $\frac{2}{3}$ as percents.

✓ QUESTION 10

...checks that you can use a fraction to estimate a percent.

10 **✓ CHECKPOINT** At the 1995 Pan American Games in Argentina, Julie Smith had 8 hits in 29 at-bats. Use a fraction to estimate the percent of hits she got.

11 Suppose a batter got a hit in 32% of her 75 at-bats. Use a "nice" fraction to estimate how many hits she got.

12 **Discussion** Which player in the table at the right had the greatest percent of hits? the least percent of hits? Explain your reasoning.

Player	Hits	At-bats
A	105	400
B	120	400
C	150	600

HOMEWORK EXERCISES ▶ **See Exs. 1–19 on pp. 445–446.**

Exploration 2

TREE DIAGRAMS

SET UP *Work with a partner. You will need:* • *Labsheets 6B and 6C* • *paper clip*

GOAL

LEARN HOW TO...
- make a tree diagram to find probabilities

AS YOU...
- play the game *Dueling Spinners*

KEY TERMS
- fair game
- tree diagram

▶ **Softball is based on skill, but there are many games that rely on a lucky roll of a die or flip of a coin. You'll predict the results of the game *Dueling Spinners* and then examine the probability of winning to see if the game is fair.**

Game Rules **You and your partner each spin a spinner. Whoever spins the greater number is the winner.**

Use Labsheet 6B for Questions 13–16.

13 Decide who will use Spinner A and who will use Spinner B. Do you think Spinner A or Spinner B will win more often? Explain your reasoning.

14 **a.** Play *Dueling Spinners* ten times. Record the winning spinner for each game on the labsheet.

b. How do your results in part (a) compare with your prediction in Question 13?

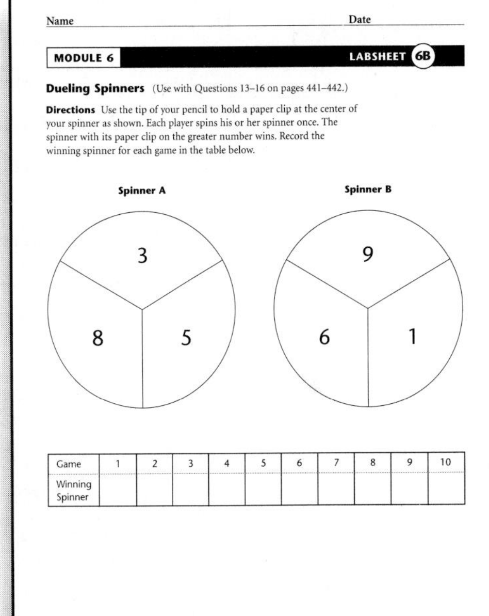

Name Date

MODULE 6 LABSHEET 6B

Dueling Spinners (Use with Questions 13–16 on pages 441–442.)

Directions Use the tip of your pencil to hold a paper clip at the center of your spinner as shown. Each player spins his or her spinner once. The spinner with its paper clip on the greater number wins. Record the winning spinner for each game in the table below.

Spinner A

3 8 5

Spinner B

9 6 1

Game	1	2	3	4	5	6	7	8	9	10
Winning Spinner										

15 **Try This as a Class** Combine your results with the results of the rest of the class.

a. How many times did Spinner A win?

b. How many times did Spinner B win?

c. How do the class results compare with your individual results and your prediction in Question 13?

▶ **In a fair game each player has an equal chance of winning. Playing a game can help you decide if it is fair, but you may need to play many times to be sure. Another way to decide if a game is fair is to list and compare all the possible outcomes.**

FOR◀HELP with *equally likely outcomes*, see **MODULE 4, p. 242**

16 **Discussion** Look at the spinners on Labsheet 6B.

a. What are the possible outcomes when Spinner A is spun?

b. Are the outcomes equally likely? Explain.

c. Suppose the outcome on Spinner A is 3. What are the possible outcomes for Spinner B? Are the outcomes for Spinner B equally likely?

d. Would your answers to part (c) be the same if the outcome on Spinner A was 5 or 8? Explain.

▶ **A tree diagram can be used to find and organize the possible outcomes for a game. The steps below show how to make a tree diagram for *Dueling Spinners*.**

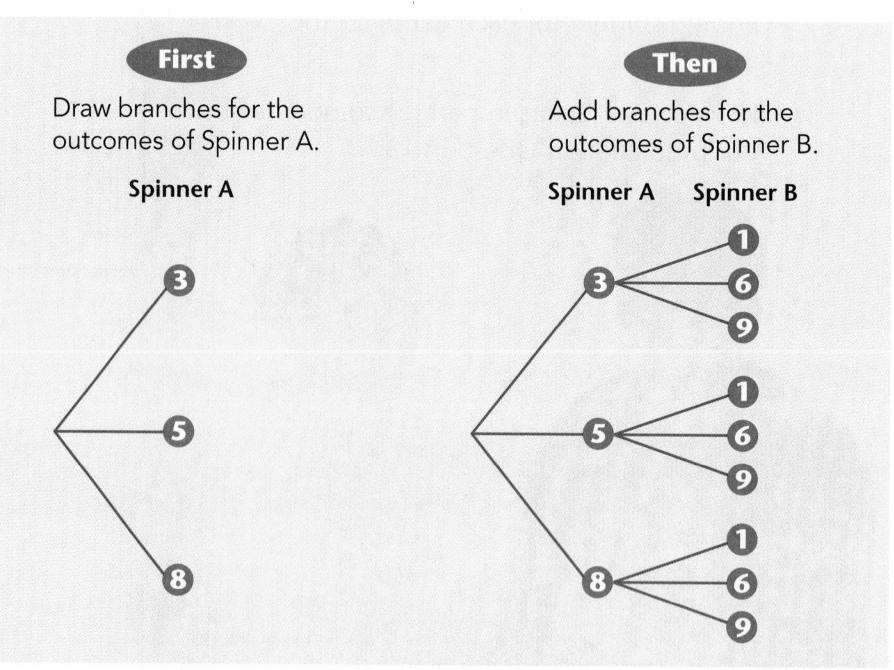

17 **Use Labsheet 6C.** Follow the directions for the *Tree Diagram.* You'll find the number of times each spinner wins and then compare probabilities to decide if the game is fair.

▶ **Suppose you are going to play the *Dueling Spinners* game using Spinner C below. Your opponent will use either Spinner D or Spinner E.**

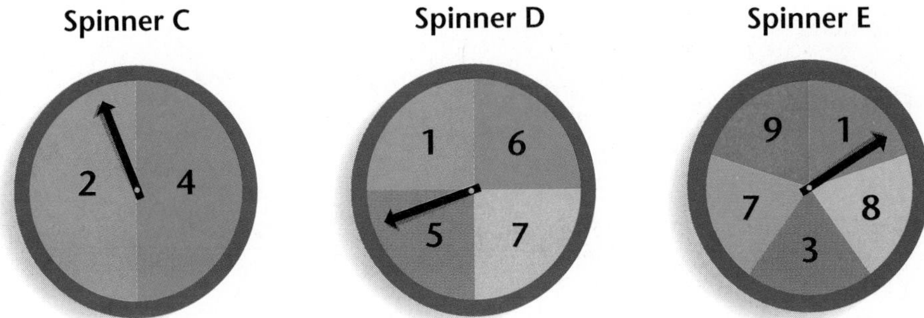

18 **Try This as a Class**

a. Make a tree diagram to show the outcomes for Spinner C versus Spinner D.

b. Find the probability that Spinner C will beat Spinner D.

19 **✓ CHECKPOINT** Use a tree diagram to find the probability that Spinner C will beat Spinner E.

...checks that you can make a tree diagram and use it to find probabilities.

▶ **Using Percent Form** **Probabilities can be written and then compared as percents.**

20 Use your answers from Questions 18 and 19.

a. What percent of the time would you expect Spinner C to beat Spinner D?

b. What percent of the time would you expect Spinner C to beat Spinner E?

c. Which spinner does Spinner C have a better chance of beating, D or E?

21 **Discussion** When you answered Question 20(c), was it easier to use the percent form of the probabilities or the fraction form that you found in Questions 18 and 19? Explain.

HOMEWORK EXERCISES ▶ See Exs. 20–28 on pp. 446–447.

Section 6 Key Concepts

Key Terms

Using Fractions for Percents (pp. 439–440)

A fraction like $\frac{2}{5}$ or $\frac{3}{4}$ can be used to find a percent of a number. "Nice" fractions can also be used to estimate a percent or a percent of a number.

Example Use a "nice" fraction to estimate 29% of 40.

29% of 40

$\frac{3}{10}$ of 40 = 12

29% is about 30%, or $\frac{3}{10}$.

Think: $\frac{1}{10}$ of 40 is 4, so $\frac{3}{10}$ of 40 is 3 x 4.

Tree Diagrams (pp. 442–443)

tree diagram

A tree diagram can be used to list outcomes of experiments and determine probabilities.

Example

This tree shows the outcomes of flipping a coin twice.

First coin flip	Second coin flip	Outcome
H	H	HH
	T	HT
T	H	TH
	T	TT

fair game

A tree diagram can help you compare probabilities to determine whether a game is fair.

22 **Key Concepts Question** Use the tree diagram for flipping a coin twice.

a. List the outcomes with at least one head. What percent of the time would you expect this to happen?

b. How many times would you expect to get at least one head in 60 rounds of flipping?

Section 6

Practice & Application Exercises

Use a fraction in lowest terms to find each value.

1. 25% of 48
2. 60% of 35
3. 10% of 90
4. 75% of 104
5. 20% of 245
6. 30% of 200
7. 5% of 380
8. 90% of 70
9. 70% of 42

10. Teams in the AAGPBL played games almost every night with about 120 games a season. How many wins would a team need to win 75% of their games?

11. **Baseball** Dottie Komenshek played for the Rockford Peaches from 1943 to 1951 and in 1953. She struck out only about 2% of the times she came to bat and had nearly 4000 at-bats in her career. About how many times did she strike out?

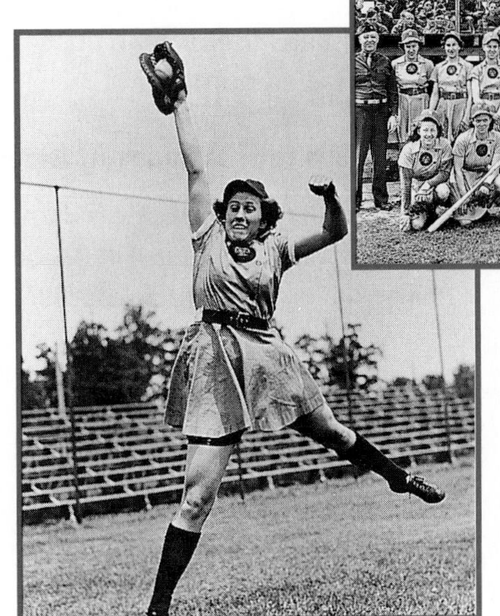

▲ The All American Girls Professional Baseball League (AAGPBL) that existed from 1943 to 1954 inspired the 1992 movie *A League of Their Own*.

12. Carlos scored in 35% of his 60 soccer games. Use a "nice" fraction to estimate the number of games in which he scored. Is your estimate higher or lower than the actual number of games? Why?

13. **Mental Math** The standard amount to leave for a tip in a restaurant is 15% of the bill. Suppose the bill is $40.00.
    a. Use mental math to find 10% of $40.00.
    b. Use mental math to find 5% of $40.00.
    c. Use parts (a) and (b) to find 15% of $40.00.

Estimate a percent for each fraction.

14. $\frac{35}{65}$
15. $\frac{31}{40}$
16. $\frac{46}{51}$
17. $\frac{19}{30}$

18. **Tennis** By the end of 1996, tennis star Pete Sampras had won 8 Grand Slam singles titles, with 3 of them at Wimbledon. About what percent of his Grand Slam titles were won at Wimbledon?

19. **Challenge** Kim Maher had 12 hits in 32 at-bats while playing in the Pan American games in 1995. Complete parts (a)–(c) to find the percent of times she got a hit.

a. Write the fraction $\frac{12}{32}$ in lowest terms.

b. Find the percent equivalents of $\frac{2}{8}$ and $\frac{4}{8}$.

c. Show how your answers from part (b) can be used to write $\frac{12}{32}$ as a percent.

20. a. Make a tree diagram showing the outcomes for flipping a coin and then rolling a die.

b. What is the probability of getting tails and a 3? of heads and an even number?

Use the die shown. It has four sides labeled 1 through 4.

21. **Geometry Connection** How many vertices does the 4-sided die have? How many edges?

22. a. Make a tree diagram showing the outcomes of rolling a 4-sided die two times.

b. What is the probability of rolling two 4's?

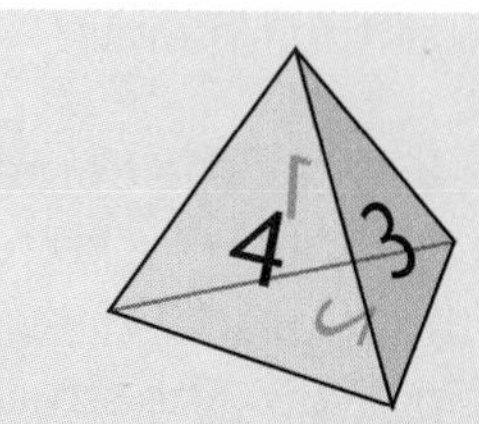

This die is a triangular pyramid with four congruent faces. This roll is counted as a roll of 2 since the die landed on 2.

In Exercises 23–26, two players are going to play *Dueling Spinners*. The first player chooses one of the spinners below. The second player chooses one of the remaining spinners.

Spinner A

9
5
1

Spinner B

Spinner C

23. Find the probability that Spinner A beats Spinner B.

24. Find the probability that Spinner B beats Spinner C.

25. Find the probability that Spinner C beats Spinner A.

26. **Challenge** Which player has the advantage—the player who chooses a spinner first, or the one who chooses second? Explain.

27. Suppose three players toss single coins in a game. The winner of the game is the player whose toss is different from the other two.

Example   

In this example, the player who tossed heads would win.

a. Draw a tree diagram to show the possible outcomes.

b. Will there always be a winner? If so, why? If not, what percent of the time should there be a winner?

c. Is this a fair game? Explain.

Reflecting on the Section

28. Suppose *Dueling Spinners* is played with Spinner A and Spinner B as shown. Find values for Spinner A and sketch a tree diagram so that Spinner A wins 40% of the time.

Visual THINKING

Exercise 28 checks that you can apply ideas about percents and probability.

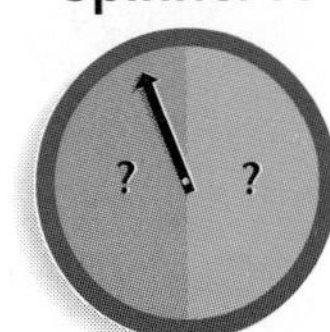

Spiral Review

29. The figures are similar. Name all the pairs of corresponding angles and corresponding sides. **(Module 6, p. 430)**

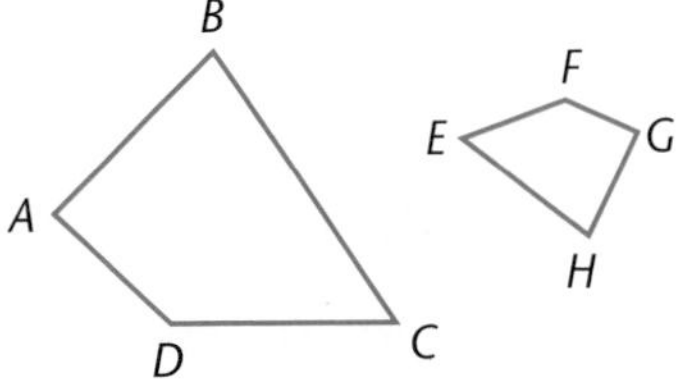

For Exercises 30 and 31, choose the form of the quotient that best answers each question. **(Module 4, p. 300)**

30. How many 4-inch bows can be made from a 35-inch piece of ribbon?

31. The bill for four people came to $35.00. What is each person's share of the bill?

A. 8.75

B. 8

C. 9

D. $8\frac{3}{4}$

32. a. Choose variables for length, width, area, and perimeter. Write rules in the form of equations for finding the area and the perimeter of a rectangle. **(Module 4, p. 288)**

b. Use your equations from part (a) to find the area and the perimeter of a rectangle with length 9.5 m and width 3 m.

Section 6 Extra Skill Practice

Use a fraction in lowest terms to find each value.

1. 25% of 72
2. 80% of 80
3. 10% of 91
4. 90% of 170
5. 5% of 60
6. 75% of 104

Estimate a percent for each fraction.

7. $\frac{19}{61}$
8. $\frac{16}{65}$
9. $\frac{3}{14}$
10. $\frac{5}{49}$

Use a "nice" fraction to estimate each value.

11. 34% of 120
12. 79% of 25
13. 48% of 90

14. Suppose you spin the spinner at the right twice.
   a. Draw a tree diagram to show the possible outcomes.
   b. What is the probability of spinning 2 twice?
   c. What is the probability of spinning two even numbers?
   d. What is the probability of spinning a 1 and a 4?

Standardized Testing ▶ Multiple Choice

1. Which is the best estimate of 67% of 60?
   (A) 42 (B) 40 (C) 36 (D) 45

2. On which item do you save the most money?
   (A) original price: $25
discount: 40% off
   (B) original price: $36
discount: 25% off
   (C) original price: $40
discount: 30% off
   (D) original price: $22
discount 50%

3. Estimate the percent of the original price that you save on each item. For which one is the percent you save greatest?
   (A) original price: $40
discount: save $10.20
   (B) original price: $19.99
discount: save $1.89
   (C) original price: $50
discount: save $9
   (D) original price: $58.99
discount: save $20

Mystery Tracks

Using Your Data In this module you collected data for your "tracks" and those of your classmates. Then you found ways to use the measurements to make predictions. To complete the module project, you'll use what you have learned to try to discover who may have made the mystery tracks below.

STATS

MYSTERY PERSON 1
Height: 5′1″

MYSTERY PERSON 2
Height: 6′8″

MYSTERY PERSON 3
Height: 5′6″

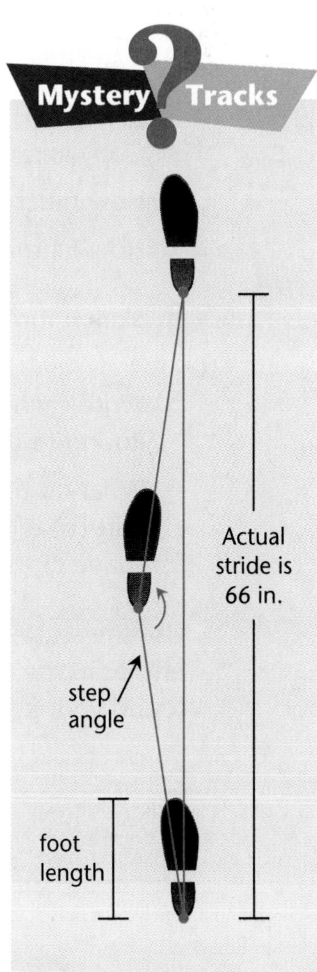

10 Use the scale drawing of the mystery tracks to predict how tall the mystery person is.

11 Do you think the person was walking or running when making the tracks?

12 Who do you think this person may be?

13 Write a report that explains how you made all your predictions. Include your results from Module Project Questions 1–9 to support your prediction methods.

MODULE 6 Review and Assessment

You will need: • *protractor* (Ex. 15)

Write each ratio in three ways. (Sec. 1, Explor. 1)

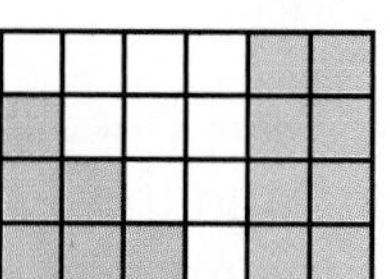

1. the ratio of red squares to blue squares
2. the ratio of blue squares to white squares

Tell whether or not the ratios are equivalent. (Sec. 1, Explor.1)

3. $\frac{2}{5}$ and $\frac{10}{15}$
4. 5 : 8 and 15 : 24
5. $\frac{3.3}{2.2}$ and $\frac{12}{8}$
6. At Super Sub, sub sandwiches are sold by the foot and you are charged the same amount for each foot. Suppose a 3-foot-long sub costs $18.00. (Sec. 2, Explor. 1)

Length (feet)	1	2	3	4
Cost (dollars)	?	?	18	?

   a. Copy and complete the table.

   b. How much does a 5-foot-long sub cost?

   c. How long is a $90.00 sub?

7. a. Sketch three rectangles that have *height to length* ratios of 4 : 7, 1 : 4, and 5 : 6. (Sec. 3, Explor. 1)

   b. Write each *height to length* ratio from part (a) as a decimal. Round to the nearest hundredth.

   c. What do the decimals you wrote for part (b) tell you about the general shape of the rectangles?

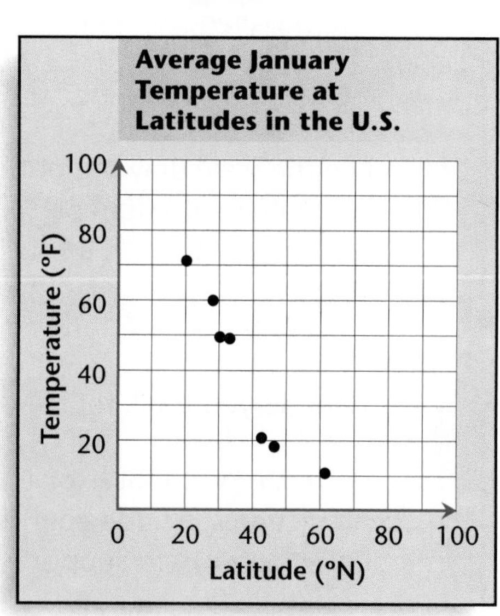

8. Use the scatter plot to estimate the missing entries in the table. Explain how you found your estimates. (Sec. 3, Explor. 3)

Latitude (°N)	25	?	44	57
Temperature (°F)	?	37	?	?

Find the missing term in each proportion. (Sec. 4, Explor. 1)

9. $\frac{4}{6} = \frac{10}{x}$

10. $\frac{3}{2.5} = \frac{y}{5}$

11. $21 : 3 = z : 18$

If appropriate, use a proportion to solve Exercises 12–13. If it is not appropriate, explain why not. (Sec. 4, Explor. 2)

12. A model of an airplane has a wingspan of 75 cm and a length of 82.5 cm. The actual airplane is 55 m long. What is its wingspan?

13. Suppose a car's gas mileage is 30 mi/gal at a speed of 30 mi/h. At what speed will the car get 60 mi/gal?

14. The triangles are similar. Use a proportion to find the missing length. (Sec. 5, Explor. 1)

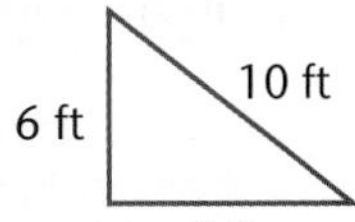

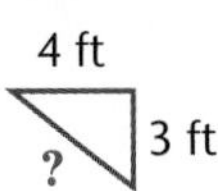

15. Use a protractor to draw an angle with each measure. (Sec. 5, Explor. 3)

a. 85°
b. 133°
c. 170°
d. 25°

For Exercises 16–18, find each value. (Sec. 6, Explor. 1)

16. 25% of 84

17. 50% of 130

18. 10% of 245

19. Raphael answered 45 of the 51 questions on the math test correctly. Use a "nice" fraction to estimate what percent he answered correctly. (Sec. 6, Explor. 1)

20. Vinh and Scott are going to play *Dueling Spinners*. The one who spins the higher number wins. (Sec. 6, Explor. 2)

Vinh's Spinner

Scott's Spinner

a. Make a tree diagram showing the possible outcomes.

b. Find the probability that Vinh beats Scott.

c. What percent of the time do you expect Scott to win?

Reflecting on the Module

21. **Open-ended** Give at least one example of how ratios, proportions, or tree diagrams help people make comparisons and predictions.

MODULE 7

WONDERS of the WORLD

Create a World Travel Poster

What places would you visit on a trip around the world? You'll create a poster that features some of the world's biggest tourist attractions. Using measurements and geometry ideas, you'll describe what makes each a "wonder of the world."

More on the Module Project

See pp. 477, 485, 519, and 521.

MATHEMATICS & The Theme

SECTION OVERVIEW

1 Area

As you explore the Taj Mahal:

- Use and convert customary units of area
- Find areas of parallelograms
- Find areas of triangles
- Find a missing dimension

2 Space Figures

As you study the Empire State Building:

- Recognize and name prisms
- Find volumes of prisms
- Use nets for space figures

3 The Great Pyramid

As you explore the Great Pyramid:

- Use and convert customary units of weight

4 Circles and Circumference

As you explore the Circus Maximus:

- Identify parts of a circle
- Find circumference

5 Circles and Cylinders

As you learn about Mesa Verde:

- Find areas of circles
- Find volumes of cylinders

6 Temperature, Integers, and Coordinate Graphs

As you learn about Marco Polo:

- Measure temperature in °F and °C
- Compare integers
- Graph ordered pairs of integers

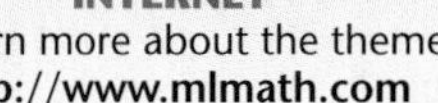

INTERNET
To learn more about the theme:
http://www.mlmath.com

Section 1 Area

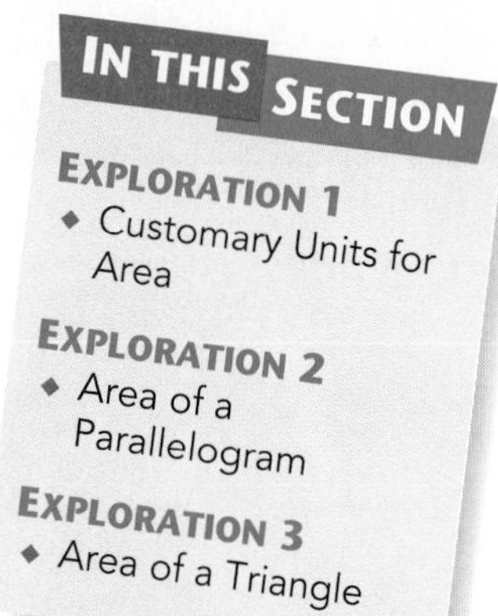

The Taj Mahal

Setting the Stage

The Taj Mahal, a gigantic domed structure, is the most visited attraction in India. In the 17th century the Emperor Shah Jahan built the Taj Mahal to honor the memory of his beloved wife Mumtaz Mahal. Its design is based on the number four and its multiples.

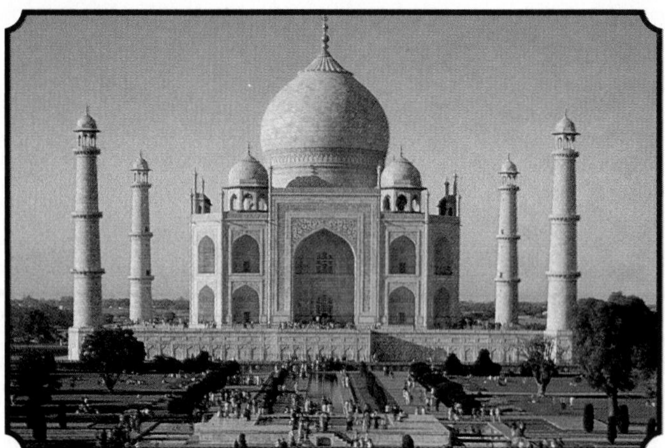

Think About It

1 The garden at the Taj Mahal was laid out in four congruent squares. Each square was divided into four flower beds, with 400 flowers in each bed. How many flowers were in the garden?

2 The central chamber of the Taj Mahal was built in the shape of an octagon. How is an octagon related to the number 4?

3 Suppose some people plan to travel to your state or town. What places do you recommend they visit? Why?

▶ **The modern Wonders of the World include structures like the Taj Mahal, the Empire State Building, and the Great Pyramid at Giza. In this module, you'll investigate the mathematics related to these and other famous Wonders of the World.**

Exploration 1

Customary U·N·I·T·S for AREA

GOAL

LEARN HOW TO...
- measure area using customary units
- convert between customary units of area

AS YOU...
- explore the size of the Taj Mahal

KEY TERMS
- square inch ($in.^2$)
- square foot (ft^2)
- square yard (yd^2)

SET UP *Work with a partner. You will need: • ruler • yard stick or measuring tape • newspaper or other large paper • scissors*

▶ **In Module 4, you learned that area is the number of square units that cover a surface. The area of the floor of the main building of the Taj Mahal is 34,596 ft^2. To find out whether the size of this floor makes the Taj Mahal "gigantic," you'll explore area.**

4 Draw two squares, one with sides 1 in. long and the other with sides 1 ft long. Cut out your squares. The area of the small square is **1 square inch (1 $in.^2$)**. The area of the large square is 1 ft x 1 ft, or **1 square foot (1 ft^2)**.

1 in.

1 in.

The area of the square is 1 in. x 1 in. = 1 $in.^2$

5 **a.** Use your model of a square foot to measure the area of the top of your desk.

b. Do you think that using your squares is a good way to find area? Explain.

6 **Discussion** The area of a rectangle is equal to its length times its width. How can you use this relationship to estimate area? to find actual area?

7 Copy the table. For each item, choose an appropriate unit of measure for its area. Next, estimate the area and then calculate the area.

Item	Unit ($in.^2$ or ft^2)	Estimated area	Actual area
this page	?	?	?
top of your desk	?	?	?
chalkboard	?	?	?

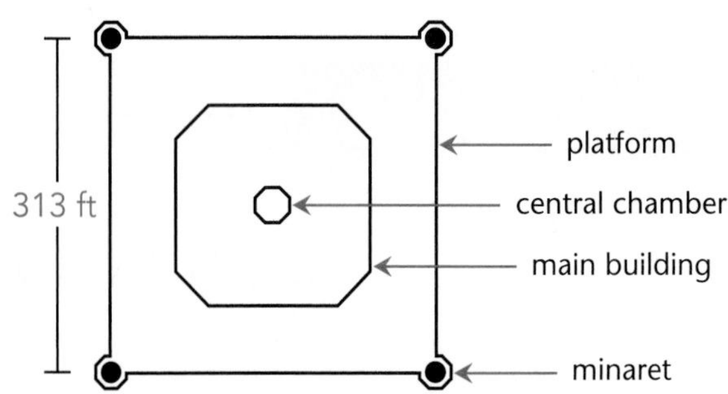

8 **a.** The Taj Mahal stands on a square platform which is 313 ft on each side. What is the area of this square in square feet?

b. What is the area of the part of the platform that is not covered by the main building? (The floor area of the main building is 34,596 ft^2.)

9 **a.** **Estimation** Estimate the area of your classroom in square feet. Explain your method.

b. Check your estimate by measuring the length and the width and finding the area.

c. About how many of your classroom areas does it take to cover the area of the main building of the Taj Mahal?

d. Would you describe the Taj Mahal as "gigantic"? Explain.

▶ **Converting Units of Area** **To express the area covered by a large building like the Taj Mahal, you may want to convert square feet to a larger unit.**

10 **Try This as a Class** Use your model of a square foot.

a. How many square feet form **1 square yard (1 yd^2)**? Make a sketch showing how to arrange square feet to form a square yard.

b. How can you convert an area measurement given in square feet to square yards?

11 Use your models of a square inch and a square foot.

a. How many square inches form one square foot?

b. How can you convert an area measurement given in square inches to square feet?

✓ QUESTION 12

...checks that you can convert between customary units of area.

12 **✓ CHECKPOINT** The floor of the main building of the Taj Mahal has an area of 34,596 ft^2. What is its area in square yards?

HOMEWORK EXERCISES **See Exs. 1–7 on p. 462.**

Exploration 2

Area of a Parallelogram

GOAL

LEARN HOW TO...
- find the area of a parallelogram

AS YOU...
- investigate geometric shapes in the tilework of the Taj Mahal

KEY TERMS
- intersect
- perpendicular
- height (of a parallelogram)
- base (of a parallelogram)

SET UP *You will need:* • *Labsheet 1A* • *scissors* • *metric ruler* • *centimeter graph paper*

Thirty-seven specialists including artists, stone cutters, engineers, architects, calligraphers, and inlayers designed the Taj Mahal and supervised the 20,000 workers who built it.

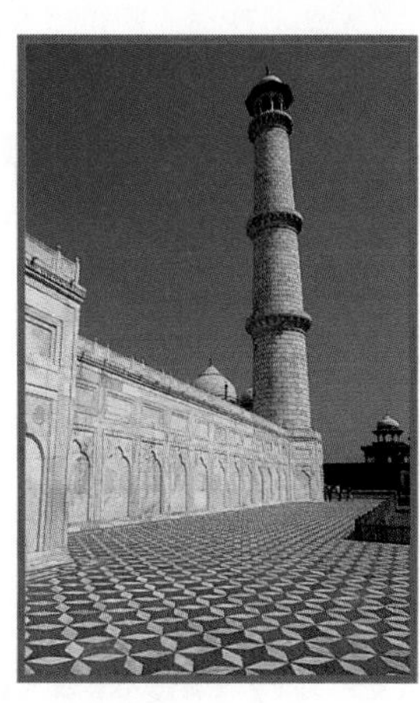

This section of flooring from a terrace at the Taj Mahal is inlaid with white marble and red sandstone tiles.

13 What geometric shapes do you see in the pattern in the floor?

▶ **The design and construction of the terrace must have involved measuring lengths and finding areas. You can use centimeter graph paper to investigate the dimensions and areas of geometric shapes.**

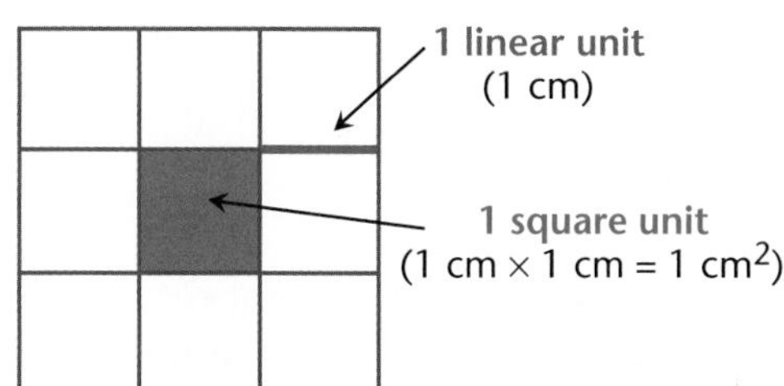

14 How are linear units and square units different?

15 **Discussion** Chen drew this parallelogram on graph paper. He says that it has an area of 3 cm^2. Is he correct? Explain.

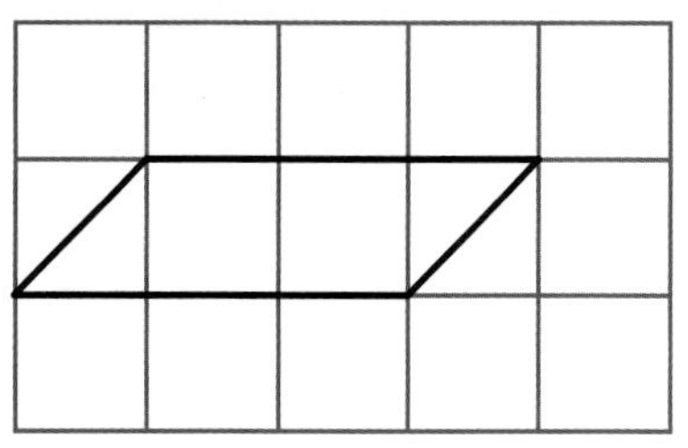

16 On graph paper, draw a different parallelogram that is not a rectangle. Estimate the area of the parallelogram.

FOR◂HELP with *parallelograms*, see **MODULE 2, p. 87**

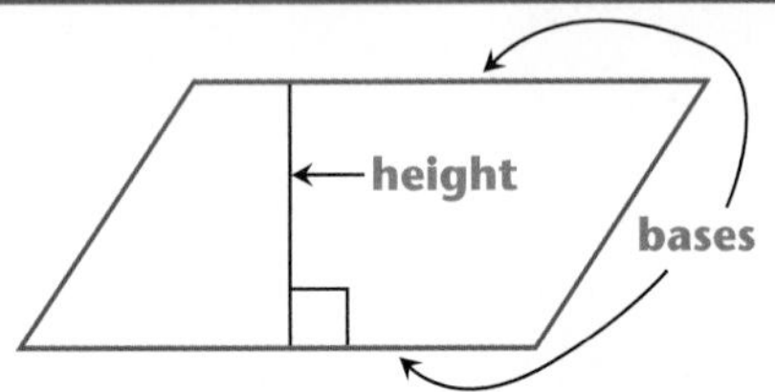

17 **a.** Lines or segments that meet at a point **intersect**. If they meet at a right angle they are also **perpendicular**. Inside the parallelogram you drew in Question 16, draw a segment that is perpendicular to a pair of parallel sides.

b. The length of the segment you drew in part (a) is called the **height** of the parallelogram. The sides that are perpendicular to the height are the **bases** of the parallelogram. Find the height and the length of a base of your parallelogram.

c. Cut out your parallelogram. Then cut it into two pieces along the segment you drew.

d. Form a rectangle using the two pieces of your parallelogram. Record the length, width, and area of this rectangle.

e. How do the length and the width of your rectangle compare with the length of a base and the height of your original parallelogram?

f. What is the area of your parallelogram? Explain.

18 **Try This as a Class** Use your results from Question 17.

a. How do the areas of the parallelograms and the rectangles constructed in Question 17 compare?

b. Use the length of the base and the height to write a formula for finding the area of a parallelogram.

c. What are two different formulas that can be used to find the area of a rectangle?

19 Draw two parallelograms that are not rectangles on graph paper, one with an area of 12 cm^2 and the other with an area of 18 cm^2. What is the length of a base and the height of each parallelogram you drew?

✓ QUESTION 20

...checks that you can find the area of a parallelogram.

20 **✓ CHECKPOINT** **Use Labsheet 1A.** You will find the areas of *Parallelograms A–D.*

21 Suppose each parallelogram-shaped marble tile in the photo on page 457 has a base length of 8 in. and a height of 4 in. What is the area of each parallelogram-shaped tile?

HOMEWORK EXERCISES See Exs. 8–15 on pp. 462–463.

Exploration 3

Area of a TRIANGLE

GOAL

LEARN HOW TO...
- find the area of a triangle
- find a missing dimension

AS YOU...
- explore geometric designs found in wall panels at the Taj Mahal

KEY TERMS
- base (of a triangle)
- height (of a triangle)

SET UP *Work with a partner. You will need: • Labsheet 1B • scissors • colored pencil • metric ruler*

▶ **Some of the shapes on this wall of the Taj Mahal can be broken into a rectangle and a triangle. You can use what you know about the area of parallelograms to help find the area of triangles.**

Any side of a triangle can be the base. The diagrams show the length of the base (*b*) and the height (*h*) of several triangles.

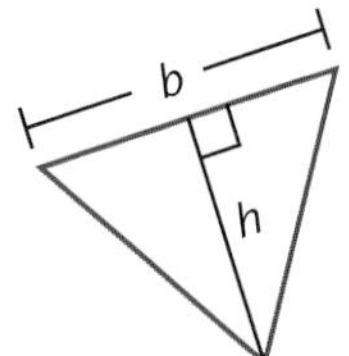

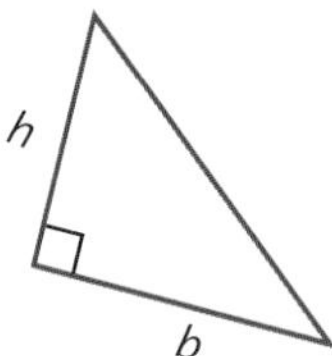

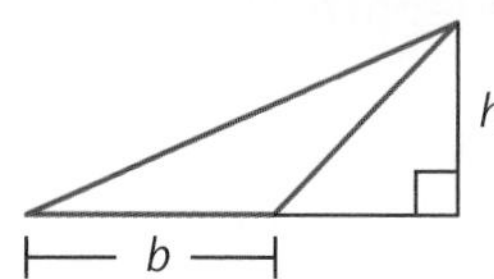

h represents the height.

b represents the length of the base.

22 How is the segment that shows the height of a triangle related to the base?

23 **a.** Draw a triangle. Start at any vertex and draw a segment perpendicular to the opposite side. Color the base. Measure the length of the base and the height to the nearest tenth of a centimeter.

b. Cut out your triangle from part (a). Trace around the triangle to make another one that is congruent to it. Cut out the second triangle. Arrange the triangles to form a parallelogram that has the colored side of the first triangle as a base.

c. Find the length of a base and the height of this parallelogram to the nearest tenth of a centimeter. Then find the area.

d. How is the area of one of the triangles related to the area of the parallelogram? What is the area of one triangle?

e. How are the length of the base and the height of the parallelogram you formed related to the length of the base and the height of your original triangle?

24 **Try This as a Class** Use your results from Question 23 to write a formula for finding the area (A) of a triangle.

25 Apply your formula to find the area of your original triangle using each of the other two sides as the bases. Measure to the nearest tenth of a centimeter.

✓ QUESTION 26

...checks that you can find the area of a triangle.

26 **✓ CHECKPOINT** **Use Labsheet 1B.** You will find the areas of *Triangles A–D.*

27 **Discussion** Suppose you know that the area of a parallelogram is 28 cm^2 and that the height is 4 cm. Explain how you can find the length of the base.

$b = ?$

4 cm

▶ **Finding Unknown Values** **When you want to find a missing dimension, you can use an equation to organize your thinking. Finding the unknown value is called solving the equation.**

EXAMPLE

Find the length of the base of the triangle.

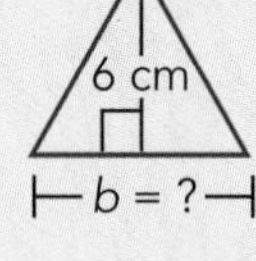

$A = 42\ cm^2$

SAMPLE RESPONSE

$A = \frac{1}{2} \cdot b \cdot h$	Use the formula for area.
$\mathbf{42} = \frac{1}{2} \cdot b \cdot \mathbf{6}$	Substitute the values you know.
$42 = \mathbf{3} \cdot b$	$\frac{1}{2} \cdot 6$ equals 3.
$42 \div \mathbf{3} = b$	To find the missing factor, you can divide.
$14 = b$	

The length of the base is 14 cm.

FOR ▶ HELP
with *number fact families*, see
TOOLBOX, p. 597

28 **Try This as a Class** The perimeter of a triangle is 120 mm.

a. Side 1 is 30 mm long and Side 2 is 42 mm long. Write an addition equation you can use to find the length of Side 3.

b. How can you use subtraction to solve your equation?

✓ QUESTION 29

...checks that you can use an equation to find a missing dimension.

29 **✓ CHECKPOINT** A parallelogram has a base 4 cm long and an area of 20.4 cm^2. Write and solve an equation to find the height.

HOMEWORK EXERCISES ▶ **See Exs. 16–27 on p. 463–464.**

Section 1 Key Concepts

Units of Area (pp. 455–456)

Area (A) is measured in square units.

You can use the relationships between units in the customary system to convert between square inches, square feet, and square yards.

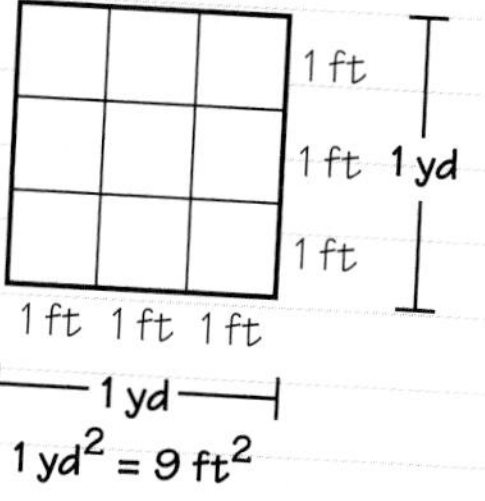

Formulas for Area

Parallelograms (pp. 457–458)

Example

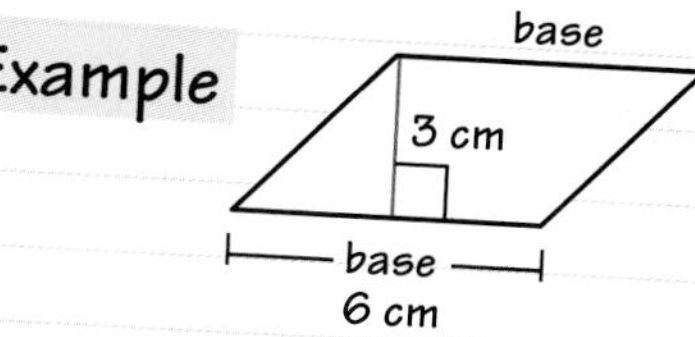

Height is measured on a segment perpendicular to the bases.

Area = length of base • height

$A = b \cdot h = 6 \cdot 3$

The area is 18 cm^2.

Triangles (pp. 459–460)

Example

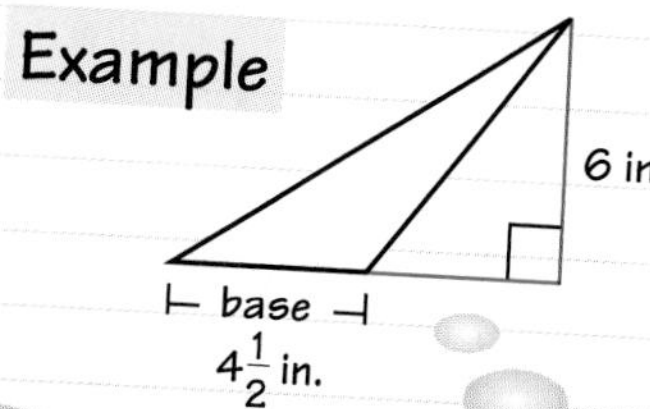

You may have to **extend the base.**

Area = $\frac{1}{2}$ • length of base • height

$A = \frac{1}{2} \cdot b \cdot h = \frac{1}{2} \cdot 4\frac{1}{2} \cdot 6$

The area is $13\frac{1}{2}$ in.^{2}

Finding Unknown Values (p. 460)

You can write and solve an equation to find a missing dimension or other unknown value.

Key Terms

square inch (in.^{2})

square foot (ft^2)

square yard (yd^2)

intersect

perpendicular

base

height

Key Concepts Questions

30 Find the area of the entire figure in square yards.

Figure *CGFE* is a parallelogram.
Figure *CDE* is a triangle.

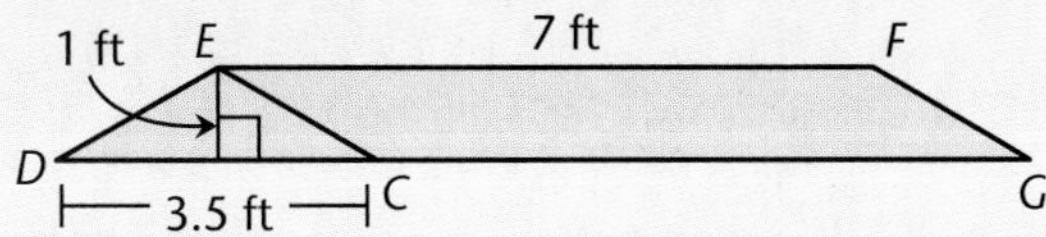

31 Find the unknown value in the equation $x + 7 = 45$.

YOU WILL NEED

For Ex. 13:
- metric ruler
- Labsheet 1A

For Ex. 15:
- centimeter graph paper
- metric ruler

For Ex. 16:
- metric ruler
- Labsheet 1B

For Ex. 26:
- graph paper

For Ex. 34:
- centimeter graph paper
- tracing paper

Section 1 Practice & Application Exercises

Estimation Estimate the area of each object in customary units and explain your method. Then measure the length and width and use the area formula to check your estimates. How did you do?

1. seat of a chair
2. a window

Replace each ? with a number to convert the measurement to the indicated unit.

3. 81 ft^2 = __?__ yd^2
4. 36 $in.^2$ = __?__ ft^2
5. 266 yd^2 = __?__ ft^2
6. 18 ft^2 = __?__ $in.^2$
7. How many square centimeters are in a square meter? Explain.

Find the area of each parallelogram.

8. $b = 3.5$ mm, $h = 2.7$ mm
9. $b = 4$ cm, $h = 5$ cm
10. $b = 4\frac{1}{2}$ ft, $h = 3$ ft

11. The groundskeeper at a high school is in charge of mowing the soccer and football fields. How many more square yards of grass does the groundskeeper have to mow on the soccer field than on the football field?

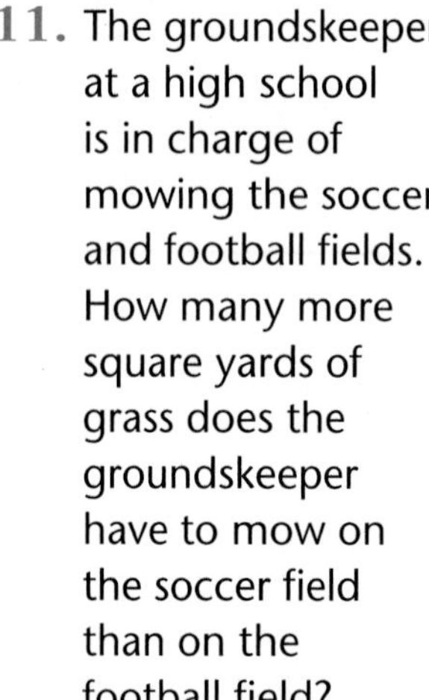

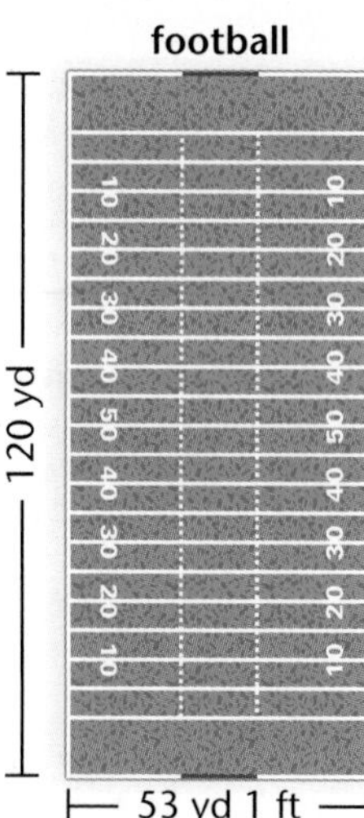

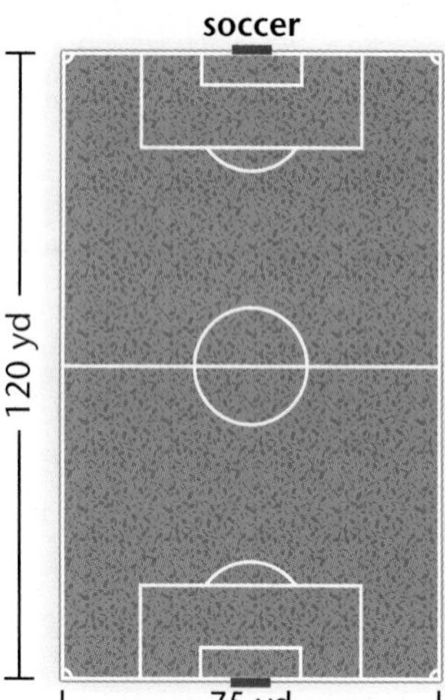

12. Shane wants to carpet his bedroom. The dimensions of his rectangular room are 12 ft × 15 ft. The carpet he has chosen costs $11.95 per square yard. How much will the carpet for Shane's room cost?

13. **Use Labsheet 1A.** Find the areas of *Parallelograms E–H.*

14. **Open-ended** Sketch two different parallelograms that each have an area of 24 cm^2 and are not rectangles. Be sure to label the length of the base and height.

15. a. Draw a parallelogram on graph paper.

b. Find the height between a pair of parallel sides. Use this measurement and the length of the corresponding base to find the area of the parallelogram.

c. Repeat part (b) using the other pair of parallel sides.

d. Are the areas in parts (b) and (c) the same? Why or why not?

16. **Use Labsheet 1B.** Find the areas of *Triangles E–H.*

Find the area of each figure.

17.

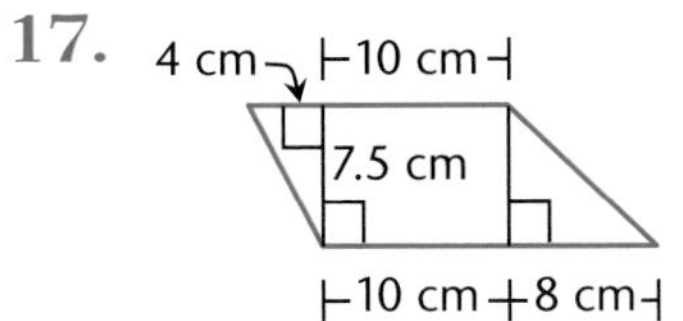

18.

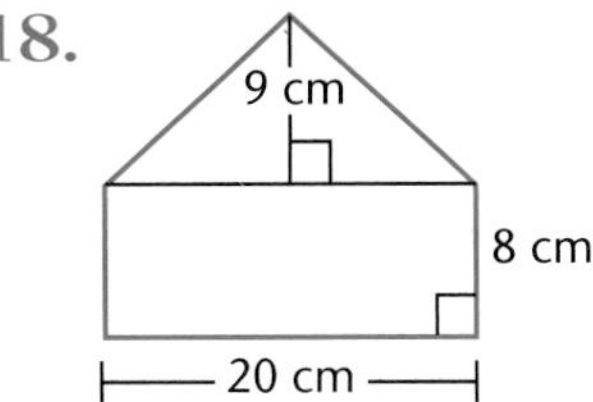

Write and solve an equation to find the missing dimension for each figure.

19.

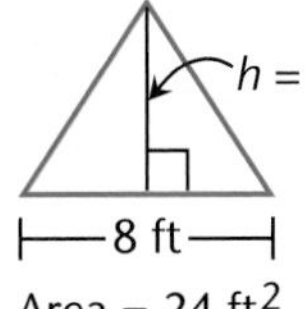

Area = 24 ft^2

20.

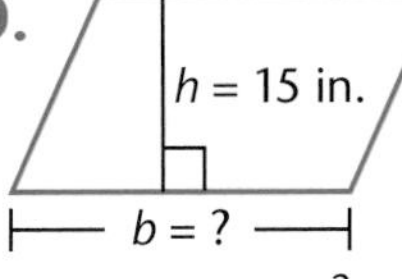

Area = 390 $in.^2$

21.

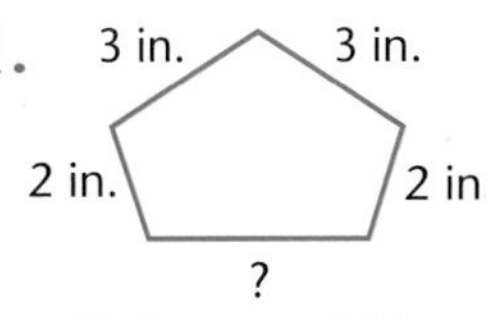

Perimeter = 14 in.

22. The multipurpose room of a school building has a rectangular floor with an area of 5828 ft^2. The length of the room is 94 ft. What is the width of the room?

Find the unknown value in each equation.

23. $19 + x = 35$

24. $5 \cdot y = 125$

25. **Create Your Own** The area of a polygon can be found by dividing it into polygons whose areas you know how to find.

a. Using one triangle, one rectangle, and one parallelogram that is not a rectangle, draw a polygon that has an area of 50 cm^2.

b. Label the base length and height of each polygon you used.

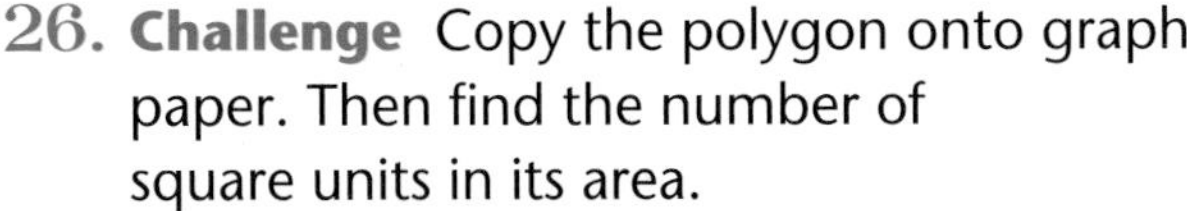

26. **Challenge** Copy the polygon onto graph paper. Then find the number of square units in its area.

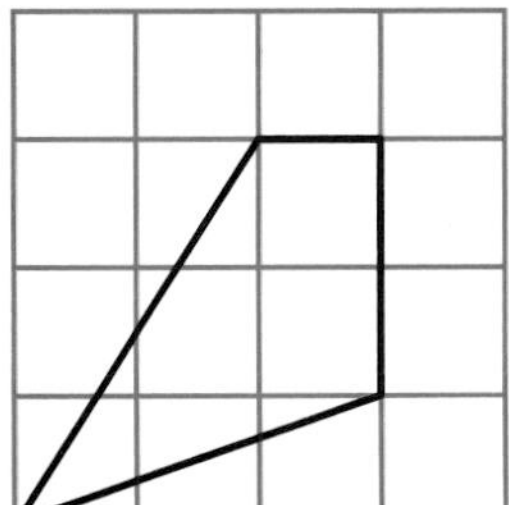

Discussion

Exercise 27 checks that you understand the relationship between the height and the base for a parallelogram and for a triangle.

Reflecting on the Section

Be prepared to discuss your response to Exercise 27 in class.

27. a. What happens if you use a segment that is not perpendicular to a base to find the height of a parallelogram or a triangle? Explain.

b. For what type of parallelogram does the height equal the length of a side? for what type of triangle? Explain.

Spiral Review

Use a fraction in lowest terms to find each value. (Module 6, p. 444)

28. 20% of 155 29. 75% of 84 30. 30% of 200

Draw an example of each polygon. (Module 2, p. 87)

31. hexagon 32. pentagon 33. trapezoid

Extension 

Area of an Irregularly Shaped Figure

You can estimate areas using grid squares.

First Trace the outline of the figure.

Next Place the tracing on a piece of centimeter graph paper.

Then Count the complete grid squares. Add on the area from the partially filled grid squares. You can use a fraction to estimate a part of a grid square or combine parts to form whole squares.

1 cm is about 200 km.

34. a. On the map, the area of Madagascar is about how many square centimeters? Explain how you made your estimate.

b. An area on the map that is 1 cm by 1 cm represents how many square kilometers? Estimate the actual area of Madagascar.

Section 1 Extra Skill Practice

Replace each ? with the number that makes the statement true.

1. $168\ ft^2 = \underline{\ ?\ }\ in.^2$
2. $5\ ft^2 = \underline{\ ?\ }\ in.^2$
3. $96\ in.^2 = \underline{\ ?\ }\ ft^2$
4. $117\ ft^2 = \underline{\ ?\ }\ yd^2$
5. $4\frac{1}{2}\ yd^2 = \underline{\ ?\ }\ ft^2$
6. $1\ yd^2 = \underline{\ ?\ }\ in.^2$

Find the area of each parallelogram.

7. $b = 38.2$ mm
   $h = 24$ mm
8. 3 ft, 12 ft
9. $b = 3\frac{1}{4}$ cm
   $h = 7$ cm

Find the area of each figure.

10.

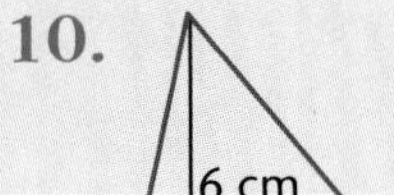

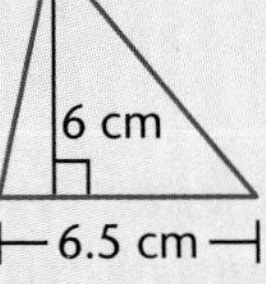

11.

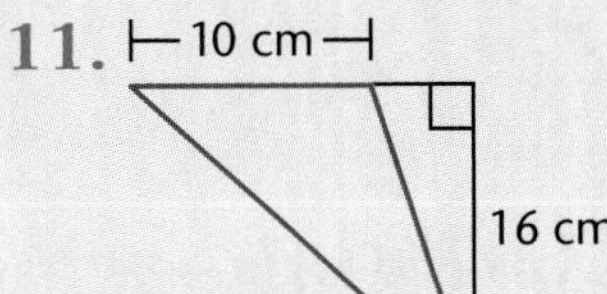

12.

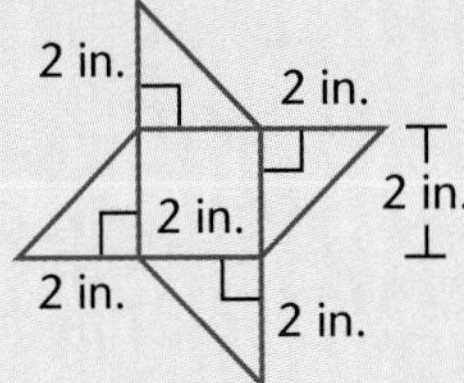

Write and solve an equation to find the missing dimension.

13. 34 in., 34 in., ?, 58 in.
    Perimeter = 148 in.

14.

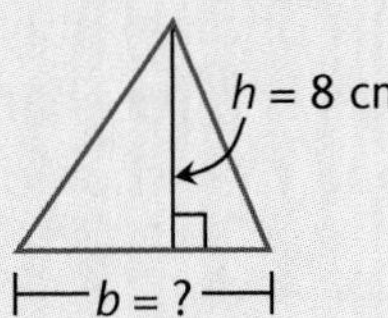

Area = 36 cm^2

15.

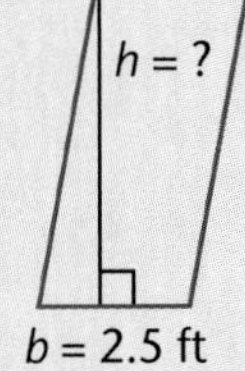

$b = 2.5$ ft
Area = 12.5 ft^2

Study Skills Graphic Organizers

Visual displays can help you relate ideas and organize information.

1. Copy and extend the concept map to connect ideas you have learned about area. Add on units of measure, formulas, and notes about relationships.

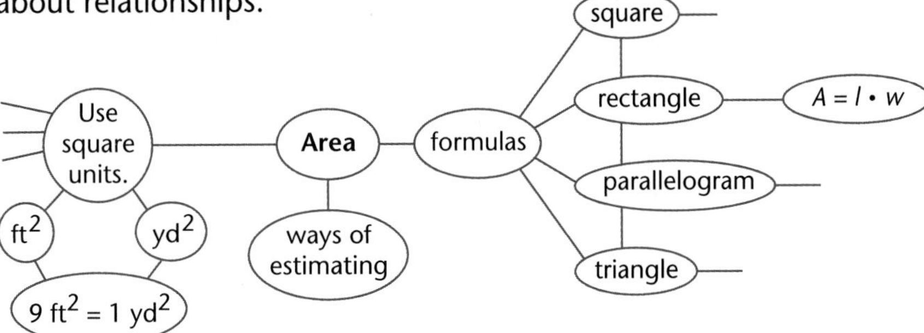

FOR ASSESSMENT AND PORTFOLIOS

ADD a Square

SET UP *You will need:* • *the Extended Exploration Labsheet* • *scissors*

The Situation

Changing the area of a figure may have a surprising effect on its perimeter. In this activity you'll explore how the perimeter changes when you add squares to a polygon made up of five squares. Begin by forming a polygon with five *1 in. by 1 in. Squares* from the labsheet. Add squares to the original polygon until the perimeter reaches 18 in. (*Note:* Added squares must share at least one complete side with another square and they should not overlap.)

The Problem

What is the least number of squares you can add to get a perimeter of 18 in.? What is the greatest number of squares you can add? Sketch the shapes that give the greatest and least areas for a polygon with a perimeter of 18 in.

Something to Think About

- Try several different polygons made with five 1 in. by 1 in. squares. You might want to try these shapes.
- Can you predict how the perimeter will change when you add a square in a certain position?
- It may be helpful to organize your work in a table which includes sketches and area and perimeter measurements.

Present Your Results

Explain what approaches you tried. Then describe your solutions. Include any tables and sketches you made. Will you get the same results if you start with *any* polygon made up of five 1 in. by 1 in. squares? Explain.

Section 2 Space Figures

IN THIS SECTION

EXPLORATION 1
- Volumes of Prisms

EXPLORATION 2
- Building with Nets

Race to the SKY

Setting the Stage

The biggest race in the 1920s and 1930s was not happening at a racetrack. In New York City, planners and builders were engaged in a frantic race to the sky. Who, everyone wondered, would build the tallest building in the world?

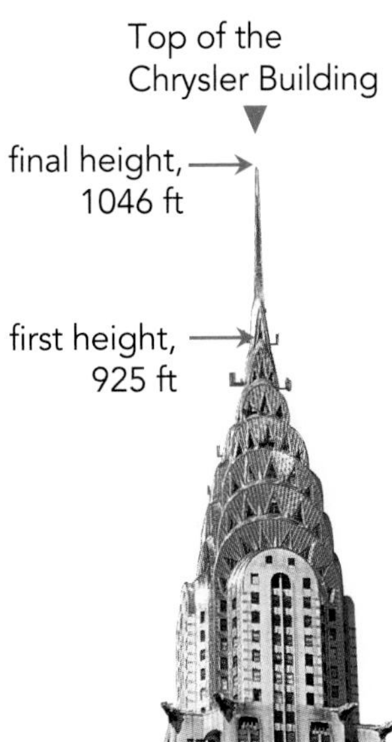

The Chrysler building seemed to be complete. Then a surprise spire "popped out" of the building's roof. The spire had been secretly assembled inside the building's fire shaft.

To compete, the Empire State Building added six stories and a 200 ft tower to its plans. With these changes, it became the world's tallest building.

Chrysler Building
Tallest Building, 1930–1931.

Empire State Building
Tallest Building, 1931–1972.

Think About It

1 The Empire State Building has 102 stories, not including the TV antenna. About how high do you think each story is?

2 In the original plan, the Empire State Building contained 36 million cubic feet of space. What do you think is meant by a cubic foot?

GOAL

LEARN HOW TO...
- recognize prisms
- find the volumes of prisms

AS YOU...
- build towers using centimeter cubes

KEY TERMS
- volume
- cubic unit
- cubic centimeter
- plane
- prism
- face
- base of a prism
- edge
- vertex (plural: vertices)

Exploration 1

Volumes of Prisms

SET UP *Work with a partner. You will need:*
- *centimeter cubes*
- *index card*

This is a centimeter cube. Its volume is 1 **cubic centimeter** (1 cm^3).

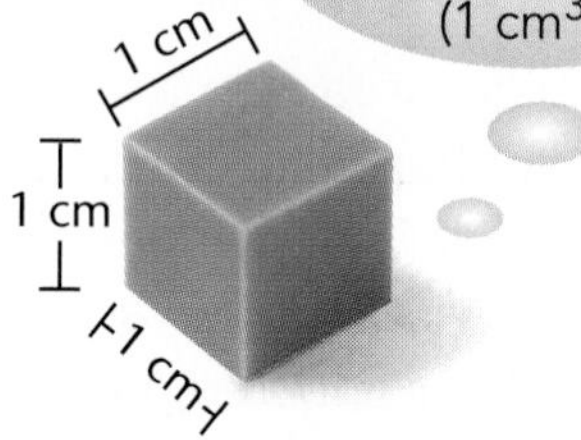

▶ **As the height of the Empire State Building increased, its *volume* also increased. The volume of an object is the amount of space it contains. Volume is measured in cubic units.**

3 On a sheet of paper, build a tower with a volume of 6 cm^3. Make the bottom, or *base*, in the shape of a rectangle, and stack identical layers of cubes above it. How many cubes did you use?

4 **a.** What is the height of your tower?

b. Trace around the base of your tower. Use your tracing, or base plan, to find the area of the base.

5 **Discussion** How are volume, area, and height different?

6 **a.** Copy the table. You will fill it in as you build towers.

Number of layers	Height (cm)	Area of base (cm^2)	Volume (cm^3)
1	?	6	?
2	?	6	?
3	?	6	?
4	?	6	?

b. Use the base plan shown. Build a tower by stacking identical layers of centimeter cubes. Each time you add a layer, fill in a row of the table.

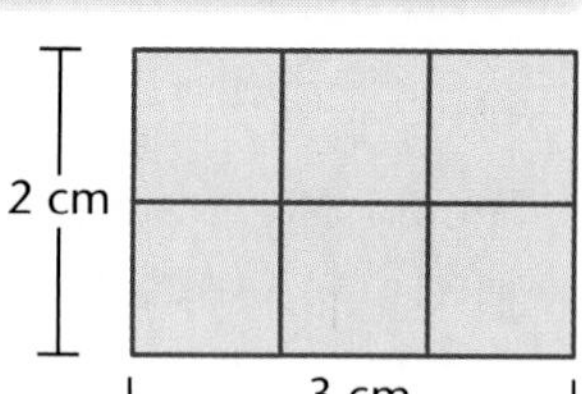

c. Use your completed table. How is the volume of your tower related to its height and the area of its base?

7 **Discussion** These towers were made from centimeter cubes. Find the volume of each tower. Explain your method.

a.  **b.**  **c.** 

▶ **Imagine stretching the top surface of one of the towers in Question 7 so that it extends forever. A flat surface that extends forever is a plane.**

8 Build a tower and place an index card on top of it. The index card models a plane. The surface your tower rests on models another plane. The two planes are parallel. What does this mean?

▶ **The towers you have built are *prisms*. A prism is a space figure made up of flat surfaces, or faces, that are shaped like polygons. Two of the faces, the bases, are congruent and lie in *parallel planes*. The other faces are parallelograms.**

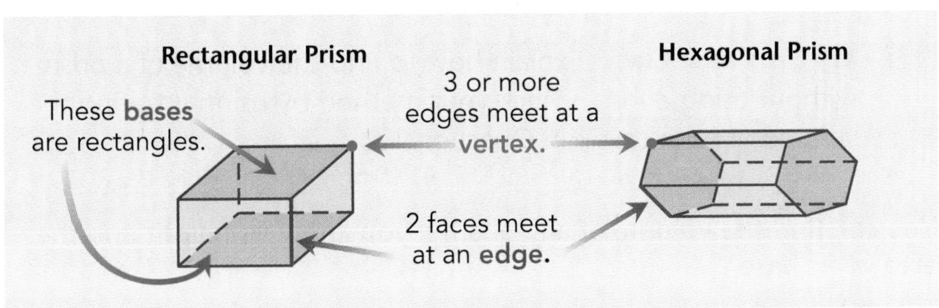

9 **a.** How many edges does the rectangular prism shown have? how many faces? how many vertices?

b. Repeat part (a) for the hexagonal prism shown.

10 **a.** Based on the prisms shown above, how do you think prisms are named?

b. What kind of prism is shown at the right?

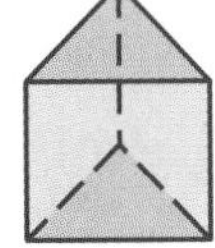

11 Is a cube a prism? If so, what type is it? Explain.

12 **Discussion** How are the prisms shown at the right different from the other prisms shown on this page?

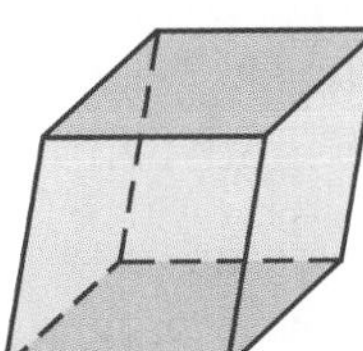

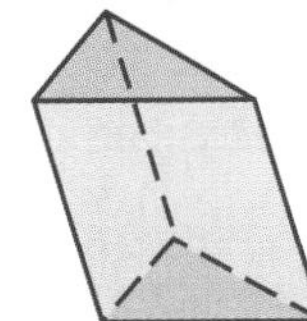

▶ **Towers that do not have rectangular bases can also be built by beginning with a base plan and stacking identical layers of centimeter cubes.**

13 **a.** For each base plan below, stack identical layers of centimeter cubes until each tower is the indicated height. Record the number of cubes you used to build each tower.

Tower 1

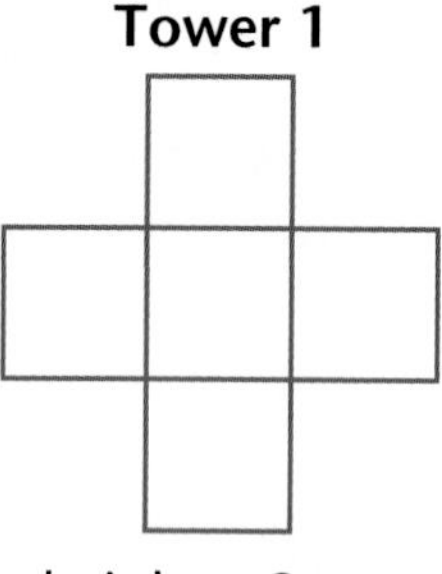

height = 3 cm

Tower 2

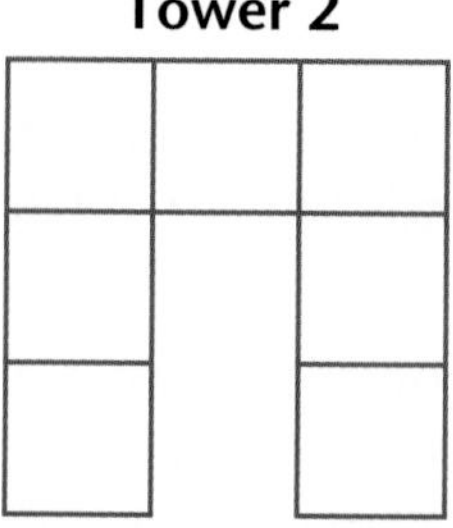

height = 2 cm

b. Towers 1 and 2 are prisms. What kind of polygon is used for the base of Tower 2? What do you call this prism?

c. The relationship you found in Question 6, part (c) for rectangular prisms is also true for these towers. Why?

14 **Try This as a Class** Explain how to find the volume of a prism without using cubes. Check your method by using it to find the volume of each tower in Question 13.

▶ **You can find the volume of any prism if you know its height and the area of its base.**

...checks that you can find the volume of a prism.

15 ✓ **CHECKPOINT** Find the volume of each prism.

a.

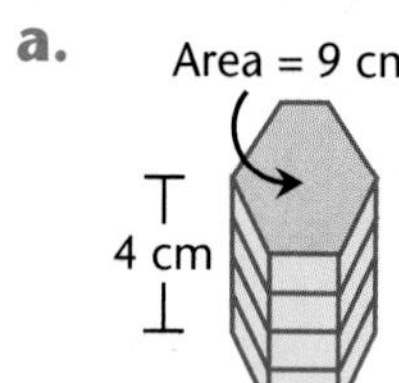

b.

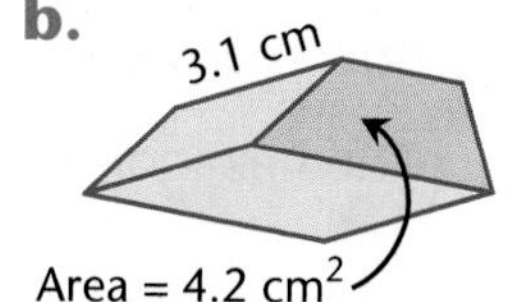

c.

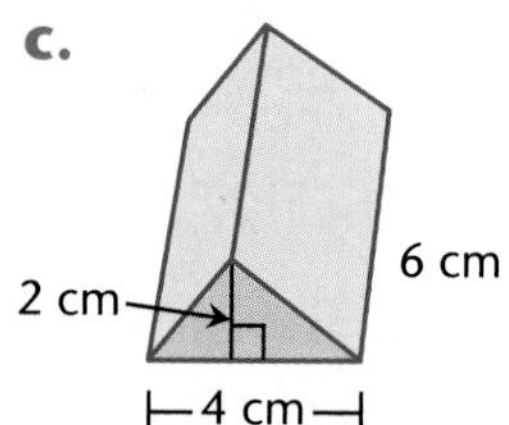

16 Although the Empire State Building is not shaped like a rectangular prism, some parts of it are. Suppose the Empire State Building can be approximated by a rectangular prism that is 1000 ft tall and has a volume of 36 million cubic feet. List three possible pairs of lengths and widths for its base plan.

HOMEWORK EXERCISES ▶ See Exs. 1–17 on pp. 474–475.

Exploration 2

SET UP *Work with a partner. You will need:* • *Labsheets 2A and 2B* • *ruler* • *tape* • *scissors* • *centimeter cubes*

GOAL

LEARN HOW TO...
- fold a flat pattern to form a space figure
- draw prisms

AS YOU...
- develop spatial visualization skills

KEY TERM
- net

▶ **Models of some space figures can be made from *nets*. A net is a flat pattern that can be cut out and folded to form a space figure. Nets can provide a useful way to model large buildings.**

17 **Use Labsheet 2A.** Use *Net 1*.

a. Predict what space figure *Net 1* will make.

b. Follow these steps to fold the net. Leave the top open.

First

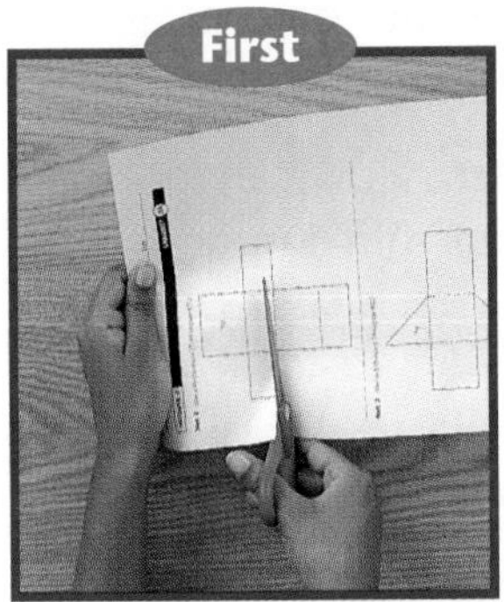

Cut on the solid lines.

Next

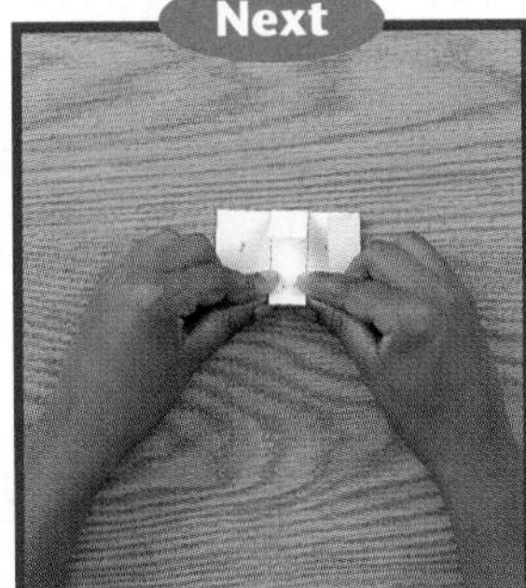

Fold on the dotted lines.

Then

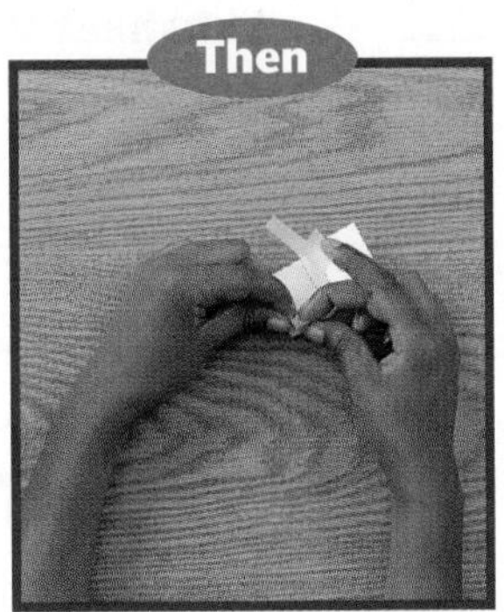

Tape the faces together.

c. Did you get the figure you expected? Explain.

18 If you can, use centimeter cubes to find the volume of the prism you made in Question 17.

19 **a.** Remove any centimeter cubes from the prism you made and tape down the top. How many faces, edges, and vertices does the prism have?

b. Describe the shapes of the faces. Which pairs of faces are congruent? Which pairs of faces could be bases for the prism?

c. How can you find the volume of the prism without using centimeter cubes? Use your method to find the volume.

20 **Use Labsheet 2A.** Repeat Questions 17–19 using *Net 2*.

▶ **Drawing Space Figures** **You may be able to understand drawings of space figures better if you learn how to draw them yourself. Here is one way to draw a prism.**

Step 1 Draw one base.

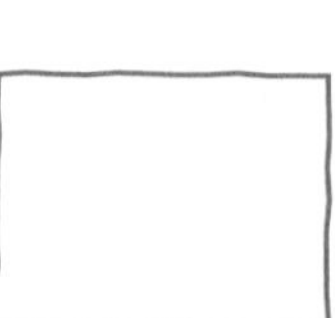

Step 2 Copy the base behind and to one side of it. The bases may overlap.

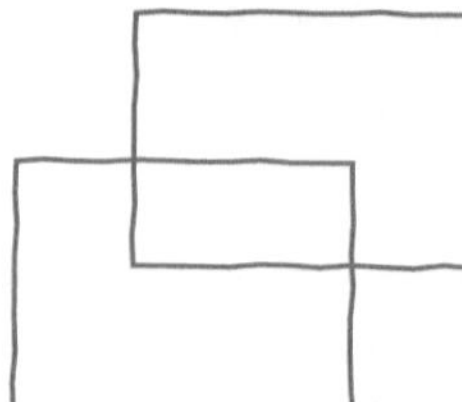

Step 3 Connect pairs of corresponding vertices. Show hidden edges with dashed segments.

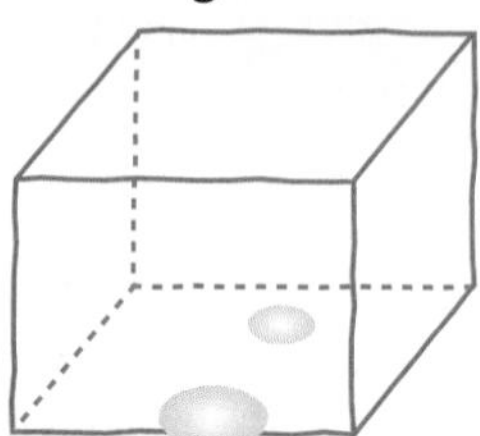

You may need to erase and redraw an edge.

21 Use the steps above to draw a triangular prism.

22 **Use Labsheet 2B.** Use *Net 3* or *Net 4*. Have your partner use the other net.

a. Predict whether each net will form a prism. How can looking at the faces help you decide? Explain your thinking.

b. You and your partner should each fold your nets to check your predictions in part (a).

c. How many faces, edges, and vertices does each figure have?

d. For each figure, describe the shapes of the faces. Are there any pairs of faces that are congruent? If so, which ones?

✓ QUESTION 23

...checks that you can use a net to visualize a space figure.

23 **✓ CHECKPOINT** Choose the letter of the space figure that can be formed with this net.

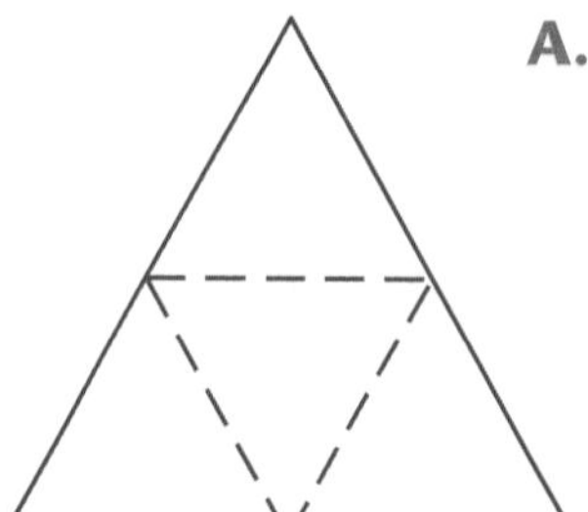

A.

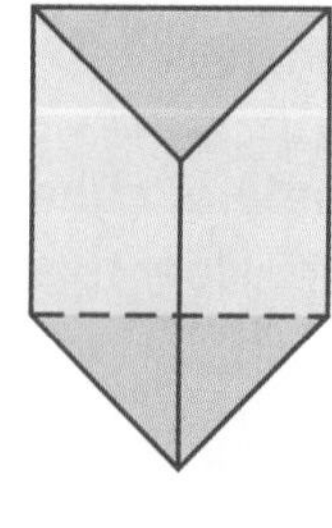

B.

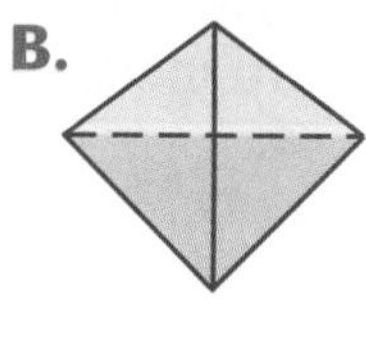

HOMEWORK EXERCISES ▶ **See Exs. 18–26 on pp. 475–476.**

Section 2
Key Concepts

Key Terms

Parts of a Space Figure (p. 469)
The flat surfaces of space figures are called faces. Pairs of faces meet in segments called edges. Edges meet in points called vertices.

face
edge
vertex

Prisms (pp. 469–470)
A prism is a space figure with two bases that:
- are shaped like polygons
- are congruent
- lie in parallel planes.

The other faces are parallelograms.

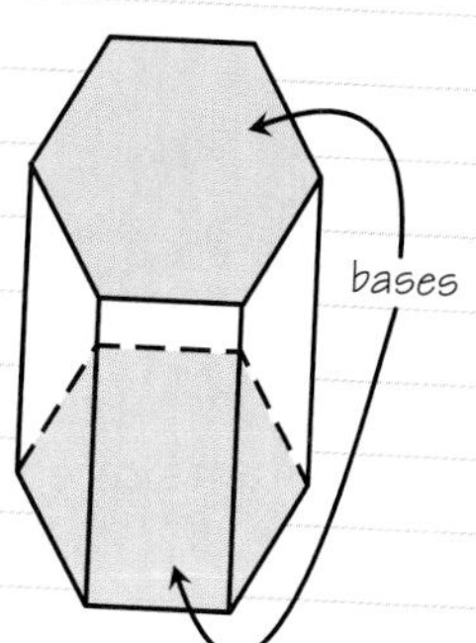

A prism is named by the shape of its bases. The prism shown is a hexagonal prism.

prism
base of a prism
plane

Volume (pp. 468–470)
The volume of a space figure is measured in cubic units such as cubic centimeters or cubic feet. To find the volume (V) of a prism, you can multiply the area of a base (B) by the height of the prism (h):

$$V = B \cdot h$$

volume
cubic unit
cubic centimeter

Drawing and Constructing Space Figures (pp. 471–472)
One way to draw a prism is to draw the bases first and then connect corresponding vertices.

A net is a flat pattern that can be cut out and folded to form a space figure.

net

Key Concepts Questions

24 **a.** Will this net form a prism? Explain.

b. Describe the shapes of the faces.

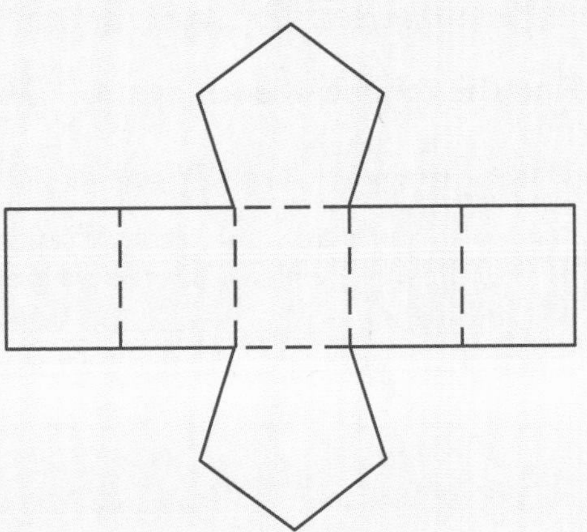

25 The area of the base of a prism is 6.25 cm^2. The height of the prism is 2.5 cm. What is the volume of the prism?

Section 2
Practice & Application Exercises

YOU WILL NEED

For Ex. 23:
- tracing paper
- scissors
- tape

For Ex. 25:
- metric ruler

Tell whether each object is shaped like a prism. If it is, name the type of prism.

1. 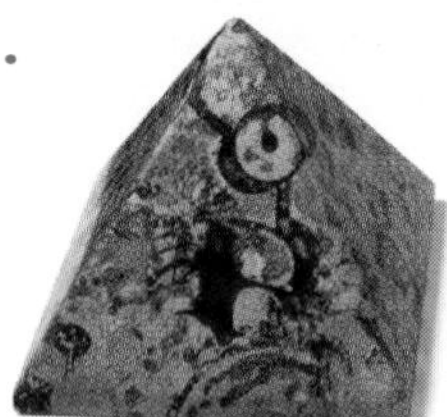

2. 

3. 

Find the volume of each tower built with centimeter cubes.

4. 

5. 

6. 

Find the volume of the prism you can build with centimeter cubes using each base plan and indicated height.

7. 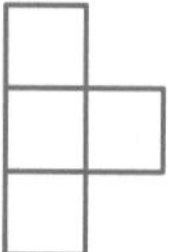

height = 4 cm

8. 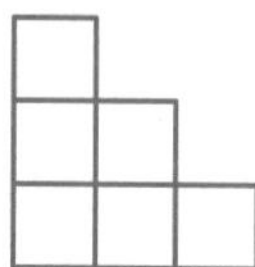

height = 5 cm

9. 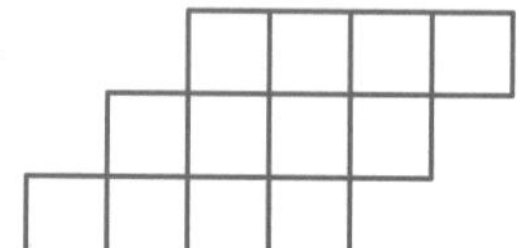

height = 8 cm

Find the volume of each prism.

10. 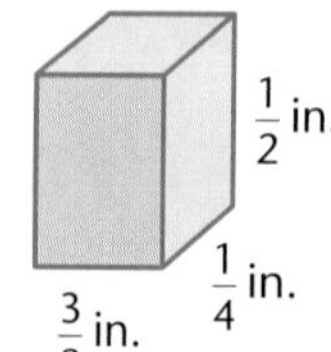

11. 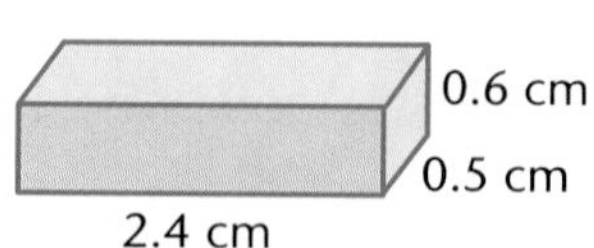

12. 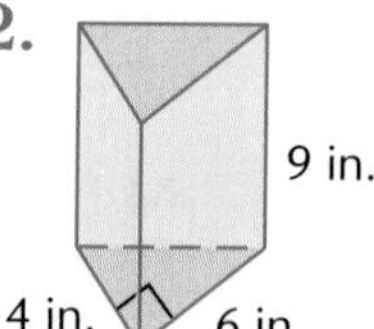

Replace each ? with the missing measurement for a prism with base area *B*, height *h*, and volume *V*.

13. $B = 40\ \text{cm}^2$
$h = 3\ \text{cm}$
$V =$?

14. $B =$?
$h = 10\ \text{cm}$
$V = 200\ \text{cm}^3$

15. $B = 18\ \text{cm}^2$
$h =$?
$V = 72\ \text{cm}^3$

16. Pet fish do better if they are kept in tanks that hold 25 gal of water or more. Since 1 gal of water takes up 231 in.^{3} of space, you can divide the number of cubic inches by 231 to find the number of gallons. Does each tank hold 25 gal or more?

17. **Visual Thinking** Use the diagram.

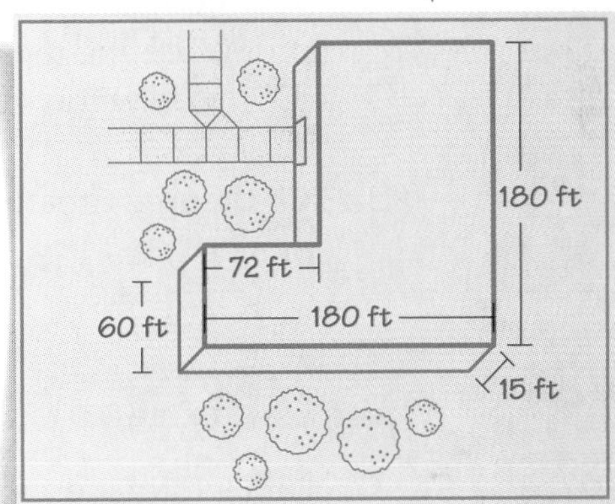

a. The shape of this building is not a rectangular prism. Why not?

b. Describe one way to separate the building into two rectangular prisms. For each prism, state the height and the length and width of a base.

c. Find the volume of the building.

Choose the letter of the space figure that can be formed with each net.

18. 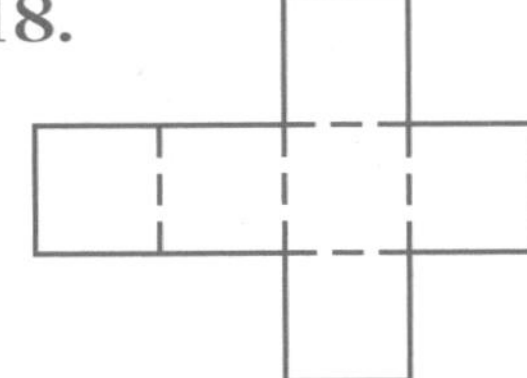

19. 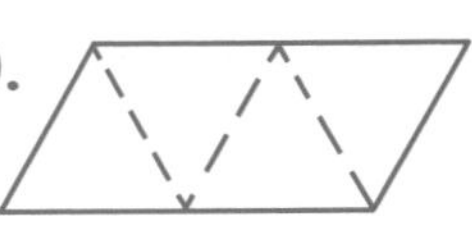

20. 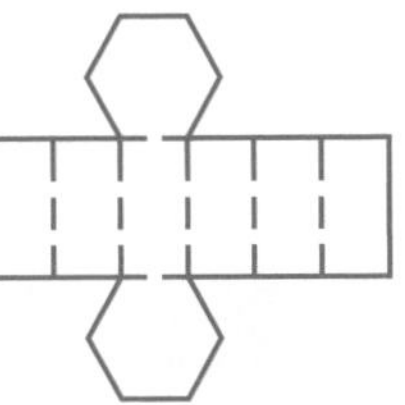

A. 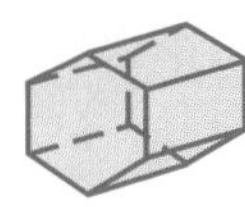

B. 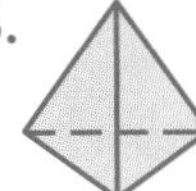

C. 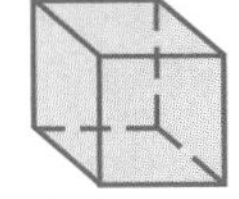

D. 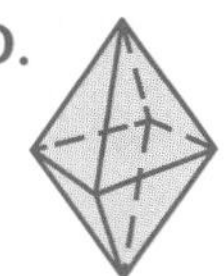

21. Name space figures A and C shown with Exercises 18–20.

22. Is space figure D shown above a prism? Why or why not?

23. a. Predict what shape this net will form. Trace the net. Then cut it out and fold it to check your prediction.

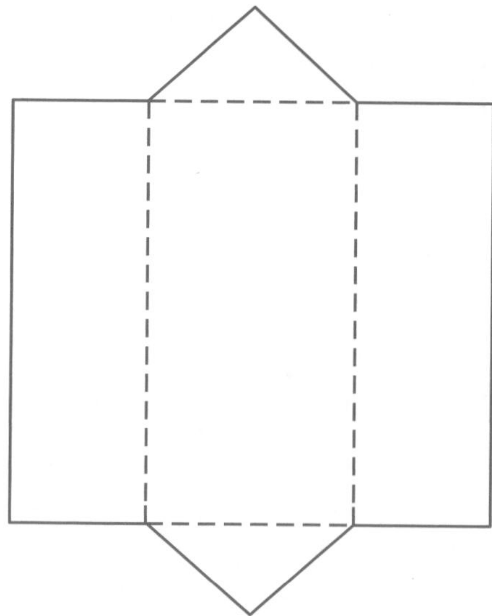

b. Name the space figure you made by folding the net.

c. How many faces, vertices, and edges does your figure have?

d. Use the method on page 472 to draw your space figure.

24. **Open-ended** Find an object in your home that is shaped like a prism. Use the method on page 472 to draw the object.

25. **Challenge** Create your own net for a prism that has a volume of 32 cm^3.

RESEARCH

Exercise 26 checks that you understand the meaning of volume.

Reflecting on the Section

26. Find information about another skyscraper, including when it was built, its height, and the area of its base. Then estimate its volume. Prepare a report on your findings. Be sure to include your sources of information and the methods you used to estimate the volume.

Spiral Review

27. Sketch and label a parallelogram that has a base of 4 cm and a height of 3.5 cm. Then find its area. (Module 7, p. 461)

28. Twelve pens cost $3.84. Use a proportion to find how much five pens cost. (Module 6, pp. 418–419)

29. a. Suppose you want to mix $1\frac{1}{4}$ qt of orange juice, $4\frac{1}{2}$ c of papaya juice, and 3 pt of pineapple juice. Can you use a 1 gal jug to mix all the juice? (Module 5, p. 358)

b. About how many servings will the mixture make? Explain.

Make a World Travel Poster

In this module you'll learn about some of the most fascinating places in the world. You'll use what you learn to create a travel poster promoting a trip around the world. To make your poster informative and eye-catching, you may include photographs, diagrams, and 3-dimensional objects as well as interesting facts.

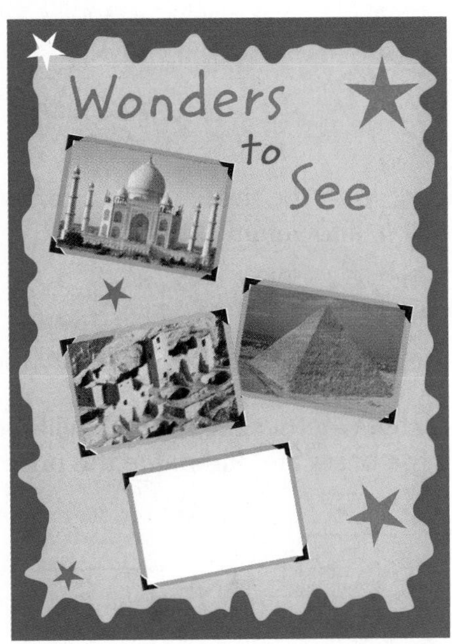

Over the next few weeks, you'll need to decide on four sites that you would like to feature on your poster and then gather information about each one. Your poster should highlight three of the wonders described in this module. The fourth site you choose should not be found in the module. As you choose your sites, think about how you would like to display each one.

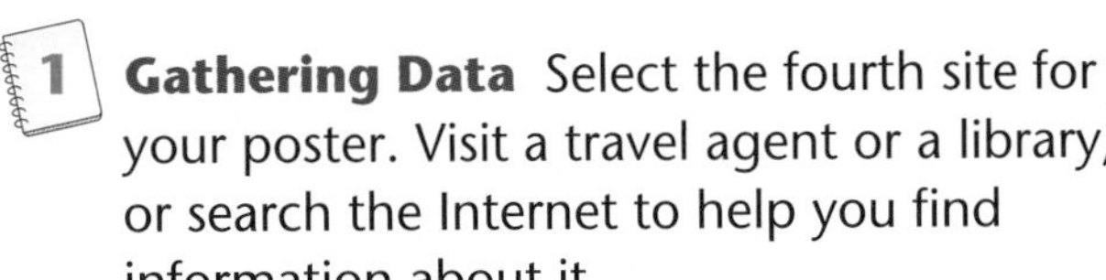

1 **Gathering Data** Select the fourth site for your poster. Visit a travel agent or a library, or search the Internet to help you find information about it.

2 **Area and Volume** The Empire State Building is world famous because it was once the world's tallest skyscraper, standing 1472 ft high. Explain why the site you chose is considered "wondrous." In particular, find out whether there is an incredible measurement that makes it world famous. If so, tell whether the measurement is related to length, area, or volume.

Section 2 Extra Skill Practice

Find the volume of each prism.

1.

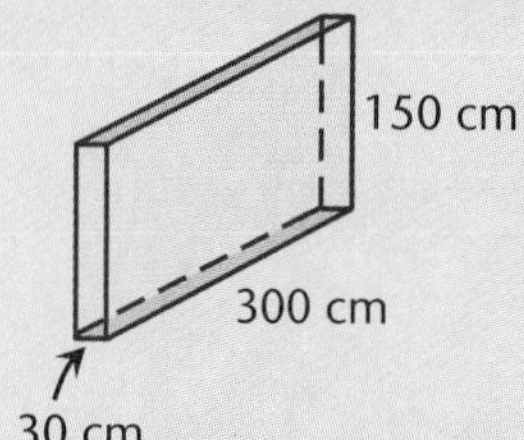

2.

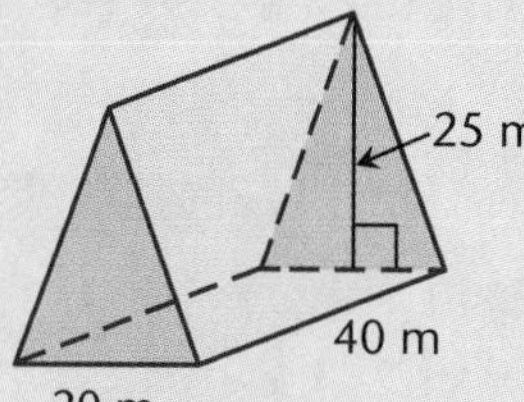

3.

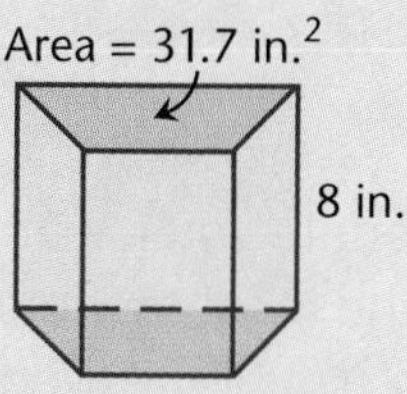

Replace each ? with the missing measurement for a prism with a base area B, height h, and volume V.

4. $B = 17\text{ yd}^2$
   $h =$?
   $V = 51\text{ yd}^3$

5. $B =$?
   $h = 28\text{ mm}$
   $V = 1400\text{ mm}^3$

6. $B = 108\text{ cm}^2$
   $h = 21\text{ cm}$
   $V =$?

For each net, tell whether the figure it will form is a prism. If it is, tell what shape the bases are and name the prism if you can.

7.

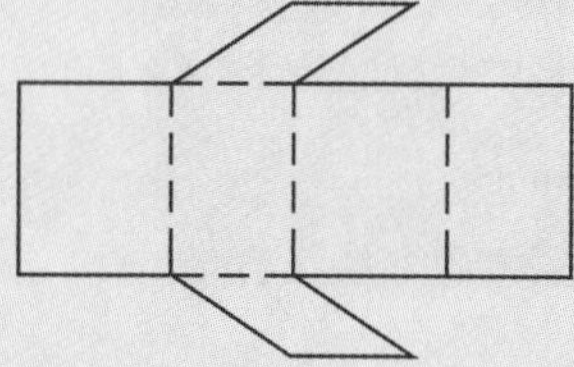

8.

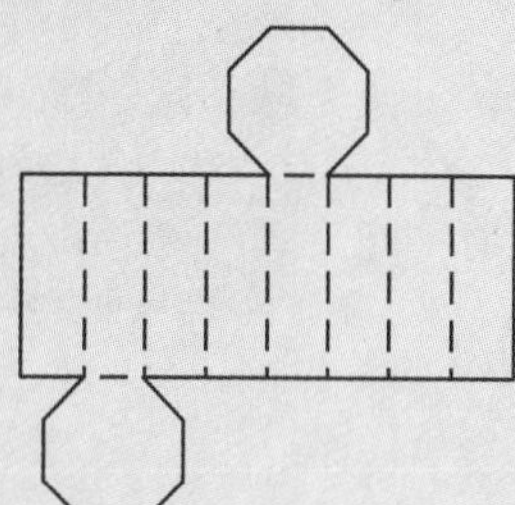

9.

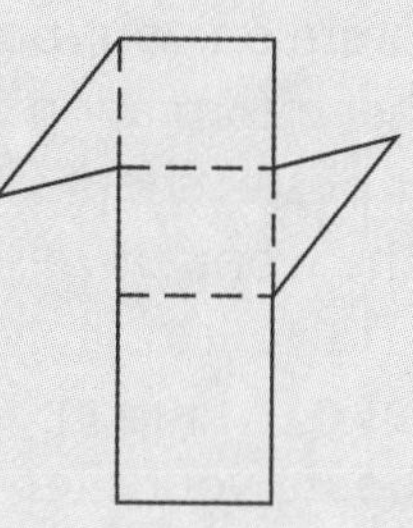

Standardized Testing ▶ Multiple Choice

Which net will form the space figure shown at the right?

A

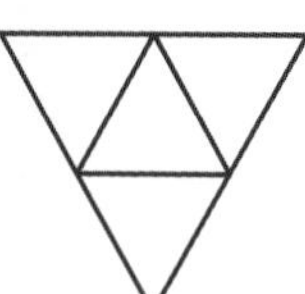

B

C

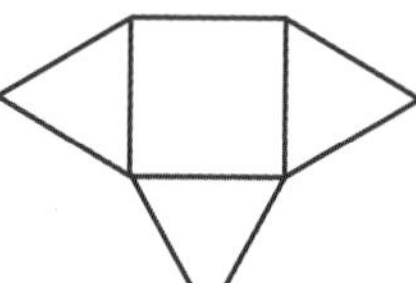

D

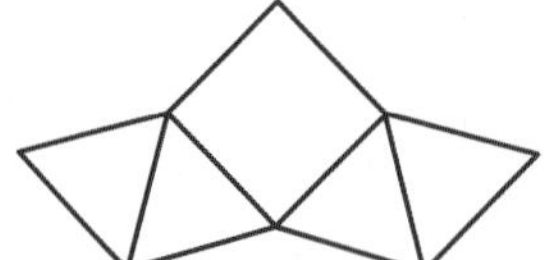

Section 3 Weight in the Customary System

IN THIS SECTION

EXPLORATION 1
- Customary Units of Weight

Setting the Stage

SET UP *You will need the space figure from Net 4 on Labsheet 2B.*

The ancient Egyptians built huge stone pyramids as tombs for their rulers, or *pharaohs*. Some pyramids contained hidden rooms and secret passages. Many also held gold and other treasure.

After 4500 years, more than eighty Egyptian pyramids are still standing. The largest, the Great Pyramid at Giza, is about 480 ft high and has a square base with sides about 755 ft long.

▲ It took 100,000 workers twenty years to build the Great Pyramid.

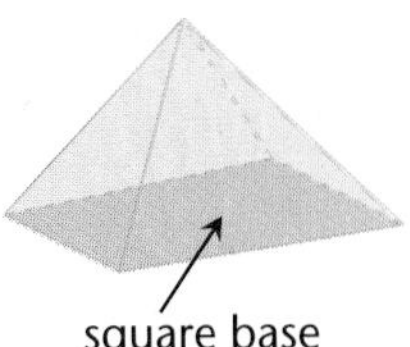

Think About It

1 On a building, a story is about 10 ft high. About how many stories high is the Great Pyramid?

2 **a.** Find the area of the base of the Great Pyramid.

b. About how many 160 ft by 120 yd football fields does it take to cover the base of the Great Pyramid?

3 The figure you folded from Net 4 on Labsheet 2B is a **pyramid**. This figure and the Great Pyramid are both square pyramids. Describe the faces. How is a square pyramid different from a square prism?

GOAL

LEARN HOW TO...
- measure weight in customary units
- convert customary units of weight

AS YOU...
- explore the building of the Great Pyramid

KEY TERMS
- pyramid
- ounce (oz)
- pound (lb)
- ton

Exploration 1

Customary Units of Weight

SET UP *You will need:* • *a scale* • *a box of chalk* • *a stapler*

Building the Great Pyramid was an amazing task. The Great Pyramid is made up of two and a half million stone blocks, each having an average weight of about $2\frac{1}{2}$ tons. After blocks were dug from a quarry miles away, they needed to be transported to the construction site and moved up to each layer of the pyramid.

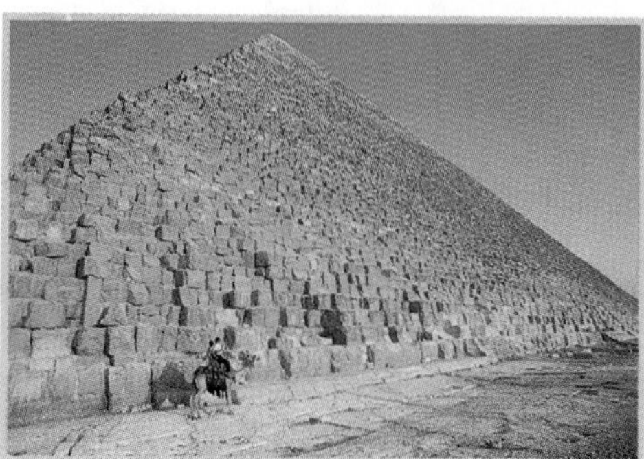

4 **a.** Write a numeral for the number of stone blocks used to build the Great Pyramid.

b. The Empire State Building weighs about 365,000 tons. Find the weight of the Great Pyramid in tons and compare it to the weight of the Empire State Building.

To better understand how heavy the blocks were, it is helpful to become familiar with units of weight in the customary system—the ounce (oz), the pound (lb), and the ton. The relationships between these units are shown below:

1 lb = 16 oz 1 ton = 2000 lb

5 **Discussion** The weight of five quarters is a good benchmark for an ounce. A compact car is a good benchmark for a ton. What can you use as a benchmark for a pound? Explain your reasoning.

6 Choose an appropriate unit *(ounce, pound, or ton)* for the weight of each item.

a. a box of cereal **b.** a person **c.** a truck

d. an orange **e.** a bicycle **f.** a vitamin pill

7 Copy the table. Use the benchmarks from Question 5 to estimate the weight of each listed item. Then weigh each item on a scale.

Item	Estimated weight	Actual weight
pencil	?	?
box of chalk	?	?
four textbooks	?	?
stapler	?	?

▶ **Converting Units Sometimes you need to convert between different units of weight. You can multiply or divide to convert one unit of weight to another.**

8 **a.** How many pounds of peanut butter are in a 48 oz jar?

b. How many pounds does a $2\frac{1}{2}$ ton stone block weigh?

c. Discussion Explain how you decided whether to multiply or divide in parts (a) and (b).

EXAMPLE

A natural foods store sells loose mint tea in 5 oz boxes. How many pounds do eight boxes of mint tea weigh?

SAMPLE RESPONSE

$8 \cdot 5$ oz = 40 oz

Multiply to find the weight of eight boxes.

40 oz = ___?___ lb

40 oz = 2 lb 8 oz, or $2\frac{1}{2}$ lb

÷ 16

Divide by 16 to convert from ounces to pounds.
16 oz = 1 lb
÷ 16

9 ✓ **CHECKPOINT** Replace each ? to convert each measurement to the indicated unit.

a. 5500 lb = ___?___ tons

b. 36 oz = ___?___ lb

c. 5 lb 6 oz = ___?___ oz

d. $3\frac{1}{4}$ tons = ___?___ lb

✓ **QUESTION 9**

... checks that you can convert customary units of weight.

10 If the average student weighs 100 lb, how many students would weigh as much as an average stone block in the pyramid?

HOMEWORK EXERCISES ▶ See Exs. 1–19 on pp. 483–484.

Section 3 Key Concepts

Key Terms

pyramid

Pyramids (p. 479)

A pyramid is a space figure that has one base. All the other faces are triangles that meet at a single vertex.

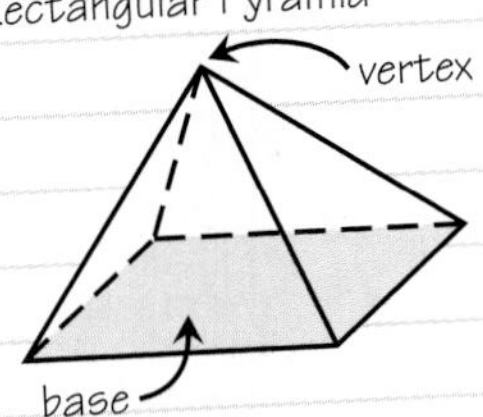

ounce (oz)

pound (lb)

ton

Customary Units of Weight (pp. 480–481)

Some commonly used units of weight in the customary system are ounce (oz), pound (lb), and ton.

- An ounce is about the weight of 5 quarters.

- A pound is about the weight of a loaf of bread.
  1 lb = 16 oz

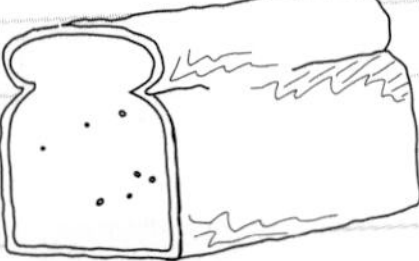

- A ton is about the weight of a compact car.
  1 ton = 2000 lb

Key Concepts Questions

11 Choose the letter of the space figure that is a pyramid.

A. 

B. 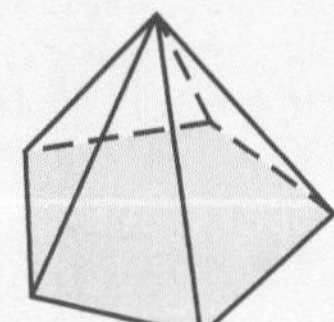

C. 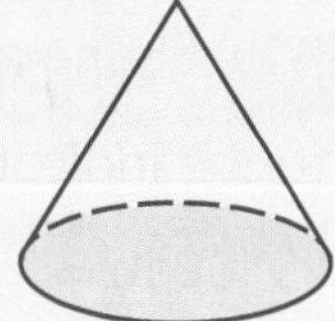

12 Suppose a museum used two and a half million one-ounce blocks to build a scale model of the Great Pyramid at Giza.

a. Should you express the weight of the scale model in *ounces*, *pounds*, or *tons*? Explain your choice.

b. How much does the scale model weigh?

Section 3

Practice & Application Exercises

Choose the best customary unit (*ounce, pound,* or *ton*) to express the weight of each object.

1. airplane
2. postcard
3. ice skates
4. fork

Open-ended **Name something that weighs about each amount.**

5. 6 oz
6. 10 lb

Replace each ? with the missing measurement.

7. 96 oz = ? lb
8. 0.75 lb = ? oz
9. 4000 lb = ? tons
10. 4 oz = ? lb
11. $5\frac{1}{2}$ tons = ? lb
12. 250 lb = ? ton

Find each weight in *pounds and ounces.*

13.

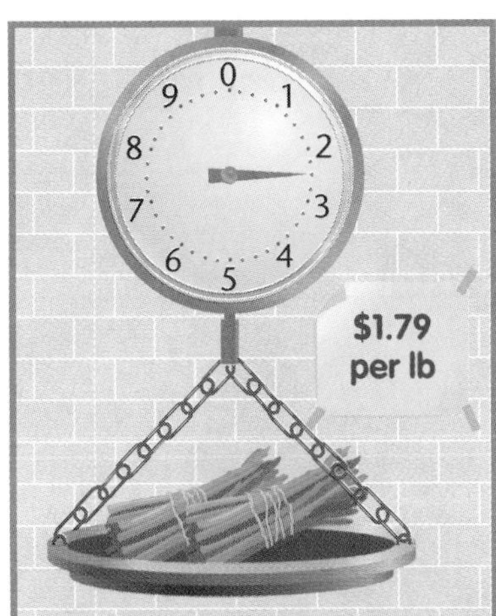

14.

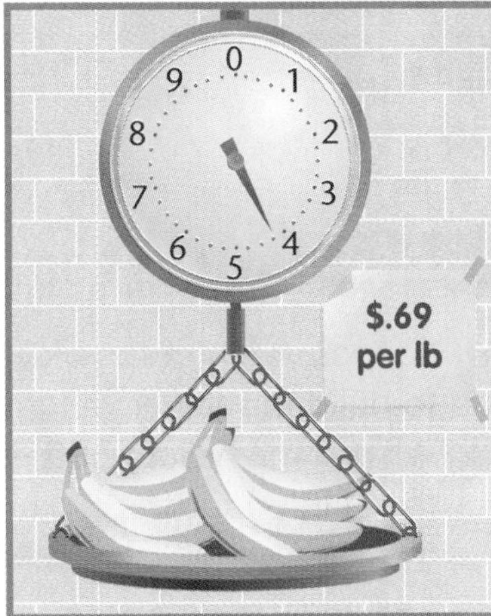

15. **Estimation** Estimate the cost of each purchase in Exercises 13 and 14. Describe your method. Then calculate the actual cost.

16. An apple pie recipe calls for 3 lb of apples. One apple weighs about 7 oz. About how many apples are in this pie?

17. **Archaeology** Tutankhamen was king of Egypt from about 1347–1339 B.C. Most of the tombs in Egyptian pyramids have had their contents stolen, but the tomb of Tutankhamen was discovered in 1922 with its magnificent treasure still in place.

    a. The solid gold mask found on Tutankhamen's mummy weighs 22 lb. What is the mask's weight in ounces?

    b. Suppose gold sells for $365 per ounce. What is the value of the gold in the mummy's mask?

Use the shipping charge table for Exercise 18.

18. Ramona wants to send a friend of hers a pair of soccer cleats that weighs 2 lb 3 oz. She also sends two shin guards that weigh 6 oz each, along with some pictures that weigh 2 oz altogether.

a. **Estimation** Estimate the shipping charge.

b. Find the total weight in pounds and ounces of the items Ramona is sending. What is the actual shipping charge?

Shipping weight	Priority Mail 2-day shipping rate
Up to 2 lb	$3.00
Up to 3 lb	$4.00
Up to 4 lb	$5.00
Up to 5 lb	$6.00

Reflecting on the Section

Visual THINKING

Exercise 19 checks that you can convert between units of customary weight.

19. Suppose each of the blocks used to build this tower weighs 3 oz. What is the weight of the tower in pounds?

Spiral Review

Find the missing measurement for each prism. **(Module 7, pp. 461 and 473)**

20. Area of base = 12 cm^2
Volume = 54 cm^3
height = ___?___

21. height = 6.2 cm
Volume = 155 cm^3
Area of base = ___?___

22. Suppose p represents a weight in pounds and n represents a weight in ounces. Write a rule in the form of an equation for converting from pounds to ounces. Use your rule to convert 15 lb to ounces. **(Module 4, p. 288)**

Career Connection

Doctor: Darrell Mease

Darrell Mease monitors the health of children from the time they are born until they become adults. He records the weights of babies because normal growth is a sign of health.

23. A normal birth weight for boys is between 95 oz. and 152 oz. Is a 9 lb 7 oz baby boy within the normal range? Explain.

24. From 10 days after birth until 3 months is a time of rapid growth for infants. During this time, doctors like to see an average weight gain of close to 1 oz per day.

    A baby weighs 8 lb 13 oz at her two-week check-up and 11 lb 7 oz at her two-month visit. Is she gaining at about 1 oz per day? Explain.

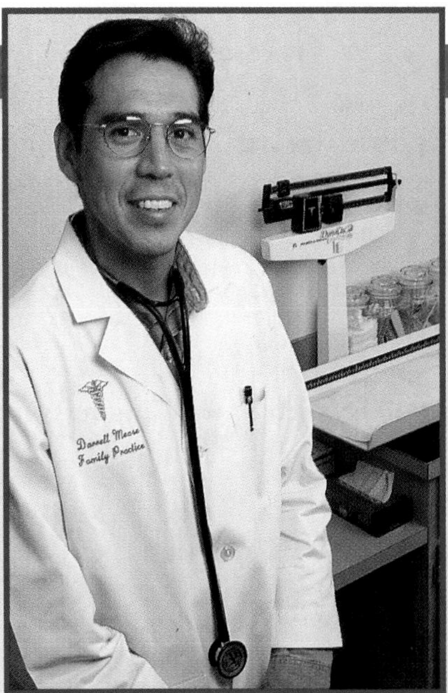

▲ Pediatrician Darrell Mease works with Native American children in his home town of Jay, Oklahoma.

Make a World Travel Poster

Nets for Space Figures To make your poster more eye-catching, you can attach 3-dimensional models of some of the sites you plan to feature.

SET UP

You will need:
- *Project Labsheet A*
- *ruler*
- *scissors*
- *tape*

3 a. **Use Project Labsheet A.** Follow the directions on the labsheet to create a net for a *Model of the Great Pyramid at Giza.*

b. How many faces, edges, and vertices does a square pyramid have?

4 Try to make a net that you can show on your poster. The 3-dimensional figure can show something about the shape of a site or it can just be used as an eye-catching way to display information.

Section 3 Extra Skill Practice

Choose the best customary unit (*ounce, pound,* or *ton*) to express the weight of each object.

1. pile of books
2. softball
3. cow
4. steamship
5. hammer
6. bag of pretzels
7. lightbulb
8. desk
9. calculator

Replace each ? with the missing measurement.

10. 7000 lb = ? tons
11. 1600 lb = ? ton
12. 32 oz = ? lb
13. $3\frac{1}{2}$ lb = ? oz
14. 10 oz = ? lb
15. 16 tons = ? lb
16. 2 tons = ? oz
17. 104 oz = ? lb
18. $4\frac{1}{4}$ lb = ? oz

Replace each ? with >, <, or =.

19. 2.5 lb ? 36 oz
20. 8500 lb ? 5 tons
21. 64 oz ? 4 lb
22. 1200 lb ? $\frac{1}{2}$ ton
23. 32,000 oz ? 1 ton
24. $4\frac{1}{2}$ lb ? 100 oz
25. $5\frac{1}{4}$ lb ? 84 oz
26. 42 oz ? 3 lb
27. 0.5 lb ? 6 oz

Standardized Testing ▶ Free Response

1. A circus parade is shown. If each elephant weighs 2.5 tons, the clown car weighs 1 ton, and the people weigh an average of 150 pounds each, should they cross the bridge together? Explain.

2. A clown juggles a can of soup (10 oz), a golf ball ($1\frac{1}{2}$ oz), a large apple ($\frac{1}{2}$ lb), and a melon ($2\frac{3}{4}$ lb). When juggling, the clown holds two objects at a time while the rest of the objects are in the air. What is the greatest amount of weight that the clown holds? the least? Explain.

Section 4 Circles and Circumference

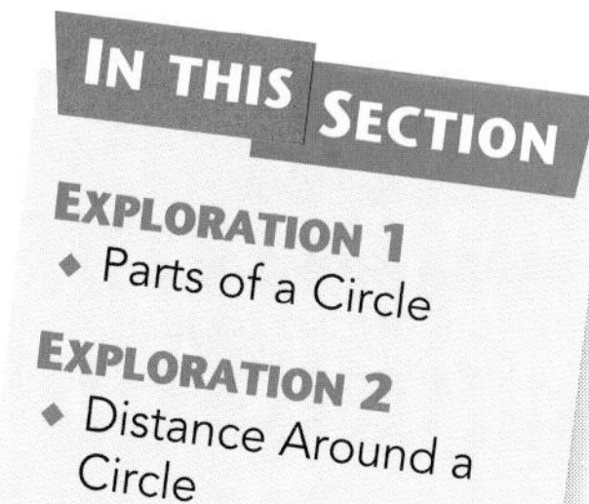

The Circus Maximus

Setting the Stage

One of the wonders of the Roman Empire was the Circus Maximus. This enormous arena was the largest gathering place in ancient Rome, seating 250,000 screaming spectators. As many as 20 four-horse chariots raced around the low wall which ran down the middle of the arena.

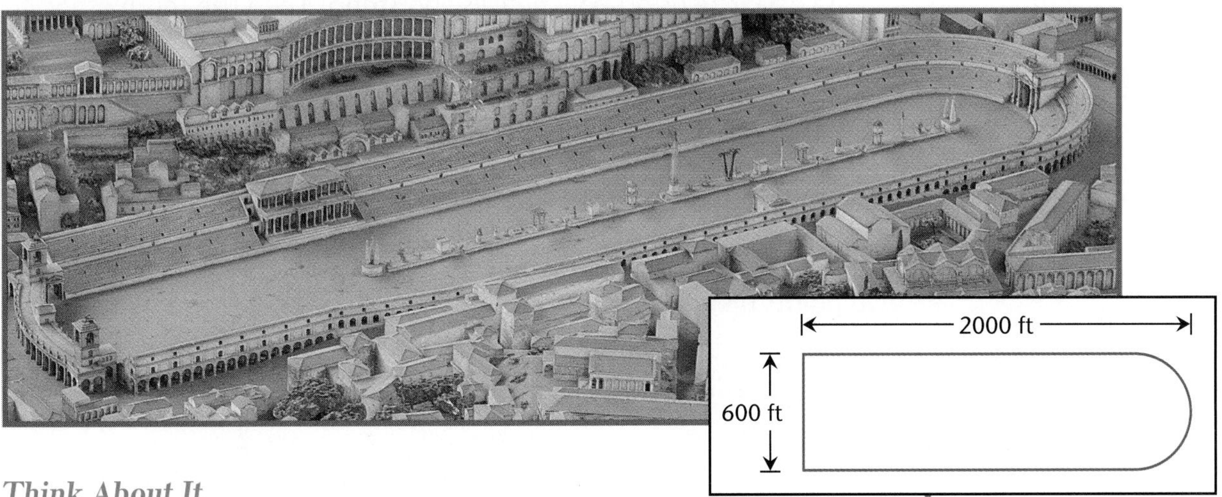

Think About It

1 Describe the shape of the track where the chariots raced.

2 How can you estimate the perimeter of the Circus Maximus? How can you estimate the length of the curved part of the building?

3 The Astrodome in Houston, Texas, holds 60,000 people. About how many times as many people did the Circus Maximus hold?

4 Estimate the area of the Circus Maximus. Explain how you estimated. How does its area compare with your classroom's area?

GOAL

LEARN HOW TO...
- identify the parts of a circle
- draw a circle

AS YOU...
- explore the Circus Maximus

KEY TERMS
- circle
- center
- radius (plural: radii)
- chord
- diameter

Exploration 1

Parts of a Circle

SET UP *You will need:* • *piece of string about 30 cm long* • *two pencils* • *compass* • *ruler*

The Circus Maximus is shaped like a rectangle with a half *circle* on one end.

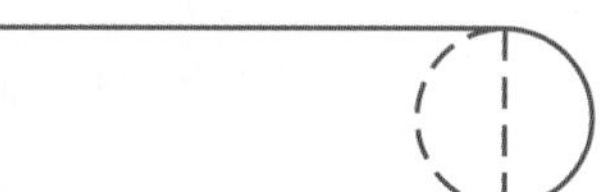

▶ **To find distances around curved paths, it is helpful to know more about circles. A circle is the set of points in a plane that are all the same distance from a given point, the center.**

5 Think about the definition of a circle. Use it to develop a way to draw a circle using only pencils and string. Then use this method to draw a circle. Label the center of your circle.

6 **Discussion** How did you draw your circle?

▶ **A radius is a segment from the center of a circle to any point on the circle. A chord is a segment that connects two points on a circle.**

Point O is the center.

B O A C

$\overline{OA}$ is a radius.

$\overline{BC}$ is a chord.

7 Draw a radius and a chord on your circle.

8 Is a radius a chord? Explain.

✓ **QUESTION 9**

...checks that you can identify radii and chords of a circle.

9 ✓ **CHECKPOINT** Look at this diagram of segments within a circle.

a. Name two chords of the circle.

b. Name two radii of the circle.

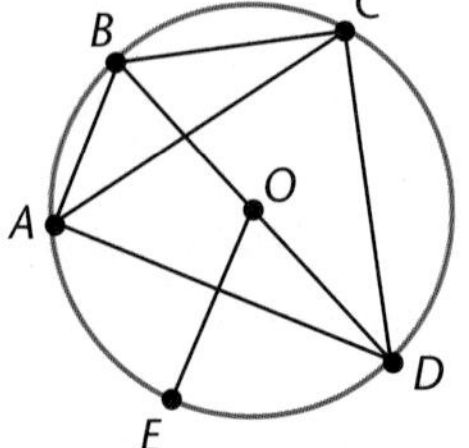

▶ **The term radius is used for length as well as for segments. Since every radius of a circle has the same length, you can say that this length is *the radius* of the circle.**

▶ **Drawing Circles** **You can use a compass to draw a circle.**

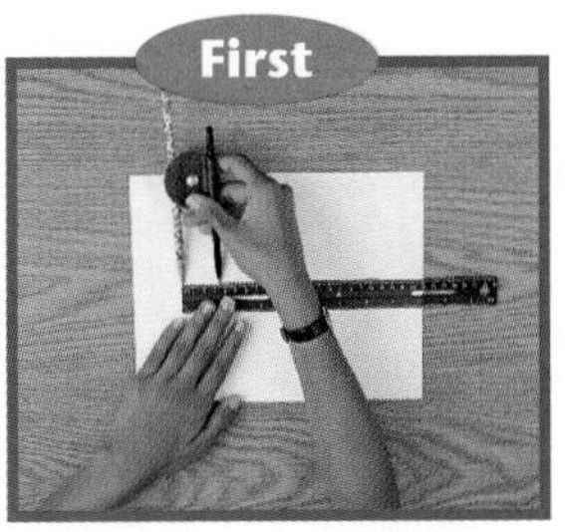

Open the compass to the desired radius.

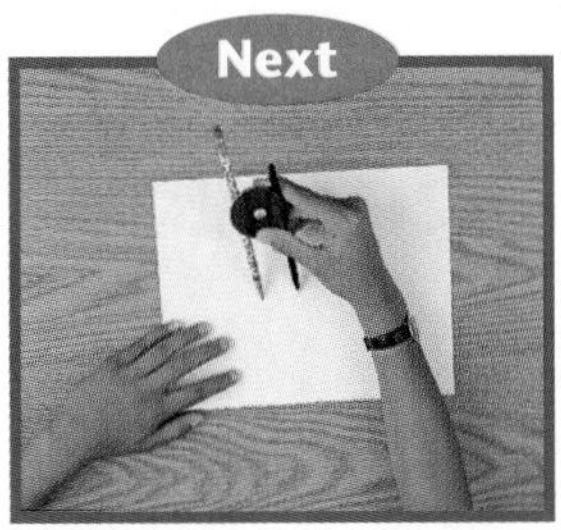

Put the point of the compass at the center of the circle.

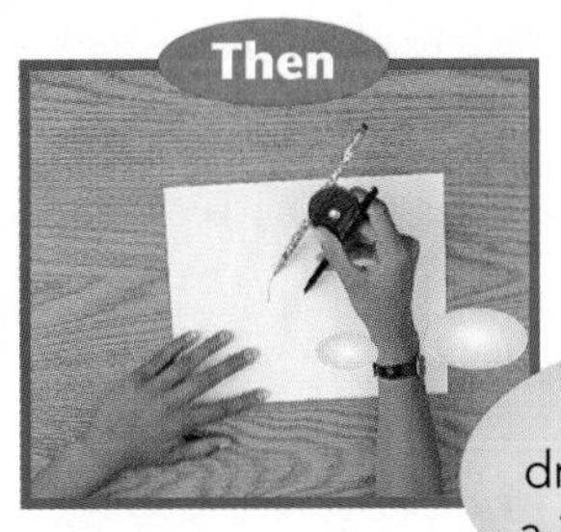

Draw the circle. Press down to hold the compass in place.

The circle drawn here has a 3.5 cm radius.

10 **a.** Draw a circle using a compass. Mark its center with a dot.

b. Draw the longest possible chord. How does the length of this chord compare with the length of the radius?

▶ **A diameter of a circle is a chord that passes through the center of the circle. Every diameter of a circle has the same length. The length of any diameter is called the diameter of the circle.**

11 **a.** How is the chord you drew in Question 10 related to a diameter?

b. How are the lengths of other chords related to the diameter?

12 ✓ **CHECKPOINT** Use the diagram of the Circus Maximus below.

a. Use what you know about circles to find the two missing dimensions.

b. Use the scale 1 in. : 200 ft and your ruler and compass to make a scale drawing of the Circus Maximus. Label your drawing with the actual measurements given and those you found in part (a). Save your drawing for use in Exploration 2.

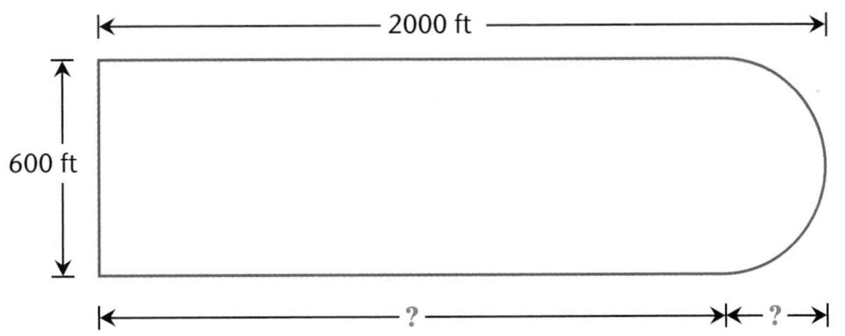

✓ **QUESTION 12**

...checks that you understand the relationships among parts of a circle and can draw a circle.

FOR◀HELP with *scale drawing,* see **MODULE 6, p. 431**

HOMEWORK EXERCISES ▶ **See Exs. 1–7 on p. 494.**

GOAL

LEARN HOW TO...
- find the circumference of a circle

AS YOU...
- investigate Roman chariot wheels and gather data about circles

KEY TERMS
- circumference
- pi (π)

Exploration 2

Distance around a Circle

SET UP *Work in a group. You will need:* • *Labsheet 4B* • *meter stick* • *4 circular objects* • *string* • *calculator* • *clear ruler*

▶ **Using spoked wheels helped chariot racers gain speed and control. To make the rim and spokes the correct lengths to form a wheel, it was important to know how parts of a circle are related.**

The rim of a Roman chariot wheel was made by bending a strip of wood to form a circle. ▶

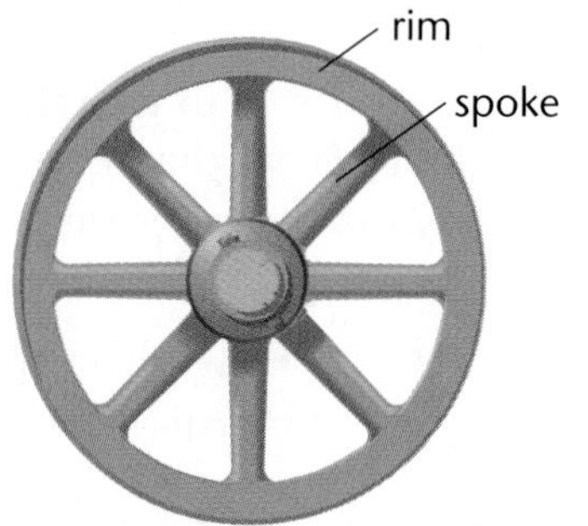

13 The distance around a circle is its **circumference**. What part of the wheel corresponds to the circumference?

Use Labsheet 4B for Questions 14–16.

14 **a.** Follow the directions for the *Data Table* to find and record the circumference and diameter of circular objects.

b. The circumference is about how many times the diameter?

c. Use your answer to part (b) to estimate the circumference of a circle with a diameter of 6 in.

FOR ◀ HELP with *scatter plots*, see **MODULE 6, p. 406**

15 **a.** Make a *Scatter Plot* of the data you collected in Question 14.

b. Use your *Scatter Plot* to estimate the diameter of a circle with a circumference of 30 cm.

16 Round decimal answers to the nearest hundredth.

a. Add a row to your *Data Table*. Find and record the decimal form of the ratio $\frac{\text{circumference}}{\text{diameter}}$ for each object.

b. What do you notice about the values of the ratios in part (a)?

c. Find the mean of the values of the ratios.

TECHNOLOGY Using Spreadsheet Software

You can use a spreadsheet to answer Question 16 on page 490. You can set up the spreadsheet to find the decimal form of each circumference to diameter ratio and to find the mean of the ratios.

Step 1 Set up your spreadsheet using the heading "circumference" for cell A1 (the box in column A and row 1), "diameter" for cell B1, and "ratio" for cell C1. Enter the circumference and diameter data you recorded on Labsheet 4B in the appropriate columns.

Step 2 In cell C2, enter a formula that will calculate the decimal form of the ratio $\frac{\text{circumference}}{\text{diameter}}$ for each object. Every formula must begin with an equals sign.

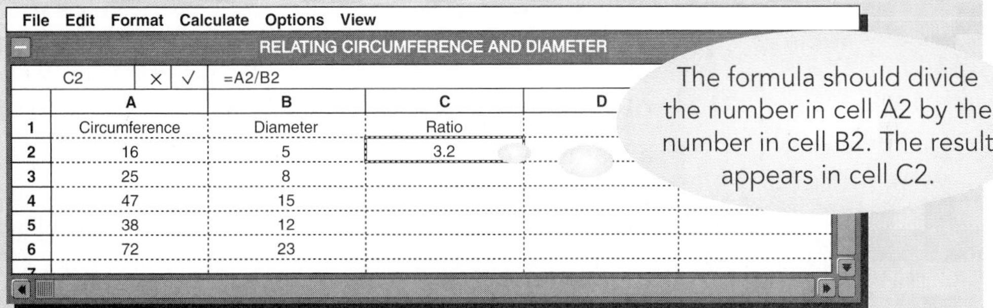

File Edit Format Calculate Options View

RELATING CIRCUMFERENCE AND DIAMETER

C2 × ✓ =A2/B2

	A	B	C	D
1	Circumference	Diameter	Ratio	
2	16	5	3.2	
3	25	8		
4	47	15		
5	38	12		
6	72	23		

The formula should divide the number in cell A2 by the number in cell B2. The result appears in cell C2.

Step 3 The formula entered in cell C2 should also be applied to the remaining cells in column C. You can use the fill down command to do this.

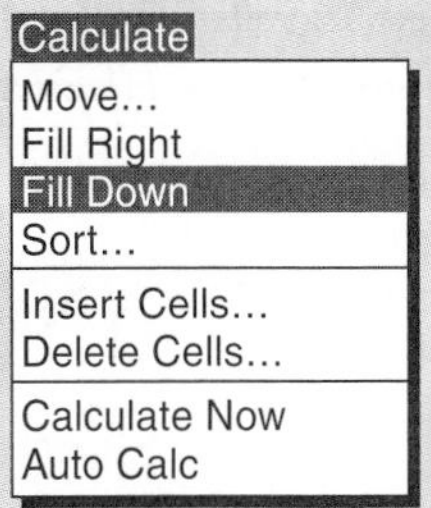

Step 4 In cell C11, enter a formula that will calculate the mean of all the ratios.

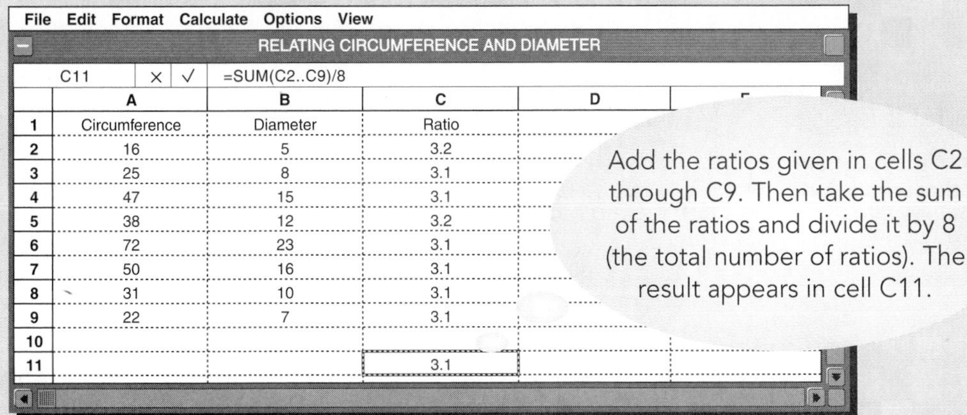

File Edit Format Calculate Options View

RELATING CIRCUMFERENCE AND DIAMETER

C11 × ✓ =SUM(C2..C9)/8

	A	B	C	D
1	Circumference	Diameter	Ratio	
2	16	5	3.2	
3	25	8	3.1	
4	47	15	3.1	
5	38	12	3.2	
6	72	23	3.1	
7	50	16	3.1	
8	31	10	3.1	
9	22	7	3.1	
10				
11			3.1	

Add the ratios given in cells C2 through C9. Then take the sum of the ratios and divide it by 8 (the total number of ratios). The result appears in cell C11.

▶ **The Ratio Pi** For any circle, the ratio of circumference to diameter is equal to the number represented by the Greek letter π, or **pi**. To estimate pi you can use 3.14 or the π key on a calculator.

17 Press the π key on your calculator. What value appears? Compare this value with your result in Question 16(c). How close are the values? How can you explain the difference?

18 **Use Labsheet 4B.** For each object named in the *Data Table*, find the product $\pi \cdot d$ to the nearest hundredth and compare it with your circumference measurement. What do you notice?

▶ **For any circle, the circumference (C) equals π times the diameter (d).**

$$C = \pi \cdot d$$

$$\text{or } C = \pi d$$

When multiplying by a variable, you can leave out the multiplication symbol.

19 **Discussion** How can you find the circumference of a circle with a diameter of 3 ft? with a radius of $\frac{1}{2}$ yd?

▶ **If you know the circumference you can solve for the diameter.**

EXAMPLE

To find the diameter of Earth at the equator, you can use the formula for circumference and substitute the values you know.

$\approx$ means "is about equal to."

$$C = \pi d$$

$$40{,}075 \approx 3.14 \cdot d$$

$$40{,}075 \div 3.14 \approx d$$

$$12{,}763 \approx d$$

The circumference of Earth at the equator is 40,075 km.

The diameter rounded to the nearest kilometer is 12,763 km.

✓ QUESTION 20

...checks that you can apply the formula for the circumference of a circle.

20 **✓ CHECKPOINT** Replace each __?__ with the missing length. Round to the hundredths place.

a. $d = \frac{1}{3}$ in., $C \approx$ __?__ **b.** $C \approx 34.54$ mm, $d \approx$ __?__

21 Use the information from your sketch in Question 12. Find the perimeter of the Circus Maximus. Round to the nearest foot.

HOMEWORK EXERCISES ▶ See Exs. 8–18 on pp. 494–495.

Key Concepts

Key Terms

circle

center

radius

chord

diameter

circumference

pi (π)

Parts of Circles (p. 488–489)

You can use a compass to draw a circle.

In any circle:

- the radius(r) is one half the diameter (d).
- the diameter is the longest chord.
- all radii are the same length.
- all diameters are the same length.

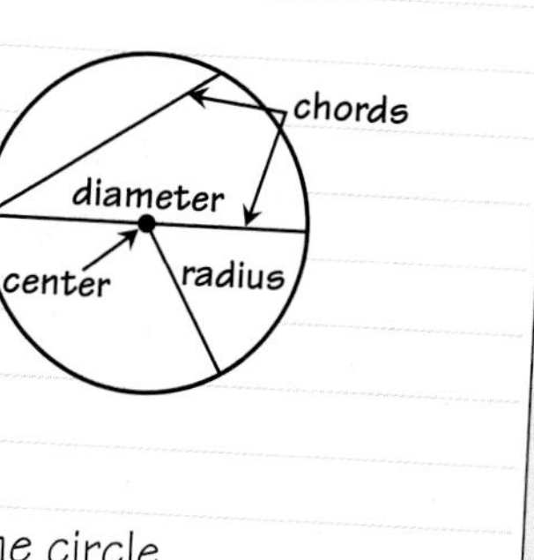

Circumference (p. 490–492)

The circumference of a circle is the distance around the circle. The ratio of the circumference of any circle to its diameter is pi (π). To find the circumference (C), multiply π by d, where d is the diameter.

You can use the value 3.14 or the π key on your calculator to estimate π.

Example

Find the circumference of a circle that has a radius of 1.5 cm.

$C = \pi d$

$C = \pi \cdot (2r)$ $2r = d$

$C \approx 3.14 \cdot 2 \cdot 1.5$

$C \approx 9.42$ cm

The circumference is about 9.42 cm.

22 Key Concepts Question Some Roman chariot wheels had a circumference of about 113 in.

a. How can you estimate the diameter of the wheel?

b. Suppose the rim of the wheel is 3 in. wide and the diameter of the hub is 9 in. About how long is a spoke to the nearest inch?

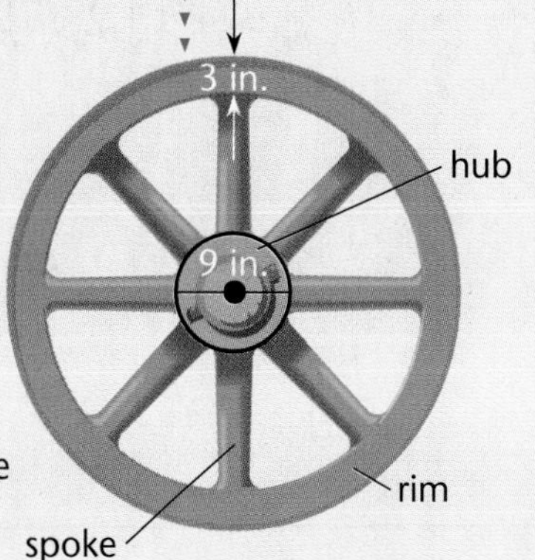

Note: The length of a spoke is not equal to the radius.

Section 4 Practice & Application Exercises

YOU WILL NEED

For Ex. 4–7:
- compass

For Ex. 7:
- Labsheet 4A

For Exs. 28–30:
- compass
- straightedge
- drawing paper
- colored pencils or markers

Name all the segments of each type shown on the circle with center O.

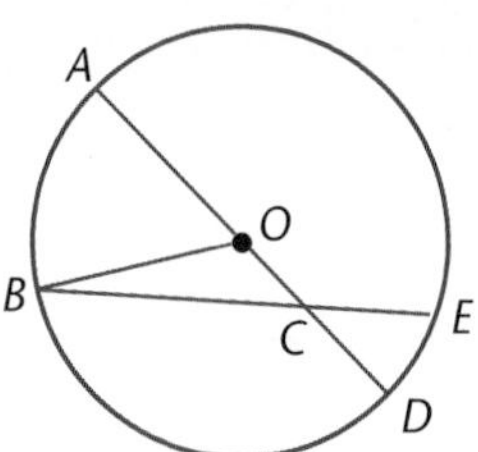

1. radii
2. diameters
3. chords

Use a compass to draw a circle with each radius or diameter.

4. radius = 2 cm
5. diameter = 8 cm
6. radius = $1\frac{1}{4}$ in.

7. **Earthquakes** A seismograph gives information about the strength and location of an earthquake. The *epicenter* of an earthquake is the point on Earth's surface directly over the place where an earthquake occurs.

   a. Readings from the seismograph at station 1 indicate that an earthquake occurred 100 km away. What do you think the circle drawn around station 1 represents?

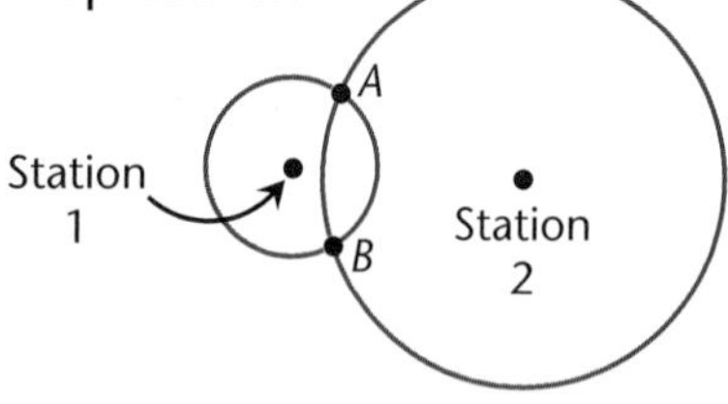

   b. A seismograph at station 2 detected the same quake 300 km away from station 2. Look at the two circles. Why do you think a scientist is interested in points *A* and *B*, where the two circles intersect?

   c. How do you think scientists can use circles to find the epicenter of an earthquake?

   d. **Use Labsheet 4A.** Use the seismograph locations and the distances in the table on the labsheet. Draw circles on the *Epicenter Map* to find the epicenter of an earthquake that occurred in the South Pacific on March 11, 1997.

A *seismograph* is an instrument used to record earthquake waves.

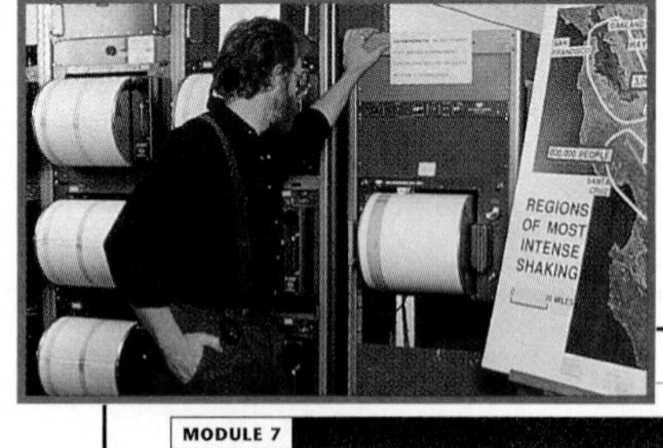

Date

MODULE 7 LABSHEET 4A

Epicenter Map (Use with Exercise 7 on page 494.)

Directions Complete the table to determine the distance on the map that each seismograph location is from the epicenter. Round your answer to the nearest tenth of a centimeter. Use a compass. Draw a circle for each seismograph location using the map distance you found as the radius. Then mark an "x" at the point on the map where the three circles intersect.

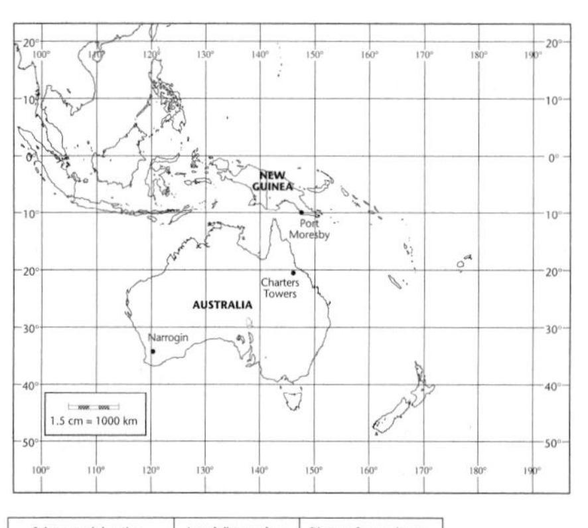

Seismograph location	Actual distance from epicenter (km)	Distance from epicenter on the map (cm)
#1: Charters Towers, Australia	3710	
#2: Port Moresby, New Guinea	2899	
#3: Narrogin, Australia	4633	

Use each answer as the radius for a circle you draw.

Find the circumference of each circle. Round to the hundredths place.

8. $d = 21$ in.
9. $d = 5$ cm
10. $r = 6$ ft

For the circle with each given circumference (C), find the missing radius or diameter. Replace each ? with the missing length. Round to the hundredths place.

11. $C = 69.08$ cm
diameter ≈ ?

12. $C = 28.26$ in.
radius ≈ ?

13. $C = 15.7$ mm
diameter ≈ ?

14. **Estimation** The trunk of an African baobab tree can grow up to 30 ft in diameter. About how many people would it take to surround the tree if the people stood with their arms fully extended and their fingertips touching? Explain your thinking.

15. **Algebra Connection** The circumference of a circle is 12.56 cm. What is the ratio of this circumference to that of a circle with a radius twice as long? three times as long?

16. Elia's bicycle wheel has a diameter of 24 inches. How far will it travel in 1 complete turn? in 4 complete turns? Explain.

17. **Challenge** The Colosseum was a large stadium in ancient Rome. Its base was shaped like an oval.

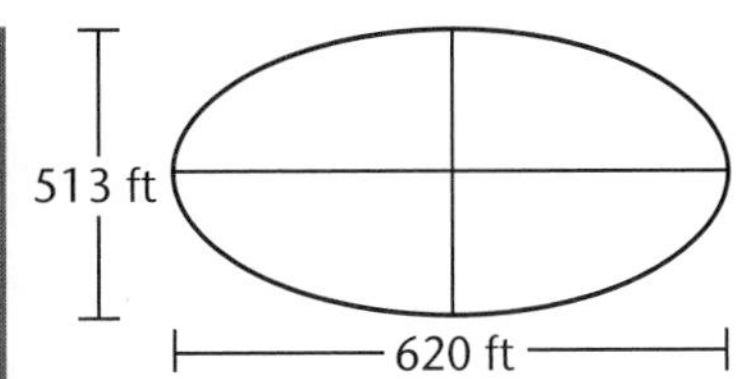

Use what you know about circles to estimate the perimeter of the base. Explain how you made your estimate.

Reflecting on the Section

Write your response to Exercise 18 in your journal.

18. The Spanish dollar was minted in Mexico during the eighteenth century. This coin had lines that allowed it to break into 8 equal sections. These *bits* were used as smaller coins.

One-eighth of a Spanish dollar is shown. Use the measurements marked to describe two ways to find the circumference of a whole coin.

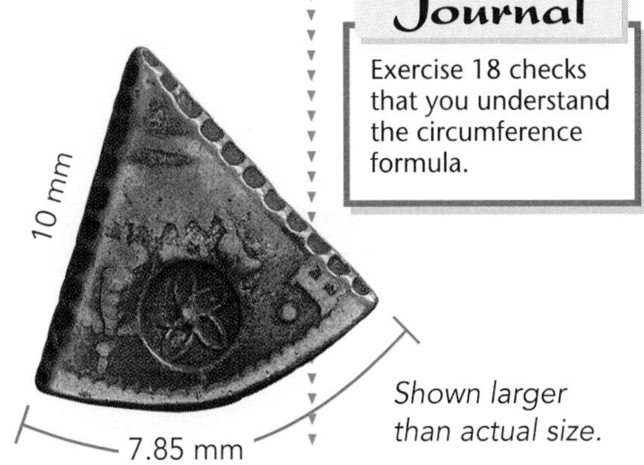

Shown larger than actual size.

Journal

Exercise 18 checks that you understand the circumference formula.

Spiral Review

Convert each measurement to pounds. (Module 7, p. 482)

19. 54 oz   20. $2\frac{3}{4}$ tons   21. 35 oz   22. $7\frac{1}{2}$ tons

23. A student's scores on five tests were 84, 86, 38, 85, and 99. Which average best describes the data: the mean, the median, or the mode? Explain. (Module 3, p. 202)

Evaluate each expression. (Module 4, p. 257)

24. 3^2 25. 2^4 26. 1^6 27. 5^3

Extension

Compass Constructions

You can make geometric figures called *constructions* using a compass and a straightedge.

28. Follow the steps to draw a circle and make a geometric figure.

Step 1

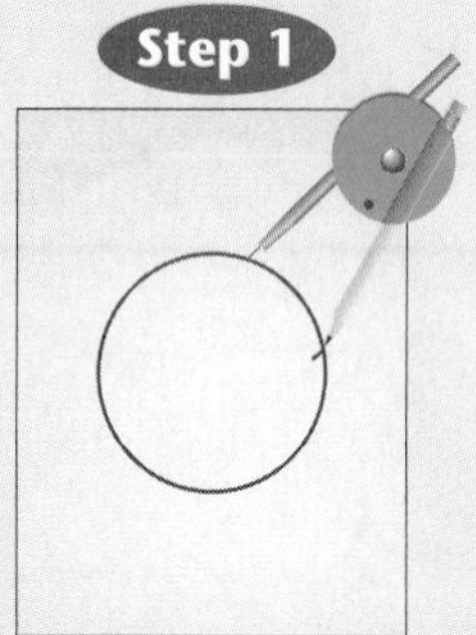

Use a compass to draw a circle. Keep the compass opening the same and put the compass on any point on the circle. Make a small mark on the circle.

Step 2

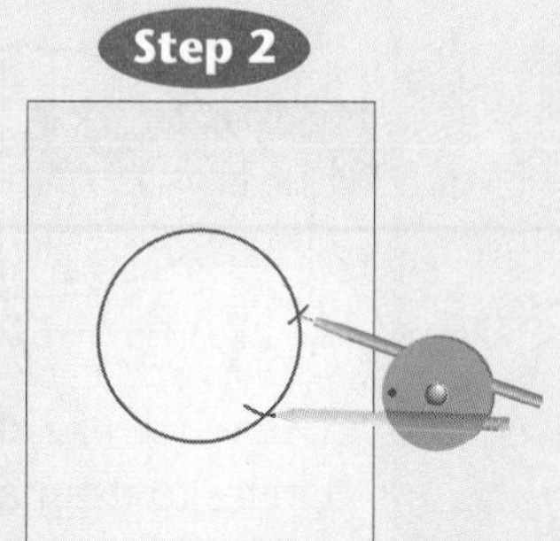

Put the point of the compass on the mark you made and make a second mark. Continue marking around the circle.

Step 3

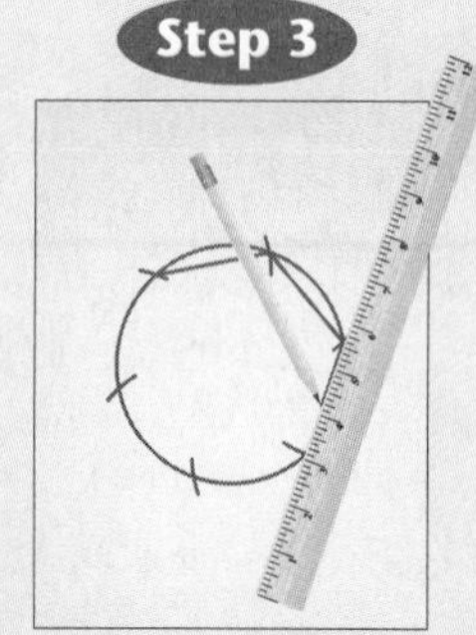

Use a straightedge to connect the marks. Name the geometric figure you made.

29. Draw and mark another circle. Use your straightedge or compass to make a design. Some examples are shown.

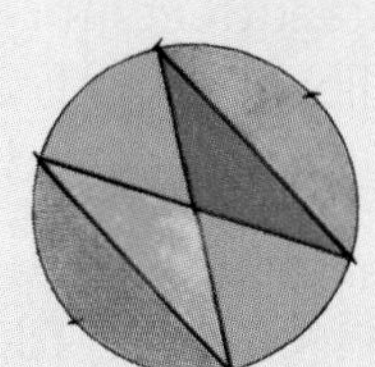

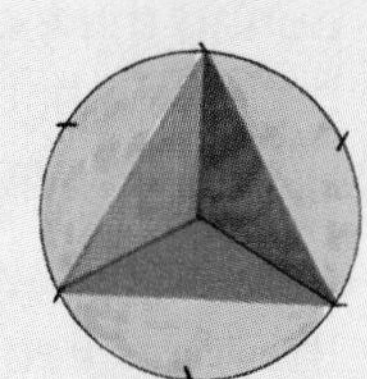

Section 4
Extra Skill Practice

Name all the segments of each type shown on the circle with center *O*.

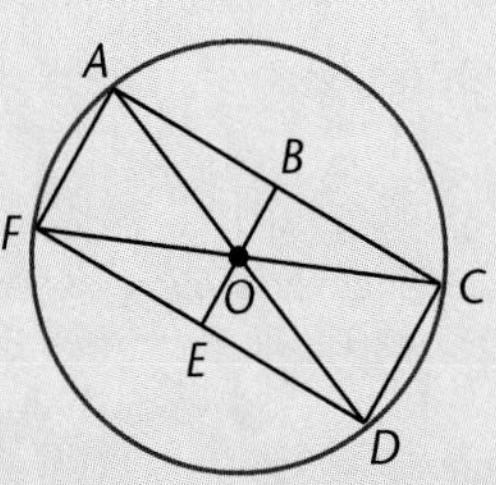

1. diameters
2. chords
3. radii

For each circle in Exercises 4–9, find the circumference. Round to the hundredths place.

4. $d = 27$ in.
5. $r = 2.5$ cm
6. $r = 53$ mm
7. 11,300 m
8. 8.125 in.
9. 13.53 ft

Replace each ? with the missing length. Round to the hundredths place.

10. $d = 5$ cm, $C \approx$ ___?___
11. $C \approx 11$ *m*, $d \approx$ ___?___
12. $C \approx 117.75$ ft, $r \approx$ ___?___
13. $r = 31$ in., $C \approx$ ___?___
14. $C \approx 55$ *m*, $d \approx$ ___?___
15. $C \approx 175.84$ cm, $r \approx$ ___?___

Standardized Testing ▶ Multiple Choice

1. Which statements about the circle are true?

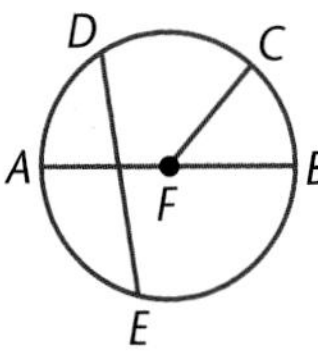

I. Segment *AB* is a radius.

II. Segment *DE* is shorter than segment *AB*.

III. Segment *FC* is exactly one half the length of segment *AB*.

(A) I and III (B) I only (C) II and III (D) II only

2. Which equation or equations are false?

I. $C = \pi d$ II. $\frac{C}{d} = \pi$ III. $\pi = Cd$ IV. $C = 2\pi r$

(A) III only (B) II only (C) II and III (D) II and IV

Section 5 Circles and Cylinders

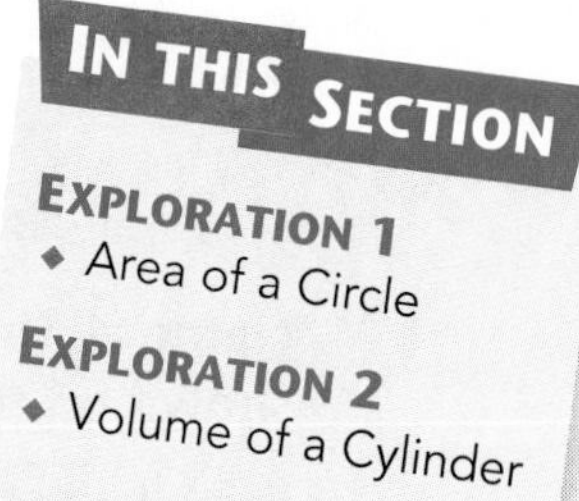

The Mystery of Mesa Verde

Setting the Stage

For many years, the ancestors of the Hopi, Zuni, and several other Native American groups lived in the stone houses they built in natural caves in the cliffs of Mesa Verde, Colorado. Then something strange happened...

> "...whole villages of people left their homes. It seems that about 650 years ago, they just walked away and left most of their belongings....Why did the ancient ones build stone houses in caves?...And why did they leave?"
>
> **Ruth Shaw Radlauer, *Mesa Verde National Park***

Although there are many theories, it is still not known for sure why the villages were abandoned.

Think About It

1 Suppose at this moment you and your classmates walked out of your classroom leaving all of your belongings behind. What do you think someone could learn about students and class activities just by looking around the room?

2 The villages contain round rooms called *kivas*. The diameter of one kiva is 4.3 m.

a. What is the radius of this kiva? the circumference?

b. How do you think the size of a kiva compares with the size of your classroom? Explain.

Exploration 1

Area of a Circle

GOAL

LEARN HOW TO...
- find the area of a circle

AS YOU...
- determine how many people can fit in a kiva

SET UP *You will need Labsheet 5A.*

In her book about Mesa Verde, Ruth Shaw Radlauer discusses the role of the kivas in the lives of the people:

> "When children were old enough, they were initiated, or proclaimed adults in a ceremony. Then they could spend some of the winter in a warm kiva. The kiva was a sort of clubhouse for adults and a place for ceremonies."

▶ **To find out how many people fit in a kiva, you need to find the area of the floor. The floor of a kiva is shaped like a circle.**

3 **Use Labsheet 5A.** Follow the directions for *Estimating the Area of a Circle* by finding the areas of the inner and outer squares.

▶ **You can use the method in Question 3 to estimate the area of any circle with radius *r*.**

4 **Try This as a Class** The diagram below can help you see the relationship between the area of the circle and *r*.

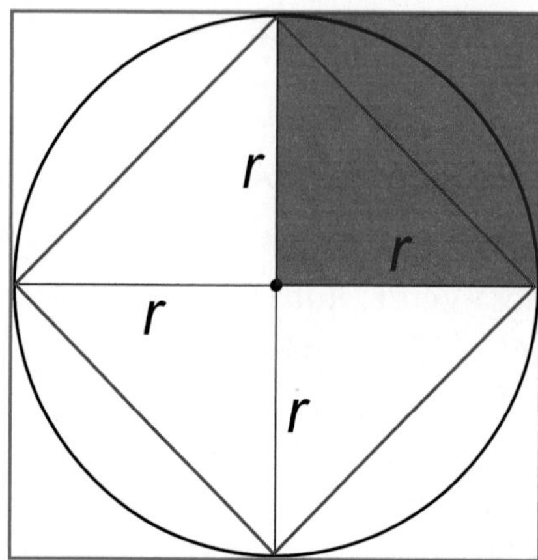

a. Use the variable *r* to write an expression for the area of a small red square.

b. How many small red squares fit in the green outer square? Use your answer to write an expression for the area of the green outer square.

c. How many small red squares fit in the blue inner square? (*Hint:* Each small red square is made up of two triangles.) Use your answer to write an expression for the area of the blue inner square.

d. Use your answers to parts (b) and (c) to write an expression that can be used to estimate the area of the circle.

5 Use your answer to Question 4(d) to estimate the area of a circle with a radius of 4 cm. How does your estimate compare with the estimate you found in Question 3?

▶ **Formula for the Area of a Circle** **In Question 4, you found an expression that can be used to estimate the area of a circle. To find the actual area of a circle with radius *r*, multiply pi by *r* to the second power.**

$$A = \pi r^2$$

You can read r^2 as "*r* squared."

6 How does the formula above compare with the expression you found in Question 4(d)?

EXAMPLE

Find the area of a circle with radius 8.5 cm. Round your answer to the nearest square centimeter.

SAMPLE RESPONSE

$A = \pi r^2 = \pi \cdot (8.5)^2$

Method 1	Method 2
To find *A*, use 3.14 for π.	To find *A*, use the π key on a calculator.
$3.14 \cdot 8.5^2 = 226.865$	π × 8.5 x^2 = 226.98...

The area is about 227 cm^2.

This key takes 8.5 to the second power.

7 In the Example, why aren't the answers the same? Which answer is more accurate?

8 **a.** Using 3.14 for π, find the area of a circle with radius 4 cm.

b. How does your answer in part (a) compare to your estimates in Questions 3 and 5?

9 ✔ **CHECKPOINT** Find the area of each circle. Use 3.14 for π. Round to the nearest hundredth.

a.

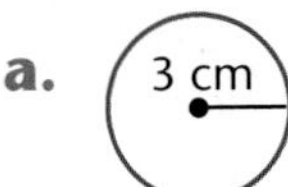

b.

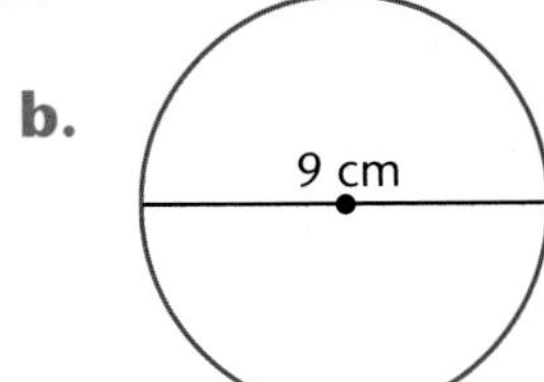

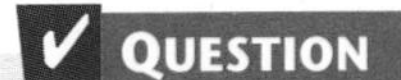

...checks that you can find the area of a circle.

▶ **The area you find when you use either 3.14 or the π key on a calculator is an estimate. To find the exact area of a circle, you need to write an expression that contains the number π.**

For example, to find the exact area of a circle with radius 4 cm, write $\pi \cdot 4^2$. Since $\pi \cdot 4^2 = \pi \cdot 16$, or 16π, the area is 16π cm^2.

10 **a.** What is the exact area of a kiva floor with diameter 4.3 m?

b. Use 3.14 for π to estimate the area of the floor of the kiva.

11 Determine how much floor space an average-sized person needs to stand comfortably. How many people can stand comfortably in the kiva in Question 10?

HOMEWORK EXERCISES See Exs. 1–13 on p. 505–506.

GOAL

LEARN HOW TO...
- recognize a cylinder
- find the volume of a cylinder

AS YOU...
- explore the size and shape of a kiva

KEY TERM
- cylinder

Exploration 2

Volume of a Cylinder

SET UP *Work in a group of three. You will need:*
• Labsheets 5B and 5C • scissors • tape • rice • ruler

In the summer of 1891, Gustaf Nordenskiöld of Sweden and his team began to uncover the ruins at Mesa Verde. Part of their task was to remove the layers of dust and rubbish that had piled up over the centuries. After digging to a depth of $\frac{1}{2}$ m at one location, they began to see a kiva take shape.

12 How do you think Nordenskiöld could have estimated the amount of dust and rubbish in the kiva without removing it?

A kiva is shaped like a circular **cylinder**. A circular cylinder is a space figure that has two circular bases that are parallel and congruent.

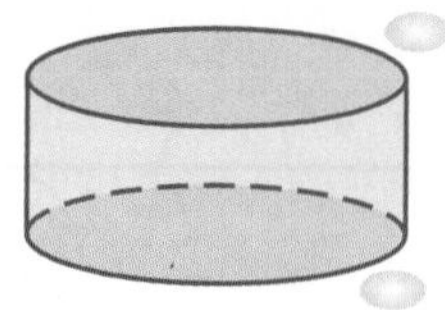

The bases are parallel and congruent.

13 **Use Labsheets 5B and 5C.** Cut out the nets for the open-topped *Prism A, Prism B and Cylinder.* Fold and tape each net.

14 How is the cylinder like a prism? How is it different?

15 Which has a larger volume, prism A or prism B? Explain.

16 Which do you think holds more, the cylinder or prism A? the cylinder or prism B? Explain your thinking in each case.

17 **a.** Fill prism B with rice and then pour the rice into the cylinder. Does the rice completely fill the cylinder, or is there too much or not enough rice?

b. Fill the cylinder with rice and then pour the rice into prism A. Does the rice completely fill prism A?

c. What can you conclude about the volume of the cylinder?

18 **a.** Place the cylinder inside the larger prism. Then place the smaller prism inside the cylinder.

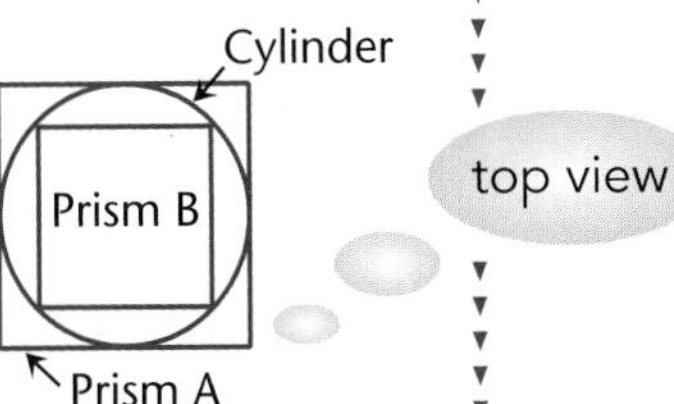

b. For each of the prisms and the cylinder, find the area of a base and the height. Make a table to record your results.

19 **Discussion** Add on to the table you completed in Question 18.

a. Find the volumes of prism A and prism B. Explain your method.

b. Use the same method you used in part (a) to find the volume of the cylinder.

c. Use your models and your results with rice to decide whether the volume you found for the cylinder is reasonable.

▶ **You can find the volume V of a cylinder with height h and a base with area B in the same way you find the volume of a prism.**

$$V = Bh, \text{ or } V = \pi r^2 h.$$

area of circular base

EXAMPLE

Find the volume of the cylinder shown to the nearest cubic centimeter. Use 3.14 for π.

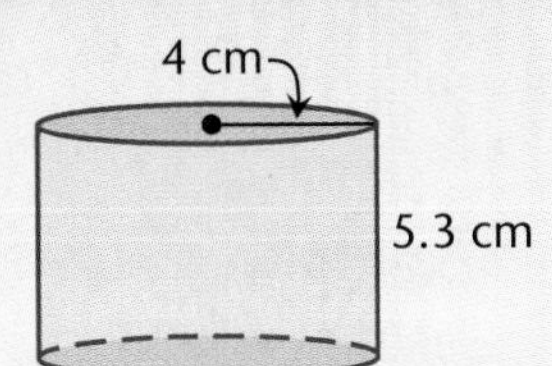

SAMPLE RESPONSE

$V = \pi r^2 h$

$\approx 3.14 \cdot 4^2 \cdot 5.3 = 266.272$

Volume is measured in cubic units.

The volume is about 266 cm^3.

20 ✔ **CHECKPOINT** Find the volume of the cylinder to the nearest cubic meter. Use 3.14 for π.

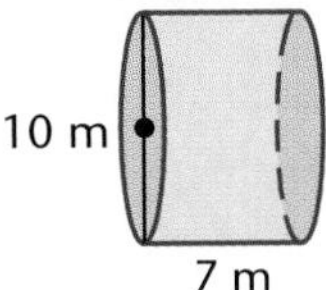

✔ **QUESTION 20**

...checks that you can find the volume of a cylinder.

21 Gustaf Nordenskiöld reported that one of the kivas he uncovered had walls 2 m high with a diameter of 4.3 m. If this kiva was completely full of dust and rubbish, about how much material did Nordenskiöld have to remove?

HOMEWORK EXERCISES ▶ See Exs. 14–22 on p. 506.

Section 5 Key Concepts

Key Terms

Area of a Circle (pp. 499–501)

To find the area (A) of a circle, multiply π by the radius (r) squared.

$$A = \pi r^2.$$

Using π (p. 501)

- To estimate the answer: Use [π] on a calculator or use 3.14 for π.
- To find the exact answer: Write an expression using the number π.

Cylinders (p. 502)

cylinder

A cylinder is a space figure that has a curved surface and two parallel, congruent bases. In this book, all the cylinders have circular bases.

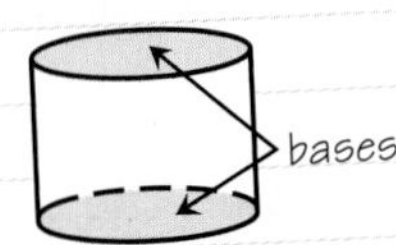

Volume of a Cylinder (pp. 502–503)

To find the volume (V) of a cylinder, multiply the area of the base (B) by the height (h).

$$V = Bh$$

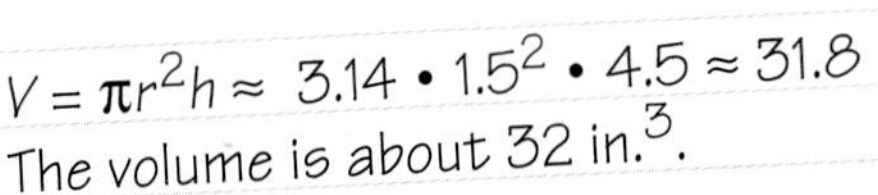

$$V = \pi r^2 h$$

Example

Find the volume of the cylinder shown to the nearest cubic inch. Use 3.14 for π.

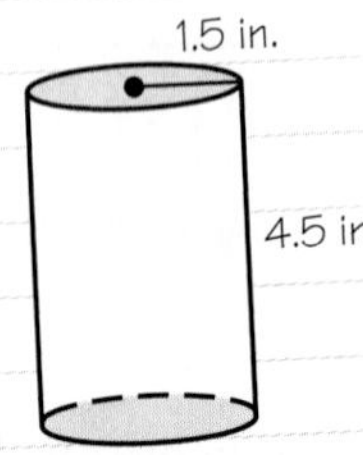

$V = \pi r^2 h \approx 3.14 \cdot 1.5^2 \cdot 4.5 \approx 31.8$

The volume is about 32 in.^{3}.

Key Concepts Questions

22 Find the volume to the nearest cubic centimeter of a cylinder that has a diameter of 16 cm and a height of 10 cm. Use 3.14 for π.

23 What happens to the volume if the diameter of the cylinder in Question 22 is doubled?

Section 5
Practice & Application Exercises

YOU WILL NEED

For Ex. 30–33:
- graph paper

For Ex. 34–39:
- Labsheet 5D
- scissors
- tape
- rice or dry cereal
- ruler

Unless you are asked to find exact areas or volumes, use the π key on a calculator or 3.14 for the value of pi. Round to the nearest hundredth.

Find the area of the circle with the given radius (r) or diameter (d).

1. $r = 2\frac{1}{2}$ in.
2. $d = 6$ ft
3. $d = 4.2$ m
4. 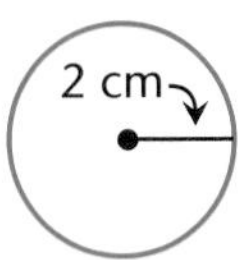

5. 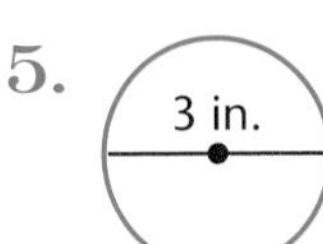

6. 

Find the exact area of the circle with the given radius (r) or diameter (d).

7. $r = 25$ mm
8. $d = 3\frac{1}{4}$ in.
9. $r = 4.6$ cm

10. The circumference of a circle is about 28.26 cm. Find the area of the circle.

11. **Archaeology** Gustaf Nordenskiöld found a piece of broken pottery at Mesa Verde. The drawing shows a whole bowl based on a broken piece. The top of the bowl is circular with a 14 cm diameter.

    If you made a flat, circular cover for a bowl this size, what would its area be?

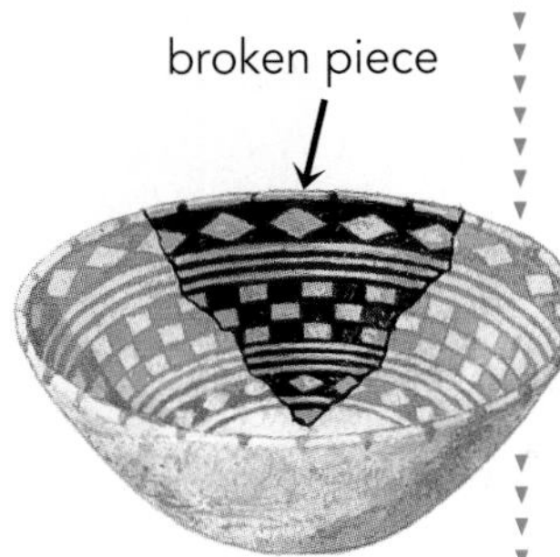

12. **Weather** One of the largest tropical storms ever recorded occurred in the Northwest Pacific on October 12, 1979. This storm, a circular typhoon named Tip, had a radius of 1100 km.
    a. About how large an area did Tip cover?
    b. **Estimation** The area of Australia is 7,614,500 km^2. Suppose Tip had reached Australia. About what fraction of this continent could Tip cover?

A severe rotating wind storm that forms in the western Pacific or Indian Ocean is called a typhoon. Similar storms in the Atlantic Ocean or Caribbean Sea are called hurricanes.

13. **Challenge** Figure *ABCD* is a square. Find the area of the shaded region.

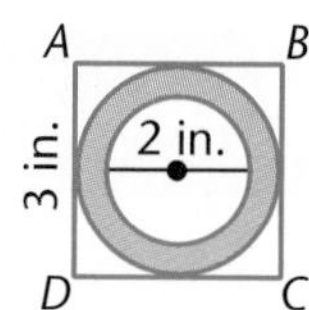

Find the volume of each cylinder.

14.
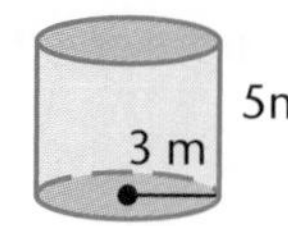

15.
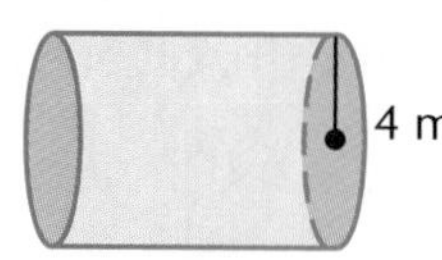

16.
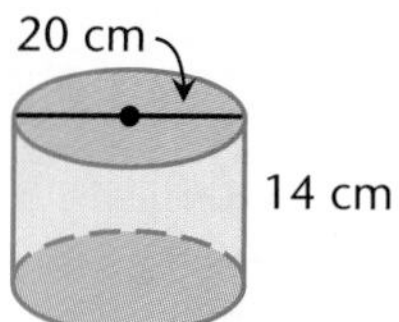

For each cylinder, replace the ? with the missing measurement.

17. $r = 2$ in.
$h = 6$ in.
$V \approx$?

18. $d = 3.5$ cm
$h \approx$?
$V \approx 57.7\text{ cm}^3$

19. $d = 5.4$ m
$h = 8$ m
$V \approx$?

20. Which swimming pool holds more water?

A.
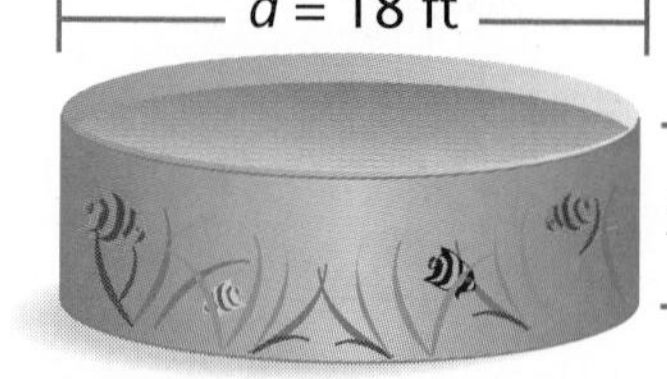

B.
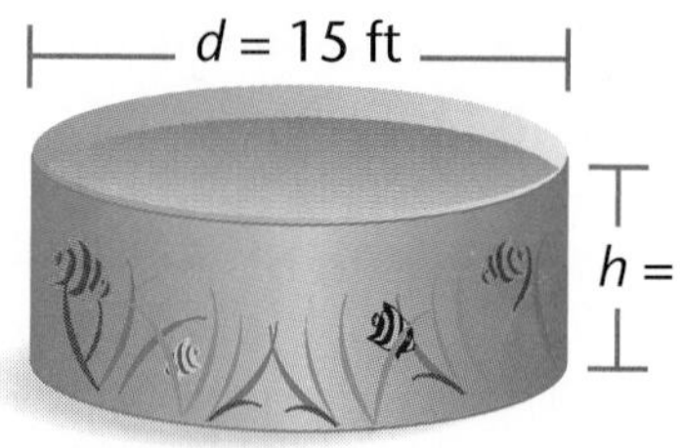

21. **Challenge** Mugs come in many different shapes and sizes.

a. What space figure are most mugs shaped like?

b. Design a mug that will hold about the same amount of liquid as the one labeled, but with different dimensions. Sketch your mug and label its height and diameter.

Visual THINKING

Exercise 22 checks that you can make connections between prisms and cylinders and the methods used to find their volumes.

Reflecting on the Section

22. Make a *concept map* that pulls together what you have learned about circles, prisms, and cylinders. Include ideas about:

- parts of a prism, a circle, and a cylinder
- formulas for area, volume, and circumference.

Spiral Review

Find the circumference of each circle. Use 3.14 for π. (Module 7, p. 493)

23. diameter = 13 ft 24. radius = 6 in. 25. diameter = 4.5 m

Write each percent as a decimal. (Module 3, p. 176)

26. 40% 27. 9% 28. 15% 29. 63%

Graph each ordered pair on a coordinate grid. (Module 4, p. 288)

30. (5, 4) 31. (0, 7) 32. (2, 6) 33. (7, 3)

Extension

Volume of a Cone

Home Involvement **Use the *Cone and Cylinder Nets* on Labsheet 5D to find the relationship between the volume of a cone and the volume of a cylinder.**

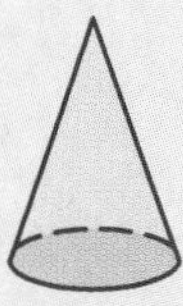

The cones you'll work with are *circular* cones because their bases are shaped like circles.

34. a. Cut out and fold the nets.

    b. How is a cone like a cylinder? a pyramid? How is it different from each?

    c. How do the heights of the cone and cylinder compare? How do the shapes and sizes of their bases compare?

35. a. Fill the cone with rice and pour the rice into the cylinder. Repeat until the cylinder is full.

    b. How many of the cones filled with rice does it take to fill the cylinder?

36. Write a formula for the volume of a cone.

Find the volume of each cone. Round to the nearest hundredth.

37.

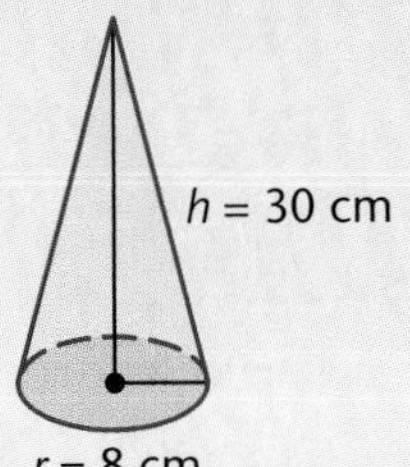

38.

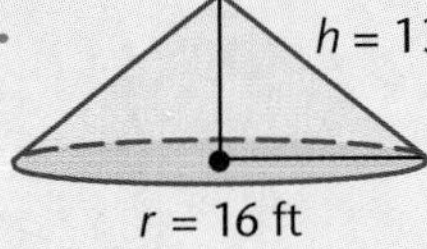

39.

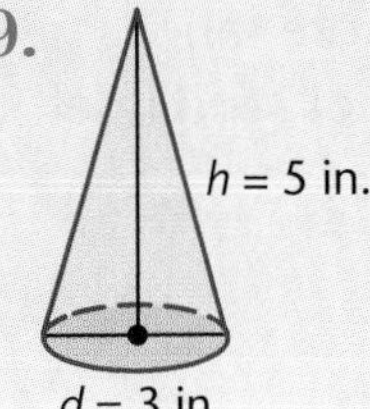

Section 5 Extra Skill Practice

Find the area of the circle with the given radius (r) or diameter (d). Use the π key on a calculator or 3.14 for π. Round to the nearest hundredth.

1. $r = 26.3$ mm

2. 

3. $r = \frac{1}{2}$ ft

Find the exact area of the circle with the given radius (r) or diameter (d).

4. 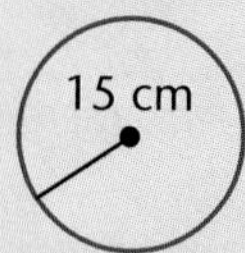

5. $d = 49$ yd

6. 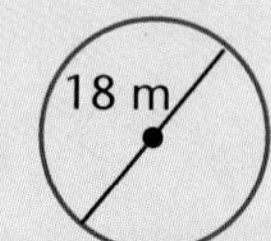

Find the volume of each cylinder. Round to the nearest hundredth.

7. 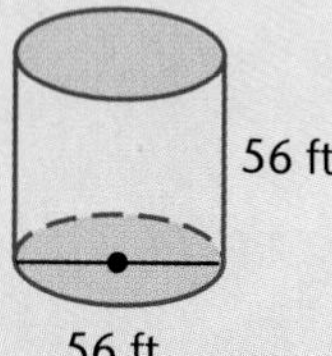

8. 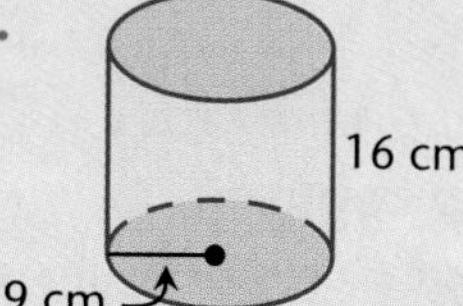

9. 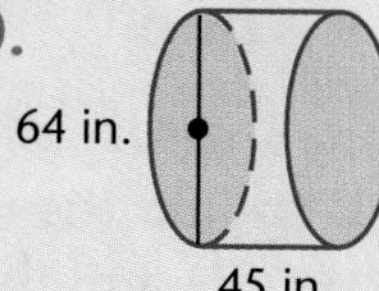

For each cylinder, replace the ? with the missing measurement. Round to the nearest tenth in Exercises 10–11 and to the nearest whole in Exercise 12.

10. $r = 4.7$ m
$h \approx$?
$V \approx 458\ m^3$

11. $d = 2.5$ ft
$h = 4.5$ ft
$V \approx$?

12. $r \approx$?
$h = 6$ cm
$V \approx 1885\ cm^3$

Standardized Testing ▶ Performance Task

Suppose the first cylinder is full of sand. If you pour sand from the first cylinder into the second cylinder, can you fill the second cylinder to the top? If not, then how much more sand is needed? If so, what volume of sand is left over in the first cylinder?

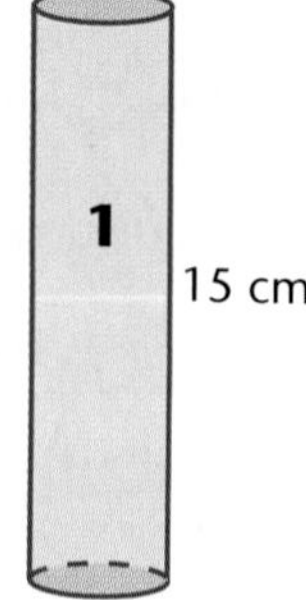

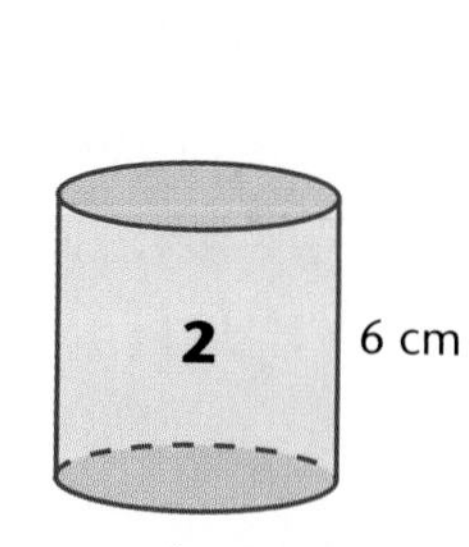

Section 6 Temperature, Integers, and Coordinate Graphs

IN THIS SECTION

EXPLORATION 1
- Temperature and Integers

EXPLORATION 2
- Graphing Ordered Pairs

World Traveler

Setting the Stage

from *The Great Travelers* by Milton Rugoff

"Of all the travelers the world has known, there is none whose name conjures up [brings to mind] more images of the exotic, of the wonder of unknown places, than that of Marco Polo.

It was in 1271 that the seventeen-year-old Marco set out from Venice with his father and uncle....it took the Polos more than three years to reach China and the fabulous court of [its ruler] Kublai Khan....Eventually [Marco] visited nearly every part of the vast empire....The Polos finally arrived in Venice after an absence of almost twenty-six years."

Marco Polo in a Tartar costume.

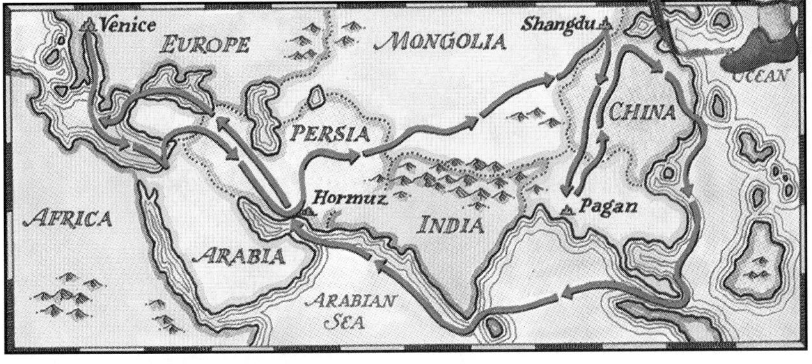

Think About It

1 How many years ago did Marco Polo begin his trip?

2 Use the map of the Polos' route. What different kinds of weather do you think the Polos experienced along the way?

GOAL

LEARN HOW TO...
- measure temperature
- compare integers

AS YOU...
- explore the climate and geography along Marco Polo's route

KEY TERMS
- Celsius (°C)
- Fahrenheit (°F)
- positive
- negative
- integer

Exploration 1

Temperature and Integers

Marco Polo's travels took him to places with a wide variety of weather conditions. During the first summer of his trip, he visited the city of Hormuz on the Persian Gulf. In Hormuz the desert wind, or *simoom,* was so hot that the people spent all morning covered up to their chins in the water of a nearby river.

3 What do you think the high temperature was on a hot day in Hormuz during Marco Polo's visit?

Student Resource

Interpreting Temperature Scales

The thermometers show two different ways to measure temperature.

Celsius Temperature Scale

Fahrenheit Temperature Scale

In **degrees Celsius (°C)**, water freezes at 0° C and boils at 100° C.

In **degrees Fahrenheit (°F)**, water freezes at 32° F and boils at 212° F.

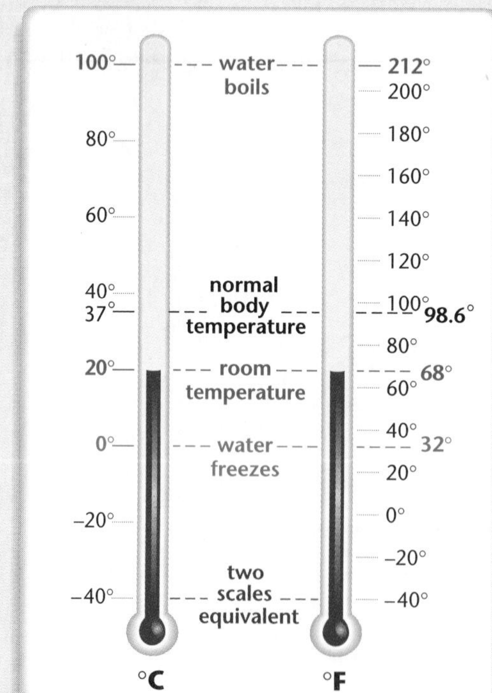

Temperatures that are *above zero* are positive. For example, you write *5 degrees above zero* as +5° or 5°.

Temperatures that are *below zero* are negative. For example, you write *5 degrees below zero* as –5°.

4 What temperature on the Celsius scale is about the same as 0° F? Will water freeze at this temperature? Explain.

▶ **The benchmark temperatures shown on the Student Resource on page 510 can help you to estimate other temperatures.**

5 **Estimation** Estimate the temperature in each scene in degrees Celsius and in degrees Fahrenheit.

a.

b.

c.

d.

6 Select the warmer temperature in each pair.

a. 30° F, 32° F **b.** –5° F, 5° F **c.** –8° F, –21° F

▶ **The numbers you have been using to describe temperature are *integers*. The integers are the numbers ..., –3, –2, –1, 0, 1, 2, 3, ... You can show integers on a number line.**

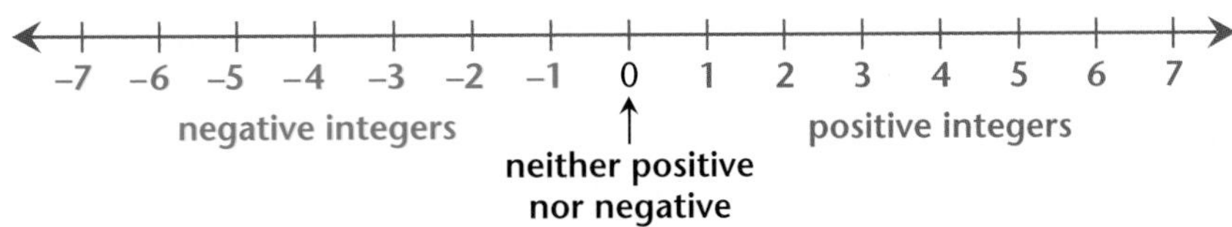

7 **a.** List the next three integers to the right of 7 on the number line. Are they *positive* or *negative* integers?

b. List the next three integers to the left of –7 on the number line. Are they *positive* or *negative* integers?

8 Integers are used to describe more than just temperatures. In the diagram, which elevations are represented by positive integers? by negative integers? by zero?

9 The Dead Sea has an elevation of 1312 ft below sea level. Write an integer for the elevation of the Dead Sea.

10 Write an integer to represent each measurement.

a. 40° below zero **b.** 10,200 ft above sea level

c. a profit of $752 **d.** a 50 point drop in stock

▶ **Comparing Integers** **When you want to compare temperatures or elevations, you can think about comparing integers using a number line.**

EXAMPLE

Use a number line to compare –2 and –6.

SAMPLE RESPONSE

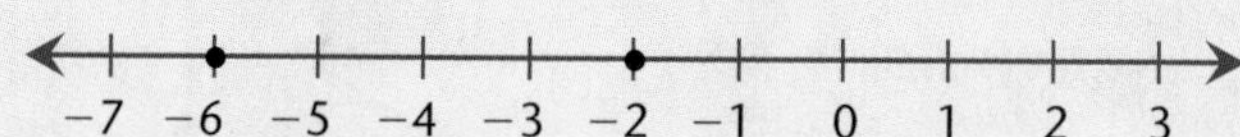

Since –2 is to the right of –6 on the number line, –2 > –6.

11 **a.** List three integers that are greater than –6.

b. The integers you listed in part (a) are three solutions to the inequality $x > -6$. List two solutions to the inequality $x < -1$.

✓ QUESTION 12

...checks that you can compare integers.

12 **✓ CHECKPOINT** Replace each ? with > or <.

a. 3 ? –4 **b.** –8 ? –2 **c.** 0 ? 4

d. 8 ? –9 **e.** –5 ? –13 **f.** 4 ? –4

13 **Discussion** After leaving Hormuz, the Polos started their long trek northeast to China. Their route crossed the Pamir Plateau, which has an elevation of 15,600 ft above sea level—so high that people call it the "Roof of the World." How much does the elevation increase from the Dead Sea to the Pamir Plateau?

HOMEWORK EXERCISES ▶ See Exs. 1–23 on pp. 517–518.

Exploration 2

GRAPHING Ordered Pairs

GOAL

LEARN HOW TO...
- graph points with integer coordinates on a coordinate grid

AS YOU...
- play the game *On the Trail of Marco Polo*

KEY TERMS
- quadrant

SET UP *Work with a partner. You will need:* • *Labsheet 6A* • *metric ruler* • *compass to draw circles (optional)* • *graph paper*

If you were to take a trip to visit all the wonders of the world, you would probably want to pack a world map.

In the thirteenth century, many parts of the world were still unknown. World travelers like Marco Polo had incomplete maps. Today's world maps show a system of lines that you can use to locate any place on Earth.

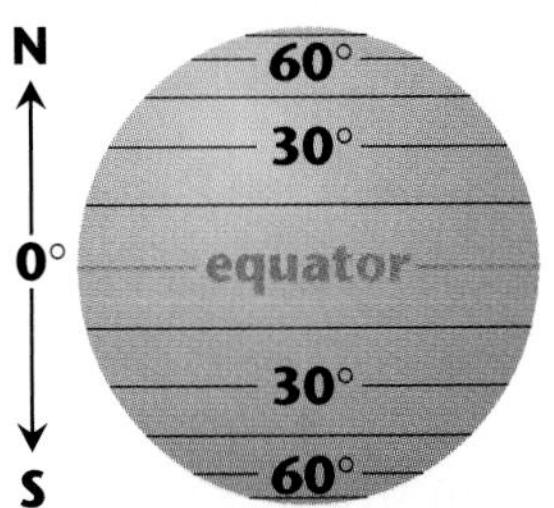

Latitude tells how far north or south of the **equator**.

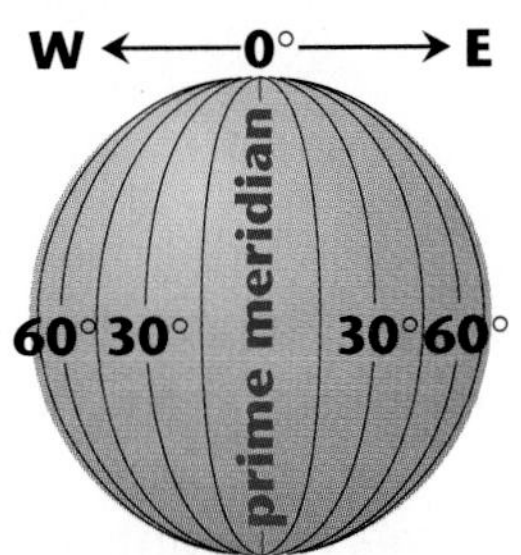

Longitude tells how far east or west of the **prime meridian**.

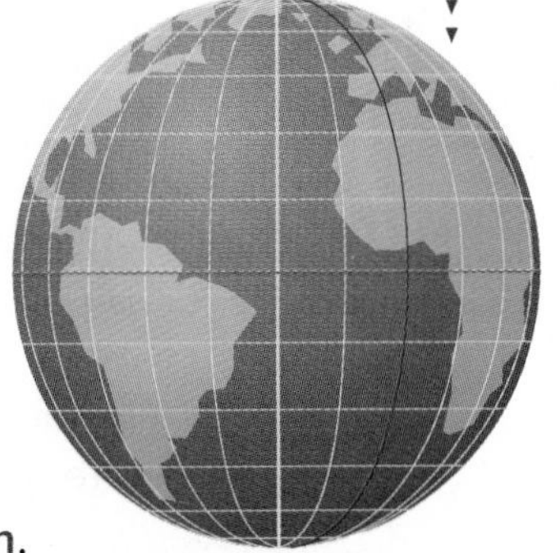

The prime meridian is the line of longitude that runs through Greenwich, England.

▶ **Latitude and longitude lines form a coordinate grid.**

14 Is the United States *north* or *south* of the equator? *east* or *west* of the prime meridian?

15 Explain how two distinct locations can both be at 30° latitude and on the same line of longitude.

▶ **In this exploration, you'll play the game *On the Trail of Marco Polo.* To play the game, you need to be able to graph ordered pairs of integers on a coordinate grid.**

The grid below extends the one you used in Module 4 to include points with coordinates that are negative integers. The axes divide the grid into four parts called quadrants.

EXAMPLE

Graph the ordered pair (–2, 3) on a coordinate grid.

SAMPLE RESPONSE

- Start at *O*, the origin.
- Since the first coordinate is **negative**, the horizontal move is to the **left**.
- Since the second coordinate is **positive**, the vertical move is **up**.

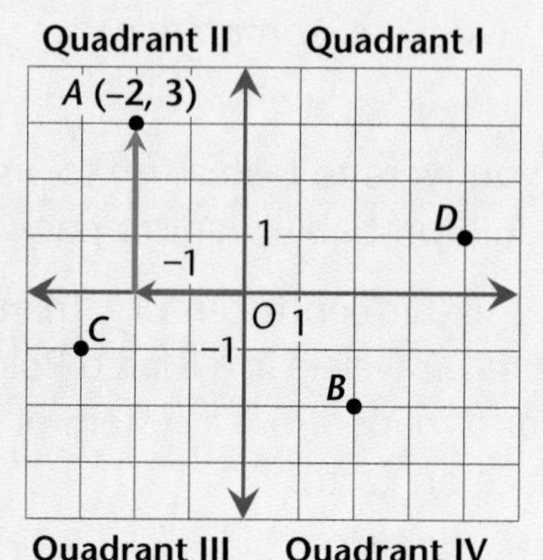

FOR ◀ HELP
with *coordinate graphing*, see
MODULE 4, p. 288

16 In Module 4 you graphed ordered pairs in which both coordinates were positive numbers. In which quadrant are the graphs of those ordered pairs located? Why?

17 What are the ordered pairs for points *B*, *C*, and *D* on the coordinate grid in the Example?

18 In which quadrant is the graph of an ordered pair located when both coordinates are negative? when only the first coordinate is negative? when only the second coordinate is negative? Explain.

19 Make a coordinate grid on graph paper. The integers on each axis should range from –10 to 10. Then plot each point on your grid.

a. (1, –5) **b.** (–6, 9) **c.** (–4, –8)

d. (4, 0) **e.** (–1, 7) **f.** (0, –10)

✓ QUESTION 20

...checks that you can locate a point on a coordinate grid.

20 **✓ CHECKPOINT** If you were to plot the point with coordinates (–3, 0) on the coordinate grid in the Example, which point on the grid—*A*, *B*, *C*, or *D*—would be closest to the new point?

21 **Use Labsheet 6A.** The object of the game *On the Trail of Marco Polo* is to find the ordered pair of integers that represents Marco Polo's location. Read the rules. Then play the game twice with your partner, so each of you has a chance to be Marco Polo.

On the Trail of Marco Polo

- Decide which player will be Marco Polo. The other player is the Searcher. Each player needs a gameboard.
- Place an upright notebook between you and your partner so that you cannot see each other's game board.

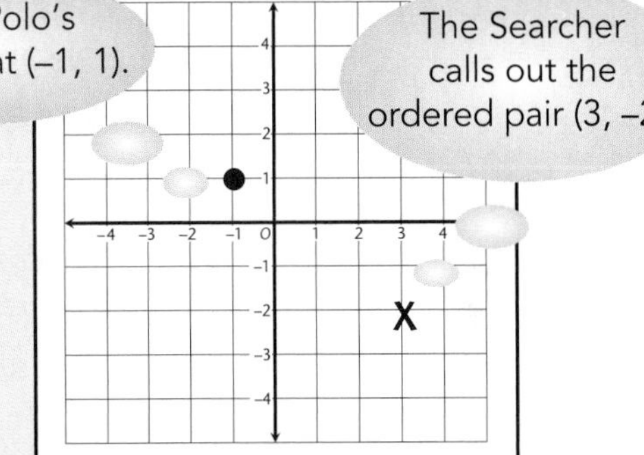

- The player who is Marco Polo should choose a point at the intersection of two grid lines to indicate Marco's location, and then mark a dot (•) at this point.
- The Searcher calls out a guess for the ordered pair that represents Marco Polo's location. Both players draw an "X" at this point.
- The player who is Marco Polo should use a metric ruler to measure how far the "X" is from the dot to the nearest millimeter, and call out the measurement.
- The Searcher has four more chances to guess the ordered pair. The game ends when the Searcher either finds Marco Polo or has no guesses left.

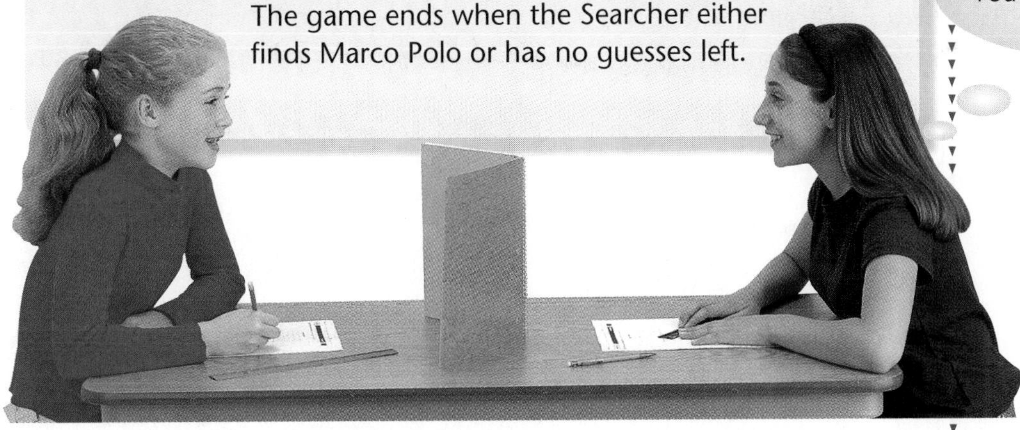

22 **Discussion** Think about how you played the game.

a. When you were the Searcher, was it helpful to know how far your guess was from Marco Polo's location? Explain.

b. What strategies did you use to play the game?

HOMEWORK EXERCISES See Exs. 24–27 on pp. 518–519.

Section 6 Key Concepts

Key Terms

Celsius (°C)

Fahrenheit (°F)

integers

positive integers

negative integers

quadrant

Temperature and Integers (pp. 510–512)

You can measure temperature in degrees Celsius or Fahrenheit. You can use integers to represent temperatures, elevations, and some other measurements.

negative integers zero positive integers

..., −4, −3, −2, −1, 0, 1, 2, 3, 4, ...

Comparing Integers:

- A positive integer is always greater than a negative integer. 5 > −6
- A negative integer that is closer to zero on a number line is always greater than a negative integer that is farther from zero. −3 > −6

Graphing Ordered Pairs of Integers (pp. 513–514)

A coordinate grid for graphing points where coordinates are integers has **four quadrants**.

Example

Write the coordinates of point A.

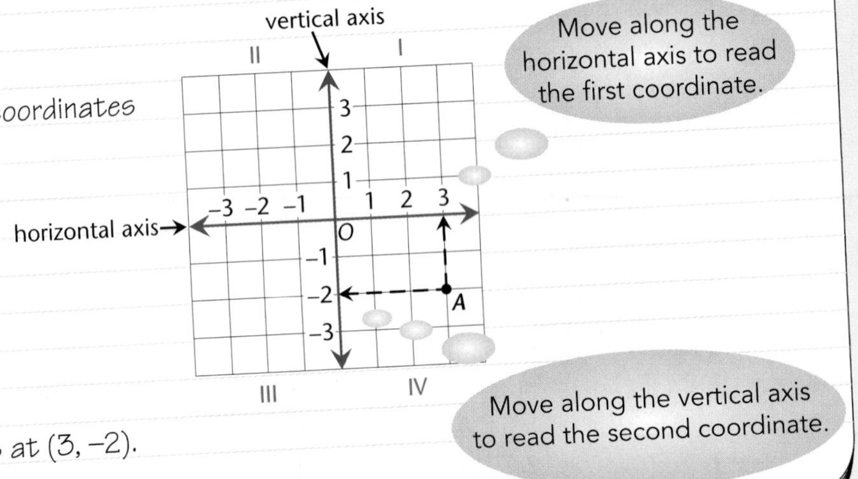

Point A is at (3, −2).

Key Concepts Questions

23 One day a thermometer read 8° F at 10 A.M. At 10 P.M. on the same day, the thermometer read –13° F.

a. Was the temperature reading higher at 10 A.M. or 10 P.M.?

b. Was the temperature at 10 A.M. *above* or *below* freezing?

24 Explain how you would graph (–5, –1) on a coordinate grid.

Section 6
Practice & Application Exercises

YOU WILL NEED

For Ex. 26:
- graph paper

For Ex. 31–34:
- protractor

Writing For each average daily temperature, describe the clothing it is reasonable to wear and the outdoor activities it is reasonable to participate in. Explain your choices.

1. 63° F
2. 32° C
3. 27° F
4. –15° C

5. While in Russia Marco Polo experienced "the greatest cold that is to be found anywhere, so great as to be scarcely bearable." Give Fahrenheit and Celsius temperatures to match this condition.

Interpreting Data Use the graph for Exercises 6–9.

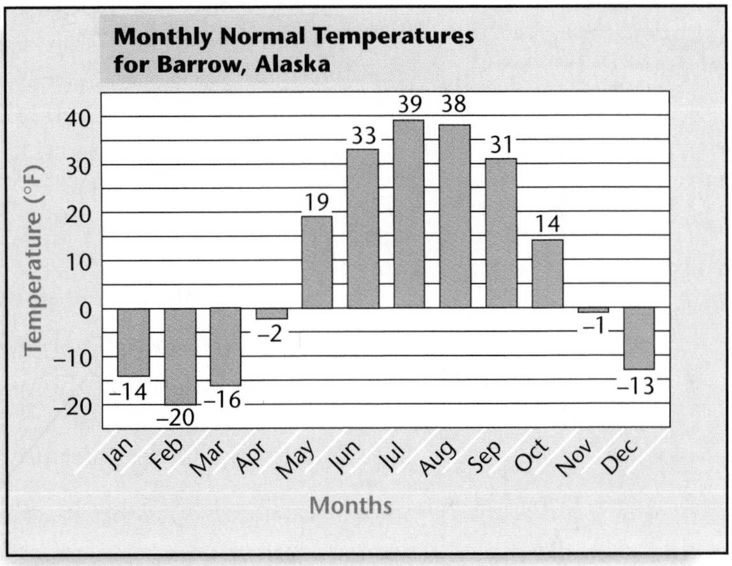

Monthly Normal Temperatures for Barrow, Alaska

Temperature (°F)

Months	Jan	Feb	Mar	Apr	May	Jun	Jul	Aug	Sep	Oct	Nov	Dec
Temperature (°F)	–14	–20	–16	–2	19	33	39	38	31	14	–1	–13

6. Which month shown is the coldest? the warmest?

7. How are the temperatures for January and October alike? How are they different?

8. List the months in order from the coldest to the warmest.

9. How much higher is the normal temperature in July than in October? in April than in January? in October than in March?

Write an integer to represent each measurement.

10. 25 yard gain in football
11. a debt of $349
12. 823 ft below sea level
13. a credit of $10

14. Draw a number line, and use a dot to locate each integer on it. Then list the integers from least to greatest.

    7, –1, –9, 3, 5, –5, 2, 4, –7

Replace each __?__ with > or <.

15. –5 __?__ 4
16. –9 __?__ –5
17. 0 __?__ –3
18. –7 __?__ –20

19. **Algebra Connection** On a number line, show two positive and two negative solutions of the inequality $x < 10$.

Social Studies *The Diving Bell* by Todd Strasser is a historical novel set in sixteenth century Mexico. In the story, a Spanish ship loaded with gold is sunk off the Mexican coast. The ship, the *Santo Cristo,* lies so deep that even the best divers cannot bring up the treasure. A young girl named Culca finds a way to do it:

> ..."If the great [church] bell were lowered into the water a diver could swim under it and breathe new air," Culca explained. [A diver] could go deeper and stay down longer...."

20. **Estimation** The sides of a ship sent to pick up the recovered treasure rise "the height of five men" above the surface. Estimate this height in feet. Then write an integer for this measurement.

21. The bell was lowered 10 fathoms below the surface to where the *Santo Cristo* was believed to be. Write an integer for this depth in feet. (1 fathom = 6 ft)

22. a. In 1733 a real Spanish ship, the *San Pedro*, sank in 18 ft of water. Write an integer for the depth of the wreck in feet.

    b. Write an inequality that compares the depth of this real wreck with the depth of the wreck in the story.

23. **Challenge** Order the numbers from least to greatest.

    $-23, 56, -12\frac{3}{4}, 2.4, -35, 25\frac{1}{3}, 25.48, 0, 13, -12.25, 25.5$

Use the coordinate grid for Exercises 24 and 25.

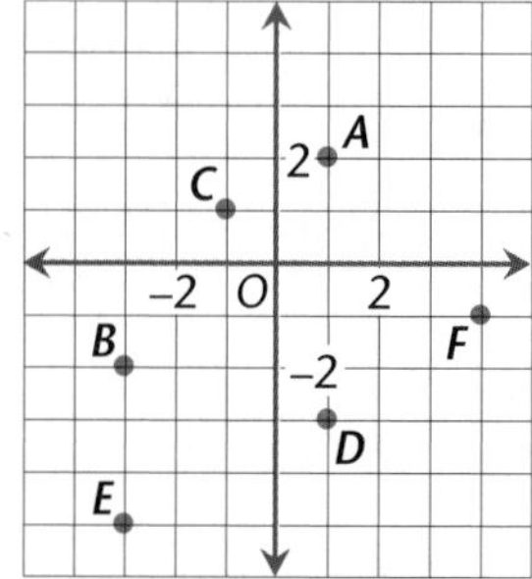

24. Write the coordinates of each labeled point *A–F*.

25. **Geometry Connection** Find the coordinates of each point.

    a. point *A* after a reflection over the vertical axis.

    b. point *B* after a reflection over the horizontal axis.

26. a. **Create Your Own** Draw a coordinate grid on graph paper. Plot points and draw segments connecting these points to create your own design. List the ordered pairs for your design in the order they need to be connected.

    b. **Home Involvement** Without showing the figure, ask a friend or family member to follow your instructions to try to make your design. How did the person do?

Reflecting on the Section

Be prepared to discuss your response to Exercise 27 in class.

27. a. Explain how number lines are used to form a coordinate grid.

b. How do the integers in the ordered pair for a point change if the point is moved to the right on a coordinate grid? to the left? up? down?

Discussion

Exercise 27 checks your understanding of integers on a number line and on a coordinate grid.

Spiral Review

Find the area of each circle. Use 3.14 for π. Round to the nearest hundredth. (Module 7, p. 504)

28. diameter = 6 in.

29. radius = 8 cm

30. diameter = 3.5 m

Use a protractor to draw each angle. (Module 6, p. 431)

31. 25°

32. 175°

33. 92°

34. 58°

35. **Choose a Method** Cherries cost $2.29 per pound. A bag of cherries weighs 1.7 lb. Would you use mental math, paper and pencil, or estimation to decide if $5 is enough money? Explain. (Module 1, p. 50; Module 4, p. 278)

Create a World Travel Poster

Writing Integers If you have not already done so, gather information on the geography and climate of the places where the sites for your poster are located.

5 For each site, write an integer to represent what you might experience as an average temperature if you traveled there in January, or write an integer to represent the elevation of each site.

6 Write an inequality comparing two of the values (two temperatures or two elevations) in Question 5.

Section 6 Extra Skill Practice

You will need: • *graph paper* (Exs. 12–19)

For each situation, give a possible temperature in degrees Fahrenheit and in degrees Celsius.

1. The snow on the ground is starting to melt.
2. The beach is crowded with swimmers.
3. People are wearing light sweaters or jackets.

Replace each ? with > or <.

4. 5 __?__ –14
5. –8 __?__ –4
6. –7 __?__ 0
7. 6 __?__ 18
8. –6 __?__ –18
9. 23 __?__ –24

Use the coordinate grid for Exercises 10–11.

10. Write the coordinates of each labeled point *A*–*H*.
11. If you were to plot the point with the coordinates (–3,1), which labeled point would it be closest to?

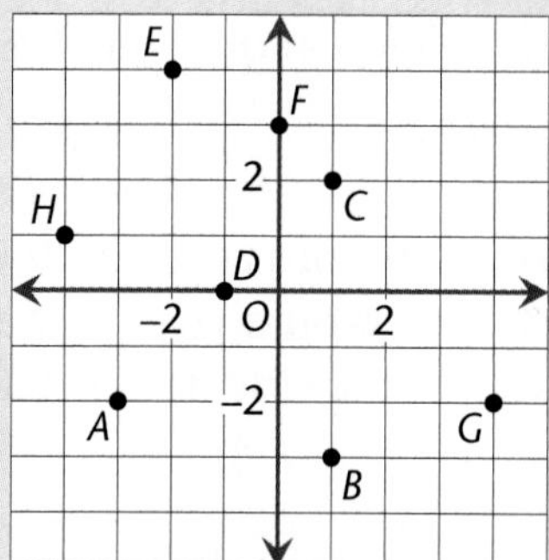

Make a coordinate grid on graph paper. The integers on each axis should range from –10 to 10. Then plot each point on your grid.

12. (–10, 0)
13. (5, –3)
14. (2, 4)
15. (–3, 5)
16. (0, –6)
17. (–2, 2)
18. (–7, –4)
19. (8, –9)

Standardized Testing ▶ Open-Ended

1. On a weekend afternoon in the summer, which temperature would you prefer, 20°C or 32°C? Explain why.
2. Here is an example of an inequality for which –5 is a solution: $x < -2$.

   Write two more inequalities for which –5 is a solution.

Create a World Travel Poster

Finishing and Sharing Your Poster In this module you have been gathering information on some of the most famous places in the world. To finish the module project, you'll use this information to complete your poster. You'll also decide which of the four sites you would most like to see.

SET UP

You will need:

- *poster board or construction paper*
- *markers or colored pencils*
- *scissors*
- *glue or tape*
- *visuals you have gathered*

7 Create your poster. Include the following:

- the name and the location of each site
- visuals that you have made or collected to help others see details of the site (See Questions 3 and 4.)
- a "Did you know?" fact for each site that applies at least one of the mathematical ideas you learned in the module and uses information you have gathered. (See Questions 2 and 5.)

8 Look back at your poster and the information you gathered. Which site would you most like to visit? Explain in a brief summary what there is about the site that attracts you.

9 Display your poster in class along with your classmates. Then look back at the presentation scale of the Assessment Scales from Module 1. What types of things make each poster unique? Is there any one poster that you found especially eye-catching? If so, explain why.

10 Think about each poster you saw. Name something you learned about a different part of the world or about one of the "world wonders" presented.

MODULE 7

Review and Assessment

You will need: • *Review and Assessment Labsheet* (Ex. 1, 2, 13–15) • *metric ruler* (Ex. 2, 8, 14) • *scissors and tape* (Ex. 4) • *graph paper* (Ex. 21)

Use the Review and Assessment Labsheet for Exercises 1 and 2. (Sec. 1, Explor. 1–3)

1. Identify each of the *Polygons.*

2. Measure and label a base and the corresponding height of each of the *Polygons* to the nearest tenth of a centimeter. Then calculate the area of each polygon.

3. A flower planter is in the shape of a rectangular prism 18 in. long, $5\frac{1}{2}$ in. high, and $6\frac{1}{2}$ in. wide. Estimate the volume of soil that the planter can hold. (Sec. 2, Explor. 1)

Use the net shown for Exercises 4–8. (Sec. 2, Explors. 1 and 2)

4. a. Predict what space figure the net will form.

   b. Trace the net. Then cut out the tracing and fold it to check your prediction.

5. Describe the shapes of the faces. Then name the space figure.

6. How many faces, vertices, and edges does the figure have?

7. Sketch the space figure.

8. a. Decide the dimensions you need to find the volume. Then find these measurements to the nearest millimeter.

   b. Find the volume.

9. Dick bought a 7 lb bag of apples for $4.97. (Sec. 3, Explor. 1)

   a. What was the cost per pound of the apples?

   b. Each apple weighed about 12 oz. About how many apples were in the bag?

Replace each ? with the missing measurement. (Sec. 3, Explor. 1)

10. $3\frac{1}{2}$ lb = ___?___ oz

11. 3500 lb = ___?___ tons

12. 80 oz = ___?___ lb

Use the Review and Assessment Labsheet for Exercises 13–15.
(Sec. 4, Explors. 1 and 2; Sec. 5, Explor. 1)

13. Name parts of the *Circle* as described.

a. the center b. two radii c. two chords d. a diameter

14. Measure the radius of the *Circle* to the nearest tenth of a centimeter.

15. Find the circumference and the area of the *Circle*.

16. The Temple of Artemis in ancient Greece was regarded as one of the Seven Ancient Wonders of the World. It dated back to 550 BC and was thought to be the most beautiful structure on earth. The structure had cylindrical columns 60 ft high. If the diameter of each column was about 15 ft, what was the volume of one of the columns? **(Sec. 5, Explor. 2)**

17. On February 21, 1918, the temperature in Granville, North Dakota, changed from –33°F to 50°F. Did the weather get warmer or cooler? Explain. **(Sec. 6, Explor. 1)**

Replace each ? with > or < to make each a true statement.
(Sec. 6, Explor. 1)

18. –5 __?__ 3 19. –10 __?__ –2 20. –5 __?__ –6

21. Make a coordinate grid on graph paper. **(Sec. 6, Explor. 2)**

a. Label the axes and the origin.

b. Plot the points (–2, 8) and (5, –4) on the grid.

Reflecting on the Module

22. **a.** Find a container that is shaped like a prism and find its volume.

b. Give the dimensions of a cylinder that has about the same volume as the container you found. Sketch it and label its height and the diameter of a base.

c. Find and label the circumference of a base of the cylinder in part (b).

MODULE 8

OUR ENVIRONMENT

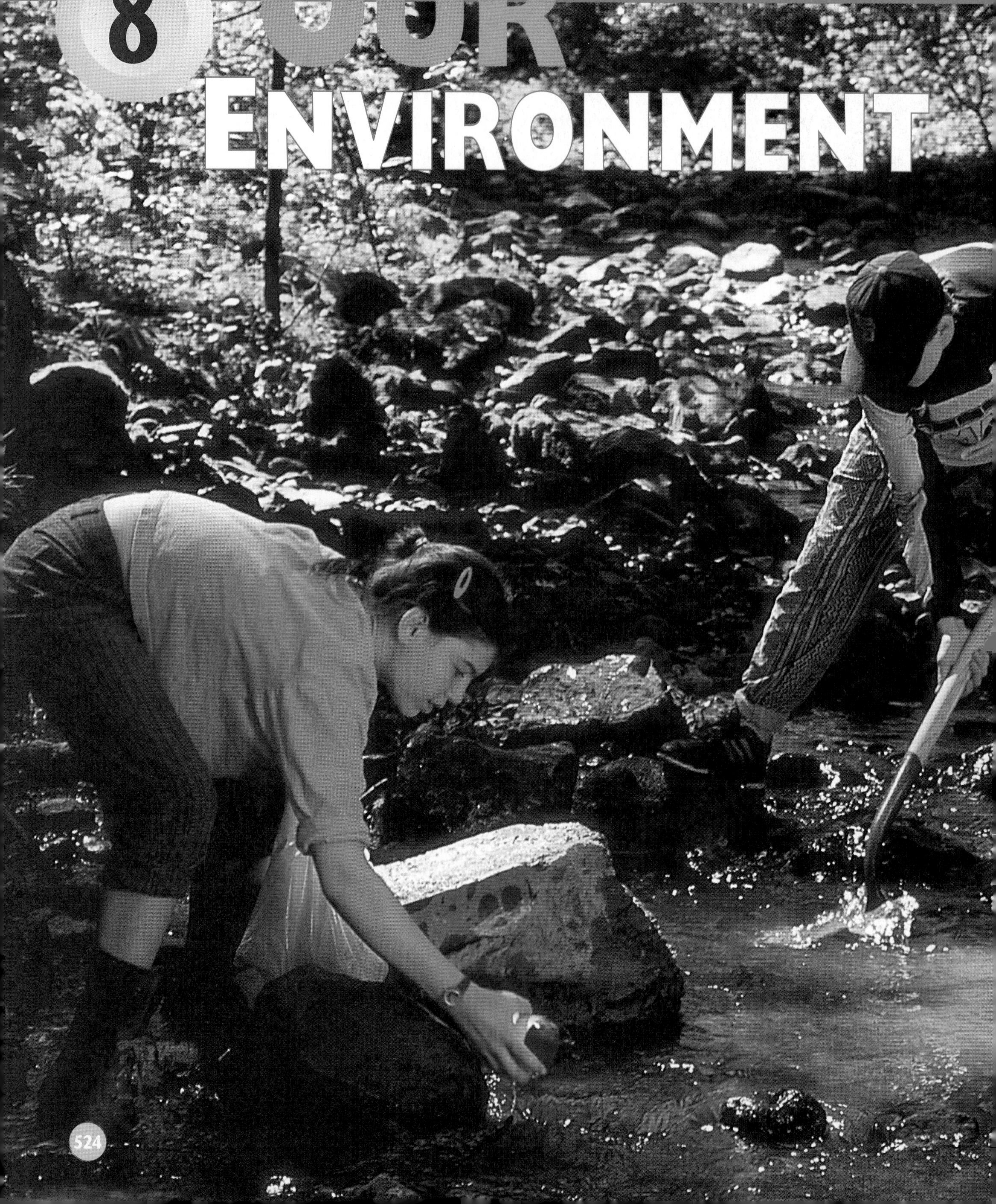

CONNECTING MATHEMATICS & The Theme

SECTION OVERVIEW

1 Adding and Subtracting Integers

As you learn about lightning and electrical charges:

- Add and subtract integers

2 Line Graphs, Scientific Notation, and Percent

As you look at the effects of population growth:

- Make and interpret a line graph
- Find population densities
- Write large numbers in scientific notation
- Multiply by a decimal to find a percent of a number

3 Metric Capacity and Percent

As you explore people's water needs:

- Relate volume and metric capacity
- Estimate capacity in metric units
- Write percents greater than 100%

4 Geometric Probability

As you simulate a meteorite's fall to earth:

- Find geometric probabilities

5 Misleading Graphs and Averages

As you learn about conserving energy and reducing pollution:

- Recognize misleading graphs and averages
- Choose an appropriate graph and average

The Module Project

Play *The Math is Right!*

A quiz game is a fun way to test your knowledge. You'll work as a team to create questions that relate to a theme and to the mathematics you have learned this year. Will your questions stump the other teams in your class? Find out when you play *The Math is Right!* at the end of the module.

More on the Module Project

See pp. 552, 571, and 585.

INTERNET
To learn more about the theme:
http://www.mlmath.com

Adding and Subtracting Integers

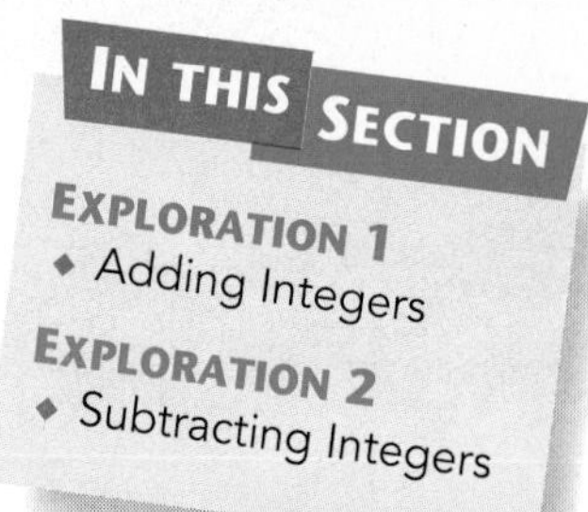

Setting the Stage

Lightning is caused by the movement of electrical charges within a cloud, between two clouds, or between a cloud and the ground.

You may think it is almost impossible to be hit by lightning, but Virginia park ranger Ray Sullivan would surely disagree. Ray was struck by lightning seven different times! The lightning knocked him out, burned off his hair, damaged his hearing, tore off a toenail, threw him in the air, melted his watch, and burned his clothing. Amazingly, Ray survived all seven lightning strikes.

A lightning bolt typically involves over 100,000,000 volts and can have enough power to light up all of New York City!

Think About It

1 Shuffling your feet on a carpet can produce up to a hundred thousand volts—enough to give you quite a shock. About how many times as many volts are there when lightning strikes?

2 **Estimation** Lightning strikes the United States about 40 million times each year. On average, about how often does it strike the United States each day?

▶ **Lightning is one of nature's most powerful forces. In this module you'll learn about how the power of nature affects people and how people affect nature.**

Exploration 1

Adding + Integers

GOAL

LEARN HOW TO...
- add integers

AS YOU...
- play the game *Thunderbolt!*

KEY TERM
- opposites

SET UP *Work with a partner. You will need:* • *Labsheet 1A* • *12 beans, each marked with a "+" on one side and a "–" on the other side* • *paper cup* • *2 game pieces*

▶ **Like other sparks of static electricity, lightning gets its power from the difference in the electrical charges of two objects. You will simulate the changing charges in a cloud by playing the game *Thunderbolt!* When the difference in charges is 10 or more—Zap!**

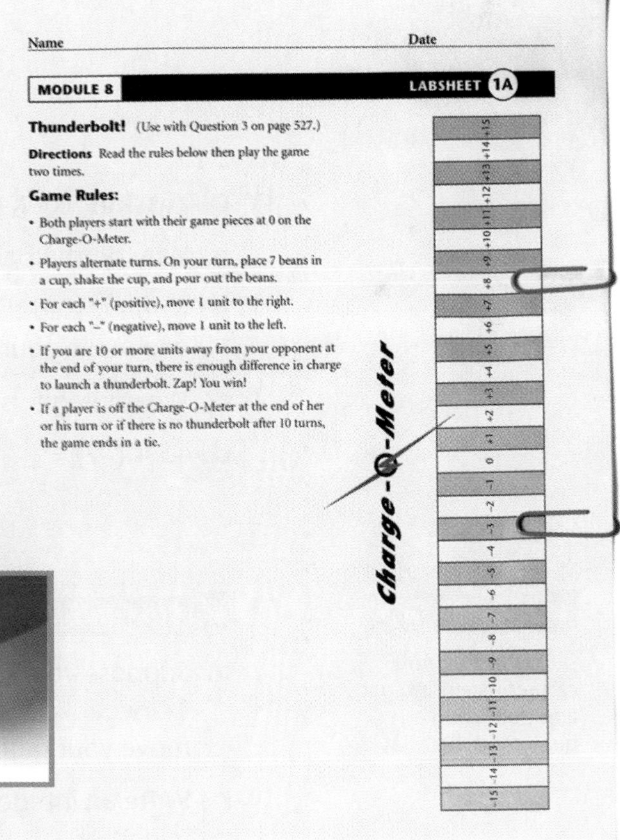
Name Date

MODULE 8 **LABSHEET 1A**

Thunderbolt! (Use with Question 3 on page 527.)

Directions Read the rules below then play the game two times.

Game Rules:
- Both players start with their game pieces at 0 on the Charge-O-Meter.
- Players alternate turns. On your turn, place 7 beans in a cup, shake the cup, and pour out the beans.
- For each "+" (positive), move 1 unit to the right.
- For each "–" (negative), move 1 unit to the left.
- If you are 10 or more units away from your opponent at the end of your turn, there is enough difference in charge to launch a thunderbolt. Zap! You win!
- If a player is off the Charge-O-Meter at the end of her or his turn or if there is no thunderbolt after 10 turns, the game ends in a tie.

3 **Use Labsheet 1A.** Follow the directions on the labsheet to play *Thunderbolt!* Play the game two times.

4 **a.** Did you find a way to quickly determine where to place your game piece after a bean toss? Explain.

b. At the end of a turn, can your game piece ever be an even number of units away from where it was at the start of your turn? Why?

c. At the end of a turn, can your game piece ever be in the same place it was when you started the turn? Why?

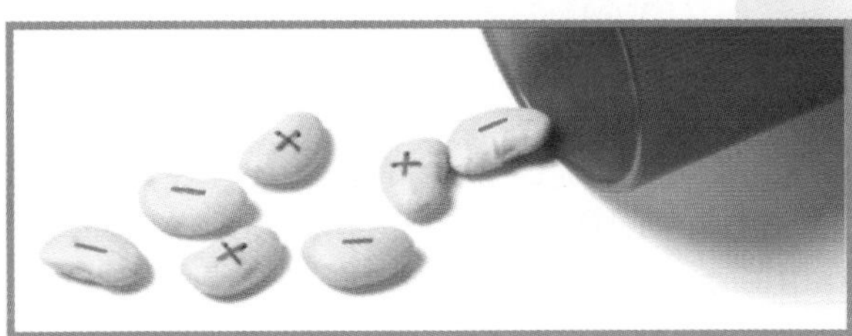

5 **a.** If you played *Thunderbolt!* with only six beans, what moves would be possible?

b. Would playing with only six beans change your answers to Questions 4(b) and 4(c)? Explain.

▶ **One strategy for quickly finding how far to move your game piece is to pair positive beans with negative beans. This strategy can also be used to model addition of integers.**

EXAMPLE

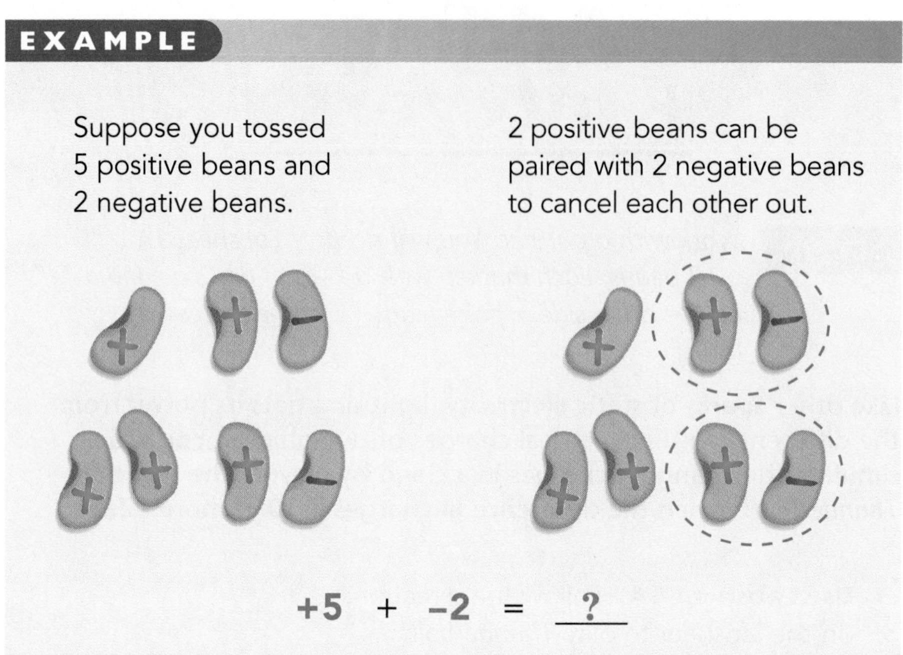

6 **Discussion** Look at the addition in the Example.

a. Why do the paired beans cancel each other out?

b. If you tossed the combination of beans shown, how far would you move your game piece and in what direction?

c. What integer is represented by the combination of beans?

d. +5 + (−2) = __?__

To avoid confusion a negative integer can be shown in parentheses.

✓ QUESTION 7

...checks that you can represent integer addition using a bean model.

7 **✓ CHECKPOINT**

a. Suppose you had 24 beans in your cup and you tossed 14 negative beans and 10 positive beans. How would you move your game piece?

b. Write an integer addition equation for the combination of beans in part (a).

8 Use a bean model to find each sum.

a. +1 + (−5) b. +6 + (−4) c. +3 + (−3) d. −5 + (−2)

Use beans to help answer Questions 9–11.

9 Try This As a Class

a. Write two different addition equations where both addends (the numbers that are added) are negative.

b. Is the sum of two negative numbers positive or negative?

c. How can you find the sum of two negative numbers without using beans?

10 Write two different examples for each case.

Case	Examples
a. one addend is positive, one addend is negative, the sum is a positive integer	
b. one addend is positive, one addend is negative, the sum is a negative integer	
c. one addend is positive, one addend is negative, the sum is zero	

11 Discussion When will the sum of a positive and a negative integer be positive? negative? equal to 0?

12 How can you find the sum of a positive and a negative integer without using beans?

13 Try This as a Class The numbers you used to answer Question 10(c) are *opposites*. What do think it means for two numbers to be **opposites**?

▶ **It is not necessary to label positive integers with a "+" sign. For example, +3 is the same as 3.**

14 ✓ CHECKPOINT Find each sum without using beans.

a. $-17 + 25$
b. $13 + (-7)$
c. $-36 + (-9)$
d. $-11 + 11$
e. $-24 + 19$
f. $12 + (-17)$

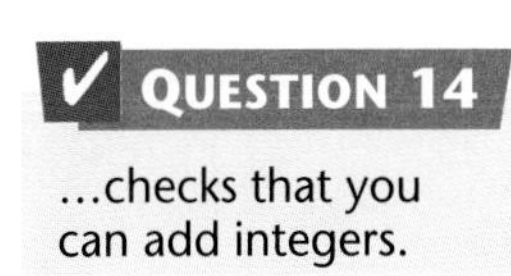

HOMEWORK EXERCISES ▶ See Exs. 1–21 on pp. 534–535.

GOAL

LEARN HOW TO...
- subtract integers

AS YOU...
- model thundercloud charges with beans

Exploration 2

Subtracting – Integers

SET UP *Work in a group. You will need the 12 beans from Exploration 1.*

Though it is not known for certain how thunderclouds become charged, scientists do know that lightning is the movement of electrical charges from a cloud.

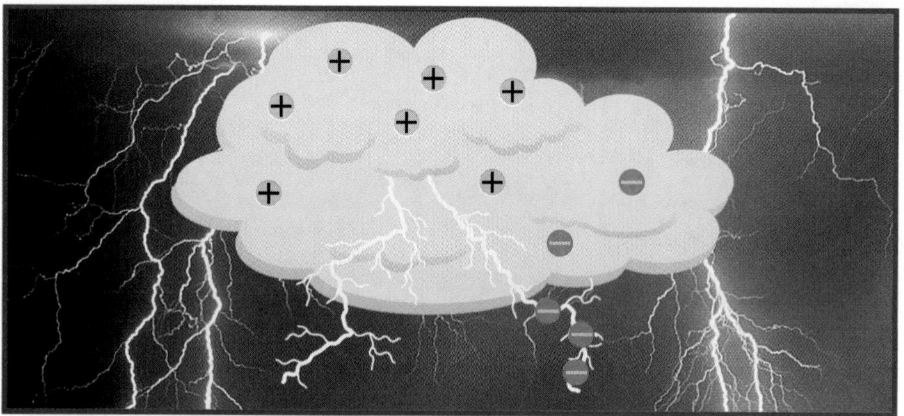

About 90% of all lightning brings a negative charge to the ground.

▶ **Integer subtraction can be modeled in a similar way by taking away beans representing positive or negative charges.**

EXAMPLE

The combination of 7 positive beans and 5 negative beans is +2. There are 3 negative beans being taken away, or +2 – (–3).

take away

+2 – (–3) = 5

15 **Try This as a Class** Use the bean model for 2 – (–3) shown in the Example on page 530.

a. Explain how 2 is modeled by the beans.

b. How is subtracting –3 shown in the model?

c. The difference is 5. How was this found?

16 Write the subtraction equation shown by each bean model.

a.

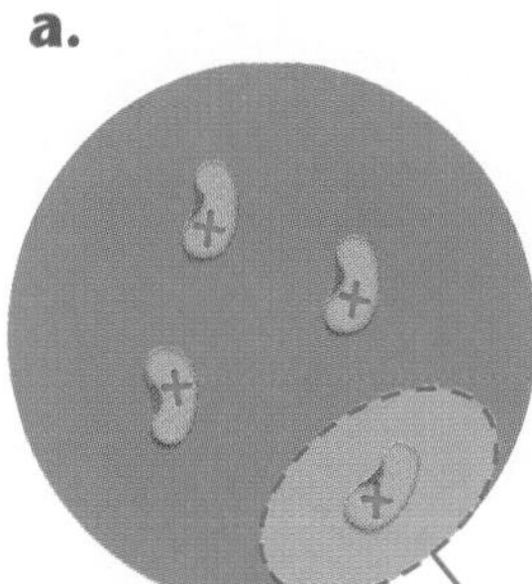

b.

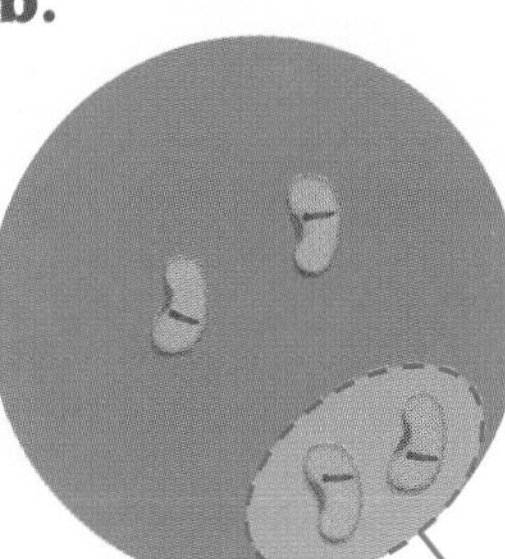

c.

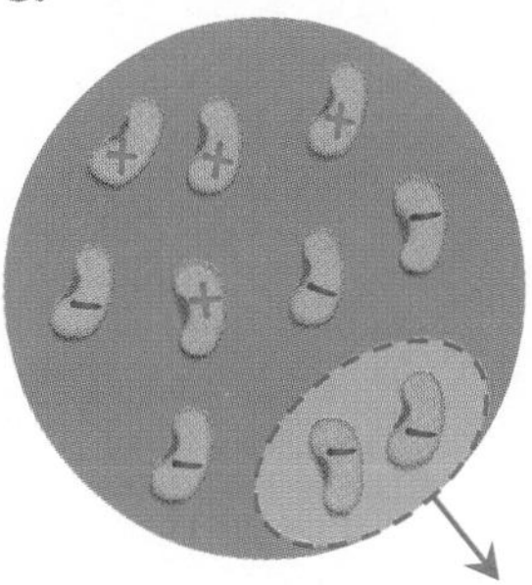

17 Use a bean model to find each difference.

a. –6 – (–3) **b.** –7 – (–2) **c.** –4 – (–4)

18 **Discussion** Think about finding 3 – 6.

a. If you modeled 3 as shown below, why would it be hard to subtract 6?

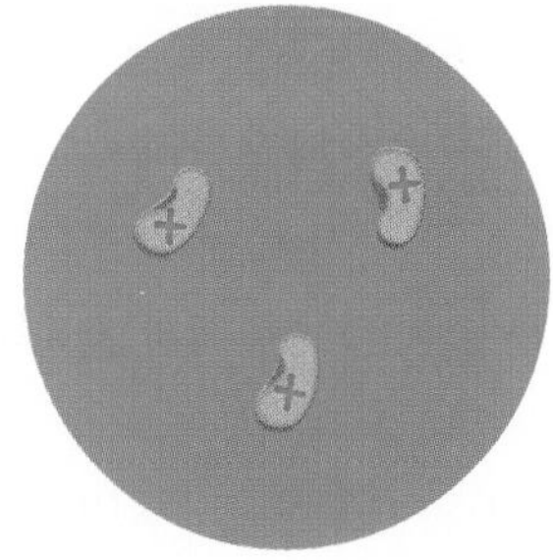

b. You can also model 3 like this. Why can this model be used to subtract 6?

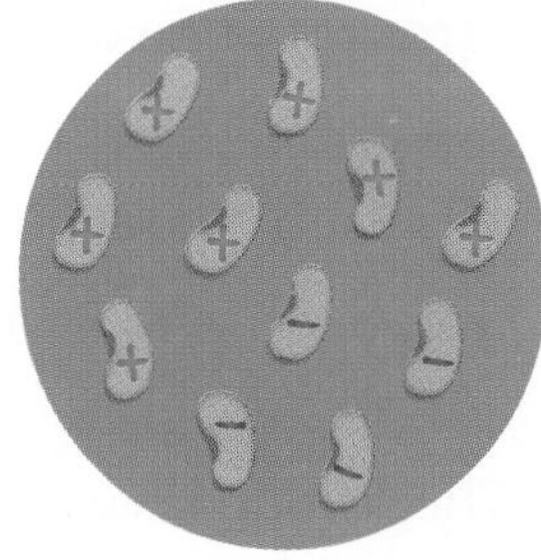

c. Use the model of 3 from part (b) to find 3 – 6.

19 ✓ **CHECKPOINT** Use a bean model to find each difference.

a. 1 – 4 **b.** –2 – (–4) **c.** 3 – (–2) **d.** 0 – (–5)

> ✓ **QUESTION 19**
>
> ...checks that you can use a bean model to subtract integers.

20 Find each sum.

a. 1 + (–4) **b.** –2 + 4 **c.** 3 + 2 **d.** 0 + 5

21 **Discussion** How do the problems and answers from Questions 19 and 20 compare?

▶ **The bean models in the Example below show the relationship between the expressions 5 – (–3) and 5 + 3.**

EXAMPLE

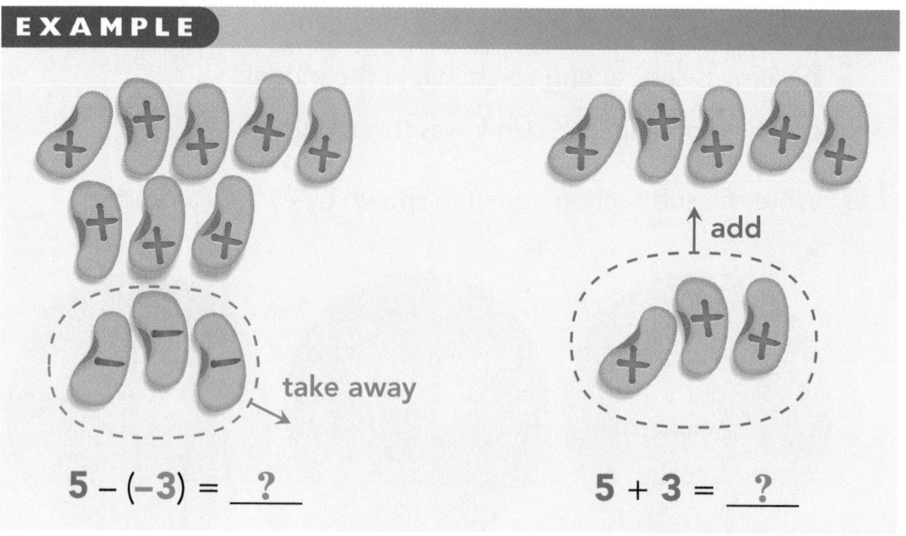

22 **a.** In the Example above, why are 8 positive beans and 3 negative beans used to model 5?

b. How are the expressions 5 – (–3) and 5 + 3 similar?

c. How are the expressions different?

d. Use the beans to find 5 – (–3) and 5 + 3. How do their values compare?

23 **Try This as a Class**

a. Use your answers from Questions 21 and 22 to write a rule for changing a subtraction problem to an addition problem.

b. Use your rule to find –2 – 3 by rewriting it as an addition problem.

c. Check your answer to part (b) by using beans to find –2 – 3.

24 Use your rule from Question 23 to find each difference. Explain your steps.

a. 22 – (–12) **b.** 15 – 72 **c.** –18 – 7

✓ QUESTION 25

...checks that you can subtract integers.

25 **✓ CHECKPOINT** Find each difference.

a. –17 – (–25) **b.** 13 – (–7) **c.** –36 – (–19)

d. –11 – 11 **e.** 49 – 78 **f.** 0 – (–13)

HOMEWORK EXERCISES See Exs. 22–44 on pp. 535–536.

Section 1 Key Concepts

Integer Addition (pp. 527–529)

- The sum of two positive integers is a positive integer. $1 + 2 = 3$
- The sum of two negative integers is a negative integer. $-2 + (-3) = -5$
- The sum of a positive and a negative integer can be positive, negative, or zero. $3 + (-2) = 1$, $2 + (-4) = -2$, $-2 + 2 = 0$

  −2 and 2 are opposites.
- The sum of an integer and 0 is that integer. $-2 + 0 = -2$

Integer Subtraction (pp. 530–532)

Subtraction of an integer can be rewritten as addition of the opposite of the integer.

Example Subtracting a negative:

8 is the opposite of −8.

$$5 - (-8) = 5 + 8$$
$$= 13$$

Example Subtracting a positive:

−7 is the opposite of 7.

$$-3 - 7 = -3 + (-7)$$
$$= -10$$

Key Term

opposites

Key Concepts Questions

26 Find each sum.

a. $-152 + 37$ b. $17 + (-41)$ c. $-23 + (-15)$

27 What integers can be subtracted from −5 so that the difference is positive? negative? zero?

YOU WILL NEED

For Exs. 45–48:
- graph paper

Section 1 Practice & Application Exercises

Write the integer that represents each combination of chips.

1.

2. 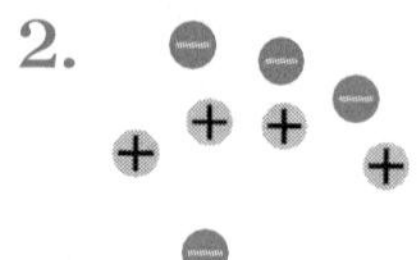

3. 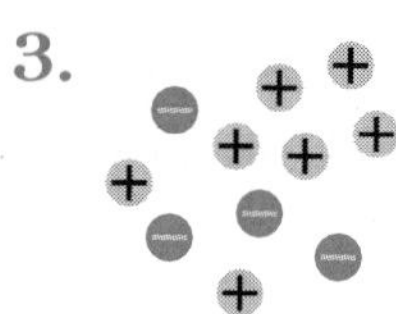

4. Draw a model that represents 4 and uses exactly two negative chips.

5. Draw a model that represents –6 and uses a total of eight chips.

6. Draw a model that represents 0 and uses a total of six chips.

7. **Writing** Is it possible to model 5 using ten chips? Explain why or why not.

Find each sum.

8. 24 + (–16)
9. –12 + (–32)
10. 0 + (–17)
11. –19 + 4
12. –8 + 22
13. 5 + (–15)
14. 12 + (–12)
15. –26 + (–6)
16. 20 + (–55)

17. The table shows monthly deposits and withdrawals from a bank account. The balance in the account on January 1 was $100. What is the balance at the end of June?

Statement of Account

MetroBank

Melissa Hernandez
23 Pine Street
Dallas, TX 75238

MetroBank
2835 West Main Street
Austin, TX 78702

Account Number 1123 886 4 | **Activity From** January | **Through** June

Summary

Month	Deposits	Withdrawals
January	$25	$50
February	$25	$0
March	$25	$40
April	$30	$30
May	$30	$35
June	$30	$20

Algebra Connection **For each expression, describe the possible values for x.**

18. $10 + x$, the sum is a positive integer

19. $-3 + x$, the sum is a negative integer

20. $x + 6$, the sum is zero

21. **Challenge** In a magic square, the sum of the numbers in each row, column, and diagonal is the same. Copy and complete the magic square using –10, –6, –4, 0, 2, 4, and 6.

Magic Square

–8	?	?
?	–2	?
?	?	?

Write the subtraction equation shown by each model.

22.

23.

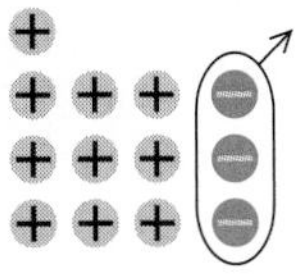

24.

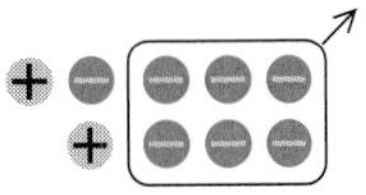

25. Draw a model of 3 that can be used to show the subtraction 3 – (–2).

Write an equivalent addition expression for each subtraction expression. Then find the sum.

26. 18 – (–33)

27. –12 – 9

28. 0 – (–28)

29. **Temperature** The greatest temperature change in one day was recorded in Browning, Montana, on January 23–24, 1916. The temperature dropped from 44°F to –56°F.

   a. Write a subtraction expression to find the range in temperature.

   b. Write an addition expression to find the range in temperature. Use the thermometer to help explain why this expression gives the same answer as your expression from part (a).

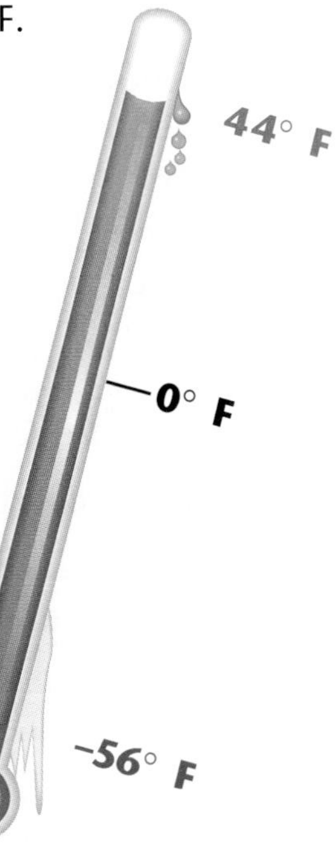

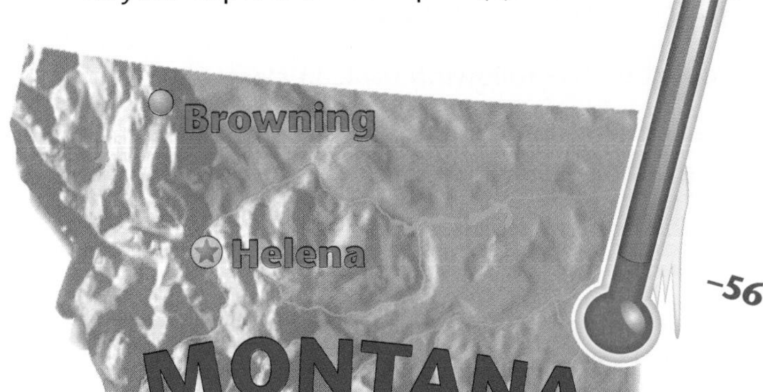

Find each sum or difference.

30. 27 – 55
31. 23 + (–18)
32. –8 – (–7)
33. –10 – 0
34. –29 – (–50)
35. –7 + 24
36. –19 – (–19)
37. –5 – 8
38. 0 – 25
39. –19 + (–19)
40. 0 – (–25)
41. 26 – (–55)

42. **Golf** In 1997, twenty-one-year-old Tiger Woods became the youngest winner of the Masters Tournament.

a. *Par* is the number of strokes it should take a very good golfer to get the ball from the tee into the hole. Of the players in the table, who took the most strokes? the fewest?

b. By how many strokes did Tiger Woods beat Tom Kite?

1997 Masters Tournament

Player	Standings
Tiger Woods	–18
Tom Kite	–6
Tommy Tolles	–5
Tom Watson	–4

–18 means 18 strokes fewer than par.

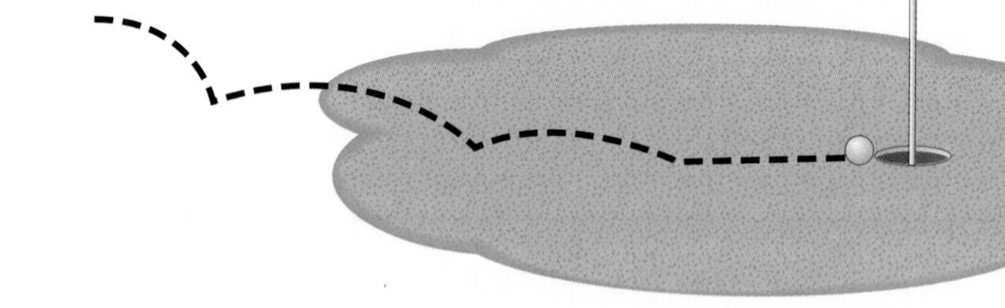

43. **Challenge** You have seen how subtraction problems can be changed to addition problems. Addition problems can also be changed to subtraction problems. Change each addition problem to a subtraction problem. Then find the difference.

a. –17 + 17
b. 23 + (–8)
c. 14 + (–22)

Oral Report

Exercise 44 checks that you understand integer addition and subtraction.

Reflecting on the Section

Be prepared to report on the following topic in class.

44. Explain how each situation could occur. You may want to draw a model for an example of each situation.

a. adding an integer to a number and getting a sum that is less than the original number

b. subtracting an integer from a number and getting a difference that is greater than the original number.

Spiral Review

Plot each pair of coordinates on a grid. (Module 7, p. 516)

45. (4, –7) 46. (0, 5) 47. (–3, –3) 48. (–2, 0)

Estimation Estimate each sum or difference. (Module 3, p. 213; Module 5, p. 347)

49. $5\frac{7}{8} + 7\frac{1}{5}$ 50. 2763 + 1287 51. $9 - 6\frac{8}{11}$

52. $2\frac{2}{7} + 3\frac{1}{8}$ 53. $16\frac{5}{9} - 4\frac{3}{4}$ 54. 15.8 + 9.2 + 7.9

Mental Math Use mental math to multiply. (Module 3, p. 164)

55. 0.137 • 1000 56. 4.23 • 100 57. 3.59 • 10,000

58. 0.2 • 10 59. 2.213 • 1000 60. 75 • 100,000

Extension 

Commutative and Associative Properties

Find the sums for each pair of expressions.

61. 2 + (–4)
    –4 + 2

62. –3 + (–2)
    –2 + (–3)

63. –8 + 15
    15 + (–8)

64. [5 + (–6)] + 2
    5 + (–6 + 2)

65. (–7 + 3) + (–5)
    –7 + [3 + (–5)]

66. 13 + [–1 + (–9)]
    [13 + (–1)] + (–9)

67. Addition of integers is *commutative.* The order in which the integers are added does not change the result. Explain which pairs of sums in Exercises 61–66 show this.

68. The addition of integers is also *associative.* The grouping of the integers does not change the result. Explain which pairs of sums in Exercises 61–66 show this.

Add the integers mentally. Explain the method you used.

69. –21 + 15 + (–9) + 5 70. –8 + 13 + (–3) + (–13)

71. Is subtraction of integers commutative? associative? Give examples to support your answers.

Section 1 Extra Skill Practice

Find each sum.

1. $-10 + (-7)$
2. $21 + (-3)$
3. $-34 + (-6)$
4. $7 + (-14)$
5. $-45 + 61$
6. $15 + (-15)$
7. $-21 + (-5)$
8. $16 + (-52)$
9. $-7 + 3$

Find each difference.

10. $6 - (-4)$
11. $-22 - (-13)$
12. $-12 - (-7)$
13. $15 - 19$
14. $-16 - 7$
15. $10 - (-12)$
16. $0 - (-72)$
17. $-51 - 12$
18. $-5 - (-5)$

For each expression, describe the possible values for *x*.

19. $-4 - x$, the difference is a positive integer
20. $x - 6$, the difference is a negative integer
21. $12 + x$, the sum is zero

Find each sum or difference.

22. $51 - 73$
23. $29 + (-35)$
24. $-96 - (-8)$
25. $0 - (-16)$
26. $-1 - (-5)$
27. $-14 + 62$
28. $-91 + (-35)$
29. $-13 - 18$
30. $12 - 44$

Study Skills Listening

Listening to the thoughts and ideas of other people can help clarify your own thoughts. It can also spark new ideas you might not have thought of otherwise.

Look at the Discussion questions on page 531. Try to remember your class discussion of these questions.

1. What were some of the comments and answers from your classmates?
2. Did any of the ideas from the discussion make you think in a new way? Explain.

Line Graphs, Scientific Notation, and Percent

IN THIS SECTION

EXPLORATION 1
- Representing Population Data

EXPLORATION 2
- Scientific Notation

EXPLORATION 3
- Applying Percent and Volume

Population GROWTH

Setting the Stage

The graph below shows how the world population has increased from the year 1000 to 1997.

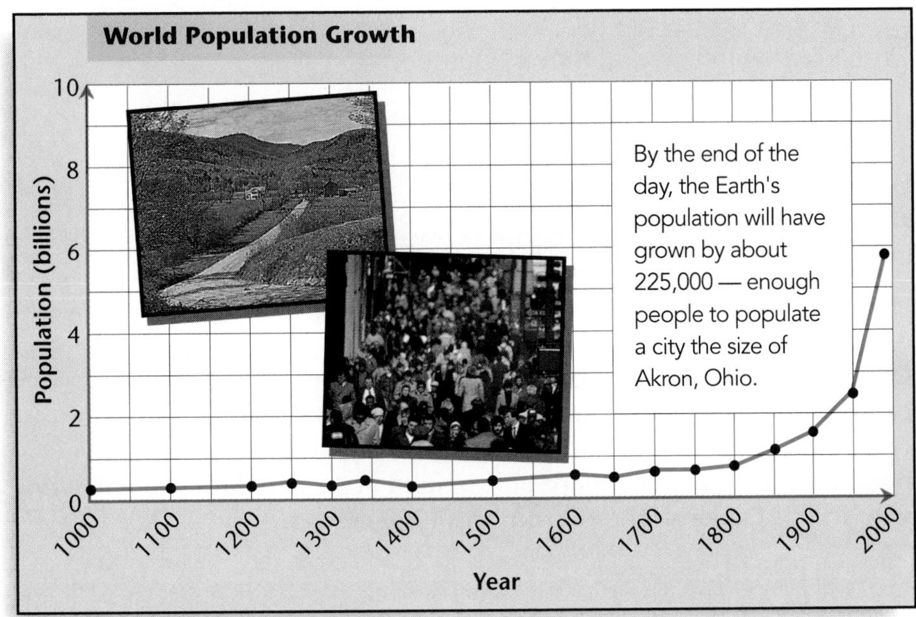

Think About It

1 About when did the world's population reach 1 billion?

2 Was the population increasing faster during the period from 1500 to 1600 or during the period from 1800 to 1900? How can you tell by just looking at the graph?

3 How do you think the growing world population affects the environment?

GOAL

LEARN HOW TO...
- make a line graph
- find population densities

AS YOU...
- explore effects of increased population

KEY TERM
- line graph

Exploration 1

Representing Population Data

SET UP *You will need:* • *Labsheets 2A and 2B*

▶ **A line graph shows changes that take place over time. The line graph in the Setting the Stage shows how the world population has increased over the past thousand years. You can also use a line graph to see how an animal population has changed.**

4 **Use Labsheet 2A.** Follow the directions on the labsheet to make a line graph of the *California Condor Population.*

5 Look at your line graph from Question 4.

a. In what year was the condor population the lowest?

b. What does your line graph tell you about the population?

6 **Discussion** How could people's awareness of the condor's near extinction help its chances of survival?

▲ The California condor is the largest bird in North America. It has been on the endangered species list since 1967.

▶ **One effect of a growing population is that people will be more crowded together. To measure how crowded a city or state is you can find its population density. *Population density* is the average number of people per square unit of land area. The data you will work with in this Exploration are from the 1990 census.**

EXAMPLE

California has a population of 29.8 million people and a land area of 156,299 mi^2. To find the population density of California:

Population density = population ÷ land area

= 29.8 million people ÷ 156,299 mi^2

= 29,800,000 people ÷ 156,299 mi^2

≈ 190.7 people per mi^2 (Rounded to the nearest tenth.)

7 **a.** In the Example, why is 29.8 million the same as 29,800,000?

b. The population of the United States is about 248,700,000. What is another way to write this number?

MODULE 8 **LABSHEET 2B**

State Population Table (Use with Questions 8–11 on page 541.)

Directions The table below shows the population and land area for eleven states and for the whole United States.

- If your state is not listed, look up its population and land area and record them in the table.
- Find what percent the population of each state is of the population of the United States. Round your answers to the nearest whole percent and record them in the table.
- Calculate the population density for each state. Round to the nearest tenth. Record the population densities in the table.

Population density = population ÷ land area

State	Population (millions)	Percent of U.S. population	Land area (mi^2)	Population density ($people/mi^2$)
California	29.8	12	156,299	190.7
Hawaii	1.1		6,425	
Mississippi	2.6		47,233	
Montana	0.8		145,388	
New Hampshire	1.1		8,993	
New Jersey	7.7		7,468	
New York	18.0		47,377	
North Carolina	6.6		48,843	
Pennsylvania	11.9		44,888	
Texas	17.0		262,017	
Vermont	0.6		9,273	
United States	248.7	100	3,539,289	70.3

your state

Use Labsheet 2B for Questions 8–11.

8 Complete the *State Population Table* to find what percent each state's population is of the total population of the United States. You'll also find the population density of each state.

9 **Discussion**

a. Will two states that have the same percent of the total United States population have the same number of people living in them? Explain your answer.

b. Will two states that have the same population density always have the same land area? Explain your answer.

c. Will regions with the greatest population always have the greatest population densities? Why or why not?

d. Will two regions that have the same land area always have the same population density? Explain.

10 If California had the same population density as North Carolina, how many people would live in California?

11 ✓ **CHECKPOINT** If everyone in Pennsylvania moved to Vermont, what would be Vermont's population density?

...checks that you can find population density.

12 **Try This as a Class** To understand how crowded a region is, it may help to think about the area available per person.

a. What is the area of your classroom in square feet? How many square feet is this per person?

b. The population density of Manhattan Borough, in New York City, is 52,415 people per square mile. How many square feet is this per person?

c. How does your answer in part (b) compare to the area of your classroom? Do you think the area in part (b) is enough space for a person to live in? Explain.

HOMEWORK EXERCISES ▶ See Exs. 1–8 on pp. 548–549.

GOAL

LEARN HOW TO...
- write large numbers in scientific notation

AS YOU...
- work with statistics about volunteering

KEY TERM
- scientific notation

Exploration 2

Scientific Notation

SET UP *You will need:* • *Labsheet 2C* • *calculator*

▶ **An increasing world population also means that there are more people that can work together to have a positive effect on the environment. In 1993, ninety million people in the United States volunteered about 19,600,000,000 hours of community service!**

13 **Estimation** Suppose that this year one billion people volunteer their time at the same rate as in 1993. Altogether, about how many hours would they volunteer?

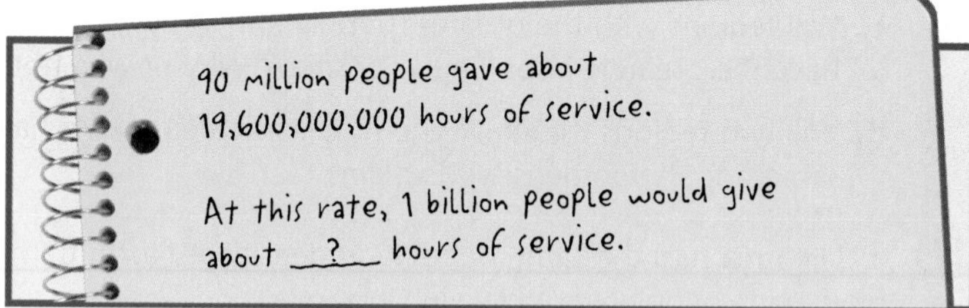

▶ **To make reading and writing large numbers easier, they are often written in *scientific notation*. Scientific notation uses powers of 10 to express the value of a number.**

Use Labsheet 2C for Questions 14–17.

14 Complete *Table 1* on Labsheet 2C.

15 **Try This as a Class** Look for a pattern in *Table 1*.

a. How can you write 90,000,000 in scientific notation?

b. What do you think $9 \cdot 10^{11}$ is in standard form?

16 Complete *Table 2* on Labsheet 2C.

17 **Try This as a Class** Look for a pattern in *Table 2*.

a. How can you write 19,600,000,000 in scientific notation?

b. What is $1.96 \cdot 10^{9}$ in standard form?

▶ **You may have noticed that the numbers you wrote in scientific notation, $9 \cdot 10^7$ and $1.96 \cdot 10^{10}$, have two parts:**

The first part is a number greater than or equal to 1 but less than 10.

$$9 \cdot 10^7$$

$$1.96 \cdot 10^{10}$$

The second part is a **power of 10.**

18 ✔ **CHECKPOINT** Tell whether each number is written in scientific notation. If a number is not in scientific notation, explain why not.

a. $60 \cdot 10^3$ **b.** $6 \cdot 10^3$ **c.** $0.6 \cdot 10^3$

d. $35 \cdot 10^1$ **e.** $3.5 \cdot 2^3$ **f.** $7.48 \cdot 10^6$

✔ **QUESTION 18**

...checks that you can recognize numbers written in scientific notation.

19 Write each number in scientifc notation.

a. 54,000,000 **b.** 1,245,000,000 **c.** 99,900

20 Calculator Shown are three different ways that a calculator could display a number in scientific notation.

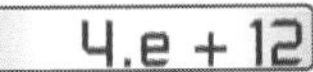

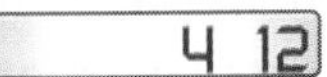

a. What number is represented in the displays? Write your answer in scientific notation and in standard form.

b. How does your calculator display numbers in scientific notation? How would the number 789,000,000 appear in scientific notation on your calculator?

▶ **So far you have used powers of 10 to write numbers in scientific notation. You can also use powers of 10 to change a number from scientific notation to standard form.**

EXAMPLE

Write $8.1 \cdot 10^3$ in standard form.

SAMPLE RESPONSE

$8.1 \cdot 10^3$

$8.1 \cdot 1000 = 8100$

$10^3 = 10 \cdot 10 \cdot 10 = 1000$

21 Write each number in standard form.

a. $2.38 \cdot 10^1$ b. $2.38 \cdot 10^2$ c. $2.38 \cdot 10^3$

d. $2.38 \cdot 10^4$ e. $2.38 \cdot 10^5$ f. $2.38 \cdot 10^6$

22 **Discussion** Look for a pattern in the problems and answers from Question 21.

a. What happened to the decimal point in each product when 2.38 was multiplied by 10^1? by 10^2? by 10^4?

b. What happens to the decimal point of a number when it is multiplied by 10^9? Test your prediction by writing $2.38 \cdot 10^9$ in standard form.

c. How can you use the exponent on each power of 10 to change a number from scientific notation to standard form?

d. What is the exponent when 23,800,000 is written in scientific notation?

$$23{,}800{,}000 = 2.38 \cdot 10^{?}$$

✓ **QUESTION 23**

...checks that you can write numbers in scientific notation and convert from scientific notation to standard form.

23 ✓ **CHECKPOINT** In the *1995 Earth Force Pennies for the Planet* campaign about 50,000 students raised money for environment improvement projects.

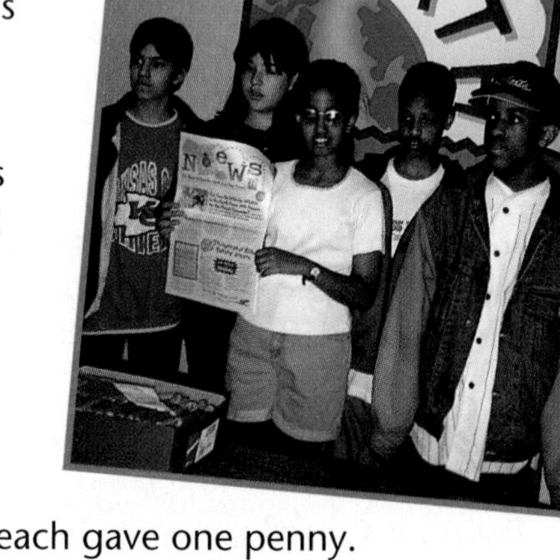

a. Write 50,000 in scientific notation.

b. On average, each student raised 350 pennies. How much is this in dollars?

c. Together the students' efforts brought in $1.75 \cdot 10^7$ pennies in one pretty amazing month! Write the number of pennies in standard form. How many dollars is this?

d. The world population will probably reach seven billion. Suppose seven billion people each gave one penny. Write this number of pennies in scientific notation.

e. How can you tell, without changing to standard form, which is more, $7 \cdot 10^9$ pennies or $1.75 \cdot 10^7$ pennies?

HOMEWORK EXERCISES See Exs. 9–25 on pp. 549–550.

Exploration 3

APPLYING Percent AND Volume

GOAL

LEARN HOW TO...
- multiply by a decimal to find a percent of a number

AS YOU...
- find the volume of trash people produce

SET UP *Work as a class. You will need:* • *yardstick* • *trash* • *cardboard box*

▶ **In just one day people in the United States throw away enough trash to fill about 65,000 garbage trucks! Most of the trash we produce ends up in landfills. The diagram below shows the percent of each type of trash that landfills contain.**

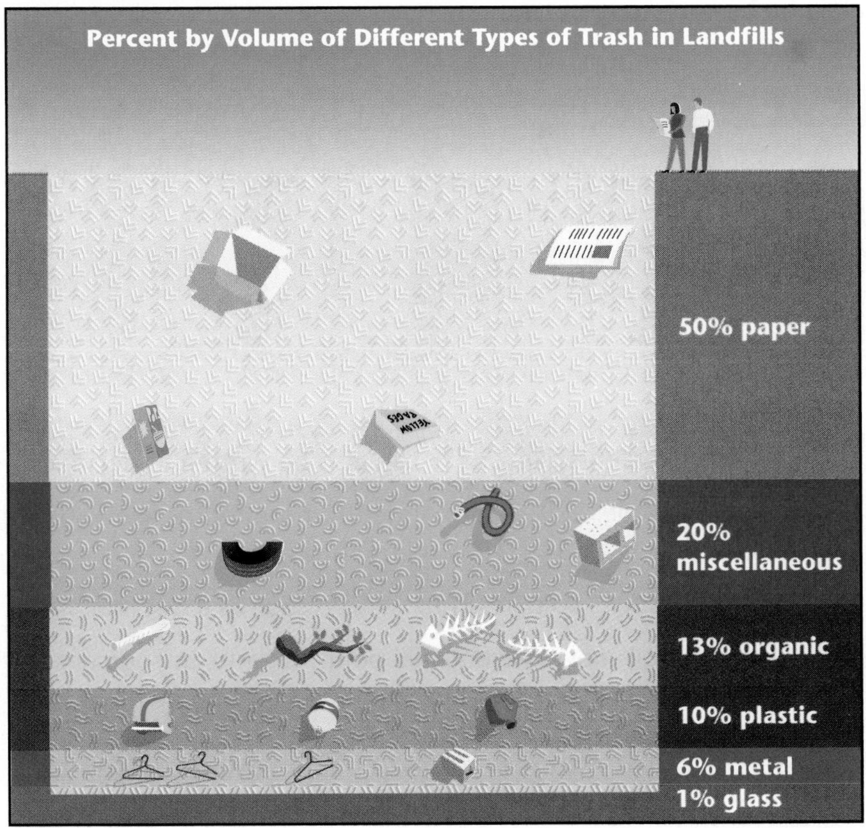

▲ In 1987 a trash barge traveled 6000 mi in search of a landfill. It was finally accepted at Islip, N.Y., where the trash was incinerated and the ash dumped.

24 Which types of trash include materials that could be recycled? About what percent of the trash in landfills is recyclable?

▶ **As our population increases, so does the amount of trash we produce. Crushing trash helps reduce the space it takes up.**

25 Try This as a Class

a. Fill a cardboard box to the top with trash. Measure the dimensions of the box. What is the volume of the trash?

b. Take the trash out of the box and compact it as much as possible by crushing it or folding it. Put the compacted trash back into the box. What is the volume of the trash now?

c. What fraction of the original volume does the compacted trash take up? About what percent is this?

Composition of Landfills	
Type of trash	Percent (by volume)
miscellaneous	20%
paper	50%
plastic	10%
metal	6%
glass	1%
organic	13%

▶ **The average person in the United States throws away 1 ton of trash every 16 months. When compacted, the trash fits in a 3 yd × 2 yd × 1 yd rectangular box. The percents in the table can be written as decimals to find how much of the 6 yd^3 is taken up by each type of trash.**

EXAMPLE

Miscellaneous items take up 20% of the 6 yd^3.

Write a decimal for 20%.
20% = 20 hundredths
= 0.20

20% of 6
↓ ↓ ↓
0.20 • 6 = 1.2

So miscellaneous items take up 1.2 yd^3 of the 6 yd^3 of trash.

26 Discussion

Percents like 25.3% can also be written as decimals.

a. In the Example, 20% was changed to hundredths. How many hundredths is 25.3%? How many thousandths?

b. Use your answer to part (a) to write 25.3% as a decimal.

c. How can you move the decimal point to write any percent as a decimal?

✓ QUESTION 27

...checks that you can multiply by a decimal to find the percent of a number.

27 ✓ CHECKPOINT

Use the percents in the table above. Find how much of the 6 yd^3 is taken up by each type of trash.

a. paper **b.** plastic **c.** metal **d.** glass **e.** organic

28 Estimation

Use your fraction or percent from Question 25(c) to estimate how many cubic yards the 6 yd^3 of trash took up before it was compacted.

HOMEWORK EXERCISES ▶ See Exs. 26–36 on pp. 550–551.

Section 2 Key Concepts

Line Graphs (p. 540)

A line graph shows a change over time. This line graph shows the population density (number of people per square unit of area) of India from 1960 to 1997.

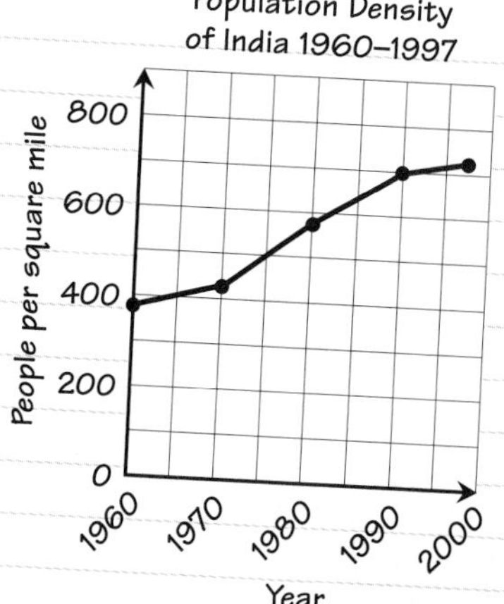

Scientific Notation
(pp. 542–544)

To write a number in scientific notation write it as a product of a power of ten.

Make the first part a number greater than or equal to 1 but less than 10.

$9,800,000,000 = 9.8 \cdot 1,000,000,000 = 9.8 \cdot 10^9$

Make the second part **a power of 10.**

To change a number in scientific notation to standard form multiply by the power of ten.

$5.32 \cdot 10^7 = 5.32 \cdot 10,000,000 = 53,200,000$

Finding a Percent of a Number (p. 546)

You can use a decimal to find a percent of a number.

Example 84% of $654 = 0.84 \cdot 654 = 549.36$

Key Terms

line graph

scientific notation

Key Concepts Questions

29 **Estimation** Use the line graph to estimate India's population density in 1997. The land area of India is 1,229,737 mi^2. What was the approximate population of India in 1997?

30 **a.** In the United States about $1.8 \cdot 10^8$ tons of trash were thrown away in 1988. Write this number in standard form.

b. Of the trash thrown away in 1988, about 13% was recycled. How many tons of trash were recycled that year? Write your answer in scientific notation.

Section 2 Practice & Application Exercises

YOU WILL NEED

For Exs. 3 and 35:
- graph paper

Use the line graph at the right to answer Exercises 1 and 2.

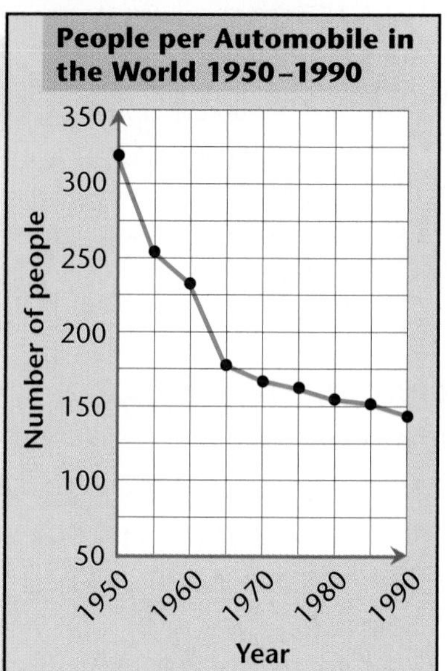

1. What does the line graph tell you about how the number of people for every automobile in the world has changed over time?

2. **Interpreting Data** If you made a line graph of the change in the number of automobiles in the world from 1950–1990, what do you think it would look like? Why?

3. Making two line graphs on one grid for the number of morning newspapers circulated and the number of evening newspapers circulated can help you compare the data.

Year	Morning newspaper circulation	Evening newspaper circulation
1980	29,414	32,788
1981	30,654	31,276
1982	33,174	29,313
1983	33,842	28,802
1984	35,425	27,657
1985	36,362	26,405
1986	37,441	25,061
1987	39,124	23,702
1988	40,453	22,242
1989	40,759	21,890
1990	41,308	21,016

a. Why would starting your scale at 0 make it difficult to graph the data?

b. Find the range of the newspaper data. Use the range to help you decide on the intervals to use for the scale. Then draw the two line graphs.

c. How has the circulation changed for morning newspapers? for evening newspapers?

d. Between which two years was the circulation of morning newspapers and of evening newspapers about the same? How does your graph make it easy to tell?

Non-numerical Graphs **Graphs that are not labeled with numerical data can still convey a message. Tell which graph best matches each situation.**

Graph 1

Time

Graph 2

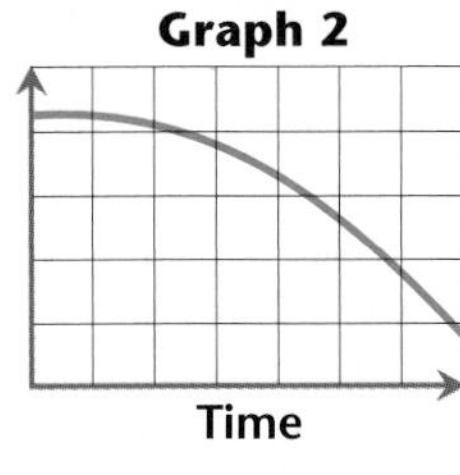

Time

Graph 3

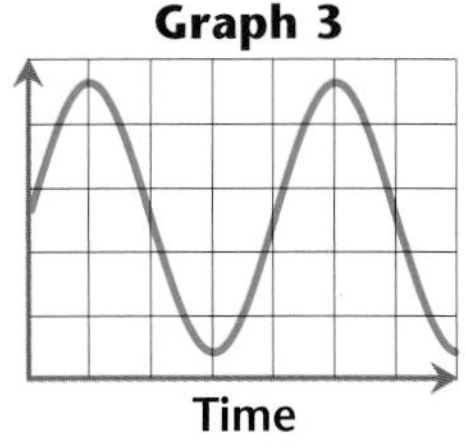

Time

4. The speed of a biker going up a hill.

5. Distance from the ground of a person on a ferris wheel.

6. Amount of water in a glass as you fill it up.

Social Studies **Use the table to answer Exercises 7 and 8.**

Metro area	Tokyo-Yokohama, Japan	Mexico City, Mexico	Hong Kong, China
Population (1995)	28,447,000	23,913,000	5,841,000
Land area (mi^2)	1089	522	23

7. Find the population density of each metro area in the table.

8. **Challenge** A rectangular parking space for a car in a parking lot is usually at least 8.5 ft wide and 18 ft long. Is there enough land in each metro area in the table to assign each person a parking space with the dimensions 8.5 ft × 18 ft?

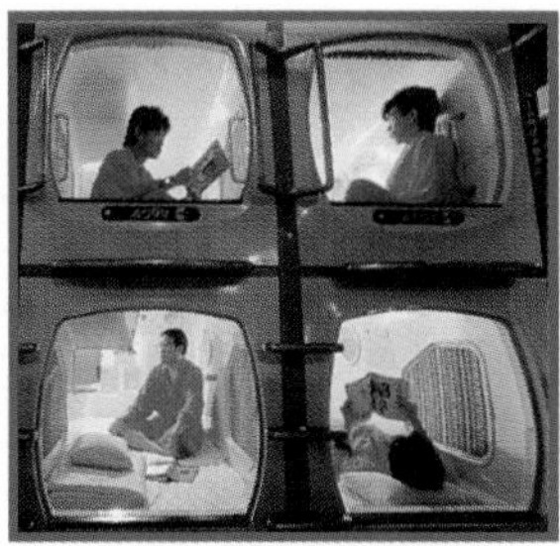

▲ Because of the limited space in Tokyo, business travelers often rent just enough space to sleep instead of getting an entire hotel room.

Write each number in scientific notation.

9. 157,000
10. 7000
11. 56,000,000
12. 10.2
13. 5600
14. 9 billion

Write each number in standard form.

15. $5.9 \cdot 10^4$
16. $1.0 \cdot 10^2$
17. $9.82 \cdot 10^5$
18. $8.1 \cdot 10^7$
19. $6.0 \cdot 10^1$
20. $3.5 \cdot 10^8$

Use scientific notation to express each fact.

21. The temperature of volcanic lava can reach 1500°F.

22. The temperature on the surface of the sun is about 10,000°F.

23. Lightning reaches temperatures of 50,000°F.

24. Write the world population for each year in standard form.

1 figure represents 10^8 people. (Note: Numbers have been rounded to show only whole figures.)

Population of the World for Selected Years

1000	1500	1900	1980	2000
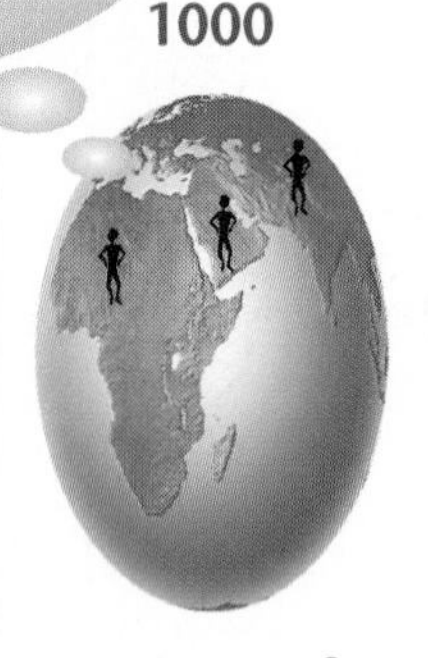				
$3.1 \cdot 10^8$	$5.0 \cdot 10^8$	$1.65 \cdot 10^9$	$4.45 \cdot 10^9$	$6.23 \cdot 10^9$ (estimated)

25. a. Without changing the numbers to standard form, tell whether more plastic or aluminum was recycled. Explain how you know.

Material	Amount discarded in 1990	Amount recycled
aluminum	$2.5 \cdot 10^6$ tons	$7.93 \cdot 10^5$ tons
plastic	$1.44 \cdot 10^7$ tons	$1.58 \cdot 10^5$ tons

b. Without changing the numbers to standard form, tell whether more plastic or aluminum was discarded. Explain how you know.

26. **Geometry Connection** Recycling 1 ton of newspaper saves 81 ft^3 of landfill space. Give the dimensions of a rectangular box that has a volume of 81 ft^3.

Find each value.

27. 30% of 120

28. 7% of \$15

29. 44% of 85

30. 6% of 72

31. 35% of 650

32. 99% of 500

33. The average person eats about 250 eggs per year. The table shows how these eggs are prepared. Find how many eggs are prepared each way.

Ways eggs are prepared	Percent of total
scrambled	34%
fried	31%
boiled	23%
in omelettes	4%
other	5%
poached	3%

By weight, a typical ton of trash in the United States is 15.6% miscellaneous trash, 37.6% paper, 6.6% glass, 8.3% metal, 9.3% plastic, and 22.6% organic. (Note: 1 ton = 2000 lb)

34. Find the number of pounds of each type of trash in 1 ton of trash.

35. a. **Choosing a Data Display** Make a visual display that shows the percents of trash types in a typical ton of trash.

b. **Writing** Explain why you chose the type of visual display you made in part (a). How does your display show how the trash percentages compare?

Some landfills are converted to living space and recreational areas such as this island in the Boston Harbor.

Reflecting on the Section

36. a. Examine a full box of cereal or pasta. Is the height of the box greater than necessary to hold the contents? If so, find the height of the box and find how much shorter the box could be and still hold all the contents. Write a percent to describe the part of the box's height which is not needed.

b. If you can, cut off the part of your box's packaging that is not needed. Fold and crush the packaging you cut off to form as small a rectangular prism as possible. What is its volume?

c. Suppose each of the 270 million people in the United States throws away a box that has extra packaging like yours each month. Use scientific notation to describe the total volume of extra trash this will be.

RESEARCH

Exercise 36 checks that you understand scientific notation and percents.

Spiral Review

Find each sum or difference. (Module 8, p. 533)

37. –18 + 7

38. –26 + (–17)

39. 15 + (–8)

40. 25 – (–18)

41. –36 – 13

42. –12 – (–3)

Find the missing term in each proportion. (Module 6, p. 418)

43. $\frac{8}{15} = \frac{x}{27}$

44. $\frac{3}{n} = \frac{22.5}{60}$

45. $a : 42 = 2 : 3$

Replace each ? with the number that makes the statement true. (Module 3, p. 165)

46. 274 m = ___?___ km

47. 38 cm = ___?___ mm

48. 9381 mm = ___?___ m

49. 7 km = ___?___ m

Play *The Math is Right!*

Have you ever watched a quiz game on TV? Players answer questions that test their knowledge. Over the next few days you'll create questions for a math quiz game. At the end of the module your team will get a chance to play *The Math is Right!* with the other teams in your class.

SET UP

Work in a team of four.

Getting Started **Your team is responsible for writing a set of eight questions. The set should include one question on the mathematics you learned in each of the eight modules. Each question must relate to one of the themes below.**

Art   Science   Music   Sports

1 Decide for which modules each team member will write questions.

2 For each of your modules, choose a mathematical concept and a theme to write a question about.

Game Format **In *The Math is Right!* your team's questions will be read aloud or shown on an overhead projector. Each of the other teams will work together to agree on an answer. No team is allowed to answer their own questions!**

3 Gather any information you may need on your theme to write your questions.

4 Write your quiz game questions. Make sure your questions are clear and ask for specific answers.

Section 2 Extra Skill Practice

Use the line graph for Exercises 1 and 2.

1. What does the line graph tell you about the number of movie screens from 1976–1996?

2. About how many more movie screens were there in 1996 than in 1976?

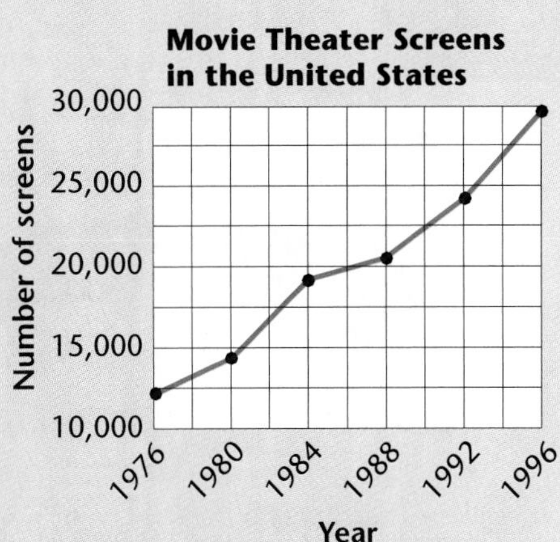

Write each number in scientific notation.

3. 49,800,000
4. 16.34
5. 32 billion
6. 958
7. 2,500,000
8. 326,000

Write each number in standard form.

9. $1.1 \cdot 10^{13}$
10. $6.08 \cdot 10^{1}$
11. $5.03 \cdot 10^{6}$
12. $4.14 \cdot 10^{3}$
13. $2.0 \cdot 10^{9}$
14. $4.1 \cdot 10^{2}$

Find each percent.

15. 5% of $22
16. 67% of 33
17. 78% of 150
18. 21.3% of 32
19. 80% of 750
20. 52.7% of 1000

Standardized Testing ▶ Multiple Choice

Write:
- **(A) if the amount in column A is greater,**
- **(B) if the amount in column B is greater,**
- **(C) if the amounts in column A and column B are equal,**
- **(D) if there is no way to tell which amount is greater.**

	Column A	Column B
1.	$1.735 \cdot 10^{6}$	$17.35 \cdot 10^{5}$
2.	30% of 5	$1.2 \cdot 10^{1}$
3.	51% of 12.8	80% of 8

Section 3 Metric Capacity and Percent

IN THIS SECTION

EXPLORATION 1
- Metric Capacity

EXPLORATION 2
- Percents Greater than 100%

Setting the Stage

Water is one of the most powerful forces in nature. Too little and we have droughts; too much and we have floods. These two stories tell about the different effects water can have on people and on the land.

> … rain was only in our dreams. The winds came every day, blowing dust through the windows and into the house until it covered the furniture and got into the food and our clothes and hair. The land got even drier, and we stopped taking baths. Every day we hauled river water for the animals in big wooden barrels.
>
> ***Skylark***
> **by Patricia MacLachlan**

> There wasn't very much left of South Oak Road. The angry streams of yellow-brown water had chewed away much of the hard surface and everywhere there was mud and the soggy debris of leaves tangled in broken twigs and branches.
>
> Seven days of heavy rain had done their damage.
>
> ***The Day It Rained Forever***
> **by Robert C. Lee**

Think About It

1 An average of 76 cm of rain falls in the United States each year.

a. Why do you think some areas experience droughts and other areas experience floods?

b. Estimate how high on your body 76 cm from the ground is.

Exploration 1

Capacity

GOAL

LEARN HOW TO...
- relate volume and metric capacity
- estimate capacity in metric units

AS YOU...
- create benchmarks

KEY TERMS
- capacity
- milliliter (mL)
- liter (L)
- kiloliter (kL)

SET UP *Work in a group. You will need:* • *Labsheet 3A* • *tape* • *scissors* • *water in a cup* • *eyedropper* • *metric ruler* • *12 straws* • *24 paper clips* • *graduated cylinder or measuring cup*

▶ **It has been estimated that a person can survive comfortably with as little as 100 *liters* of water each day. This includes water for washing, drinking, and cooking. To get an idea of how much water this is you will first look at a more familiar unit—a cubic centimeter.**

2 **Use Labsheet 3A.** Follow the directions on the labsheet to construct a *Cubic Centimeter.*

3 **a.** How do you know that the volume of the cube you made is 1 cm^3 (one cubic centimeter)?

b. Use an eyedropper to fill your cube with water.

c. Pour your cubic centimeter of water into the graduated cylinder.

d. How many cubic centimeters of water did your class pour into the cylinder?

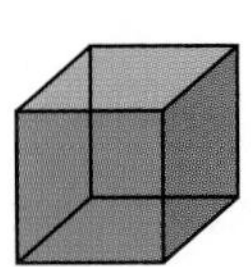
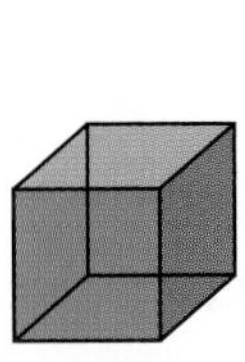

Volume

Capacity

▶ **The capacity of a container is the amount of liquid it can hold. In the metric system, a container that can hold 1 cm^3 of liquid has a capacity of 1 milliliter (mL).**

4 **a.** How many milliliters of water did your class pour into the cylinder?

b. Is your answer to part (a) the same as the reading on the cylinder? If not, why might they be different?

▶ **Since a milliliter is such a small amount, many liquids, such as juice and soda, are measured in *liters*. The picture at the right shows the size difference between a cube that could hold a liter (L) of fluid and one that could hold a milliliter.**

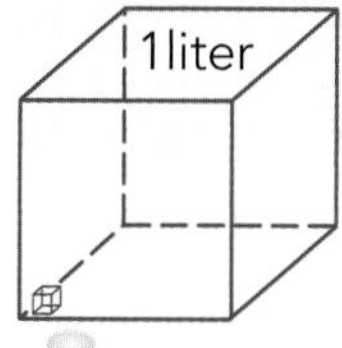

5 **a.** The prefix "milli" means *one thousandth*. How many milliliters are there in a liter?

b. How many centimeter cubes filled with water would you need to make a liter of water?

✔ **QUESTION 6**

...checks that you understand how to determine the dimensions of a liter-sized cube.

6 ✔ **CHECKPOINT** Determine the dimensions of a liter-sized cube.

7 Follow the steps below to create a liter-sized cube.

First

Measure and cut your straws. Use the dimensions you found in Question 6.

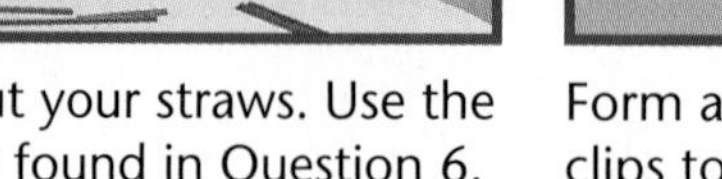

Then

Form a liter-sized cube by using paper clips to connect the straws.

8 **a.** Place your centimeter cube inside your liter-sized cube to visually compare the sizes of these two benchmarks.

b. Give a different set of dimensions that could be used to create a liter-sized rectangular box.

9 **Try This as a Class**

a. "Kilo-" means *one thousand*. How many liters are there in a **kiloliter (kL)**?

b. Give a set of dimensions that could be used to create a kiloliter-sized rectangular box.

✔ **QUESTION 10**

...checks that you can estimate capacity in metric units.

10 ✔ **CHECKPOINT** Use your liter and milliliter cubes to help you choose the best estimate.

a. capacity of a can of soup	300 mL	3 mL	300 L
b. capacity of a bathtub	1.8 kL	800 L	180 L
c. a dose of children's liquid medicine	5 mL	100 mL	1 L

11 Tell whether or not each container could hold a liter of water. Explain your reasoning.

12 **a.** Besides the cube you made in Question 7, what type of container could you use as a benchmark to estimate 1 L?

b. What benchmark could you use for 1 kL?

13 A person needs about 100 L of water each day for drinking, washing, and cooking.

a. Would 100 L fill a *pond*, an *outdoor swimming pool*, a *large fish tank*, or a *sink*? Explain.

b. Do you think that 100 L of water per day is a good estimate of *your* needs? Explain.

HOMEWORK EXERCISES See Exs. 1–17 on pp. 560–561.

Exploration 2

PERCENTS GREATER THAN > 100%

GOAL

LEARN HOW TO...
- model and write percents greater than 100%

AS YOU...
- describe rainfall

SET UP *You will need Labsheet 3B.*

▶ **In March of 1983, Wilmington, Delaware received about 17 cm of rainfall. Wilmington's usual March rainfall is only about 10 cm. You can use percents to compare 17 cm with the usual rainfall.**

14 If Wilmington received 100% of its usual rainfall, how many centimeters of rain would Wilmington receive?

FOR ◀ HELP with *using percent grids*, see **MODULE 3, p. 176**

▶ **The fraction $\frac{17}{10}$ compares Wilmington's rainfall in March 1983 with its usual March rainfall. To show the relationship as a percent, you can write a fraction or decimal in hundredths or use a 100-square grid.**

As a fraction:

$$\frac{17}{10} = \frac{17 \cdot 10}{10 \cdot 10} = \frac{170}{100}$$

As a decimal:

$$\frac{17}{10} = 1.7 = 1.70$$

With a 100-square grid model:

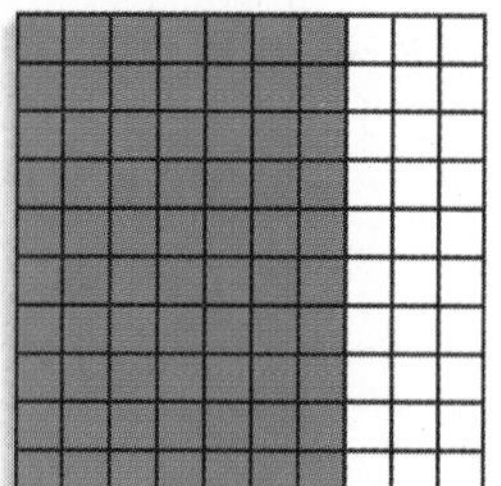

15 What percent is represented by the completely shaded 100-square grid? by the partially shaded grid? by the two grids together?

16 **Use Labsheet 3B.** Fill in the missing fractions, decimals, or percents. Then *Shade the Grids* to represent each percent.

▶ **You can use a proportion to help find a percent.**

EXAMPLE

The actual rainfall for Wilmington in March 1983 was 17.3 cm. This is what percent of the city's usual March rainfall of 9.8 cm?

SAMPLE RESPONSE

	rainfall		percent
March 1983 → / Usual March →	$\frac{17.3}{9.8}$	=	$\frac{p}{100}$
	$17.3 \cdot 100$	=	$9.8p$
	1730	=	$9.8p$
	177	≈	p

Think of writing the fraction in hundredths.

You can divide to find the missing factor, *p*.

The March 1983 rainfall is about 177% of the usual March rainfall.

QUESTION 17

...checks that you can write a percent greater than 100%.

17 ✓ **CHECKPOINT** In a typical February, Oslo, Norway receives 4.8 cm of rainfall. In February of 1995 Oslo received 9.2 cm of rainfall. Oslo received what percent of its typical rainfall? Round your answer to the nearest whole percent.

HOMEWORK EXERCISES ▶ See Exs. 18–33 on pp. 561–562.

Section 3 Key Concepts

Key Terms

Capacity (pp. 555–557)

Capacity is the amount of fluid that a container can hold. Volume and capacity are related in the metric system. One cubic centimeter of water has a capacity of one milliliter.

capacity

Unit of measure	Symbol	Relationship to other units
milliliter	mL	$1 \text{ mL} = \frac{1}{1000} \text{ L} = 0.001 \text{ L}$
liter	L	$1 \text{ L} = 1000 \text{ mL}$ $1 \text{ L} = \frac{1}{1000} \text{ kL} = 0.001 \text{ kL}$
kiloliter	kL	$1 \text{ kL} = 1000 \text{ L}$

milliliter (mL)

liter (L)

kiloliter (kL)

Percents Greater than 100% (pp. 557–558)

You can use a percent greater than 100% to describe how one value compares to a lesser value.

Example In January of 1995, Munich, Germany received 5.6 cm of rainfall rather than its normal rainfall of 4.5 cm.

rainfall percent

Jan. 1995 → normal →

$$\frac{5.6}{4.5} = \frac{x}{100}$$

$$124 \approx x$$

Munich received about 124% of its normal rainfall.

Key Concepts Questions

18 A 40 cm × 20 cm × 20 cm fish tank is filled with water. What is its capacity in liters?

19 During January of 1995, Paris, France received 11.3 cm of rainfall. Usually its total January rainfall is about 4.9 cm. What percent of its normal rainfall did Paris receive in January of 1995? Round to the nearest whole percent.

Section 3

Practice & Application Exercises

The containers in Exercises 1–4 are shaped like rectangular prisms. What is the capacity of each in milliliters and in liters?

1. 5 cm × 20 cm × 10 cm
2. 2 cm × 5 cm × 2 cm
3. 25 cm × 20 cm × 8 cm
4. 8.5 cm × 10 cm × 12.3 cm

Replace each _?_ with the number that makes the statement true.

5. 1800 L = _?_ kL
6. 3 kL = _?_ L
7. 892 mL = _?_ L
8. 0.62 kL = _?_ L
9. 2.5 L = _?_ mL
10. 700 L = _?_ mL

Choose the best estimate for each capacity.

11. capacity of a kitchen sink:
    60 mL   30 L   300 L

12. amount of water you can hold in your hands:
    100 mL   1 L   100 L

13. capacity of a small carton of milk:
    250 mL   250 L   250 kL

14. **Home Involvement** Have a friend or relative help you find a container at home. Estimate the metric capacity of the container. How can you check your estimate?

15. a. The amount of water in all the rivers and lakes in the world totals about $2.0 \cdot 10^{14}$ kL. Write this in standard notation.

    b. How many liters of water is your answer to part (a)? Write your answer in scientific notation.

16. **Geography** The Baltic Sea has a surface area of 381,705 km^2. The average depth of this sea is 55 m. Estimate the capacity of the Baltic Sea in kiloliters. Explain how you made your estimate.

◄ The Baltic Sea is a gulf of northern Europe.

17. **Challenge** A soda can has a capacity of 355 mL. Soda is also packaged in 2-liter bottles. Which is a better value: a 2-liter bottle of soda for $1.20 or a can of soda for 30¢? Explain.

One grid represents one whole. Write a percent for the shaded part of each group of grids.

18.

19. 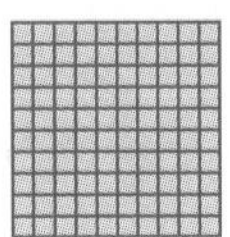 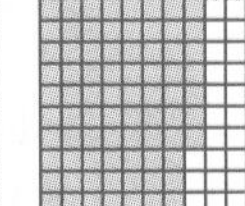

20. A photo copy machine can shrink or enlarge a picture to a certain percent of its original size.

  a. Suppose you set a photo copy machine at 130% and make a copy of a picture. Do you think the copy will be bigger or smaller than the original picture? Explain.

  b. If you have a picture that has a length of 8 in. and you want a copy that is 10 in. long, by what percent of the original should you enlarge it?

Write each fraction or decimal as a percent.

21. 6.3 22. $\frac{21}{15}$ 23. 3.01 24. $\frac{275}{250}$

25. $\frac{45}{30}$ 26. $\frac{2.5}{1.25}$ 27. $\frac{600}{250}$ 28. $\frac{52}{16}$

29. **Science** The pupil of your eye gets larger at night to let in as much light as possible. This helps you see when it is dark.

  a. For each age in the table, write a percent to describe how the pupil diameter at night compares to the pupil diameter during the day. Round to the nearest whole percent.

  b. What effect do you think aging has on the pupil's ability to enlarge?

	Diameter of Pupil (millimeters)	
Age	**Daylight**	**Night**
20	4.7	8.0
30	4.3	7.0
40	3.9	6.0
50	3.5	5.0
60	3.1	4.1
70	2.7	3.2
80	2.3	2.5

The diameter of a pupil in daylight.

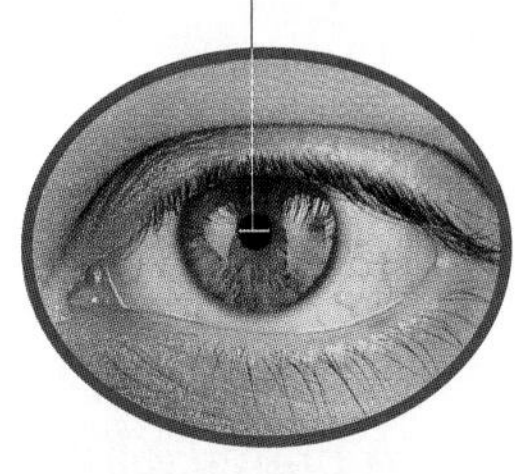

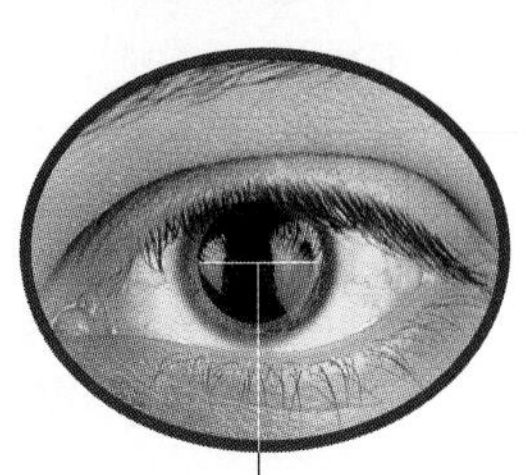

The diameter of a pupil at night.

Without doing any written calculations, tell whether each value can be written as a percent *less than 100%* or *greater than 100%*. Explain your reasoning.

30. 0.92 31. $\frac{85}{84}$ 32. 11 out of 17

Visual THINKING

Exercise 33 checks that you understand percents greater than 100%.

Reflecting on the Section

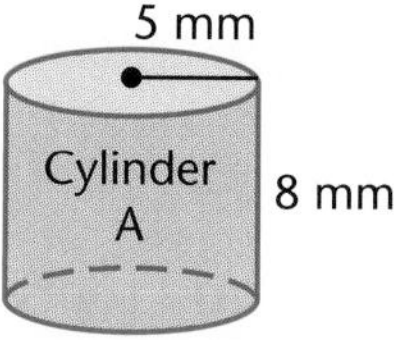

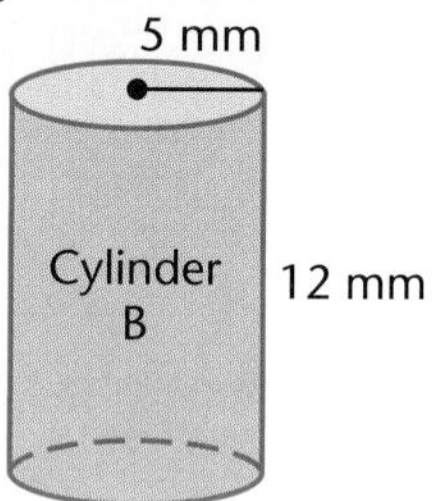

33. **Visual Thinking** Imagine that Cylinder A shows the amount of rainfall in a typical year and Cylinder B shows the rainfall two years ago.
    a. The rainfall shown by Cylinder B is what percent of the normal rainfall shown by Cylinder A?
    b. Last year the rainfall was 75% of the average. Draw a cylinder to represent the amount of rainfall.

Spiral Review

Find each value. (Module 8, p. 547)

34. 23% of 80 35. 35% of 42 36. 6% of 18

Evaluate each expression when $x = 4$ and $y = 9$. (Module 4, p. 288)

37. $7 \cdot x$ 38. $y - 3.4$ 39. $8\frac{5}{6} \div x$ 40. $y \cdot 2.5$

41. Suppose a coin is tossed 50 times and lands with a head showing 29 times. What is the experimental probability of heads? of tails? (Module 4, p. 242)

Career Connection

Chemist: Lynda Jordan

When experimenting with the cells in proteins, Dr. Jordan creates a *buffer solution*. A buffer solution is a liquid that is close to the normal environment of the cell.

▲ Dr. Jordan is studying the protein phospholipase A2. This protein may be linked to many diseases, including asthma and arthritis.

42. Dr. Jordan plans to mix 5 L of a buffer solution. Dimensions are given for two containers shaped like rectangular prisms. Tell whether each one can hold 5 L.
    a. 10 cm × 20 cm × 26 cm
    b. 165 mm × 122 mm × 240 mm

43. Once the buffer solution is mixed, the experiment may only require 300 mL of the solution. How many liters is this? How much of the solution is left?

Section 3 Extra Skill Practice

Replace each ? with the number that makes the statement true.

1. 3400 L = __?__ kL
2. 4200 mL = __?__ L
3. 12 kL = __?__ L
4. 750 mL = __?__ L
5. 14 L = __?__ mL
6. 628 L = __?__ kL

Choose the best estimate for each capacity.

7. capacity of a beach pail	2 L	200 mL	20 L
8. capacity of a swimming pool	10 L	16 kL	600 mL
9. capacity of a vase	700 mL	5 L	20 mL

Write each fraction as a percent.

10. $\frac{5}{2}$
11. $\frac{147}{105}$
12. $\frac{27}{18}$
13. $\frac{18}{27}$
14. $\frac{510}{170}$
15. $\frac{48}{20}$
16. $\frac{650}{1000}$
17. $\frac{20}{16}$

Write each fraction or decimal as a percent. Round to the nearest whole percent.

18. 51.7
19. $\frac{72}{13}$
20. $\frac{4.1}{2.22}$
21. 1.65
22. $\frac{96}{92}$
23. 2.009
24. $\frac{8.5}{1.2}$
25. 0.8
26. Last week Aisha earned $20 baby sitting. This week she earned $35. What percent of Aisha's earnings last week are her earnings this week?

Standardized Testing ▸ Free Response

Angelique had a cubic centimeter filled with water. Stacey had a larger container filled with water. Stacey said her container held more than 1000% of what Angelique's held. For Stacey to be correct, how large must her container be? Give your answer in liters.

FOR ASSESSMENT AND PORTFOLIOS

DROP by DROP

The Situation

Each day, the average person in the United States uses about 400 L of water. It is estimated that a person could live comfortably using only 100 L of water.

The Problem

How much water do you use each day? Keep a tally of the activities you do that require water. The information in the table can help you estimate the amount of water you use. Think about how you could cut down on the amount of water you need, then devise a plan to save water.

Average Water Use	
Activity	**Average (liters each time)**
get a drink (letting water run)	1
brush teeth	1
wash hands or face	7
cook a meal	18
flush toilet	22
do dishes (1 meal)	30
take shower (5 min)	75
wash clothes (washer)	90
take a bath	110

Something to Think About

- Since some water-using activities are not done every day, you may want to keep track of your water use for at least a week.
- Washing clothes or cooking might involve the whole family. How can you count your own water use for these activities?
- How does your water use compare to 400 L? to 100 L?

Present Your Results

Describe your plan to save water. Show any charts or tables you made to organize your data. Is 100 L enough for your water needs each day?

◀ The *Peanuts* character Pigpen, "conserves" water by not washing!

Section 4 Geometric Probability

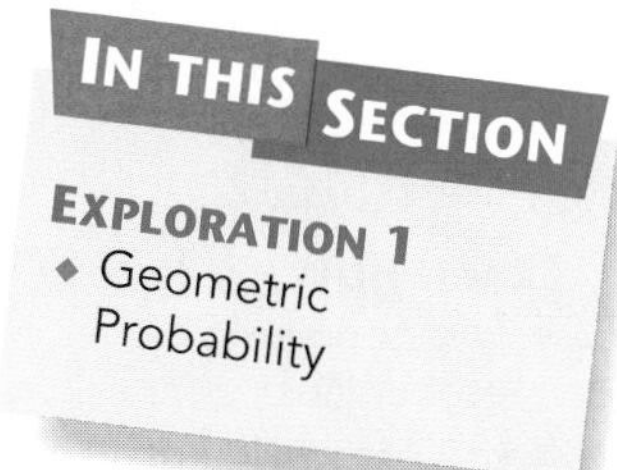

HEADS UP!

Setting the Stage

Although most meteoroids that enter Earth's atmosphere burn up completely, about 500 strike Earth each year. Fifty thousand years ago a meteoroid traveling 25,000 mi/h hit Earth to form Meteor Crater, a bowl-shaped hole about 4000 ft across and 650 ft deep.

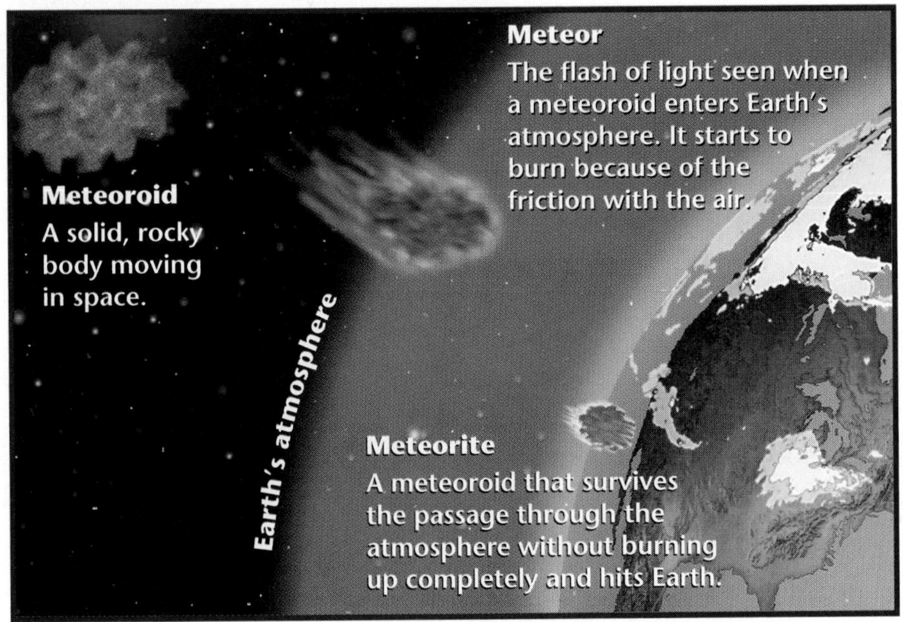

▲ Meteor Crater, Arizona

Think About It

1 **a.** The meteorite that formed Meteor Crater was about 150 ft in diameter. About how many times bigger is the diameter of Meteor Crater?

b. How might you explain the difference in size between the crater and the meteorite that formed it?

GOAL

LEARN HOW TO...
- find geometric probabilities
- use probability to predict

AS YOU...
- describe the chance of an object falling in a particular area

KEY TERM
- geometric probability

Exploration 1

GEOMETRIC Probability

SET UP *Work as a class. You will need an inflatable globe.*

▶ **A meteorite has an equally likely chance of hitting anywhere on Earth. To find the probability that a meteorite will hit land you will conduct an experiment with a globe.**

2 **Try This as a Class** Follow the steps below to simulate a meteorite falling to Earth.

First Make a table like the one shown to record the results of your experiment.

Next Carefully toss an inflated globe from one person to another. Each time the globe is caught, make a tally mark to record whether the left index finger is touching land or touching water before tossing it again. Record the results of 30 tosses.

Then Complete your table by calculating the percent of the tosses that hit land and the percent that hit water.

	Tally	Number of tosses	Percent of tosses
Land			
Water			
Total		30	

FOR ◀ HELP with *finding probabilities*, see **MODULE 4, p. 242**

3 Discussion Use the results of the globe-tossing experiment.

a. What percent of Earth do you think is covered by water?

b. Estimate the probability that a meteorite will hit water. Estimate the probability that it will hit land. These events are *complementary*. They cover all the possibilities for the situation.

c. What is the probability that a meteorite will hit either land or water?

4 Try This as a Class Use the probabilities you found in Question 3.

a. It is estimated that 500 meteorites hit Earth each year. About how many meteorites would you expect to hit water each year? Explain.

b. About how many meteorites would you expect to hit land each year?

Objects in space travel at such great speeds that an aluminum sphere 1 cm in diameter orbiting Earth can cause the same damage to a spacecraft as a 400 lb safe traveling 60 mi/h on Earth!

▶ **In addition to meteoroids, space junk—such as pieces of satellites and rockets—can be harmful to orbiting spacecraft. In 1990, the Long Duration Exposure Facility was brought back to Earth. It had been in space for nearly six years and had thousands of small dents caused by orbiting space junk.**

5 Try This as a Class Suppose a rectangular sensor is placed in the middle of a rectangular panel on a spacecraft as shown.

a. If a piece of space junk randomly hits the panel, how can you find the probability that it hits the sensor? What is the probability?

b. What is the probability that a piece of space junk hits the panel but *not* the sensor? How did you find the probability?

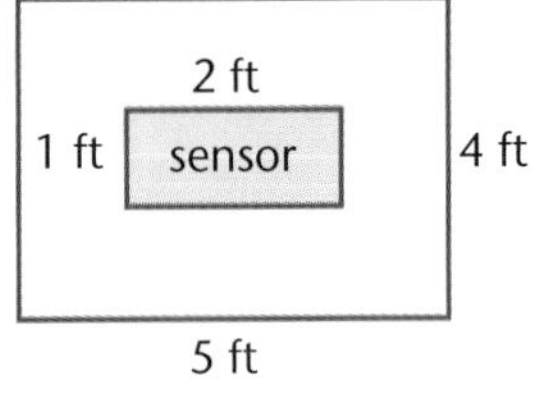

▶ **In Question 5, you used areas to find a probability. Probabilities that are based on lengths, areas, or volumes are called geometric probabilities.**

6 ✓ CHECKPOINT Suppose an object randomly hits within the circle to the right.

a. What is the probability that it will hit within the square?

b. If 200 objects hit randomly within the circle, about how many would you expect to hit within the square?

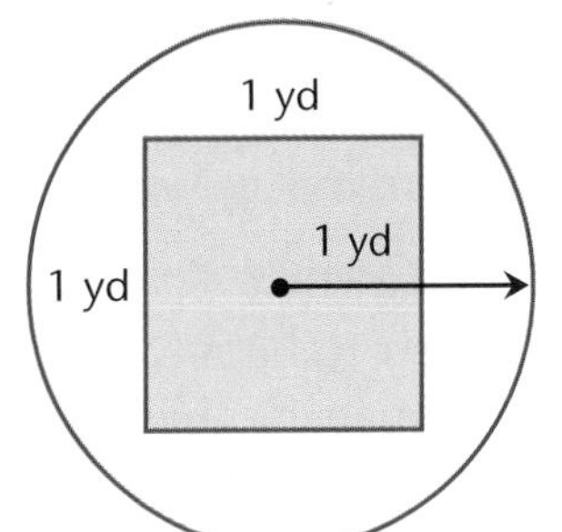

✓ QUESTION 6

...checks that you can find geometric probabilities and use them to make predictions.

HOMEWORK EXERCISES ▶ See Exs. 1–12 on pp. 569–570.

Section 4 Key Concepts

Key Term

geometric probability

Geometric Probability (pp. 566–567)

A probability that is based on lengths, areas, or volumes is a geometric probability.

Example

A dart that hits the target is equally likely to hit any point on the target.

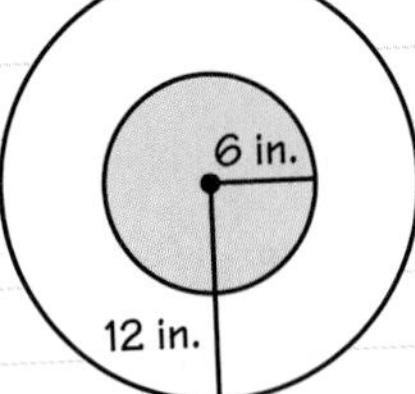

Probability that the dart hits the shaded region $= \frac{\text{Area of shaded region}}{\text{Total area of target}}$

$$= \frac{\pi \cdot 6^2}{\pi \cdot 12^2} = \frac{36\pi}{144\pi} = \frac{1}{4}$$

Probability that the dart hits the white region $= 1 - \frac{1}{4}$

$$= \frac{3}{4}$$

1 minus the probability that the dart hits the shaded region

You can use the probability $\frac{3}{4}$ to predict the number of times a dart will hit the white region in 80 tosses that hit the target.

$\frac{3}{4}$ of $80 = 60$

Key Concepts Questions

7 A dart that hits the target at the right is equally likely to hit any point on the target. What is the probability that the dart hits the shaded region?

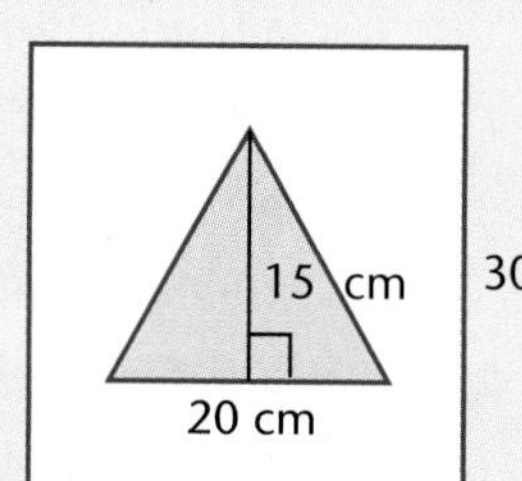

8 In the Example, why does the probability that the dart hits the white region equal 1 minus the probability that the dart hits the shaded region?

Practice & Application Exercises

Suppose an object falls at random onto each target shown below. For each target, what is the probability the object will land in a shaded region?

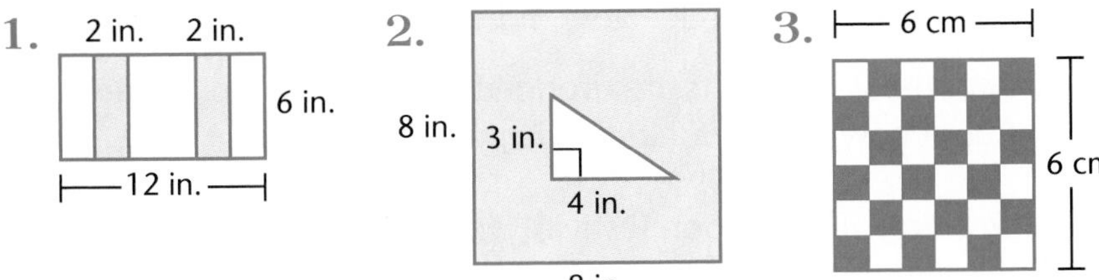

Shuffleboard **In a game of shuffleboard players take turns sliding plastic disks onto a scoring area. Players gain or lose the number of points marked on the space their disk is on.**

4. If you randomly slide your disk so that it lands somewhere on the court shown, what is the probability that it will land within the triangle that is outlined in black?

5. If you randomly slide your disk so that it lands within the black triangle, what is the probability that you will score 10 points?

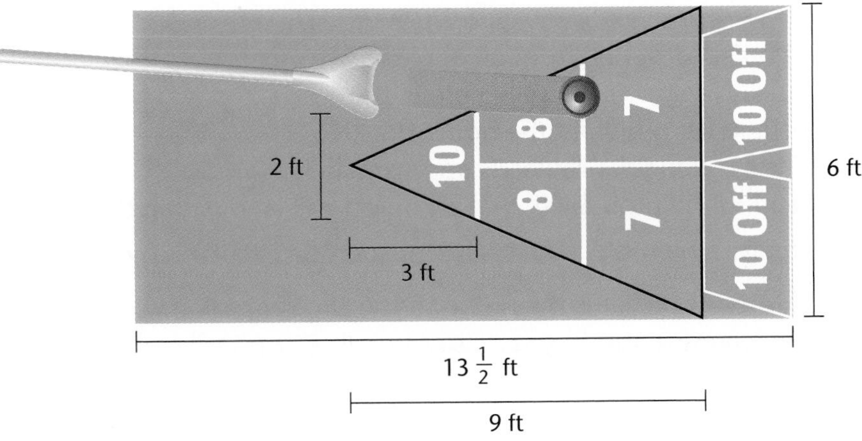

6. At a fair there is a jug filled with water with a small glass at the bottom. To win a prize you must drop a quarter into the jug and have it land in the glass. If the quarter falls randomly to the bottom, what is the probability of winning a prize?

7. **Create Your Own** Draw and shade a target. Include at least two different geometric shapes in your design. Find the probability of a dart hitting a shaded part of your target.

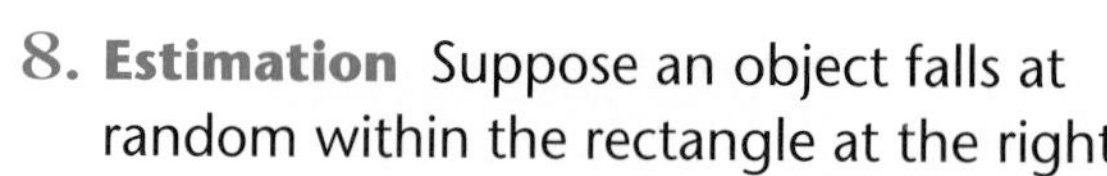

8. **Estimation** Suppose an object falls at random within the rectangle at the right.

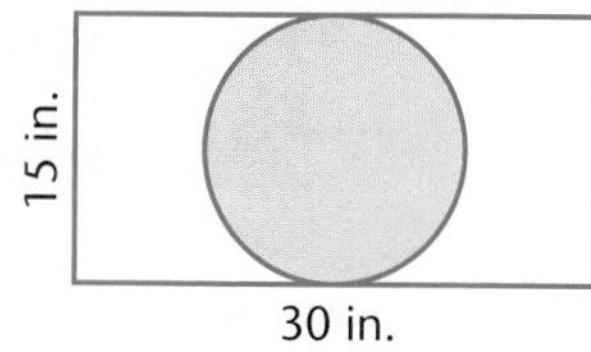

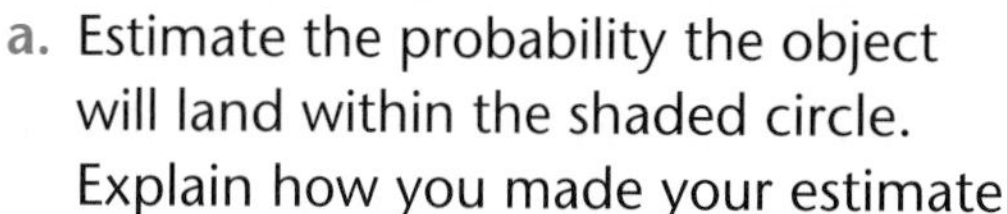

a. Estimate the probability the object will land within the shaded circle. Explain how you made your estimate.

b. Estimate the probability the object will land within the white area around the circle. How did you make your estimate?

c. Suppose 250 objects are dropped at random onto the rectangle. About how many would you expect to land within the circle?

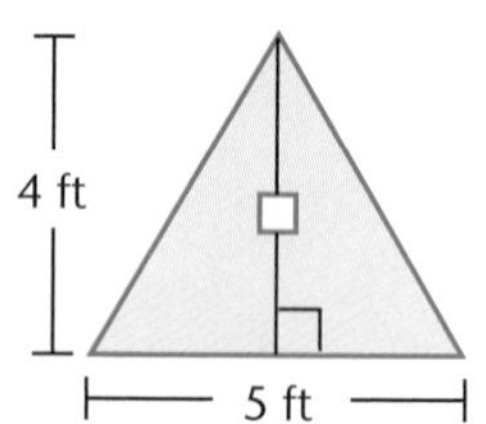

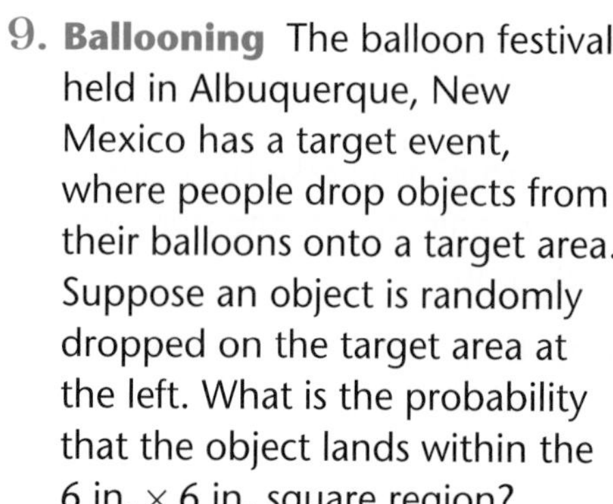

9. **Ballooning** The balloon festival held in Albuquerque, New Mexico has a target event, where people drop objects from their balloons onto a target area. Suppose an object is randomly dropped on the target area at the left. What is the probability that the object lands within the 6 in. × 6 in. square region?

10. The land area of the United States is about 1.8% of the area of Earth. If 500 meteorites hit Earth each year, about how many would you expect to hit the United States each year?

11. a. An object dropped from an airplane is equally likely to land anywhere in the rectangular region at the right. The area of the rectangular region is approximately 75 mi^2. The probability that an object will land within the circular region is $\frac{1}{6}$. What is the area of the circular region?

b. **Challenge** What is the radius of the circular region? Round to the nearest tenth.

Journal

Exercise 12 checks that you can find geometric probabilities.

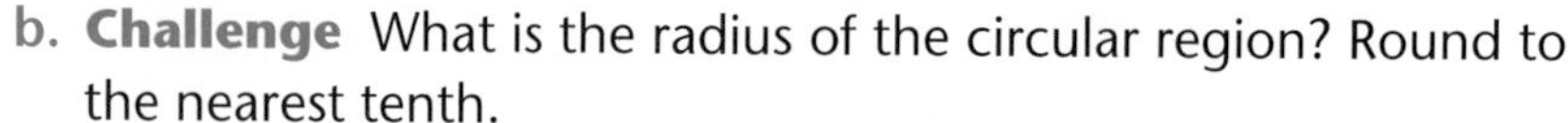

Reflecting on the Section

Write your response to Exercise 12 in your journal.

12. In 1954, Mrs. E. H. Hodges was resting on a sofa when a 4 kg meteorite broke through her roof, ricocheted off a radio, and hit her leg. The probability of a person being hit by a meteorite is actually very small because of the small fraction of the earth that is covered with people. Estimate this probability and explain how you did it.

Spiral Review

Convert each measurement to liters. (Module 8, p. 559)

13. 3425 mL 14. 97 kL 15. 250 cm^3 16. 0.84 kL

17. Find the least common multiple of 15 and 9. (Module 4, p. 300)

Month	Jan	Feb	Mar	Apr	May	Jun	Jul	Aug	Sep	Oct	Nov	Dec
Number of days	31	28	31	30	31	30	31	31	30	31	30	31

18. a. Make a line plot for the data in the table. (Module 3, p. 188)
    b. Use your line plot to find the mode and the median for the number of days in the twelve months.

Play *The Math is Right!*

Revising Your Questions Now that you have written your questions, you can test them out on your teammates.

Take turns reading your quiz questions to your teammates. Make sure that everyone understands each question and agrees on an answer. Rewrite any questions that are not clear.

Write each question on an index card or overhead transparency. Write your team number at the top of the card and the answer on the bottom.

Review your team's questions and decide which one you think is the most challenging. Mark this question with a star. This will be used as a bonus question in *The Math is Right!*

SET UP

Work with your team. Your team will need:

- *8 index cards or 8 overhead transparencies*
- *markers*

Section 4

Extra Skill Practice

Suppose a dart thrown at random hits each target. What is the probability that it hits the white region?

1.

80 cm

60 cm 80 cm 60 cm

area of white square = 1600 cm^2

2.

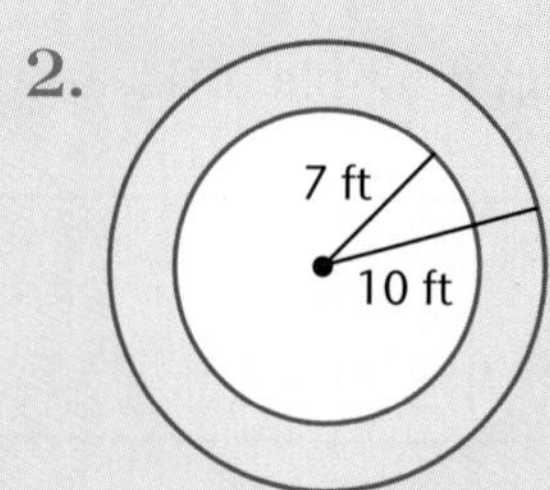

3.

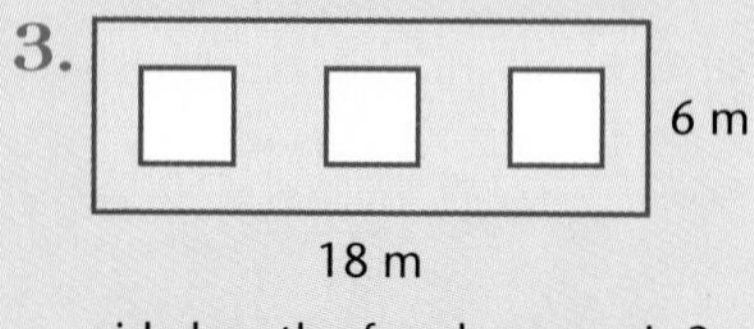

side length of each square is 3 m

4.

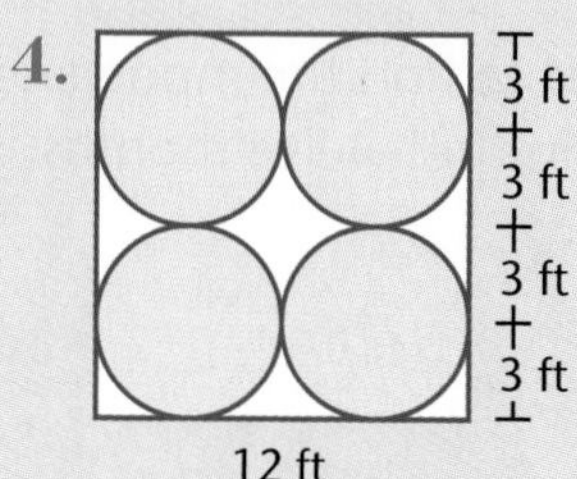

5.

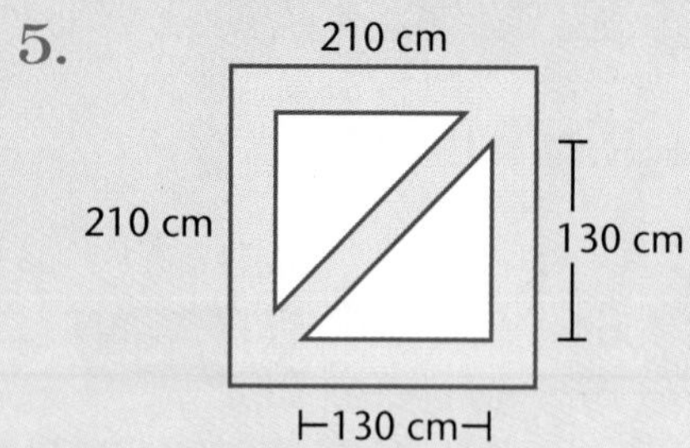

6.

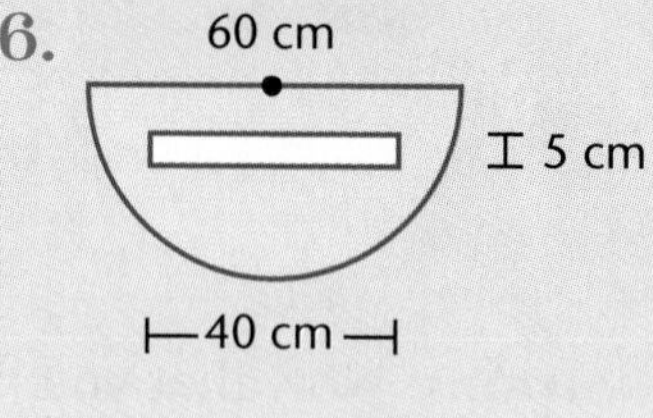

Standardized Testing ▸ Performance Task

You are designing a dart game where a player will throw darts at a 1 ft × 1 ft board with three to five separate squares drawn on it. Suppose that the squares are all the same size and that a dart thrown at random hits the board.

1. Find the probability that a dart hits a square if there are three squares and each has a side length of 2 in. Write your answer as a whole percent.

2. Suppose you want players to have about a 30% chance of hitting one of the squares. How many squares would you include and how long would you make each side? Explain.

Misleading Graphs and Averages

IN THIS SECTION

EXPLORATION 1
- Misleading Graphs

EXPLORATION 2
- Misleading Averages

Setting the Stage

Carbon monoxide (CO) is a pollutant produced by burning gasoline in cars, trucks, and buses. Finding ways to reduce the amount of CO in the atmosphere has been an ongoing battle. How well have we fought the CO war? Both graphs show the amount of CO in the atmosphere over nine years.

Graph 1

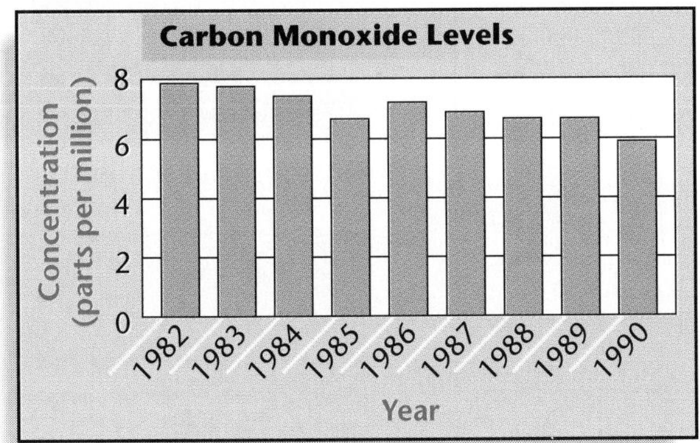

Graph 2

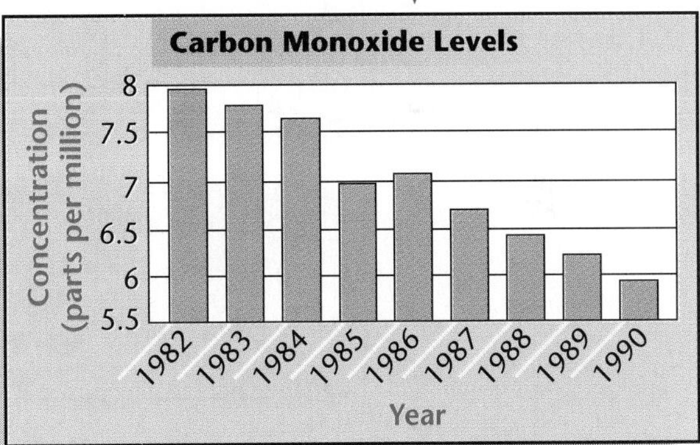

Think About It

1 **a.** Data for what years are shown in each graph?

b. In which year was the CO level lowest? highest?

2 Which graph seems to show little change in the CO level? Which seems to show that the CO level has dramatically decreased?

3 How was the vertical scale of Graph 1 adjusted to create a different view of the data in Graph 2?

GOAL

LEARN HOW TO...
- recognize misleading graphs
- choose an appropriate graph

AS YOU...
- compare graphs that give different pictures of data

KEY TERM
- circle graph

Exploration 1

Misleading GRAPHS

SET UP *You will need Labsheet 5A.*

By carpooling and using public transportation, people help reduce the amount of carbon monoxide in the atmosphere and conserve our limited supply of oil. A survey was done to find out how people get to work. The double bar graph shows the percent of people who carpooled or used public transportation and the percent who drove alone.

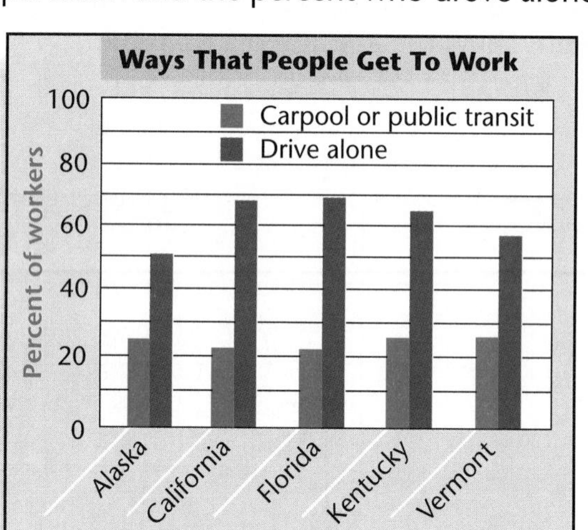

San Francisco, California

Boston, Massachusetts

Seattle, Washington

Burlington, Vermont

4 **a.** In Kentucky about 26% of workers carpooled or used public transportation. About what percent drove alone?

b. Why do you think the two percents in part (a) have a sum that is less than 100%?

In some cities people can also get to work by walking, taking a trolley or ferry, or by biking.

Use Labsheet 5A for Questions 5 and 6.

5 The commuter data used to create the graph on page 574 is given on the labsheet. Use the *Commuter Data and Blank Grid* to create a different picture of how people commute.

6 **Try This as a Class** Use your graphs of the commuter data.

a. In Vermont the percent of commuters who carpooled or used public transportation is about one half the percent of commuters who drove alone. Do both graphs show this relationship? Explain.

b. Which graph seems to show that very few people carpooled or used public transportation? How does it show this?

c. Which graph would you use if you wanted to show that a large percent of workers in these five states carpooled or used public transportation? Why?

d. How are the scales different for each graph?

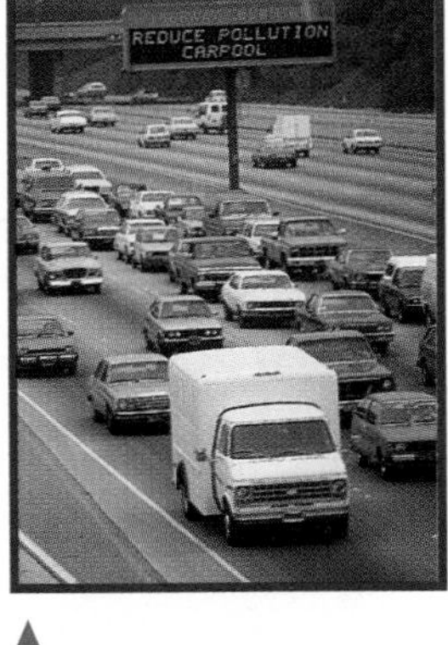

▲ There is a limited supply of fossil fuels like coal, oil, and natural gas. By burning less fossil fuels, we can reduce the amount of pollutants in the air.

▶ **Line graphs can also show different pictures of data. The two line graphs below show the use of petroleum (oil) in the United States.**

One Btu (British thermal unit) is about the same as the heat energy in one lighted match.

Graph 1

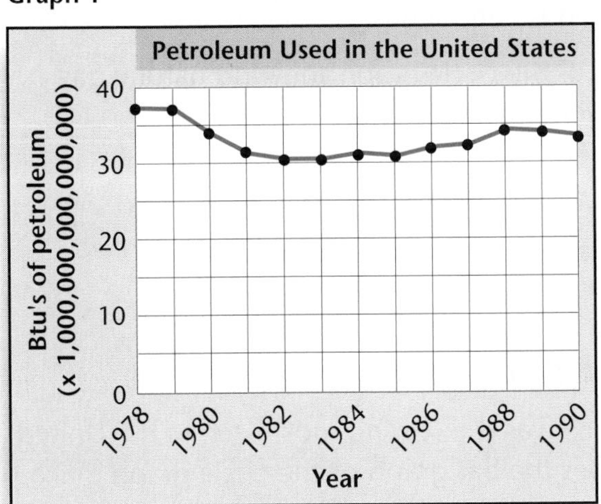

Graph 2

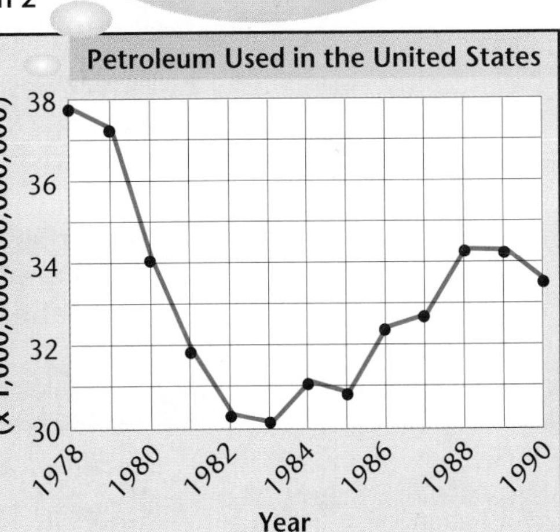

7 **a.** In which year was the least petroleum used in the United States?

b. Which graph did you use to answer part (a)? Why does this graph make it easier to find the lowest point on the graph?

c. How are the scales for the two graphs different?

d. Which graph seems to show that the amount of petroleum used in the United States has stayed about the same? What does the other graph seem to show?

▶ **The amount of energy used in the United States in 1993 is shown below in a bar graph and in a *circle graph*. A circle graph shows the part to whole relationship between data. The whole circle represents 100%.**

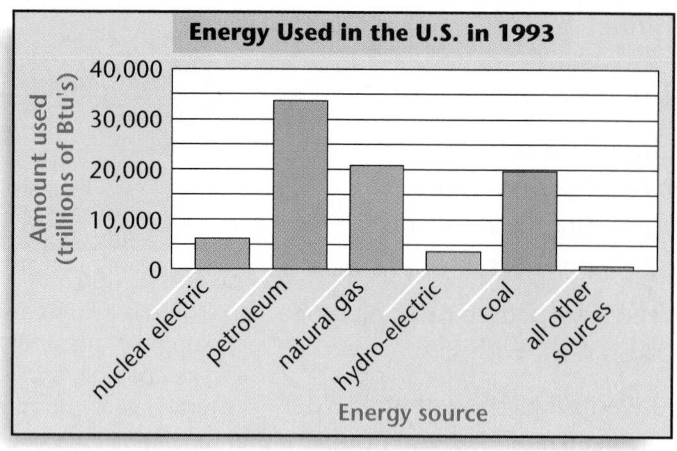

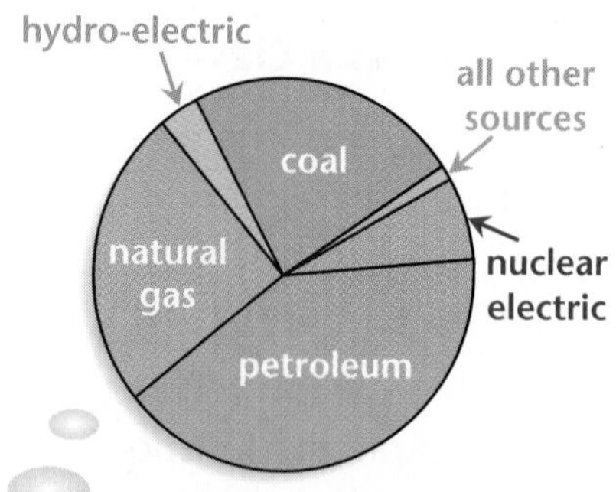

The whole circle represents the total amount of energy used in the United States.

8 **Discussion**

a. Use the bar graph to estimate the total amount of energy used in the United States in 1993. Explain how you made your estimate.

b. Use your estimate from part (a) to find about what percent of the total energy used is natural gas.

c. How does the part of the circle graph showing natural gas relate to your answer to part (b)?

▶ **Choosing a Graph** **Some ways of displaying data are more appropriate than others, depending on the type of data you have and the information you need.**

...checks that you can choose a graph to find information.

9 ✓ **CHECKPOINT** Use the bar graph and the circle graph.

a. Which energy source was the second most used in the United States in 1993? Does the bar graph or the circle graph make it easier to find this information? Explain.

b. About what fraction of the energy used in the United States in 1993 was petroleum? Which visual diplay did you use?

10 **Discussion** Look back at the double bar graph on page 574 and your answer to Question 4. Do you think it would be appropriate to show the commuter data in a circle graph? Explain.

HOMEWORK EXERCISES ▶ See Exs. 1–12 on pp. 580–581.

Exploration 2

Misleading AVERAGES

GOAL

LEARN HOW TO...
- choose an appropriate average

AS YOU...
- compare the fuel efficiency of prototype cars

▶ **To conserve oil, people have also developed automobiles that use less fuel. In the 1970s the average car in the United States had a fuel efficiency of 14 mi/gal. By 1985, the average fuel efficiency for new cars had risen to 27 mi/gal. Prototype cars have been designed that have fuel efficiencies of 100 mi/gal or more!**

11 **Try This as a Class** Suppose after examining the data on the fuel efficiencies of prototype cars, a reporter began an article with the following headline.

FOR ◀ HELP with *mean, median, and mode,* see **Module 3, p. 202**

Ultra-Fuel-Efficient Prototype Cars Get an Average of 81 Miles on Every Gallon of Gas

DETROIT, Mi.- For several decades, major car companies have researched and developed designs for more fuel efficient cars. Although companies have been able to build prototypes of these cars, several advancements in technology will have to happen simultaneously in order for them to be cost efficient enough to reach consumers.

a. Do you think the average 81 mi/gal is the *mean*, the *median*, or the *mode*? Why?

b. Does the average of 81 mi/gal contradict the statement that prototype cars have been designed that have fuel efficiencies greater than 100 mi/gal? Explain.

c. What else might you want to know about the fuel efficiencies of the prototype cars that the average does not tell you?

▶ **The reporter used the information in the table below to create a stem-and-leaf plot and determine the average highway fuel efficiency of prototype cars.**

Model name	Number of passengers	Fuel efficiency (mi/gal)		Type of fuel used
TPC	2	61 city	74 hwy	gasoline
ECV-3	4–5	41 city	52 hwy	gasoline
Auto 2000	4–5	63 city	71 hwy	diesel
VW-E80	4	74 city	99 hwy	diesel
LPC 2000	2–4	63 city	81 hwy	diesel
EVE+	4–5	63 city	81 hwy	diesel
Vesta2	2–4	78 city	107 hwy	gasoline
VERA+	4–5	55 city	87 hwy	diesel
ECO2000	4	70 city	77 hwy	gasoline
un-named	4–5	57 city	92 hwy	diesel
AXV	4–5	89 city	110 hwy	diesel

Highway Fuel Efficiency of Prototype Cars

Stem	Leaves
5	2
6	
7	1 4 7
8	1 1 7
9	2 9
10	7
11	0

7 | 4 → means 74 mi/gal

12 **a.** Find the mean, the median, and the mode of the highway fuel efficiencies of the prototype cars.

b. Did the reporter use the *mean*, the *median*, or the *mode* in Question 11? Why do you think that average was used?

✓ QUESTION 13

...checks that you can choose an appropriate average and make an appropriate graph for a set of data.

13 **✓ CHECKPOINT** The fuel efficiencies of prototype cars are much lower when driving in the city.

a. If you had to give a number that is typical of the fuel efficiencies of prototype cars when driving in the city, what number would you use? Why?

b. Write a headline for the fuel efficiencies of the prototype cars when they are driven in the city.

c. Make a graph to display the fuel efficiencies of the prototype cars. Explain why you think your graph is an appropriate way to display the data.

HOMEWORK EXERCISES ▶ See Exs. 13–21 on pp. 581–582.

Section 5

Key Concepts

Key Term

Misleading Graphs (pp. 574–575)

- Changing the numerical scale on a bar graph and on a line graph can give a very different impression of the data.

Choosing a Graph (pp. 574–576)

- A circle graph shows the part to whole relationship between data. The entire circle represents one whole or 100%, so the parts must add up to one whole.

circle graph

- A line graph shows a change over time.

Choosing an Average (pp. 577–578)

- The mean is the most commonly used average. The mean is affected by extreme data values.
- The median is rarely affected by extreme data values, but if the data are clustered around two different numbers with a large gap between, the median may give you a false impression of the typical data value.
- The mode is best used with categorical data. Shoe sizes and favorite colors are examples of categorical data.

Key Concepts Question

14 **a.** How could you change the numerical scale on the bar graph to make it look like a lot more money was made on the weekend than on weekdays?

b. Do you think the mode would be an appropriate average to use to describe the fundraiser data? Why or why not?

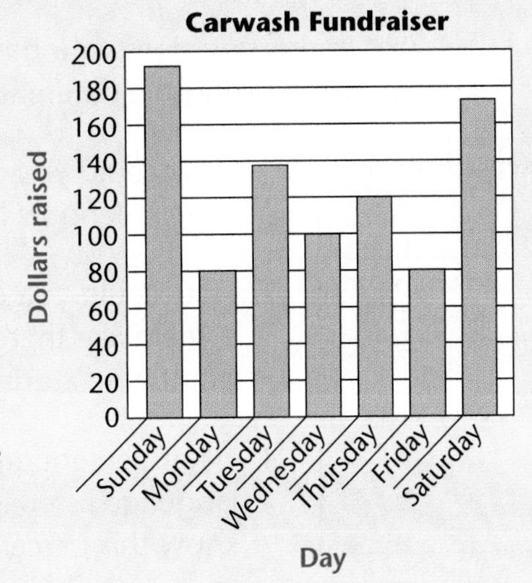

Section 5 Practice & Application Exercises

Graph 1

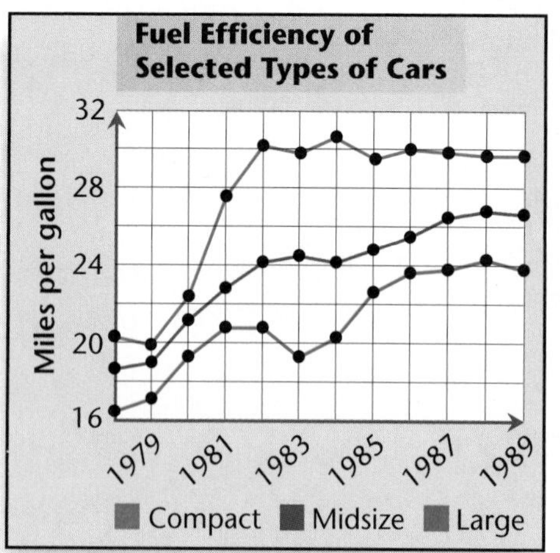

Graph 2

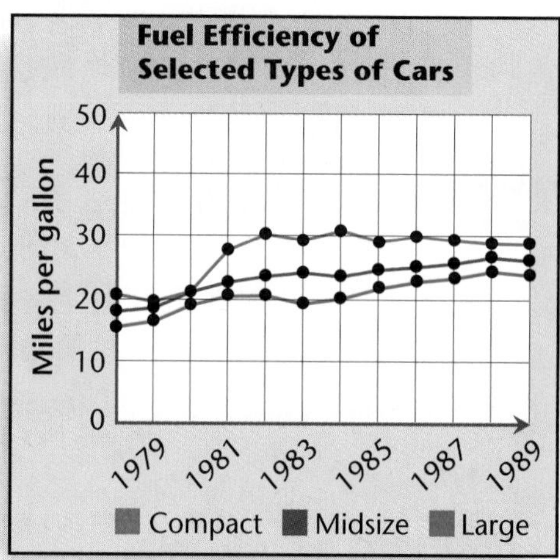

Displaying Data Choose the graph that best supports each statement. Explain your choice.

1. The fuel efficiencies of automobiles did not change much during the years 1978–1989.

2. Around 1983 there was a drop in the fuel efficiency of compact and large cars.

3. The fuel efficiency of compact cars is significantly higher than the fuel efficiency of large cars.

World Languages Use the table showing the percent of students taking a foreign language for Exercises 4–8.

4. Draw a bar graph to display the foreign language data.

5. What impression does your bar graph give about the percent of students taking the different languages?

High School Students Taking World Languages in the United States in 1993

World language	Percent of students
French	10.5
German	3.3
Japanese	0.4
Spanish	25.0

6. How could you change the percent scale so that the bar lengths look more even?

7. How could you change the percent scale to make it seem like there is a huge difference between the number of students taking each language?

8. What percent of students did not take a world language listed in the table? Why would you need to know this percent in order to make a circle graph?

Writing **Tell whether you would use a *line graph*, a *bar graph*, or a *circle graph* for each situation. Explain your choice.**

9. You took a survey of students' favorite video games and want to make a graph that helps you determine the top ten games picked.

10. Your principal wants to see how the number of students in your grade has changed over the past six years.

11. Six different instruments are played in the band. You want to compare the part of the band taken up by each instrument.

12. **Visual Thinking** It is estimated that 10% of all people are left-handed.
    a. Without finding an actual angle measure, sketch and label a circle graph to show the percent of people who are left-handed and the percent of people who are right-handed.
    b. How did you estimate the angle measures for your circle graph?
    c. If you were in a class of 32 students, about how many would you expect to be left-handed?

13. **Science** The chart lists the number of moons for each planet in our solar system.
    a. Find the mean, the median, and the mode of the data.
    b. Which, if any, of the averages would you use to describe the typical number of moons for a planet in our solar system? Why?

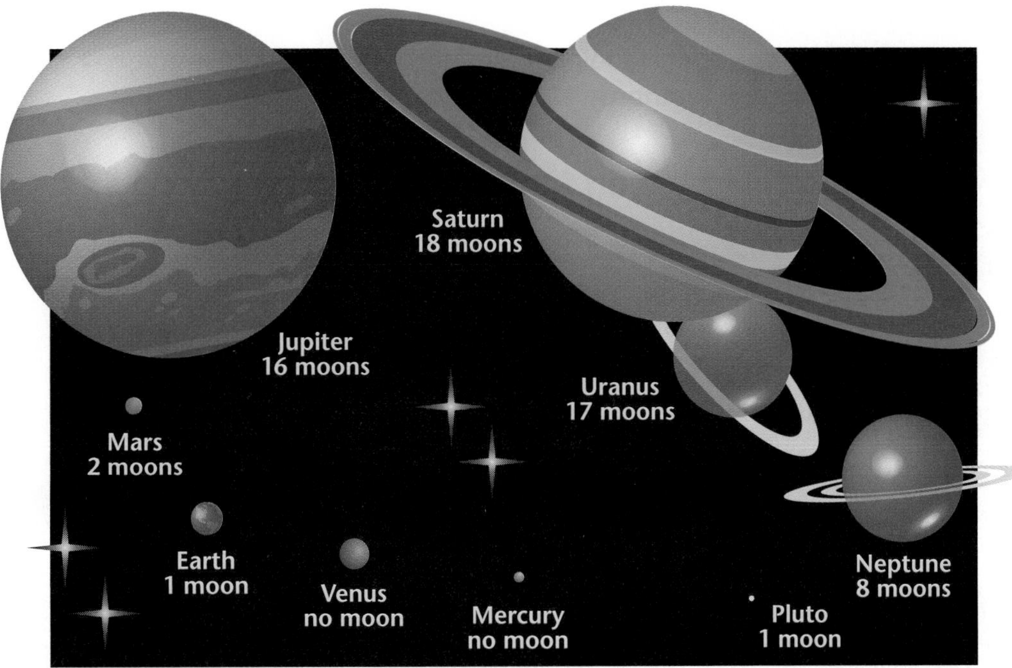

Tell whether the *mean*, the *median*, or the *mode* best describes each set of data. Explain your choice.

14. Number of bees in eight hives:

293	355	25	92	470	600	71	50

15. Number of ants in five colonies:

8200	7004	5216	60,000	8991

16. Number of students in nine college classes:

18	14	52	15	20	61	21	22	22

17. **Open-ended**

a. List the ages of five people in your family. Explain which type of average you think is most appropriate to use to describe the data.

b. List the ages of five of your friends. Which average best describes these ages?

c. Combine your lists from parts (a) and (b). Which average would you use to describe the ages?

Challenge Tell which type of average you think was used to make each statement. Explain your reasoning.

18. More students at Glenmore Middle School chose swimming as their favorite sport than chose any other sport.

19. The Swansons just had their first child. The average height of the mother, father, and baby is 5 ft 6 in.

20. A group of students took a survey and found that the average person uses a toothbrush 2.8 times a day.

RESEARCH

Exercise 21 checks that you understand how graphs and averages can be misleading.

Reflecting on the Section

21. a. Find a bar graph or a line graph in a magazine or newspaper.

b. What is the graph trying to show about the data? How could you change the scale on the graph so that it gives a different message?

c. Was an average used with the graph? If so, does the average give the same message as the graph?

Spiral Review

22. A dart thrown at random hits the target at the right. Find the probability that it hits the shaded area. (Module 8, p. 568)

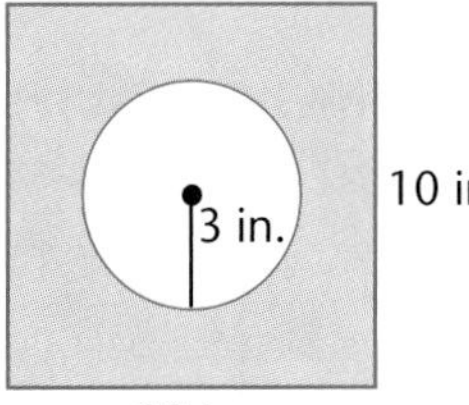

Find each product or quotient. (Module 5, pp. 358 and 370)

23. $5 \cdot 2\frac{1}{3}$

24. $6\frac{3}{5} \div 4$

25. $\frac{5}{12} \cdot 2\frac{3}{8}$

26. $8 \div 2\frac{1}{4}$

27. $3\frac{2}{7} \cdot 5\frac{1}{2}$

28. $10\frac{2}{5} \div 4\frac{1}{4}$

Find each sum or difference. (Module 2, p. 147; Module 5, p. 347)

29. $16.35 - 9.07$

30. $5\frac{3}{8} + \frac{7}{12}$

31. $3.74 + 26.83$

32. $12\frac{4}{9} - 7\frac{5}{6}$

33. $28.6 - 4.29$

34. $7\frac{5}{6} + 2\frac{2}{3}$

Extension

Three-Dimensional Misleading Graphs

The graph below is from a 1979 magazine. It uses different-sized barrels to show the change in price of crude oil from 1973–1979.

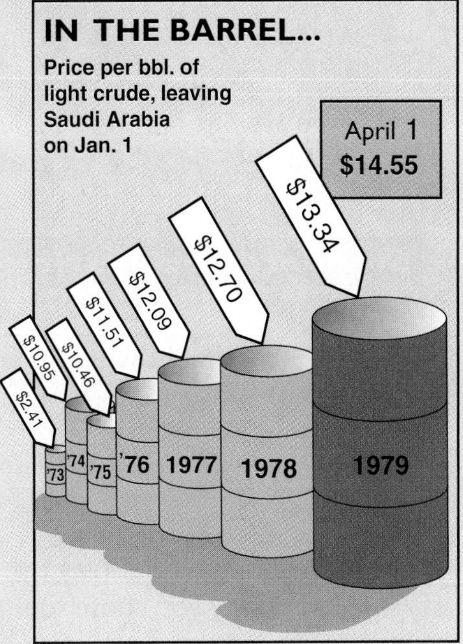

35. a. If the barrels were real objects, about how many times would the 1973 barrel fit inside the 1979 barrel? About how many times as great was the 1979 price as the 1973 price?

b. In the picture, the diameter of the 1973 barrel is about 3.5 mm and the diameter of the 1979 barrel is 19 mm. The height of the 1973 barrel is about 6 mm, and the height of the 1979 barrel is 33 mm. Is the relationship between the measurements of the barrels about the same as the relationship between the prices?

c. Use the dimensions from part (b) to find the volumes of both barrels. Explain why the relationship between the volumes is misleading when being used to show the change in oil price.

36. Make a bar graph and a line graph for the data. Be sure neither graph is misleading. Compare the graphs.

Section 5 Extra Skill Practice

The bar graph shows the number of drive-in movie screens from 1976–1996. Use the graph and the table for Exercises 1–5.

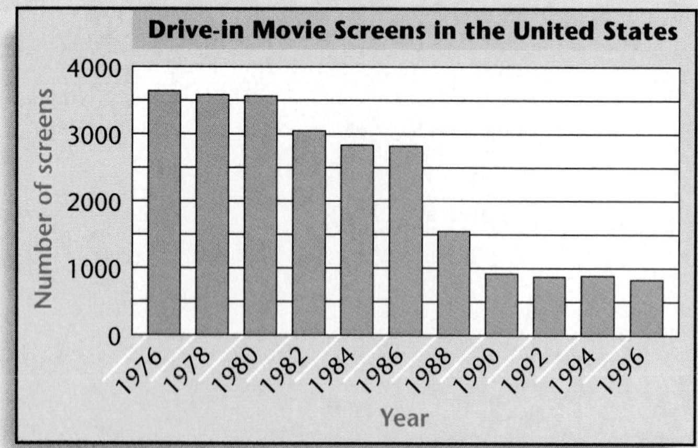

Drive-in Movie Screens in the United States	
Year	**Number of screens**
1976	3635
1978	3580
1980	3561
1982	3043
1984	2832
1986	2818
1988	1545
1990	915
1992	872
1994	885
1996	826

1. What impression does the bar graph give you about the number of drive-in movie screens from 1976–1996?
2. Describe a way that you could change the vertical scale to create a different impression of the data.
3. Use the table and the method you described in Exercise 2 to draw another bar graph for the data.
4. Would a line graph be an appropriate way to display this data? a circle graph? Explain why or why not.
5. If the average number of drive-in movie screens from 1976–1996 is reported to be 2818, what average do you think is being used? Explain.

Standardized Testing Open-ended

High and Low Temperatures for Three Cities in January			
City	Chicago	Miami	New York City
High (°F)	29	72	37
Low (°F)	14	66	26

1. Make a graph to display the temperature data in the table. Explain why you chose to make that type of graph.
2. What impression does your graph give about the high and low January temperatures for the three cities?

Play *The Math is Right!*

Now that you have written the quiz questions, it is time to play the game!

Getting Ready

Sit in a group with your team. Make sure each player has paper and a pencil. Your teacher should have each team's questions in separate, shuffled piles.

Playing

- Your teacher picks a card from Team 1's pile, reads it out loud, then sets a timer for two minutes. Team 1 is not allowed to answer the question.
- When time is up each team puts their pencils down and then shows their answer. All answers must be written down. Each team gets 10 points for a correct answer.
- The next question read is from Team 2's pile and Team 2 is not allowed to answer. Questions continue to be read in this manner.

Bonus Questions

If a bonus question is drawn, teams answering the question decide how many points they want to risk on the question before it is read. Each team writes the point value on a piece of paper and then turns it over. A team without any points can risk up to 10 points.

Each team gets the number of points they risked for a correct answer to a bonus question. Teams with incorrect answers to bonus questions lose the number of points they risked.

Winning the Game

The team with the most points when all the questions have been read (or the class period ends) wins. Now play *The Math is Right!*

MODULE 8 Review and Assessment

You will need • *graph paper* (Ex. 9)

Find each sum or difference. (Sec. 1, Explor. 1 and 2)

1. $-19 + 25$
2. $-36 - 3$
3. $0 - (-18)$
4. $-12 + (-12)$
5. $42 - 68$
6. $-7 - (-6)$
7. $56 - (-34)$
8. $-21 + 15$
9. Make a line graph for the data in the table. (Sec. 2, Explor. 1)

Fuel Efficiency of New Automobiles in the United States								
Year	1955	1960	1965	1970	1975	1980	1985	1990
Mi/gal	16.0	15.5	15.4	14.1	15.1	22.6	26.4	26.9

Write each number in standard form. (Sec. 2, Explor. 2)

10. $5.67 \cdot 10^3$
11. $1.002 \cdot 10^5$
12. $7 \cdot 10^8$
13. $4.2 \cdot 10^6$
14. $2.3 \cdot 10^1$
15. $9.11 \cdot 10^6$
16. $1.833 \cdot 10^4$
17. $8.9 \cdot 10^2$

Write each number in scientific notation. (Sec. 2, Explor. 2)

18. 4,400,000
19. 7700
20. 789
21. 331,000
22. 62,000
23. 5,000,000,000
24. 377,125
25. 88,000,000

Find each value. (Sec. 2, Explor. 3)

26. 22% of 542
27. 89% of 50
28. 72% of 90
29. 8% of 241
30. It is recommended that people drink about 4 L of water a day. Give the dimensions of a rectangular container that has a capacity of exactly 4 L. (Sec. 3, Explor. 1)

Write each fraction or decimal as a percent. Round to the nearest whole percent if neccessary. (Sec. 3, Explor. 2)

31. $\frac{80}{50}$
32. $\frac{1242}{540}$
33. $\frac{185}{125}$
34. $\frac{75}{25}$
35. $\frac{480}{250}$
36. 2.6
37. 5.315
38. 1.22
39. 3.0
40. 6.004
41. The snack bar at the beach made a profit of \$153.50 last week. This week it made a profit of \$165.78. This week's profit is what percent of last week's? (Sec. 3, Explor. 2)

For each target a dart that hits the target is equally likely to hit any point on the target. Find the probability that the dart hits the shaded area. (Sec. 4, Explor. 1)

42. 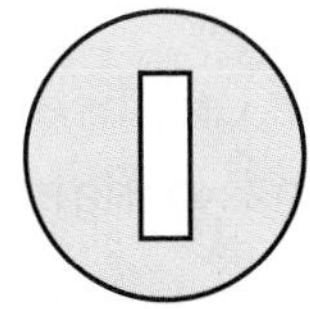

area of rectangle = 5 cm^2
diameter of circle = 7 cm

43. 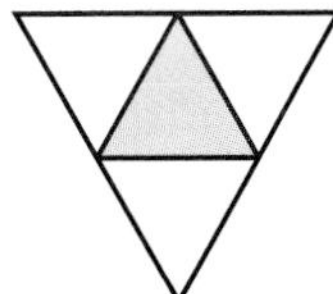

The four small triangles are all the same size.

44. 5 in. 3 in. 1 in.
10 in.
8 in.
6 in.

Use the graphs to answer Exercises 45–47. (Sec. 5, Explor. 1)

Graph 1

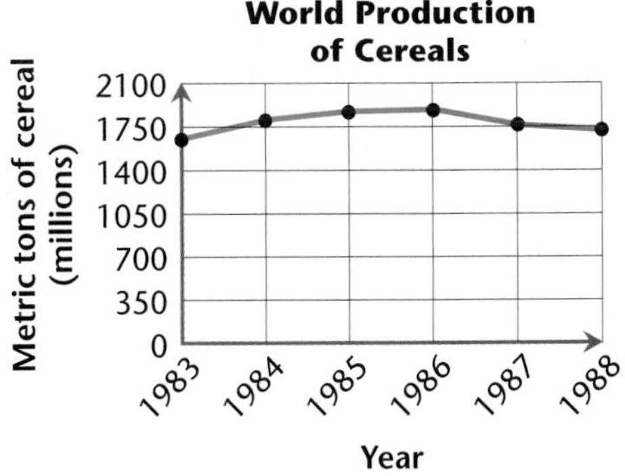

Graph 2

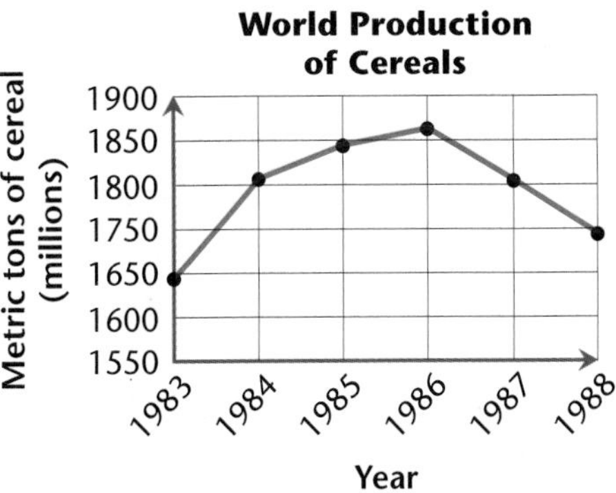

45. The median annual cereal production in the world was $1.8 \cdot 10^9$ metric tons in the years 1983 through 1988. Which graph do you think shows this fact the best? Why?

46. Which graph would you use to try to show that the cereal production in the world has changed dramatically in the years 1983 through 1988? Why?

47. What changes were made in Graph 1 to create a different view of the data in Graph 2?

48. A teacher says that 12 is the average age of the students in his class. What type of average do you think the teacher is using? Explain. (Sec. 5, Explor. 2)

Reflecting on the Module

49. **Writing** Mathematics can be a powerful tool. Explain how you think people use mathematics to discover and to show how the population and the environment change.

CONTENTS

STUDENT RESOURCES

STUDENT RESOURCES

TOOLBOX

NUMBERS and OPERATIONS

Whole Number Place Value

Each digit in a number has a place. To find the value of a digit, multiply the digit by the value of the place.

Millions			Thousands			Ones		
Hundreds	Tens	Ones	Hundreds	Tens	Ones	Hundreds	Tens	Ones
	8	3	2	9	5	0	4	1

The places are grouped into periods.

Period: millions
Place: one millions
Value: **3,000,000**

83,295,041 ← standard form

In expanded form 83,295,041 is written as:
80,000,000 + 3,000,000 + 200,000 + 90,000 + 5,000 + 40 + 1

In words, 83,295,041 is expressed as:
eighty-three million, two hundred ninety-five thousand, forty-one

EXAMPLE

Write the place and the value of each underlined digit.

	$\underline{1}$,248,630	2$\underline{2}$5,000	85,6$\underline{9}$9
SOLUTION	place: **one millions**	place: **ten thousands**	place: **tens**
	value: **1,000,000**	value: **20,000**	value: **90**

Write the place and the value of each underlined digit.

1. $\underline{8}$41,670
2. 33$\underline{5}$,928
3. $\underline{5}$6,831,000
4. 2$\underline{8}$
5. 9$\underline{9}$3,671
6. 403,$\underline{2}$00

Give the following information about the number 469,224.

7. the place of the 6
8. the value of the digit in the tens place

Write each number in standard form.

9. fifteen million, nine hundred forty-six thousand, six hundred nineteen
10. two hundred twenty thousand, nine

Write each number in words.

11. 518
12. 23,400
13. 70,000,624
14. 450,672

Comparing Whole Numbers

The symbols below are used to compare numbers:

> (is greater than) **< (is less than)** **= (is equal to)**

Thinking about place value will help you compare two numbers and put a list of numbers in order.

EXAMPLE

To compare 23,760 and 23,748, first line up the digits of each number by place value. Then compare the digits in each place, starting at the left. If the digits are equal, compare the digits in the next place to the right, and so on until you come to different digits.

Compare digits from left to right since the leftmost place has the greatest value.

same	same	same	different: 6 > 4	
2	3	7	6	0
2	3	7	4	8

23,760 is greater than 23,748 because it has a greater digit in the first place that is different, the tens place.

EXAMPLE

Write the list of numbers in order from greatest to least.

2,227 21,237 20,080 1,919 450,900 34,888

SOLUTION Compare the digits in each place starting with the greatest place value.

		2	2	2	7
	2	1	2	3	7
	2	0	0	8	0
		1	9	1	9
4	5	0	9	0	0
	3	4	8	8	8

hundred thousands: The only number with a digit in the hundred thousands place is 450,900 so 450,900 is the greatest number.

ten thousands: 3 > 2 so 34,888 is greater than both 21,237 and 20,080. Check the next digit of 21,237 and 20,080. 1 > 0 so 21,237 > 20,080.

thousands: 2 > 1 so 2,227 > 1,919.

450,900 > 34,888 > 21,237 > 20,080 > 2,227 > 1,919

Replace each ? with >, <, or =.

1. 2224 ? 1810
2. 20,111 ? 19,991
3. 3,201,999 ? 419,963
4. 37,011 ? 370,110
5. 897,500 ? 190,001
6. 5,402,320 ? 5,410,320
7. 198,999 ? 199,000
8. 891,450 ? 340,232
9. 50,777,760 ? 51,666,700

Write each list of numbers in order from greatest to least.

10. 239,400; 47,777; 24,000; 79,899
11. 6,150,762; 892,570; 7,902,500; 937,400

Rounding Whole Numbers and Money

To round a number to a given place, look at the digit to the right of that place to decide whether the number is greater or less than the halfway point.

If the digit in the place to the right is less than 5 (0, 1, 2, 3, or 4) round down.

If the digit in the place to the right is 5 or greater (5, 6, 7, 8, or 9) round up.

EXAMPLE

Round 5839 to the nearest hundred.

SOLUTION 5839 is between 5800 and 5900.

Look at the digit to the right of the hundreds place: the 3 in the tens place. 3 is less than 5, so 39 is less than half of 100. Round down to the nearest hundred, 5800. 5839

5839 rounded to the nearest hundred is 5800.

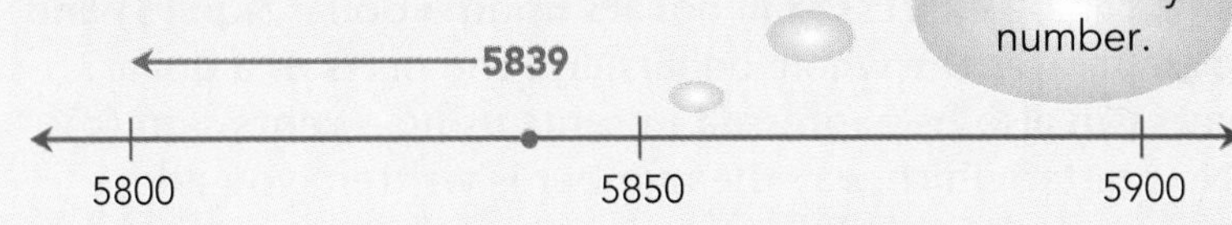

EXAMPLE

Round $42.61 to the nearest one dollar.

SOLUTION $42.61 is between $42 and $43.

6 is the digit to the right of the dollars place. 6 is greater than 5, so 61 cents is greater than half of a dollar. Round up to the nearest dollar, $43. $42.61

$42.61 rounded to the nearest one dollar is $43.

Round each number to the given place.

1. 888 (nearest ten)
2. 94,575 (nearest hundred)
3. 85,920 (nearest thousand)
4. 27,380,573 (nearest million)
5. 602 (nearest hundred)
6. 43 (nearest ten)
7. 298,722 (nearest ten thousand)
8. 68,274 (nearest hundred)

Round each amount to the given place.

9. $949.50 (nearest dollar)
10. $4369.75 (nearest ten dollars)
11. $52.05 (nearest dollar)
12. $644.00 (nearest hundred dollars)

Adding Whole Numbers and Money

To add whole numbers, add place by place. First add the ones, then the tens, then the hundreds, then the thousands, and so on.

EXAMPLE

Find 206 + 58.

SOLUTION Rewrite the numbers, lining up the ones, the tens, and the hundreds.

Add the ones and trade if needed.	Add the tens and trade if needed.	Add the hundreds.
$\begin{array}{r} {}^{1} \\ 206 \\ +\ 58 \\ \hline 4 \end{array}$	$\begin{array}{r} {}^{1} \\ 206 \\ +\ 58 \\ \hline 64 \end{array}$	$\begin{array}{r} {}^{1} \\ 206 \\ +\ 58 \\ \hline 264 \end{array}$

Trade 14 ones for 1 ten and 4 ones.

206 + 58 = 264

Money amounts can be expressed in dollars using a dollar sign ($) and a dot. The dot separates the whole dollars and the parts of a dollar. Money amounts can also be expressed in cents using a cents sign (¢) and no dot. No matter which way the number is written, you add money place by place. First add the pennies, then the dimes, then the one dollars, then the ten dollars, and so on.

EXAMPLE

Find $3.80 + $9.44 + $.75.

$.75 means 75 cents, or 7 dimes and 5 pennies.

SOLUTION Line up the pennies, the dimes, and the dollars.

Add the pennies, dimes, and dollars separately. Trade as needed.

Trade 19 dimes for 1 dollar and 9 dimes.

$$\begin{array}{r} {}^{1} \\ \$3.80 \\ \$9.44 \\ +\ \ \$.75 \\ \hline \$13.99 \end{array}$$

Add.

1. 2767 + 465
2. 8219 + 4499
3. 66,405 + 35,511
4. 2,082 + 58,875
5. 35,294 + 62,472
6. 77,996 + 5,687 + 5,434
7. $8.14 + $3.97
8. $20.87 + $18.17
9. $27.40 + $16.75
10. $54.25 + $66.65
11. $31.24 + $11.83
12. $26.50 + $88.95

Mental Math

When you want to use mental math to add, it helps to break numbers into parts.

To add two-digit numbers, you can break up at least one of the numbers you are adding into tens and ones and add on these parts separately.

EXAMPLE

Find 38 + 15.

SOLUTION Break 15 into tens and ones: 15 = 10 + 5

38 + 10 = 48 ← Add the tens to 38.

48 + 5 = 53 ← Add the ones to the result.

38 + 15 = 53

Sometimes it is helpful to add enough to reach a number that ends in 0 and then add the rest.

EXAMPLE

Find $5.75 + $1.50.

SOLUTION You need $.25 to get $5.75 to reach $6.00, so break $1.50 into $.25 + $1.25.

$5.75 + $.25 = $6.00 ← Add the $.25 to the $5.75.

$6.00 + $1.25 = $7.25 ← Add the remaining $1.25 to the result.

$5.75 + $1.50 = $7.25

Use mental math to find each sum.

1. 56 + 67
2. 35 + 47
3. 452 + 29
4. 253 + 68
5. 49 + 322
6. 796 + 35
7. 428 + 67
8. 634 + 157
9. 181 + 494
10. $6.90 + $5.35
11. $4.20 + $14.37
12. $6.28 + $4.10
13. $8.35 + $5.00
14. $2.45 + $11.95
15. $3.99 + $4.98
16. $15.50 + $4.75
17. $9.84 + $3.56
18. $17.69 + $5.36

Subtracting Whole Numbers and Money

To subtract whole numbers, subtract the ones, then the tens, then the hundreds, and so on. Trade before each step if necessary.

EXAMPLE

Find 3001 – 1953.

SOLUTION Rewrite the numbers, lining up the ones, the tens, and so on.

Since there are no tens or hundreds, trade 1 thousand for 9 hundreds, 9 tens, and 10 ones to get more ones.

You need to trade to get more ones.

```
  2 9 9 11
  3 0 0 1
-   1953
```

Now you can subtract.

```
  2 9 9 11
  3 0 0 1
-   1953
    1048 ← difference
```

3001 – 1953 = 1048

Check your answer with addition. The difference plus the number subtracted should equal the number you started with: 1048 + 1953 = 3001.

When you subtract money, first subtract the pennies, then the dimes, then the one dollars, then the ten dollars, and so on.

EXAMPLE

Find $5.45 – $2.86.

SOLUTION Line up the dollars and cents.

Subtract the pennies. Trade first if needed.

```
     3 15
  $5.45
– $2.86
      9
```

Subtract the dimes. Trade first if needed.

```
  4 13 15
  $5.45
– $2.86
     59
```

Subtract the dollars.

```
  4 13 15
  $5.45
– $2.86
  $2.59
```

Put in a dot to separate dollars and cents.

$5.45 – $2.86 = $2.59

Your answer can be checked with addition.
$2.59 + $2.86 = $5.45

Subtract.

1. 8712 – 134
2. 506 – 318
3. 9501 – 4688
4. 2500 – 379
5. 7211 – 709
6. 6040 – 2199
7. $46.26 – $17.18
8. $401.40 – $13.00
9. $183.50 – $119.42
10. $333.25 – $299.86
11. $501.00 – $180.67

Multiplying Whole Numbers and Money

To multiply whole numbers, begin by lining up the numbers you are multiplying. Multiply the entire first number by the ones of the second number, by the tens of the second number, and so on.

EXAMPLE

Find 583 × 304.

SOLUTION Rewrite the numbers, lining up the ones, the tens, and the hundreds.

0 tens × 583 = 0, so no product is written.

```
              583
            × 304
             2332   ← 4 × 583      ← Multiply by 4 ones.
         + 174900   ← 300 × 583    ← Multiply by 3 hundreds.
product → 177,232   ← 304 × 583
```

Zeros are used to hold the ones and tens place.

When multiplying with money, you can think of dollars and cents as just cents and multiply as you do with whole numbers.

EXAMPLE

Find 7 × $3.25.

SOLUTION $3.25 is equal to 325 cents.

```
 325¢
 ×  7   ← Multiply 325 by 7.
2275¢
```

Think of 2275 cents as 22 hundred cents and another 75 cents. Each hundred cents is worth one dollar so you have 22 dollars and 75 cents.

7 × $3.25 = $22.75

Multiply.

1. 25 × 38
2. 96 × 504
3. 146 × 260
4. 655 × 337
5. 158 × 29
6. 14 × 2048
7. 6 × $38.18
8. 22 × $16.01
9. 41 × $2.72
10. 60 × $31.50
11. 2 × $54.82
12. 303 × $9.95

Dividing Whole Numbers

Dividing whole numbers is the same as finding how many times the divisor goes into the dividend.

Sometimes when you divide there will be a remainder. The remainder is a number that is leftover after the divisor goes into the dividend as many times as possible.

$$\begin{array}{r l} 9 & \leftarrow \text{quotient} \\ \text{divisor} \rightarrow 5\overline{)45} & \leftarrow \text{dividend} \end{array}$$

EXAMPLE

Find 968 ÷ 27.

SOLUTION Rewrite the division in columns to organize your work. Try to divide 27 into each place or combination of places in 968, starting at the left.

You will need to multiply and subtract each time you write a digit in the quotient. Be careful to keep columns lined up.

hundreds place	tens place	ones place
27 does not go into 9.	Divide 27 into 96. It goes in 3 times.	Divide 27 into 158. It goes in 5 times.
$27\overline{)968}$	$\begin{array}{r} 3 \\ 27\overline{)968} \\ -81 \\ \hline 15 \end{array}$	$\begin{array}{r} 35 \text{ R}23 \\ 27\overline{)968} \\ -81\downarrow \\ \hline 158 \\ -135 \\ \hline 23 \end{array}$

27 × 3 = 81 Subtracting 81 from 96 gives a remainder of **15**.

Combine the 15 tens remaining and the 8 ones from the dividend to get 158.

27 × 5 = 135 Subtracting 135 from 158 gives a remainder of **23**.

968 ÷ 27 = 35 R23 (35 remainder 23)

To check the answer, multiply the quotient by the divisor and add the remainder.

35 × 27 = 945   945 + 23 = 968

Divide.

1. 3205 ÷ 8
2. 500 ÷ 64
3. 9875 ÷ 4
4. 269 ÷ 21
5. 7852 ÷ 26
6. 8080 ÷ 15
7. 741 ÷ 36
8. 520 ÷ 45
9. 6800 ÷ 42
10. 350 ÷ 102
11. 1208 ÷ 34
12. 344 ÷ 26

Number Fact Families

The following is an example of a number fact family for addition and subtraction:

$7 + 9 = 16$ $9 + 7 = 16$ $16 - 7 = 9$ $16 - 9 = 7$

You can use a number fact family to find missing numbers. For example, suppose you want to find the missing number in $7 + \underline{?} = 16$. If you know that $16 - 7$ will give you the same number, you can subtract to find the missing number.

A number fact family for multiplication and division is given below:

$6 \times 2 = 12$ $2 \times 6 = 12$ $12 \div 6 = 2$ $12 \div 2 = 6$

You can use this family to complete the number sentence $12 \div \underline{?} = 2$.

EXAMPLE

addends (3, 5) — sum (8)

Complete the number fact family for 3 + 5 = 8.

SOLUTION You can write the other addition fact in the family by switching the order of the addends. You can write the related subtraction facts by starting with the sum and taking away each addend.

$3 + 5 = 8$ $5 + 3 = 8$ $8 - 3 = 5$ $8 - 5 = 3$

EXAMPLE

Find the missing number: $18 \div \underline{?} = 2$

SOLUTION You know from the multiplication and division number fact families that the missing number is the same for $18 \div \underline{?} = 2$ as for $18 \div 2 = \underline{?}$.

$18 \div 2 = 9$. Therefore $18 \div 9 = 2$.

Complete each number fact family.

1. $6 + 3 = 9$ $3 + \underline{?} = 9$ $9 - \underline{?} = 6$ $9 - \underline{?} = \underline{?}$
2. $16 \div 2 = \underline{?}$ $\underline{?} \div \underline{?} = 2$ $\underline{?} \times 8 = 16$ $\underline{?} \times \underline{?} = 16$

Find each missing number.

3. $23 + \underline{?} = 35$
4. $344 - \underline{?} = 320$
5. $\underline{?} + 12 = 65$
6. $62 - \underline{?} = 37$
7. $\underline{?} - 4 = 77$
8. $\underline{?} + 51 = 83$
9. $\underline{?} - 8 = 95$
10. $\underline{?} \times 4 = 52$
11. $\underline{?} \div 7 = 9$
12. $7 \times \underline{?} = 56$
13. $\underline{?} \div 3 = 13$
14. $6 \times \underline{?} = 72$
15. $\underline{?} \div 4 = 12$
16. $28 \div \underline{?} = 7$
17. $\underline{?} \times 3 = 42$

Multiplying and Dividing by Tens

You can use mental math to multiply by 10, 100, 1000, and so on, by thinking about place value.

EXAMPLE

To find 100×23, think: 1 hundred taken 23 times is 23 hundreds.

$100 \times 23 = 2300$

You can use what you know about multiplying by 10, 100, or 1000 to multiply other numbers that end in one or more zeros.

EXAMPLE

To find 200×80, first multiply the non-zero digits then put on the extra zeros.

$200 \times 80 = 2 \times 100 \times 8 \times 10 = 16 \times 1000 = 16{,}000$

$2 \times 8 = 16$

$100 \times 10 = 1000$, so you need 3 zeros at the end.

The mental math strategies shown for multiplying numbers ending in zeros can also help you to divide numbers ending in zeros. Think about the relationship between division and multiplication.

EXAMPLE

To find $670{,}000 \div 1000$, think: $\underline{?} \times 1000 = 670{,}000$.

$670{,}000 \div 1000 = 670$

To find $48{,}000 \div 60$, think about the zeros and the non-zero digits separately.

$48{,}000 \div 60 = 800$

Think: $\underline{?} \times 6 = 48$

Think: $\underline{?} \times 10 = 1000$

Multiply and divide.

1. 100×500
2. 200×30
3. 5000×300
4. 400×4000
5. 3000×200
6. 5000×100
7. $200 \times 60{,}000$
8. $10{,}000 \times 2{,}000$
9. $8{,}000 \times 40{,}000$
10. $800{,}000 \div 2$
11. $10{,}000 \div 1{,}000$
12. $10{,}000 \div 200$
13. $3900 \div 30$
14. $20{,}000 \div 400$
15. $250{,}000 \div 50$

Perimeter and Using a Ruler

The perimeter (*P*) of a figure is the distance around it. You can find the perimeter by adding the lengths of the sides together.

EXAMPLE

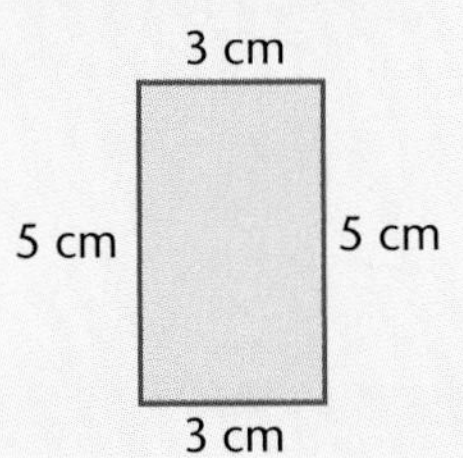

3 cm
5 cm
5 cm
3 cm

$3 + 5 + 3 + 5 = 16$
***P* = 16 cm**

2 m
2 m
4 m
6 m
4 m
6 m

$4 + 2 + 2 + 6 + 6 + 4 = 24$
***P* = 24 m**

5 ft
3 ft
4 ft

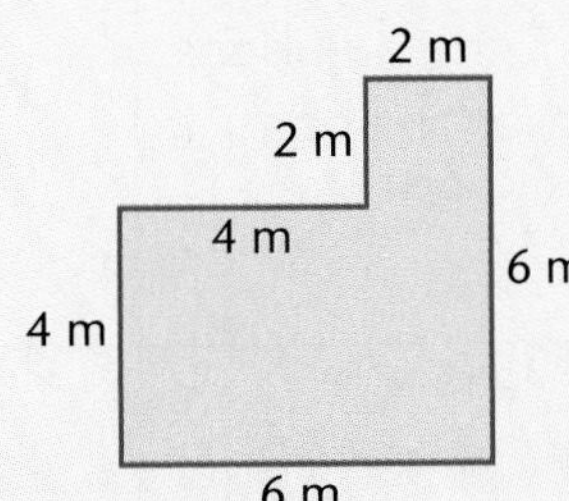

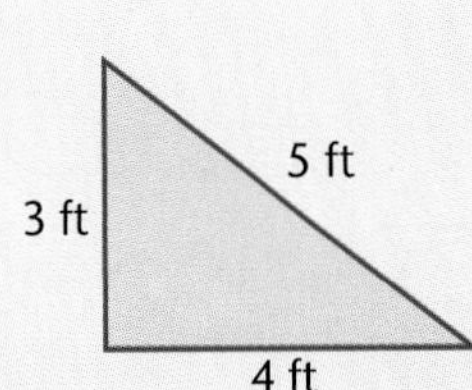

$3 + 5 + 4 = 12$
***P* = 12 ft**

A ruler is a tool that is used to measure length. A United States customary ruler shows measurements in inches.

EXAMPLE

The other end of the pencil is between 3 in. and 4 in. It does not reach the halfway mark, so round down.

Use a ruler to measure the pencil to the nearest inch.

Line up one end of the pencil with the 0 mark on the ruler.

0
1
2
3
4

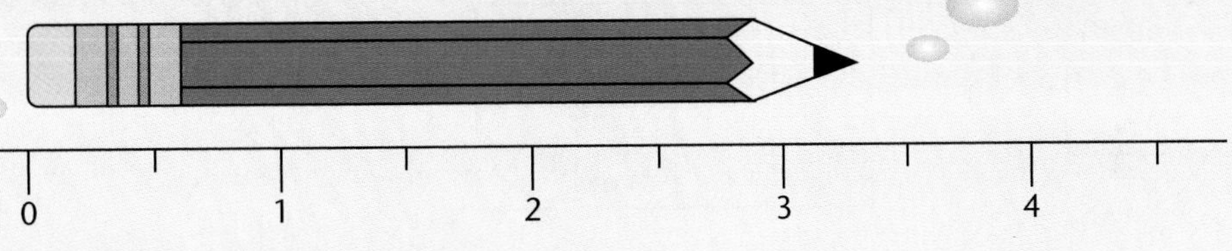

The pencil is about 3 in. long.

For Exercises 1–5, find the perimeter of each figure.

1.
6 in.
3 in.
3 in.
6 in.

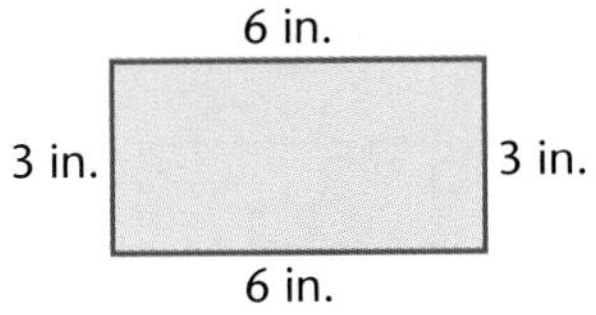

2.
4 cm
4 cm
5 cm
5 cm

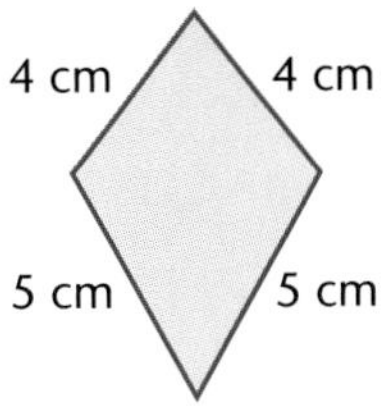

3.
3 ft
3 ft
3 ft
3 ft

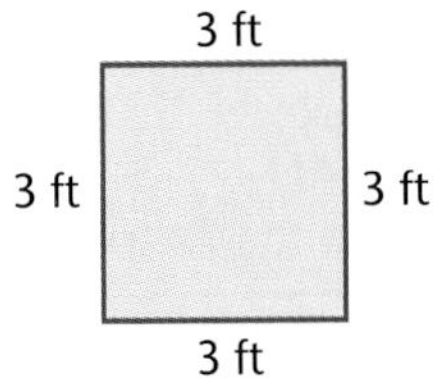

4. a square with sides 5 cm long

5. a triangle with sides 3 in., 5 in., and 6 in. long

Use a ruler to measure each nail to the nearest inch.

6.

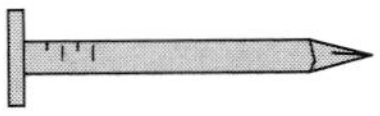

7.

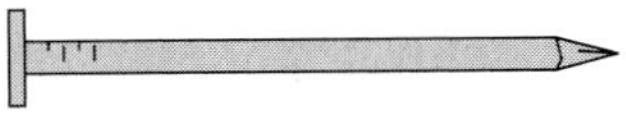

Area

The area of a figure is the amount of surface it covers. Area is measured in square units. The square units used may be square inches, square centimeters, square feet, or squares of any other size.

EXAMPLE

This square is a square inch.

1 in.

1 in.

You can count the number of square inches to find the area.

The area of the figure is 4 square inches.

EXAMPLE

This square is a square centimeter.

1 cm

1 cm

Add 4 square centimeters in each row to get 8 square centimeters.

The area of the figure is 8 square centimeters.

Find the area of each figure. Each small square is 1 centimeter by 1 centimeter.

1.

2.

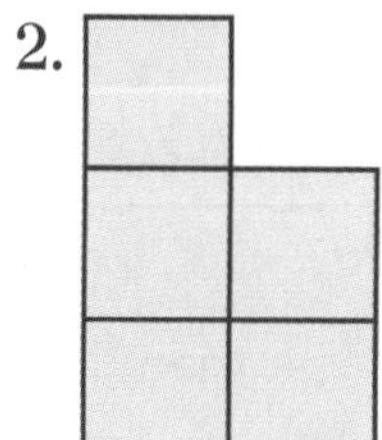

3.

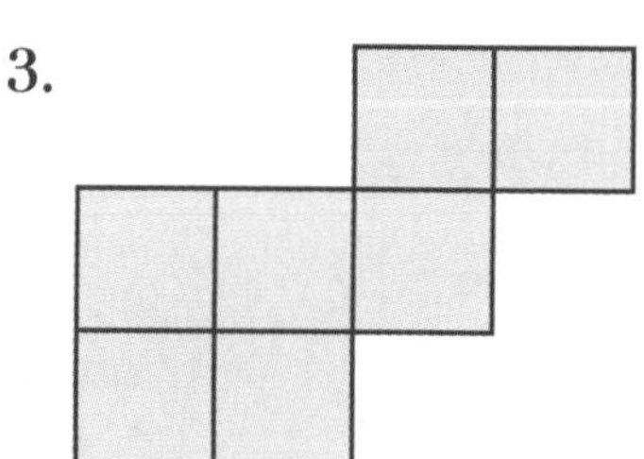

Time Conversions and Elapsed Time

The chart below can help you convert time measurements. You can also use these relationships when you subtract to find elapsed time.

60 seconds (s) = 1 minute (min)
60 minutes (min) = 1 hour (h)
24 hours (h) = 1 day
7 days = 1 week

EXAMPLE

Find the missing number: 20 min = ? seconds

SOLUTION Every 1 min equals 60 seconds.
20 min = 20 × 60 seconds = **1200 seconds**

EXAMPLE

How much time has elapsed between 8:30 A.M. and 10:15 A.M.?

SOLUTION

10:15 A.M.	→	~~10~~ (9) h ~~15~~ (75) min	
− 8:30 A.M.	→	− 8 h 30 min	
		1 h 45 min	

Trade 1 h for 60 min. Then combine the 60 min with the 15 min already there.

EXAMPLE

How much time has elapsed between 3:00 P.M. and 1:30 A.M.?

SOLUTION

1:30 A.M.	→	13 h 30 min
− 3:00 P.M.	→	− 3 h 00 min
		10h 30 min

To get to 1:30 A.M. you need to go another hour and a half past 12:00 midnight. Add 1 h 30 min to 12 h to get 13 h 30 min.

Change each time measurement to the given unit of time.

1. 8 h to minutes
2. 72 h to days
3. 180 seconds to minutes

Find how much time has elapsed between the given times.

4. 12:40 P.M. and 5:35 P.M.
5. 9:30 A.M. and 11:23 P.M.
6. 6:10 P.M. and 9:06 P.M.
7. 10:45 P.M. and 12:20 A.M.

Reading a Graph

A graph is a visual display of data. Different types of graphs are used depending on the type of data and the relationship you are showing.

EXAMPLE

To read a bar graph, find the bar that represents the information you are looking for. Think of extending a line from the end of the bar to the numbers on the scale.

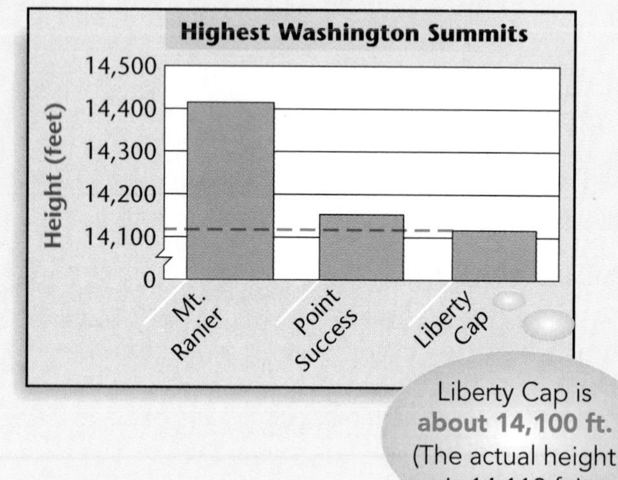

To see what each point represents on a line graph, think of drawing a line across or down to each of the scales.

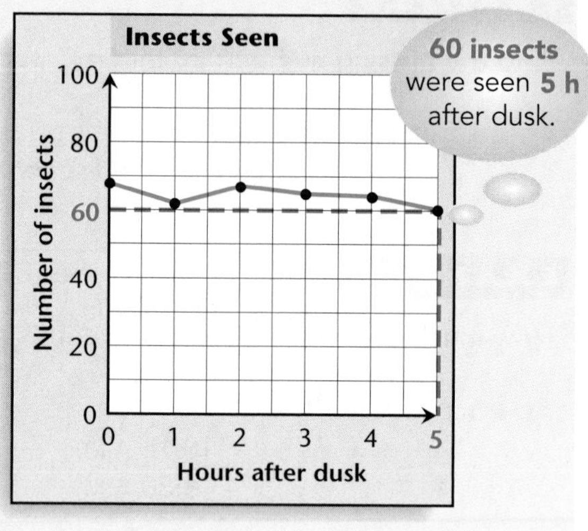

Use the graph to estimate each value.

1. By the end of 1998, how many World Cup tourneys had Brazil played? had France played?

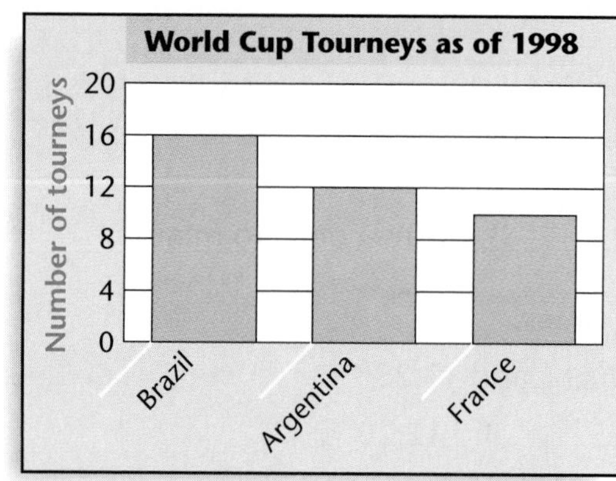

2. What was the population of Birmingham, Alabama, in 1990? in 1994?

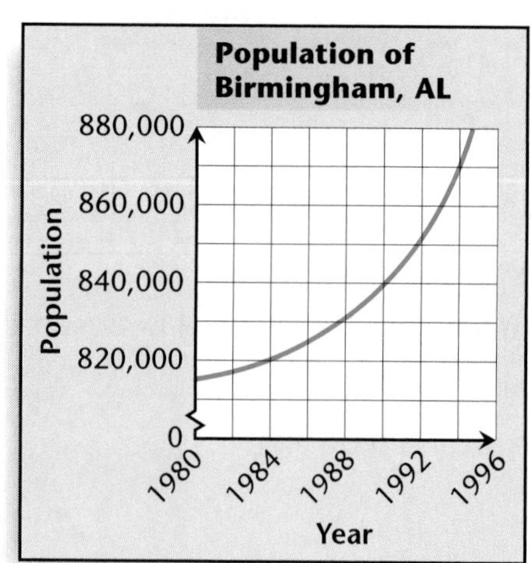

Making a Pictograph

A pictograph can be used to display data. Usually a symbol is used to represent a given number of items.

EXAMPLE

Make a pictograph to represent the number of campers each summer.

Year	1993	1994	1995	1996	1997	1998
Campers	600	640	690	655	700	750

SOLUTION You can use 1 triangle for each 100 campers. You can also use part of a triangle to show part of 100.

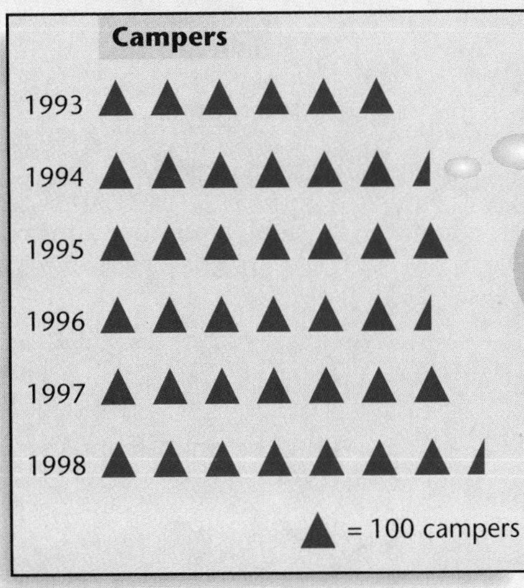

There are 6 hundreds in 600, so use 6 full triangles to show 600 campers. There are 40 campers left and 40 is almost half of 100, so you can show half of another triangle.

1. Make a pictograph to represent the students studying music in each grade.

Grade	6th	7th	8th
Students studying music	71	90	85

2. Make a pictograph to represent the money spent on advertising in 1994. The dollar amounts have been rounded to the nearest billion.

Advertising medium	newspapers	magazines	television	radio	direct mail
Billions of dollars	34	8	34	10	29

TABLE OF SYMBOLS

SYMBOL		Page
...	and so on	**4**
$\times$	times	**8**
=	equals	**8**
−	minus	**11**
+	plus	**11**
$\overleftrightarrow{AB}$	line *AB*	**15**
$\overline{AB}$	segment *AB*	**15**
$\overrightarrow{AB}$	ray *AB*	**15**
$\angle A$	angle *A*	**18**
°	degree(s)	**18**
∟	right angle	**19**
$<$	is less than	**26**
$>$	is greater than	**26**
•	times	**47**
÷	divided by	**49**
( )	parentheses—grouping symbol	**49**
⟌	divided into	**69**
R	remainder	**69**
$\frac{3}{4}$	3 equal parts of 4	**95**
′	feet	**105**
″	inches	**105**
1.2	decimal point, separates whole numbers from parts of a whole number	**134**

SYMBOL		Page
%	percent	**174**
$\frac{3}{4}$	3 divided by 4	**200**
$\geq$	is greater than or equal to	**202**
2^3	3rd power of 2	**255**
(x, y)	ordered pair of numbers	**284**
1 : 2	ratio of 1 to 2	**382**
AB	length of $\overline{AB}$	**425**
$\triangle ABC$	triangle *ABC*	**426**
π	pi, a number approximately equal to 3.14	**492**
$\approx$	is about equal to	**492**
−1	negative 1	**510**
−1	the opposite of 1	**533**

TABLE OF MEASURES

Time

60 seconds (s)	=	1 minute (min)
60 minutes	=	1 hour (h)
24 hours	=	1 day
7 days	=	1 week
4 weeks (approx.)	=	1 month
365 days 52 weeks (approx.) 12 months	=	1 year
10 years	=	1 decade
100 years	=	1 century

METRIC

Length

10 millimeters (mm)	=	1 centimeter (cm)
100 cm 1000 mm	=	1 meter (m)
1000 m	=	1 kilometer (km)

Area

100 square millimeters (mm^2)	=	1 square centimeter (cm^2)
10,000 cm^2	=	1 square meter (m^2)
10,000 m^2	=	1 hectare (ha)

Volume

1000 cubic millimeters (mm^3)	=	1 cubic centimeter (cm^3)
1,000,000 cm^3	=	1 cubic meter (m^3)

Liquid Capacity

1000 milliliters (mL)	=	1 liter (L)
1000 L	=	1 kiloliter (kL)

Mass

1000 milligrams (mg)	=	1 gram (g)
1000 g	=	1 kilogram (kg)
1000 kg	=	1 metric ton (t)

Temperature — **Degrees Celsius (°C)**

0°C	=	freezing point of water
37°C	=	normal body temperature
100°C	=	boiling point of water

UNITED STATES CUSTOMARY

Length

12 inches (in.)	=	1 foot (ft)
36 in. 3 ft	=	1 yard (yd)
5280 ft 1760 yd	=	1 mile (mi)

Area

144 square inches ($in.^2$)	=	1 square foot (ft^2)
9 ft^2	=	1 square yard (yd^2)
43,560 ft^2 4840 yd^2	=	1 acre (A)

Volume

1728 cubic inches ($in.^3$)	=	1 cubic foot (ft^3)
27 ft^3	=	1 cubic yard (yd^3)

Liquid Capacity

8 fluid ounces (fl oz)	=	1 cup (c)
2 c	=	1 pint (pt)
2 pt	=	1 quart (qt)
4 qt	=	1 gallon (gal)

Weight

16 ounces (oz)	=	1 pound (lb)
2000 lb	=	1 ton (t)

Temperature — **Degrees Fahrenheit (°F)**

32°F	=	freezing point of water
98.6°F	=	normal body temperature
212°F	=	boiling point of water

GLOSSARY

A

acute angle (p. 19) An angle with a measure greater than 0° but less than 90°. *See also* angle.

acute triangle (p. 20) A triangle with three acute angles.

angle (p. 18) A figure formed by two rays that have a common endpoint.

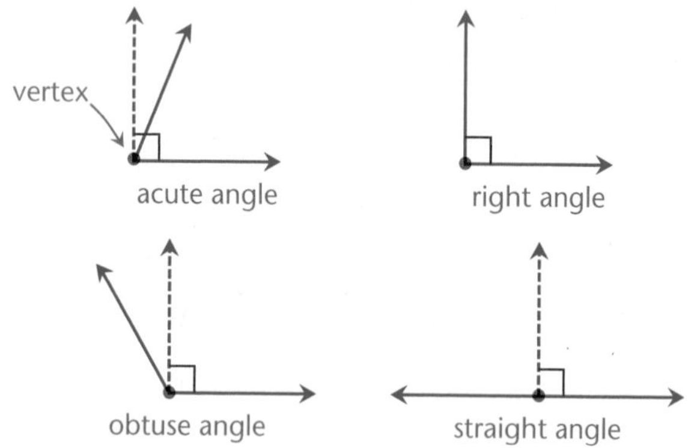

area (p. 287) The number of square units of surface a figure covers.

average (p. 196) A single number used to describe what is typical of a set of data. *See* mean, median, *and* mode.

axes (p. 284) *See* coordinate grid.

B

back-to-back stem-and-leaf plots (p. 227) A stem-and-leaf plot that compares two related sets of data.

bar graph (p. 183) A graph used to compare data by comparing the lengths of bars.

base (p. 255) *See* exponential form.

base of a polygon (pp. 458, 459) *See* parallelogram *and* triangle.

base of a space figure (pp. 469, 479, 502) *See* prism, pyramid, *and* cylinder.

benchmark (p. 161) An item whose measure you know that can be used to estimate lengths. For example, you could use your height to estimate the height of a doorway.

C

capacity (pp. 354, 555) The amount of liquid a container can hold.

center (p. 488) *See* circle.

certain event (p. 241) An event that must happen. It has a probability of 1.

chord (p. 488) A segment that connects two points on a circle. *See also* circle.

circle (p. 488) The set of points in a plane that are all the same distance from a given point, the center.

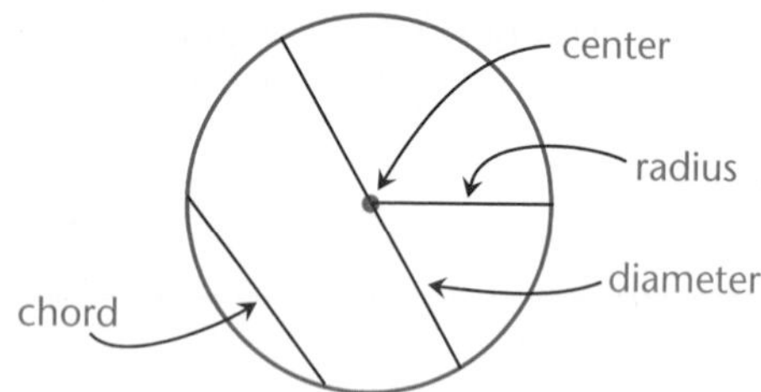

circle graph (pp. 434, 576) A circular-shaped graph that shows the part to whole relationship between data. A whole circle represents 100%.

circumference (p. 490) The distance around a circle.

common denominator (p. 314) A common multiple of the denominators of two or more fractions.

compatible numbers (p. 46) Numbers that have sums, products, or quotients that are easy to find and compute with.

composite number (p. 252) A whole number greater than 1 that has more than two factors.

congruent (p. 85) Having the same size and shape.

congruent figures (p. 426) Figures that have the same shape and the same size.

connections (p. 67) Similarities that relate two patterns, problems, ideas, or applications.

coordinate grid (p. 284) A grid formed using two number lines as axes. The axes intersect at the point (0, 0) called the *origin*.

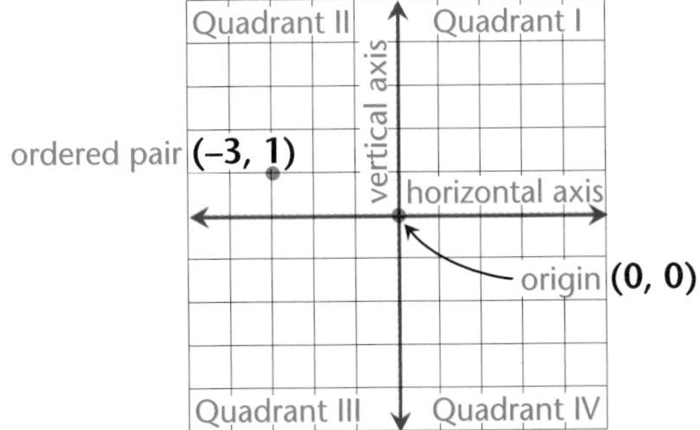

corresponding parts (p. 424) When two figures are similar, for each angle or side of one figure there is a similar angle or side on the other figure.

cross products (p. 414) Equal products formed from a pair of equivalent ratios by multiplying the numerator of each fraction by the denominator of the other fraction.

proportion	cross products
$\frac{2}{3} = \frac{4}{6}$	$2 \cdot 6$ $3 \cdot 4$

cubic unit (p. 468) A unit for measuring volume.

cylinder (p. 502) A space figure that has a curved surface and two parallel, congruent bases.

circular cylinder

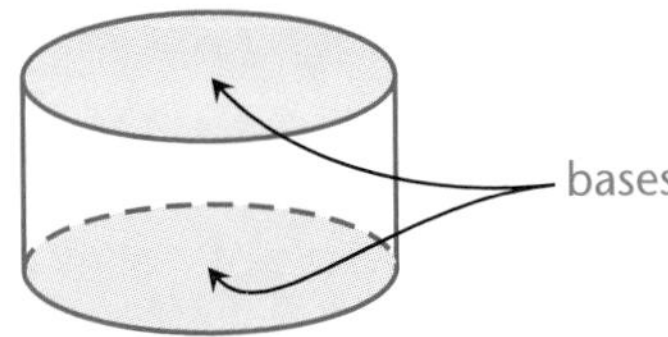

D

decimal point (p. 134) The dot that separates whole numbers and parts of a whole number.

decimal system (p. 134) A system of numbers based on 10.

denominator (p. 95) The bottom number in a fraction that tells how many equal-sized parts the whole is divided into.

diameter (p. 489) A chord that passes through the center of a circle and the length of such a chord. *See also* circle.

difference (p. 594) The result when two numbers are subtracted.

distributive property (p. 356) Each addend inside a set of parentheses can be multiplied by a factor outside the parentheses. For example, $3 \cdot (4 + 2) = 3 \cdot 4 + 3 \cdot 2$.

divisible (p. 248) When a number can be evenly divided by another number, it is divisible by that number.

E

edge (p. 469) A segment on a space figure where two faces meet. *See also* prism.

empty set (p. 159) A set with no objects in it.

equally likely (p. 237) Outcomes are equally likely if they have the same chance of occurring.

equation (p. 287) A mathematical sentence that uses the symbol "=" between two expressions to show that they have the same value.

equilateral triangle (p. 16) A triangle with three sides of equal length.

equivalent decimals (p. 137) Two decimals that represent the same amount.

equivalent fractions (p. 109) Fractions that name the same part of a whole.

equivalent ratios (p. 383) Ratios that can be written as equivalent fractions.

estimate (p. 43) An answer that is not exact.

evaluate an expression (p. 286) To substitute a number for each variable, then carry out any operations in the expression.

event (p. 240) A set of outcomes for a particular experiment.

experiment (p. 235) An activity whose results can be observed and recorded.

experimental probability (p. 236) The ratio of the number of times the outcome happened to the number of times the experiment was repeated.

exponent (p. 255) A raised number that tells how many times a base is used as a factor. *See also* exponential form.

exponential form (p. 255) A way of writing a number using exponents. A number that can be written using an exponent and a base is a power of the base.

8 is a power of 2

standard form $8 = 2 \cdot 2 \cdot 2 = 2^3$ exponential form (3: exponent; 2: base)

expression (pp. 48, 285) A mathematical sentence that can contain numbers, variables, and operation symbols.

F

face (p. 469) A flat surface of a space figure. *See also* prism.

factor (p. 249) When a whole number is divisible by a second whole number, the second number is a factor of the first.

factor tree (p. 252) *See* prime factorization.

fair game (p. 442) A game in which each player has an equal chance of winning.

fitted line (p. 402) A line that passes near to most of the data points in a scatter plot, so that close to half of the data points fall above the line and close to half fall below the line.

fraction (p. 95) A number that compares a part with a whole.

front-end estimation (p. 211) A method of estimation that focuses on the left-most digits, since they have the greatest value.

G

general case (p. 68) When you solve a problem for one situation and extend it to any such situation, you are extending the solution to the general case.

general rule (p. 6) A rule that tells you how to find any term in a sequence.

geometric probability (p. 567) A probability that is based on length, area, or volume.

greatest common factor (GCF) (p. 250) The greatest number that is a factor of each of two or more numbers.

H

height of a polygon (pp. 458, 459) *See* parallelogram, triangle.

I

impossible event (p. 241) An event that cannot happen. It has a probability of 0.

inequality (p. 312) A mathematical sentence that uses symbols such as > (greater than) or < (less than) to compare values.

integer (p. 511) Any number in the set {..., –3, –2, –1, 0, 1, 2, 3, ...}.

intersect (p. 458) Two segments or figures that meet at a common point intersect.

isosceles triangle (p. 16) A triangle with two or more sides of equal length.

L

least common denominator (p. 314) The least common multiple of the denominators of two or more fractions.

least common multiple (LCM) (p. 296) For two or more numbers, the least number in the list of their common multiples.

line (p. 15) A straight arrangement of points that extends forever in opposite directions.

line graph (p. 540) A graph on which the plotted points are connected with line segments. It may show changes that take place over time.

line plot (p. 187) A plot displaying data above the appropriate points along a scale. The scale must include the greatest and least values of the data.

line symmetry (p. 86) A figure has line symmetry when it can be folded in half so that the two halves fit exactly on each other. The fold line is called the *line of symmetry*.

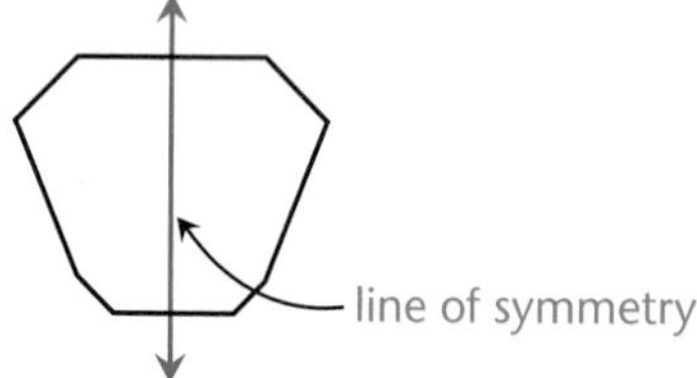

lowest terms (p. 113) A fraction is in lowest terms when 1 is the greatest whole number that will divide both the numerator and the denominator evenly.

M

mean (p. 196) The sum of a set of numerical data divided by the number of data items.

median (p. 198) The middle data item in a set of data in numerical order. If there is no single middle item, the number halfway between the two data items closest to the middle.

mixed number (p. 97) The sum of a whole number and a fraction.

mode (p. 197) The data item or items that occur most often in a set of data.

multiple (p. 295) A multiple of a whole number is the product of that number and any nonzero whole number.

N

negative (p. 510) Less than zero.

net (p. 471) A flat pattern that can be cut out and folded to form a space figure.

"nice" fraction (p. 400) A fraction like $\frac{1}{3}$, $\frac{1}{4}$, or $\frac{2}{5}$ that can be used to estimate a ratio or percent, making computation easier.

numerator (p. 95) The top number in a fraction that tells how many parts of the whole to consider.

O

obtuse angle (p. 19) An angle with a measure greater than 90° but less than 180°. *See also* angle.

obtuse triangle (p. 20) A triangle with one obtuse angle.

opposites (p. 529) Two numbers whose sum is equal to 0; one addend is positive, one addend is negative.

order of operations (p. 48) The order to follow when performing operations: simplify inside parentheses, multiply or divide left to right, and finally add or subtract left to right.

ordered pair (p. 283) The numbers that give the location of a point on a coordinate grid. The first number gives the horizontal position and the second number gives the vertical position. *See also* coordinate grid.

origin (p. 284) *See* coordinate grid.

outcome (p. 235) The result of an experiment.

P

parallel lines (p. 82) Lines on a flat surface that do not meet.

parallel planes (p. 469) Planes that do not intersect.

parallelogram (p. 83) A quadrilateral with two pairs of parallel sides.

The perpendicular distance between bases of a parallelogram is the height.

bases

percent (p. 174) "per hundred" or "out of 100."

perfect number (p. 258) A number that equals the sum of all its factors, not including the number itself.

perimeter of a polygon (p. 287) The sum of the lengths of the edges of a polygon.

perpendicular (p. 458) The relationship between lines or segments that meet at a right angle.

pi (π) (p. 492) The ratio of circumference to diameter for any circle. The value of π is approximately equal to 3.14.

place value (p. 134) The numerical value assigned to the different positions of digits in a number that is written in decimal form.

plane (p. 469) A flat surface that extends forever.

point (p. 15) A specific location in space.

polygon (p. 81) A closed figure made from segments that are drawn on a flat surface and do not cross.

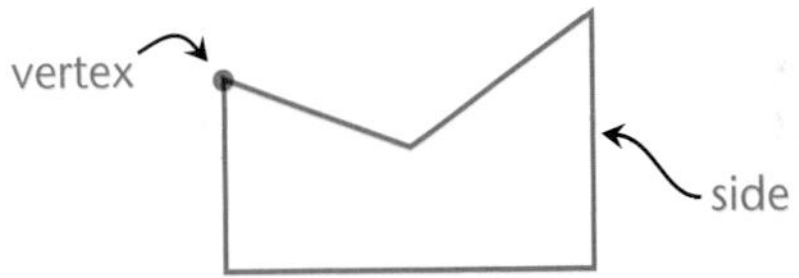

A polygon can have 3 or more sides. Some types of polygons are:

pentagon (5 sides)	hexagon (6 sides)
octagon (8 sides)	decagon (10 sides)

population (p. 172) A whole set of objects being studied.

positive (p. 510) Greater than zero.

power (p. 255) *See* exponential form.

prime factorization (p. 252) A number written as the product of prime factors. A factor tree helps to find the prime factorization.

factor tree

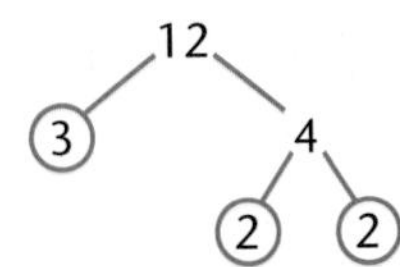

The prime factorization of 12 is 2 · 2 · 3

prime number (p. 252) A whole number greater than 1 that has exactly two factors, 1 and the number itself.

prism (p. 469) A type of space figure made up of flat surfaces that are shaped like polygons. It has two bases that are congruent and lie in parallel planes. The other faces are parallelograms. A prism is named for the shape of its bases.

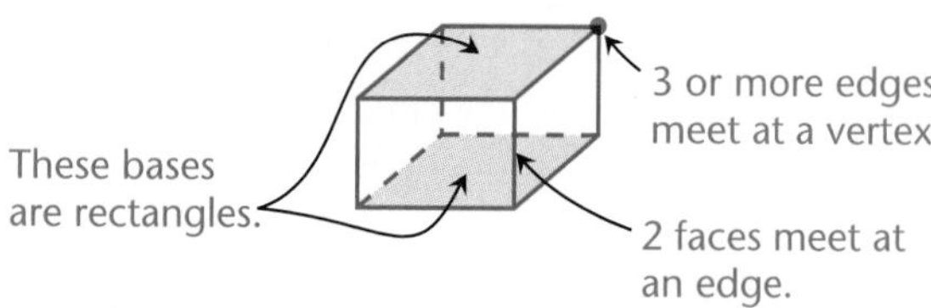

probability (p. 236) A number from 0 to 1 that tells you how likely something is to happen.

product (p. 595) The result when two or more numbers are multiplied.

proportion (p. 414) An equation stating that two ratios are equivalent.

protractor (p. 429) A tool used to measure an angle.

pyramid (p. 479) A space figure that has one polygon-shaped base. All the other faces are triangles that meet at a single vertex.

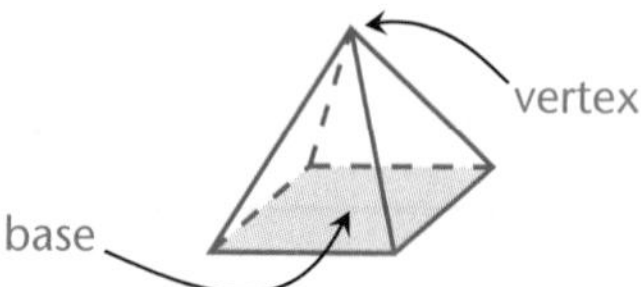

Q

quadrant (p. 514) The four parts of a grid divided by the axes. *See also* coordinate grid.

quadrilateral (p. 83) A polygon with four sides.

quotient (p. 596) The result when two numbers are divided.

R

radius (plural: radii) (p. 488) A segment from the center of a circle to any point on the circle and the length of such a segment. *See also* circle.

range (p. 184) The difference between the greatest and the least values of a set of numerical data.

rate (p. 390) A ratio that compares two quantities measured in different units. Rates describe how one measure depends on another measure.

ratio (p. 382) A type of comparison of two numbers or measures. Ratios can be written several ways. For example the ratio of 8 and 12 can be expressed as 8 to 12, 8 : 12, or $\frac{8}{12}$.

ray (p. 15) A part of a line that starts at a point and extends forever in one direction.

reciprocals (p. 357) Two numbers whose product is equal to 1.

reflection (p. 123) A change made to a figure by flipping it across a line.

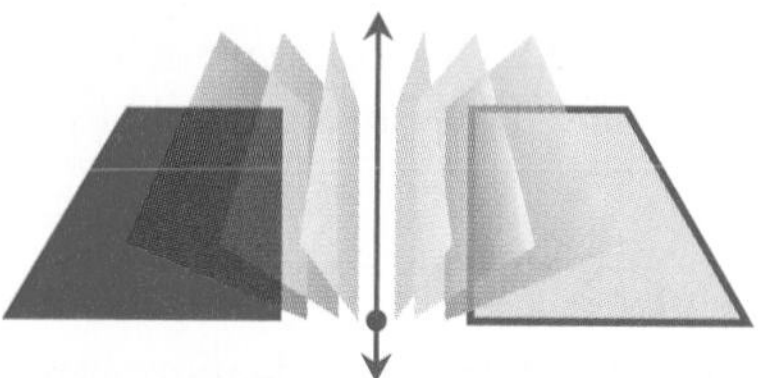

regular polygon (p. 85) A polygon that has sides that are all of equal length and angles that are all of equal measure.

rhombus (p. 83) A parallelogram with all sides the same length.

right angle (p. 18) An angle with a measure of 90°. *See also* angle.

right triangle (p. 20) A triangle that has one right angle.

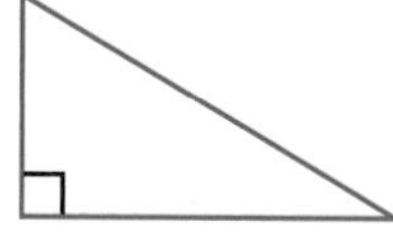

rotation (p. 122) A change made to a figure by turning it around a fixed point. The point of rotation can be any fixed point outside, inside, or on the figure.

round (p. 43) To approximate a number to a given place. For example, 28 rounded to the nearest ten is 30.

rule (p. 3) An explanation of how to create or extend a pattern.

S

sample (p. 172) Part of a whole set of objects being studied.

scale (p. 428) The ratio of a measurement on a model or a drawing to the corresponding measurement on the actual object.

scalene triangle (p. 16) A triangle with no sides of equal length.

scatter plot (p. 403) A graph that shows the relationship between two sets of data. The data is represented by points and a fitted line can be drawn through the points.

scientific notation (p. 542) A form of writing a number using a number between 0 and 10 and a power of 10.

segment (p. 15) Two points on a line and all points between them.

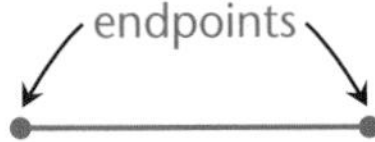

sequence (p. 4) An ordered list of numbers or objects.

set (p. 159) Any collection of objects.

similar figures (p. 424) Figures that have the same shape but not necessarily the same size.

standard form (p. 255) A number written without using exponents. *See also* exponential form.

stem-and-leaf plot (p. 219) A display of data where each number is represented by a *stem* (the leftmost digits) and a *leaf* (the rightmost digits).

straight angle (p. 19) An angle with a measure of 180°. *See also* angle.

sum (p. 597) The result when two or more numbers are added.

T

term of a sequence (p. 5) An individual number or object in a sequence.

term number (p. 5) Indicates the order or position of a term in a sequence.

theoretical probability (p. 240) The ratio of the number of outcomes in the event to the total number of possible outcomes.

trading off (p. 212) A method that involves taking away from one number and adding the same amount to another number, to have numbers that are easier to add using mental math.

transformation (p. 123) A change made to a figure or its position.

translation (p. 122) A change made to a figure by sliding every point of it the same distance in the same direction.

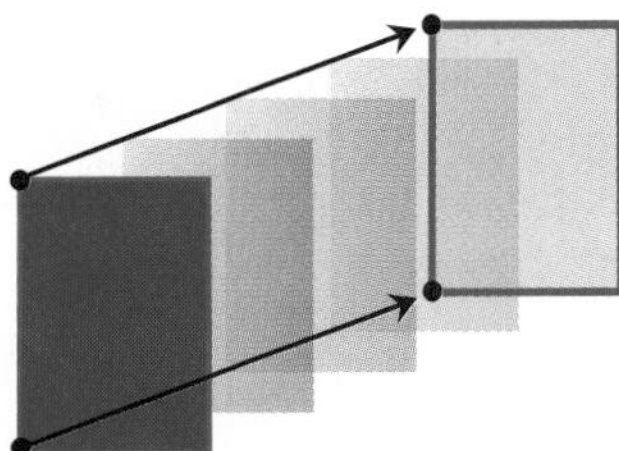

trapezoid (p. 83) A quadrilateral with exactly one pair of parallel sides.

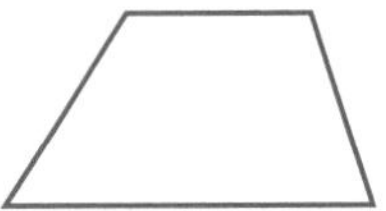

tree diagram (p. 442) A diagram that organizes the possible outcomes for an experiment.

triangle (pp. 16, 81) A polygon with three sides.

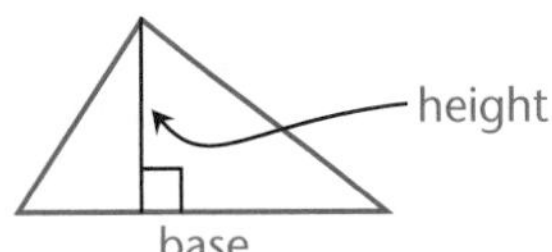

U

unit rate (p. 392) A form of a rate that gives an amount per one unit.

V

variable (p. 285) A letter or symbol that represents a quantity that is unknown or that can change.

Venn diagram (p. 160) A diagram that uses geometric shapes to show how sets are related.

vertex of an angle (p. 18) The endpoint of the rays of an angle. *See also* angle.

vertex of a polygon (p. 459) A point at which two sides meet. *See also* polygon.

vertex (plural: vertices) of a prism (p. 469) A point where three or more edges meet. *See also* prism.

volume (p. 468) The amount of space an object contains.

INDEX

A

G

M

N

Q

R

CREDITS

ACKNOWLEDGMENTS

24 Graphic and text from *Puzzles and Brain Twisters* by Fred Walls. Copyright © 1970 by Franklin Watts, Inc. By permission of Grolier Publishing Company. **94 and 195** Excerpts and illustration from *The Phantom Tollbooth* by Norton Juster and illustration by Jules Feiffer. Text copyright © 1961 and renewed 1989 by Norton Juster. Illustration copyright © 1961 by Jules Feiffer. Reprinted by permission of Random House, Inc. **310** Excerpt and illustration from *Sadako and the Thousand Paper Cranes,* text copyright © 1977 by Eleanor Coerr, illustrations copyright © 1977 by Ronald Himler. Reprinted by permission of G. P. Putnam's Sons. **360** Excerpt and illustration from *Justin and the Best Biscuits in the World* by Mildred Pitts Walter, illustrated by Catherine Stock. Text copyright © 1986 by Mildred Pitts Walter, illustration copyright © 1986 by Catherine Stock. By permission of Lothrop, Lee & Shepard Books, a division of William Morrow & Company, Inc. **380** "One Inch Tall" poem and art from *Where the Sidewalk Ends* by Shel Silverstein. Copyright © 1974 by Evil Eye Music, Inc. By permission of HarperCollins Publishers. **389** Excerpt from "The Great Flood of 1993" by Barbara Brownell, from *National Geographic World* magazine, Oct. 1993 issue National Geographic Society. Reprinted with permission.

COVER PHOTOGRAPHY

Front (Clockwise from top left) Bob Daemmrich/Stock Boston; Melanie Carr, Courtesy of Southern Stock Uniphoto International; Lynda Richardson; Louis Psihoyos/Matrix; Joshua Singer; Robert Frerck/Odyssey Productions; Kristin Finnegan/Tony Stone Images; Didier Givois. **Back** Photo of STEM pilot students: Randall Hyman.

STOCK PHOTOGRAPHY

iii RMIP/Richard Haynes; **iv** Didier Givois; **v** Joshua Singer; **vi** Lynda Richardson; **vii** © Melanie Carr, Courtesy of Southern Stock Uniphoto International; **viii** Bob Daemmrich/Stock Boston; **ix** Louis Psihoyos/Matrix; **x** Robert Frerck/Odyssey Productions; **xi** Kristin Finnegan/Tony Stone Images; **xii-xiii** Louis Psihoyos/Matrix; **xiii** RMIP/Richard Haynes (br); **xiv** Breck P. Kent/Animals Animals (t); School Division, Houghton Mifflin Company; **xvi** Doris DeWitt/Tony Stone Images (tl); ©Buena Vista Pictures Distribution (bl); Owen Seumpewa/Native Shadows (tr); **xx** Jeffrey N. Becom/Photo 20-20 (t); Rhoda Sidney/Photo Edit (c); Robert Tinney/The Stock Market (b); **1** Didier Givois; **3** Richard Howard Photography; **4** Frame (br); R. Phillips/The Granger Collection (inset); Michael Freeman/Bruce Coleman, Inc. (bl); **10** Cabisco/Visuals Unlimited (center all); Richard T. Nowitz/Photo Researchers (bl); **15** Walter Bibikow/FPG International; **18** Phyllis Picardi/Stock South (l); Jan Halaska/Tony Stone Images, Inc. (r); **36** Joachim Messerschmidt/Bruce Coleman, Inc.; **37** Joachim Messerschmidt/Bruce Coleman, Inc.; **39** Courtesy of Bryan Ellis; **52** Jeff Greenberg/Photo Edit; **53** Paul J. Sutton/Duomo; **58** SuperStock; **60** Will Steger/Adventure Photo & Film; **64** Rick Rappaport/Westlight (l); Focus on Sports (r); **68–69** Joshua Singer; **71** International Stock Photo (t); Paul Thompson (c); Neville Fox Davies/Bruce Coleman, Inc. (b); **80** Alex MacLean/Landslides; **82** Tom Bean/Tony Stone Images; **88** John Pontier/Animals Animals; **89** Tracey Wheeler; **90** Carlos Merida "The Mestizo Race of Guatemala"/Sherlyn Bjorkgren; **91** Tracey Wheeler; **95** Bill Ross/Westlight; **98** Tracey Wheeler; **100** Gene Stein/Westlight; **102** William Waterfall/The Stock Market (l); Jay Syverson/Stock Boston (r); **104** Alex MacLean/Landslides; **105** Courtesy of Mark Beckwith; **107** Courtesy of E.P. Dutton; **111** Tracey Wheeler; **115** Albano Guatti/The Stock Market; **117** National Portrait Gallery, Smithsonian Institution/Art Resource, NY; **118** Tracey Wheeler; **120** Bill Stanton/International Stock (r); **128** David Madison (l); Chris Cole/Duomo (r); Grant Heilman (b); **130** Joe Carini/Pacific Stock (t); Mealii Kalama/Peter French (b); **131** Tracey Wheeler; **133** Tracey Wheeler; **137** George W. Yarrall, Spectrum Quilt, 1933–1935, Kentucky Museum, Western Kentucky University; **139** Yellowish Asante cloth quilt, Asante textile/National Museum of African Art (t); Whitish Asante cloth quilt, Asante textile/ National Museum of African Art; **142** Ron Kimball Studios (t,c); Michael Newman/Photo Edit (b); **156–57** Lynda Richardson; **158** A. & M. Shah/Animals Animals (l); Thomas Dressler/DRK Photo (r); **164** M.P. Kahl/DRK Photo (l); Thomas Dressler/DRK Photo (r); **166** Royal Tyrrell Museum/Alberta Community Development; **175** Courtesy of Kathleen Matthews; **177** Peter Menzel/Stock Boston; **186** Clive Bromhall/Animals Animals; **191** Mitchell Layton/Duomo; **197** Jack Wilburn/Animals Animals; **198** Mitsuaki Iwago/Minden Pictures; **200** E. R. Degginger/Animals Animals; **203** Ventura County Star; **204** Simon Bruty/Allsport; **210** North Wind Picture Archives; **211** Niller/Gamma; **212** Sovfoto; **214** Photo Researchers, Inc.; **225** AW&ST/Gamma-Liaison; **227** Courtesy of Lizette Cruz-Watko; **232–233** Melanie Carr, Courtesy of

Southern Stock Uniphoto International; **234** David Madison (l); American Numismatic Association (r); **258** Kenneth W. Fink/Photo Researchers; **263** Jose Carillo/Photo Edit (br); **269** Joseph Pobereskin/Tony Stone Images (l); Richard T. Nowitz (r); **285** Tom Van Sant/Geosphere Project/Santa Monica Science Photo Library/Photo Researchers; **289** Bryan Mullennix/Tony Stone Images; **291** Jeremy Spiegel; **301** Sue Pashko/Envision; **303** Courtesy Emiko Tokunaga; **308–09** Bob Daemmrich/Stock Boston; **321** D.E. Cox/Tony Stone Images; **324** Trip/Viesti Associates, Inc.; **326** Kathleen Campbell/Tony Stone Images, Inc.; **329** Alan Oddie/Photo Edit; **332** Laura Somersol/Impact Images (l); Mickey Pfleger/Photo 20-20 (r); **341** Lawrence Migdale; **344** John Running/Stock Boston (r); **348** Gayna Hoffman (l); **350** Bongarts/Mark Sandte; **353** Chester Chronicle; **357** Richard Howard; **360** Bert Andrews/Courtesy of Mildred Pitts (l); Courtesy of Catherine Stock; **362** Courtesy of Bobby Flay; **372** Anthony Mercieca/Natural Selection (l); Rod Planck/Photo Researchers, Inc. (r); **378–79** Louis Psihoyos/Matrix; **385** PhotoDisc, Inc. (t, all); Corbis-Bettman (b); **386** Marcee Watkins Hopper/Southeastern Kentucky Physical Therapy; **389** Richard H. Bliesner/National Geographic World; **394** Gayna Hoffman; **407** Tsugumi Joiner; **409** O. Louis Mazzatenta/National Geographic Image Collection; **412** Jeffrey N. Becom/Photo 20-20 (t); Rhoda Sidney/Photo Edit (c); Robert Tinney/The Stock Market (b); **413** Breck P. Kent/Animals Animals; **417** Mike Powell/Duomo; **420** Doris DeWitt/Tony Stone Images (t); © Buena Vista Pictures Distribution (l); **421** Owen Seumpewa/Native Shadows; **423** "Study for Square Limit" by M.C. Escher © 1997 Cordon Art - Baarn - Holland. All rights reserved.; **424** "Study for Square Limit" by M.C. Escher © 1997 Cordon Art - Baarn - Holland. All rights reserved.; **427** Korczak Ziolkowski/Rob DeWall, Crazy Horse Memorial; **429** The Purcell Team; **434** Roberto McGrath/© Lucasfilm Ltd. All rights reserved.; **435** Motts Miniature Museum; **436** Courtesy of Marcia McNutt; **438** Rusty Jarret/Allsport (t); Brad Mangin/Duomo (b); **439** Norm Schindler/UCLA; **440** Glen Johnson/Texas A&M; **445** National Baseball Hall of Fame; **452–453** Robert Frerck/Odyssey Productions; **454** Telegraph Colour Library/FPG International, Inc.; **457** Ine Harrington III/The Stock Market; **459** Jon Brenneis/Photo 20-20; **467** Rafael Macia/Photo Researchers, Inc.; **477** Tracey Wheeler; **479** Michael J. Howell; **480** Timothy O'Keefe/Bruce Coleman, Inc.; **485** Courtesy of Dr. Mease; **487** Museo della Civilta Romana/Art Resource; **494** Cindy Charles/Photo Edit; **495** Renault/Photo Researchers (c); National Audobon Society/Photo Researchers (t); American Numismatic Society (b); **499** Alan Kearney/Viesti Associates Inc.; **502** Kenneth Murray/Photo Researchers; **505** NOAA/Science Library/Photo Researchers (b); **509** Giraudon/Art Resource; **521** Tracey Wheeler; **524** Kristin Finnegan/Tony Stone Images; **526** Ralph H. Wetmore II/Tony Stone Images; **536** William R. Sallaz/Duomo; **539** Peter D'Angelo/Comstock (r); Brown Brothers (l); **540** M. Amsterman/Animals Animals; **544** Earthforce; **545** Robert Brenner/Photo Edit; **549** Paul Chesley/Tony Stone Images; **551** Michael A. Dwyer/Stock Boston; **561** Diane Hirsch/Fundamental Photo; **562** Courtesy of Lynda Jordan; **563** United Features Syndicate; **565** Michael Collier/Stock Boston; **567** NASA; **570** Wendy Stone/Gamma Liaison (t); Bachmann/Stock Boston (r); **574** John Coletti/Stock Boston (r); Nik Kleinberg/Stock Boston (t); Tim Crosby/Liaison International (c); William Gray/Westlight (b); **575** Mark Richards/Photo Edit; **577**, **578** Courtesy Ford Motor Company; **583** © 1979 Time, Inc.

ASSIGNMENT PHOTOGRAPHY

RMIP/Richard Haynes 14, 30, 32, 42, 74 (c), 108, 148, 159, 160, 171, 180, 184, 185, 196, 197 (c, br), 229 (t), 235, 245, 273, 277, 282, 287, 298, 303, 311, 313, 323, 328, 330, 334, 344 (l), 359 (r), 364 (l), 375, 382, 387, 390, 398, 401, 402, 429, 441, 449, 458, 471, 477, 489, 515, 552, 556, 566, 571, 582, 585.

ALL OTHER PHOTOGRAPHY

School Division, Houghton Mifflin Company 6, 7, 13, 16, 17, 29, 36, 37, 48, 62, 66, 72, 73, 74, 85, 86, 96, 111, 116, 117 (t), 120 (l), 121, 124, 125, 129, 133, 134, 148, 178, 180, 192, 199, 201, 203, 229, 237, 239, 247, 263 (bl), 310, 318, 322, 333, 335, 342, 344 (c), 346, 356, 359 (l), 364 (r), 383, 447, 468, 469, 474, 484, 505 (c), 527, 529, 534, 548, 557, 563.

ILLUSTRATIONS

2 Sara Mintz Zwicker; **9** Sara Mintz Zwicker; **89** Scott Kim; **94** David Shepherd; **195** Jules Feiffer; **264, 321** David Ballard; **310** Ronald Himler; **360** Catherine Stock; **380** Shel Silverstein; **397, 406** Hannah Bonner; **410, 456, 499, 509** Chris Costello; **433** John Sanderson; **505** Matthew Pippin.

ALL OTHER ILLUSTRATIONS

School Division, Houghton Mifflin Company, or McDougal Littell Design Group.

SELECTED ANSWERS

MODULE 1

Section 1, Practice and Application

1. a. Samples: bear, deer, bear; yes, the first and third sets. **b.** Check students' drawings. **3.** 63, 54, 45, 36; Subtract the term number from 12 and multiply by 9, or start with 99 and subtract 9 from each number to get the next number. **5.**  Draw an X. It determines four open spaces. Start with a dot in the space at the left. Move the dot in each figure one space clockwise to get the next figure.

7. a. Classes begin at 7:40 A.M. and every 50 minutes after that.

b.

Term no.	Term
1	7:40 A.M.
2	8:30 A.M
3	9:20 A.M.
4	10:10 A.M.
5	11:00 A.M.
6	11:50 A.M.
7	12:40 P.M.

9. a.

Term no.	1	2	3	4
Term	1	2	4	8

b. Each term is twice the previous term. **c.** 16 cells

11. a.

Term no.	Term
1	99
2	98
3	97
4	96
5	95
6	94
7	93
8	92

11. b. Each term is 100 minus the term number. **c.** 70

13. Sample:

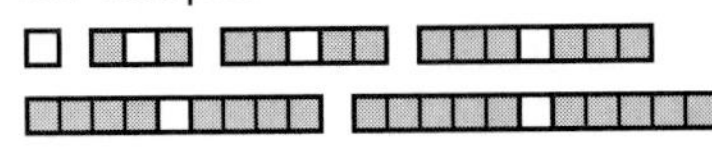

Spiral Review

16. three thousand, six hundred seventy-two
17. six hundred seventy-one thousand, five hundred ninety-eight **18.** twenty-three thousand, eight hundred fifty-six **19.** 1216 **20.** 135 **21.** 8129 **22.** 4875
23. 23,328 **24.** 502 **25-27.** Samples responses are given.

25.  **26.**  **27.** 

Extra Skill Practice

1. 125, 150, 175, 200, 225; multiply the term number by 25, or start with 25 and add 25 to each term to get the next term. **3.** 96, 84, 72, 60, 48; subtract the term number from 13 and multiply by 12, or start with 144 and subtract 12 from each term to get the next term.
5. 81, 243, 729, 2187; multiply each term by 3 to get the next term.

7.

Term no.	10	11	12	13	14	15	16	17
Term	100	110	120	130	140	150	160	170

Multiply the term number by 10, or start with 100 and add 10 to each term to get the next term; 400.

Study Skills, Getting to Know Your Textbook

2. See page 588. **3.** page 591

Section 2, Practice and Application

1. Sample: The character consists of a circle and three segments, two short and one longer. The longer segment is placed horizontally on the bottom of the figure with the two shorter segments placed vertically beside each other on top of the longer segment. The circle is then placed directly above the two short segments. **3.** $\overline{XY}$, $\overline{XZ}$, and $\overline{YZ}$; they include different points and have different endpoints. **5.** segment
7–9. Samples are given.

7.

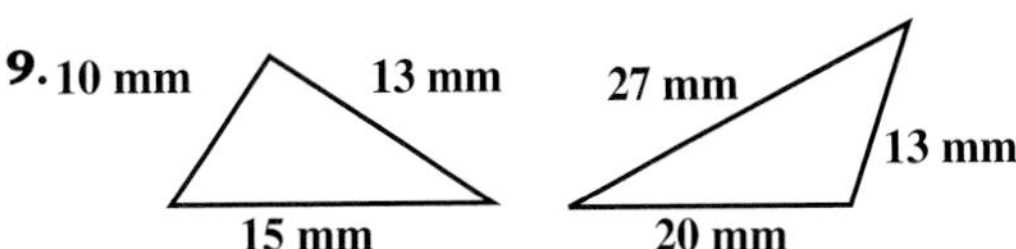

9.

11. cannot **13.** cannot **15.** From left to right the examples are: pink isosceles, blue equilateral, black scalene, purple equilateral, yellow scalene, green isosceles
17. right **19.** acute **21.** acute, isosceles **23.** acute, scalene **25.** acute, equilateral **29.** $\overline{AB}$ is part of the ray; the name must be $\overrightarrow{AB}$ or $\overrightarrow{AC}$. **31.a.** Sample: No; I would add "and the triangles are obtuse, scalene triangles."
b. Sample: 2; The caller used the appropriate term triangles but did not describe the triangles in any mathematical way.

Spiral Review
33. 24 **34.** The money symbol is used incorrectly. ".99¢" means 99 hundredths of a cent. **35.** < **36.** > **37.** 3000 **38.**180

Extra Skill Practice
1. D **3.** B **5.** can **7.** cannot **9.** True. **11.** True. **13.** straight **15.** obtuse

Standardized Testing, Free Response
Samples are given: **a:** 1, 3, 4 or 2, 5, 6 **b:** 1, 2 or 4, 5 or 1, 2, 3, 4, 5, 6 **c:** 1, 2 or 4, 5 or 1, 2, 3, 4, 5, 6 **d**: 1, 4 or 2, 5 **e:** 1, 3, 4 or 2, 5, 6 **f:** 1, 4 or 2, 5

Section 3, Practice and Application
1., 3. Sample responses are given. **1. a.** Which of two monthly service contracts for 8 to 10 hours a month on line is a better buy? **b.** the monthly fee, number of included hours, hourly rate for hours beyond the number included, and discount information **c.** whether there are limits on the total number of hours, or available times, and whether either has cheaper telephone access **3. a.** How many times does a given event occur? **b.** the time periods over which the tour runs, and the frequency and length of the trips **c.** whether there is more than one double-hulled canoe (If not, the times given could not be exact. There would need to be time to load and unload.) **7.** If you are on line 8 h, the standard contract is cheaper. For 9 h, the costs are the same. For 10 h, the frequent user contract is cheaper. **9.** Sample: Try a simpler problem, make a table, and look for a pattern; draw chains of triangles with 1, 2, 3, and 4 triangles and find the perimeter. Enter the values in a table. Make a prediction based on the table.
11. 25 times **13.** no later than 6:45 A.M.
16. right-isosceles **17.** obtuse-scalene
18. acute-equilateral **19.** 5600 **20.** $40 **21.** $7
22. 35,000 **23.** 900 **24.** 45,000 **25.** 10,000
26. 100,000 **27.** 6000 **28.** 560 **29.** 21,000
30. 72,600 **31.** 32,000 **32.** 1,000,000 **33.** 63,000,000

Career Connection
35. make a plan

Extra Skill Practice
1. too much; the cost of markers and pens **3.** too little; Jose's age, ticket price **5.** 4 mi; Make a picture or diagram. **7.** $83.50; Work backward.

Section 4, Practice and Application
1. a. about $5 **b.** Yes; I rounded two items up by a total of $.20 and one item down by $.09, so my estimate is $.11 too high. The actual sum is $4.89. I don't have enough money. **3.** about 200; hard to tell **5.** about 1800; greater than **7.** about 60,000; hard to tell **9. a.** Sample: about 210; I looked at the beads in the upper right-hand corner of the second abacus and compared them to those in the first. There were 2 more in the first row and 1 more in the second, so the number added is about 210. **b.** 751 **c.** 209; 542 + 209 = 751
11. 40 **13.** 120 **15.** 600 **17–19.** Ex. 17 and 19 do not involve compatible numbers. **17.** 4941 **19.** 364
21. No; $4 \div 2 = 2$, but $2 \div 4 = \frac{2}{4}$ and $5 - 3 = 2$, but $3 - 5 \neq 2$. **23.** $15 \cdot 2 \cdot 40 = 1200$ **25.** $325 + 75 = 400$ **27. a.** 355 **29.** 36 **31.** 10 **33.** 7 **35.** 3 **37. a.** the number of non-leap years in the 70 years **b.** 3600 s **c.** about 90,000 s **d.** about 36,000,000 s **e.** Yes; to estimate the number of seconds in either type of year, you would probably round the number of days to 400.
39. $(11 + 5) \div 4$ **41.** $50 - 4 \cdot 6$

Spiral Review
43. 6 different ways; 1 quarter and 1 dime, 1 quarter and 2 nickels, 3 dimes and 1 nickel, 2 dimes and 3 nickels, 1 dime and 5 nickels, 7 nickels **44.** 25, 29 **45.** 20, 27 **46.** Sample: 3 cm and 4 cm

Extension
47. Samples are given. $5 - 2 \times 2 = 1$; $2 \times 2 - 2 = 2$; $5 - 2 = 3$; $2 \times 2 = 4$; $5 \times 2 - 5 = 5$; $2 \times 2 \times 2 - 2 = 6$; $2 \times 2 \times 2 \times 2 - 2 \times 2 - 5 = 7$; $5 \times 2 - 2 = 8$; $5 \times 5 - 2 \times 2 \times 2 \times 2 = 9$; $5 \times 2 = 10$

Extra Skill Practice
1. about 300; greater than **3.** about 100; less than **5.** about 1800; hard to tell **7.** about 280; hard to tell **9.** about 2600; greater than **11.** about 4500; greater than **13.** 40 **15.** 90 **17.** 1200 **19.** 1800 **21.** 26 **23.** 13 **25.** 15 **27.** 5 **29.** 37 **31.** 14

Standardized Testing, Multiple Choice
1. A **2.** C

Section 5, Practice and Application
1. Samples: The team members had to be able to communicate well to share their skills. Also, they had to be able to share responsibility to use each person's training and ability to the best advantage. **3. a.** not appropriate; The figure is not divided into two right triangles.
b. appropriate; The figure is a square and it is divided into two right triangles. **c.** not appropriate; The figure is not a square.
5. 4 mi 

Spiral Review
10. 43 **11.** 45 **12.** 36 **13.** No. **14.** Yes.
15.

Term no.	1	2	3	4	5	6
Term	4	8	12	16	20	24

General rule: (1) The term is 4 times the term number. (2) Start with 4 and add 4 to each term to get the next term.

Extra Skill Practice

1–5. Samples are given. **1.** 2 blocks north, 6 blocks west

1.

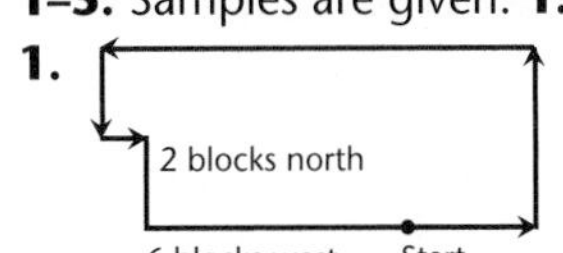

3. Sue is the President.

	Pres	VP	Sec	Treas
John	No	Yes	No	No
Sue	Yes	No	No	No
Lisa	No	No	No	Yes
Fernando	No	No	Yes	No

5. The small cubes that have two painted faces are on the edges of the cube but not at the corners. There are 12 such cubes.

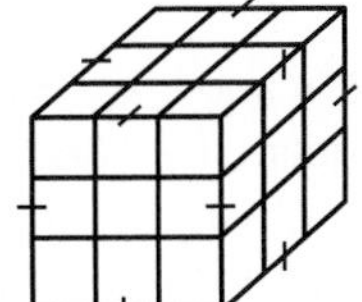

Standardized Testing, Multiple Choice

C

Section 6, Practice and Application

1. 8 days **3. a.** C = 2, E = 5, D = 7, G = 1, K = 3 **b.** Substitute the numbers for the letters and verify that the multiplication is correct. **5. a.** 52 ft; 76 ft **b–c.** Sample responses are given. **b.** Multiply the number of panels by 24 and add 4. **c.** 5; I extended the ideas in the solution to the general case.

Spiral Review

8. 16 posts

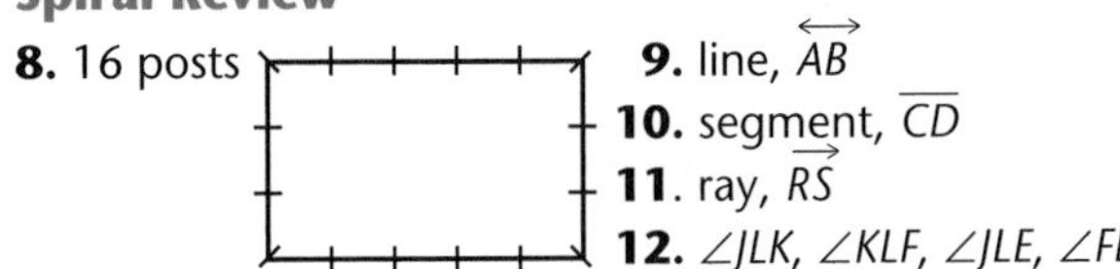

9. line, $\overleftrightarrow{AB}$ **10.** segment, $\overline{CD}$ **11.** ray, $\overrightarrow{RS}$ **12.** $\angle JLK$, $\angle KLF$, $\angle JLE$, $\angle FLE$

Extra Skill Practice

1. 7 large tables, 6 large tables and 2 small tables, 5 large tables and 4 small tables, 4 large tables and 6 small tables, 3 large tables and 8 small tables, 2 large tables and 10 small tables, 1 large table and 12 small tables, 14 small tables **3.** 56°F **5.** 78

Standardized Testing, Free Response

Yes; Each person can carry 31 lb. There are a number of ways to divide the weight.

Review and Assessment

1. 176, 173, 170; Start with 188 and subtract 3 from each term to get the next term, or subtract 3 times the term number from 191 to get each term. **2.** 75, 90, 105; Start with 15 and add 15 to each term to get the next term, or multiply the term number by 15 to get each term. **3. a.**

Term no.	1	2	3	4	5
Term	2	3	4	5	6

b. Add 1 to the term number. **4.** Yes; the sum of the lengths of the two shorter sticks is greater than the length of the longest stick.

5. Sample: (4 in., 4 in.) **6.** not possible **7–11.** All possible answers are given. **7.** $\angle ACB$, $\angle DCE$ **8.** $\overline{AC}$, $\overline{BC}$, $\overline{DC}$, $\overline{CE}$, $\overline{BE}$ **9.** $\overrightarrow{CA}$, $\overrightarrow{CB}$, $\overrightarrow{CE}$, $\overrightarrow{CD}$, $\overrightarrow{BC}$, $\overrightarrow{EC}$ **10.** $\angle ACD$ **11.** $\angle BCD$, $\angle ACE$ **12.** $\overleftrightarrow{BE}$ **13.** A, B, C, D, E

14.

President	Vice President	Secretary
Gail	Lita	Ben
Gail	Ben	Lita
Lita	Gail	Ben
Lita	Ben	Gail
Ben	Gail	Lita
Ben	Lita	Gail

15. about 40 • 70 = 2800 **16.** about 250 – 190 = 60 **17.** about 3100 + 900 = 4000 **18.** about 260 + 30 + 90 = 380 **19.** about 200 • 10 = 2000 **20.** about 3500 – 2100 = 1400 **21.** greater than; He rounded $47.98 up and $22.31 down; both increased the difference. **22.** Use compatible numbers 67 and 143 and 19 and 31: 210 + 50 = 260. **23.** Use compatible numbers 7 and 5 and 4 and 25: 35 • 100 = 3500. **24.** Use compatible numbers 5 and 2: 10 • 46 = 460. **25.** Use compatible numbers 34 and 66: 100 + 158 = 258. **26.** 45 **27.** 47 **28.** 6 **29.** 21 **30.** 19

31. He can walk 3 blocks west, then 2 blocks north, or 2 blocks north, then 3 blocks west.

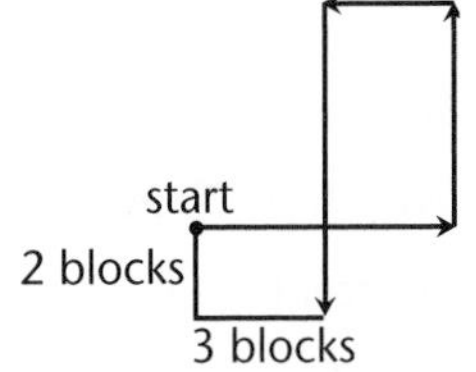

32. a. 36 squares **b.** Sample: Make a table and notice that the sequence of perimeters increases by 4 while the sequence of numbers of squares is the sequence of triangular numbers. So for any perimeter, divide the perimeter by 4 and find the resulting triangular number. For example, for a perimeter of 24, divide 24 by 4 and find the 6th triangular number, 21.

MODULE 2

Section 1, Practice and Application

1. Yes. **3.** Yes. **5.** regular pentagon **7.** A polygon; five of the six shapes are polygons, so the probability that the shape pulled out is a polygon is $\frac{5}{6}$. The probability that it is a pentagon is $\frac{2}{6}$ and that it is a quadrilateral is $\frac{2}{6}$. **9.** Only the polygon in Ex. 5 is a regular polygon. The rhombus in Ex. 4 does not have angles of equal measure. The rectangle in Ex. 6 does not have sides of equal length. **11.** trapezoid **13.** regular hexagon

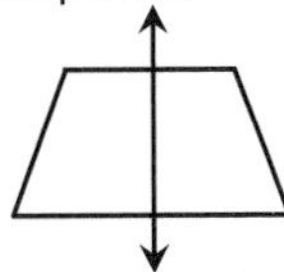

15. one line of symmetry

Spiral Review

19. 86,050 **20.** 4007 **21.** 537 **22.** 1021 **23.** acute **24.** right **25.** acute **26.** obtuse **27.** 3 **28.** 1, 2

Extra Skill Practice

1. Yes. **3.** Yes. **5.** regular polygon **7.** not a regular polygon; angles are not all of equal measure

9. rectangle

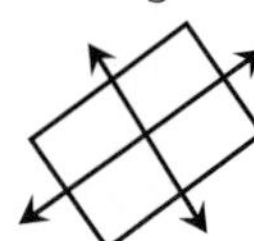

11. regular pentagon

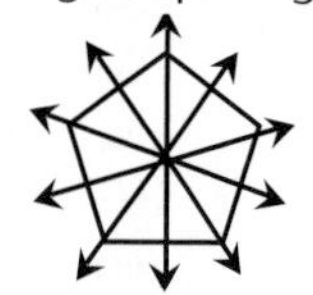

13. one line of symmetry **15.** no lines of symmetry

Study Skills, Taking Notes

1. the classifications of quadrilaterals according to the number of parallel sides, the number of sides of equal length, and the number of right angles

2. Sample:

Angle Name	Measure
acute	greater than 0°, less than 90°
right	90°
obtuse	greater than 90°, less than 180°
straight	180°

Section 2, Practice and Application

1. $\frac{1}{2}$ **3.** $\frac{4}{12}$ **5. a.** $\frac{3}{8}$ **b.** $\frac{5}{8}$ **c.** 1; the two fractions together represent the whole. **7.** $\frac{4}{3}$, $1\frac{1}{3}$ **9.** $\frac{5}{2}$, $2\frac{1}{2}$ **11.** $\frac{3}{4}$, $\frac{5}{9}$, $\frac{7}{16}$, $\frac{9}{25}$, $\frac{11}{36}$ **13.** The figures are congruent because they have the same size and shape. **15.** The figures are congruent because they have the same size and shape.

17. a. four times **b.** $\frac{2}{4}$ mi; $1\frac{2}{4}$ mi **c.** $\frac{1}{8}$

Spiral Review

20. regular pentagon **21.** parallelogram **22.** quadrilateral **23.** Add 3 and 2, then multiply the sum by 4. **24.** Divide 10 by 2, then add the quotient to 7. **25.** Multiply 3 and 2, then subtract the product from 8. **26.** 340 **27.** 15,900 **28.** 43,890,000 **29.** red, green, blue, yellow

Career Connection

31. Sample:

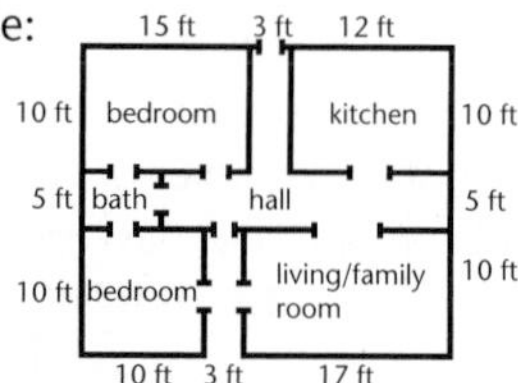

Extension

33. a.

b.

Extra Skill Practice

1. False; the two parts of the triangle do not have the same size and shape. **3.** True **5.** $\frac{5}{2}$, $2\frac{1}{2}$ **7.** The shapes are not congruent; one is longer than the other. **9.** The shapes are congruent; they have the same size and shape.

Standardized Testing, Free Response

1. A.

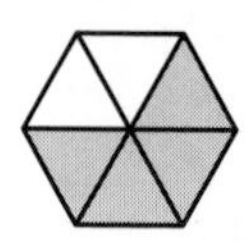

B.

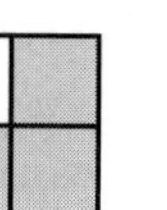

C.

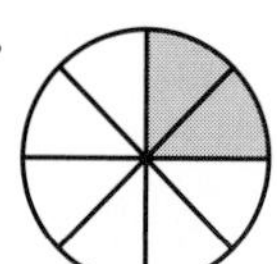

2. A and B are true. Since the triangle fits on top the square, the "bottom" of the triangle has the same length as the "top" of the square. The triangle is equilateral, so all sides of the shape have the same length. The figure has five sides, so it is a pentagon. C and D are not true. The area of the triangle appears to be about half that of the square. The angles of the figure are not all of the same measure.

Section 3, Practice and Application

1. a. $\frac{1}{2}$ **b.** $\frac{3}{6}$ **3–7.** Sample responses are given. **3.** $\frac{2}{5}$, $\frac{4}{10}$ **5.** $\frac{2}{3}$, $\frac{4}{6}$ **7.** $\frac{1}{3}$, $\frac{2}{6}$ **9.** Samples: $\frac{4}{16}$, $\frac{2}{8}$, $\frac{1}{4}$ **11.** 21 **13.** 2 **15.** 9 **17.** $\frac{10}{15}$, $\frac{12}{18}$, $\frac{14}{21}$ **19.** $\frac{3}{20}$ **21.** $\frac{4}{9}$ **23.** $\frac{2}{3}$ **25.** $\frac{1}{12}$

Spiral Review

29. Sample responses are given. **a.** triangles, quadrilaterals, pentagons, hexagons, heptagons, octagons, nonagons, and decagons, as well as polygons with 16 and 32 sides **b.** $\frac{1}{2}$, $\frac{1}{4}$, $\frac{1}{8}$, $\frac{1}{16}$, $\frac{1}{32}$ **30.** No; the circle is not divided into four congruent parts. **31.** 135 **32.** 8497 **33.** 1293 **34–35.** Sample sketches are given.

34.

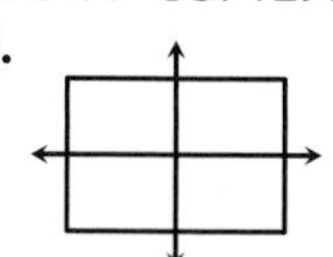

35.

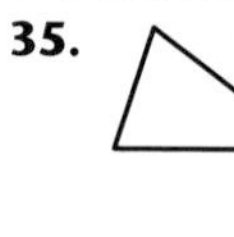

Extra Skill Practice

1. $\frac{2}{10}$, $\frac{1}{5}$ **3.** $\frac{4}{8}$, $\frac{1}{2}$ **5–19.** Sample responses are given. **5.** $\frac{4}{10}$, $\frac{6}{15}$, $\frac{8}{20}$ **7.** $\frac{1}{4}$, $\frac{2}{8}$, $\frac{3}{12}$ **9.** $\frac{1}{3}$, $\frac{2}{6}$, $\frac{3}{9}$ **11.** $\frac{4}{14}$, $\frac{6}{21}$, $\frac{8}{28}$ **13.** $\frac{2}{10}$, $\frac{3}{15}$, $\frac{4}{20}$ **15.** $\frac{2}{5}$, $\frac{12}{30}$, $\frac{18}{45}$ **17.** $\frac{6}{14}$, $\frac{9}{21}$, $\frac{12}{28}$ **19.** $\frac{4}{5}$, $\frac{16}{20}$, $\frac{24}{30}$ **21.** 36 **23.** 24 **25.** 12 **27.** 1 **29.** 11 **31.** 4 **33.** $\frac{1}{6}$ **35.** $\frac{1}{5}$ **37.** $\frac{7}{16}$ **39.** $\frac{4}{15}$ **41.** $\frac{3}{8}$

Standardized Testing, Multiple Choice

1. B **2.** B

Section 4, Practice and Application

1. translation **3.** translation **5.** translation **7.** reflection **9. a.** reflection; rotation or reflection; rotation **b.** Quarter A can be moved to Quarter B in the middle Hex symbol by rotation or reflection.

11. **13.** **17.**

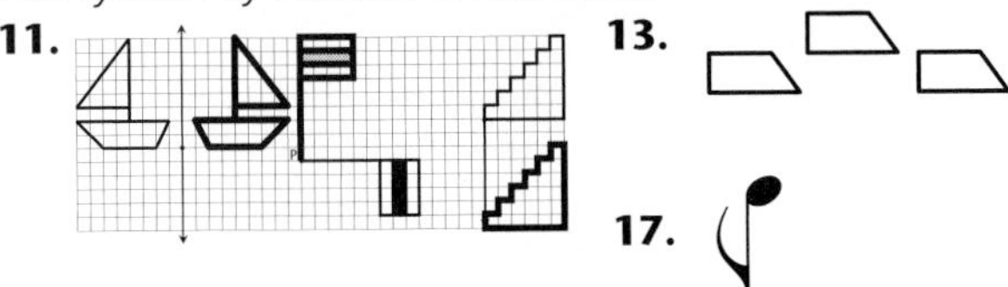

Spiral Review

21. $\frac{1}{3}$ **22.** $\frac{4}{5}$ **23.** $\frac{3}{5}$ **24.** $\frac{1}{3}$ **26.** < **27.** > **28.** < **29.** = **30.** > **31.** >

Extra Skill Practice

1. reflection **3.** translation **5.** translation **7.** rotation **9.** translation **11.** C **13.** A

Standardized Testing, Open-ended

1. A; B: The crops in the two upper sections are rotated one section clockwise. The lower left crop is replanted in the same section, while the lower right crop is moved to the upper left; C: reflection across a vertical line dividing the field

Section 5, Practice and Application

1. tens **3.** tenths **5.** thousandths **7.** eight and three tenths, $8\frac{3}{10}$ **9.** one and two thousandths, $1\frac{2}{1000}$ **11.** 0.03 **13.** 0.0205 **15.** dime; penny **17.** Show that 40 pennies have the same value as four dimes. **19.** $\frac{1}{10}$ **21.** 0.03, 0.16, 0.3, 0.51 **23.** 0.008, 0.105, 0.17, 0.717 **25.** < **27.** >

Spiral Review

30. translation **31.** reflection or rotation **32.** reflection or rotation **33.** about $20 **34.** about $123 **35.** about $9 **36.** I would use the fact that if I took 1¢ from the 41¢ and gave it to the 29¢, the sum would be the same and I would be adding 40¢ and 30¢. Then the sum is $27.70. **37.** I would add 7¢ and 33¢ first, then add the sum to 66¢. The sum is $1.06. The sum of the dollar amounts is $10, so the sum of the three amounts is $11.06. **38.** I would add 75¢ and 50¢ to get $1.25, then add that to the sum of the dollar amounts. The sum of the two amounts is $15.25.

Extra Skill Practice

1. five thousandths **3.** two tenths **5.** two **7.** five tenths **9.** 0.2, $\frac{2}{10}$ **11.** 356.40, $356\frac{40}{100}$ or $\frac{35,640}{100}$ **13.** 1.25, $1\frac{25}{100}$ **15.** twenty-six thousandths **17.** ten and two hundred five thousandths **19.** one and four thousandths **21.** eleven and one hundred thousandths **23.** > **25.** > **27.** < **29.** 0.123, 1.233, 12.3, 123.1, 124 **31.** 7.0652, 7.526, 75.024, 75.24

Standardized Testing, Multiple Choice

1. D **2.** B

Section 6, Practice and Application

1. 13.841 **3.** 78.91 **5.** 20.692 **7.** $9.51 **9.** 0.74, 0.85, 0.96 **11.** 0.75 + 0.25 = 1; 2 + 3 + 1 = 6 **13.** 0.35 + 0.65 = 1; 5 + 1 = 6; 6 + 1 = 7; 7 + 2.8 = 9.8 **15.** 0.036 = 0.035 + 0.001; 0.045 + 0.035 = 0.080; 0.080 + 0.001 = 0.081 **17. a.** 7.7 **b.** one decimal place; since 7.700 = 7.7, the calculator does not display the zeros. **19.** 29.27 **21.** 2.2 **23.** 0.0046 **25.** 2 **27.** It appears that the whole numbers were subtracted and the decimal parts were added. The correct answer is 4.259.

29. The problem solved was 11.689 – 0.689. The correct answer is 116.201. **31.** 13.44; add 13.44 and 2.85 to see if the sum is 16.29. **33.** No; 1.280 – 1.099 = 0.181 > 0.025. **35.** Yes; 2.010 – 2.008 = 0.002 < 0.010. **37.** 90.5, 97.1, 104.8

Spiral Review

39. one and twelve hundredths **40.** eight hundred three thousandths **41.** three and four tenths **42.** fifty and twenty-eight hundredths **43.** 69, 87 **44.** 2800 **45.** 1490 **46.** 386,000 **47.** 28 **48.** 729 **49.** 720

Extension

51. 0.00001, 0.00009, 0.00015, 0.0008, 1.00002 **53.** 0.00009 and 0.00001

Extra Skill Practice

1. 21.46 **3.** 51.423 **5.** 245.97 **7.** 31.617 **9.** 0.075 **11.** 36.307 **13.** 0.77 **15.** 34.72 **17.** 71.685 **19.** 141.886 **21.** 8.5 **23.** 71.08 **25.** 34.196 **27.** $23.10 **29.** 6.4, 6.9, 7.5 **31.** 1.42, 1.52, 1.62

Standardized Testing, Performance Task

1. The first three terms of the sequence of payments are $.10, $.20, and $.40. Jim interprets this as a sequence in which each term is twice that of the previous term. Jim's dad intends it to be a sequence in which the increase from term to term increases by $.10 each time. The payments in dollars for each plan are shown in the table.

Time mowed	Pay (Jim's plan)	Pay (Dad's plan)
1	0.10	0.10
2	0.20	0.20
3	0.40	0.40
4	0.80	0.70
5	1.60	1.10
6	3.20	1.60
7	6.40	2.20
8	12.80	2.90
9	25.60	3.70
10	51.20	4.60

Review and Assessment

1. Samples are shown: square *DGPA*; parallelogram *FGSA*; rectangle *FGPR*

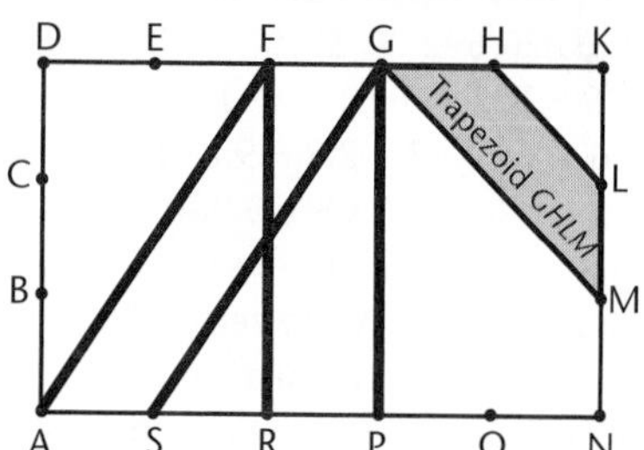

2. Sample responses are given for parallel lines.

a. regular hexagon **b.** pentagon **c.** square

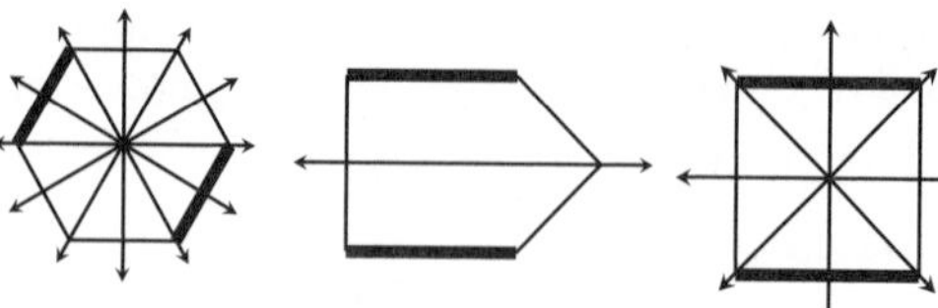

d. parallelogram **e.** trapezoid **f.** octagon

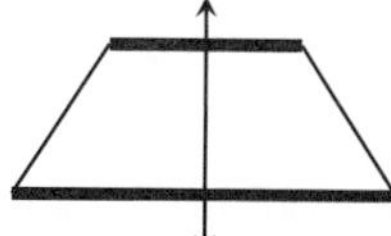
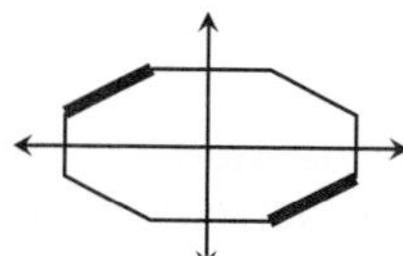

3. False; the figure is not divided into congruent parts. **4.** True. **5.** False; the circle is not divided into congruent parts. **6.**  **7.** **8.** 

9. b and c; $\frac{2+2}{4+2} = \frac{4}{6} \neq \frac{2}{4}$; $\frac{2 \cdot 2}{4 \cdot 2} = \frac{4}{8} = \frac{2}{4}$; $\frac{2 \div 2}{4 \div 2} = \frac{1}{2} = \frac{2}{4}$; $\frac{2-2}{4-2} = \frac{0}{2} \neq \frac{2}{4}$ **10. a.** $\frac{4}{20}, \frac{2}{10}, \frac{1}{5}$ **b.** 0.2 **11.** $\frac{1}{4}$ **12.** $\frac{3}{4}$ **13.** $\frac{5}{6}$ **14.** $\frac{1}{2}$ **15.** $\frac{3}{8}$ **16.** $\frac{3}{4}$ **17.** $\frac{7}{8}$ **18.** $\frac{3}{11}$

19. Sample responses are given.

A. Each petal can be produced (roughly) by rotating a petal to every other petal or by reflecting the flower across one of the dashed lines.

B. Each petal can be produced (roughly) by reflecting another petal across the dashed line.

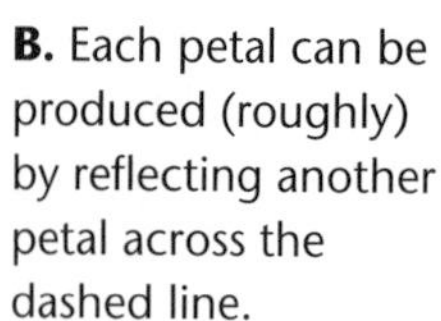

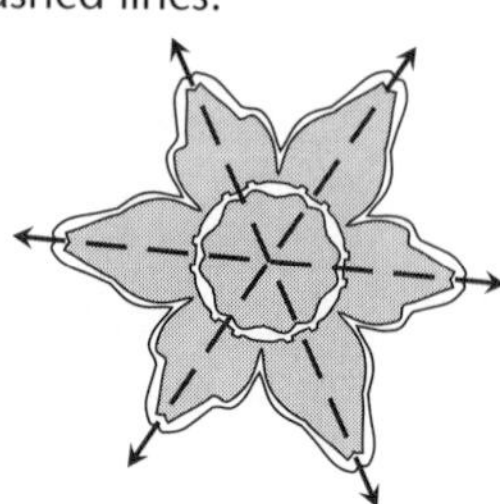

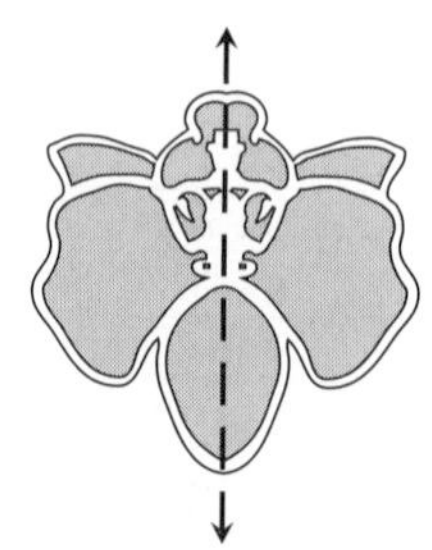

C. Each petal can be produced (roughly) by rotating any other petal.

20. six and fifty-six hundredths **21.** seven thousandths **22.** one thousand two hundred eight and three tenths **23.** thirty-five and one tenth **24.** one hundred twenty-three thousandths **25.** twenty-five thousand one and five hundredths **26.** five hundred twenty-one and sixty-three hundredths **27.** one and twenty-two thousandths **28.** six hundred and seven hundredths **29.** < **30.** < **31.** = **32.** > **33.** < **34.** = **35.** 9.077 **36.** 15.17 **37.** 6.1 **38.** 2.212 **39.** 500.92 **40.** 11 **41. a.** Max: $3.85, Rachel: $1.51, Alisha: $2.98 **b.** $8.34

MODULE 3

Section 1, Practice and Application

1. 8 kinds; 7 kinds **3.** 12 kinds **5.** 20 kinds **9.** Nearest centimeter; measuring to the smaller unit provides a more exact measurement. **11.** 7 m **13.** 1 mm **15.** gram or kilogram **17.** 15 kg **19.** 0.5 g **21.** 0.0034 **23.** 0.07 **25.** 0.0001 **27.** 650 **29.** 2.540 **31.** 720 **35.** > **37.** > **39.** <

Spiral Review

41. 2.512 **42.** 11.13 **43.** 1.997 **44.** Beth: France, rabbit; Karen: Australia, Chihuahua; Steve: Brazil, iguana **45.** 12 **46.** 75 **47.** 5

Extension

49. 42 students **51.** 5 students **53.** 3 students **55.** 4 students

Extra Skill Practice

1. 7 animals **3.** A lobster has both legs and a tail. **5.** 0.0025 **7.** 0.003 **9.** 34.8 **11.** 250 **13.** 2.930 **15.** 400

Study Tip, Preparing to Do Homework

1. The example on page 162 shows how to write a measurement involving decimals. The example on page 164 shows how to convert a measurement in millimeters into meters. **2.** set, empty set, Venn diagram, meter, centimeter, millimeter, benchmark, gram, milligram, kilogram, metric ton; sample: A set is a collection of objects.

Section 2, Practice and Application

1. 8 **3.** 8 **5.** 6 **7.** 15 **9.** 4 cards **11.** 8 mammals

13. pine: 216 grains; grass: 162 grains; oak: 135 grains; cactus: 27 grains **15.** about 4 **17.** 7 cards **19.** $\frac{30}{100}$ or $\frac{3}{10}$, 0.30 **21.** $\frac{72}{100}$ or $\frac{36}{50}$ or $\frac{18}{25}$, 0.72 **25.** $\frac{4}{10}$ or $\frac{2}{5}$, 40% **27.** $\frac{2}{100}$ or $\frac{1}{50}$, 2% **29.** $\frac{3}{10}$, 30% **31.** $\frac{1}{100}$, 1% **33.** 0.36, 36% **35.** 0.8, 80% **37.** 0.85, 85% **39.** 0.23, 23% **43.** < **45.** > **47.** > **49.** 50; 25; 12.5; 12.5

Spiral Review

53. 7 **54.** 9000 **55.** 3 **56.** 200 **57.** 0.5 **58.** 8 **59.** The term is 7 times the term number. **60.** 420

Extra Skill Practice

1. 8 **3.** 9 **5.** 49 **7.** 93 **9.** 35%, $\frac{35}{100}$ or $\frac{7}{20}$ **11.** 28%, $\frac{28}{100}$ or $\frac{7}{25}$ **13.** 60%, $\frac{6}{10}$ or $\frac{3}{5}$ **15.** 5%, $\frac{5}{100}$ or $\frac{1}{20}$ **17.** 0.07, 7% **19.** 0.32, 32% **21.** 0.9, 90% **23.** 0.05, 5% **25.** < **27.** > **29.** > **31.** =

Standardized Testing, Free Response

1. 55%; 65%; 20%

2.

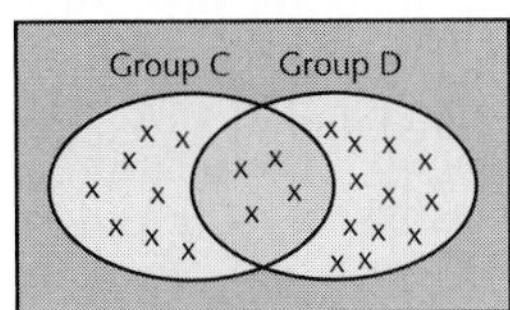

Section 3, Practice and Application

1. 145 Sample graph:

Weights of Four Members of the Cat Family

Weight (lb): 0, 40, 80, 120, 160

Cat: bobcat, ocelot, cheetah, mountain lion

3. about 25% (The bar for 1989 is about one-fourth as long as the bar for 1979.) **5.** Central African Republic, Kenya, and Mozambique appear to have had about an equal number. **7.** Sample: Between 1979 and 1989, the number of elephants in each of the selected countries dropped sharply. The countries with the largest numbers of elephants in 1979 seemed to experience the sharpest decreases. The double bars show the drastic change in the numbers of elephants for each country in each year.

9.

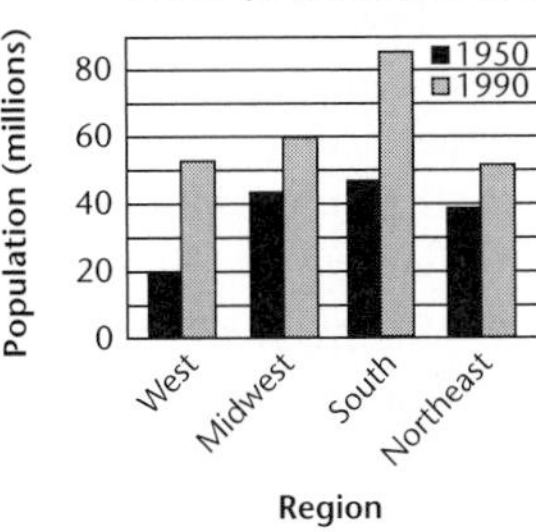

11. West

13. a. the first bar graph; the heights of the bars are relatively close. **b.** Sample: the graphs use different scales. Using the second graph makes it seem like there are about $3\frac{1}{2}$ times as many deer as antelope or bison.

15. 9 players **17. a.** 5 **b.**

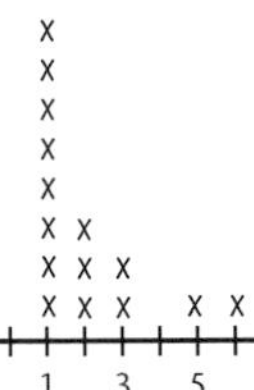

19. Yes; 12 years. **21.** Sample: The average life span of the animals is about 10 years.

Spiral Review

23. $\frac{1}{2}$ **24.** $\frac{9}{10}$ **25.** $\frac{3}{4}$ **26.** $\frac{2}{5}$ **27.** 10 **28.** 25 **29.** 7 **30.** 800 **31.** 5410 **32.** 1000

Extra Skill Practice

1. royal albatross; arctic tern **3.** about 225 **5.** 8 types

Standardized Testing, Open-ended

Sample: I would use a bar graph; by comparing the lengths of the bars, I could get a feeling for how the temperature varied over the month.

Section 4, Practice and Application

1. 14, 14, 18 **3.** 6, 6, 4 **5.** 61, 79, no mode **9.** The mode; no; the mode implies Thom will probably get an A. The mean (about 82) and the median (80) are better descriptions of his grades. The teacher will probably use the mean. **11.** 0.73 **13.** 0.83 **15.** 1.13 **17.** 1.75

19.

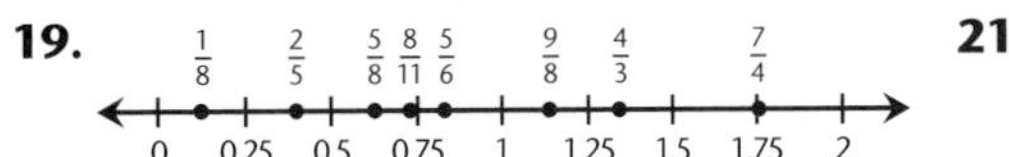

21. 0.396

23. 4.3 **25.** 102.34 **27.** C; you can measure $3\frac{1}{8}$ in. sections with a ruler.

Spiral Review

30.

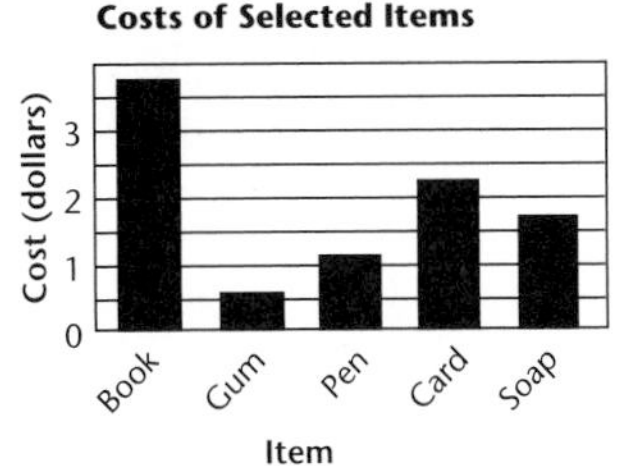

31. about \$3.00. (\$3.15) **32.** one hundred thousandths **33.** 4.12 **34.** 7.9 **35.** 1.016 **36.** 258 **37.** 451 **38.** 6 R 49

Extra Skill Practice

1. 11, 11, 12 **3.** 22, 22, 22 **5.** 345, 283.5, no mode **7.** Samples: (1) All three; they are nearly identical. (2) and (3) All three; they are identical. (4) The mean or the median; the mode is lower than four of the seven data items. (5) The mean and the median are both reasonable; there is no mode. (6) The mean is slightly better than the median because it is a bit higher. However, they are so close, neither is significantly better. The mode is too low. **9.** 5.0 **11.** 2.785 **13.** 679.00 **15.** 22 **17.** 0.53 **19.** 1.33 **21.** 0.81 **23.** 0.57 **25.** 2.67 **27.** 0.69

Standardized Testing, Multiple Choice

C

Section 5, Practice and Application

1. 800 ÷ 4 = 200; 195.8 **3.** 21 ÷ 7 = 3; 3.02 **5.** 0.08; 0.6 ÷ 6 = 0.1 **7.** 1.09; 12 ÷ 12 = 1 **9.** 9.325; 36 ÷ 4 = 9 **11.** 1.3075 cm **13.** 0.875 **15.** 1.8 **17.** about 3500 **19.** about 1000 **21.** 84 **23.** 115 **25.** 78 **31.** Sample: 1,700,000; about 5,100,000; the median is about 1,700,000. One of the numbers is a little higher and one is a little lower than that, so I chose 1,700,000 and 3(1,700,000) = 5,100,000.

Spiral Review

34. 64 **35.** 13.40 **36.** 3.0 **37.** 0.361 **38.** Can form a triangle; the sum of any two side lengths is greater than the third. **39.** Can't form a triangle; 5 + 3 = 8. **40.** Can't form a triangle; 20 + 13 < 35. **41.** Can form a triangle; the sum of any two side lengths is greater than the third. **42.** 21 **43.** 72 **44.** 21

Extra Skill Practice

1. 0.09; 0.5 ÷ 5 = 0.1 **3.** 6.23; 12 ÷ 2 = 6 **5.** 3.454; 27 ÷ 9 = 3 **7.** 4.015; 12 ÷ 3 = 4 **9.** 17.801; 126 ÷ 7 = 18 **11.** not correct; 7.22 **13.** not correct; 5.2 **15.** not correct; 58.96 **17.** about 12 **19.** about 800 **21.** about 220 **23.** 1.03 **25.** 5.9 **27.** 6.7 **29.** 186

Standardized Testing, Multiple Choice

1. B **2.** D

Section 6, Practice and Application

1. 62; 100 **3.** 84.1 (to the nearest tenth), 86, 86 **5.** They represent the integers between the least stem and the greatest. The 0 is included to represent the digit in the tens place of a one-digit number.

7. Meat Consumption by Small and Medium-Sized Predatory Dinosaurs

Stem	Leaves
0	4
1	9
2	1 1 6 7
3	
4	6 7 8

4 | 8 means 48 kg per day

9. The United States; the bar graph; the stem-and-leaf plot doesn't identify countries. **11.** China; the bar graph; the stem-and-leaf plot doesn't identify countries. **13.** 60 **15.** 2.8 **17.** 18.75 **19.** 285.5 **21.** 0.902 **23.** 775.5 times

Spiral Review

27. about 5000 **28.** about 27 **29.** about 1700 **30.** No; the figure is not closed. **31.** Yes. **32.** No; the figure is not made from segments. **33.** No; the figure has sides that intersect. **34.** 80% **35.** 30% **36.** 25% **37.** 12%

Extension

39. men: 10.1, 10.05, 10.0; women: 11.05, 11.05, 11.0 and 11.1. **41.** Sample: Because the plots line up according to stems, you can easily compare the data. For example, it is clear that the median for the men's scores is lower than the median for the women's scores and that more men than women scored times between 10 and 11 s.

Career Connection

43. 0.215 in.

Extra Skill Practice

1. 77 **3.** 2 tests **5.** 17 **7.** 3.4 **9.** 12 **11.** 4.8 **13.** 9.3 **15.** 45.2

Standardized Testing, Performance Task

Sample: Dividing by a number is the same as multiplying by its inverse. If the divisor is between 0 and 1, its inverse is greater than 1. Then dividing by the number is the same as multiplying by a number greater than 1, so the quotient is greater than the dividend. For example, $0.5 = \frac{1}{2}$, so $0.5\overline{)12}$ or 12 ÷ 0.5 is the same as $12 \times \frac{1}{0.5} = 12 \times 2 = 24$.

Review and Assessment

1. green and yellow vegetables, sweet potatoes, butter, liver, fish liver, milk, eggs, oils **2.** four foods **3.** Nuts and fruits are not main sources of either vitamin. **4.** 8000 **5.** 23 **6.** 1.3 **7.** 4000 **8.** 500 **9.** 2300 **10.** 9 **11.** 20 **12.** 50 **13.** 49 **14.** 0.6, 60% **15.** 0.32, 32% **16.** 0.45, 45% **17.** 0.69, 69%

18. Typical Monthly Rainfall in Seattle, WA (rounded to the nearest inch)

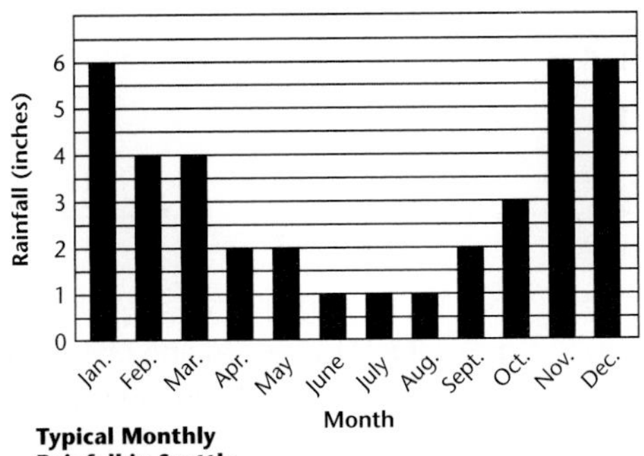

Typical Monthly Rainfall in Seattle, WA (rounded to the nearest inch)

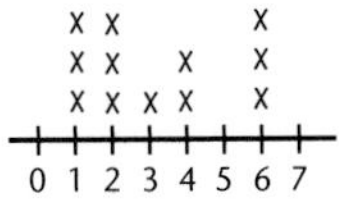

bar graph; The bar graph shows the month associated with each data value. The line plot does not.

19. 3.2, 2.5, 2 and 6 **20.** 3.505 **21.** 19.525 **22.** 19.705 **23.** 0.625 **24.** 3.75 **25.** 0.36 (to the nearest hundredth) **26.** about 1000 **27.** about $40 **28.** about 18 **29.** 102 **30.** 6.04 **31.** 1.85 **32.** 91 cm **33.** 30 cm **34.** 79.5 cm, 77 cm and 86 cm **35.** 65.1 **36.** 6.44 **37.** 1.2

MODULE 4

Section 1, Practice and Application

1. a. red, green, blue; red and green, red and blue; green and blue **b.** Yes. **3.** $\frac{25}{60}$ or $\frac{5}{12}$; 42% **5.** $\frac{1}{5}$
7. Yes; all outcomes have the same chance of occurring.

Spiral Review

12. 58, 50.5, no mode **13.** 8.73, 9.05, no mode **14.** 2000 **15.** 0.065 **16.** 34,000 **17.** 256, 1024 **18.** 6.3, 6.0

Extra Skill Practice

1. $\frac{15}{80} = \frac{3}{16}$ **3.** 62.5% **5.** $\frac{1}{8}$ **7.** $\frac{2}{8} = \frac{1}{4}$
9. Yes; the event "The spinner stops on B"; No.

Section 2, Practice and Application

1. divisible by 2 and 3 **3.** not divisible by 2, 3, 5, 9, or 10 **5.** divisible by 2 and 3 **7.** divisible by 3 **9.** 1, 2, 7, 14; 1, 2, 4, 7, 14, 28; 14 **11.** 1, 3, 7, 21; 1, 3, 17, 51; 3 **13.** 1, 2, 3, 6, 9, 18, 27, 54; 1, 2, 3, 4, 6, 9, 12, 18, 36; 1, 2, 3, 4, 6, 8, 9, 12, 18, 24, 36, 72; 18 **15.** $25 \cdot 4 \cdot 12 = 100 \cdot 12 = 1200$ **17.** $16 \cdot 125 = 4 \cdot 4 \cdot 25 \cdot 5 = 4 \cdot 100 \cdot 5 = 20 \cdot 100 = 2000$ **21.** prime **23.** composite **25.** composite **27.** $2^4 \cdot 3^2$
29. $2^3 \cdot 5 \cdot 7$ **31.** $2^3 \cdot 5 \cdot 7 \cdot 3$ **35.** 25 **37.** 243

39. 6^2 **41.** 10^2 **43. a.** 8 bits; 1024 bytes **b.** 524,288 bytes; 4,194,304 bits **45.** 3^{10}

Spiral Review

50. $\frac{1}{10}$; 0 **51.** Sample: 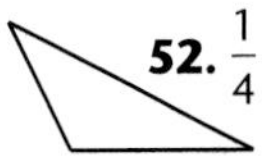 **52.** $\frac{1}{4}$ **53.** $\frac{1}{3}$ **54.** $\frac{1}{4}$ **55.** $\frac{2}{3}$

Extra Skill Practice

1. divisible by 2 **3.** divisible by 2 and 3 **5.** divisible by 3 **7.** 1 **9.** 9 **11.** 8 **13.** composite **15.** composite **17.** $2 \cdot 3^2$ **19.** 3^3 **21.** $2^2 \cdot 5^2$ **23.** 343 **25.** 256 **27.** <; $2^3 = 8$, $3^2 = 9$ **29.** >; $3^4 = 81$, $4^3 = 64$ **31.** $2^2 \cdot 3 \cdot 5^2$ **33.** 2^8 **35.** 5^2 **37.** 10^3 **39.** 11^2

Standardized Testing, Performance Task

1. a. Sample: 20, 40, 60, 80, 100, 120, 140, 160, 180, 200 **b.** Sample: The last digit must be zero, the other digits must represent an even number.
2. a. $2 \cdot 5$; $2^2 \cdot 5^2$; $2^3 \cdot 5^3$ **b.** $2^8 \cdot 5^8$

Section 3, Practice and Application

1. a. $\frac{5}{24}$ **b.** $\frac{5}{24}$ **c.** They are the same. **3.** $\frac{5}{8}$ **5.** $\frac{2}{5}$ **7.** $\frac{10}{27}$ **9.** $\frac{1}{144}$ **11.** $\frac{3}{8}$ **13.** $\frac{4}{7}$ **15.** No; if $\frac{1}{5}$ of the crop was destroyed by hail, $\frac{4}{5}$ remained. Then $\frac{1}{3}$ of that, or $\frac{4}{15}$ was eaten.

Spiral Review

18. $2^2 \cdot 11$ **19.** 5^3 **20.** $2^3 \cdot 7$ **21.** $3^2 \cdot 13$
22. Congruent; they are the same size and shape.
23. Not congruent; they are neither the same size nor the same shape. **24.** 390 **25.** 9168 **26.** 16,160

Extension

27. $\frac{1}{9}$

Extra Skill Practice

1. $\frac{1}{2}$ **3.** $\frac{1}{9}$ **5.** $\frac{3}{4}$ **7.** $\frac{2}{3}$ **9.** $\frac{3}{4}$ **11.** $\frac{2}{5}$ **13.** $\frac{1}{3}$ **15.** $\frac{1}{10}$ **17.** $\frac{3}{16}$ **19.** $\frac{3}{10}$ **21.** $\frac{7}{15}$ **23.** $\frac{2}{9}$ **25. a.** about $\frac{2}{15}$ **b.** about $\frac{2}{5}$

Standardized Testing, Free Response

1. a. $\frac{1}{12}$ **b.** $\frac{6}{14}$, or $\frac{3}{7}$ **c.** $\frac{1}{14}$ **2. a.** $\frac{9}{24}$, or $\frac{3}{8}$ **b.** $\frac{15}{24}$, or $\frac{5}{8}$ **c.** 0 **d.** 1

Section 4, Practice and Application

1. 53.55 **3.** 1.029 **5.** 0.036; $0.3 \cdot 0.1 = 0.03$
7. 4.68; $8 \cdot 0.6 = 4.8$ **9.** 8.928; $25 \cdot 0.4 = 10$ **13.** 0.67
15. 2.635 **17.** about $510 **19.** less than; $0.87 < 1$
21. greater than; $1.5 > 1$

Spiral Review

26. $\frac{3}{32}$ **27.** $\frac{2}{15}$ **28.** $\frac{1}{3}$ **29.** 21.2 cm **30.** 19.6 cm
31. 16 **32.** 92 **33.** 32

Extra Skill Practice

1. 198.74 **3.** 0.092 **5.** 2.76 **7.** 5.349 **9.** 8.37 **11.** 2.349 **13.** 0.0504 **15.** 0.75 **17.** 0.35; 35 ÷ 100 = 0.35 **19.** 6.31; 176 ÷ 28 ≈ 168 ÷ 28 = 6

Standardized Testing, Open-ended

1. Sample: Sam bought 2.5 lb of fish at $8.99 per pound. How much did Sam pay for the fish?
2. Sample: 0.75 (Any number between 0.5 and 1 is an acceptable answer.) **3.** Sample: 0.5 • 0.1 = 0.05

Section 5, Practice and Application

1. (1, 5) **3.** (8, 26) **5–12.**

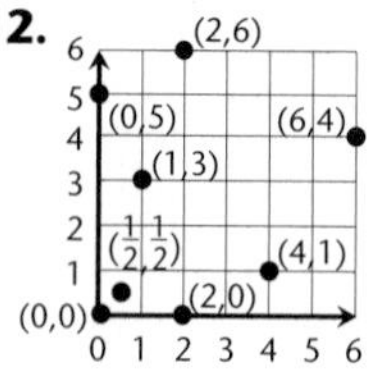

13. a, b.

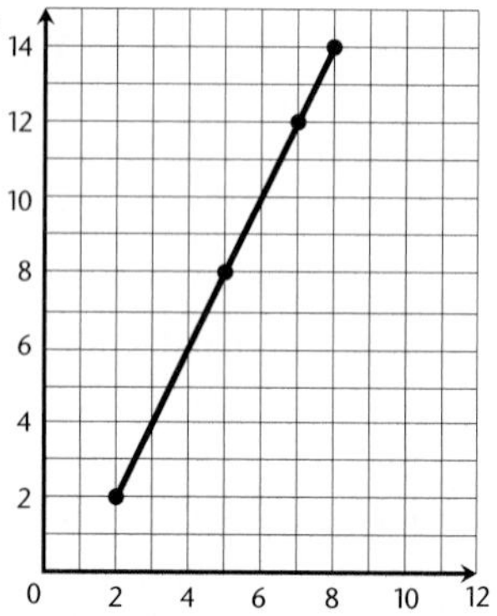

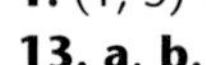

c. 7; 6 **d.** (2, 2), (5, 8), (7, 12), (8, 14); Sample: For every increase of 1 in the input, the output increases by 2. To find the output for $4\frac{1}{2}$, notice that $4\frac{1}{2} - 2 = 2\frac{1}{2}$ and $2\frac{1}{2} \cdot 2 = 5$; 2 + 5 = 7. Compare the ordered pair with output 10 to (5, 8). The output increased by 2, so the input must have increased by 1. Then the input is 6.

15. a, b.

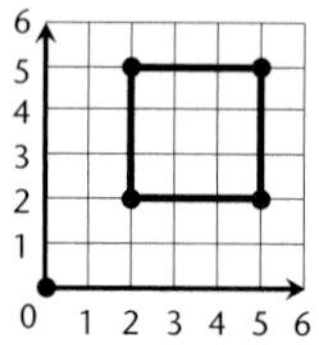

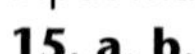

c. square

17. 6 • 10 **19.** $n \div 5$ or $\frac{n}{5}$ **21.** C **23.** B **25.** 20

27. 10.3 **29.** 6 **31.** 60 ft²; 34 ft **35.** (a) 5596, (b) 78, (c) 8, (d) 5682

Spiral Review

38. 0.09 **39.** 5.27184 **40.** 9.423 **41.** 3 quarters and 4 dimes **42.** $\frac{13}{8}$; $1\frac{5}{8}$

Extra Skill Practice

1. G **3.** A **5.** (5, 0) **7.** $n - 5$ **9.** $n + 12$ **11.** 24 **13.** 8 **15.** 40 cm²; 26 cm **17.** 1 ft²; 5 ft

Standardized Testing, Multiple Choice

1. C **2.** B

Section 6, Practice and Application

1. 7, 14, 21, 28, 35, 42, 49 **3.** 99, 198, 297, 396, 495, 594, 693 **5.** a, c, d **7.** 36 **9.** 80 **11.** 105 **13.** $5\frac{1}{4}$ **15.** $6\frac{5}{6}$ **17.** $\frac{21}{5}$ **19.** $\frac{23}{2}$ **21.** $\frac{39}{5}$ **23.** $\frac{47}{7}$
25–28.

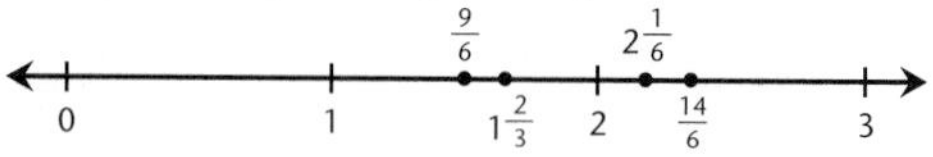

29. $5\frac{1}{5}$ **31.** $9\frac{8}{10}$ or $9\frac{4}{5}$ **33.** Choices (b) and (c) are both reasonable; both clearly represent a dollar and a half.

Spiral Review

35. 94.5 cm², 41 cm **36–39.** Samples are given.
36. 60%; mental math **37.** 83%; paper and pencil or calculator **38.** 65%; mental math **39.** 36%; paper and pencil or calculator **40.** 40 **41.** 1 **42.** 2

Career Connection

43. a. a multiple of 12; for example, 12, 24, 36
b. Sample: The same piece of music can be used if the measures are multiples of 4, 8, and 12, or multiples of 24. For example, 24, 48, and 72 measures can be used.

Extra Skill Practice

1. 4, 8, 12, 16, 20, 24, 28 **3.** 33, 66, 99, 132, 165, 198, 231 **5.** 36 **7.** 150 **9.** 120 **11.** $3\frac{1}{3}$ **13.** $4\frac{1}{4}$ **15.** $10\frac{1}{2}$ **17.** $\frac{49}{9}$ **19.** $\frac{24}{7}$ **21.** $2\frac{1}{5}$ **23.** $4\frac{2}{4}$ or $4\frac{1}{2}$

Standardized Testing, Multiple Choice

1. B **2.** A **3.** C **4.** C

Review and Assessment

1. 24% **2.** 49% **3.** 0 **4.** (1) $\frac{1}{4}$, 25%; (2) $\frac{1}{2}$, 50%; (3) 0, 0% **5.** 0, 2, 4, 6, 8 **6.** 0, 5 **7.** 0, 3, 6, 9 **8.** 3
9. No; He missed 6 and 18. Sample: I used a factor tree to find the prime factors, then I found all the possible combinations. **10.** 12 **11.** 1 **12.** 26 **13.** composite

14. composite **15.** prime **16.** composite **17.** >; $2^5 = 32$, $5^2 = 25$ **18.** =; $4^3 = 2^6 = 64$ **19.** <; $3^3 = 3 \cdot 3 \cdot 3 = 27$, $3 \cdot 3 \cdot 3 \cdot 3 = 3^4 = 81$ **20.** 2^5 **21.** 97^1 **22.** $2^2 \cdot 3 \cdot 5^2$ **23.** $3 \cdot 7 \cdot 11$ **24.** $\frac{1}{10}$ **25.** $\frac{10}{21}$ **26.** $\frac{5}{18}$ **27.** $\frac{3}{8}$
28. 0.128; 0.4 • 0.3 = 0.12 **29.** 1851.3; 40 • 50 = 2000
30. 0.0282; 5 • 0.006 = 0.03
31. a,b.

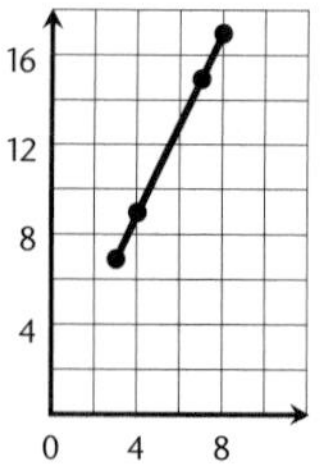

c. 12; $4\frac{1}{2}$ **32. a.** $2 \cdot w$
b. $2 \cdot w^2$ or $2w \cdot w$
33. 7.2; 25.92 **34.** Sunday
35. 33 **36.** 3 **37.** 7 **38.** 7

MODULE 5

Section1, Practice and Application

1. No; The sections of the strip are not equal in length. **3.** $\frac{2}{4} = \frac{1}{2}$ **5.** $\frac{5}{12} < \frac{1}{2}$ **7.** $\frac{2}{3}, \frac{9}{10}, \frac{49}{50}, \frac{99}{100}$ **9.** > **11.** > **13.** > **17.** < **19.** > **21.** = **23.** > **25.** < **27.** > **29. a.** 4 **b.** 4 **c.** 2 **31.** > **33.** > **35.** Trinja

Spiral Review

39. $5\frac{1}{2}$ **40.** $2\frac{3}{12}$ or $2\frac{1}{4}$ **41.** $4\frac{3}{7}$ **42.** $4\frac{1}{3}$

43. Daily High Temperatures for July

Stem	Leaves								
5	6	9							
6	1	4	8	9	9				
7	1	2	2	7	7	8	8	8	8
8	0	2	2	2	4	5	5	7	7	9
9	0	1	1	8					
10	1								

7 | 1 means 71

44–45. Samples are given. **44.**

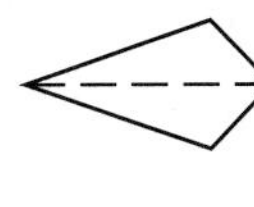

45.

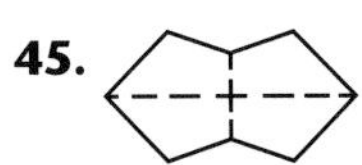

Extension

47–49. Sample responses are given.

47. $\frac{1}{2}$ **49.** $\frac{1}{2}$

Extra Skill Practice

1. > **3.** > **5.** > **7.** > **9.** < **11.** > **13.** < **15.** > **17.** < **19.** < **21.** <

Study Tip, Reviewing for Assessment

1. pages 314–315

Section 2, Practice and Application

1–7. Sample responses are given. **1.** about 1 in. **3.** about 2 ft **5.** an unsharpened pencil **7.** the length of my living room **9.** feet **11.** inches **13.** $1\frac{1}{2}$ in,; $1\frac{2}{4}$ in.; $1\frac{3}{8}$ in. **15.** 7 **17.** $4\frac{1}{2}$ **19.** 99 **21.** $\frac{2}{3}$ yd **23.** $\frac{18}{36}$ yd or $\frac{1}{2}$ yd **25.** 6 yd 2 ft 1 in. **27.** 1 mi 1198 yd **29.** 1 yd 1 ft 10 in. **31.** 7 yd 1 ft

Spiral Review

34. < **35.** < **36.** > **37.** 10 ways (2 quarters; 1 quarter, 2 dimes, 1 nickel; 1 quarter, 1 dime, 3 nickels; 1 quarter, 5 nickels; 5 dimes; 4 dimes, 2 nickels; 3 dimes, 4 nickels; 2 dimes, 6 nickels; 1 dime, 8 nickels; 10 nickels)

Extra Skill Practice

1. 2 in. **3.** $1\frac{3}{4}$ **5.** 27 **7.** $4\frac{1}{6}$ **9.** $\frac{1}{2}$ **11.** $11\frac{1}{4}$ **13.** 180 **15.** $\frac{2}{3}$ **17.** 5 yd 1 ft 7 in. **19.** 2 ft **21.** 11 yd 2 ft **23.** 1 mi 71 yd **25.** 2 yd 1 in.

Standardized Testing, Performance Task

1. Sample: To measure 1 in., place the longest strip on top of the midsize strip with the left ends meeting. Mark the right end of the midsize strip on the longest strip. The mark will be 2 in. from the end. Fold the 2 in. strip in half. You now have a 1 in. measure. You can use it to mark off a 3 in. piece or any combination that adds to 3 in. to overlap the strips. The total length will be 3 ft 2 in + 2 ft 9 in. + 3 ft 4 in. – 3 in. = 3 yd.

Section 3, Practice and Application

1. $\frac{7}{9}$ **3.** $\frac{21}{20}$ or $1\frac{1}{20}$ **5.** $\frac{7}{9}$ **7.** $\frac{4}{7}$ **9.** $\frac{1}{8}$ **11.** $\frac{7}{45}$ **15. a.** about $\frac{5}{6}$ **b.** about $\frac{1}{6}$ **c.** In April 1996, about $\frac{1}{6}$ of the users of the World Wide Web were between the ages of 5 and 20.

Spiral Review

18. $1\frac{3}{4}$ **19.** 3520 **20.** $5\frac{1}{3}$ **21.** four cities, six cities, one city, nine cities, one city **22.** 35 **23.** 85 **24.** 49

Extra Skill Practice

1. $\frac{7}{15}$ **3.** $\frac{17}{18}$ **5.** $\frac{35}{33}$ or $1\frac{2}{33}$ **7.** $\frac{37}{60}$ **9.** $\frac{87}{80}$ or $1\frac{7}{80}$ **11.** $\frac{13}{40}$ **13.** $\frac{3}{4}$ **15.** $\frac{49}{60}$ **17.** $\frac{1}{2}$ **19.** $\frac{37}{30}$ or $1\frac{7}{30}$ **21.** $\frac{11}{12}$ **23.** $\frac{7}{6}$ or $1\frac{1}{6}$ **25.** $\frac{41}{30}$ or $1\frac{11}{30}$ **27.** $\frac{14}{9}$ or $1\frac{5}{9}$ **29.** $\frac{37}{72}$ **31.** $\frac{10}{7}$ or $1\frac{3}{7}$ **33.** $\frac{7}{8}$

Section 4, Practice and Application

1. about 10 **3.** about 5 **5.** $10\frac{1}{6}$ **7.** $8\frac{23}{24}$ **9.** $5\frac{13}{18}$ **11.** $8\frac{4}{5} + 1\frac{1}{5} = 10$ and $4\frac{3}{8} + 2\frac{5}{8} = 7$; $10 + 7 + 6\frac{1}{3} = 23\frac{1}{3}$

13. a. $3\frac{3}{8}$ is closer to $3\frac{1}{2}$ than to 3. **b.** high; Both numbers were rounded up. **c.** $8\frac{7}{40}$; The sum is lower than the estimate. **15.** $1\frac{3}{20}$ **17.** $\frac{3}{8}$ **19.** $7\frac{6}{11}$ **21.** $3\frac{2}{3}$; $3\frac{1}{3} + \frac{2}{3} = 4$, so $3\frac{1}{3} + 3\frac{2}{3} = 7$ **23.** $1\frac{3}{4}$; $1\frac{1}{4} + \frac{3}{4} = 2$, so $1\frac{1}{4} + 1\frac{3}{4} = 3$ **25. a.** Sharon; $\frac{1}{4}$ in. **b.** $3\frac{1}{8}$ in. **27. a.** $1\frac{1}{2}$ in. **b.** $\frac{3}{4}$ in. **29.** $\frac{3}{4}$ in.

Spiral Review

32. $\frac{9}{25}$ **33.** $\frac{1}{12}$ **34.** $\frac{41}{30}$ or $1\frac{11}{30}$ **35.** neither **36.** certain **37.** impossible **38.** 9 **39.** 6 **40.** 40

Extension

41.a. 4:16 – 1:37 = 3:76 – 1:37 = 2:39; 2 h 39 min **b.** Sample: The regrouping is the same because I had to change a whole (1 hour) into parts (60 minutes). The regrouping is different because the parts (minutes) can be represented by whole numbers.

Extra Skill Practice

1. $8\frac{1}{4}$ **3.** $10\frac{1}{10}$ **5.** $4\frac{7}{60}$ **7.** $2\frac{1}{18}$ **9.** $4\frac{17}{28}$ **11.** $8\frac{11}{18}$ **13.** $3\frac{1}{4}$ **15.** $2\frac{5}{16}$ **17.** $18\frac{1}{2}$ **19.** $16\frac{5}{6}$ **21.** $\frac{17}{20}$ **23.** $2\frac{43}{45}$ **25.** $3\frac{17}{42}$ **27.** $14\frac{8}{35}$

Standardized Testing, Multiple Choice

1. D **2.** E

Section 5, Practice and Application

1. D **3.** C **5.** E **7.** 22 **9.** 5 **11.** 3 **13.** $15\frac{3}{4}$ **15.** 32 **17.** $25\frac{5}{6}$ **19.** $7\frac{7}{15}$ **21.** $1\frac{7}{20}$ **23.** $10\frac{3}{4}$ **25.** $3\frac{2}{3} \cdot 5 = \frac{11}{3} \cdot \frac{5}{1} = \frac{55}{3} = 18\frac{1}{3}$; $3\frac{2}{3} \cdot 5 = \left(3 + \frac{2}{3}\right) \cdot 5 = (3 \cdot 5) + \left(\frac{2}{3} \cdot 5\right) = 15 + \frac{10}{3} = 15 + 3\frac{1}{3} = 18\frac{1}{3}$ **27.** $\frac{1}{10}$ **29.** $\frac{3}{2}$ **31.** 3 **33.** less than; $\frac{2}{3}$ is less than 1; $3\frac{1}{5}$ **35.** greater than; $\frac{9}{8}$ is greater than 1; $5\frac{2}{5}$ **37.** 4 half lives **39.** between 0 and 1; Samples: $\frac{1}{4} \cdot \frac{1}{2} = \frac{1}{8}$, $\frac{5}{8} \cdot \frac{2}{3} = \frac{10}{24} = \frac{5}{12}$, $\frac{1}{10} \cdot \frac{9}{10} = \frac{9}{100}$

Spiral Review

41. $10\frac{5}{6}$ **42.** $\frac{1}{2}$ **43.** $15\frac{7}{8}$ **44.** about $4000 **45.** about $120 **46.** about $50 **47.** $2\frac{1}{6}$ **48.** $5\frac{7}{11}$ **49.** $8\frac{1}{3}$

Extra Skill Practice

1. 16 **3.** $\frac{1}{2}$ **5.** $3\frac{1}{2}$ **7.** $1\frac{3}{4}$ **9.** 8 **11.** $12\frac{4}{5}$ **13.** $7\frac{1}{32}$ **15.** $\frac{15}{16}$ **17.** $5\frac{3}{5}$ **19.** 6 **21.** $\frac{1}{32}$ **23.** 6

Standardized Testing, Free Response

$3\frac{1}{3}$ c

Section 6, Practice and Application

1. 2 **3.** $10\frac{2}{3}$ **5.** $2\frac{1}{2}$ **7.** 9 **9.** 13 pieces; Yes; $\frac{1}{4}$ ft or $\frac{1}{3}$ of a piece **11. a.** The first indicates 8 divided by 5 and the second indicates 8 multiplied by the reciprocal of 5 or $\frac{1}{5}$; Yes; $0.1 = \frac{1}{10}$, the reciprocal of 10. The relationship is the same. **b.** Move the decimal place to the left as many places as there are zeros in the divisor. **13.** $1\frac{17}{28}$ **15.** $\frac{11}{24}$ **17.** $3\frac{3}{20}$ **19.** 4 times; Yes. **21. a.** less than; Sample: $2 \cdot 6 = 12$ and $\frac{3}{4} > \frac{1}{2}$, so $2 \cdot 6\frac{3}{4} > 13$. **b.** $1\frac{23}{27}$

Spiral Review

25. 21 **26.** $43\frac{1}{5}$ **27.** 21 **28.** (4, 6) **29.** (1, 3) **30.** (6, 0) **31.** 14 **32.** 15 **33.** 5

Extra Skill Practice

1. 8 **3.** 20 **5.** $3\frac{3}{7}$ **7.** $3\frac{3}{5}$ **9.** $25\frac{2}{3}$ **11.** $1\frac{3}{4}$ **13.** $3\frac{3}{5}$ **15.** $1\frac{1}{2}$ **17.** $9\frac{1}{3}$ **19.** $2\frac{1}{4}$ **21.** $\frac{12}{23}$ **23.** $\frac{1}{20}$

Standardized Testing, Multiple Choice

1. C **2.** D

Review and Assessment

1. $\frac{3}{100}, \frac{4}{7}, \frac{2}{3}, \frac{5}{3}$ **2.** $\frac{4}{5}, \frac{9}{10}, \frac{19}{20}, \frac{99}{100}$ **3.** $\frac{1}{7}, \frac{1}{4}, \frac{4}{5}, \frac{7}{8}$ **4.** $\frac{1}{4}, \frac{1}{2}, \frac{2}{3}, \frac{5}{6}$ **5.** $>$ **6.** $>$ **7.** $<$ **8.** $<$ **9.** $>$ **10.** $<$ **11.** $>$ **12.** 1 in. **13.** $\frac{3}{4}$ in. **14.** $\frac{7}{8}$ in. **15.** 126 **16.** $2\frac{5}{6}$ **17.** 63 **18.** $8\frac{2}{3}$ **19.** 6030 **20.** $1\frac{3}{22}$ **21.** $\frac{12}{8}$ or $1\frac{1}{2}$ **22.** $\frac{19}{21}$ **23.** $5\frac{7}{8}$ **24.** $3\frac{7}{15}$ **25.** $6\frac{2}{3}$ **26.** $5\frac{7}{24}$ **27.** $10\frac{3}{40}$ **28.** $6\frac{1}{2}$ **29.** $23\frac{1}{6}$ h **30.** $8\frac{1}{2}$ **31.** $6\frac{1}{4}$ **32.** $1\frac{1}{4}$ **33.** $5\frac{15}{16}$ **34.** $1\frac{1}{6}$ mi **35.** $\frac{3}{8}$ **36.** $6\frac{1}{15}$ **37.** $6\frac{6}{7}$ **38.** $2\frac{3}{5}$ **39.** $1\frac{4}{5}$ **40.** $\frac{13}{24}$ **41.** $2\frac{1}{12}$ **42.** $\frac{39}{40}$ **43.** A, C, or D **44.** $12\frac{1}{4}$ c; $6\frac{1}{8}$ pt; 98 fl oz **45.** $11\frac{1}{4}$ **46.** $8\frac{1}{3}$ **47.** $\frac{13}{24}$ **48.** $2\frac{9}{10}$ **49.** 7 **50.** 34 **51.** 16 **52.** 26 **53.** Yes; $8 \div \frac{3}{4} = 10\frac{2}{3}$ **54.** $1\frac{5}{9}$ **55.** 24 **56.** $1\frac{2}{5}$ **57.** $\frac{19}{24}$ **58.** $1\frac{1}{8}$ **59.** $\frac{4}{9}$ **60.** $1\frac{1}{2}$ **61.** $\frac{13}{24}$

MODULE 6

Section 1, Practice and Application

1. a. $\frac{1}{4}$ **b.** $\frac{4}{16}$ **c.** Yes; $\frac{1}{4} = \frac{4}{16}$ **3.** Yes. **5.** No. **7.** No. **9. a.** 3 to 1, 3 : 1; $\frac{3}{1}$ **b.** 27 steps **c.** 4 steps **11.** Sample: If you were only one inch tall, you couldn't ride a bike. And climbing into bed would be a terrifying hike. You never could play basketball, Or safely stroll around the mall. A summer walk would take till fall, If you were one inch tall.

Spiral Review

14. $9\frac{3}{5}$ **15.** $1\frac{1}{6}$ **16.** $23\frac{3}{5}$ **17.** 0.8 **18.** 0.0524 **19.** 87.2 **20.** 0.027 **21.** 9 **22.** 0.608 **23.** 3 **24.** 5 **25.** 20

Extra Skill Practice

1. 256 to 120, 256 : 120, $\frac{256}{120}$ **3.** 32 to 37, 32 : 37, $\frac{32}{37}$

5. ★ ★ ★ ★ ★ ■ ■ ■ **7.** 🍎 🍎 🍎 🍎 🍎 🍐 🍐 🍐 🍐 🍐 🍐 **9.** Yes.

11. No. **13.** Yes. **15.** No. **17.** Yes.

Study Skills, Using Mathematical Language

1. A ratio is a special type of comparison of two numbers or measures. **2.** "8 : 12" means "the ratio of 8 to 12." **3.** The length of 1 m equals 100 cm or 1000 mm. **4.** The book covers both customary and metric measurement, including length, area, and volume.

Section 2, Practice and Application

1. Yes. **3.** Yes. **5.** No. **7.** Yes. **9.** \$3/h **11.** $1\frac{1}{2}$ ft per step **13.** $3\frac{2}{5}$ pages per min **15.** \$3.80 for 10 pens; Those pens cost \$.38 apiece, while the others cost \$.44 apiece. **17.** about 900 mi; about 54,000 mi **19.** \$30

Spiral Review

22. 3 : 5 ▲▲▲ ■■■■■ ▲▲▲ ■■■■■ **23.** 0.83 **24.** 0.52 **25.** 0.73 **26.** 0.72 **27.** 80 **28.** $58\frac{5}{6}$

Extension

29. a.

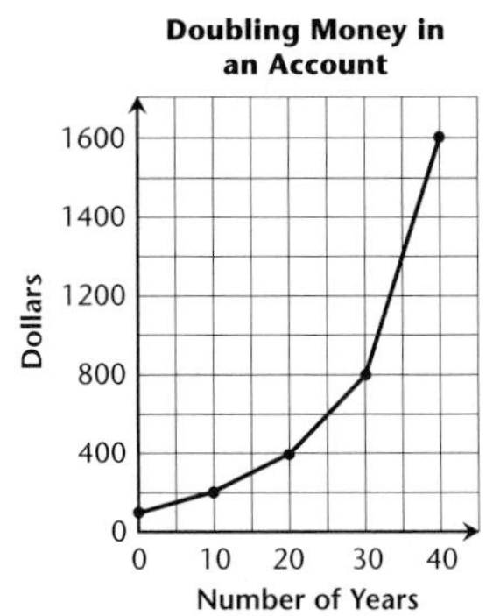

b. Instead of being a constant rate of change like the rates in this section, the rates are multiplied and the ratios of years to money are not the same. The rates are $\frac{0}{100} = 0$, $\frac{10}{200} = \frac{1}{20}$, $\frac{20}{400} = \frac{1}{20}$, $\frac{30}{800} = \frac{3}{80}$, $\frac{40}{1600} = \frac{1}{40}$, so the rates are not equivalent.

Extra Skill Practice

1. No. **3.** Yes. **5.** No. **7.** Yes. **9.** Yes. **11.** 8 km/h **13.** \$7.50 per book **15.** 28 mi/gal **17.** \$5.76 for 12 oranges **19.** about 360 mi; about 21,600 mi

Standardized Testing, Performance Task

1. a. warm air **b.** 82 ft/s **2.** 16,530 ft

Section 3, Practice and Application

1. a. about 10 cm, about 40 cm, about 80 cm **3.** 0.78 **5.** 0.29 **7. a.** Sample: The ratio of the projected number of computers in Australia to the projected number of computers in Japan will be about 1 : 5. **b.** about 2; about 3 **c.** The ratio in part (b) doesn't give any message about the number of personal computers, but if you thought the populations in the two countries were about the same, you might think there would be about $1\frac{1}{2}$ times as many computers in Japan. **9–13.** Sample responses are given. **9.** $\frac{1}{5}$ **11.** $\frac{1}{3}$ **13.** $\frac{3}{2}$ **17. b.** Use 1:6 as the ratio for length of radius to height; 20, 25, 30; 144, 192

19. a. Sample graph: **b.** about 16 pages **c.** about 25 pages

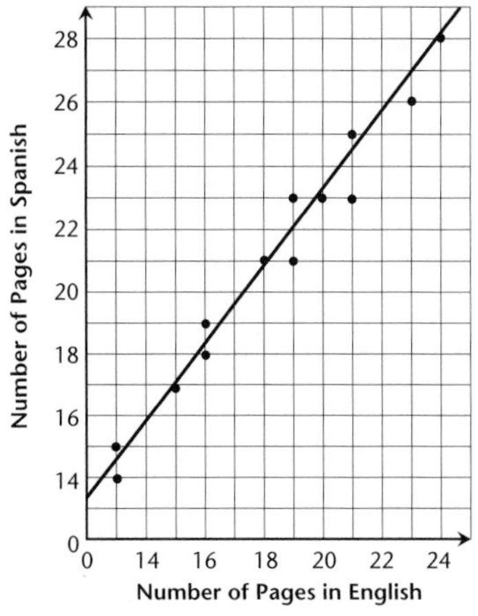

Spiral Review

21. 33 mi/gal **22.** about \$2.83 per lb **23.** 53 heartbeats per min **24.** $\frac{14}{30} = \frac{7}{15}$ **25.** 9 **26.** 12 **27.** 37 **28.** 153 **29.** 15 **30.** 23

Extra Skill Practice

1. a. 0.74, 0.74, 0.74, 0.76, 0.75, 0.74, 0.75, 0.73 **b.** about 0.74 **c.** $\frac{3}{4}$ **d.** 99, 105; 125, 116

Section 4, Practice and Application

1. $\frac{15}{60}, \frac{75}{300}$, and $\frac{3.5}{14}, \frac{24}{32}$ and $\frac{21}{28}$ **3.** 20 **5.** 8 **7.** 1.8 **9.** 12 **11.** 5 **13. b.** $\frac{1 \text{ mi}}{20 \text{ min}} = \frac{3.2 \text{ mi}}{x}$ **c.** 64 min **15.** $\frac{5}{24}$; about 13 times **17.** 72 steps

Spiral Review

19. a. $\frac{1}{4}$ **b.** about 15 in. **20–24.** Sample responses are given. **20.** **21.** **22.** **23.**

24.

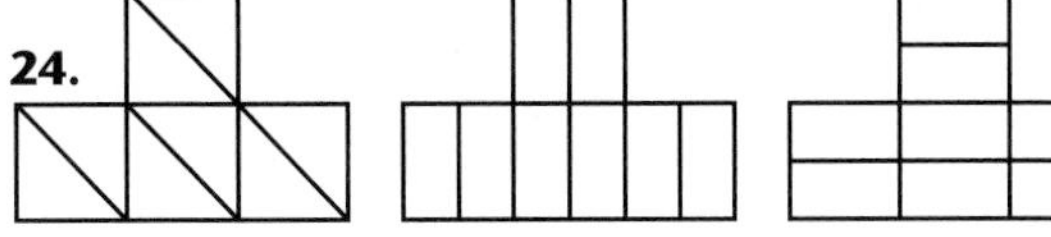

Extra Skill Practice

1. Yes. **3.** No. **5.** 48 **7.** 39 **9.** 2 **11.** $7\frac{1}{2}$ **13.** \$2.70 **15.** $6\frac{2}{3}$ yd

Standardized Testing, Multiple Choice

1. D **2.** B

Section 5, Practice and Application

1. $\angle A$ and $\angle F$; $\angle B$ and $\angle D$; $\angle C$ and $\angle E$; $\overline{AB}$ and $\overline{FD}$; $\overline{AC}$ and $\overline{FE}$; $\overline{BC}$ and $\overline{DE}$ **3.** congruent; Corresponding angles have the same measure and corresponding sides have the same length. **5.** similar; Corresponding angles have the same measure and the ratios of the lengths of corresponding sides are equivalent. **7.** F; 1 : 2 **9.** A and C; The ratios of the corresponding measures are equivalent. They are all 1 : 3. **11.** $ST = 9$, $TQ = 13.5$, $QR = 13.5$ **13.** 15 ft **15.** 15 ft **17.** 400 mi **19. a.** about 1 ft : 16.3 ft **b.** about 3.7 ft long and about 2.5 ft wide **21.** 35° **23.** 75° **25.** 148°; 142°; 138°; 133°; 120°

27. **29.**

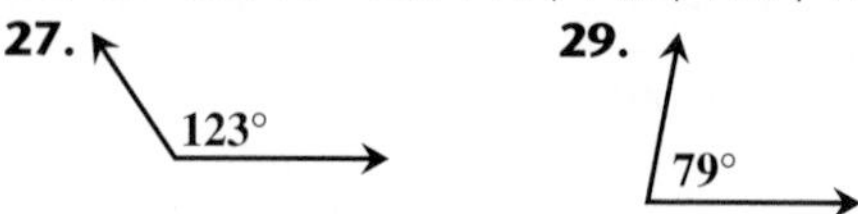

Spiral Review

31. No. **32.** Yes. **33.** Yes. **34.** $3\frac{3}{5}$ **35.** 9.20 **36.** $8\frac{5}{6}$ **37.** 40% **38.** 30% **39.** 75% **40.** 50%

Career Connection

41. a. 1 cm = 132 km **b.** 64 km

Extra Skill Practice

1. similar **3.** 32.4 cm **5.** 48 in. **7.** 80 ft

9. **11.**

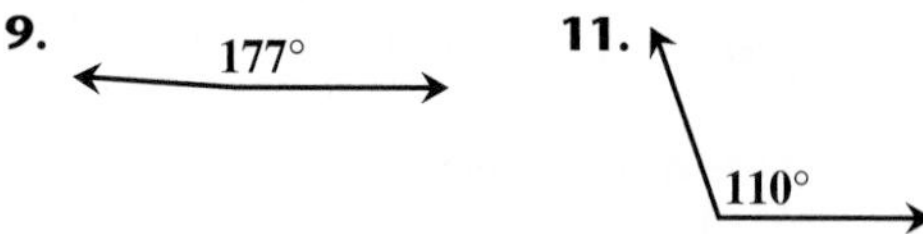

Section 6, Practice and Application

1. 12 **3.** 9 **5.** 49 **7.** 19 **9.** 29.4 **11.** about 80 times **13. a.** \$4 **b.** \$2 **c.** \$6 **15.** about 75% **17.** about $66\frac{2}{3}$ % **21.** 4 vertices; 6 edges **23.** $\frac{5}{9}$ **25.** $\frac{5}{9}$

27. a. First Coin Second Coin Third Coin Outcome

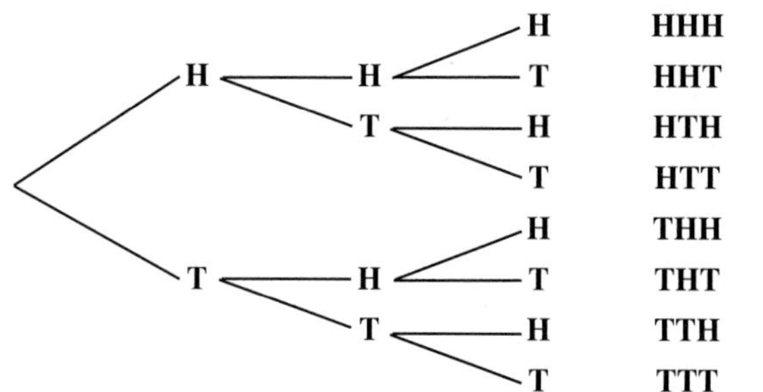

b. No; about 75% of the time. **c.** Yes; Each of the three players has an equal chance of winning.

Spiral Review

29. $\angle A$ and $\angle G$, $\angle B$ and $\angle H$, $\angle C$ and $\angle E$, $\angle D$ and $\angle F$; $\overline{AB}$ and $\overline{GH}$, $\overline{BC}$ and $\overline{HE}$, $\overline{CD}$ and $\overline{EF}$, $\overline{DA}$ and $\overline{FG}$ **30.** B **31.** A **32. a.** Sample: Let ℓ = length, w = width, A = area, and P = perimeter; $A = \ell \cdot w$, $P = 2 \cdot \ell + 2 \cdot w$ or $2(\ell + w)$ **b.** 28.5 m², 25 m

Extra Skill Practice

1. 18 **3.** 9.1 **5.** 3 **7.** about $33\frac{1}{3}$ % **9.** about 20% **11.** about 40 **13.** about 45

Standardized Testing, Multiple Choice

1. B **2.** C **3.** D

Review and Assessment

1. 8 to 6, 8: 6, $\frac{8}{6}$ **2.** 6 to 10, 6 : 10, $\frac{6}{10}$ **3.** No. **4.** Yes. **5.** Yes. **6. a.** 6, 12, 24 **b.** \$30 **c.** 15 ft

7. a.

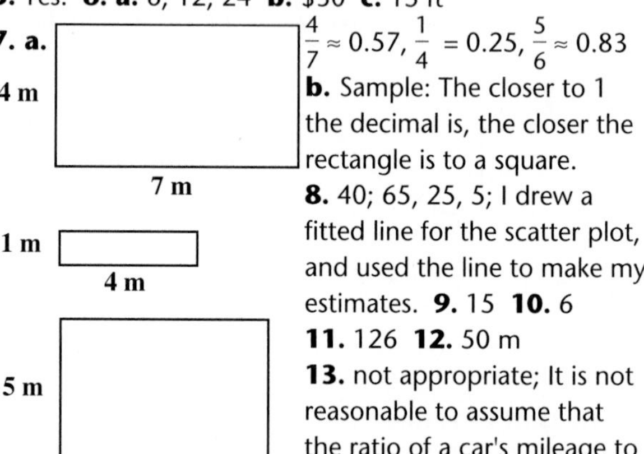

$\frac{4}{7} \approx 0.57$, $\frac{1}{4} = 0.25$, $\frac{5}{6} \approx 0.83$ **b.** Sample: The closer to 1 the decimal is, the closer the rectangle is to a square. **8.** 40; 65, 25, 5; I drew a fitted line for the scatter plot, and used the line to make my estimates. **9.** 15 **10.** 6 **11.** 126 **12.** 50 m **13.** not appropriate; It is not reasonable to assume that the ratio of a car's mileage to its speed is always the same. **14.** 5 ft **16.** 21 **17.** 65 **18.** 24.5 **19.** about 90%.

20. a. Vinh's spin Scott's spin Outcome Winner

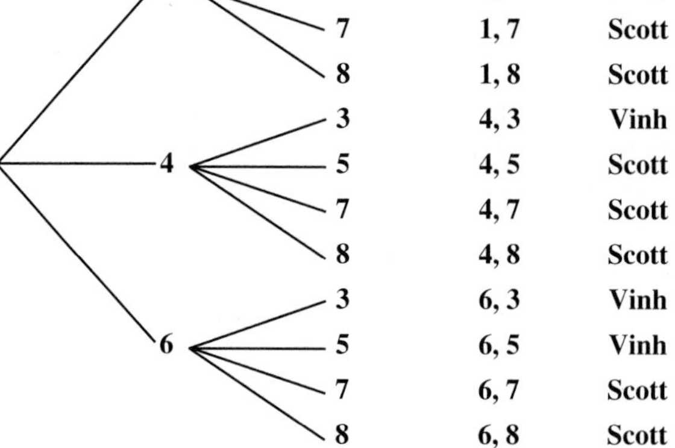

b. $\frac{1}{4}$ **c.** 75%

MODULE 7

Section 1, Practice and Application

3. 9 **5.** 2394 **7.** 10,000 cm^2; 1 m = 100 cm, so the area of a square that is 1 m on a side is 100 • 100 = 10,000 cm^2. **9.** 20 cm^2 **11.** 2600 yd^2
13. E: 12.5 cm^2 ; F: 3.38 cm^2; G: 5.2 cm^2; H: 5.46 cm^2
15. a. Sample: 3 cm 2.4 cm 2.5 cm 2.5 cm 2 cm 3 cm **b.** 3 • 2 = 6; 6 cm^2
c. 2.5 • 2.4 = 6; 6 cm^2 **d.** Yes; They represent the area of the same figure. **17.** 120 cm^2 **19.** 6 ft **21.** 4 in. **23.** 16

Spiral Review

28. 31 **29.** 63 **30.** 60 **31–33.** Sample responses are given. **31.** **32.** **33.**

Extra Skill Practice

1. 24,192 **3.** $\frac{2}{3}$ **5.** $40\frac{1}{2}$ **7.** 916.8 mm^2 **9.** $22\frac{3}{4}$ cm^2
11. 80 cm^2 **13.** 148 = 34 + 34 + 58 + x; x = 22 in.
15. 12.5 = 2.5 • h; h = 5 ft

Section 2, Practice and Application

1. No. **3.** Yes; triangular **5.** 32 cm^3 **7.** 16 cm^3
9. 96 cm^3 **11.** 0.72 cm^3 **13.** 120 cm^3 **15.** 4 cm
17. a. The bases are not congruent rectangles.
b. Sample: Draw a line from the concave corner near the 72 ft label to the right side of the building. The two rectangular prisms are 60 ft by 180 ft by 15 ft and 108 ft by 120 ft by 15 ft. **c.** 356,400 ft^3 **19.** B **21.** A: hexagonal prism, C: square prism or cube **23. a.** triangular prism **b.** triangular prism **c.** 5 faces, 6 vertices, 9 edges
d. Sample

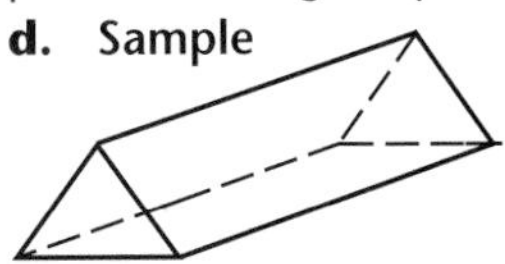

Spiral Review

27. area = 14 cm;^{2} Sample: 3.5 cm 4 cm

28. $1.60
29. a. Yes.
b. about fifteen 8 oz servings; The total number of ounces is 124 and 124 ÷ 8 = 15.5.

Extra Skill Practice

1. 1,350,000 cm^3 **3.** 253.6 in.^{3} **5.** 50 mm^2 **7.** Yes; parallelograms **9.** Yes; triangles; triangular prism

Standardized Testing, Multiple Choice

D

Section 3, Practice and Application

1. ton **3.** pound **7.** 6 **9.** 2 **11.** 11,000 **13.** 2 lb 8 oz
15. (13) estimate: about \$4.50, since 2 lb 8 oz = 2.5 lb and 2.5 × 1.8 = 4.50, actual cost: \$4.48; (14) estimate: about \$2.98, since 4 lb 4 oz = 4.25 lb and 4.25 × .70 = 2.98, actual cost: \$2.93

Spiral Review

20. 4.5 cm **21.** 25 cm^2 **22.** n = 16 • p; 240 oz

Career Connection

23. Yes; 9 lb 7 oz = 151 oz and 95 oz < 151 oz < 152 oz

Extra Skill Practice

1. pound **3.** pound **5.** ounce or pound **7.** ounce
9. ounce **11.** 0.8 **13.** 56 **15.** 32,000 **17.** $6\frac{1}{2}$ **19.** >
21. = **23.** = **25.** = **27.** >

Standardized Testing, Free Response

1. Yes; The total weight is 13,800 lb which is less than 7 tons (14,000 lb) **2.** greatest: 54 oz; least: 9.5 oz; The melon and the soup can weigh 54 oz together. The golf ball and apple weigh 9.5 oz together.

Section 4, Practice and Application

1. $\overline{OA}$, $\overline{OB}$, $\overline{OD}$ **3.** $\overline{AD}$, $\overline{BE}$ **7. a.** a circle with a radius of 100 km **b.** These are the possible locations for the epicenter. **c.** Use 3 circles; The point of intersection of all 3 circles is the position of the epicenter. **9.** 15.7 cm
11. 22 cm **13.** 5 mm **15.** $\frac{1}{2}$; $\frac{1}{3}$

Spiral Review

19. $3\frac{3}{8}$ lb **20.** 5500 lb **21.** $2\frac{3}{16}$ lb **22.** 15,000 lb
23. the median; Four of the scores are higher than the mean (78.4), while four of the scores are close to the median (85). There is no mode. **24.** 9 **25.** 16 **26.** 1 **27.** 125

Extra Skill Practice

1. $\overline{AD}$, $\overline{FC}$ **3.** $\overline{OA}$, $\overline{OF}$, $\overline{OD}$, $\overline{OC}$ **5.** 15.71 cm **7.** 35,482 m
9. 84.97 in. **11.** 3.50 m **13.** 194.68 in. **15.** 28 cm

Standardized Testing, Multiple Choice

1. C **2.** A

Section 5, Practice and Application

1. 19.63 in.^{2} **3.** 13.85 m^2 **5.** 7.07 in.^{2} **7.** 625π mm^2
9. 21.16π cm^2 **11.** 49π cm^2 or about 153.86 cm^2
15. 452.16 m^3 **17.** 75.36 in.^{3} **19.** 183.12 m^3
21. a. cylinder **b.** Sample:

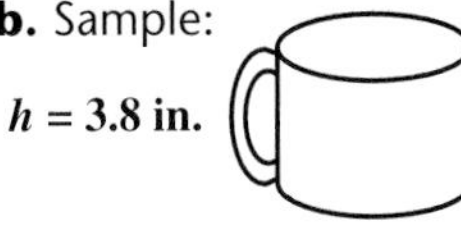

Spiral Review

23. 40.82 ft **24.** 37.68 in. **25.** 14.13 m **26.** 0.4 **27.** 0.09 **28.** 0.15 **29.** 0.63 **30–33.**

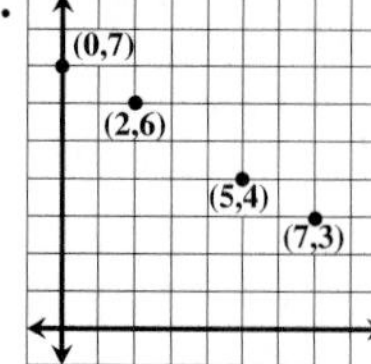

Extension

35. b. 3 cones **37.** 2009.62 cm^3 **39.** 11.78 $in.^3$

Extra Skill Practice

1. 2171.91 mm^2 **3.** 0.79 ft^2 **5.** 600.25π yd^2 **7.** 137,858.56 ft^3 **9.** 144,691.2 $in.^3$ **11.** 22.1 ft^3

Standardized Testing, Performance Task

No; about 63.59 cm^3 more sand is needed.

Section 6, Practice and Application

1–5. Sample responses are given. **1.** lightweight clothing such as long pants and a shirt; tennis, jogging, hiking; It is warm but not hot. **3.** heavy clothing such as a winter coat, hat, scarf, gloves, boots; ice skating, skiing; It is quite cold. **5.** –60° F or –50° C **7.** The number of degrees is the same, but one is negative and one is positive. **9.** 25° F; 12° F; 30° F **11.** –349 **13.** 10 **15.** < **17.** > **19.** Sample:

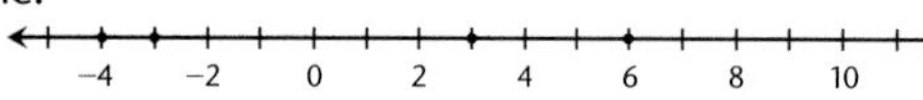

21. –60 **25. a.** (–1, 2) **b.** (–3, 2)

Spiral Review

28. 28.26 $in.^2$ **29.** 200.96 cm^2 **30.** 9.62 m^2

35. Sample: I would use estimation. I could round \$2.29 up to \$2.50 and 1.7 up to 2. Then 2 • \$2.50 = \$5. Since both numbers are rounded up, I know the estimate is higher than the actual cost and I have enough money.

Extra Skill Practice

1–3. Sample responses are given. **1.** 41°F or 5°C **3.** 59°F or 15°C **5.** < **7.** < **9.** > **11.** *H*

12–19.

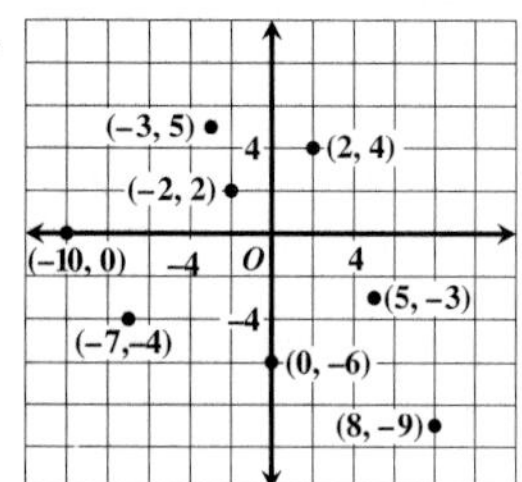

Standardized Testing, Open-ended

1. Sample: I would prefer 32°C because it is hot enough to go swimming. **2.** Samples: $x < 0$, $x > -10$

Review and Assessment

1. rectangle, triangle, parallelogram **2.** Choices of base and corresponding height may vary. rectangle: b = 3.5 cm, h = 2 cm, A = 7 cm^2; triangle: b = 5.4 cm, h = 1 cm, A = 2.7 cm^2; parallelogram: b = 3.7 cm, h = 2.4 cm, A = 8.88 cm^2 **3.** about 643.5 $in.^3$

4. a. a pentagonal prism **5.** two congruent pentagons and five rectangles, four of which are congruent to each other and one that is not congruent to any other face; pentagonal prism **6.** 7 faces, 10 vertices, 15 edges

7. **8. a.**

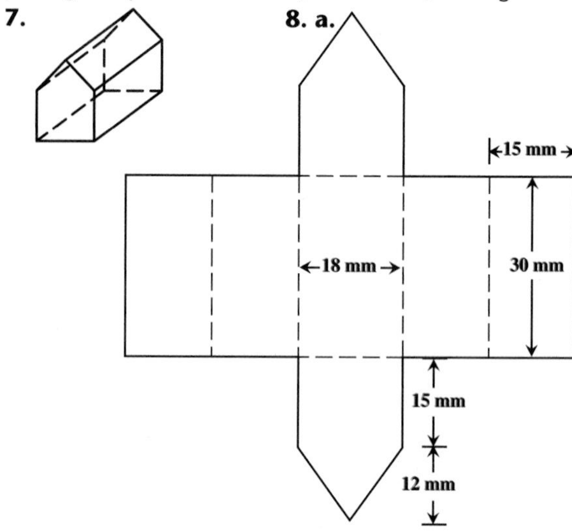

b. 11,340 mm^3 **9. a.** \$.71 per pound **b.** about 9 apples **10.** 56 **11.** $1\frac{3}{4}$ **12.** 5 **13. a.** *O* **b.** any two of $\overline{OB}$, $\overline{OE}$, and $\overline{OD}$ **c.** $\overline{AC}$ and $\overline{BE}$ **d.** $\overline{BE}$ **14.** 2.5 cm **15.** circumference: about 15.7 cm; area: about 19.625 cm^2 **16.** about 10,598 ft^3 **17.** warmer; Positive integers represent greater values than negative integers. **18.** < **19.** < **20.** >

21. a, b.

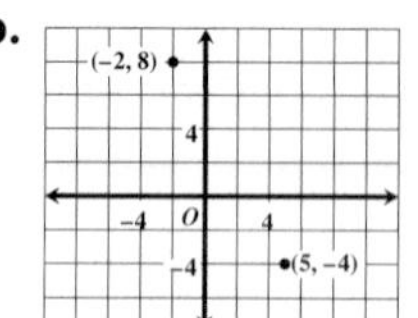

MODULE 8

Section 1, Practice and Application

1. –2 **3.** 3 **5.** **7.** No; five of the chips would have to total 0 and that is not possible. **9.** –44 **11.** –15 **13.** –10 **15.** –32 **17.** \$90 **19.** integers less than 3 **23.** 7 – (–3) = 10 **25.** Sample: **27.** –12 + (–9); –21 **29. a.** 44 – (–56) **b.** 44 + 56 = 100; Sample: The thermometer shows there are 44° between 44°F and 0°F and 56° between 0°F and –56°F, so the total number of degrees between the two temperatures is 44 + 56 = 100. **31.** 5 **33.** –10 **35.** 17 **37.** –13 **39.** –38 **41.** 81

Spiral Review

45–48.

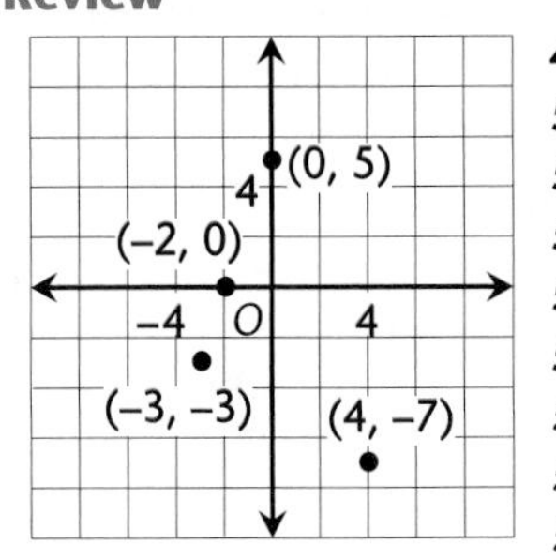

49. about 13
50. about 4000
51. about 2
52. about 5
53. about 12
54. about 33
55. 137
56. 423 **57.** 35,900
58. 2 **59.** 2213
60. 7,500,000

Extension

61. –2; –2 **63.** 7; 7 **65.** –9; –9 **67.** Each of Exs. 61–63 includes a pair of expressions in which the same addends are added in different orders and the answers are the same. **69.** –10; Sample: Group –21 with –9 and 15 with 5 to get –30 + 20 = –10. **71.** No; No; 5 – 7 = –2 and 7 – 5 = 2; 10 – (8 – 3) = 5 and (10 – 8) – 3 = –1.

Extra Skill Practice

1. –17 **3.** –40 **5.** 16 **7.** –26 **9.** –4 **11.** –9 **13.** –4 **15.** 22 **17.** –63 **19.** integers less than –4 **21.** –12 **23.** –6 **25.** 16 **27.** 48 **29.** –31

Section 2, Practice and Application

1. Sample: From 1950 to 1965, the number decreased sharply. After that the number declined steadily, but less sharply. **3. a.** Since the numbers range from 21,016 to 41,308, if the scale started at 0, the graph itself would either have to be enormous or the units would have to be so large the graph would not be meaningful.

b. 20,292

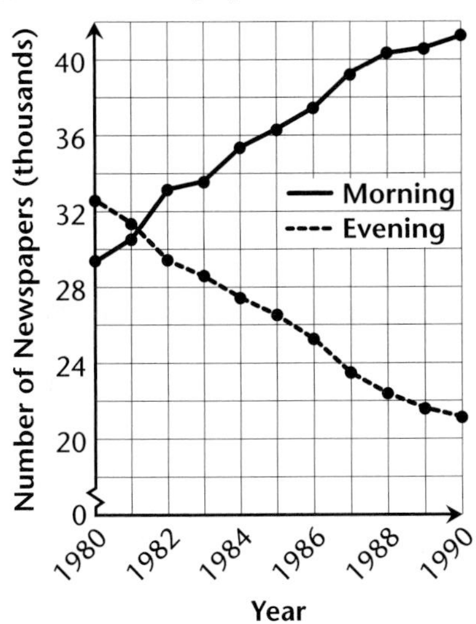

c. morning circulation increased; evening circulation decreased **d.** 1981 and 1982; The graphs cross between those two years. **5.** Graph 3 **7.** Answers are rounded to the nearest whole number. Tokyo-Yokohama: 26,122 people/mi^2; Mexico City: 45,810 people/mi^2; Hong Kong: 253,957 people/mi^2

9. $1.57 \cdot 10^5$ **11.** $5.6 \cdot 10^7$ **13.** $5.6 \cdot 10^3$ **15.** 59,000 **17.** 982,000 **19.** 60 **21.** $1.5 \cdot 10^3$ **23.** $5 \cdot 10^4$ **25.** Sample explanations are given. **a.** aluminum; $7.93 > 1.58$, so $7.93 \cdot 10^5 > 1.58 \cdot 10^5$. **b.** plastic; $1.44 \cdot 10^7 = 14.4 \cdot 10^6$ and $14.4 > 2.5$, so $1.44 \cdot 10^7 > 2.5 \cdot 10^6$. **27.** 36 **29.** 37.4 **31.** 227.5 **33.** Answers are rounded to the nearest whole number. scrambled: 85; fried: 78; boiled: 58; in omelettes: 10; other: 13; poached: 8 **35. a.** Sample:

Spiral Review

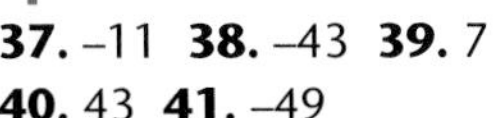

37. –11 **38.** –43 **39.** 7
40. 43 **41.** –49
42. –9 **43.** 14.4
44. 8 **45.** 28
46. 0.274 **47.** 380
48. 9.381
49. 7000

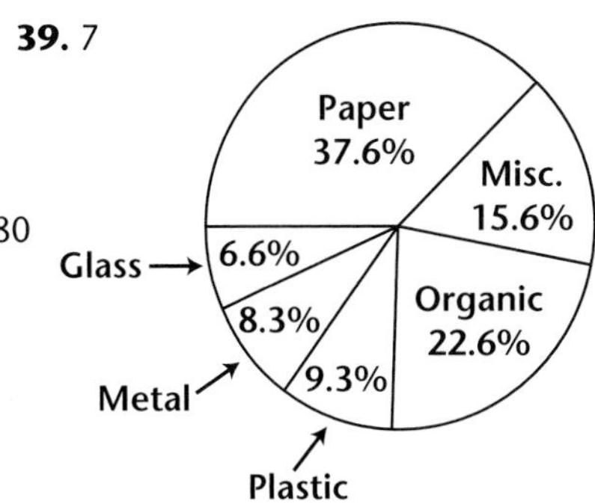

Extra Skill Practice

1. Sample: It increased fairly steadily and sharply. **3.** $4.98 \cdot 10^7$ **5.** $3.2 \cdot 10^{10}$ **7.** $2.5 \cdot 10^6$ **9.** 11,000,000,000,000 **11.** 5,030,000 **13.** 2,000,000,000 **15.** \$1.10 **17.** 117 **19.** 600

Standardized Testing, Multiple Choice

1. C **2.** B **3.** A

Section 3, Practice and Application

1. 1000 mL, 1 L **3.** 4000 mL, 4 L **5.** 1.8 **7.** 0.892 **9.** 2500 **11.** 30 L **13.** 250 mL **15. a.** 200,000,000,000 kL **b.** 2.0×10^{17} L **19.** 277% **21.** 630% **23.** 301% **25.** 150% **27.** 240% **29. a.** 20: 170%; 30: 163%; 40: 154%; 50: 143%; 60: 132%; 70: 119%; 80: 109% **b.** It appears from the table that age decreases the pupil's ability to enlarge.

31. Sample: greater than; $\frac{85}{84} > 1$

Spiral Review

34. 18.4 **35.** 14.7 **36.** 1.08 **37.** 28 **38.** 5.6 **39.** $2\frac{5}{24}$ **40.** 22.5 **41.** $\frac{29}{50}$; $\frac{21}{50}$

Career Connection

43. 0.3 L; 4.7 L

Extra Skill Practice

1. 3.4 **3.** 12,000 **5.** 14,000 **7.** 2 L **9.** 700 mL **11.** 140% **13.** $66\frac{2}{3}$ % **15.** 240% **17.** 125% **19.** 554% **21.** 165% **23.** 201% **25.** 80%

Standardized Testing, Free Response

greater than 0.01 L

Section 4, Practice and Application

1. $\frac{1}{3}$ **3.** $\frac{1}{2}$ **5.** $\frac{1}{9}$ **9.** $\frac{1}{40}$ **11. a.** 12.5 mi^2

Spiral Review

13. 3.425 L **14.** 97,000 L **15.** 0.25 L **16.** 840 L **17.** 45
18. a.

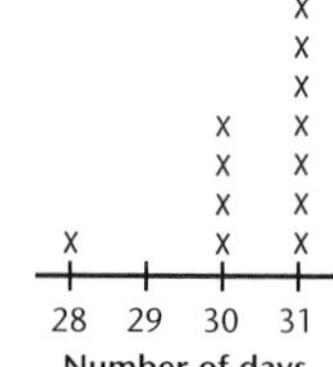

b. 31; 31

Extra Skill Practice

1. $\frac{1}{7}$ **3.** $\frac{1}{4}$ **5.** $\frac{169}{441}$

Standardized Testing, Performance Task

1. about 8% **2.** The combined area of the 11 squares should be about 44 in.^{2}. For example, 11 squares, each 2 in. on a side.

Section 5, Practice and Application

1. Graph 2; The scale on Graph 1 is spread out and makes the change look greater. **3.** Graph 1; The scale on Graph 1 is spread out and emphasizes the difference. **5–7.** Sample responses are given. **5.** The percent of students studying Spanish is much greater than the percent for any other language. **7.** Make 1 unit represent, say, 1% instead of 2%. **9–11.** Sample responses are given. **9.** bar graph; You can compare the popularity of the games by comparing the lengths of the bars. **11.** bar graph; You can compare the number of students playing the instruments by comparing the lengths of the bars. **13. a.** 7; 2; 0 and 1 **b.** Sample: None; The median and mode make it seem like most planets have only 0, 1, or 2 moons. The mean makes it seem as if most planets have 7 moons, but only Neptune is close to this. **15.** Sample: the median; There is no mode and the mean will be affected by the one extreme data value.

Spiral Review

22. about $\frac{18}{25}$ **23.** $11\frac{2}{3}$ **24.** $1\frac{13}{20}$ **25.** $\frac{95}{96}$ **26.** $3\frac{5}{9}$ **27.** $18\frac{1}{14}$ **28.** $2\frac{38}{85}$ **29.** 7.28 **30.** $5\frac{23}{24}$ **31.** 30.57 **32.** $4\frac{11}{18}$ **33.** 24.31 **34.** $10\frac{1}{2}$

Extension

35. a. about 200 times; about 5.5 times. **b.** Yes. **c.** 1973: about 57.7 mm^3; 1979: about 9356.4 mm^3; The volume of the 1979 barrel is about 162 times the volume of the 1973 barrel, not about 5.5 times as great.

Extra Skill Practice

1–3. Sample responses are given. **1.** The number decreased steadily.

3.

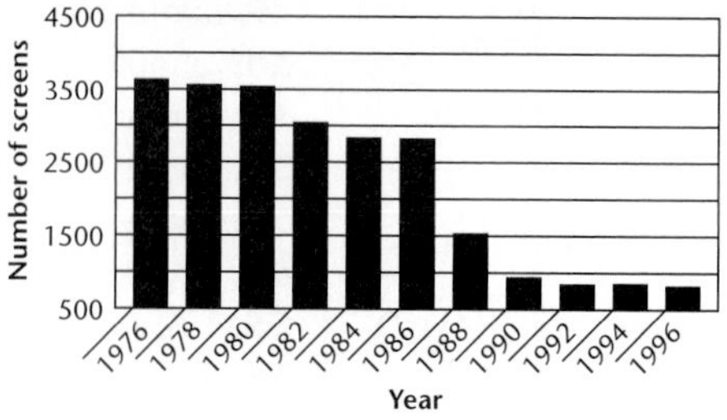

5. Sample: the median; You can tell from the table that 2818 is the middle data item.

Standardized Testing, Open-ended

1–2. Sample responses are given. **1.** A bar graph makes it easy to compare the data values. **2.** For each city individually, the high and low temperatures do not vary greatly, but the high and low temperatures for Miami are much greater than the high and low temperatures for Chicago or New York City.

Review and Assessment

1. 6 **2.** –39 **3.** 18 **4.** –24 **5.** –26 **6.** –1 **7.** 90 **8.** –6
9.

Fuel Efficiency of New Automobiles in the United States

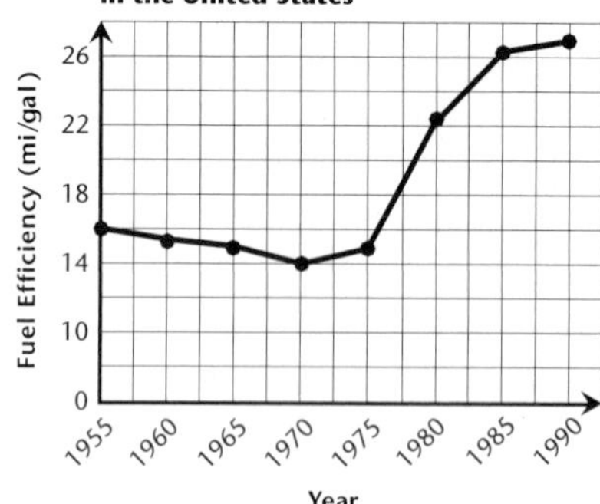

10. 5670 **11.** 100,200 **12.** 700,000,000 **13.** 4,200,000 **14.** 23 **15.** 9,110,000 **16.** 18,330 **17.** 890 **18.** $4.4 \cdot 10^6$ **19.** $7.7 \cdot 10^3$ **20.** $7.89 \cdot 10^2$ **21.** $3.31 \cdot 10^5$ **22.** $6.2 \cdot 10^4$ **23.** $5 \cdot 10^9$ **24.** $3.77125 \cdot 10^5$ **25.** $8.8 \cdot 10^7$ **26.** 119.24 **27.** 44.5 **28.** 64.8 **29.** 19.28 **30.** Sample: 10 cm by 10 cm by 40 cm **31.** 160% **32.** 230% **33.** 148% **34.** 300% **35.** 192% **36.** 260% **37.** 532% **38.** 122% **39.** 300% **40.** 600% **41.** 108% **42.** about $\frac{33}{38}$ **43.** $\frac{1}{4}$ **44.** $\frac{9}{25}$ **45.** Graph 2; The scale is easier to read. **46.** Graph 2: The scale is spread out, so the changes are emphasized. **47.** The scale was spread out by changing the starting value from 0 to 1550 and changing the number of million metric tons each unit represented. **48.** Sample: I think the teacher would use the most common age, the mode.

TOOLBOX ANSWERS

NUMBERS AND OPERATIONS

Whole Number Place Value

1. place: one hundred thousands; value: 800,000 **2.** place: one thousands; value: 5,000 **3.** place: ten millions; value: 50,000,000 **4.** place: ones; value: 8 **5.** place: ten thousands; value: 90,000 **6.** place: hundreds; value: 200 **7.** ten thousands **8.** 20 **9.** 15,946,619 **10.** 220,009 **11.** five hundred eighteen **12.** twenty-three thousand, four hundred **13.** seventy million, six hundred twenty-four **14.** four hundred fifty thousand, six hundred seventy-two

Comparing Whole Numbers

1. > **2.** > **3.** > **4.** < **5.** > **6.** < **7.** < **8.** > **9.** < **10.** 239,400; 79,899; 47,777; 24,000 **11.** 7,902,500; 6,150,762; 937,400; 892,570

Rounding Whole Numbers and Money

1. 890 **2.** 94,600 **3.** 86,000 **4.** 27,000,000 **5.** 600 **6.** 40 **7.** 300,000 **8.** 68,300 **9.** $950.00 **10.** $4370.00 **11.** $52.00 **12.** $600.00

Adding Whole Numbers and Money

1. 3232 **2.** 12,718 **3.** 101,916 **4.** 60,957 **5.** 97,766 **6.** 89,117 **7.** $12.11 **8.** $39.04 **9.** $44.15 **10.** $120.90 **11.** $43.07 **12.** $115.45

Mental Math

1. 123 **2.** 82 **3.** 481 **4.** 321 **5.** 371 **6.** 831 **7.** 495 **8.** 791 **9.** 675 **10.** $12.25 **11.** $18.57 **12.** $10.38 **13.** $13.35 **14.** $14.40 **15.** $8.97 **16.** $20.25 **17.** $13.40 **18.** $23.05

Subtracting Whole Numbers And Money

1. 8578 **2.** 188 **3.** 4813 **4.** 2121 **5.** 6502 **6.** 3841 **7.** $29.08 **8.** $388.40 **9.** $64.08 **10.** $33.39 **11**. $320.33

Multiplying Whole Numbers and Money

1. 950 **2.** 48,384 **3.** 37,960 **4.** 220,735 **5.** 4582 **6.** 28,672 **7.** $229.08 **8.** $352.22 **9.** $111.52 **10.** $1890.00 **11.** $109.64 **12.** $3014.85

Dividing Whole Numbers

1. 400 R5 **2.** 7 R52 **3.** 2468 R3 **4.** 12 R17 **5.** 302 **6.** 538 R10 **7.** 20 R21 **8.** 11 R25 **9.** 161 R38 **10.** 3 R44 **11.** 35 R18 **12.** 13 R6

Number Fact Families

1. 6; 3; 6, 3 **2.** 8; 16, 8; 2; 8, 2 **3.** 12 **4.** 24 **5.** 53 **6.** 25 **7.** 81 **8.** 32 **9.** 103 **10.** 13 **11.** 63 **12.** 8 **13.** 39 **14.** 12 **15.** 48 **16.** 4 **17.** 14

Multiplying and Dividing by Tens

1. 50,000 **2.** 6000 **3.** 1,500,000 **4.** 1,600,000 **5.** 600,000 **6.** 500,000 **7.** 12,000,000 **8.** 20,000,000 **9.** 320,000,000 **10.** 400,000 **11.** 10 **12.** 50 **13.** 130 **14.** 50 **15.** 5000

MEASUREMENT

Perimeter and Using a Ruler

1. 18 in. **2.** 18 cm **3.** 12 ft **4.** 20 cm **5.** 14 in. **6.** 1 in. **7.** 2 in.

Area

1. 6 cm^2 **2.** 5 cm^2 **3.** 7 cm^2

Time Conversions and Elapsed Time

1. 480 min **2.** 3 days **3.** 3 min **4.** 4 h 55 min **5.** 13 h 53 min **6.** 2 h 56 min **7.** 1 h 35 min

DATA DISPLAYS

Reading a Graph

1. 16; 10 **2.** about 840,000; about 870,000

Making a Pictograph

1. **Students Studying Music**

6th grade	● ● ● ● ● ● ●
7th grade	● ● ● ● ● ● ● ● ●
8th grade	● ● ● ● ● ● ● ● ◐

● = 10 students

2. Money Spent on Advertising in 1994

Newspapers	■ ■ ■ ■ ■ ■ ■
Magazines	■ ■
Television	■ ■ ■ ■ ■ ■ ■
Radio	■ ■
Direct Mail	■ ■ ■ ■ ■ ■

■ = 5 billion dollars